Saskatchewan
POLITICS
CROWDING THE CENTRE

Canadian Plains Research Center
University of Regina
Regina, Saskatchewan S4S 0A2
Canada
Tel: (306) 585-4758/Fax: (306) 585-4699
e-mail: canadian.plains@uregina.ca
http://www.cprc.uregina.ca

Library and Archives Canada Cataloguing in Publication

Saskatchewan politics : crowding the centre / edited by Howard A. Leeson.

(University of Regina publications, ISSN 1480-0004 ; 21)
Includes bibliographical references and index.
ISBN 978-0-88977-234-2

1. Saskatchewan--Politics and government--21st century.
2. Saskatchewan--Politics and government. I. Leeson, Howard A., 1942-
II. University of Regina. Canadian Plains Research Center III. Title.
IV. Series: University of Regina publications ; 21

FC3528.2.S268 2009   320.97124   C2009-903306-2
Cover, DVD face and interface design: Duncan Campbell, Canadian Plains Research Center, University of Regina
Cover photos by Don Healy, courtesy of the Regina *Leader-Post*.
Index prepared by Adrian Mather (amindexing@shaw.ca)
Printed and bound by Marquis.
Recorded debates provided with the permission of the Speaker of the Legislative Assembly of Saskatchewan.
DVD master authoring by Java Post Production, Regina, SK.

Publisher's Note:
We acknowledge the financial support of the Government of Canada through the Book Publishing Industry Development Program (BPDIP) for our publishing activities. We also acknowledge the support of the Canada Council for the Arts for our publishing program.

Saskatchewan
POLITICS
CROWDING THE CENTRE

edited by HOWARD A. LEESON

UNIVERSITY OF
REGINA

CPRC
PRESS

Dedication

This book is dedicated to my children and grandchildren, who continue to be a joy in my life.

Contents

Acknowledgements

Any book involves the collaboration of a large number of people. An edited volume is dependent upon a large number of authors and their staff. Thank you to all who have taken time, without remuneration, to contribute to this book.

I would also like to thank the Canadian Plains Research Center, and in particular Brian Mlazgar, who at a crucial time provided me with office space, a computer, and the wherewithal to complete the volume.

Special thanks to Aydon Charlton, Elsa Johnson, and Jacques Rodgers for a fine job of proofreading the various articles. As usual, the CPRC Press did a wonderful job in preparing the book. Thank you all.

Finally, special thanks to my wife Ede for all of her help and support, including reading various articles and offering suggestions.

Howard Leeson
Regina, Saskatchewan
May 2009

Introduction

Howard Leeson

Broken Skyline

Grain elevators
shoulders hunched against the wind
towers marking towns
guarding the prairie scene
no longer needed just standing there
hanging around.

Not worth their lumber
bounden steel cables
pulled and yanked
groaning and thrashing, they tumble
in tattered heaps on the ground.

My brush is still.
It's hard to paint on empty space
against a dwindling plain
its nature lost
flat without a sound.[1]

This small poem by Madeleine Reid, who spent most of her life in rural Saskatchewan on a farm, graphically captures the feeling of change and loss in the rural areas of the province. Change was the theme of the first volume on Saskatchewan politics published in the year 2001. Writing in the introduction I said "the old Saskatchewan is gone forever, lost in the welter of changing industries, ideologies, and peoples. A new Saskatchewan continues to be born with new players and perhaps new goals … maybe, just maybe, we will get the best of both change and continuity."[2] In many ways this volume demonstrates not just continued change, but a massive convergence in political attitudes that would have been unthinkable even 20 years ago. Not only elevators are gone, but many of the political attitudes that underpinned the mythology of Saskatchewan have disappeared as well. For better or for worse Saskatchewan has truly entered into the global village.

In an era where the internet and instant communication dominate the world it is inevitable that local communities will lose some of their uniqueness. Saskatchewan has not been immune to that process. Issues of national security, terrorism, and international conflict now dominate much of the politics of the world. These images have flooded into our province, changing the focus from local and national politics to the international scene.

Thus, for most people provincial governments have become less important, less in the forefront of their consciousness. Whereas we used to turn to
the provincial government for solutions to social and economic problems, we
now assume that these problems must be solved at the national or international level. Few people now ask for the provincial government to use the public
sector to regulate or correct excesses in the private economy. When it comes to
matters like regulating gasoline prices, providing social housing, or dealing
with the ups and downs of the agricultural economy, almost no one thinks
that the provincial government can do much to help them. Indeed, most
believe that these matters are beyond the reach of national governments, and
a sizeable group, perhaps a majority, believe that government ought not to
involve itself at all. In part this is the result of 25 years of ideological pressure
on the role of government in general. Ironically, the economic collapse of the
last few months may serve to change these attitudes in a profound way.

Seven years ago I concluded that the reality of a global economy and a
dominant ideology of corporatism would serve to create a new Saskatchewan.
I also concluded that the politics of the past would look "jarringly antiquat-
ed." In my opinion, that process is now largely complete. As you will see the
articles in this volume reflect that change. Indeed, the word "convergence"
has replaced the word "change" in many of the articles, especially those dealing with the political parties.

THE ARTICLES IN THIS VOLUME

The articles in this volume were written after the 2007 provincial election
which saw the New Democratic Party lose office for the first time since 1991.
In itself this change would have been significant. The fact that the NDP lost
office to a new political party, the Saskatchewan Party, formed less than 10
years prior, makes that change even more significant. Thus, many of the articles deal in whole or in part with that election. Certainly the articles on the
political parties concentrate on its impact on the party system. However,
many deal with institutions and structures, issues and policies, which are
somewhat immune to the results of any individual election.

The first section of this book, which deals with institutions, reveals that little has changed in some areas over the last several years. In his article on the
role of the Crown in Saskatchewan Michael Jackson reaffirms the trend that he
illustrated in his article eight years ago. That is, the role of the Crown in
Saskatchewan is not only secure, but probably more entrenched than at any
time since Saskatchewan became a province. His interviews with current and
former premiers provide an interesting insight into how the relationship has
further developed since he wrote his first article eight years ago. Of course, as
before, anti-monarchists will find little comfort in this trend, or in his article.

In her second article about the Legislature Merrilee Rasmussen returns to
two themes that permeated the first one and continue to be important today.
The first is that in the constant tug-of-war between the legislative and executive branches of government, the executive branch continues to become more

and more dominant. However, she points out that legislatures continue to lose power not only to the executive branch but to external agencies through trade agreements like the Agreement on Internal Trade and the creation of quasi-independent agencies like Enterprise Saskatchewan. Most importantly, however, she returns in more detail to the whole question of the relationship between First Nations governments, and the Legislature of Saskatchewan. As she says, "more significant because of the potential transformative impact, on both government as well as business interests in the province, is the growing influence and power of Aboriginal governments."[3] She concludes that this relationship will become even more important in the future. The obvious implication of the above is that the legislature of Saskatchewan will continue to lose power and influence to the executive branch, to aboriginal governments, and to international agencies as a result of globalization.

While Merrilee Rasmussen concentrates on the role of the legislature, Dan Perrins, former Deputy Minister to Premier Calvert, examines how the relationship between the public service and legislative committees has changed, especially during the last decade. In order to do so he concentrates on the role of the Public Accounts Committee. He provides us not only with a history of the committee, but important detail on how recent changes have affected the relationship between public servants and their political masters. He concludes that this relationship has been changed, probably to the detriment of the elected official. In the tug-of-war between the premier's office on one side, and the senior public service on the other, it would appear that Ministers are losing out.

In their article John Whyte and Thomas Gusa examine the justice system in the province from two points of view. The first has to do with the availability of legal services for all, regardless of affordability, and the second has to do with the prosecutorial system and the causes of crime. In both cases the authors find the system is lacking. They worry about the impact of this deficiency on the reconciliation and restorative functions of the law. This leads them to the conclusion that remedies are required, which if not undertaken, could lead to larger and more difficult problems for the whole community.

Not surprisingly, given the central role that the cabinet plays in our form of government, the interview with former premier Roy Romanow about cabinet making in Saskatchewan is extremely interesting. Mr. Romanow gives us a unique insight into the many facets of how a cabinet is constructed and maintained in Saskatchewan. In particular, he gives us a glimpse into some of the more human aspects involved, both as to those being appointed, and by the premier doing the appointing. As well, we learn about the differences between appointing first cabinets, succeeding cabinets, and cabinets in a coalition government. In providing an interview and not an article, Mr. Romanow has extended the reach of our understanding considerably.

Taken together these five articles on the institutions of the province tell us about how stable our arrangements are. No institution has been radically changed or disappeared during the past several decades. Although there have been trends toward the centralization of power it is quite apparent that our institutions are flexible enough to accommodate provincial and global changes to our society. They remain, for good or ill, anchors in often turbulent social waters.

The same cannot be said for the second section of the book which deals with the political parties in the province. As noted at the beginning of this Introduction change and convergence are the orders of the day in terms of our political parties. The contrast with the political party system of 50 years ago could not be more dramatic.

As David McGrane tells us in his article, the NDP in Saskatchewan has undergone a substantial ideological transformation, especially in the last 15 years. In explaining this change the author provides an excellent analysis of traditional Social Democracy on the one hand, and the so-called "Third Way" on the other. His application of this analysis to the Saskatchewan NDP is compelling in its detail and its logic. While he concludes that both Romanow and Calvert were basically "Third Way" premiers, in large part explained by the pressures of globalization, he also concludes that there were differences between them. He believes that the Calvert government did a better job of balancing between the needs of remaining economically competitive and striving for more social equality. At the end of his article he has a number of prescriptions which he thinks would be useful should the NDP conduct an extensive self examination. Most importantly for us, McGrane believes there are still ideological differences between the NDP and the Saskatchewan Party.

By contrast Raymond Blake believes that there has been substantial convergence between the NDP and the Saskatchewan Party, and that there is now little to choose between them. He comes to this conclusion after a thorough examination of the evolution of the Saskatchewan Party. His article gives us valuable detail on how the Saskatchewan party was formed, its policy directions in the early years, and how it changed under the current leader Brad Wall. He points out that under Mr. Wall the Saskatchewan Party abandoned a number of policy directions that had formed the bedrock of the party under Mr. Hermanson. He calls this process a "re-branding" of the party, with the final step taking place in October of 2007 when the election platform was released. He goes so far as to say that under Brad Wall the party has become a flexible non-ideological vehicle, dedicated to becoming the new "government" party.

Together with my article on the election the three of us come to some similar conclusions. The first is that the major parties in Saskatchewan have crowded toward what is now in Canada the ideological centre of the spectrum. Second, we all believe that the NDP and the Saskatchewan Party will remain the two major parties in the party system for the foreseeable future. Last, we all conclude that Saskatchewan may be entering a new and different economic and social era. That is, not only has the party system changed, but it has changed as a result of changing economic and social imperatives. Put another way, globalization has successfully invaded our province.

No book on Saskatchewan politics would now be complete without a look at the impact of First Nations and other aboriginal peoples on the politics of the province. In this volume we decided to devote an entire section to First Nations and aboriginal politics, in order to provide students with a better understanding of how the political process functions in this important area. Of course, almost all politics for First Nations people in Canada begins with the treaties that were negotiated with Great Britain and Canada since the first settlers arrived in our part of North America. In his article David Arnot, now the head of the Human Rights Commission in Saskatchewan, outlines both the background and importance of these treaties in our province. He concludes that the obligations under these treaties have not been met, either in substance or in spirit, and that if we are to have harmony in the future these treaties will have to be a bridge to a new understanding.

In her article Dr. Bonita Beatty provides us with a clear understanding of how the executive and legislative structures of First Nations function. This should be particularly valuable for most students who unfortunately have little understanding of the constitutional basis for these structures, and less understanding of how they operate. Dr. Beatty also provides us with a sense of how challenging it is to build political structures within the strictures of social and economic challenge. She concludes that failures to fulfill treaty obligations and to recognize inherent rights are the basis for many of the problems facing First Nations people in the province.

The final article in this section, written by Marilyn Poitras, outlines the extreme difficulties faced by the Métis people in Saskatchewan. Most will be familiar with some of the political challenges that have plagued the Métis in Saskatchewan during the last few years, in particular around forming a stable electoral and political structure. The jubilation at being recognized in the constitutional settlement of 1982 has since been replaced by a sense of frustration and disillusionment at the seeming inability of the Métis people to become masters in their own house. Ms. Poitras outlines in detail how the failure of political structures has affected the ability of her community to deal with the very real problems of unemployment, education, and social services. At the core of much of the problem for this community is an inability to define who is Métis. This problem, she says, together with the inability to set their own agenda, constitute the most important issues for the Métis in the near future. In particular, she concludes that if the Métis community is unable to escape the dependency trap, the future will be bleak indeed.

In previous volumes on Saskatchewan politics there has been a tendency to ignore the municipal level, mostly because interest has centred on the socialist/non-socialist dimension of provincial politics. In this volume Dr. Joe Garcea provides us with a full history of municipal development and change in southern Saskatchewan. It is perhaps one of the most complete articles on the subject in many years. As you read through the article you soon become struck by how vital a sector this has been, both in terms of its impact on provincial politics, and its impact on the people of the province. Dr. Garcea is particularly qualified to write this article given his role in recent attempts at restructuring rural municipalities in the province. Nowhere is the impact of changing demographics and economic structures more apparent than in rural

Saskatchewan. However, attempts at finding new and innovative ways to accommodate this change have been largely unsuccessful. At the end of his article Dr. Garcea concludes that change will likely come from outside, but only if there are incentives to do so.

No volume of this nature would be complete without a look at federal-provincial relations and its impact on the politics of the province. In his article David Smith provides us with an historical view of the overall relations with the federal government. Instead of concentrating on the usual list of variables that have affected federal provincial relations he concentrates on leadership, administrative infrastructure, and other matters like resourcefulness. He concludes that Saskatchewan, although a small province, has often "punched above its weight" on the national stage because of the unique combination of these kinds of attributes in a setting that has been called "Executive Federalism."

The last five articles in the book deal with some of the major issues that will face provincial politicians in the coming years. Not surprisingly, the economy, healthcare, and education continued to top the list of important matters. In this volume they are joined by two relatively new issues, inner-city problems, and the environment. It isn't that they have been unimportant in the past, rather, it is because they have vaulted to the front ahead of some matters, such as agriculture. It is not surprising that they have done so, given their importance worldwide.

As we know from the economic problems that developed in the last few months of 2008, and promise to continue into the foreseeable future, the economy and the province will probably become the most important issue for decision-makers during the next three years. In his article Dr. Gary Tompkins outlines the major problems facing the provincial government, and how they are different from those faced by governments in the past. Surprisingly, though many issues remain the same, such as the role of aboriginal people in the provincial economy, the role of Crown corporations, and stabilizing the fiscal structure of the province. Interestingly, as we see from the title of his article, one of the problems facing the province is managing expectations and resources in a period of prosperity. However, he concludes by warning us that the current prosperity may be fragile, and that we may be too dependent on natural resource revenue. Given the current situation in Canada and around the world, and given our increasing integration into the global economy, it will be interesting to see how accurate he is.

In their article on health care Drs. Marchildon and Macintosh remind us of how important health care is for any provincial government, but especially Saskatchewan's government. Their article provides us with an interesting review of health-care changes during the last eight years, especially with regard to how the provincial governments have handled the recommendations of the Fyke commission. They end by examining the three most important challenges that face the Wall government in this area, workforce planning, promoting "upstream" as opposed to "downstream" health initiatives, and dealing with aboriginal health needs in the province. They note at the end of their article that these are not the only problems that will confront the government, but they are critical to how the government will treat other health issues in the future.

In her look at post-secondary education in the province Andrea Rounce provides us with a history and analysis of the place of post-secondary education amongst political issues in the province, and examines in some detail the role of this issue in the last election. In this chapter the connection between educational institutions, training, and the global economy is quite marked. Our understanding of the role of universities and colleges has changed profoundly in the last two decades. Post-secondary institutions have become intimately linked to the economy and to economic growth in a way which would have disturbed many educators in the past. Ms. Rounce provides us with detail on how this change occurred. She outlines as well the convergence between the political parties on this linkage, which now treats education as an economic good as well as a social good. In this area, she expects the political parties to remain convergent.

Part of the mystique and the myth of Saskatchewan involves its rural past. For most Canadians who have not visited the province, there is a general belief that it is mostly rural farmland, with happy rural socialist small towns. However, as we know, the reality of the province is now quite different. Both Regina and Saskatoon are complex urban areas that face many of the same problems that confront other cities in Canada. In his article Dr. Ryan Walker examines the question of housing in the inner-city areas of the major cities in the province. In particular, he outlines how housing policy has changed dramatically and, frankly, how those changes have failed to provide adequate housing for those who need it most. Once again we see a convergence of policy between the major parties in the province. As Dr. Walker notes, in his opinion, both parties have failed on this issue. Interestingly, he concludes by saying that the spirit of "social democracy" needs to be revived in this area.

The last, but certainly not least, article in the book is written by the long time environmental activist and former MLA Peter Prebble. It is both informative and provocative. Mr. Prebble is neither a nattering nabob of negativism, nor someone wedded to "airy fairy" solutions to problems. In a detailed and common sense way he outlines the arguments for immediate action on a number of environmental concerns in Saskatchewan, and in the world. Moreover, he puts forward interesting and practical suggestions for change which would be instrumental in amending our economic, social, and political attitudes and practices. Most of what he says is backed up by solid science, and his suggestions for change are deeply rooted in a good knowledge of what is possible in the political system.

Perhaps no other area of social and economic change demonstrates the need for global action. Saskatchewan does have an environmental impact on the entire world, and conversely, the rest of the world certainly has an impact on us. While the term globalization is ordinarily thought of in the context of economic change, there is little doubt that it could and should be applied to the area of the environment.

This leads to some final comments on the shape and context of this volume of work. We began by pointing out the massive change in political, economic, and social attitudes in the province. The inevitable question arises as to whether this is good or bad. Of course, the answer depends upon how you view change. Many say that these changes will bring greater prosperity, a more secure life, and more individual freedom. Others, however, will point out that much of what has traditionally characterized Saskatchewan has been lost, including our sense of uniqueness in terms of social policy, our caring for each other, and our collective traditions. This uniqueness, they will argue, has been sacrificed on the altar of globalization and profit. Thus how you answer the question about change will depend largely on how and what you value most. It is not a matter of left wing or right wing politics. Perhaps the dilemma is best characterized by George Grant who had the following to say:

> Those who loved the older traditions of Canada may be allowed to lament what has been lost, even though they do not know whether or not that loss will lead to some greater political good.[4]

NOTES

1. This piece was written by Madeleine Reid and is taken from a small collection called *Reflections*, which she published in 2007. Madeline spent most of her life as a prairie farm woman who eventually came to the city and counseled single mothers. Her small collection deals almost entirely with her experiences in rural Saskatchewan.

2. Howard Leeson, "Introduction" in *Saskatchewan Politics: Into the Twenty-First Century* (Regina, Saskatchewan, Canadian Plains Research Center, 2001), xii.

3. See page 43 in this publication.

4. George Grant, *Lament for a Nation: The Defeat of Canadian Nationalism* (Princeton, NJ: D. Van Nostrand Co., 1965), 96.

INSTITUTIONS

The Crown in Saskatchewan: An Institution Renewed

D. Michael Jackson

The institution of the Crown in Saskatchewan, particularly as seen through the Office of Lieutenant Governor, regained and enhanced its prestige from the 1970s after many years of decline.[1] Indeed, the Crown played a more positive role in the province's political culture than it had since the 1930s. The symbolic dimension of the Crown was particularly evident to the citizenry. The constitutional function of the lieutenant governor may not have been as well appreciated; arguably, however, its importance increased.

INTRODUCTION: THE CANADIAN CROWN

Reduced to its simplest terms, the Crown is the institution of constitutional monarchy, in Canada embodied by the Queen, the governor general and the lieutenant governors. It incarnates the executive branch of government in Canada's Westminster-style parliamentary democracy. Compared to the presidential or gubernatorial positions in the United States, the monarchical headship of state in Canada is not well understood and its significance tends to be underestimated.

Underestimated or not, the Crown pervades Canada's constitutional order and political culture. The leading scholar on the subject, David E. Smith, entitled his definitive 1995 book, tellingly, *The Invisible Crown: The First Principle of Canadian Government*.[2] The Crown may indeed seem invisible because it is so discreet, but Dr. Smith sees it as "an organizing principle of government."[3] "The Crown," he says, "is no icon. It permeates daily government."[4] An Australian scholar has a similar view of the Crown in that country: "despite being a fundamental institution in Australia's constitutional system [the Crown] has been little understood and is the subject of widespread misconceptions."[5]

POWERS OF THE CROWN

The Sovereign and her representatives are the most visible component of this semi-visible and little understood institution. To adapt a cliché, they are the tip of a constitutional iceberg. Their powers are almost always exercised on what is called "advice," given by the ministers of the Crown, and fall into two categories: *statutory*, that is, by legislation; and *prerogative*—traditional non-statutory powers wielded in the name of the Sovereign by the first minister and cabinet through the orders-in-council, writs, proclamations and warrants signed by the Queen's representative. The royal prerogative includes preparation of budgets and legislation. It also includes a myriad of administrative decisions and a vast range of appointments, ranging from deputy ministers to judges, lieutenant governors, diplomats, and members of boards, commissions and agencies. David Smith emphasizes that, in addition to its symbolism, the Crown makes a "practical contribution" to "the primary feature of Canadian government—executive dominance."[6] Another Australian scholar, Peter Boyce, in a penetrating study of the Crown in Canada, Australia and New Zealand, points out the profound constitutional implications of the monarchical system in all three countries: "the enshrining of state authority in 'the Crown' has provided an effective mask for the steady expansion of power within the political executives."[7]

However, the Crown's representatives, despite popular opinion to the contrary, are not merely decorative, nor are they entirely powerless. For legislation to be valid it must receive royal assent. For government orders to be effective they must be signed by the vice-regal incumbent. For first ministers and their cabinets to legitimately hold office they must be invited to do so by the Crown. The governors' constitutional duties, although essential to the functioning of the political system, are normally routine in nature. Yet there are circumstances—albeit rare—where the Crown's representatives may exercise personal discretion, invoking what are known as the "reserve" powers.

THE CROWN AND FEDERALISM
In Canada and in Australia, the Crown plays another important role: reinforcing the powers of the sub-national units—the Canadian provinces and the Australian states. David Smith asserts that Canada is a "compound monarchy" and points out that the Crown has contributed enormously to the strength of provincial jurisdiction by investing the provincial cabinets with the powers embedded in the royal prerogative.[8] This is despite the fact that, under the British North America Act of 1867, the lieutenant governors are appointed, paid, and theoretically subject to direction, by the federal government. Australia, in preparing for its confederation in 1901, deliberately rejected the Canadian model of *lieutenant* governors appointed by the governor general in favour of *governors* appointed by the Queen, on the grounds that the Canadian system was incompatible with federalism.[9]

Indeed, one of the powers of the lieutenant governors under the 1867 BNA Act was "reservation"[10]: lieutenant governors could "reserve" royal assent to provincial bills and refer it to the governor general for consideration, which meant in effect a veto for the governor general's advisors—the federal cabinet. (There was also another form of federal veto called disallowance, through which the federal cabinet could simply declare a provincial law to be invalid.[11])

Despite such centralizing devices, the Canadian provinces gradually emerged from the subordinate status to which the British North America Act appeared to have relegated them and by the late twentieth century functioned, and saw themselves, as co-sovereign jurisdictions. What is of interest to those studying the Crown is that its provincial manifestation, the Office of Lieutenant Governor, was a key element in the series of court decisions which buttressed provincial autonomy. The most significant of these were the judgements of the Judicial Committee of the Privy Council in London, Canada's final appeal court until 1949.[12]

As early as the end of the 19th century "the principle of coordinate federalism was generally accepted" by the courts, and the Judicial Committee had "authoritatively asserted the independent status of the lieutenant governor as the representative of the crown for all purposes of provincial government."[13] In short, provincial autonomy revolved around the Office of Lieutenant Governor.

VICE-REGAL APPOINTMENTS

The appointment of lieutenant governors solely by the federal government, despite—indeed in contradiction with—this "independent status," has perplexed the Canadian provinces. Contrary to popular belief, provincial governments have no say in the selection of their lieutenant governors, although, depending on the good graces of the federal prime minister, informal consultation may be offered to the extent of sounding out a premier on the acceptability of a candidate. The recurrent pattern for most provincial vice-regal appointments until the 1970s was for the prime minister to select an active politician or supporter of the governing party in Ottawa.

This was as true in Saskatchewan as elsewhere. However, the appointment of Stephen Worobetz in 1970 by Prime Minister Pierre Trudeau as the first lieutenant governor of Ukrainian origin signalled a changing approach to the provincial vice-regal office. As noted in the author's 2001 essay,

> A Saskatoon surgeon, Dr. Worobetz was a supporter of the Liberal Party […]. But in a distinct break with the usual practice of the last six decades, he was not active politically and had not held political office, either elected or within the party. In another break with previous practice, he was first approached by Premier Ross Thatcher to see if he would accept the post, before Prime Minister Pierre Trudeau called to offer it.[14]

Allan Blakeney, NDP premier from 1971 to 1982, considered that the appointment of Stephen Worobetz marked a turning-point in the fortunes of the vice-regal office[15]: the lieutenant governor was no longer a blatantly partisan, patronage appointee but someone chosen and respected for his own merits.

To succeed Worobetz in 1976 the Trudeau government appointed another person with exemplary war service and without political baggage: 72-year-old George Porteous of Saskatoon, who had worked for the YMCA. Attached to the Canadian Army in Hong Kong, he was a Japanese prisoner of war from 1941 to 1945 and was made a Member of the Order of the British Empire for service to his fellow-prisoners. Allan Blakeney respected this lieutenant governor as he had Worobetz and endeavoured to persuade the frugal Porteous to accept more resources from the provincial government.[16] But since Porteous died in office in 1978, he made relatively little impact on the vice-regal position.

This was not the case for Porteous' replacement, hastily chosen only days after his death, again by Trudeau: C. Irwin McIntosh, a newspaper publisher in North Battleford. While from a prominent Liberal family—his father had been a Liberal MP for 15 years—McIntosh had not held elected or party office. Although he started out being too outspoken for the government's taste, he soon earned their approval for his rock-solid support for the national unity campaign after the election of the first Parti Québécois government in Quebec. He also worked tirelessly for the 75th anniversary of the Province of Saskatchewan in 1980. By the time Irwin McIntosh left office in 1983 the lieutenant governor's role in public life had stabilized and even regained momentum.

Trudeau's fourth vice-regal appointee was to build on this momentum. Frederick W. Johnson was the archetype of the respected citizen: war veteran, former teacher, school trustee and superior court judge, he was at the time of his appointment Chief Justice of the Court of Queen's Bench. His attempts to run for the Liberals federally and provincially had receded into the past. Johnson's appointment emerged only after internecine squabbling in the provincial Liberal establishment over potential candidates. The rumours exasperated Johnson to the point where he considered turning down the appointment if it was offered.[17] But it *was* offered, and Johnson accepted. During the Conservative government of Grant Devine he was to inaugurate a veritable renaissance of vice-regal prestige in the province.

The only Saskatchewan vice-regal appointment by Progressive Conservative Prime Minister Brian Mulroney was that of Johnson's successor in 1988. As in 1983 among local Liberals, there was manoeuvring among Saskatchewan Conservatives for the job. However, Mulroney chose to appoint as the first woman lieutenant governor a non-partisan academic, Sylvia Fedoruk, who had just retired from a distinguished career in cancer research at the University of Saskatchewan. For this appointment Mulroney very likely accepted the advice of Saskatoon cabinet minister Ray Hnatyshyn, later to become governor general, who was an admirer of his fellow Ukrainian-Canadian. Fedoruk was a popular lieutenant governor. While she had no political experience, she quickly learned the ropes and, as we shall see, proved to be an asset to governance in the province.

Grant Devine's nine years as Progressive Conservative premier (1982–91) overlapped with the terms of Lieutenant Governors McIntosh, Johnson and Fedoruk. In 1983 he received a telephone call from Prime Minister Pierre Trudeau asking for his comments on the proposed appointment of Frederick Johnson, a choice which Devine welcomed. He did not recall a similar approach by Prime Minister Mulroney in 1988; instead, the Prime Minister's Office called him to inform him of the selection of Sylvia Fedoruk. Again, however, Devine was pleased with the choice.[18]

Roy Romanow was NDP premier at the time of the appointments of Jack Wiebe in 1994 and Lynda Haverstock in 1999. In both cases Liberal Prime Minister Jean Chrétien "consulted" him, in the sense of telling him the name of the person he proposed to appoint and giving him an opportunity for input. Romanow was satisfied with both.[19] Jack Wiebe's was the easier one. Although he once been a Liberal MLA and continued to be active in the Liberal Party, he had been out of electoral politics for some time. A popular farmer from the Swift Current area, Wiebe was well liked by people of all political persuasions.[20]

Lynda Haverstock, on the other hand, still had political baggage. She had become provincial Liberal leader in 1989, the first woman to head a political party in Saskatchewan. After her election to the legislature in 1991 she led the party from one MLA to eleven in 1995, when the notoriously fractious Saskatchewan Liberals ousted her in a caucus revolt. She served as an independent member of the Assembly until retiring in the 1999 election. There was some concern on the part of both Chrétien and Romanow that Haverstock had not been out of partisan politics long enough. However, Chrétien believed, and Romanow knew Haverstock well enough to agree, that her exceptional skills and intelligence would soon enable her to overcome this drawback. This is exactly what happened. A university teacher, clinical psychologist and expert on farm stress, Dr. Haverstock was energetic, persuasive, even inspiring in her public role. By the end of her six-and-a-half years in office she was acclaimed as one of the best lieutenant governors in recent memory.

In 2006, Romanow's successor as premier, Lorne Calvert, experienced a different form of consultation with Conservative Prime Minister Stephen Harper. It was Harper's first vice-regal appointment after the election of his minority government that year. The Prime Minister telephoned Calvert and asked for his assessment of half-a-dozen names from a variety of backgrounds. Harper wanted to maintain the Saskatchewan tradition of non-political appointments; he was also of the view that appointees should be at the end of their careers, thus avoiding the problem of what younger incumbents such as Lynda Haverstock could do after leaving office. The Prime Minister eventually called Calvert to let him know about the appointment of Gordon Barnhart as lieutenant governor. This was a pleasant surprise to Calvert, as Dr. Barnhart had not been on the original list.[21]

It was a solid appointment. Originally from the town of Saltcoats in eastern Saskatchewan, Gordon Barnhart had been Clerk of the Legislature for twenty years, from 1969 to 1989. After five years as Clerk of the Senate in Ottawa, he returned to his home province to teach history at the University of Saskatchewan and turned his 1998 PhD thesis on Saskatchewan's first premier into a definitive biography of Walter Scott.[22] Barnhart filled Harper's two criteria: he was at the end of his career, having retired from the university in 2005; and he was rigorously non-partisan, to the point that, as Clerk of the

Legislative Assembly, he had refused to vote in elections.[23] He was also an acknowledged authority on parliamentary government and an international consultant on democratic institutions, which would be an asset in the vice-regal constitutional role.

POLITICS AND THE CONSTITUTION

ROYAL ASSENT

The most frequently used vice-regal powers, signing government orders-in-council and giving royal assent to legislation, are hardly ever contentious. Although lieutenant governors did refuse royal assent to a number of bills between 1870 and 1945 (assent has never been refused by a Canadian governor general),[24] the practice was considered obsolete after that and never occurred in Saskatchewan. The reservation of royal assent for the governor general was also considered an obsolete reserve power. Then, in 1961, Saskatchewan Lieutenant Governor Frank Bastedo stunned the nation by reserving royal assent to a bill, the first time this had happened in Canada since 1937, in Alberta.[25] It was the only use of the power of reservation in Saskatchewan and the last in the country. The exercise of this prerogative by Bastedo was therefore an aberration and roundly denounced as such. As noted elsewhere by the author,[26]

> The Bastedo incident had two consequences. Constitutionally, it confirmed that the power of reservation in Canada was indeed obsolete and would not be used again. [...] In terms of the perception of the vice-regal office in Saskatchewan, the incident cast a chill on relations between the lieutenant governor and the CCF/NDP which lasted two decades. [...] According to Allan Blakeney, in 1961 the CCF cabinet was apprehensive that Bastedo, given his exaggerated opinion of his vice-regal powers, might go so far as to dismiss their administration.[27]

Indeed, during the crisis over medicare in 1962, Premier Woodrow Lloyd, on receiving a telephone inquiry at home about the situation from Bastedo, feared the worst.[28]

DISSOLUTION AND DISMISSAL

What vice-regal power could cause such concern? We have already noted that both the statutory and the prerogative powers of the Crown are almost always exercised "on advice" of the first minister and cabinet. The catch is "almost," for there are vaguely-defined cases where the vice-regal incumbent may exercise his or her own discretion, using the "reserve" powers. Dismissal of the government is one such power; refusal of dissolution of Parliament or the Legislature to the first minister is another. Both prerogatives were used in Canadian provinces only a very few times and in the early years of confederation.[29] Thus, if Bastedo had actually attempted to dismiss the government, there would have been a major constitutional crisis.

The power of *dismissal* has been used once in modern times in Australia, where in 1975 Governor General Sir John Kerr dismissed the Labor government of Prime Minister Gough Whitlam to overcome a deadlock over supply between the two houses of Parliament. Opinions have been expressed vigorously for and against this action.[30] What is undoubted is that the dismissal was highly unusual and very controversial.

The power of *dissolution* was invoked once in Ottawa, in 1926. Soon after an election Governor General Lord Byng refused a dissolution of Parliament to Prime Minister Mackenzie King, which King had requested in order to avoid a confidence vote he expected to lose. Instead Byng invited the Leader of the Opposition, Arthur Meighen, to form a government. Although constitutional experts concluded that Byng was justified,[31] politically the Governor General was the loser when Meighen's government promptly fell and King's Liberal party was returned in the ensuing election. Yet the "King-Byng" episode does indicate a potential use of vice-regal discretion in a minority government situation.

For it is indisputable that the governor general or lieutenant governor exercises the royal prerogative of calling on someone to become first minister and form a government. Normally this person is the leader of the party with a majority of seats. If, however, like Mackenzie King's Liberals in 1926, no one party secures a majority in the election, other options come into play. The practice is that, again like King's Liberals, the existing government is entitled to meet the House and seek its confidence. This is what happened in Saskatchewan after the 1929 election when Premier James Gardiner's Liberals were reduced to a minority and were immediately defeated in the Legislature. Lieutenant Governor Henry Newlands then called on the opposition leader, Dr. J.T.M. Anderson, to form a government from a coalition of Conservatives, Progressives and Independents, which, unlike Meighen's, survived for five years. There was a similar case in Ontario in 1985 when the Progressive Conservatives, in a minority after an election, were defeated in the Legislature and the lieutenant governor invited the Liberal leader to form a government with the support of the New Democratic Party members. This example was followed four years later in the Australian state of Tasmania.[32]

In neither case did the lieutenant governor have to override "advice" to dissolve the legislature, as had Governor General Byng. It is nonetheless conceivable that such a situation might arise. Minority governments have become more frequent in Canada: in Ottawa in 2004 and 2006, in Quebec in 2007, previously in Saskatchewan, Manitoba and Nova Scotia. In a minority situation a vice-regal person might soon after an election, decide to refuse dissolution to the first minister and ask another person to attempt to pull together a government. If proportional representation is ever introduced into the electoral system, minority governments will occur more often. The New Zealand adoption of multi-member proportional representation in 1995 has in fact resulted in more "hung parliaments" and focused attention on the role of the governor general in that country.[33] Even in the present system, the unusual granting of dissolution and then prorogation by Governor General Michaëlle Jean to Prime Minister Stephen Harper's minority government in 2008 placed the vice-regal representative in the spotlight.

When Roy Romanow's New Democrats were in a minority after the 1999 Saskatchewan election, Lieutenant Governor Jack Wiebe did not have to face this prospect, since the NDP formed a coalition with the Liberals. It must have been a relief for him, given the constitutional issues his two immediate predecessors had to deal with.

A CONSTITUTIONAL CONUNDRUM: SPECIAL WARRANTS

One of the statutory powers of the lieutenant governor is to authorize "special warrants," approving government expenditure outside the normal budgetary process.[34] Usually this is done near the end of the fiscal year when the legislature is not in session, to cover any shortfall between actual expenditure and the estimates, and is then retroactively approved by the Assembly. But in 1987 the Progressive Conservative government of Premier Grant Devine did not recall the legislature in the early spring as was the custom, nor did it introduce a budget. Instead it asked the Lieutenant Governor Frederick Johnson to sign a series of special warrants. This flaunted parliamentary convention and was close to the borderline of unconstitutional behaviour. It was not quite close enough for Johnson to intervene, but he apparently warned the premier the situation could not continue indefinitely.[35] Eventually the government did recall the legislature to pass a budget.

Four years later, in 1991, near the end of its legal five-year mandate, the same government tried a similar tactic. In order to avoid a non-confidence vote it anticipated losing, it abruptly prorogued the legislature without passing the budget and again operated through special warrants. Lieutenant Governor Sylvia Fedoruk was in an extremely difficult situation. She could have refused prorogation of the Assembly, but that would have been a highly controversial use of the reserve power. Or she could have refused to sign the special warrants; but that would have brought public administration grinding to a halt. However, she knew that the government would have to call an election within months. It is believed she told the premier that if he didn't call the election very soon she would.[36] He did—and he lost.

In November 1991 Roy Romanow's NDP government inherited the problem. What were they to do so late in the fiscal year? Continue until the next spring with special warrants? Fedoruk asked to meet with the new premier and told him she had constitutional concerns about the use of special warrants, to the extent that she had consulted the provincial and federal justice departments. She made it clear that she did not wish a budget to be postponed to the following spring. Romanow accepted her advice: his government convened the legislature and passed Devine's suspended budget intact.[37]

The result of the special warrant saga appears to be that the lieutenant governor does have the power to refuse his or her signature *in extremis*, but is more likely to use confidential persuasion to protect the constitutional order.[38]

TO BE CONSULTED, TO ENCOURAGE AND TO WARN

On taking office, Roy Romanow had assumed that regular meetings with the lieutenant governor were part of his obligations as premier—unaware that this had not been the previous practice. Then Sylvia Fedoruk asked to see him to discuss special warrants. "It was an issue," said Romanow, "which propelled us together."[39] The issue cemented the relationship between lieutenant governor and premier and regular meetings became the norm.

The 19th-century British expert on the constitution, Walter Bagehot, stated in a now-classic aphorism that the Sovereign retained three rights in a constitutional monarchy: "the right to be consulted, the right to encourage, the right to warn." In the United Kingdom the Queen exercises these rights by meeting weekly and privately with the prime minister—an opportunity greatly valued by British first ministers.[40] The governor general of Australia meets approximately monthly with the prime minister.[41] In Canada the governor general met regularly, even weekly, with prime ministers until the 1980s.[42] This pattern began unravelling when Brian Mulroney was prime minister. From 2006, when Stephen Harper was in that position and Michaëlle Jean was governor general, it had virtually ended.

Practice in the Canadian provinces, as in the Australian states, varies. In Nova Scotia the premier meets every two months with the lieutenant governor. In Prince Edward Island the two meet quarterly. By contrast, in Manitoba the lieutenant governor and the premier have not had meetings since the 1960s.[43] A similar disconnect between premier and lieutenant governor prevailed in Saskatchewan until the 1980s, due in large part to the perceived partisan nature of the vice-regal appointments and latterly the hostility of the CCF-NDP to the office. Even Allan Blakeney, premier from 1971 to 1982, favourable as he was to the institution, did not have meetings with his three lieutenant governors.[44]

While his Progressive Conservative successor, Grant Devine, did not schedule regular appointments as Romanow was to do, he met often with the three lieutenant governors under whom he served. He always found these meetings helpful. The lieutenant governor was, he said, like a "travelling representative sponge," absorbing the nuances of public opinion. Devine recalled three critical moments when he especially valued his private discussions with the lieutenant governor: the interest rate crisis in 1982–83 with Irwin McIntosh, the prairie drought in 1988 with Frederick Johnson, and the provincial deficit at the end of the decade with Sylvia Fedoruk. For Devine, all three served as a "great sounding board" for the premier. They were people of integrity, discreet, confidential, comfortable in their position. Devine recommended that all premiers take advantage of the lieutenant governor's role. "There is," he said, "no downside."[45]

In making these meetings systematic from 1992, Roy Romanow was to find them even more helpful than he had expected. The 1992–94 period was a difficult one for the NDP government as it pulled the province back from the verge of bankruptcy. Due to the severe fiscal measures that had to be taken, support for the government in the caucus and party was dropping, as was public confidence. In those critical days, says Romanow, Lieutenant Governor Sylvia Fedoruk was "very insightful and wonderfully intelligent. I needed somebody completely removed from the situation and I could tell her point-blank in confidence what I felt."

Frustration within the NDP came to a head during the preparation of the 1994 budget. There was an impasse in caucus and Romanow realized to his consternation that he did not have a consensus to present a budget to the legislature. At this point he told the caucus that the province deserved a government which could put together a responsible budget. Going from the caucus meeting to Government House to see Fedoruk, he explained his dilemma to the lieutenant governor and told her he was considering advising her to call an election on the issue of putting the public finances in order. In their discussion Fedoruk put a number of questions to him about the consequences of such a drastic action. For Roy Romanow this was a "seminal moment" in his appreciation for the vice-regal office. "If there had not been a lieutenant governor," he said, "emotion might have got the better of my reason."[46] In the end he returned to his caucus and the issue was resolved.

Roy Romanow's relationship with Jack Wiebe was especially warm, going back many years to when Wiebe was a rural Liberal MLA. Jack Wiebe had astute political insights and knew the municipal sphere, an important asset at a time when the NDP was reforming health care and wanted to reform rural government. Lynda Haverstock, installed early in 2000, was lieutenant governor for only a year of Romanow's time as premier and by then Romanow himself had been on the job for eight years. Still, he greatly valued his monthly meetings with Haverstock given her own political experience, which was to benefit Romanow's successor, Lorne Calvert.

The lieutenant governors, in Romanow's view, all gave solid, honest, helpful advice in the best interest of the province. They had "no axe to grind, no election to be concerned about, no hidden agenda." They filled the role of a "house of sober second thought" and served as a steadying hand for a person pulling together a cabinet. Romanow gave them the fullest picture possible of legislation, budgets and major issues. He saw three consistent characteristics in his three lieutenant governors: they were committed to the province and the public good; they had external qualifications, including intellect; and they were keen on strengthening the vice-regal office through their relationship with the premier.[47]

Premier Lorne Calvert came to treasure his meetings with Lieutenant Governor Lynda Haverstock, which took place approximately every six weeks. Her office was, he said, the one room in the province where a premier could speak freely in absolute confidence. As Roy Romanow had found with Jack Wiebe, it was helpful that she had political experience, including that of being a party leader. "I would seek her counsel on public policy issues because she had that experience. I could even talk to her about the cabinet!" Given her public contacts she would bring 'case work' to the meetings, matters she could not raise publicly but could in confidence. The relationship with the lieutenant governor was a "refreshing surprise" to Calvert. "We worked as a team," he said, "for example on the provincial centennial and on the bid for holding the Juno Awards in Saskatchewan." Calvert continued the practice of regular meetings with Haverstock's successor Gordon Barnhart. Echoing Grant Devine, he said, "I would recommend this practice to all my colleagues." Calvert also saw the role of the lieutenant governor as helping reduce the "erosion of the parliamentary system"—an interesting comment on the place of the Crown as constitutional guarantor in parliamentary democracy.[48]

When Brad Wall was first elected to the Legislature in 1999 for the fledgling Saskatchewan Party, he had admittedly been a sceptic about the Crown. However, when Lieutenant Governor Jack Wiebe spoke to the new MLAs about the role of the vice-regal office during their orientation, he changed Wall's view on the institution. By the time Wall took office as premier in November 2007 he needed no further convincing. His first meeting with the Lieutenant Governor Barnhart, when he was formally asked by the Queen's representative to form a government, was, he recalled, a "surreal event" which underscored for him the intrinsic value of constitutional monarchy.

Premier Wall had no hesitation in continuing the practice of regular meetings with the lieutenant governor. "I have found my meetings [with Dr. Barnhart] to be invaluable. In the greatest of confidence we can talk about anything and everything," Wall said after four months in office. He learned much from Barnhart, given his experience as parliamentary clerk, historian and author. The new Premier took "solace and counsel" from the meetings. He considered that Bagehot's three "rights" were genuinely achieved by Gordon Barnhart, "without any pretence, in no way interfering with the democratic system, and by only doing what was proper."[49]

THE DECORATIVE FUNCTIONS OF THE CROWN

Walter Bagehot placed much emphasis on what he called the "dignified" aspect of the constitution, represented by the monarchy, as distinct from the "efficient" or practical side fulfilled by the elected government. The view of some Canadian scholars is similar. "The Crown," wrote Frank MacKinnon, "acts as the repository for the decorative and emotional functions which are inevitable in any state."[50] He went on to say that "the duties of the Queen, Governor General, and Lieutenant-Governors include the decorative functions to facilitate the conduct of public business."[51]

However, David Smith cautions that there is a need to "reclaim the institution of the Crown from Bagehot's dignified limbo [...] the Crown and its prerogatives empower the political executive and make it efficient in the very sense Bagehot intended when he used that term to describe the non-dignified elements of the constitution: that is to produce an effect."[52] "The Crown," he concludes, "is dignified *and* efficient."[53]

With this caveat, that the dignified and efficient functions are two sides of the same monarchical coin, it is of interest to see how the decorative role of the Crown played out in Saskatchewan after 1970.

STATE CEREMONIAL AND SYMBOLS

The ceremonial aspect of the Crown, the "pomp and circumstance" at which the British monarchy excels, has its Canadian counterpart not only in visits of the Royal Family but in the public profile of the governor general and lieutenant governors. Examples are the opening of Parliament or Legislature, provincial visits of the governor general, vice-regal installations, presentations of honours, Remembrance Day ceremonies and state funerals. Uniforms, music, guards of honour, gun salutes, parades, flags and other décor form part of the ambiance of what, using a religious analogy, can loosely be called "civil liturgy."

In the Canada of the 1960s and 1970s civil liturgy was on the decline as a more casual, egalitarian society emerged. Nowhere was this more evident than in Saskatchewan, where the trend was exacerbated by the official coolness to the vice-regal office. Lieutenant Governor Frank Bastedo, he who revived the obsolete power of reservation of royal assent, also attempted to restore the ceremonial formality of his office, for example by riding in the historic horse-drawn landau at the opening of the legislature. Any initiative by Bastedo, however, was discredited by the 1961 reservation controversy and after he left office the decorative functions of the Crown dwindled away.

By the time Irwin McIntosh took office in 1978 the "dignified" role of the lieutenant governor was a shadow of its former self. Gone were the landau and military guard of honour at the opening of the legislature - McIntosh arrived at the Legislative Building virtually unnoticed to deliver the Speech from the Throne. The swearing-in of new lieutenant governors took place with little publicity in a perfunctory ceremony in the Legislative Library. The NDP government grudgingly provided the ceremonial minimum for an institution with which it had to co-exist but barely tolerated.

With the province's 75th anniversary celebrations in 1980 came a shift in the attitude towards the vice-regal office. That year the landau and guard of honour were restored for the Opening of the Legislature, and historic Government House, the former vice-regal residence, was restored as a museum. In 1981 Premier Blakeney presided at the inauguration of the lieutenant governor's flag; until then Saskatchewan had been the only Canadian jurisdiction without a vice-regal standard. In 1982 Blakeney, for the first time, personally met with the Lieutenant Governor to request the writ for the election of that year. In 1983 Premier Grant Devine's Progressive Conservative government staged the first public, televised swearing-in of a lieutenant governor for Frederick Johnson in the Legislative Chamber—a pattern to be followed for his successors. The following year Devine returned the vice-regal office to Government House.

In 1985, Devine's government launched a provincial honours program in which the lieutenant governor played a key role. In 1986 the Conservative government secured a provincial coat of arms from the Queen, replacing for formal purposes the bland wheat sheaf logo which Blakeney's government had introduced in 1977 to pre-empt the traditional shield of arms dating from 1906.

At the installation of his government in 1991 Roy Romanow inaugurated a new Great Seal bearing the coat of arms. Romanow soon began the practice of swearing in new cabinet ministers at Government House.

His successor Lorne Calvert saw to it that Saskatchewan was the first juris-diction in Canada to plan celebrations for the Queen's Golden Jubilee in 2002—the 50th anniversary of the reign of Queen Elizabeth II. Calvert's gov-ernment co-sponsored a bronze equestrian statue of the Queen, which the Sovereign unveiled in front of the Legislative Building during her visit for the provincial centennial in 2005. As a sequel to 1980, the showcase "built legacy" of the centennial was a major addition to Government House Heritage Property, also opened by the Queen in 2005. In 2007 Brad Wall's Saskatchewan Party government was sworn in by Lieutenant Governor Gordon Barnhart at Government House, the first time for a new administration. In 2008, Wall made a small but symbolic change: henceforth the Clerk of the Executive Council personally brought orders-in-council to Government House for signa-ture instead of sending them by messenger—and briefed the lieutenant gov-ernor on their content.[54]

This litany of changes may appear to be one of form rather than content, of detail rather than substantive policy. However, it represented a consistent approach to the Crown over thirty years by five successive premiers from three different political parties. In conjunction with six lieutenant governors they cumulatively raised the Saskatchewan vice-regal office from the weakest in the country to one of the strongest.

UPS AND DOWNS: THE STORY OF GOVERNMENT HOUSE[55]

The most obvious physical presence of the Crown in Saskatchewan is Government House in Regina. Built in 1891 as the residence and office of the lieutenant governors of the Northwest Territories, this substantial mansion was designed by Thomas Fuller, architect of the Parliament Buildings in Ottawa, to be an imposing symbol of national and imperial rule over the vast Canadian western plains and northern territories. At the height of the territo-rial empire, two-thirds of present-day Canada was administered from Government House—all of Saskatchewan and Alberta, much of northern Manitoba, Ontario and Quebec, the Northwest Territories, Nunavut and, until 1898, Yukon.

When Saskatchewan became a province in 1905 it inherited Government House. For 40 more years Government House and its ample grounds served as a social hub for Regina society and the Saskatchewan political class. However, with the Second World War came major changes, social, economic—and polit-ical. The CCF, born of the Depression, swept into office in 1944. Sceptical of the vice-regal office, the government of Premier T.C. Douglas decided to close Government House as an unwanted symbol and unnecessary expense and in 1945 most of its furnishings were sold by auction at bargain-basement prices.[56] For the next four decades the lieutenant governors functioned out of a small suite in the Hotel Saskatchewan in Regina, the smallest, cheapest vice-regal operation in the country. Visiting diplomats could not help noting the contrast with the other provinces. It did nothing to help Saskatchewan's image in the protocol-sensitive sphere of international relations.

Meanwhile Government House lurched through several crises. From 1946 to 1957 it was leased to the federal government as a veterans' rehabilitation centre. In 1958 the provincial government resumed operation of the facility under the name "Saskatchewan House" as a centre for continuous learning. Demolition of the building was seriously considered in the late 1960s under Ross Thatcher's Liberal government, but was forestalled thanks to the efforts of a citizens' coalition which eventually became the Government House Historical Society. Then the NDP government of Allan Blakeney decided to restore the building for the province's 75th anniversary in 1980 as a historic property and museum, although not for the offices of the lieutenant governor.

It was left to Allan Blakeney's successor, Grant Devine, to take the next, logical step. Encouraged by his wife Chantal, and by their joint friendship with Lieutenant Governor Johnson and his wife Joyce, Devine directed that the north wing of Government House be converted into a suite of offices for the lieutenant governor. The new office was inaugurated on Canada Day, July 1, 1984. Vice-regal ceremonies and entertainment resumed in their historic venue, including a revival of the traditional New Year's Day levee.

Then negative officialdom reared its head. The provincial heritage staff responsible for operating Government House resented the return of the lieutenant governor's offices. Friction between the two occupants grew, the situation exacerbated by inadequate funding for maintenance and museum programming. In 1991, ironically marking the centennial of the historic property, Devine's administration proposed to "privatize" the House by transferring it to the Government House Historical Society, a task well beyond the capabilities of the volunteer group. Then the House was, again, rescued by a newly-elected NDP government.

Soon after assuming office late in 1991, Roy Romanow, picking up on the legacy of Allan Blakeney, made it clear that Government House Heritage Property was a prized public asset and that he would not countenance its privatization. Instead, Romanow created a management committee of stakeholders to advise the government on a long-term strategy for the facility.[57] While progress was made, it became increasingly evident that the heritage and vice-regal tenants were incompatible.[58] In 1996 matters came to ahead when Lieutenant Governor Jack Wiebe submitted a proposal to Premier Romanow for further development of Government House, including an interpretive centre. Hostile heritage officials lobbied against Wiebe, leaked his proposal, and tried to rally outside support. This time Romanow had had enough. In 1998 his government transferred responsibility for the House to the Office of Provincial Secretary, the agency already looking after the lieutenant governor's office, protocol and honours.[59] This was to mark another, major turning point in the history of Government House.

The new administration tackled the long-neglected task of obtaining adequate operating funding for the heritage property. More significantly, responding to Premier Romanow's earlier call for a long-range vision, it commissioned a study on the future of Government House. A consultant's report in 2000 identified considerable potential for expanded tourism, school programs, government functions and vice-regal activities, and recommended construction of new facilities for administrative offices, a coach house, a gift shop and an interpretive centre. It also recommended creating a Crown foundation to raise some of the funding from the non-governmental sector, on the understanding that the federal and provincial governments would contribute the balance.

The government of Premier Lorne Calvert approved the proposal. A Government House Foundation was established and architects were hired to design an addition to the original building. In 2004 the Princess Royal (the Queen's daughter, Princess Anne) laid the cornerstone for the new Queen Elizabeth II Wing of Government House and by the end of the year the addition was complete, incorporating offices, an elegant hall named after Lieutenant Governor Sir Richard Lake, and a coach house for the landau. Above the 1928 ballroom was installed the J.E.N. Wiebe interpretive centre on the Crown, the only one of its kind in the country and named in tribute to the lieutenant governor who had contributed the idea. The original building was designated the Queen Victoria Wing and other facilities were named after former lieutenant governors, emphasizing the links to Saskatchewan's vice-regal history. In 2005, during her visit for the provincial centennial, an evidently pleased Queen Elizabeth II officially opened the wing named in her honour as well as the interpretive centre. In 2008 the government of Premier Brad Wall announced that the Edwardian gardens of 1906 would be restored, thus completing the initial centennial project, and Lieutenant Governor Gordon Barnhart instituted a Canada Day garden party in the grounds.

The number of visitors, school groups, government functions, conferences and vice-regal events substantially increased, vindicating the consultant's predictions. Thus, 60 years after its humiliation, 40 years after its near-death, and a quarter-century after its rescue and restoration, Government House, reborn and renewed, realized its potential. So in a sense had those for whom it was built in 1891: the lieutenant governors.

HONOURS OF THE CROWN

One of the symbolic acts accomplished by Queen Elizabeth during her 2005 visit to Government House was her signature of approval on the emblems of three Saskatchewan honours of the Crown. It capped a 20-year evolution in formal provincial recognition of deserving citizens.

In 1967, marking the centennial of Confederation, the Canadian government launched a national honours program with the Order of Canada. This was later expanded into a comprehensive system of orders, decorations and medals.[60] The Canadian provinces, however, were excluded from consultation and participation in the program, apart from occasional presentations of medals by lieutenant governors. This was in contrast with Australia, where the states and their governors were directly involved in national honours from their introduction in 1975—once again, the Australians had learned from the Canadian experience and decided to do things differently.[61]

Given the dynamics of Canadian federalism, it was not surprising that all ten provinces eventually entered the field of honours.[62] For Saskatchewan, the 75th anniversary in 1980 proved to be the key moment, as it had been for Government House. With the support of then intergovernmental affairs minister Roy Romanow, a study of honours and awards was undertaken. Its conclusion was that Canadian provinces had the right to create honours and that Saskatchewan should do so. Significantly, the study recommended that these be honours of the provincial Crown, bestowed by the lieutenant governor. The report was adopted in principle by Allan Blakeney's government and implemented in 1985 by Grant Devine's Conservative government with the creation of the Saskatchewan Order of Merit.[63]

In its first decade the Saskatchewan Order of Merit had indubitable success in recognizing outstanding people such as former premier Tommy Douglas, Aboriginal painter Allen Sapp, cancer researcher and later lieutenant governor Sylvia Fedoruk, historian Dr. John Archer, businessman George Morris, poet Anne Szumigalski, former lieutenant governor Frederick Johnson, First Nations Chief Samuel Bunnie and medical researcher Dr. Ali Rajput. Roy Romanow's NDP government added the Saskatchewan Volunteer Medal in 1995 as a decoration to recognize the province's crucial volunteer sector. In 2003 the government of Lorne Calvert announced two further honours: the Saskatchewan Protective Services Medal, awarded for 25 years of exemplary service to police, firefighters, emergency medical personnel, corrections workers, Canadian Forces members and others; and the Saskatchewan Centennial Medal, which was presented in 2005 and 2006 to 4,200 recipients.

Two factors characterized the provincial honours system. One was the symbolism of the Crown as a non-partisan source of recognition, distinct from the political programs of the elected government. Successive premiers firmly supported this policy, first, through the selection of recipients by an arms-length Saskatchewan Honours Advisory Council chaired by a distinguished citizen,[64] a practice started for the Order of Canada and followed by all Canadian provinces; second, by separating government awards from honours of the Crown[65]; and third, by providing for the lieutenant governor to confer the honours, a practice followed by all Canadian jurisdictions except Quebec.

The other factor was the coolness of official Ottawa, led by the governor general's office at Rideau Hall. Following the exclusion of the provinces from the national system, the federal government refused to recognize the legitimacy of provincial honours and discouraged provinces, including Saskatchewan, from establishing them. The provinces ignored Ottawa's objections, but were faced with an awkward situation where recipients of their honours could not wear their medals with those of national honours. The situation was partially resolved in 1991, when Ottawa granted official status to provincial orders, and further in 1998 when this recognition was extended to some other honours such as the Saskatchewan Volunteer Medal. In 2005 similar recognition was granted to the Saskatchewan and Alberta Centennial Medals. It was refused, however, for the Saskatchewan Protective Services Medal, on the grounds that it duplicated equivalent federal awards. This was why, in her 2005 visit to Government House, the Queen could approve the insignia of only three of the four Saskatchewan honours of the Crown.

PUBLIC INITIATIVES AND CIVIL SOCIETY

By definition, constitutional monarchs and their representatives do not play a direct role in public policy. This is the purview of their "advisors," the first ministers and cabinets. However, by what they say and do, monarchs and governors can exercise influence well beyond their closed-door meetings with prime ministers and premiers. In Saskatchewan, as the vice-regal office recovered from its low point in the 1960s, so did its influence.

PUBLIC INITIATIVES

The process did not start well. In 1978, newly appointed Lieutenant Governor Irwin McIntosh publicly expressed support for capital punishment; Premier Allan Blakeney admonished the lieutenant governor for taking a public stand on a controversial issue. But, as we have already noted, McIntosh quickly redeemed himself through his firm support for the national unity initiative in which Blakeney was a leader, following the 1977 election victory of the separatist Parti Québécois government in Quebec. The lieutenant governor also worked tirelessly to promote the province's 75th anniversary celebrations in 1980, which were a successful public relations coup for the NDP government. McIntosh sketched out a more active role for the vice-regal office, as long as the incumbent did not stray into contentious matters.

Frederick Johnson concentrated his efforts on the return of the vice-regal office to Government House, the provincial honours system, and otherwise strengthening the Crown in the province. His successor, Sylvia Fedoruk, began a practice of touring schools and First Nations communities in northern Saskatchewan each autumn. Supported by the provincial education department, the lieutenant governor presented awards to leading, mostly Aboriginal, high school students in a move to promote role models and reward academic success. It was entirely consonant with the government's emerging focus on Aboriginal social and economic development as the First Nations and Métis grew in population and profile. Like Johnson, Jack Wiebe focused on reinforcing the role of the Lieutenant Governor. He contributed to the renewal of the administration of Government House, supported the expansion of the provincial honours system, and persuaded Premier Romanow that the government should produce an educational video on the Crown.[66]

It was Lynda Haverstock who developed the lieutenant governor's influence into a fine art. Like her federal counterpart, Governor General Adrienne Clarkson (1999–2005), she moved vice-regal speech-making from traditionally cautious, feel-good bromides into substantive commentaries on social, cultural and economic issues of the day, while carefully avoiding any hint of

partisan politics. Lynda Haverstock's impact was especially felt in the Saskatchewan centennial, celebrated in 2005. She gave of herself tirelessly to the
Centennial Medal program, personally presenting the vast majority of the
4,200 medals at 80 events around the province in 2005–06, impressing thousands of people with her charisma. As patron of the Government House
Foundation she backed the fund-raising campaign which eventually raised
more than $2 million, a third of the cost of the centennial project. When
provincial and federal heritage officials tried to block the design for the Queen
Elizabeth II Wing, the lieutenant governor convened a meeting of parties to
the project and knocked heads together until a compromise was reached.

She closely followed the development of the Queen's Golden Jubilee statue, a bronze sculpture portraying Queen Elizabeth II on her favourite horse,
Burmese, born and raised in Saskatchewan for the RCMP Musical Ride and
given to the Queen in 1969. Haverstock played a key role with the committee
which oversaw both the artistic side of the project and public fund-raising,
and she helped overcome the resistance of government officials who wanted
the statue relegated to an obscure location. In 2005 the Queen, obviously
delighted, unveiled the statue in the Queen Elizabeth II Gardens directly in
front of the Legislative Building. It immediately became a much-pho-
tographed artistic and tourist attraction.

Lynda Haverstock's influence on the centennial did not stop there. She
organized a program for recognition of volunteers in the arts. She also personally conceived and brought to fruition one of the most spectacular events of
the year: a Centennial Gala of the Arts. The Lieutenant Governor convened a
blue-ribbon committee to raise funds and by sheer persistence overcame the
scepticism of officials in Lorne Calvert's government. Televised live nationally by the CBC from Saskatoon, the lavish production brought together per-
formers like Buffy Sainte-Marie, Joni Mitchell, Gordon Tootoosis, Brent Butt
and the Amati String Quartet. Leading the more than 9,000 spectators were
none other than Queen Elizabeth and Prince Philip. The gala sent reverbera-
tions across a Canada accustomed to considering Saskatchewan as a cultural
backwater.

PROMOTING CIVIL SOCIETY

Lynda Haverstock also extended the lieutenant governor's reach into "civil
society," a term used to describe the intricate web of non-governmental organizations and worthy causes. As we have seen, Sylvia Fedoruk had emphasized
outreach to Aboriginal people and northern Saskatchewan. The First Nations
were undergoing rapid change as their population grew and they sought to
overcome endemic poverty, discrimination and lack of education. "Indians"
had been traditionally regarded as wards of the federal government, which
indeed they were as long as most resided on reserves. But as more and more
First Nations people moved off reserve, the balance shifted: provincial and
municipal involvement increased and the lieutenant governors devoted much
attention to Indian and Métis people and communities. The vice-regal affinity
for the First Nations derived from their traditionally close relationship with

the Crown dating back to the 19th-century treaties with Queen Victoria. Although this relationship was primarily with the monarch and with the federal Crown represented by the governor general, the lieutenant governors began playing a more prominent role.

Lynda Haverstock made it a priority to attend treaty days in First Nations reserves. Like her Ontario counterpart,[67] she focused on the north of the province. Noticing the large number of stray dogs in Aboriginal communities, she organized a spay-neutering program across the north, obtaining *pro bono* veterinary services. This also helped her goals of promoting education for First Nations youth. Indeed, literacy and citizen recognition were among Haverstock's constant themes.[68]

Her successor, Gordon Barnhart, took up civil society issues immediately upon assuming office. In 2007 he launched his first major initiative, a Lieutenant Governor's Leadership Forum for youth. Gathering promising young people from across the province, half of them from northern Saskatchewan, the Forum introduced them to major figures in the public and private sectors. It was Barnhart's way of helping prepare the leadership of tomorrow.

ROYAL SASKATCHEWAN

The bond between the First Nations and the monarchy came to the fore whenever members of the Royal Family visited Saskatchewan.[69] A visit to Regina by the Queen and Prince Philip for the RCMP centennial in 1973 proved attractive enough to Allan Blakeney's NDP government that they invited the Royal Couple and their youngest son, Prince Edward, in 1978. The "royal visit business" blossomed in the 1980s as governments, whatever their political stripe, realized that members of the Royal Family were hard-working, consummate professionals, willing and able to lend credence to provincial policy objectives.

During the 75th anniversary year of 1980 the Queen's sister Princess Margaret was royal guest for the celebrations. Grant Devine's Conservative government was host for the Queen's daughter Princess Anne in 1982; Queen Elizabeth the Queen Mother in 1985; the Queen and the Duke of Edinburgh in 1987; and their second son, Prince Andrew, Duke of York, and the Duchess of York in 1989. While during the decade of the 1990s there was only one visit by a member of the Royal Family, a low-key "working visit" in 1994 by Prince Edward, it was to be very different in the first decade of the new millennium.

Lorne Calvert, taking over as premier in 2001, hosted that year the first visit of the Prince of Wales. Prince Charles charmed everyone with his self-deprecating sense of humour and his empathy for civil society causes: disadvantaged youth, the inner city, the First Nations, environment, health care, sustainable agriculture and the heritage movement.[70] Calvert quipped to hither to sceptical members of his cabinet that if the media-savvy Prince of Wales were in politics none of them would want to run against him.[71]

Other royal visits followed in quick succession. Prince Edward, now Earl of Wessex, came back in 2003 and 2006 and Princess Anne, now the Princess Royal, in 2004 and 2007. The centennial tour of the Queen and Duke of

Edinburgh in 2005 drew together all the strands of "royal Saskatchewan." Elizabeth II appeared to relish the position of "Queen of Canada," which had been promoted since her 1953 coronation to differentiate the Sovereign from her otherwise predominantly British role. It was essential if the monarchy was to survive in the bilingual, multicultural, multi-racial Canada of the second millennium.

CONCLUSION

There is a certain anomaly in a monarch domiciled in the United Kingdom acting as the formal Canadian head of state. From the 1960s Canada's "British" character rapidly declined as Quebec nationalism and multicultural immigration redefined the nation.[72] The federal government responded by de-emphasizing monarchical symbols.[73] David Smith observes that "Canadians have witnessed the separation of the person of the monarch from the concept of the Crown." On the other hand, he says, "the Crown is an integral part of a practical form of government."[74] Could one conceive then of a Crown without a monarch?

Under the guise of "canadianizing" the monarchy, the governor general's office emerged in as the principal foyer of a move to effectively "de-monarchize" Canada by, for example, referring to the governor general as head of state and banishing royal portraits from the governor general's official residence at Rideau Hall.[75] While this may not have played well in "outer Canada," it seemed to appeal to the political elite whose gaze focused on Ottawa and Quebec. According to an opinion poll taken in 2007, about half of Canadians favoured ending the monarchy - a similar ratio to polls a decade earlier, although the results were skewed by the much higher negative response from Quebec. A majority of Australians, but only about a quarter of New Zealanders, are of the same view, although the proportion rises in all three countries if the monarchy were to end following the present Queen's reign.[76]

And yet... Canada has been reluctant to tamper more than superficially with the monarchy and there has been little organized opposition to it.[77] This is in contrast with Australia, where a strong republican movement forced a referendum on the issue in 1999. The republican option was defeated by a substantial margin, due largely to the failure of its proponents to offer a credible replacement for the monarchy.[78] In the putative republic, how would the head of state be chosen—by direct election or by some form of appointment? Would that person hold the prerogatives now vested in the monarch's representative, including the reserve powers of dismissal and dissolution?

And what of the status of the Australian states[79]—and the Canadian provinces? Would their constitutionally guaranteed autonomy survive intact the disappearance of their own Crown with its supra-federal origin? It is no coincidence that the lieutenant governors of Saskatchewan have, like their counterparts in most other provinces, peppered their speeches with references to the Crown and asserted their status as the Queen's representative, at a time when Canadian governors general have avoided even mentioning the monarchy. And what about the increasingly influential and vocal First Nations, with their historic, emotional, deep-rooted loyalty to the Sovereign based on the treaty relationship?

Stephen Harper's Conservative government was at least aware of these factors, judging from positive references to the monarchy in Parliament and the invitation to the Queen to preside at the 90th anniversary of the battle of Vimy Ridge in France in 2007. While the federal bureaucracy and Rideau Hall continued their efforts to "de-monarchize" the country, in 2008 the Harper government produced an educational publication on the Crown[80]—something that had not been seen in Ottawa for decades, although it had been done by some provinces.[81]

Despite this national ambivalence, at the beginning of the 21st century Saskatchewan appeared to have resolved the issues of the Crown to its satisfaction. Two factors were key: appropriate vice-regal appointments from 1970 and the active support of the premiers. From 1980 the decorative functions of the Crown made a remarkable come-back. Saskatchewan governments supported the process in word and deed, not only giving prominence to Government House and royal visits, but producing educational material on the Crown at a time when Canadian schools were woefully lax in teaching Canadian history.[82]

Perhaps the most intriguing development was the realization that the Crown could, after all, be a useful element in governance. The vice-regal reserve or emergency powers may not have been wielded after the anachronistic reservation of royal assent in 1961. But the awareness of their potential after the special warrant issues of 1987 and 1991 was a healthy reminder that, as a British Columbia lieutenant governor said, "the lieutenant governor exists to deny the government absolute power."[83]

Saskatchewan premiers found that the most helpful role of the lieutenant governor was that of confidential sounding board - exercising the triple Bagehotian rights of consultation, warning and encouragement. Premiers Devine, Romanow, Calvert and Wall have shed some light on the exercise of these rights in their closed-door meetings with the lieutenant governors, but most of it will remain unknown beyond the two people in that room in Government House. And that is as it should be.

To again paraphrase David Smith, the Crown is invisible, yet a basic principle of Canadian government; it is dignified, but efficient. One might add that, in common with many Canadian institutions, the Crown survives through ambiguity. It adapts to its context, in a striking Australian image, like a chameleon.[84] Reverting to a musical simile, the Province of Saskatchewan has since 1970 orchestrated the subtle royal and vice-regal themes of the Canadian Crown like a maestro and with brio.

NOTES

The author wishes to thank the following for their co-operation in his research: Lieutenant Governor Gordon Barnhart and former Lieutenant Governor Lynda

Haverstock; Premier Brad Wall and former Premiers Allan Blakeney, Grant Devine, Roy Romanow and Lorne Calvert; and Dr. David E. Smith. Responsibility for the text is, of course, entirely the author's.

1. For an account of the vice-regal office in Saskatchewan, see D. Michael Jackson, "Political Paradox," in Howard A. Leeson (ed.), *Saskatchewan Politics: Into the Twenty-First Century* (Regina: Canadian Plains Research Center, University of Regina, 2001), 56–60.

2. David E. Smith, *The Invisible Crown: The First Principle of Canadian Government* (Toronto: University of Toronto Press, 1995).

3. Ibid., 176.

4. Ibid., xi.

5. Anne Twomey, *The Chameleon Crown: The Queen and Her Australian Governors* (Sydney: The Federation Press, 2006), 272.

6. Smith, *The Invisible Crown*, 179.

7. Peter Boyce, *The Queen's Other Realms: The Crown and Its Legacy in Australia, Canada and New Zealand* (Sydney: The Federation Press, 2008).

8. Smith, *The Invisible Crown*, 11. See also Dr. Smith's article "Empire, Crown and Federalism," in *Canadian Journal of Political Science* 24, no. 3 (September 1991): 451–73.

9. The Australian governors were directly appointed by the Sovereign on the advice of the British government from 1901 to 1986, when the Australia Acts provided for this advice to be given by the state premiers. For the complete story of the appointment process for the Australian governors, see Twomey, *The Chameleon Crown*.

10. The Constitution Act, 1867, Section 90.

11. Ibid., Section 91.

12. For the Judicial Committee's role, see John T. Saywell, *The Lawmakers: Judicial Power and the Shaping of Canadian Federalism* (Toronto: University of Toronto Press, for The Osgoode Society for Canadian Legal History, 2002).

13. Ibid., 114.

14 D. Michael Jackson, "Political Paradox," 60.

15. Interview with Hon. Allan Blakeney, 1999.

16. Ibid.

17. Confidential information.

18. Interview with Grant Devine, March 2008.

19. Interview with Hon. Roy Romanow, March 2008

20. After retiring as lieutenant governor in 2000, Jack Wiebe was appointed by Chrétien to the Senate.

21. Interview with Lorne Calvert, March 2008.

22. Gordon L. Barnhart, *"Peace, Progress and Prosperity": A Biography of Saskatchewan's First Premier, T. Walter Scott* (Regina: Canadian Plains Research Center, University of Regina, 2000).

23. Conversation with the author.

24. See John T. Saywell, *The Office of Lieutenant-Governor* (Toronto: University of Toronto Press, 1957; revised edition, Toronto: Copp Clark Pitman, 1986), 221–23.

25. Following the disallowance by Ottawa of several controversial bills of the Social Credit government of Premier William Aberhart in 1937, the Lieutenant Governor

reserved three more, which were later declared *ultra vires* by the Supreme Court of Canada. See Saywell, ibid., 215–18.

26. Jackson, "Political Paradox," 53–54.

27. Interview with Hon. Allan Blakeney, 1999. See his political memoirs, *An Honourable Calling* (Toronto: University of Toronto Press, 2008), 54–55.

28. Confidential information.

29. See Saywell, *The Office of Lieutenant-Governor*, chapters V, "The Prerogative of Dismissal," and VI, "The Prerogative of Dissolution."

30. For a strong view in favour, see Sir David Smith, *Head of State: the Governor-General, the Monarchy, the Republic and the Dismissal* (Sydney: Macleay Press, 2005). For the opposing view, see George Winterton, *Parliament, the Executive and the Governor-General* (Melbourne University Press, 1983) and *Monarchy to Republic* (Melbourne: Oxford University Press, 1986).

31. See Eugene A. Forsey, *The Royal Power of Dissolution in the British Commonwealth* (Toronto: Oxford University Press, 1943; reprinted with corrections as an Oxford in Canada Paperback, 1968).

32. See Boyce, *The Queen's Other Realms*, 162.

33. Ibid., 180–81.

34 The current legislative provision in Saskatchewan is found in section 14 of The Financial Administration Act, 1993. Other provinces and the federal government have similar legislation.

35 Confidential information.

36 Confidential information.

37 Interview with Hon. Roy Romanow, March 2008.

38. For the issue of special warrants, see Merrilee D. Rasmussen, "The Decline of Parliamentary Democracy in Saskatchewan" (MA thesis, University of Regina, 1994).

39. Interview, with Hon. Roy Romanow, March 2008.

40. For comments by Prime Ministers Tony Blair and Gordon Brown, see Robert Hardman, *A Year with the Queen* (New York: Simon & Schuster, 2007), 168–70.

41. Source: Malcolm Hazell, Official Secretary to the Governor-General of Australia, March 2008.

42. For positive comments on this practice by Prime Ministers Lester Pearson and Pierre Trudeau, see Frank MacKinnon, *The Crown in Canada* (Calgary: Glenbow Alberta Institute/McClelland and Stewart West, 1976), 103, and Jacques Monet, *The Canadian Crown* (Toronto/Vancouver: Clarke, Irwin & Company, 1979), 66–70.

43. Information provided by the Offices of the Lieutenant Governors.

44. See Jackson, "Political Paradox," 60.

45. Interview with Grant Devine, March 2008.

46. Interview with Hon. Roy Romanow, March 2008.

47. Ibid.

48. Interview with Lorne Calvert, March 2008.

49. Interview with Hon. Brad Wall, March 2008.

50. MacKinnon, *The Crown in Canada*, 47.

51. Ibid., 136.

52. Smith, *The Invisible Crown*, x–xi.

53. Ibid., 181.

54. Information from Fredrick D. Mantey, Clerk of the Executive Council, March 2008.

55. The complete story of Government House is well told in Margaret Hryniuk, edited by Garth Pugh, *"A Tower of Attraction": An Illustrated History of Government House, Regina* (Regina: Government House Historical Society/Canadian Plains Research Center, 1991). See also Robert H. Hubbard, *Ample Mansions: The Vice-Regal Residences of the Canadian Provinces* (Ottawa, London, Paris: University of Ottawa Press, 1989), 172–89.

56. See Hryniuk and Pugh, *"A Tower of Attraction,"* 106–07.

57. The author was chair of this committee from 1993 to 2006.

58. Similar problems characterized "Old Government House" in Fredericton, New Brunswick, when it was restored and returned to vice-regal use in 1998, a century after it was decommissioned.

59. The author, then chief of protocol, also served as executive director of Government House Heritage Property from 1998 to 2005.

60. For the history and a description of Canadian honours see Christopher McCreery, *The Order of Canada: Its Origins, History and Development* (Toronto: University of Toronto Press, 2005), and *The Canadian Honours System* (Toronto: Dundurn Press, 2005). See also John Blatherwick, *Canadian Orders, Decorations and Medals*, Fifth Edition (Toronto: The Unitrade Press, 2003).

61. See Michael Jackson (ed.), *Honouring Commonwealth Citizens: Proceedings of the First Conference on Commonwealth Honours and Awards* (Toronto: Ontario Ministry of Citizenship and Immigration, 2007), especially Malcolm Hazell, "The Australian Honours System: An Overview," and Michael Jackson, "Honours in the Federal State."

62. Ontario was the first to create medals, starting in 1973. Quebec established the first provincial order in 1984, followed by Saskatchewan in 1985, Ontario in 1986, British Columbia in 1989, Prince Edward Island in 1997, Alberta in 1998, Manitoba in 1999, and Nova Scotia, New Brunswick, and Newfoundland & Labrador in 2001.

63. For the story of Saskatchewan honours, see D. Michael Jackson, "The Development of Saskatchewan Honours" (unpublished research paper for the Senior Management Development Program of the Saskatchewan Public Service Commission, 1990); Jackson, "Political Paradox," 67–68; and "Honours in the Federal State," in *Honouring Commonwealth Citizens*, 115–19.

64. Former Chief Justice Edward Culliton; Dr. William Riddell and Dr. Lloyd Barber, former presidents of the University of Regina; Marguerite Gallaway, president of the Saskatchewan Council of Cultural Organizations; Ted Turner, former president of the Saskatchewan Wheat Pool; Dr. Terence McKague, former Chancellor of the University of Regina; and Hon. Frank Gerein, former Chief Justice of the Court of Queen's Bench.

65. Three government awards were established, to be presented by the premier or a designated minister: the Saskatchewan Distinguished Service Award for non-residents of the province (1997), the Premier's Award for Excellence in the Public Service (2003), and the Saskatchewan Youth Award (2006).

66. *From Palace to Prairie: the Crown and Responsible Government in Saskatchewan* (Regina: Saskatchewan Intergovernmental Affairs and Saskatchewan Communications Network, 1997).

67. Hon. James Bartleman, Lieutenant Governor of Ontario from 2002 to 2007 and himself a First Nations person, organized a highly-successful campaign to promote

literacy among Aboriginal youth in northern Ontario by collecting books for them from across the province.

68. See Lynda Haverstock, "Bestowing Honours—the Other Side," in Jackson, *Honouring Commonwealth Citizens*, 158–61.

69. For royal visits to Saskatchewan, see Michael Jackson, "Royal Visits," in *The Encyclopedia of Saskatchewan* (Regina: Canadian Plains Research Center, University of Regina, 2005), 785–86.

70. For an account of the Prince of Wales' visit, see *Saskatchewan Royal Reflections: The Visit of the Prince of Wales, April 2001* (Regina: Government of Saskatchewan, 2001).

71. Conversation with the author.

72. On this subject see Phillip Buckner (ed.), *Canada and the End of Empire* (Vancouver: UBC Press, 2005), in particular Phillip Buckner, "The Last Great Royal Tour"; and Phillip Buckner, "The Long Goodbye: English Canadians and the British World," in Phillip Buckner and R. Douglas Francis (eds.), *Rediscovering the British World* (Calgary: University of Calgary Press, 2005).

73. For the relationship between Saskatchewan and the governors general, and the trends in official Ottawa, see Jackson, "Political Paradox," 69–71.

74. Smith, *The Invisible Crown*, 25–26.

75. Some of these portraits were rescued by Quebec Senator Serge Joyal and are now displayed in the Senate foyer in the Parliament Buildings.

76. Boyce, *The Queen's Other Realms*.

77. See David E. Smith, *The Republican Option in Canada, Past and Present* (Toronto: University of Toronto Press, 1999), and "Canada's Republican Silence" in Linda Cardinal and David Heaton (eds.), *Shaping Nations: Constitutionalism and Society in Australia and Canada* (University of Ottawa Press, 2002), 260–69.

78. See Sir David Smith, *Head of State*.

79. See Twomey, *The Chameleon Crown*.

80. Kevin S. MacLeod, *A Crown of Maples: Constitutional Monarchy in Canada* (Ottawa: Department of Canadian Heritage, 2008).

81. For example, Province of Ontario, *Loyalty in a Changing World* (Toronto: n.p., 1985); George F.G. Stanley, *The Role of the Lieutenant Governor in New Brunswick* (Fredericton: n.p., 1992); and a British Columbia video, "On Behalf of Her Majesty" (Victoria, 1991).

82. D. Michael Jackson, *The Canadian Monarchy in Saskatchewan* (1989 and 1990); the video "From Palace to Prairie"; Saskatchewan, *Royal Reflections; Images of a Province: Symbols of Saskatchewan* (2002); *The Monarchy in Saskatchewan* (2005); D. Michael Jackson, *Royal Saskatchewan: The Crown in a Canadian Province* (2007).

83. Hon. David Lam, in the video *On Behalf of Her Majesty. The Story of British Columbia's Government House and the Lieutenant-Governor* (Victoria: British Columbia Government House Foundation, 1991).

84. "Like a chameleon, the Crown is a unique and unusual creature within Australia's constitutional law. It takes great care to protect itself by blending into its background, so carefully that its presence is barely perceptible. It can, of its own volition, change its colour to suit its environment and deceive others as to its nature." Twomey, *The Chameleon Crown*, 272.

Legislatures in Saskatchewan: A Battle for Sovereignty?

Merrilee Rasmussen

INTRODUCTION

The Glorious Revolution in England over 300 years ago marked the humbling of a monarchy that purported to rule by virtue of the divine right of kings and the explicit recognition of a sovereign Parliament.[1] The ancient Bill of Rights[2] articulates the fundamental principles that are the hallmarks of the parliamentary system of government: the abolition of the suspension power[3] and the requirement that money needed by the Crown can only be secured with the prior consent of the people's representatives in Parliament. And while the enactment of the ancient Bill of Rights marks the end of the struggle between the Crown and Parliament, it marks the beginning of the struggle between Parliament and the executive arm of government. This is a struggle played out in various ways in different jurisdictions, including in Saskatchewan.

THE STRUGGLE BETWEEN LEGISLATIVE AND
EXECUTIVE BRANCHES OF GOVERNMENT IN SASKATCHEWAN

The Saskatchewan Legislature was created with the stroke of a pen through the enactment of the Saskatchewan Act by the Canadian Parliament, which came into force on July 20, 1905. The creation of the province occurred, in the words of Saskatchewan political scientist David Smith, "*de novo*, within invisible, geometrically determined boundaries" in which "state preceded society."[4] The new province inherited a parliamentary legacy that reaches back to England and the Glorious Revolution. Indeed, the ancient Bill of Rights remains in force in Saskatchewan and Canada today.[5]

For the first 40 years of the province's existence, the Legislature was dominated by Liberal governments and the Saskatchewan Grain Growers Association. As Professor Smith described it: "The Legislature's job was to ratify the [executive] government's decisions and by its assent to lay the foundation on which an electoral majority might be sustained."[6] From its creation, the Saskatchewan Legislature has operated in the shadow of the executive, struggling to assert itself, by exercising the power obtained for it in the ancient Bill of Rights, and to attain the status of Parliamentary institutions at their zenith.[7]

The Co-operative Commonwealth Federation (CCF) was first elected to form government in Saskatchewan in 1944, under the premiership of Tommy

Douglas. According to Saskatchewan historian Evelyn Eager, "the Liberals said responsible government had ended after 1944 and a regime of rule by experts had taken its place."[8] Nevertheless, the CCF elected in the mid-1940s took a number of steps to provide accountability by executive government both to the CCF Party that got it elected as well as through the Legislature to the people who elected the CCF to form the executive government. In some respects, it could be said that the CCF took the Legislature seriously.

The CCF Party established a Legislative Advisory Committee empowered to meet with the government caucus and report to the Party's Council and to the Party in Convention. On the government side, the CCF established the Crown Corporations Committee of the Legislature at the same time that it brought the first Crown Corporations Act to be enacted in the province before the Legislature. The purpose of the committee was to provide a forum in which the various Crown corporations could be called to account before the Legislature. Without the committee, the arm's length nature and structure of the Crown corporation would have mitigated more strongly against accountability. Premier Douglas also insisted that a Cabinet Minister chair the board of directors of each Crown corporation to ensure a two-way line of communication between government and the corporation and, therefore, accountability by the Minster to the Legislature.[9] The committee was an innovative solution devised in Saskatchewan to address the problem of managing government control over increasingly complex matters while at the same time retaining legislative accountability. In this way, as Evelyn Eager described it, "the CCF during the Douglas regime in Saskatchewan achieved a unique juxtaposition of two opposing principles: the operation of party democracy while in power and adherence to the traditions of parliamentary government."[10]

This legacy was continued under Premier Woodrow Lloyd when, in 1963, legislation to provide for the central filing and publication of regulations[11] was first enacted. A special committee[12] of the Legislature was established to conduct a review of all regulations and professional bylaws[13] filed. The committee was mandated to analyze regulations from a number of perspectives and, in particular, to examine them on the broad grounds of appropriateness by inquiring as to whether, even if legal, a regulation relies on an unexpected— and therefore, perhaps, improper—use of the legal power. The committee was chaired by an Opposition Member and was authorized to report to the Legislature and to recommend that regulations be amended or repealed. The committee thus provided an all-party mechanism by which the use of delegated law-making power could be supervised and controlled by the Legislature.

In 2003, with the adoption of new rules for the Legislative Assembly, these duties were transferred to the four policy field committees, each of which conducts a review of the regulations and bylaws associated with its particular portfolio. The criteria used by the previously established regulations committees are now contained in the orders of reference of the policy field committees.[14] As before, the policy field committees may make recommendations to the Legislature based not just on the legality of the regulations or bylaws, but also on broad grounds of public policy. The committees may also hold public hearings to receive public input on issues that may arise with respect to regulations or professional bylaws.[15] However, the chair of the policy field committees must be a government member, other than a Minister.[16]

Although the Liberals formed government under Ross Thatcher from 1964 to 1971, there was little during this period in the way of fundamental change in the relationship between executive and legislative arms of government. However, fundamental change did occur during the 1980s under the Conservative government of Grant Devine, most dramatically in the illegal use of special warrants to purportedly authorize executive expenditures,[17] the revival of the suspension power[18] and the use of prorogation to avoid a humiliating defeat in the Legislature.[19]

This is not to suggest that the move by executive governments to wrest power away from the legislative arm is necessarily ideologically motivated. A cursory look at the use of special warrants[20] by various governments across Canada demonstrates this point. When an NDP government was elected in British Columbia in 1991, it continued to use special warrants to authorize ordinary government spending, as had the Social Credit government that it defeated.[21] In contrast, the NDP government—elected at almost the same time in Saskatchewan—moved to meet the Legislature to obtain legislative approval to government expenditure without delay,[22] but after the prorogation of the Legislature by the previous Conservative administration without passing a final Appropriation Act. In Nova Scotia, on June 28, 1993, a newly elected Liberal government convened the Nova Scotia House of Assembly for only a few minutes in order to meet the Charter's requirement that a legislature sit every 12 months, but didn't bother to request interim supply while the Legislature was sitting and available. In Manitoba in 1994, a Conservative government with a one-seat majority obtained a special warrant to authorize its expenditures during the period before the Legislature was called into session and also for a period of several weeks after the Legislature would be sitting and available to grant interim supply.[23]

Because new and old governments across Canada of varying political stripes have all used special warrants inappropriately and perhaps illegally, neither inexperience in government nor ideology provides an answer to the question of why they do so. One is driven to conclude that executive governments generally, whatever their political complexion and wherever they are, take whatever opportunities for control that present themselves. Eugene Forsey made this prescient observation more than 50 years ago, when he said:

> The danger of royal absolutism is past; but the danger of Cabinet absolutism, even of Prime Ministerial absolutism, is present and growing.[24]

DEVOLUTION OF POWER THROUGH TRADE AGREEMENTS

The Cabinet absolutism about which Forsey warned us represents a movement of power within government. More recently, the Legislature's loss of power in Saskatchewan is not to the executive but to powers outside government altogether.

For example, the Agreement on Internal Trade (AIT)[25] and the related Trade, Investment and Labour Mobility Agreement (TILMA)[26] move power away from the executive and into the hands of private interests outside the province. Although TILMA is an agreement between Alberta and British Columbia, other provinces have been invited to join as parties to the agreement, and Saskatchewan as the nearest neighbour is a prime prospect (some would say target) for TILMA's expansion. TILMA is intended to go further than the AIT by reversing the presumption of its applicability. Under the AIT, the agreement applies only to those sectors that are specifically identified in the agreement and subject to the limitations contained in the agreement. Under TILMA, the agreement applies to anything that is not specifically exempted. The question of whether or not Saskatchewan would become a party to the agreement became an issue not long before the 2007 election in Saskatchewan, and both the NDP and the Saskatchewan Party announced that they would not sign on to the agreement automatically without question nor without public consultation.

After having decided to investigate the issue on May 1, 2007, the Saskatchewan Legislature's Standing Committee on the Economy submitted its Ninth Report pursuant to Rule 146(2) to the Assembly on June 28, 2007, after having held nine days of public hearings in Regina and Saskatoon, and having received submissions from 81 representatives from 47 organizations, institutions, and associations, as well as nine private citizens. The Report summarizes what the Committee heard and makes no recommendations. Perhaps its most striking feature is that one of the recurring comments made by those who appeared before it was that they were grateful for the fact that they were being consulted, unlike what had occurred in Alberta and British Columbia. On the other hand, many raised concerns that there had not been much time to prepare submissions for the Committee's consideration, and, of course, hearings were held only in the two major cities and not throughout the province.[27]

ENTERPRISE SASKATCHEWAN

The creation of Enterprise Saskatchewan[28] has the potential to move power into the hands of private interests within the province. In the Speech from the Throne opening the first session after the Saskatchewan Party was elected in 2007, the Lieutenant Governor described it as follows:

> Enterprise Saskatchewan will be a unique and innovative public-private partnership designed to replace the top-down, government-driven economic schemes of the past. It will return direction of the economy to the hands of people who create the jobs, invest the dollars and build the labour force of the future. It will be tasked with the ongoing development of—and reporting on—economic goals and targets. Enterprise Saskatchewan will ensure we remain a competitive and attractive home for investment and job creation.[29]

It was established by one of the first pieces of legislation enacted by the newly elected Saskatchewan Party government. The Act contains a preamble (something of a rarity in modern Canadian legislation, usually reserved for the making of political statements) that sets out what might be described as the new government's principles guiding its relationship with the business sector. These include a commitment to a "competitive" tax structure, removal of barriers to economic growth, "balanced" labour laws, a promise to not provide government hand-outs to "mature" businesses, tax incentives to stimulate economic growth, a balanced budget, reduction of the debt, and respect for The Crown Corporations Public Ownership Act.[30] (This Act was enacted by the previous NDP administration, and requires that legislation be enacted to privatize certain listed Crown corporations and that any such legislation can not come into force until after the next provincial general election.)

Enterprise Saskatchewan is itself established as a corporate agency with a mandate to monitor various identified sectors of the economy and to make recommendations and provide advice to government generally with respect to the Saskatchewan economy. The board of directors consists of persons appointed by Cabinet, including two ministers and nominees of business, labour, Aboriginal persons, rural municipalities, urban municipalities, post-secondary educational institutions, co-operatives, the resource industry and agriculture, as well as one other person, with the Minister designated as its chair. The hiring of an executive director and other staff is stated to be "notwithstanding The Public Service Act, 1998." Section 23 of The Enterprise Saskatchewan Act allows Cabinet to transfer to the agency "any personal property, assets, liabilities, debts, interests, rights, obligations, and contracts of the Crown, a Crown corporation or agent of the Crown" or "any lands, interests in lands, mortgages, charges, encumbrances or other real property interests of the Crown, a Crown corporation or agent of the Crown." In addition, the Chair of the Public Service Commission can transfer "any employees or class of employees in the public service, as defined in The Public Service Act, 1998, to and cause them to become employees of the agency." As well, the "president, chief executive officer or other head of a Crown corporation or other agent of the Crown may, by agreement with the agency, transfer any employees or class of employees of the Crown corporation or agent of the Crown to and cause them to become employees of the agency." All of these powers can be exercised "notwithstanding any other Act or law or any provision of any contract."

In other words, the executive government can rearrange the Crown corporations by moving their assets and staff to Enterprise Saskatchewan, a Crown corporation that is *not* listed in The Crown Corporations Public Ownership Act.[31] Arguably, this permits circumvention of this legislation by Cabinet order, but it remains to be seen what the impact of the preamble's statement that Enterprise Saskatchewan is to "further the economic goals of the Government of Saskatchewan in a manner that is consistent with" the principle of respect for The Crown Corporations Public Ownership Act. However, these provisions do not relate just to Crown corporations, but to executive government as a whole. This leads to the further possibility, at least on the face of the statute as drafted, that the entire operations of government could be transferred into the hands of a board of directors appointed by Cabinet.[32]

The first announcement of such a transfer occurred on August 1, 2008, when a government press release said that the staff of the Ministry of Enterprise and Innovation would now be formally transferred to the new operating agency.[33] The formal transfer was effective on November 1, 2008, when The Enterprise Saskatchewan Regulations were amended to authorize Enterprise Saskatchewan to "carry on activities that serve to provide the structure wherein and whereby the powers, responsibilities and functions of the Minister of Enterprise and Innovation may be exercised and carried out."[34] At the same time, the regulations under The Government Organization Act were amended to repeal The Ministry of Enterprise and Innovation Regulations, 2007[35] and to amend The Ministry of Finance Regulations, 2007[36] to authorize Finance "to provide administrative and financial support services to the Minister of Enterprise and Innovation in that Minister's capacity as Minister responsible for" The Ethanol Fuel (Grants) Regulations, The Labour-sponsored Venture Capital Corporations Act, and The Small Business Loans Association Program Regulations.

Because these changes were made by regulation, they were made in private, by Cabinet order, in spite of the fact that the Saskatchewan Legislature is presently sitting at the same time that the Legislature has under consideration amendments to The Labour Market Commission Act.[37] The Act establishes an advisory board consisting of representatives from various sectors who are appointed by Cabinet. It was enacted by the former NDP government and came into force on February 1, 2007, not long before the last election that saw the administration change. The amendments, among other things, would change the mandate of the Commission.[38] At present, the Commission provides advice to the Minister "on provincial, regional and sectoral labour market issues, trends and strategies." Once the amendment is enacted, it will provide advice also to Enterprise Saskatchewan, in effect a government department run by an unelected committee.

All of these initiatives respond to the pressures on government from business and economic interests. Their focus is on removing barriers to trade, investment and mobility and providing a more hospitable provincial climate for those interests. Prior to 1944, the economic interests of the day, in the form of the Saskatchewan Grain Growers Association, had such close ties to the government of the day as to be seen as synonymous with it. Critics of the AIT, TILMA and Enterprise Saskatchewan fear a similar anti-democratic hold on power.

POTENTIAL JURISDICTION OF ABORIGINAL GOVERNMENTS

However, more significant because of the potential transformative impact, on both government as well as business interests in the province, is the growing influence and power of Aboriginal governments. The potential for their exercise of a constitutionally protected inherent right of self-government, which, given the demographic realities of Saskatchewan,[39] could result in a much more significant shift in power in practical terms, away from the Legislature created by the Saskatchewan Act and into the hands of other types of governmental institutions and legislating bodies within the province.

The enactment of the Canada Act, 1982 brought to Canada a constitutional amending formula, the Charter, and section 35, which provides:

> 35(1) The existing aboriginal and treaty rights of the aboriginal peoples of Canada are hereby recognized and affirmed.
>
> (2) In this Act, "aboriginal peoples of Canada" includes the Indian, Inuit and Métis peoples of Canada.[40]
>
> (3) For greater certainty,[41] in subsection (1) "treaty rights" includes rights that now exist of land claims agreements or may be so acquired.
>
> (4) Notwithstanding any other provision of this Act, the aboriginal and treaty rights referred to in subsection (1) are guaranteed equally to male and female persons.

Section 35 is accompanied by section 25, which is a provision in the portion of the Canada Act, 1982 that contains the Charter. It provides as follows:

> 25. The guarantee in this Charter of certain rights and freedoms shall not be construed so as to abrogate or derogate from any aboriginal, treaty or other rights of freedoms that pertain to the aboriginal peoples of Canada including:
>
> (a) any rights or freedoms that have been recognized by the Royal Proclamation of October 7, 1763; and
>
> (b) and rights or freedoms that now exist by way of land claims agreements or may be so acquired.

Thus, section 25 provides a direction to the courts when interpreting the scope of the individual rights contained in the Charter, as opposed to establishing what Aboriginal rights are, and section 35 recognizes and affirms those rights that exist.

The issue of what rights were "existing" was the first issue to be addressed by the Supreme Court of Canada in unpacking the content of section 35. In its landmark decision in *R. v. Sparrow*,[42] the Court held that rights that had not been extinguished prior to 1982 were existing rights, and that they were not frozen in the form in which they happened to be exercised in 1982, but were to be understood flexibly so as to permit their evolution over time. The Court also held that mere regulation of a right did not extinguish it; extinguishment could only occur where there was a "clear and plain intention" on the part of the federal[43] government to do so. Finally, the *Sparrow* decision is notable for having established that the fiduciary relationship between the Crown and

Aboriginal peoples requires government to justify any infringement of an existing Aboriginal right that is protected by s. 35 and thus operates as a restraint on Parliament's exercise of legislative power in relation to "Indians, and lands reserved for the Indians" under s. 91(24) of the Constitution Act, 1867.[44]

One of the rights that is widely viewed—certainly by Aboriginal peoples themselves—to be protected by s. 35 is an inherent right of self-government. Only one case has so far found its way to the Supreme Court of Canada where a claim of self-government was central to the issue to be decided. The case is *R. v. Pamajewon*,[45] and it involved a claim to regulate high-stakes gambling on reserve lands. The Shawanaga First Nation and the Eagle Lake First Nation had both passed bylaws dealing with lotteries on reserve lands. Neither of them had a provincial licence authorizing gambling operations as required under the Criminal Code provisions relating to gambling. The Shawanaga First Nation asserted an inherent right to self-government and the Eagle Lake First Nation asserted the right to be self-regulating in its economic activities. Certain individuals were charged and convicted under the Criminal Code of a number of gambling offences. They argued that the Criminal Code provisions did not apply to them because they interfered with the Aboriginal rights of the First Nations to make their own laws, and those rights are protected by s. 35.

The Supreme Court arrived at its conclusion on the assumption that an inherent right of self-government does exist and is protected by s. 35. However, the Court concluded that the general test to determine whether an Aboriginal right exists applies also in the case of a claim to an Aboriginal right of self-government. This test was described by the Court as requiring that the Aboriginal peoples who assert the right claimed must show that the activity to which their claim attaches is an "element of a practice, custom or tradition integral to [their] distinctive culture."[46] The Court went on to state that the claim to a general right of self-government in the context of high stakes gambling was "overly broad" and itself recast the claim as a right to regulate gambling. As a result, it was necessary for the First Nations to demonstrate that gambling or the regulation of gambling was integral to their culture. The Court found that there was no evidence to establish this link and therefore the defence of the accused to the charges against them failed and their convictions stood.

The Court's approach to self-government in *Pamajawon* has been strongly criticized by academic commentators. Professor Peter Hogg, a noted Canadian constitutional expert, described it as "singularly inappropriate."[47] He argues that to require Aboriginal peoples to prove that specific activities were regulated in a formalistic sense prior to European contact effectively emasculates the right and, in effect, freezes it in time—something the Court itself said was inappropriate in its decision in *Sparrow*. As Professor Hogg points out, the Court was "obviously concerned about the ability of aboriginal peoples to immunize themselves from the rules of the Criminal Code," but he concludes that it would be more appropriate to address that issue head on.

Once an Aboriginal right protected by s. 35 is established, it then falls to the government that has enacted legislation that infringes on that right to justify the infringement. The question of whether or not the Criminal Code provision at issue should prevail in the face of the Aboriginal right is one that can and should be dealt with specifically under the justification requirement. In other words, the Court should not hide behind an unexplained conclusion about how to characterize a claim as a means of avoiding difficult decisions regarding balancing interests.

Professor Brian Slattery argues that the Court's decision in *Delgamuukw*[48] has changed the situation. In that case, the Court rejected the argument of non-Aboriginal governments that Aboriginal title was just a bundle of specific rights that each group of Aboriginal peoples was required to establish at law in accordance with the test set out in *R. v. Van der Peet*.[49] Instead, the Court held that Aboriginal title gives an Aboriginal group the right to exclusive use and occupation of land, in effect a general right and not a specific one. He describes these "generic" rights of Aboriginal peoples as "uniform rights that operate on an abstract level and reflect broader normative considerations"[50] than do the specific rights that are distinctive to particular Aboriginal groups. Slattery argues that the same considerations that led the Court to conclude that Aboriginal title is a generic right of universal application lead to the conclusion that self-government is also a right. He concludes that:

> The generic right of self-government gives an Aboriginal group the power to establish and amend its own constitution within the overarching framework of the Canadian federation. So, the abstract right engenders a range of specific governmental powers detailed in particular Aboriginal constitutions.[51]

However, as Slattery points out, it is not sufficient to simply recognize Aboriginal rights, including the right of self-government, it is also necessary to address the issue of reconciliation of those rights in the context of modern-day Canada. His principles of reconciliation include the need to distinguish between what he describes as the "inner core" of rights, which may be implemented by Aboriginal peoples on their own and with recognition from the courts, and the "penumbra" of rights that must be defined through negotiation with non-Aboriginal governments.[52]

The issue of the inherent right to self-government has also been dealt with by the Saskatchewan courts in two different contexts. The first context is similar to that in *Pamajewon*. In 1993, the RCMP raided a casino that had been established by the White Bear First Nation on its reserve near Carlyle, Saskatchewan. Criminal charges against two corporate defendants and several individuals were ultimately dismissed for the reason that the provincial court judge hearing the case was not convinced "beyond a reasonable doubt" that the defendants had the requisite criminal intention to be found guilty because, the judge said, he was:

> [...] left with the inference that they possessed the legal capability to do what they did because they honestly believed they

did not surrender their right to self-government. In conclusion, I find that their actions and their belief that the *Criminal
Code* gaming provisions did not apply to their on-reserve gaming activities, may be considered as reasonable.[53]

The Crown appealed the acquittal and, while it is true that a conviction and
absolute discharge were subsequently entered by agreement, this occurred
after and as a result of the Government of Saskatchewan negotiating an
arrangement with First Nations in the province in relation to gaming.[54] That
agreement resulted in the establishment of several casinos on reserve lands
and the enactment of legislation by the Saskatchewan Legislature, as well as
by the Legislative Assembly of the Federation of Saskatchewan Indian
Nations (FSIN) to provide a framework for Indian gaming. This set the stage
for the second context in which Aboriginal peoples have asserted an inherent
right of self-government before the courts in this province.

In *Saskatchewan Indian Gaming Authority (SIGA) v. National Automobile,
Aerospace, Transportation and General Workers Union of Canada (CAW-Canada)*,[55]
the issue was whether or not the Saskatchewan Labour Relations Board had
the authority to certify the CAW as the bargaining agent for employees of the
Saskatchewan Indian Gaming Authority Inc. (SIGA) at the Northern Lights
Casino in Prince Albert, one of four casinos operated by SIGA in the province.

Smith J. acknowledged that the framework for Indian gaming was created
as a result of the White Bear situation in 1993 and that the agreement that the
Government of Saskatchewan and First Nations reached in 1994 was, in effect,
to "park" their disagreement in relation to jurisdiction and to enter into a dual
system of regulation that was put into place by the simultaneous enactment of
both provincial and First Nations laws. However, their agreement did not
address the issue of labour relations. SIGA argued that the matter fell within
federal jurisdiction under s. 91(24) or under the inherent right of self-government protected by s. 35. Smith J. undertook a careful and reasoned analysis,
and ultimately concluded that the application of the provincial Trade Union
Act was not ousted by the Canada Labour Code because the provincial legislation did not bear on the essential character of the federal jurisdiction under
91(24).[56] She also found that there was a lack of evidence to establish an
Aboriginal right to regulate gaming. Her decision was upheld by the Court of
Appeal in a brief oral decision endorsing her reasoning.[57]

However, one is left to speculate what her decision may have been if First
Nations, through their own Legislative Assembly, had adopted a labour relations law. The argument advanced by SIGA was an attempt to avoid a Labour
Relations Board decision about certification by asserting the application of
federal law, in effect a choice between two non-Aboriginal jurisdictions with
essentially similar approaches to the issues and also a transparent effort at
avoiding certification. If she had had a choice between applying such a non-
Aboriginal law to a First Nation entity employing largely First Nation persons
and operating on First Nation lands, or applying a law fashioned by First
Nations for themselves, she would have been confronted with a much more
difficult jurisdictional question. On the basis of Professor Slattery's argument

that self-government is a generative right, the issue would instead have been a question of whether or not the First Nation law primarily affected First Nations, and thus fell within the inner core of Aboriginal jurisdiction, to be enacted by First Nations without the consent of other governments.

And at least one more recent case in Saskatchewan suggests that there may be an evolution in judicial regard for the status of First Nations and their related ability to self-regulate. In *Battlefords Tribal Council Inc. (c.o.b. Battlefords Tribal Council) v. Federation of Saskatchewan Indians Inc.*[58] Popescul J. was faced with an application from the Battlefords Tribal Council to restrain certain actions of the FSIN on the basis that the FSIN, a federation of First Nations in Saskatchewan, and the FSI Inc., a non-profit corporation incorporated under provincial law, are one and the same entity. The FSIN argued that these were two distinct entities, and Popescul J. accepted this argument, describing the FSIN as a "political organization with, as yet, undetermined legal status."[59] He went on to state:

> The Saskatchewan government, while not expressly recognizing the FSIN as a self-governing body, has most definitely acknowledged its existence by consistently treating the FSIN as some form of recognizable entity. This is evidenced by the fact that the various casino agreements are between the Saskatchewan government and the FSIN, not the FSI, Inc. It is obvious that a conscious decision was made to refer the institution with whom the Saskatchewan government chose to sign agreements with pertaining to the operation of casinos was the FSIN and not the FSI, Inc. This approach is consistent and can be seen manifesting itself in other areas. For example, the Saskatchewan government has expressly recognized and referred to the FSIN as some type of distinct entity, in legislation including The Saskatchewan Gaming Corporation Act, S.S. 1994, c. S-18.2 (s. 25.01(c)) and The Police Act, 1990, S.S. 1990-91, c. P-15.01 (s. 38(2)(c)).
>
> The essence of the actions complained of were those of the First Nations Legislature and not those of a non-profit corporation. Resolution 1511 was passed by the FSIN, in accordance with its practices and procedures, and not by the FSI, Inc. The passage of that resolution emanated from the authority created by the "The Conventions Act, 1982" and not by virtue of the practices and procedures found within any bylaws of the FSI, Inc. or any provision contained in The Non-Profit Corporations Act.[60]

Because the court's jurisdiction to act on the application before it was limited to powers provided to it under The Non-profit Corporations Act, Popescul J. held that he had no authority to make the order applied for and dismissed the application.

On the political front, all governments in Canada indicated their support of an inherent right of self-government for Aboriginal peoples in their support of the Charlottetown Accord in 1992. Although the Accord was defeated in a nation-wide referendum, First Ministers and Aboriginal leaders had agreed to include amendments to s. 35 to explicitly recognize its existence and to provide for the negotiation of self-government agreements and resort to the courts if negotiation failed. Nevertheless, in March of 1994, the Department of Indian and Northern Affairs released the following statement:

> The Government of Canada announced in a recent Speech from the Throne that it will forge a new partnership with Aboriginal peoples. Recognition of the inherent right of self-government is the cornerstone of this new partnership. Implementation of the inherent right of self-government will enable aboriginal peoples to become full partners in Canada, govern themselves and make decisions concerning their own affairs.

In Saskatchewan, in the same year, the provincial government adopted an Aboriginal Policy Framework that, while not a wholesale endorsement of the right of self-government, acknowledged the possibility in appropriate circumstances.[61] More currently, the 2007–08 annual report for the Saskatchewan Ministry of First Nations and Métis Relations states that the province "recognizes the inherent right to self-government for First Nations people."[62]

ABORIGINAL SELF-GOVERNMENT AGREEMENTS

As a result, the federal and provincial governments have continued to engage in self-government negotiations with Aboriginal peoples, regardless of the defeat of the Charlottetown Accord, and a number of final agreements have been concluded.[63] One of the most well-known of these is the Nisga'a Agreement, which became effective in 1999, between Canada, British Columbia and the Nisga'a Nation.[64] When it was concluded, the Leader of the Opposition of the day, Gordon Campbell (now Premier of British Columbia), launched a legal action challenging its validity.[65] Because the Nisga'a Agreement was described by the parties to it as a "treaty," the case was not concerned with determining whether or not an Aboriginal right existed; the issue was whether or not the Nisga'a Treaty is a treaty constitutionally protected by s.35 of the Constitution Act, 1982.

Campbell argued that the treaty violated the Canadian Constitution because parts of the treaty purport to provide the governing body of the Nisga'a Nation with legislative jurisdiction. Campbell said this was inconsistent with the "exhaustive" division of powers granted to Parliament and the Legislative Assemblies of the provinces by sections 91 and 92 of the Constitution Act, 1867. He also argued that the legislative powers set out in the treaty interfered with the concept of Royal Assent and that non-Nisga'a Canadian citizens who reside in or have other interests in the territory subject to Nisga'a government are denied rights guaranteed to them by section 3 of the Canadian Charter of Rights and Freedoms, which provides every citizen with the right to vote for members of Parliament and the legislatures.

The Nisga'a had been attempting to negotiate a treaty with Canadian authorities for over 100 years, ever since 1887 when the Nisga'a people first sent a delegation of their Chiefs to Victoria. It was also the Nisga'a who initiated the litigation that resulted in the Supreme Court's decision in *R. v. Calder*[66] and paved the way for modern treaty negotiations. In reviewing briefly the history of the Nisga'a and their dealings with the Crown, Williamson J. noted what he described as two important facts: 1) the Nisga'a had never ceded their rights or their land to the Crown; and 2) both the federal and provincial Crowns, in negotiating the agreement with the Nisga'a, recognized that the Nisga'a had the authority to bargain with the state and that they had rights that were negotiable. He described Campbell's position in this way:

> The heart of this argument is that any right to such self-government or legislative power was extinguished at the time of Confederation. Thus, the plaintiffs distinguish Aboriginal title and other Aboriginal rights, such as the right to hunt or to fish, from the right to govern one's own affairs. They say that in 1867, when the then British North America Act (now called the Constitution Act, 1867) was enacted, although other Aboriginal rights including Aboriginal title survived, any right to self-government did not. All legislative power was divided between Parliament and the legislative assemblies. While they concede that Parliament, or the Legislative Assembly, may delegate authority, they say legislative bodies may not give up or abdicate that authority. To do so, they argue, is unconstitutional.[67]

But Williamson rejected that argument. He held that Aboriginal rights, including an inherent right of self-government providing the jurisdiction to make laws survived "as one of the unwritten 'underlying values' of the Constitution outside of the powers distributed to Parliament and the legislatures in 1867. The federal-provincial division of powers in 1867 was aimed at a different issue and was a division 'internal' to the Crown."[68]

Williamson concluded:

> For the reasons set out above, I have concluded that after the assertion of sovereignty by the British Crown, and continuing to and after the time of Confederation, although the right of Aboriginal people to govern themselves was diminished, it was not extinguished. Any Aboriginal right to self-government could be extinguished after Confederation and before 1982 by federal legislation which plainly expressed that intention, or it could be replaced or modified by the negotiation of a treaty. Post-1982, such rights cannot be extinguished, but they may be defined (given content) in a treaty. The Nisga'a Final Agreement does the latter expressly.

> I have also concluded that the Constitution Act, 1867 did not distribute all legislative power to the Parliament and the legislatures. Those bodies have exclusive powers in the areas listed in Sections 91 and 92 (subject until 1931 to the Imperial Parliament). But the Constitution Act, 1867, did not purport to, and does not end, what remains of the royal prerogative or Aboriginal and treaty rights, including the diminished but not extinguished power of self-government which remained with the Nisga'a people in 1982.
>
> Section 35 of the Constitution Act, 1982, then, constitutionally guarantees, among other things, the limited form of self-government which remained with the Nisga'a after the assertion of sovereignty. The Nisga'a Final Agreement and the settlement legislation give that limited right definition and content. Any decision or action which results from the exercise of this now-entrenched treaty right is subject to being infringed upon by Parliament and the legislative assembly. This is because the Supreme Court of Canada has determined that both Aboriginal and treaty rights guaranteed by s.35 may be impaired if such interference can be justified and is consistent with the honour of the Crown.[69]

In other words, the mere fact of Confederation could not extinguish the right of self-government, because the purpose of that legislation was to provide for a structure of governance as between federal and provincial governments. It did not intend to nor did it deal with the question of what authority Aboriginal peoples might have through their governments. It concerned itself only with the question of what authority was provided to the federal and provincial governments, and intended to allocate authority exhaustively as between *them*. Perhaps significantly, thereafter, and until the constitutional changes in 1982, the authority to legislate in relation to the rights of Aboriginal peoples was allocated to the federal government under s. 91(24).

The *Campbell* decision, while it is sometimes dismissed by federal officials as "just a lower level court decision," is important not only because it upholds the validity of a self-government agreement, but also because the reasoning it employs also supports the validity of laws that might be adopted by the governments of Aboriginal peoples even in the absence of such agreements. Since the right of self-government may be an existing Aboriginal right that is protected by section 35, the agreement of federal and/or provincial governments may not be necessary to its exercise in some circumstances. First Nations in Saskatchewan have been positioning themselves for this exercise of power for some time.[70]

SELF-GOVERNMENT NEGOTIATIONS IN SASKATCHEWAN

First Nations in Canada began to organize as early as 1919 when returning veterans came home and found that they were not treated in the same was as other Canadians who fought in the Great War. The Union of Saskatchewan

Indians was established in 1946.[71] In the early 1980s, Saskatchewan Indian Chiefs met to discuss the formation of a Legislative Assembly. On April 16, 1982, they implemented The Federation of Saskatchewan Indian Nations' Convention Act. The Convention was signed by 74 Saskatchewan Chiefs representing their respective bands and it defines the Federation of Saskatchewan Indian Nations as "the provincial political organization recognized by the Convention of April 16, 1982 and whose structure and representation is described herein." The Convention Act established a Legislative Assembly whose members are the First Nations in Saskatchewan who are signatories to the Convention. The Legislative Assembly meets three times annually—in fall, winter and spring, and in special sessions when required. The Legislative Assembly has the authority to enact laws for and on behalf of the member First Nations.

The Common Table process[72] established in 1996 led to extensive self-government negotiations between the Federation of Saskatchewan Indian Nations and Canada, in which Saskatchewan participated technically as an observer. Saskatchewan's position is based on the province's view that because of the existence of s. 91(24) the federal government has primary jurisdiction and responsibility in relation to First Nations and, as a matter of law, would be able to implement self-government together with First Nations and without the involvement of the province. First Nations generally support this view. Most First Nations in Saskatchewan have concluded Treaties with the federal Crown, and regard the Treaties as acknowledging, among other things, their right to govern themselves. However, because of the practical overlap of laws, services and program delivery that would occur when Aboriginal peoples assume responsibility for their members living within the borders of Saskatchewan, both the provincial government and First Nations have an interest in ensuring that practical arrangements and conflict of laws provisions are in place in those areas of overlap.

By 2003, the negotiators had reached draft agreements in principle[73] that each of them was prepared to recommend to their principals for signature. The agreements would have provided the parties with a blueprint for negotiations to conclude a final agreement that would have been province-wide in scope. Although the agreements stalled at the draft stage, they provide an important insight into the potential for the exercise of the power to make laws by First Nations governments in Saskatchewan via the governmental structures First Nations have created for themselves, at the province-wide, regional and community levels.[74] One of the key features of the agreements was the provisions relating to "relationship of laws"—that is, the rules for resolving questions about which order of government has jurisdiction to enact a law and in what circumstances.[75]

POTENTIAL SCOPE OF FIRST NATIONS GOVERNANCE

The draft agreement in principle did not address all possible areas of First Nation jurisdiction comprehensively. It addressed the key areas of families and children and education, and provided a process for concluding negotiations in relation to those areas that remained. However, the First Nations took the position that the relationship of laws principles to be applied should be based on their potential scope of law-making authority and therefore it was necessary to look at the existing scope of provincial ability to make laws applicable to Aboriginal peoples.

As constitutional law has developed in Canada, provincial laws can apply to First Nations on their own (*ex proprio vigore*) as a result of the exercise of provincial jurisdiction under s. 92 of the Constitution Act, 1867, where they do not affect the essential character of federal jurisdiction in relation to Indians under s. 91(24).[76] They can also apply because of s. 88 of the Indian Act, which provides:

> Subject to the terms of any treaty and any other Act of the Parliament of Canada, all laws of general application from time to time in force in any province are applicable to and in respect of Indians in the province, except to the extent that such laws are inconsistent with this Act or any order, rule, regulation or by-law made thereunder, and except to the extent that such laws make provision for any matter for which provision is made by or under this Act.[77]

Thus, unless a provincial law interferes with treaty rights or other federal legislation, it applies to First Nations because the federal government has (via s. 88) exercised its jurisdiction to enact laws in relation to Indians under s. 91(24) of the Constitution Act, 1867 to effectively adopt provincial laws and make them applicable to them. In practical terms, this has meant that courts have not often had to decide what the exact scope of the federal jurisdiction under s. 91(24) is, since one way or another the provincial law in question will apply. However, in the face of the exercise of First Nation jurisdiction, the difference is critical in the context of the relationship of laws question. In those situations in which provincial laws apply by virtue of s. 88, First Nation laws should have priority in the case of a conflict because the province doesn't actually possess the jurisdiction necessary to make provincial laws applicable. Thus, in the areas where significant negotiation did occur—families and children and education—the draft agreements in principle provide for priority of First Nation law.

EXERCISE OF JURISDICTION THROUGH ABORIGINAL GOVERNMENTAL INSTITUTIONS

Whether one looks at the scope of an inherent Aboriginal right to self-government as one delineated by a core and periphery of jurisdiction, as articulated by RCAP, or a generative right consisting of an inner core and penumbra, as Brian Slattery has theorized, or as defined by the range of things about which provinces cannot legislate in relation to Aboriginal peoples by virtue of s. 91 and s. 92, the result is the same. There is a range of law-making authority that Aboriginal governments must possess because Aboriginal peoples have the right to exist as peoples. This authority must include at least the ability to adopt constitutions, to regulate relationships within the group, and to engage in inter-governmental relationships with other governments. It is only a matter of time before First Nations will assert their jurisdiction to act, especially when negotiations to conclude self-government agreements with other governments take so long and use up so much of their scarce financial resources.

At the same time that First Nations and Métis peoples in Saskatchewan continue to develop their governmental institutions and their own laws, they are becoming a larger part of the population in the province. As they become a majority, will they be more interested in their institutions or ours? It has perhaps been assumed that Aboriginal peoples will aspire to gain control of our institutions as they become a majority, but they are also likely to wish to develop their own. The important issues that they will deal with in relation to their own communities can only gain greater significance for the rest of us. Their views of appropriate economic development may lead to very different relationships with economic interests in the province, most of which are largely non-Aboriginal.

CONCLUSION

Executive governments in parliamentary systems have worked diligently to wrest control from the legislative branch since the legislative high-water mark of 1688. In doing so, they have impoverished legislatures to the extent that they have been able to turn them into a rubber stamp for executive decisions. Provincial legislatures are at an additional disadvantage in relation to Aboriginal peoples because Aboriginal peoples view their primary relationship with non-Aboriginal governments to be with the federal government and, indeed, the Canadian Constitution does not allow provinces to enact laws in relation to them. It cannot be assumed that Aboriginal peoples in Saskatchewan will necessarily turn to the provincial legislature as they become a dominant force in the province numerically. It is equally likely that they will be interested in the further development of their own legislatures, as they have already created them.

The concentration of power in the Cabinet or with the Premier that Forsey wrote about more than 60 years ago serves to feed the general cynicism that people have about government and a view that legislatures really don't matter that much. It may lead in Saskatchewan to a legislature that is diminished not just by cynicism, but by a reduction in real power over a significant portion of the population. Since the golden age of Parliament in 19th-century Britain, parliamentary reform has centred on finding ways to enhance the role of the individual member and access by members of the public to legislative processes. In Saskatchewan, the most recent venture of this type was the overhaul of the Rules in 2003. But it will be necessary for the Legislature to have more than the occasional public hearing to revive a public attitude of trust and respect.

More than 400 years ago, the presumption of the Tudor monarchs that they ruled by divine right led to their downfall and to the rise of Parliament. In modern times, the presumption of executive governments that they rule because they control through party discipline a majority of the seats in the House may lead to a quieter revolution. As the Legislature continues to be de-legitimized in the minds of those who are not of the "political class," the advent of different legislating bodies with more relevance to a growing pro-portion of the people residing within the boundaries of Saskatchewan may well lead to a significant loss of power in practical terms, for the provincial government generally and for the legislature in particular. It may well be that, in future, the important role of the Saskatchewan Legislature will be in its rela-tionship with other, Aboriginal governments within the boundaries of the province.

NOTES

1. James II prorogued Parliament in 1685 when it refused to grant him money to main-tain his army and refused to repeal the Test Acts, which restricted public office to those who had taken the sacrament of the Church of England. James II continued to rule by royal prerogative, that is, without the consent of Parliament, and declared the Test Acts to be no longer in force. Ultimately, as a result, William of Orange was invited to invade England and James II fled the country. William and Mary were then invited to take the throne on the terms mentioned. See Philip Norton, "The Glorious Revolution of 1688 and 1689: Its Continuing Relevance," *Parliamentary Affairs* 42, no. 2 (April 1989).

2. The Bill of Rights 1688-89 was adopted on February 2, but after its enactment the beginning of the year was moved from March 1 to January 1. By the old manner of reckoning time it was enacted on February 2, 1688, but by the new manner it was on February 2, 1689.

3. The suspension power is the power asserted by James II in declaring the Test Acts to be inoperative. The abolition of the suspension power is an important confirmation of the supremacy of Parliament; the law is what Parliament enacts, not what the monarch might declare. This topic is discussed in more detail by Merrilee Rasmussen "The Role of the Legislature," in Howard Leeson (ed.), *Saskatchewan Politics: Into the Twenty-First Century* (Regina: Canadian Plains Research Center, 2001), 18–20 and 31–33.

4. David E. Smith, "Saskatchewan: Approximating the Ideal," in Gary Levy and Graham White (eds.), *Provincial and Territorial Legislatures in Canada* (Toronto: University of Toronto Press, 1989), 49.

5. See the decisions of the Supreme Court of Canada in *Re Anti-Inflation Act*, [1976] 2 S.C.R. at p. 433 and *Reference re Amendment of the Constitution of Canada (Nos. 1, 2 and 3)* (1982), 125 D.L.R. (3d) 1 at 30.

6. David E. Smith, "Saskatchewan: Approximating the Ideal," in Levy and White, *supra* note 4 at 50.

7. The Parliament of the 19th century at Westminster may be regarded as something of a "golden age" in that it apparently exerted real power or, perhaps more accurately, individual Members of Parliament did. In part, this power was due to the nature of the legislation that typified the era. Most of it was legislation relating to specific public works in particular locations. Members had to lobby one another for support for the

measures desired for their constituencies. Legislation in the present time is quite different. It deals with matters of more general public policy and in a context in which governments generally are more active. Individual members are also subject to party discipline, and the party machine ensures that members who do not support the party's legislative proposals are deprived of the personal rewards available, such as Cabinet posts and support in election campaigns.

8. Evelyn Eager, *Saskatchewan Government: Politics and Pragmatism* (Saskatoon: Western Producer Prairie Books, 1980), 47.

9. This reasoning has fallen out of favour in recent years, as government has provided greater autonomy to the Crowns through measures such as ensuring that no Cabinet Minister even sits on the board of directors.

10. Evelyn Eager, "The Paradox of Power in the Saskatchewan CCF, 1944-1961," in J.H. Aitchison (ed.), *The Political Process in Canada* (Toronto: University of Toronto Press), as quoted in Doris French Shackleton, *Tommy Douglas* (Toronto: McClelland and Stewart, 1975).

11. "Regulations" are laws enacted by statutory delegates, most often Cabinet or a Minister. In theory, regulations provide the operational details to enable practical implementation of the law; they put the flesh on the bones of the statutory framework. On occasion, the statutory framework may be very thin, and the regulations arguably deal with more than the details of filling in practical gaps. However, regulations are enacted outside the Legislature in private, and most of the time they do not come to public knowledge until after they are made, unlike the bill procedure in the Legislature which is a public process providing for opposition to the enactment of a proposed law. In addition, regulations, even if they concern themselves with details, are important to access in addition to the statute in order to understand the complete law. The Regulations Act facilitates access to regulations by providing a systematic process for filing them in a central registry and publishing them in the *Saskatchewan Gazette*.

12. A "special committee" was established because, under the rules of the Legislature at that time, a special committee was able to work during the time between sessions, while a standing committee was not.

13. Strictly speaking, bylaws enacted by the councils of self-regulating professions are not "regulations" as defined by The Regulations Act. They are thus not subject to the central filing and publication requirements of that Act. However, each of the statutes establishing the self-regulating professions requires that bylaws be tabled in the Legislature and, in the case of what are described as regulatory bylaws, published in the *Saskatchewan Gazette* (although not as regulations). See for example, The Paramedics Act, S.S. 2007, c. P-0.1, the most recently enacted professional Act. Subsection 14(8) provides for publication of regulatory bylaws and subsection 45(2) requires all bylaws to be tabled in the Legislature. Such bylaws may "cease to have any effect and [are] deemed to have been revoked" if the Legislative Assembly finds them to be "beyond the powers delegated by the Legislature or in any way prejudicial to the public interest."

14. Rule 145(2), *Rules and Procedures of the Legislative Assembly of Saskatchewan*, accessible online at http://www.legassembly.sk.ca/publications/Docs/Rules_2007_2008.pdf

15. Ibid., Rule 145(4).

16. Ibid., Rule 122(2).

17. See Merrilee Rasmussen, "The Decline of Parliamentary Democracy in Saskatchewan" (MA thesis, University of Regina, 1994), 64 to 128.

18. See Rasmussen, "The Role of the Legislature," *supra* note 3.

19. Ibid., 31 to 33.

20. A special warrant is an approval to executive government expenditure obtained from the Lieutenant Governor when the Legislative Assembly is not available to provide its consent, as required by the ancient Bill of Rights (and confirmed by more modern statutes in all Canadian jurisdictions). It is a statutory exception to that rule, enacted in Canada as a result of Fenian raids in the mid-1800s, and copied in all provincial and territorial jurisdictions since then. It does not exist in the United Kingdom or in other Commonwealth countries, since the reason for the enactment of the special warrant power was peculiar to Canada.

21. The British Columbia Legislature sat from March 11 to 22, 1991, but did not deal with obtaining consent to executive expenditures, even on an interim basis, in spite of the fact that the fiscal year would begin on April 1 and funds would be needed for the ordinary processes of government. Interim supply was granted on June 1 and again on June 27. About one-third of the provincial budget for the entire 1991–92 fiscal year was authorized by special warrants after the Legislature was dissolved on September 19, 1991.

22. The Romanow government was sworn into office on November 1, 1991 and the Legislative Assembly was called into session on December 2, 1991. Two significant pieces of legislation were enacted in that brief session: The Mortgage Protection Act and The Appropriation Act, 1991 (No. 2). The former enacted the change to the level of mortgage interest subsidies that the Devine government had simply "declared" to be the law when its own amendment died on the Order Paper after it suddenly prorogued the House after the resignation of a member of the Devine Cabinet on June 17, 1991. While the Act legitimated what the Devine government had merely announced, it was an important recognition of the fact that only the Legislature has the authority to make law. The latter provided the consent of the Legislature to executive government spending on an interim basis, and thus recognized the second important principle stemming from the ancient Bill of Rights.

23. The Manitoba Legislature did not commence sitting until April 7, 1994, and the budget was not presented until April 20. Special warrants in the amount of approximately $1.6 billion were issued on March 23, 1994, for the fiscal year to begin on April 1, pursuant to Order in Council 188/94.

24. Eugene Forsey, *The Royal Power of Dissolution of Parliament in the British Commonwealth* (Toronto: University of Toronto Press, 1943), 259.

25. Signed by all First Ministers in Canada on July 18, 1994, and effective on and from July 1, 1995. Its objective is "to reduce barriers to the movement of persons, goods, services and investments within Canada." See online at http://www.ic.gc.ca/epic/site/ait-aci.nsf/en/home.

26. Signed by British Columbia and Alberta April 28, 2006 and effective on and from April 1, 2007.

27. See the Committee's Report and transcripts of the public hearings online at http://www.sfl.sk.ca/pdfs/Standing_Committee_on_the_Economy_Report_June_2007.pdf

28. The Enterprise Saskatchewan Act, S.S. 2007, c. E-10.02, came into force on July 28, 2007.

29. First Session, Twenty-Sixth Legislature of the Legislative Assembly of Saskatchewan, *Debates and Proceedings (Hansard)*, December 10, 2007, 3.

30. S.S. 2004, c.C-50.102.

31. Subclause 2(b)(xiii) does permit the making of regulations to add a Crown corporation to the legislated list, but no such regulations have been promulgated at this time.

32. These issues and others were raised in questions in the Legislature just prior to the introduction of the legislation. See First Session, Twenty-Sixth Legislature of the Legislative Assembly of Saskatchewan, *Debates and Proceedings (Hansard)*, December 13, 2007, 71 to 73.

33. See online at: http://www.gov.sk.ca/news?newsId=6a04e1c9-6efd-4529-bcd5-bd01a631e9cf

34. The Enterprise Saskatchewan Amendment Regulations, SR 104/2008, published in Part II of the *Saskatchewan Gazette*, November 14, 2008 at 779.

35. Ibid., SR 106/2008 at p. 780, effective December 1, 2008.

36. Ibid., SR 105/2008 at p. 779-80, effective December 1, 2008.

37. S.S. 2006, c. L-0.11.

38. See The Labour Market Commission Amendment Act, 2008, Second Session, Twenty-Sixth Legislature, Bill 46.

39. Current provincial projections indicate that by 2045, one-third of the population of Saskatchewan will be Aboriginal. The median age in the First Nations population is 18.4 while in the non-Aboriginal population it is 38.8. See online at: http://www.fnmr.gov.sk.ca/demographics/.

40. The Constitution Act, 1867 refers to "Indians" as a head of federal jurisdiction under s. 91(24). In 1930, the Supreme Court of Canada determined, in its decision in *In re Eskimo*, that the Inuit people were "Indians" within the meaning of the term as used in 1867. While no judicial decision has dealt specifically with the issue of whether or not the term "Indian" includes the Métis, most writers in this field have concluded that it does. The term "Indian" has come to be viewed by many as a negative term, and in 1982 it was jettisoned in favour of "Aboriginal peoples." However, the drafters also found it necessary to clarify that the phrase was intended to refer to all three groups of Aboriginal peoples and not just to those known as "Indians" in 1867. Section 35 refers to "aboriginal peoples" rather than "Aboriginal peoples," which has been a matter of criticism by some who are of the view that the term should be capitalized in the same manner as the terms "English" or "French" are capitalized. Although not a constitutional term, the current term, "First Nation," is used to refer to communities of Status Indians, that is as defined under the Indian Act, and the term "Aboriginal" is usually associated with Métis. However, in the language of the constitution, "aboriginal peoples" and "Indians" are the same. The terms "Indian" and "Aboriginal peoples" are used throughout this article in their constitutional sense, although "Aboriginal" is capitalized.

41. "For greater certainty" is a drafting convention that is intended to signal that the drafter does not believe that the definition that follows is an addition to the meaning that should be taken from the term as originally used. In this case, the message is that the addition of the specific reference to land claims agreements does not mean that land claims agreements are not treaties or that the rights they provide for are not treaty rights.

42. [1990] 1 S.C.R. 1075.

43. And only the federal government was capable of extinguishing aboriginal rights, not the provinces, since extinguishment was a power contained within the legislative authority assigned to Parliament through s. 91(24) of the Constitution Act, 1867.

44. This constraint on the exercise of legislative power applies to provincial governments too, but because of the existence of s. 91(24), there is not a very broad scope of jurisdiction that provincial governments are constitutionally able to exercise "in relation to" Aboriginal peoples. While many provincial laws apply to Aboriginal peoples in the same way that they apply to others, it is arguable that a provincial law that infringes constitutionally-protected Aboriginal rights is either invalid or inoperable because it interferes with the essential nature of the federal jurisdiction. See Merrilee Rasmussen, "Prairie First Nations and Provinces: Is There a Fiduciary Relationship That Gives Rise to Fiduciary Obligations?" (LLM thesis, University of Saskatchewan, 2001). In Saskatchewan, however, the province has jurisdiction to make laws relating to hunting applicable to "Indians" subject to the limitations of paragraph 12 of the Natural Resources Transfer Agreement, 1930.

45. [1996] 2 S.C.R. 821.

46. *R. v. Van der Peet* [1996], 2 S.C.R. 507.

47. Peter Hogg, *Constitutional Law of Canada* (Toronto: Thomson Carswell, 2007), para. 27.5(c).

48. *Delgamuukw v. British Columbia,* [1997] 3 S.C.R. 1010.

49. Supra, note 41.

50. "The Generative Structure of Aboriginal Rights," in John D. Whyte (ed.), *Moving Toward Justice: Legal Traditions and Aboriginal Justice* (Saskatoon: Purich Publishing Limited, 2008), 22.

51. Ibid., 29.

52. Ibid., 46. This "inner core" and "penumbra" is very similar to the "core" and "periphery" of rights that the Royal Commission on Aboriginal Peoples described in similar terms. In the core of jurisdiction, Aboriginal peoples can make their own laws without permission; in the periphery, the intersection between the two cultures, they must negotiate with other governments to give effect to their laws.

53. *R. v. Bear Claw Casino Ltd.,* [1994] 4 C.N.L.R. 81.

54. *See Saskatchewan Indian Gaming Authority (SIGA) v. National Automobile, Aerospace, Transportation and General Workers Union of Canada (CAW-Canada),* [2000] S.J. No. 266, at para. 12.

55. Ibid.

56. This is the usual test applied by the courts in determining whether or not an otherwise valid provincial law must be read down so as to be rendered inapplicable because it affects in a significant was a head of federal jurisdiction. This is called the doctrine of interjurisdictional immunity and can render a provincial law inapplicable even when there is no federal law in place. See Hogg, *Constitutional Law of Canada,* chapter 15.

57. [2000] SKCA 138. Her reasoning was also adopted in a subsequent case involving the question of whether or not The Saskatchewan Human Rights Code applied to a human rights complaint involving a SIGA casino. See *Saskatchewan Indian Gaming Authority v. Drew,* [2000] SKCA 19.

58. [2007] SKQB 339.

59. Ibid., at para. 32.

60. Ibid., at paras. 33 and 34.

61. The provincial concern was to avoid "overlap and duplication" through the proliferation of governments and also provincial liability in the case of systems failures.

62. Ministry of First Nations and Métis Relations, 2007-2008 Annual Report, at p. 14; accessed online at http://www.fnmr.gov.sk.ca/annualreports/FNMR2007-08.pdf

63. See the Government of Canada's website at http://www. ainc-inac.gc.ca/pr/agr/index_ .html#Self-GovernmentAgreements

64. The Meadow Lake Tribal Council in Northern Saskatchewan has been engaged in self-government negotiations with the province and the federal government since 1994. Agreements in principle were reached among the parties in 2001. However a self-government agreement has not yet been concluded.

65. *Campbell v. British Columbia (Attorney General)*, [2000] 4 C.N.L.R. 1.

66. [1973] S.C.R. 313. The Nisga'a asked the Court for a declaration that their Aboriginal title had never been lawfully extinguished. Three of the judges of the Supreme Court of Canada held that the sovereignty exercised by the Colony of British Columbia and later by Canada was inconsistent with the continuation of Aboriginal title and dismissed the Nisga'a's appeal. Three other judges dissented, pointing to a number of precedents in which it was established that the common law recognizes the rights of Aboriginal inhabitants. They also pointed to the Royal Proclamation of 1763. They concluded that the Nisga'a title could only be surrendered to a competent legal authority, which had not occurred. The seventh judge held that the court had no jurisdiction to make a declaration because, as it was a claim against the Crown, the fiat (or permission to proceed) of the Lieutenant-Governor of British Columbia had not been obtained. Technically, the Nisga'a lost the case, but the powerful dissent of Justices Hall, Spence and Laskin paved the way for a change in government policy and ultimately, through subsequent cases, in the law.

67. *Supra* note 43, at para. 59.

68. Ibid., at para. 81.

69. Ibid., at paras. 179 to 181.

70. The Métis Nation – Saskatchewan (MNS) has also made efforts to organize its governmental structures, but internal difficulties have resulted in its being at a more preliminary developmental stage. Although Saskatchewan's Métis Act, S.S. 2001, c. M-14.01, recognizes the contributions of the Métis to the province and commits the province to bilateral discussions, it also establishes as a corporate creature of provincial law, the Métis Nation—Saskatchewan Secretariat Inc., as the "administrative body" by which the programs and policies of the MNS are to be carried out. As such, the focus of this article is on First Nations, who have at this time a more stable and entrenched governmental structure, established in accordance with their own laws.

71. See a brief history online at the FSIN website: http://www.fsin.com/aboutfsin/historicalformation.html

72. See online at http://www.fnmr.gov.sk.ca/relations/fn-governance/fsin/

73. There were two "agreements" that were negotiated: a bilateral agreement between Canada and First Nations and a tripartite agreement between Canada, First Nations and Saskatchewan. This approach satisfied the concerns of First Nations, who were engaged in a Treaty-based process of self-government implementation that could only involve Canada as their Treaty partner, and Saskatchewan, who saw its role as providing room for self-government implementation in a practical sense.

74. That is, through the FSIN Legislative Assembly province-wide, by Treaty area or Tribal Council on a regional basis, or by individual First Nations, all of which have structures that provide for the making of laws.

75. For a more comprehensive description of the Treaty self-government negotiations process and the agreements in principle, see Ian Peach and Merrilee Rasmussen, "Federalism and the First Nations: Making Space for First Nations' Self-determination in the Federal Inherent Right Policy," paper submitted to the University of Edinburgh's Centre for Canadian Studies conference on First Nations, First Thoughts, May 2005; online at http://www.cst.ed.ac.uk/2005conference/papers/Peach_Rasmussen_paper.pdf

76. I would argue also that provincial legislation that infringes Aboriginal jurisdiction that is recognized or affirmed under section 35 of the Constitution Act, 1982 is not applicable to the Aboriginal peoples to whom that jurisdiction belongs, whether or not it can be justified in accordance with the *Sparrow* test articulated by the Supreme Court of Canada in *R. v. Sparrow,* [1990] 1 S.C.R. 1075, on the basis that provincial legislation that infringes is also trenching on the essential character of the federal jurisdiction under 91(24).

77. R.S.C. 1985, c. I-5.

Forming Shadow Cabinets and Cabinets in Saskatchewan from 1987 to 2001

Honourable Roy Romanow, Former Premier of Saskatchewan[1]

INTRODUCTION

This article provides key insights on the processes and criteria used by the Honourable Roy Romanow in appointing members of the shadow cabinet and cabinet while he served as Leader of the Opposition, and Premier. His responses to a series of questions provide very interesting and important information about these matters at the provincial level. It is based on his experience as Leader of Saskatchewan's New Democratic Party for fourteen years from November 7, 1987 until February 2001. During that time he served as Leader of the Official Opposition from November 7, 1987 to October 30, 1991 and as Premier of the province of Saskatchewan from November 1, 1991 until February 2001.

The article consists of four parts. Part one deals with appointing a shadow cabinet during his time as Leader of the Official Opposition in Saskatchewan. The subsequent three parts deal with the appointment of cabinet members during his time as Premier. Whereas part two deals with appointing a cabinet for the first time, and part three deals with appointing a cabinet after an election in which the government is returned to office with a reduced majority, part four deals with appointing a cabinet for a coalition government in his last term as Premier.

Notable themes regarding appointing shadow cabinets include: the importance of appointing enough members to cover all the government ministries; the importance of choosing people who are intelligent, articulate and strong; and the importance of using a shadow cabinet as training for future cabinet ministers.

Notable themes regarding appointing cabinets include: the need to juggle numerous values or factors related to representational issues and personal qualities in appointments; the need for extreme care in vetting prospective candidates; and the need to exercise considerable care and attention in managing the ambitions and sensitivities of those who are appointed to cabinet, those who are shuffled within the cabinet, those who are dropped from cabinet, and those who never make it into cabinet.

The article is cast in a question and answer format.

APPOINTING OPPOSITION CRITICS

Q: As Leader of the Opposition, did you appoint people to a shadow cabinet or critic positions in the legislature?

A: Yes, I did. I had a shadow cabinet which essentially followed, in terms of responsibility and numbers, the makeup of the cabinet of the day. In some ways, this was challenging because Premier Grant Devine's cabinet was very large in those days. Virtually everybody was either a Cabinet Minister or a Legislative Secretary. Nonetheless, I appointed a complete shadow cabinet because it was important that virtually all our members in opposition gain experience critiquing the actions of government.

Q: When you appointed people to the shadow cabinet, on what basis were the appointments made? For example, did you include such considerations as legislative experience, region, constituency, gender, age, occupation, ethnic or language background, education, professional affiliation, religious affiliation, or status within the party? If so, can you elaborate on how you might have ranked these considerations or whether any of them were relevant at all?

A: All of these considerations were relevant, and I believe them to still be relevant with respect to the appointment of opposition critics in the legislature. I think you have identified all of the key factors that ran across my table and to which I gave some considerable personal consideration before making the decisions to nominate somebody.

However, there is another important factor that I considered. I was looking for men and women who could credibly stand up in the House, pose the questions or make the appropriate statements, both in opposition to, and as alternatives to, some of the plans of the government of the day. I was also looking for them to be able to communicate our core messages to the journalists, which is very important for obvious reasons, and to the party and to the public at large.

Legislative experience is important in appointing critics. In some ways it is tied to years of service. Senior members often expect to get senior assignments regardless of gender or age and the like. This makes for a very complex juggling process. It is a little bit easier to juggle things when in Opposition because generally no one who was assigned a critic's role really expected to continue to perform in that same policy area when our caucus formed the government. But still, you want to make sure that competence is a key factor in appointing any members of the shadow cabinet. And, one hopes that members of the shadow cabinet begin to build up their confidence, in preparation to becoming a full-fledged Minister of the Crown when that caucus forms the government.

In short, I was looking for people with the ability or competence either to perform key roles or to learn how to perform key roles very quickly. The ability or competence for this purpose is composed of some indefinable characteristics, including mental toughness, an ability to be quick witted and sharp on one's feet at the time of a heated exchange in the legislature, and timely and sound decision making when the Leader is not around.

Q: Would it be fair to say that the things that you have described embrace the ability of a person to perform mentally and verbally in pressure situations?

A: Yes, let me expand a little bit on this point regarding the importance of such a person also being able to think as well as being able to speak in policy terms. An MLA can be popular at home and be very good at serving the constituency. Such an MLA looks after the needs of the members of the constituency effectively and promptly for a variety of reasons, not the least of which is knowing what government or agency to approach if there is a need to solve a problem. But, it does not necessarily follow that such a person has the ability to think in policy terms to formulate or advance policy for debate within the caucus or the party, or even exhibit mental agility or toughness of thinking in the course of a particular exchange. I might also add that the reverse can be true. A very good performer in the legislature and in caucus, who is policy oriented and has done the policy homework, may not be a very good constituency person. Ideally, you wish for people with both sets of abilities.

So it is an imperfect piece of business putting together critic's roles. At the end of the day, to use that overused phrase, you rely on a lot on your intuition even after having processed and considered objectively, the skills, the backgrounds and the experiences that are required to be either a critic or eventually a cabinet minister.

Q: How important is "media savvy," as part of that package in serving as a member of the shadow cabinet?

A: In today's world the good six-second response is absolutely necessary. But again, that individual may not bring to the table the skills of deliberation, careful thought, or perhaps even party or public sensitivity. As in all matters, there are people who sometimes have certain capacities but not others.

I remember specifically a number of MLAs while Premier Allan Blakeney was leader of the NDP, one of whom is a very close personal friend of mine, whose wit in legislative debate was unmatched. The particular individual was kind of a modern day Will Rogers, from a Saskatchewan point of view, and everybody loved hearing from him. In advancing his arguments, he was very witty and would often demolish, through humour, the opposition's point of view. But in caucus it would be impossible to get him to contribute no matter how many times you spoke to him privately or even urged him publicly to do so. But none of us is blessed with having all of the qualities, at all the right times, and in all the right positions.

Q: What other considerations do you think are important for members of the shadow cabinet?

A: Members of a shadow cabinet must be loyal to the leader. Loyalty is always important. But it has been said many times that being an Opposition leader is probably one of the most difficult of all the tasks in our parliamentary system. You really do not have any power. Your authority stems from the fact that you have been selected as party leader by a party convention democratically selecting you. There is also a continual requirement to ensure that you listen to backbench members' views, identify problems, and propose possible solutions.

During my time in Opposition I was criticized sometimes for lacking a vision for the NDP. This criticism came from some members of the NDP, and even some members of the press. In this circumstance it is very easy to get derailed as an opposition group in the Legislature. I think loyalty is important to an effective opposition. I don't say blind loyalty—far from it. I welcomed members coming to me and saying, "You did not approach this in the right way." I didn't mind it in caucus. But when things get a little bit tight for the Opposition and everybody gets a little bit panicky, I have seen some Oppositions come apart. These are times when some MLAs don't remain steadfast in supporting the leader to get over a particularly difficult hurdle or crisis.

Q: Would you describe this as a team loyalty that is needed more in opposition than it is in government?

A: I found it to be more important in opposition than in government, but others probably would not agree with me. During our government years, we had some very difficult problems to tackle—particularly related to the finances of the province. Loyalty was not a major problem. Part of the reason for this is that when you are on the government side of the Legislature the sweet scent of being in power makes it easier to stay loyal. However, when in opposition some caucus members who think change is required either in policy or in leadership find it difficult to remain loyal either to the leader or the caucus. This is particularly true when a substantial proportion of the party is restless and questions the direction and performance of the leader or the caucus.

Q: In making an appointment to a critic position when you were in opposition did you ever consider such things as whether or not the person had been a supporter of your leadership bid, whether or not the person was a leadership candidate in the past, or whether or not the person came from another party?

A: Essentially, I did not. In my case I became the party leader by acclamation. This can be dangerous because you don't have opposing views openly debated. Sometimes they fester in the back rooms. The duty of the leader of an opposition party is to make sure that the factions of the caucus and the party are brought together as a team. You want the brightest and the best and the hardest working members around you, regardless of whom they have supported. In an uncontested leadership this is even more important. You have to make everyone part of the team to make the whole stronger.

The leader has to be able to bond with caucus colleagues in a warm and collegial manner regardless of who they supported. Still, the leader has to be cautious and reserved when appointing members to the shadow cabinet. After all, the leader must be free to make changes to the critic's roles or to try to convince the party or the caucus to go a different direction. In caucus the matrix is very complex as you try to weave a team which has purpose, direction and a meaningful message, which, you hope, will see you elected.

APPOINTING THE CABINET FOR THE FIRST TERM

Q: Thinking about the formation of your first cabinet—please elaborate on the major considerations in the appointment of cabinet ministers. Are there any considerations such as region or constituency experience that weren't a consideration in the appointment of cabinet member?

A: I tried to be guided by one important principle in the formation of the first cabinet. First and foremost, I wanted to keep the first cabinet small, numerically. I had a large caucus that came into office with me in 1991. I did not want to immediately fill 14 or 16 cabinet positions when I did not know the talents of the new MLA's. So flexibility dictated a small cabinet in its first stages.

Q: How large was your first cabinet?

A: I believe it was 10 plus me for a total of 11. Of the 11, seven were men and four were women.

Q: Was gender an important consideration?

A: It was a very important consideration, but it wasn't the most essential consideration at that time. We discovered very quickly that we had major financial problems on our hands. We needed ministers who could handle the pressure resulting from the very difficult decisions that would have to be made. This included program cutbacks and tax increases which would likely alienate our party supporters, and many members of the Saskatchewan public.
I also believed that we needed to have the ability to act quickly. A smaller cabinet permitted us to do this. And so the guiding principle for me was to have a cabinet which was capable, determined, and intelligent enough to acknowledge our fiscal crisis, advise as to how to handle it, communicate it to the public, and translate it to both the civil service and the public at large. And we needed to act quickly. Our political capital would be used up quickly and the bankers and financial institutions, not to mention Ottawa, demanded quick and decisive action.

So, gender was a factor but I knew that a bigger factor was ability to deal with this particular crisis.

With a small cabinet, regional representation became a problem. We could only have a few ministers from Saskatoon and Regina so that we could ensure some representation from other regions. Thus, it was a very tough cabinet to put together.

Q: Where would you rank previous cabinet experience as a factor in appointing that first cabinet?

A: I didn't think it was the key factor. Certainly, someone who had some knowledge of the legislative process and policy knowledge was given careful consideration. What was really needed, however, were people with an ability to grasp quickly the complexity and the gravity of our fiscal crisis who possessed the toughness who had the ability to come to a common decision, to implement, and explain it in the face of strong criticism. So cabinet experience was a factor but was not the most important factor. The most important factor was to find the most competent group of Ministers who could overcome the province's grave fiscal crisis.

Q: Do you remember how many of your first cabinet actually had sat in a cabinet before and how many had previous legislative experience?

A: I believe that out of the 11, including me, there were three with previous cabinet experience.

Q: Was there a premium on whether these people could carry through a necessary program as opposed to putting a premium on having served in a previous cabinet?

A: Absolutely. The enormity of the problem outweighed virtually all other considerations. Eventually other considerations would catch up. How long nine or ten people could work on this problem was a big factor. And then there were growing pressures from some members of caucus to get in to Cabinet. But, in my opinion, we needed a "war cabinet," in the first months. It is a rather unfortunate term but at least it communicates the level of importance to which we attached the gravity of the situation.

Q: Is it fair to say that things like occupation, ethnic background, education, political affiliation, or professional background were secondary?

A: It is fair to say that. For example, Carol Carson was a member of our first cabinet. She was a former mayor of Melfort. I do not know whether she ever previously held an NDP card. I may have looked it up at some point or other but I can't remember today whether she had been a longtime member of the New Democratic Party. It wasn't important to me. From the very first time that I met Carol Carson, I was impressed by her intelligence, her practical experience derived from her time as Mayor of Melfort, and her mental toughness.

Q: In making your selections to cabinet what matters constrained you the most?

A: Well, the size of cabinet was one of the constraints as I stated. At all times, and later as the cabinet expanded, I was constrained by my sense of a person's abilities. I did succumb occasionally to regional representation as the sole criterion for early entry into cabinet when it was necessary to do so.

Q: Would that include the urban/rural representation balance?

A: Yes, the urban/rural balance was important. However, equally important was the balance between the two largest cities. One of the constraints in this regard revolved around the choice of deputy premier. Since during my years as Premier, I represented Saskatoon, I chose a deputy premier from Regina. In doing so, I was following the Blakeney model of having the premier from one of the largest cities and the deputy premier from the next largest city. The deputy premier initially, was Ed Tchorzewski, from Regina. He had seniority over Dwain Lingenfelter, but after Ed fell ill Lingenfelter took it over. Those kinds of balances were required. Another important position in terms of representational balance was to include someone from the north of Aboriginal ancestry. To achieve this I expanded the cabinet later to bring in Keith Goulet from the north, who was highly competent person of native ancestry. My goal was to put together a cabinet of 14–16 people who were as representative of Saskatchewan as possible given the caucus that we had at that time.

Q: Was regional representation a major factor here?

A: It was more of a factor in the subsequent cabinets than in the first one. But I repeat, in those first years, speaking of the first cabinet, the major goal was forming a team that was willing and able to deal with the deficit. I was quite prepared to be defeated because of the measures we were going to take, if that was the will of the people. I was convinced that it absolutely had to be done. "Taming the deficit" and doing it quickly with all the hardship. If it meant defeat, I wouldn't like it, for both the party and myself, but, I was prepared for it. To get it done I needed conviction, discipline and support from cabinet and caucus.

Q: Given the constraints that you have mentioned, how did you cope with saying no to some people who may have thought that they should also be represented in the cabinet.

A: This is a very good question. For example, in Moose Jaw I had two excellent MLAs, one of whom ended up being Premier. In Prince Albert, the same situation … two very competent people, as well as others in the regions. But if you're constrained in the size of cabinet you go ahead and make the selections. You make a selection for cabinet, the first one, and then you provide a meaningful role for the other MLAs. And so I would make a very deliberate effort to ask somebody who did not make it into the cabinet to take on another important position such as chair of caucus or caucus committees, Speaker of the Legislative Assembly and so on. I was not keen in those early days on legislative secretaries because it was so abused by the previous administration.

Q: Would you have to indicate to people that they might be put into cabinet in the future?

A: No. I tried very hard not to hint at a future appointment because hinting and not fulfilling that perceived commitment would have been worse than never suggesting it. But you had to always give an MLA some sense of hope and opportunity.

But I would like to believe that MLAs were not involved mainly to get a cabinet position. Generally, most of them saw it as a privilege to be a part of the legislature and the government which they believed was an important task. So I really cannot think of ever telling somebody: "If you stick around long enough, I am going to make you a cabinet minister after I give this particular minister three or four years in recognition of previous service." I do not remember ever doing that.

Q: Did you ever make such a promise in the period leading up to an election? Did you indicate to any individuals that they could expect to be in cabinet and if so, was this most of the future cabinet, or only a few?

A: No. Not to that specific question. I did have conversations with two at the most. I made no commitments to any appointment to cabinet or specific portfolios. I merely indicated to them that I knew of their contribution to the province, to the party, and their qualifications. But no future offer of a particular position was made.

Q: *In the selection of your first cabinet, how much advice did you take from any of the following: legislative colleagues, party officials, trusted friends, academic advisers, future senior civil service appointees, and transition committee or committees? And if all or most of the above, can you just try ranking them in order of importance?*

A: I would say the number one source of information and advice came from the transition team—which was fairly small but was somewhat fluid. Without a doubt I took advice from trusted friends and advisers. I am going to mention one name here, former Premier Allan Blakeney, who knew a lot about good government and governance and knew a lot of the players. He was also very discreet in his observations.

Q: *Did you reach out to academic advisers?*

A: No, I did not reach out to academic advisers as such. I did not reach out to legislative colleagues with the exception of the two most senior ones, and NDP officials only a day or so before the swearing in of the cabinet. Once decided I would say to the party president and the advisory committee to the caucus, "Here is what I propose to do with the cabinet, do you have any objection to this?" Theoretically there could be some veto power there but none was ever used. But in the actual formation of the cabinet, the transition committee, and a few close friends and colleagues were the sources of advice I relied upon.

Q: *In constructing any cabinet, some individuals who hope to be in cabinet are left out. Would you please elaborate on the major considerations for people being left out of cabinet and secondly, the process by which they were eliminated from consideration.*

A: Well, the first hurdle that had to be overcome would be the selection process that I went through with the advice of transition team members. But after the transition team was gone, in subsequent cabinets, I would inform the prospective cabinet member of my intention to invite them to join the cabinet. I would tell the MLA of the cabinet assignment I intended to give them; I would not engage in any negotiations with that member about some other cabinet position. I would then make it very, very clear that the actual appointment was subject to the results of a clearing and vetting process which I had established. I made it clear to the would-be nominee that they were free to subject themselves to this process or not. But if they didn't, they would be excluded from cabinet.

Q: *What else can you say regarding the vetting process?*

A: The vetting process involved having the nominee interviewed for a lengthy period of time by a lawyer who also was a long-time member of the party. This person was an experienced lawyer with political experience, who worked on a confidential basis with the prospective cabinet members to determine whether there was anything about them, of a criminal, civil or personal nature, which could conceivably impair their ability to serve as cabinet ministers. With the approval of the prospective cabinet members, the lawyer would report to me any important information from the vetting process that had a bearing on their ability to serve as cabinet members. At the end of the process, the lawyer who conducted the vetting process would give me an overview of the important questions and answers. The lawyer would be given the freedom to withhold from me some matters which on a solicitor/client basis the prospective nominee might want to keep confidential. At that point the adviser would provide me with a general recommendation saying, "Premier, I have seen nothing in this person's past that would bar him or her from nomination to cabinet," and in fact, sometimes, would often go one step further and say, "I found him or her to be very knowledgeable in this area or very engaging or a good communicator." That was the kind of vetting and clearance I sought before making cabinet appointments.

Q: In your opinion did the process work well?

A: It worked reasonably well. I thought it was a very thorough process but the reality is that even after the process was completed there was yet another informal vetting process by the caucus advisory committee of the party as it is set out by the NDP constitution. By then you've done all that you can do to make sure you had a good nominee. But as I found out, even that was not a foolproof guarantee against some problem or issue arising, making what looked like a good nomination, a questionable one.

Q: In hindsight, given the process that you set in place, what extra steps would you have taken to ensure that something did not come up later?

A: I cannot think of any other step. I felt that the lawyer responsible for the vetting was an experienced person in both the legal and the political world. He was an experienced, knowledgeable, highly reputable lawyer who knew the ethical demands on him to do the job appropriately, and he was an honest and faithful adviser to me. I had absolute confidence in him. His reports were very thorough. He was extremely objective and fair. There was no better process.

   The focus was on important legal and ethical matters, including potential conflict of interest situations that could have an adverse effect on the person being an effective cabinet member. I did not wish to know about personal matters not relevant to cabinet duties. Dealing with personal matters not relevant to cabinet duties would have been too cumbersome and undesirable.

Q: Did this trusted lawyer give you advice as to the ability of the nominee to do the job?

A: That was not his mandate, however at the end of the conversations, occasionally, this adviser would say, "By the way, I think this is a good nominee because he or she struck me as…" and make an observation pertinent to the selection. He would never say, and I can say this without any equivocation, "You're trying to put a round peg in a square hole," or vice versa. "This is the wrong person for the wrong portfolio." His job was, and he carried it out very faithfully with extensive notes—probably destroyed now, to check the integrity, the skeletons in the closet, the medical issues, carefully and delicately, any of which could be barriers to getting entry in the first place. We all know that once you get entry into a cabinet position you can still get into a pile of trouble. Nobody can foresee that.

Q: Could you elaborate just a bit more on the process as to how people were informed that they would be included within cabinet?

A: The MLA was notified about 72 hours before being sworn in. Secrecy was paramount. Sometimes there would be a bit of bargaining … "What did you have in mind, Premier? Well, I did not think this was the portfolio, I had some other portfolio in mind." Those kinds of general comments were sometimes made. Almost all ultimately said yes to the offer to be a cabinet member in the position which I was offering, although one said no. That was a rather rancorous moment. But, it was eventually resolved with the nominee accepting my position.

Q: This person agreed to sit in cabinet but just not in that portfolio?

A: That's right.

Q: What else can you share regarding the appointment of the first cabinet?

A: The first cabinet was one that I had about 10 days to assemble. I think the election was October 21, in 1991 and I was sworn in on November 1 so it was about a 10-day transition period. A number of us, including the transition team went through a number of names and eventually it was left with me. Late at night I compiled the nine or 10 that I wanted in cabinet. This would change frequently. I remember one of the big issues for me in that first 10-day period was whether it was to be a 10-person or an 11-person cabinet. I remember one of the nominees who entered into the first cabinet was always number 10 or 11, either just barely in or just barely out. I did not feel that person had the prerequisite toughness to take the heat which was going to flow from the decisions that we were going to take. I was proven wrong, by the way. But that was one consideration and one pleasant surprise that came to mind.

Q: Were there a number of small things that still had to be done as well?

A: Yes, the Lieutenant Governor had to be notified of the date on which the cabinet would be sworn in. The prospective cabinet ministers had to be notified regarding the event, and they had to communicate with their families about the event. The actual event had to be planned and various things had to be in place. All of this had to be done within about three or four days from the final decisions regarding the prospective cabinet ministers and the actual swearing in ceremony. It was done within a relatively short time to minimize the risk of leaks regarding the appointments.

Q: Were there any media leaks regarding the appointment of your first cabinet?

A: No, not that I can recall. In fact I cannot think of a leak involving the appointment of any cabinet.

Q: In constructing a cabinet, did you ever turn to members of your family for advice?

A: No, never.

Q: Is there anything about making a cabinet in Saskatchewan that might be different from somewhere else?

A: Yes, I think there is. It may be the same, albeit for different reasons, in other provinces. But for Saskatchewan it is a feeling for what it means to be a prairie person. The combination of rural life, the history of our hardships, the expectations which were sometimes very high, all comprise an understanding of the province. The impact of weather, of external market forces, the history of Premiers Tommy Douglas and Jimmy Gardiner and all those other like them who shaped Saskatchewan in Canada. You have to have some knowledge and some sense about that. That doesn't mean you have to be a PhD student in Saskatchewan politics but you have to be aware of our history. Some of my best ministers were those people who were the sons and daughters of people who had worked or were still working our prairie soil.

Q: Could you elaborate on any specific considerations that shaped particular appointments to the first cabinet?

A: About the only thing that I felt was a specific requirement was that the Attorney General who, in our constitutional parliamentary democracy holds a very distinct position, had to be a lawyer. He or she is the Attorney General responsible for prosecutions and as such holds a different position from other cabinet ministers, and one which requires legal training.

Q: Was this because of your own experience as Attorney General?

A: Undoubtedly, I was influenced by my ten and a half years as the Attorney General but also by my legal training. The Attorney General holds a special constitutional position and that needs a sensitive person, who is very knowledgeable of what must be done to perform the key functions. I think, as well, since prosecutions and justice matters are always very sensitive, there is more public confidence in a person who is a lawyer. I do not think that applies, for example, to health. I think the art of healing and implementing policies to assist us in remaining healthy and living a life of well being, is of a different nature. I would actually be quite worried about appointing a Minister of Health who is a doctor or a professional healthcare service provider. The reason for this is that there is a risk of such a professional having too many close ties within the health care system that it would make it very difficult to deal with some important issues in an objective manner.

APPOINTING A CABINET FOR THE SECOND TERM

Q: What do you recall regarding the cabinet appointments for your second term in office, which lasted from 1995 to 1999?

A: The first thing I recall is that following the 1995 election the number of seats shrunk from 55 to 42. Consequently both the number of people and the pool of experienced legislators from which to draw cabinet ministers were diminished. I lost a number of very experienced and competent people in the 1995 election and again in the 1999 election, therefore the cabinet construction was more difficult following those elections.

Q: In the transition to the second cabinet, what weight did you give to the fact that you wanted to put a new face on cabinet?

A: When we won in 1995 I took the message from the public—which was obviously that we had won but had a significantly reduced number of voters voting for us. And I tried to be very careful as to why that was. I tried to restructure the cabinet to be more reflective of that. Thus it meant that some of the original, more experienced ministers in the more senior portfolios required a change from their portfolios to take over new responsibilities in new areas where they would not only freshen up their own images and their own experiences but contribute more to cabinet and the government as a whole. Also I wanted the public to view this as being reflective of a responsive government that didn't get quite the glowing voter support that it did initially in 1991.

Q: When you say lessons from the election itself, would these relate to the original considerations such as region or were there other messages from the election?

A: Yes, there were messages in the election and I would think that the most prominent message said, in effect, the voters are tired of cutbacks to programs, tired of 52 rural hospitals or more being closed or converted, and tired of paying more taxes. You have now balanced the budget. We want to see some reward and some reinvestment. That was my interpretation of the 1995 election result. In fact, the theme of our campaign was, "It's Morning Again in Saskatchewan." We had balanced the budget and we were now out to build what I dreamt I might build when I first entered politics—a social democratic, modern approach to governance for building a prosperous and fair-minded province.

It is difficult, however, when you have been a messenger for four years telling the people, "Look you are just going to have to live with this closed hospital because I promise you what you will eventually see will be as good, if not better." Well you can only ask for that patience and that loyalty for so long and then you have to produce some results. You have to have a new messenger doing that. So I brought in, for example, a new Minister of Finance very early after 1995.

I will add that this sometimes was not easily accomplished. A minister gets comfortable in a position, and sometimes wants to be there for the next phase when there may be a little more latitude to do things that he or she wanted to do in the previous phase. The cabinet changes were difficult to make, but eventually, there was acceptance.

Q: Thinking back to the earlier question about who you took advice from, who advised you primarily on cabinet shuffles of this nature?

A: Well, this is an interesting question but essentially it came down to two or three people, one of which would be the Chief of Staff who would be in daily contact with the ministers and would know how they performed. There was also my Deputy Minister. Occasionally a major issue would come to me via a senior member of the party who would say, "Look, this Minister just simply is not carrying the load very well."

Q: Was there a formal role for the Deputy Premier in this process?

A: I would invariably consult with the Deputy Premier once the issues were determined and the likely outcomes were clear.

Q: Not in the early process?

A: I'm sure there must have been some occasions when we would sit down over coffee. I would say, "I intend to do this, what do you think?" Sometimes the Deputy Premier would come to me, rarely, and urge me to include or exclude someone from cabinet. Generally, I would not consult other elected members because, like me, they had strong personal relationships with some of their colleagues. It would just have compounded my difficulties to consult other elected MLAs.

Q: What types of situations or considerations led to changes in the membership of cabinet? In particular what led you to drop or add someone to the cabinet?

A: There were essentially three types of situations or considerations that led to changes in the composition of cabinet. One was to change cabinet ministers either to improve the management of a portfolio or at least the communication regarding important issues within that portfolio. A second was to change ministers as a means of sending a message that the government was modifying its approach in dealing with a portfolio or problem. A third was to drop ministers from cabinet either because they were not up to the job or failed serious standards of conduct.

Q: What was the process for shifting cabinet ministers from one portfolio to another?

A: The process for shifting cabinet ministers was basically to sit down with them and say, "Look, I am looking at a cabinet shuffle. I am looking at rejuvenating the cabinet. I want to bring in some of the people who have been in the backbenches for the past four or five years. You have had a good run of four or five years at it. I would like you to take a backbench role or a new position in cabinet. Interestingly, sometimes asking ministers to change of portfolio is just as tough as asking them step out of cabinet. The reason for this is that ministers tend to get wedded to their favorite job, their favorite deputies and either do not favour or even fear change. Frequently, when dealing with such cases I would be met with criticism and opposition regarding my decisions. The ministers involved would indicate that I had somehow misread the situation, and they inquired as to what motivated my decision. I would try to assure them that it was a genuine effort to make a change. I do not think I ever said that they were somehow deficient or incompetent in performing the duties either as a cabinet minister in general or for a particular portfolio.

Q: What was the process for dropping ministers from cabinet?

A: If it was an issue of competence, then, it was handled as I've described. However, when it became absolutely clear to me that a Minister was facing serious allegations of conflict of interest, allegations of improper personal conduct or any criminal charges, my policy was that the Minister immediately leave cabinet. To do otherwise would have seriously encumbered the ability of the Minister and cabinet to perform their functions effectively. Communicating this message to a cabinet colleague facing charges or allegations was very difficult. My policy was to request an urgent meeting with the minister involved to which they invariably consented. Two documents were prepared for the meeting. One was a simple letter of resignation by the minister to me. The other was an Order-in-Council which as I advised the minister, would be immediately signed by me, removing him or her from cabinet. Invariably, the letter of resignation was signed by the Minister. Those rare situations were among the least pleasant moments in my time as Premier.

APPOINTING A CABINET FOR THE THIRD TERM

Q: What can you say regarding the appointment of a cabinet during the third term in which you formed the coalition government?

A: Let me say that I believe that the coalition government worked quite well. We actually entered into a formal written agreement with the Liberal Party members. The terms included, amongst others, that the agreement should be ratified by the provincial executives of each respective party so that there would be party legitimacy granted to the coalition.

For my party, there was a little bit of opposition to the coalition but not very much. Most caucus and party members believed that we were doing the right thing in seeking the coalition. I cannot speak with certainty about the Liberal Party but my guess is that they had a little more difficulty in achieving the same degree of consent. Nevertheless the actual agreement was a fairly expansive and it set out the fact that the Premier had the unfettered authority to make the appointments to cabinet in the normal or usual way. If you read the text of the coalition government agreement, it is clear that it is a model agreement with respect to the recognition of traditional parliamentary rules except for the requirement for it to be ratified by leadership of the provincial political parties.

However, there is another aspect to this, namely, the personal relationships. They are always important, especially in a coalition. Those who joined the coalition as the minority partners were under tremendous pressure from some in their party not to do so both because they would be the minority group in cabinet, and because publicly they would likely see a loss of their identity as Liberal party members. We had to be sensitive to these pressures. We had to make sure that there was an important role for them to play. Not only for their own self-esteem but also for the validation to their party that they were, in fact, advancing some of the ideals and some of the vision of the Liberal Party.

We all knew that we would have some significant differences between the members of the two parties in the coalition cabinet. However, we thought we could find common ground and a very good working relationship both with the Leader of the Liberal Party and with the other members of the Liberal caucus who entered cabinet. I wanted to bring in the Leader of the Liberal Party as well as one of his caucus members into cabinet right away and to assign the third Liberal as Speaker of the Legislature. There was no quarreling about portfolios or bargaining about policy positions. I was dealing with an intelligent man as leader of the Liberal party and we came to a very quick understanding as to, not only roles, but how we were going to function as a coalition government.

But it was not easy either for the Liberal leader or for me In fact, I think it was more difficult for him. For example, he had been publicly against some of the major innovations that we implemented in health care. So when he actually took the position in cabinet and had to have his previous statements read back to him in the legislature, it was very difficult for him. Many of his own party members, as it turned out, did not like it. But he took the criticism and he did it with loyalty to the coalition- caucus-cabinet decision-making processes, and with a very high degree of competence.

I made him Minister of Finance and he was a very thorough and knowledgeable Minister of Finance. He got a very quick handle on Treasury Board processes, Budget Bureau processes and understood the tough job that a Minister of Finance had to fulfill. Somehow, he was able to do it with a smile on his face.

The coalition government arrangement came apart after I left as leader, though this was not due to my successor as NDP leader, Premier Lorne Calvert. I think what happened was that the initial personal working relationship we had developed was difficult to carry forward. Some in caucus, on our side, became more wary of the new minority partners. During my time our people worked very hard at trying to understand Liberal policy and seek compromises. So, we did not have any major disagreements on policy matters. We did not have as many contentious policies either. The deficit had been conquered and the economy was coming back, so we had a little more freedom to spend money on programs. After my departure, however, one Liberal member left the cabinet. Perhaps this would have also happened if I had still remained as premier. The Liberal Party eventually selected a new leader who was strongly opposed to the coalition and gave the other two Liberal members the ultimatum of abandoning the coalition if they wanted to remain members of the Liberal Party.

Q: Was there ever a situation where the Liberal caucus members threatened to remove their support?

A: Not during my term. Not once during my term was there ever a communication of withdrawal on any policy issue at all. Look, I am a New Democrat. I have a certain ideology and a philosophy, and the coalition was not the easiest thing for me. Forget for the moment about Mr. Melenchuk's problems. I am sure it was very difficult for the Liberal leader but it wasn't easy on me either to have Liberals sitting around the cabinet table with full access to cabinet secrets and records. But I learned very quickly that this was an unwarranted fear in this circumstance.

Q: Of course we have very little experience with this here in Canada.

A: Exactly. That may be a case for proportional representation. But leaving that larger argument aside, our coalition worked well and collegially.

Q: Were there other notable differences in constructing the coalition cabinet? Were some factors emphasized or de-emphasized when appointing members of the Liberal Party to a cabinet post? Were they vetted in the same way as other cabinet ministers had been vetted?

A: Everybody was vetted by the adviser, including new coalition team members. But, there were constraints on me. There were unspoken constraints insofar as one cannot have the leader of the Liberal Party take a very junior portfolio. There was an additional constraint. There was always an uncertainty about how he might react to some issues that you felt very strongly about by virtue of your own philosophy and background. But, happily, that dissipated very quickly. I had confidence in the advice that the coalition cabinet gave me. This may be more the result of the personal chemistry than anything else. Still, if I had had my druthers, I would rather have had four more New Democrats in caucus so that we could have formed a majority government. Having said that I believe that the coalition worked out quite well for our citizens. We made it work.

CONCLUDING OBSERVATIONS

Q: Is there anything that we have not covered about cabinet making from the perspective of a premier?

A: It is, to use the old cliche, one of the most important tasks a premier must carry out. It is difficult. It is time consuming, and it is nerve wracking. It requires constant nurturing, listening, learning, some modifications, patience, of which I must confess at times I had very little, and it requires a very careful assessment of the character and ability of your people. A premier has to be close to the cabinet, to know them, but not so close to them that you can not do what is right in the interests of the government, the party, or the province. It is a very complicated piece of business and I am not saying that I fulfilled it admirably—that is for others to judge. But there is this undefined quality of making some of these judgments as objectively as you can, but knowing full well that sometimes they are going to have to be made intuitively as well. And even with all that, it still goes wrong from time to time.

NOTE
I would like to thank Dr. Howard Leeson for his assistance, encouragement and support for the production of the thoughtful questions in this article. His contribution was invaluable and appreciated.

The Administration of Justice in Saskatchewan: Seeking Political Accountability for Justice

John D. Whyte and Thomas Gusa

INTRODUCTION

Our aspiration for public goods delivered by the liberal democratic state is that they be efficient, effective and just. We want our roads to be safe, our doctors and hospitals to improve health, our police services to keep us safe, our schools to educate and our justice system to respond fairly and efficiently to social conflicts and social harms. Of course, none of these public institutions is able to live up to our ambitions all of the time. Both human frailties and human demands are ceaseless and the apparatus of the state struggles to keep up. The relationships between social phenomena and downstream effects, between costs and benefits, and between public policies and their outcomes are, notwithstanding the aspirations of social studies methodologies, beyond our calculation. In short, good public government is confounded by diversity, a rich array of social pathologies, our constantly refined anxieties, globalization, new technologies, increased mobility and the accumulation of demands.

In the metrics of state failure it is unlikely that one public good has failed to reach its goals more severely than the others. However, citizens seem to express most alarm over the breakdown of law and order. When they know that crimes against the innocent and rapacious acts against the vulnerable will not be remedied because of overburdened and insufficiently funded police and justice services, or because the real sources of crime and disorder lie beyond the state's means, then their sense of a general state collapse grows more pronounced. This sense of direness becomes lodged in rumours of gangs and cycles of gang homicides and home invasions, the ubiquity of drugs, and the sense of a rapidly deteriorating social responsibility. In truth, the checking of lawlessness has never been anywhere near to being comprehensively effective. It seems we have always had a low grasp of how to arrest social deviance before it is expressed or how to identify illnesses that lead to harming others or how to remedy the social pathologies that produce crime. The administration of justice inevitably betrays our hopes for a perfectly secure world and this is most true in communities, like Saskatchewan, in which inter-cultural conflict has led to dangerous levels of exclusion and anger.

But this is not the complete story. The administration of justice has its strengths and its general reliability and steadiness—at least as experienced in many communities—giving us the sense that we are living within a long and successful tradition of lawfulness. Our formal commitments are enforced, our disputes over dissolutions of all sorts are resolved peaceably, the public and private harms we experience ground claims that are impartially adjudicated, our losses are indemnified and, often enough perhaps, the people who commit crimes are held accountable through processes that are diligent and fair. The structures and institutions of justice have proven to be durable and the underlying ideology of the rule of law is the foundation of our conception of the good state.

In this paper we look at two features of the administration of justice in Saskatchewan that reasonably provide cause for concern. The first of these is the problem of how the benefits of our justice system are made available to those who need them. It is true that our structure of court adjudication has been built with assiduous attention paid to: ensuring fair procedures; constantly increasing legal expertise in those who judge our disputes; creating stronger guarantees of judicial impartiality; and encouraging developments in law that allow new classes of claims to be made against wrongful conduct. However, notwithstanding these elements of effective justice, legal representation in the prosecution of claims in our legal system is not a widely available public good. This means that the justice system that we want to trust—that we need to trust—is not actually available to meet the justice needs of a large segment of society. The justice system is designed to be effective but it is made available on a basis that defeats justice. When there is substantial denial of access to justice then our system of rules and our panoply of rights lead, for many, to no remedies for the legal abridgements that they experience.[1]

The second problem to be looked at is the unresponsiveness of the formal administration of criminal justice, initiated through the public prosecutions mechanism, to the complex and diverse challenges of criminal offending. Criminal prosecutions carry the imprint of public affairs and public interest and, indeed, criminal offending does disturb the public sense of security and well-being. It is for this reason that we bring prosecutions in the name of the state—specifically in the name of the head of state. And it is for this reason that we consider victim's rights in sentencing hearings following a conviction to be a criminal justice innovation. Victims of crime are not parties to criminal proceedings and victims' statements about the impact on them of crimes are only one factor—and not an overwhelming factor—in deciding appropriate punishment. However, in actual lived experience, criminal offending is often an expression of anger over, or of indifference to, one's local relationships— neighbourhood or domestic relationships—or to one's feelings of worth, value and respect. In other words, crime comes from social and psychological spaces that are local and private. If we are serious about reducing crime we need to care about the personal places where crime is born as much as we care about the formal expressions of public value. Of course, a good society will administer criminal justice as a way to protect every person through the deterring effect of public condemnation of crime. But it will also seek to respond to conditions of individual harms, private needs and broken relationships. In the second part of this chapter we will look at how the challenge of restoring the social health and well-being that is undermined by criminal behaviour could be better met through careful reform of prosecutorial responsibility.

ACCESS TO JUSTICE

Our justice system is a valuable state instrument for only some citizens. It is a public good that is distributed unfairly. The cost and complexity of obtaining formal dispositions of disputes means that many, many people do not use the justice system when their interests are placed in jeopardy through decisions and acts that could well be challenged in the legal process. Or, if they do venture to become engaged in the justice system, both their understanding of the process they are in and the costs of engagement inflict substantial transactional injuries on them. The distributional effect of this is that only some people have effective access to the justice system.[2] Moreover, this situation occurs in the context of every taxpayer—even the most modest consumer and almost every steady worker—being required to contribute to the costs of the justice system. Of course, the state is not completely indifferent to this unfairness in the delivery of a vital public good and a number of initiatives have been developed to respond. The most obvious are the development of legal aid programs and the use of specialist governmental agencies and tribunals to take up representation on behalf of individual claimants. These include such agencies as labour relations boards, human rights commissions, residential tenancy commissions, consumer protection agencies and, to name a uniquely Saskatchewan innovation, the Provincial Mediation Board that acts on behalf of persons with significant debt. A much smaller investment in improving access to law is found in the partial public financing of non-governmental legal clinics (e.g. Seniors Legal Assistance Service, Equal Justice for All), student clinics (e.g. CLASSIC (Community Legal Assistance Services for Saskatoon Inner City), and rights-based NGOs (e.g. the Elizabeth Fry and John Howard societies). Notwithstanding these initiatives, a basic fact of the administration of justice is that if court proceedings are necessary in order to vindicate a legal entitlement—especially proceedings in the province's high court, the Court of Queen's Bench—the cost of legal action means that most people with this level of dispute are warned off that course of action because of high expense. In other instances, disputes arising from marriage dissolution, for example, when the persons affected often have little choice but to proceed, can lead to financial devastation.

Confidence in the provincial administration of justice depends on it satisfying core precepts of justice in modern liberal democratic states, namely, equality before the law and due process.[3] Neither of these precepts is realized in a justice system that either excludes from court-administered justice those people who are too poor to bear the costs of legal representation or imposes court processes (normally through charging with a criminal offence) on people who are compelled to go through proceedings without representation. The principle behind publicly funded legal aid schemes is that access to legal representation in serious matters is a right and it should not be dependent on the accused person's ability to pay. The importance of this principle is underscored by convincing evidence that the poor experience a different quality of justice than the well-off.[4] For example, this is revealed by the fact that in criminal cases, the poor are more likely to be convicted and to receive a harsher sentence.[5]

Saskatchewan's legal aid plan was not initiated until 1967, and then only for those charged with criminal offences. Even today the plan makes only a very small dent in tackling the need for legal representation in civil law disputes. Prior to 1967, lawyers in private practice sometimes offered free legal services (or *pro bono* legal representation) to accused persons. In Ontario, lawyers' "*pro bono* services" were facilitated by a governmental agency for a decade or more before Ontario Legal Aid was created—in the same year that Saskatchewan began its program. In Saskatchewan, *pro bono* legal services have never enjoyed public recognition or (until very recently) significant encouragement. In 1972, Saskatchewan, in response to the Attorney General's Committee on Legal Aid (the Carter Committee) restructured legal aid to be delivered by legal aid staff lawyers instead of the initial structure of lawyers in private practice being compensated by the province for acting on behalf of legal aid clients. The hope was that the staff lawyer system would generate higher levels of expertise in legal matters that affect the poor, would build a mutually supportive relationship with communities being served, and would generate a structural or social understanding of legal difficulties that might make Legal Aid an effective agency in promoting reforms. It is doubtful that the last two goals have been significantly achieved. For one thing, the legal staff has never had the time or capacity to participate in either the analysis or the mobilization that meeting these goals would entail. It would require both a re-conception of lawyers' responsibilities and a significantly larger legal staff for these roles to emerge under the current legal aid scheme.

In all provinces, except Prince Edward Island, an independent organization is directly responsible for the administration of legal aid.[6] The motivation for the neutrality of these organizations stems from the need to establish the independence of legal services from the state since many applicants requiring representation are involved in litigation against the state either as defendants in criminal prosecutions or as litigants in civil suits against the government. With respect to the scale of public financing, in 2006, over $659 million was spent on legal aid in Canada, which amounts to just $20 for every Canadian.[7] Slightly trailing the national expenditure level, Saskatchewan Legal Aid Commission, in fiscal year 2007–08, implemented a budget of $19 million[8] for legal services and the administration of 157 staff positions (82 lawyers, one articling student, 17 legal assistants and 57 administrative staff) located in 15 offices throughout the province.

Multiple criteria must be met before a resident of Saskatchewan can access provincial legal aid.[9] The applicant must meet financial criteria based on a two-part test: the asset test and the income test. The financial situation of applicants will be examined to determine if they can be deemed to have enough money, including any spousal income, or assets (e.g. vehicles, RRSPs) to afford a lawyer without recourse to legal aid. Generally, applicants will qualify if they receive social assistance, or if their financial resources are at social assistance levels, or if the costs of obtaining the services from a private lawyer would reduce their financial resources to social assistance levels. The most recent Legal Aid Commission Annual Report identifies the very low income levels required in order to qualify for legal aid. It states: "To illustrate with a couple of examples, in 2007–08, financially eligible persons included single people making less than $12,000 (net) per year and families with four children with incomes less than $23,000 (net) per year."[10]

The next impediment to obtaining legal representation is that claims will proceed only if the legal matter for which service is needed falls within the range of cases that are taken on by the Saskatchewan Legal Aid Commission and then only if the matter has professional merit. According to the Saskatchewan Legal Aid Commission, professional merit has a multi-faceted definition.[11] Some or all of the following are considered: is the case one that a reasonable person of modest means would commence or defend; are the legal costs of commencing or defending an action reasonable when compared to the relief asked for; how serious to the applicant's interests is the potential legal or economic outcome of the action; what are the potential benefits to the client; is there a plausible defence to a charge; has the client been cooperative, such as keeping appointments or keeping in touch with the office after a move; and has the client accepted all reasonable professional advice from the assigned lawyer?

The range of services provided includes representation in criminal proceedings for both adult and youth applicants and in some civil law cases, but there are severe restrictions.[12] In the criminal law realm, legal aid will be available to applicants charged with indictable offences under the Criminal Code or other federal laws and to those charged with summary offences when there is a likelihood of imprisonment or loss of livelihood. Legal aid will only be provided for trials under the Youth Criminal Justice Act if the offence falls within the same criteria of the charge being for a serious offence and there is likelihood of imprisonment. Furthermore, as the 2007–08 Annual Report notes, the number of cases that legal aid is able to take has decreased due to the increasing complexity of criminal trials, the increased practice of multiple charges being laid and, perhaps most disturbingly, the much longer time it is taking criminal cases to get to trial.[13] In the civil law realm, the Commission limits its service to family law and will provide assistance to applicants in matters such as child custody, spousal support payments, separation and divorce.[15] As is evident, there is a very broad range of court proceedings that affect vital interests of individuals for which there is no legal aid assistance. This gap means that: the court processes that poorer people find themselves involved in unfold in the context of process mystification. These litigants experience lost opportunities to challenge proceedings against them. They are frequently ineffective in confrontating damaging evidence and they have a low capacity to plead their cases—

especially, to conduct them on the basis of existing statute and case law. The closing of the large gap between the promise of due process and the reality of court proceedings for poor litigants has been slight.

The range of legal administration that bears on important interests for which there is no state-aided legal assistance is broad. This means that there is a significant portion of the public that simply does not have access to state aid with respect to important areas of legal regulation. A very partial list of what is not covered by publicly funded legal aid includes lawyers' services for proceedings related to matrimonial property, wrongful dismissal and other employment law claims, actions based on municipal bylaws, driving offences other than impaired driving charges, private prosecutions, small claims actions (or, in fact, most civil claims for damages), welfare appeals, foreclosures, matters under the Immigration and Refugee Protection Act, parole hearings and inmate discipline hearings in correctional centres and penitentiaries. The sorts of regulatory legal processes for which legal help is often needed but is not available from legal aid include property transfers, tenancy contracts, wills, estate administration, income tax and compliance with business legislation.

Perhaps, what is most disturbing is that in Saskatchewan there is no system for obtaining legal representation in the context of the administration of poverty law.[15] New Brunswick and Prince Edward Island are the only other provinces that share this deficiency. A non-exhaustive list of poverty law issues includes administration of Employment Insurance, the Canada Pension Plan, Old Age Security, income assistance, public housing, landlord and tenant law, workers' compensation and debtor and creditor rights. Residents of Saskatchewan requiring services in any of these poverty law areas are instead referred to organizations such as the Office of the Rentalsman, the Workers' Compensation Board, and the provincial Ministry of Social Services. While this arrangement is far better than total non-representation, often the agencies that people are able to resort to are the very agencies that have already made decisions that have rejected claimants' claims.

Notwithstanding these gaps in state funded legal aid, the greater defect of the program is the stringent financial criterion for qualifying for legal aid. Because an applicant needs to be virtually at social assistance levels to be eligible for Saskatchewan Legal Aid, this means that the "working poor" and "middle class" do not receive assistance in pursuing claims or in defending themselves from criminal charges. Only the extremely poor and the wealthy are certain to gain the benefits from Saskatchewan's justice system. In other words, access to justice in Saskatchewan follows a "j-curve" with availability to legal services declining as one gets richer until one's income moves beyond working class levels.[16] A majority of the population is left to two equally unattractive choices when faced with court proceedings or when needing to initiate court proceedings. They must either forgo defending themselves, or prosecuting their claims, or they must proceed through representing themselves and that is without doubt a desperate strategy bound to be experienced by the person acting on his or her own behalf as a further stage of disempowerment and a deeper sense of exclusion from the experience of social justice.

This sense of exclusion from the realm of justice is most acute in those cases of criminal prosecution for which legal aid is not provided. Most accused persons are not highly adept at social functioning, especially in formal and complex processes. They may be poorly educated, have low levels of literacy and live lives that are challenging in many ways. Legal aid will not offer assistance to first time offenders who commit minor offences, especially when they are not likely to be jailed. However, these offenders will likely receive a criminal record which will have deeply negative consequences on their lives, their sense of self and their prospects. They may not even be aware of the implications of a conviction for employment, security clearances, volunteering, foreign travel, and the operation of vehicles, and, even if they do recognize these sorts of implications, there is very little that they can do to minimize the injury.

Although Legal Aid is Saskatchewan's most comprehensive response to the moral challenge of unequal access to justice, it is, in truth, a meagre response. Furthermore, for a very long time there has been neither any re-consideration of the scope of legal services covered by Legal Aid (notwithstanding the increased regulatory complexity of most people's lives)[17] nor any real increase in the budget allocation for legal aid services or the expansion of legal aid staff. The federal Department of Justice has pointed out that following a period of strong growth in legal aid case approvals and expenditures in Canada during the 1980s and 1990s there is now a steadily decreasing trend, including in Saskatchewan, in the number of cases that are approved for legal aid and in the per capita expenditure on legal aid in Canada.[18] The province does not have a current reform policy process relating to legal aid or, more generally, to access to justice. One might ask: what can the province do? The income eligibility criteria could not be raised to sensible levels (every family earning less than $40,000, for instance)[19] and the service range could not be expanded to cover the matters listed above without, at a rough guess, increasing the budget four- or five-fold to as much as $100 million.[20] Is this a reasonable expectation? On the one hand, state supported legal services would still be miniscule compared to universal programs like health care and education but, on the other hand, fair access to the legal process may matter less to the well-being of the province. At the level of the impact on individuals, determinations of legal liability (criminal or civil) can be as life-defining as educational experience but, of course, they are not normally as directly injurious to persons as inadequate health care. If the provincial calculation is that the province's social well-being is not as negatively affected by markedly uneven access to legal services as it would be by poor education and health care—and it seems that this has been the calculation—this means that we have decided that our long and deep commitments to justice for all and the rule of law are to be achieved only partially and that it is satisfactory if these values are realized only rhetorically or symbolically. Apart from the corrosive effect on confidence in the provincial justice system when it is a public good that is distributed so narrowly and with such advantage to the already wealthy, the failure to enable so many people to use the justice system mocks the foundations of civil society—that people should live together under common conditions of legal restraint and legal responsibility.

In a May 2007 speech on the topic of access to justice for Canadians that fall outside legal aid coverage and lack the financial capacity to engage in litigation, Chief Justice McLachlin of the Supreme Court of Canada observed that " their options are grim: use up family assets … become their own lawyer, or give up."[21] The choice that many lower- to upper-middle class Canadians make when confronted by the need to make, or defend against, a legal claim is to act for themselves in legal proceedings. Although self-representation in legal proceedings is a consequence of meagre state-assisted legal representation, it is hardly a solution to the access to justice challenge. For one thing, the term "self-representation" is actually a euphemism which disguises the reality that self-representing litigants are actually unrepresented; The common law adversarial system is premised on two equally matched parties vigorously presenting and challenging the other before an impartial judge and these conditions are simply not the reality when one side is self-represented.[22]

Both the courts of Saskatchewan and the Saskatchewan Legal Aid Commission have acknowledged the plight of the unrepresented litigant and have taken steps to provide minimal levels of service—minimal not because of lack of will so much as the difficulty of developing information that fits the virtually infinite array of contexts in which litigation takes place. On the websites of both the courts and the Commission, links are provided to pages that give instructions on how one should go about representing himself or herself. The instructions are divided into self-representation in civil litigation and in criminal defence. At the top of the web page for criminal charges, written in italics, is the statement: "This is general information and is not intended to take the place of legal advice from a qualified lawyer." At the bottom is the statement: "This information is for general educational purposes and is not meant to be used as advice in respect to the conduct of any particular case or proceeding against a person. Please contact a lawyer for specific information." Fair warning, certainly, but hardly relevant to the person for whom legal counselling is not affordable. The web page for criminal charges includes key definitions and procedural information pertaining to pre-court and court proceedings as well as information on sentencing. It is fair to conclude that the web information simply does not enable an accused person to conduct an effective defence or, more importantly, to understand what the process is going to be like or how they should prepare for it. With respect to civil cases, the websites describe the Small Claims Court process in more detail—likely so much detail as to confuse the unsophisticated. While this last form of assistance does not break new ground in expanding self-representation since self-representation has been the norm for small claims court actions, this effort made by Saskatchewan courts to assist unrepresented litigants is laudable. What is of concern is that by mid-2008 the courts of Saskatchewan website did not contain help with respect to family litigation, the very matter that engages all income groups and which entails the greatest losses to private well-being, both financial and familial.

Most of the research on problems in the area of self-representation has been carried out in criminal courts and there has been limited, if any, research done on self-representation in civil matters. However, this research can be extrapolated into civil matters since many of the pitfalls transcend the precise nature of the dispute being adjudicated. With respect to the imagined narrative, it needs to be recognized that accused persons are likely to be relatively poorly educated and have lower levels of literacy.[23] In Saskatchewan, many criminally accused persons will also face language and cultural barriers and this is especially so for Aboriginal defendants and immigrants. In many courts, including those in Saskatchewan, there is also a significant number of accused who suffer from mental disorders. Going to criminal court will be intimidating and stressful and the culture of adversarial advocacy, even when muted by accommodating prosecutors and judges, is likely to sap persons of the sense that they can control—or even have any say—in events. The only thing that may be fully understood—and this, unfortunately, is certainly not always the case—is the costly consequences of not being effective. This condition of being filled with the senses of high risk, low capacity to protect one's interest, confusion and alienation is, one can assume, a common daily occurrence for self-represented litigants in Saskatchewan courts.

The first problem that self-represented persons face is lack of knowledge of the relevant area of law. In studies of self-representation, litigants have been described as suffering from "lack of" problems—lack of experience, lack of knowledge of relevant law, court ritual and form, procedural rules that constrain presentation and the rules of evidence, lack of ability to intervene to limit damaging effects and lack of understanding of the adversarial culture.[24] Though information about laws and the legal process can be accessed through the internet, the ability to process it and to apply it effectively in a courtroom takes legal professionals years to acquire. Likewise, knowing how to perform in a courtroom and being able to express positions with confidence and with full grasp of the contingencies in play at any given moment takes a great deal of experience. A courtroom is an intimidating place in which the audience—the judge and counsel representing your opponent—is innately critical and challenging. Added to these difficulties is the specific burden in self-representation of high emotional affect around the issues, the evidence and the outcome. This emotional condition impairs both concentration and judgment. As a result of all these factors working together the overwhelming view of many lawyers and judges is that self-represented litigants lack the ability to function in the adversarial and expertise-driven environment of criminal courts.[25]

With respect to areas of civil litigation, it is unlikely the situation would be markedly different. Whether the proceedings deal with family law disputes, claims under tort law or small claims, the self-represented litigant suffers from the same disadvantage. As one judge in a recent study on self-represented litigants explained, "Most don't have a clue. They don't understand how trial is conducted [...] They don't have the advocacy skills, and who is to blame them for that? A lot of them are poorly educated people and people who are on the margins. But, even people who have been generally more fortunate and better-educated do not have the advocacy skills. They don't know how to ask questions and don't know which questions to ask."[26] Regardless of the sociodemographic characteristics of the litigant, or of the type of litigation, the self represented person will be at a disadvantage.

The ability- and knowledge-based deficiencies of self-represented litigants lead to further problems that affect their chances of receiving access to justice. Even though most criminal matters are disposed of without a full trial, the unrepresented litigant must appear at earlier stages of the criminal justice process and these preliminary stages can be highly adversarial. In civil litigation as well, self-represented litigants must go through a combative discovery process and an adversarial mediation process and may be subjected to many pre-trial motions (possibly driven by the strategy of dissuading the self-represented person from pursuing a court action or legal defence). In both civil and criminal cases the unrepresented litigant is opposed by counsel in complex legal procedures that are unfamiliar to lay persons. Interviews in criminal courts with lawyers and judges indicate that virtually all unrepresented litigants make mistakes in court proceedings that harm their legal position.[27]

The mixture of client-based deficiencies in ability and knowledge, along with the obvious disadvantages and mistakes committed by unrepresented litigants, creates a situation that is cause for deep concern. While there are no empirical studies that exist on the issue, qualitative data reveals that virtually no accused persons who appear unrepresented in criminal courts can represent themselves without making errors that place them at a disadvantage.[28] It has been found that in some situations, depending on the jurisdiction, and the state at which the plea was entered, over 50% of accused were convicted without the benefit of legal representation. Furthermore, depending on the jurisdiction, and the type of offence, up to 30% of those who are unrepresented and convicted are then incarcerated.[29] There are no specific statistics with regard to Saskatchewan, but if our numbers are even close to these it should be cause for alarm. But the problem does not stop and start with conviction rates and the resulting incarcerations. There are several other complications that lead to the unrepresented litigant's failure. To begin with, many unrepresented accused do not realize that not being represented precludes them from certain court processes. Crown prosecutors will rarely, if ever, plea bargain with the unrepresented because prosecutors are concerned that dealing directly with an accused that is representing him or herself can lead to situations, such as their becoming a witness to an accused's damaging statement or admission of guilt that would jeopardize their position as prosecutor. As a result, the unrepresented accused does not benefit from reduced or dropped charges. Furthermore, in most courts throughout Canada, a significant number of unrepresented litigants plead guilty "just to get it over with," without understanding the weaknesses of the Crown's case or the repercussions of conviction. It has also been shown that many unrepresented accused plead guilty (in the hope of avoiding jail time) because they cannot comply with bail restrictions or afford time for numerous court appearances because of the l impact these can have on their families and on their income. Legal representation would ensure that these concerns were raised and, in many instances, accommodated by the court. Many accused may plead guilty, even when they have a legal defence, because they are ashamed or embarrassed and they wish to minimize publicity and their shame over the charges against them. This is especially the case for immigrants and members of visible minority groups that may experience more than usual community stigma or personal shame over a criminal charge and may feel particularly vulnerable over involvement with the criminal justice system.[30]

Problems and consequences faced by self-represented defendants in criminal cases are also experienced by the self-represented in civil cases. Strategizing, knowledge of court procedure, and the ability to process and apply the law will be areas of shortcoming. Lack of confidence and a sense of inability to direct events will be suffered by any self-represented litigant. Failure to understand rules of evidence and the fact that many self-represented litigants cannot afford the numerous court appearances will also be problems. The consequences of these inadequacies will not differ from their effect in criminal courts. The damaging effects of civil decisions, perhaps especially decisions relating to matrimonial property and child custody, in which not all relevant evidence is presented and all relevant claims made, can be easily envisaged.

Besides these serious concerns over the quality of justice self-represented people can expect, and hence concern over the real efficacy of our criminal and civil laws, there is the added problem of what self-representation is doing to the administration of justice. Chief Justice McLachlin has commented on the negative impact of self-representation on the courts. She said: "The judge is faced with telling them what the law is, telling them what procedures are available to them, and trying to help that person while remaining an impartial arbiter."[31] The actual effect of these litigants on the court system is a much debated. For instance, it is maintained that a self-represented litigant in a court proceeding will jeopardize fairness, complicate consideration of the issues, delay proceedings because of the need to explain procedures and legal points and lead to time being spent on matters not relevant to the precise legal claim that the court is charged with deciding. Many judges and prosecutors claim that the presence of unrepresented litigants forces them to act outside of their normal roles in the adversarial process in order to offer assistance. In some criminal trials, judges feel they must be punctilious in the extreme and ample in their direction of every aspect of the proceedings in order to avoid improper situations and to compensate for the accused persons' lack of counsel. Judges are required to intervene on behalf of accused persons if they believe it is required to ensure that their rights are protected. This creates concerns over the fairness and impartiality of the trial.[32] As stated by Ontario Court of Appeal Justice Borins in *R. v. Tran*: "It is not an enviable task for a trial judge to conduct a criminal trial where the defendant is without counsel. Accommodating the inexperience of a self represented litigant presents a challenge to a trial judge who must balance the need to preserve his or her neutrality with the duty to ensure that the accused receives a fair trial."[33] Practising lawyers also express displeasure in dealing with a self-represented litigant. They state that it is difficult to engage with someone who doesn't know the law and doesn't understand the legal process and court procedures. They claim that it adds to their workload and increases stress. In a study carried out by the Nova Scotia Department of Justice on self-represented litigants, court staff described the impact of self-represented litigants in these terms: frustrating, anxiety creating, time consuming, stressful, obstructs performance of other duties and exhausting.[34]

The public policy argument that the presence of self-represented litigants in the court system creates costs that would not be borne had the litigant had legal counsel is premised on the claim that clogging the courts with amateurs is costly and burdensome. Some researchers claim that self-represented litigants prohibit access to justice for all because their cases take more time than cases with counsel. The trickle-down effect is that other cases are delayed and fewer cases can be heard. This is compounded by the fact that self-represented litigants rarely settle without a court hearing and this uses up more court time than cases which involve counsel who are normally very alert to the possibility of reaching a settlement before a matter goes to trial, or during the trial.[35] However, some researchers claim that self-represented litigants do not interfere with other court parties or prevent the court system from running effectively. Professor Robert Flannigan points out that these concerns are misguided as delay and frustration are common features of litigation. Furthermore, Flannigan states that self-represented litigants are not more responsible for delay or frustration than lawyers themselves are.[36] These claims are supported by research that shows that, contrary to expectations, the quantitative data does not support the claim that self-represented litigants create an increased burden on the courts. In most provincial criminal courts in Canada, appearances in pre-trial hearings by unrepresented litigants were typically shorter than those with legal counsel. It was also found that in most of these courts, unrepresented litigants made fewer pre-trial appearances than accused with legal representation. In general, in a majority of Canadian courts, trials involving unrepresented litigants did require more time to resolve than cases represented by duty counsel. However, cases in which the accused was represented by private lawyers were found to take longer than those without counsel.[37]

However, the main point is not that court operations are, or are not, hindered by self-representation, but that the current situation of poor access to legal representation for all but the reasonably well-off has led to a recent significant increase in defendants and claimants going to court without legal counsel and, generally, this has weakened their ability to have their legal rights vindicated. Therefore, self-representation is a product of access problems in our justice system, as well as an exacerbation of them. It is a consequence that adds to society's failure to deliver justice to all on more or less equal terms. There is no easy or cheap solution to this problem. At the level of public policy analysis it receives a great deal of intelligent attention.[38] Imaginative and multi-faceted initiatives are proposed to avoid litigation, to simplify litigation, to create stronger networks of support for litigants and, of course, to increase public expenditures so that ordinary Canadians can pursue their legal entitlements and get their full share of due process. However the nation's governmental and judicial institutions are providing little assistance in meeting this justice pathology. Legal aid programs are not being restructured or re-thought in the light of a palpable breakdown in adequate representation. There are few new policies or significant new funds. The federal government (one might say, outrageously) cancelled the Court Challenges Program that funded public interest constitutional litigation, thereby cutting off access to the courts for all those seeking Charter remedies unless they are very wealthy or are part of a well-funded interest group.[39] That decision mocks our commitment to equal justice for all. The Supreme Court of Canada in two recent cases[40] and in a recent refusal to hear an appeal[41] has defeated attempts to bring access to justice into the realm of protected constitutional rights. We can only conclude that justice mechanisms sometimes work to support practices of injustice by denying people a real capacity to engage in legal proceedings.

Of course, the inadequacy of legal aid and the inefficacy of self-representation do not exhaust all the dimensions of the access to justice issue. There are other strategies and policies. These include broader use of alternative dispute resolution measures such as: mediation; attempts to demystify law and procedure; more test case litigation; greater use of specialized clinics in areas such as immigration law; radically simplified rules of procedure; legal expenses insurance, at least for employees of large firms and institutions; and more extensive free legal advice given by members of the private bar on a *pro bono* basis. Consideration and development of these sorts of initiatives are necessary, if only because of the sense that the state cannot meet every social need through more and more services. Sadly, however, it is a mistake to think that any of these represents a breakthrough in enabling ordinary citizens to gain access to legal processes. Of the above ideas, the most promising may be significant expansion in law firms' *pro bono* work. However, not surprisingly, there is a natural limit to this, and it does mean that, for the poor, legal assistance becomes, like food, another charity. At the end of the day it will be public money spent on something closer to universal legal aid and not administrative reforms or lawyers' charity that will overcome today's injustice in the distribution of legal services.

CRIMINAL PROSECUTIONS AND EFFECTIVE JUSTICE

We live in an age where we should no longer be satisfied simply because state agencies perform their specific duties well. We used to believe that if each agency or institution were true to its internal code the sum effect of all proper administration would be a good state and a good society. But the rise of the critical perspective of deconstruction has taught us that institutions' moral codes can sometimes limit their social success—that they were formed when cause and effect were simpler and the context of applying fixed rules and procedures was stable and well understood. Today, we care less about constancy to the forms and more about results, especially the unintended consequences that arise from our heterogeneity and our barely understood social interactions. Perhaps a key area in which this conflict for primacy between form and substance is played out is in the area of criminal prosecutions, especially in a society that experiences every kind of social crack—cracks that make the labelling of deviance a complex social science and devising constructive responses a soup of hopeful policies and good intentions. In short, we have reasonably come to wonder if the formal and traditional processes of accountability for criminal prosecutions now meet our needs for creating a peaceable society.

However, we do not forget the basic statecraft truth that each constitutionally recognized agency brings its own set of political virtues to governance. (For that matter, so do the more recent, non-constitutionalized state agencies such as specialized tribunals, and officers of the legislature such as election administrators, auditors and ombudsmen.) The virtues that legislatures and cabinets bring to public government have seemed unconnected to the prosecutorial process. In fact, much of the intellectual energy behind the academic writing on the Attorney General is directed to purging from the prosecutorial function the vice of political interest—the vice that we call partisanship. It is claimed that the normal political virtue of responsiveness to political interests that governs the political branches of government becomes a deviant influence when present in the context of administering criminal justice.

However, before we conclude that this simple division between purity and danger is essential to prosecutorial legitimacy, we must ask why it is in our system that the Attorney General is usually a member of the legislature and always a member of the cabinet. And, why is it usual in Canada for the criminal prosecution services to be located within departments of justice and under the administrative supervision of those departments? The answer to these questions is simply that criminal prosecutions are a part—a key part—of the criminal justice system, and the criminal justice system deserves, and needs, both justice policy and political accountability. The apparent and traditional instruments of justice policy are: statutorily defined offences; common law developed elements of crime; professional police investigation and charging; prosecution by a politically independent service; investigations and trials that meet the conditions of sections 7 to 14 of the Canadian Charter of Rights and Freedoms, including a trial before an independent and impartial tribunal; dispositions that meet rigorous legal standards; and defensible sentencing and corrections administration that satisfies the law, fulfils the sentence that was given and meets national and international standards of humane treatment for prisoners. As extensive—and as expensive—as these basic conditions for justice are, this cannot be the complete picture of justice policy. The reason is that criminal justice policy, understood solely in terms of these key elements of the legal process, too often does so little social good and so often does much personal and social harm.

The cause of the basic criminal justice system's capacity for social harm is that, for all its care, all its constraints and all its refined analysis, it fails to reflect the complexity of the social expression that lies behind criminal acts—

that lie behind the many acts of callousness and harming that result in social disorder. Criminal guilt is presented as a declaration of moral and legal imperfection but it is, in so many cases, more profoundly a manifestation of a broader social failure. Its real messages are: social exclusion, the systemic construction of minorities—usually visible minorities—as a misunderstood and disrespected other, persistent patterns of oppressive inter-societal relations and colonialism. Crime tells us that people in our political society have experienced immense social dislocation and social devaluation. It tells us that the great political virtue of self-determination is unknown to both the individuals and the political collectives that comprise our minorities. It tells us that there is a class of dispossessed and they have been robbed by the social and economic structures of a valued social role; they have experienced a history of abuse and they look into their future without hope and without any idea of what a successful strategy for inclusion might be. It tells us that, for many, contemplation of their place engenders only despair, and (since it is only sensible to seek to mask despair) for them the best choices are destructive choices with harm distributed without reason or purpose to self, spouse, children, parents, neighbours, community and strangers.

To place the phenomenon of crime so unequivocally within the operation of social determinants and, hence, away from the impact of personal choice, character and morals is a political stand and, like most political positions, lacks the nuance and balance that refined social criticism requires. But, social order and control of crime is a political project—one of the vital aims of the good and effective state—and, as a matter of politics, it is prudent to form a generally plausible political understanding of criminal offending—of the social practices and conditions that erode public safety and public security— and to form a public strategy that reflects that understanding. Our modest claim is that a highly plausible (and compelling) political conclusion for some political societies, and their elected leaders, to reach is that they simply should not decide to do nothing (other than what they are doing without much good effect through formal criminal justice) to address disorder. Such political societies cannot sensibly choose to pursue the goal of order and safety through eschewing strategies such as restorative justice, community-based justice, therapeutic diversion for treating addictions and mental disorders, programs for controlling the effects of fetal alcohol syndrome disorders, and community empowerment, to say nothing of the broader strategies that are appropriate in these jurisdictions of decolonization and Aboriginal self-government. These sorts of initiatives need to be seen as logical and fully legitimate justice policies for responding to crime in some jurisdictions. This, we claim, is true for Saskatchewan.

Justice departments and Attorney General ministries should not place these sorts of justice policy analysis outside the box of controlling crime, reducing offending and promoting safe communities. They should attempt to create a seamless administrative mechanism for allocating the state response to offending between the two major paradigms of charging and diversion to processes leading to social reconciliation. Similarly, they should build strong and mutually respectful linkages between the central state apparatus for justice administration and community based initiatives for responding to offending and crime reduction. They need to refrain from seeing their role in managing the response to crime as that of the senior partner, licenser, coordinator, uniquely legitimate voice, or sole contractor.[42] Justice departments should not choose to say nothing to the police services with which they must co-ordinate nor should they choose to say nothing to their prosecutors about the need to develop and apply mechanisms for promoting community engagement with offending. Justice departments need to adopt a flexible sense of how to respond to offending and develop a deeper understanding of the community whose interests need to be met in the response to offending, the capacity of that community for creative intervention and the processes that the community feels might most effectively meet needs. These kinds of political insights should be communicated to prosecutors so that they will inform their exercises of discretion and not be seen as external and improper influences. When these political ideas cannot be introduced into the relationship between Attorneys General and prosecutors, or between Department of Justice administrators and prosecutors, there will ultimately be a political reckoning. This interest in more effective responses to social disorder will emerge through more overt political discourse that will ultimately force their way into prosecutorial administration. This political influence is not inappropriate; it demands that those at the heart of the administration of criminal justice be attentive to the political need for efficacy in fighting crime, for the state of social health, for the fiscal consequences of not managing to reduce high rates of offending and, even, for Canada's reputation as a fair and orderly state. These are, most certainly, elements of political accountability but they must also come to inform the prosecutorial function.

The means by which this sort of political direction normally enters into prosecutorial decision-making is Attorney General-issued prosecutorial guidelines.[43] Sometimes these guidelines have a rhetorical function and cannot guide the professional exercise of the prosecutorial discretion. For instance, zero tolerance guidelines cannot remove the inevitable prosecutorial consideration of the factors of de minimis harm or the unlikelihood of obtaining a conviction. These factors must continue to govern decisions. However, other guidelines, such as those relating to community and therapeutic options in responding to offences, can properly have an impact on charging decisions that are made.

Perhaps one should not be overly confident about their influence. These guidelines are hard to administer. They can be difficult to apply because some believe that Attorney General guidelines with respect to the laying of charges erode the rule of law in the sense that the guideline directs that not all offenders be treated equally according to the law.[44] The guidelines are based on the view that treating all offenders according to federally prescribed laws and procedures does not lead to reform for whole classes of offenders, nor is any social benefit produced, and that something else—something more informal and more flexible—will do more good for both the offender and the community that he or she is a part of. The message of Attorney General prosecutorial guidelines may seem to cast doubt on whether the precept of treating all people equally according to the law is being valued and, as a general position with respect to public administration, this is not a doubt that is initially positive for the rule of law. However, accepting the inherent conflict between efficacy in responding to crime and subscription to narrow conceptions of the rule of law is exactly the sort of political responsibility that those charged with the administration of justice must accept and must express administrative principles about. It is not enough for justice administrators and ministers of justice to say that the social efficacy of criminal administration is of no concern and that the process of building safe and responsible communities is the business of other departments. Criminal justice is precisely the place where public administration has a very large impact—an impact that if performed in a way that is oblivious to social context and need simply compounds social disintegration, but if performed imaginatively and in the spirit of community development can make a positive contribution to community well-being. Of course, the needs for social development go far beyond changing the norms that guide criminal prosecutions—and far beyond altering the mechanisms of justice—but crime is a central expression of social condition and how we respond to it reveals our real interest in promoting social capacity and health.

In making criminal justice adapt to the political idea of improving our social response to offending and improving the state of social order there is a strong case for making the administration of criminal justice responsive to broader justice policy. The efficacy of this project depends significantly on the sense of responsibility that resides in prosecutors. It also depends on their belief that the democratic legitimacy of the Attorney General as a member of the government needs to be honoured, especially when that office holder—that member of the cabinet—concludes that the traditional administration of justice is failing society, or at least, is not getting to the heart of underlying social challenges faced in many communities.[45] In this way, we can see that the earlier identified idea against interfering with the prosecutorial function through political direction, which is based on preserving the utmost impartiality and integrity in decision-making, collapses under the basic truth that, in the exercise of the power of the state, more than one strategy for, or one idea about, good government is required. The inevitable truth about the state is that its efficacy and its justice depend on personal and public commitments to its basic political goals: extending due process, of acting legally and of respecting the dignity of each member of the polity, and of providing government that is effective. As a political society, we want prosecutors to respect their professional commitments, including the commitment to promote a genuine social order that is based on doing justice.

CONCLUSION

Our legal system's prestige—perhaps even it majesty—rests on its transcendent quality, existing above, and avoiding corruption by, the exigencies of daily demands and passions. Its constancy is its strength. Its content and its processes have developed slowly over time and are not to be battered by the demands of our current situation. And, yet, it seems that our legal system responds to our needs, including our need to see justice done, so imperfectly. The administration of justice faces no greater challenge than to preserve the rigour and impartiality in the way that law works in our society while subjecting it to the changes that will make it an effective social instrument for all people in all their vastly different social contexts and with all their vastly different social needs. Certainly two places where this adaption must take pace is in having the legal system available to all on a more equal footing and in the response to social disorder through the administration of criminal justice..

Law, after all, is manifestation of the self-determination ideology that has shaped both our political system and our sense of personal entitlement. Both as individuals and as a political community we can make choices with the confidence that when those choices are expressed in law they will be honoured and that these attempts to shape our future condition will be vindicated. But if law is in this way so closely tied to our public and private integrity it must itself have integrity. That is to say that law—the mechanism of justice—must itself meet the underlying conceptions of justice which are: the right of all to be treated with dignity (with respect for personal capacity and not to be enslaved through poverty, poor health, low status, or dispossession) and the right to equal treatment. Law's challenge is to reflect in its operation the political values that led to its development, values of respect, dignity and equality. These values ground the connection between people in our political society and govern the way we act and develop as a political community. When law is not serving these values, either because it is not available to some or because it is detached from the reconciling and restorative function it is meant to perform, then it has become hollow and sterile and our political community is vulnerable to the diseases of low commitment, resentment over tyranny and bitterness over being rendered invisible and insignificant. When we worry about inadequacies in the administration of justice we are doing nothing less than worrying about the future of our community.

NOTES

1. See Faisal Bhabha, "Institutionalizing Access-to-Justice: Judicial Legislative and Grassroots Dimensions," *Queen's Law Journal* 139, no. 33 (2007): 140.

2. For an analysis and statistics on legal aid's shortcomings, see Melina Buckley, *The Legal Aid Crisis: Time for Action* (Ottawa: Canadian Bar Association, 2000) at: http://www.cba.org/CBA/Advocacy/pdf/Paper.pdf. See, also, Neil McCartney, "Permanent Legal Aid Crisis May Infect Justice System," *Lawyers Weekly* 28, no. 23 (October 17, 2008): 9.

3. These abridgements of basic conditions for justice were recognized by the Supreme Court of the United States in *Gideon v. Wainwright* in 1963 (372 U.S. 335) The Court was re-asserting what it had said in *Powell v. Alabama* in 1932 (287 U.S. 45).Of course, the American decisions were mandated by the terms of the U.S. Constitution. At that time, the Canadian constitution did not contain due process and equality rights but this

simply means that courts could not have ordered legal aid; it does not mean that policy makers and legislators could not have responded to an unjust condition.

4. Robert G. Hann, Colin Meredith, Joan Nuffield and Mira Svoboda, *Legal Aid Research Series: Court Site Study of Adult Unrepresented Accused in the Provincial Criminal Courts, Part 1: Overview Report* (Ottawa: Department of Justice Canada, 2000), 1; http://www.justice.gc.ca/eng/pi/rs/rep-rap/2003/rr03_la2-rr03_aj2/rr03_la2.pdf

5. Ibid.

6. Lorne D. Bertrand, Joanne J Paetsch, Joseph P. Hornick and Nicholas M.C. Bala, *Legal Aid Research Series: A Profile of Legal Aid Services in Family Law Matters in Canada* (Ottawa: Department of Justice Canada, 2002), 3; http://www.justice.gc.ca/eng/pi/rs/rep-rap/2003/rr03_la12-rr03_aj12/rr03_la12.pdf

7. Erin Smith, *Legal Aid in Canada: Resource and Caseload Statistics 2006/2007* (Ottawa: Minister of Industry, 2008), p. 6; http://www.statcan.ca/english/freepub/85F0015XIE/85F0015XIE2007000.pdf

8. Saskatchewan, Saskatchewan Legal Aid Commission, *Annual Report 2007–2008*, 1; http://legalaid.sk.ca/assets/pdf/2008%20Annual%20Report.pdf

9. Saskatchewan, Saskatchewan Legal Aid Commission, *Financial Eligibility* (March 2006): 1; http://legalaid.sk.ca/assets/pdf/2006%20Financial%20Eligibility%20letter%20size.pdf

10. Saskatchewan Legal Aid Commission, *Annual Report 2007–2008*, 3.

11. "Definition of Terms" online: Saskatchewan Legal Aid Commission; http://www.legalaid.sk.ca/defterm.html

12. "Frequently Asked Questions" online at Saskatchewan Legal Aid; http://legalaid.sk.ca/freqques.html

13. Saskatchewan Legal Aid Commission, *Annual Report 2007–2008*, 19–20.

14. "What Services Do We Provide" online at Saskatchewan Legal Aid; http://legalaid.sk.ca/services.html

15. Social Planning and Research Council of B.C, "Executive Summary," *Legal Aid Research Series: An Analysis of Poverty Law Services in Canada* (Ottawa: Canada, Department of Justice, 2002).

16. See Herbert M. Kritzer, "Access to Justice for the Middle Class," in Julia Bass, W.A. Bogart and Frederick Zemans (eds.), *Access to Justice for a New Century: The Way Forward* (Toronto: The Law Society of Upper Canada, 2005), 157.

17. This can be compared with the extensive review of Legal Aid Ontario conducted by Professor Michael Ttrebilcock of the University of Toronto Faculty of Law. See, Michael Trebilcock, *Report of Legal Aid Review, 2008* (Toronto: Ministry of the Attorney General, 2008) at: http://www.attorneygeneral.jus.gov.on.ca/english/about/pubs/trebilcock/legal_aid_report_2008_EN.pdf

18. Hann, Meredith, Nuffield and Svoboda, *Overview Report*, 1.

19. Trebilcock, *Report of Legal Aid Review, 2008*, recommended that "… financial eligibility criteria … significantly raised to a more realistic level that bears some relationship to the actual circumstances of those in need. They should be simplified and made more flexible so that services could be provided along a sliding scale of eligibility with broadened rules for client contributions. The criteria also need to be brought into line with anti-poverty measures used elsewhere in the social welfare system and adjusted on a regular basis" (p. xiii).

20. Put forward as a response to the serious inaccessibility to the legal system, this

suggested expenditure is not compelling. An increase in funding to this degree would prompt an array of both civil law reforms that might simplify procedures and legal aid delivery reforms. A good source for the former is the website of the University of Alberta's Canadian Forum on Civil Justice at: http://cfcj-cfjc.org/inventory. It cannot be overstressed, however, how resistant the legal process – and the professionals who are engaged in it – has been to simplification or abridgement of the stages of litigation. With respect to legal aid delivery, the Trebilcock Report, ibid. contains many suggestions relating to efficiencies, although not all of them appropriate to Saskatchewan's legal aid structure.

21. Philip Slayton, "The Self-representation Problem," *Canadian Lawyer* 30, no. 31 (November 2007): 30; quoting Chief Justice Beverly McLachlin, "The Challenges We Face" (Speech presented to the Empire Club of Canada, Toronto, March 8, 2007).

22. Lee Steusser, "Dealing with the Un-represented Accused," *Criminal Reports* 9 (2003): 82.

23. Hann, Meredith, Nuffield and Svoboda, *Overview Report*, 9.

24. Marguerite Trussler, "A Judicial View of Self-represented Litigants: Principles, Interests and Agendas," *Canadian Family Law Quarterly* 19, no. 547 (2002).

25. See, Ab Currie, "The Nature and Extent of the Unmet Need for Criminal Legal Aid in Canada," *International Journal of the Legal Profession* 11, no. 192 (2004); Robert Flannigan, "Costs for Self-Represented Litigants: Principles Interests and Agenda," *Advocates Quarterly* 33, no. 447 (2007).

26. Currie, "The Nature and Extent of the Unmet Need for Criminal Legal Aid in Canada," 202.

27. Ibid., 207. On p. 201, Currie provides a list of 40 serious mistakes that unrepresented defendants commonly make. Any one of them can be fatal to his or her position. These include such basic things as not calling essential witnesses, not understanding available defences and not being aware of the significance of the other side's evidence.

28. Ibid., 202.

29. Hann, Meredith, Nuffield and Svoboda, *Overview Report*, iv.

30. These risks are described in detail in Currie, "The Nature and Extent of the Unmet Need for Criminal Legal Aid in Canada," 200.

31. McLachlin, "The Challenges We Face," 21.

32. These problems have been identified in Currie, "The Nature and Extent of the Unmet Need for Criminal Legal Aid in Canada," 25; Hann, Meredith, Nuffield and Svoboda, *Overview Report*, 4.

33. Quoted in Nora Rock, "Challenges for Unrepresented Defendants," *Law Times* (June 6, 2005): 9.

34. Nova Scotia Department of Justice, Self-Represented Litigants in Nova Scotia: Needs Assessment Study (Halifax: Department of Justice Court Services, 2004), 11.

35. These problems are identified in Trussler, "A Judicial View of Self-represented Litigants," 24.

36. Flannigan, "Costs for Self-Represented Litigants."

37. This series of findings are reported in Hann, Meredith, Nuffield and Svoboda, *Overview Report*, v.

38. For example, see these two superb articles on Canada's serious access to justice deficiencies: Bahba, "Institutionalizing Access-to-Justice," and Roderick A.

Macdonald, "Access to Justice in Canada Today: Scope, Scale, Ambitions" in Bass, Bogart and Zemans, *Access to Justice for a New Century*, 19.

39. See Bahba, "Institutionalizing Access-to-Justice," 162–66.

40. See *Little Sisters Book and Art Emporium v. Canada (Commissioner of Customs and Revenues)*, [2007] 1 S.C.R.38 and *British Columbia (Attorney General) v. Christie*, [2007] 1 S.C.R. 873.

41. Leave to appeal B.C. Court of Appeal decision in *Canadian Bar Association v. Her Majesty the Queen* denied by Supreme Court of Canada (2008).

42. Naturally this last condition for integrating community based diversion into the state's criminal justice administration is overly idealistic. Every regime, even a regime that is progressive, empowering and based on shared values, requires some basic rules of recognition and coordination. The question is whether, if the essential condition relating to the recognition of partners is met, the partnership can operate on the basis of shared authority and responsibility. A proposal for integrating community justice with the state's formal administration of criminal justice is discussed in G. Seniuk and J. Borrows "The House of Justice: A Single Trial Court," *Criminal Law Quarterly* 48, no. 126 (2003). I doubt, however, that the proposal advanced by Seniuk and Borrows in the concluding paragraphs of their paper for the management of the interface between state responses and community based responses (pp. 139–40) escapes placing community justice under the authority of the traditional governmental agencies.

43. Prosecutorial guidelines with respect to general policies of diversion and community justice do not run afoul of the great dread concerning political interference—the Attorney General interfering in the prosecutorial decision in a specific case. This problem is discussed in B. MacFarlane, "Sunlight and Disinfectants: Prosecutorial Accountability and Independence through Public Transparency," *Criminal Law Quarterly* 45, no. 272 (2001).

44. This characterization of the Attorney General's guidelines as counter to the rule of law is a complex claim. It is arguable that the guideline is itself a rule of general application that serves as a general legal condition to the application of the Criminal Code. Furthermore, there is an inevitable area of discretion in legal application in deciding whether a statutory provision properly applies to the specific context.

45. The tension between the legal mandate of Attorneys General and their political responsibilities is well explored (in the context of Charter litigation) in M.A. Hennigar, "Conceptualizing Attorney General Conduct in Charter Litigation: From Independence to Central Agency," *Canadian Public Administration* 51, no. 193 (2008).

From In Camera to On Camera:
The History of Legislative Committees
in Saskatchewan and the Role of the Public Servant

Dan Perrins

INTRODUCTION

The first decade of this century has seen many changes in how the Legislative Assembly of Saskatchewan conducts its business. These changes, amongst others, have included the creation of fixed election dates, the adoption of a permanent calendar, revisions to sessional sitting times and revisions to the committee system. This paper will examine the changes to the committee structure and how these changes have affected senior public servants' interaction with elected officials, as well as the overall implications for accountability in government.

Historically, public servants have supported the elected officials in the Public Accounts Committee (PAC), the Committee of the Whole (legislative process) and the Committee of Finance (budget process).

PUBLIC ACCOUNTS COMMITTEE

The committee with the longest documented history of public servant involvement is the Public Accounts Committee, which developed from a standing committee formed in 1888 by the Assembly of the North West Territories. When the province of Saskatchewan was created in 1905, the functions of the Select Committee on Public Accounts and Printing were continued.[1] The terms of reference for the committee empowered it "to examine and inquire into all such matters and things as may be referred to [it] by this Assembly, and to report from time to time [its] observations therein; with power to send for persons, papers and records, and to examine witnesses under oath."[2]

Normally, the only matter referred to the committee was a public account document prepared by the Treasury Department, which contained approximately 650 pages of detailed expenditures for each department. Under the direction of the chair, the committee, which consisted of 35 members, proceeded through the accounts page by page. The minister of the department whose accounts were being considered was present to answer questions. The minister was supported by a deputy minister and by one or two other senior administrators. No records of the questions asked or the answers received were kept.[3] The chair was a government member and was responsible for determining proper procedure.

In 1923, the Select Committee on Public Accounts and Printing began, for the first time, to look closely at how they conducted their business:

> During the discussions the question arose as to the duty of the committee in the matter of the investigation of any particular item in the Public Accounts and it was agreed to leave this matter in the hands of the chairman to ascertain the proper procedures.[4]

Apparently, no satisfactory resolution was found, and the same kinds of questions were asked repeatedly over the next 40 years. In 1963, the Legislative Assembly brought this issue to a head by passing the following motion:

> That Mr. Johnson as Chairman together with Messrs. Brocklebank, Thiessen, Strum (Mrs.), Berezowsky, Thatcher, McDonald, and Gardiner be constituted a Special Committee to examine into and evaluate the function, terms of reference and methods of the Select Standing Committee on Public Accounts and Printing, and the adequacy of the information and assistance provided to the Committee in its work of examining the public accounts, and to report thereon with recommendations at the next session; the said Special Committee to be empowered to consult with the Provincial Auditor, officials of the Treasury and other departments, to gather information from other jurisdictions, and to sit after prorogation.[5]

The Special Committee produced a report that led to the most significant and clearly articulated changes to the Public Accounts Committee (PAC) in the history of Saskatchewan. If the present day PAC in Saskatchewan can be characterized as well functioning, the roots of its effectiveness can be found in the work of the 1963 Special Committee.

The report of the Special Committee had two major parts: the first part contained descriptions of the PAC of Britain and Canada, and the second part compared the Saskatchewan PAC with those of Britain and Canada. From this comparison, it was clear to the Special Committee that the Saskatchewan PAC did not have the characteristics that made the British and Canadian PACs effective. As the report states:

> On reflection it appeared surprising that the Saskatchewan Public Accounts Committee should be so different from the British and Canadian committees when the principles of British parliamentary government are taken for granted in so many other aspects of the conventions and procedures of the Legislative Assembly.[6]

The Special Committee concluded that the members of the Saskatchewan PAC did not have a clear statement of purpose and recommended the following:

> The purpose of the examination by the public accounts committee is to determine systematically and thoroughly whether the government has in fact acted within and according to the legal authority granted it by the legislature and where it has not, to find out why and deter the government from future misuse of funds. The public accounts committee completes the circle of control: it makes certain that the government is held truly responsible to Parliament for its use of funds and authority.[7]

The Special Committee went on to stress that:

> The public accounts committee is important because it is a committee of Parliament in a parliamentary system of government. In such a system the direction of all financial legislation is the responsibility of the cabinet—the real holder of the executive power that was formerly exercised by the Crown. The cabinet prepares an annual budget and submits it to the legislature. The cabinet is responsible for the spending of funds appropriated by the legislature. The cabinet is also responsible for the handling of funds from the time they are raised by taxation to the time they are spent. The cabinet, not the legislature, collects taxes, makes contracts, borrows money, and issues cheques. The cabinet in turn, however, is subject to the control of legislature, a control exercised formally through the legislative process of law-making and accounting, and actually through discussion, examination, and criticism.[8]

To achieve the stated purpose of the report, the Special Committee proceeded to observe on the role of the auditor, the membership of the committee, the witnesses before the committee, and the reports, publicity and follow-up procedures.

AUDITOR

With respect to the auditor the report noted that the provincial auditor had the duty of approving expenditures before they were made. As a result, when the Public Accounts Committee received the accounts of government, the provincial auditor had already approved them:

> If the provincial auditor in Saskatchewan were to prepare a report like those prepared by the Auditors General of Britain and Canada, which contains criticisms and descriptions of selected significant financial transactions of the government, he would be criticizing transactions which he must by statute have approved already.[9]

MEMBERSHIP OF THE COMMITTEE

The chair of the Public Accounts Committee was a government member, as compared to the British and Canadian committees where the chair was an opposition member and was "keenly interested in making a critical examination of the government's accounts…. [K]nowing that the government majority can overrule him or prevent inquiry, he has every incentive to be fair and thorough in his investigation."[10]

WITNESSES

Although the minister acted as the witness before the Saskatchewan Public Accounts Committee, the report observed that the permanent head of the department would be a more satisfactory witness for the following reasons:

> His attendance tends to preclude policy debates; he may say what the policy is, he may discuss the administrative aspects of policy but he will not debate policy.

> His evidence is based on a more intimate knowledge of the facts.

> The information he provides is less likely to be subjected to the same political screening as that obtained from a minister.

> [T]he selection of the permanent head or deputy minister as the principal witness before the public accounts committee, builds right into the civil service a pressure in the direction of a strict observance of propriety, lawfulness, custom, convention, and the rights of Parliament.[11]

PUBLICITY

The Special Committee noted that there were strong arguments for holding the meetings of a Public Accounts Committee open to the press and the public. At the same time, it also argued that there were strong arguments against having meetings in public:

> If meetings are in public, it is possible for an investigation by the committee to receive wide attention from the press before it is completed, giving the public only a part, and perhaps a distorted part, of the whole story. Public meetings encourage the committee to seek for sensational material and ignore more important but less entertaining matters, a process which can reduce the committee's ability to make a systematic and thorough investigation. Public meetings deter civil servants from speaking freely before a committee because they might become involved in political controversy. In camera meetings enable the committee to examine witnesses more freely and impartially.[12]

SIZE OF THE COMMITTEE

The Saskatchewan Public Accounts Committee had 35 members, which equaled over half of the members of the Legislative Assembly (MLA). This committee appears to have grown so large because the opposition could nominate as many members as it wished and then the government would add enough to outvote them. In comparison, the British PAC had 15 members out of 650 members of Parliament.[13]

REPORTS AND FOLLOW-UP

Unlike Britain and Canada, the Saskatchewan PAC rarely produced reports containing specific recommendations and, as a result, did not develop follow-up procedures.

   The Special Committee concluded that change was needed and should be based on the experience of the British and Canadian PAC. As a result, the committee made the following recommendations:

> 1. That an independent legislative auditor, responsible only to the assembly, be appointed, and to this end:
>
>> a. that the duties of the provincial auditor be changed to those of an independent legislative auditor, auditing the accounts of the government on behalf of the legislature after expenditures have been made, and reporting to the legislature on the results of his audit, and
>>
>> b. that the present duties of the provincial auditor in control over disbursement be transferred to the Saskatchewan Treasury Department.
>
> 2. That the chairman of the public accounts committee be a member of the opposition, while representation on the committee be based on the voting strength of parties in the legislature,
>
> 3. That the permanent heads of departments be called as the principal witnesses before the committee; at the same time it being recognized that any other persons may be called when necessary,
>
> 4. That the meetings of the public accounts committee be held in camera,
>
> 5. That an official verbatim report of the proceedings of the committee be maintained and submitted to the legislature as an appendix to the committee's report,
>
> 6. That the public accounts committee have not more than eleven members,
>
> 7. That the Treasury Department implement or see to the

implementation of recommendations or state, in writing, reasons for not adopting such recommendations: the Treasury to report in either case at the next session, and the public accounts committee to review at each session its earlier recommendations and the Treasury's reports thereon, and

8. That the formal title of the public accounts committee be changed to the "Select Standing Committee on Public Accounts" and the committee to be relieved of its duties for sessional printing.

These recommendations were implemented in 1967 and form the basis for the PAC to the present day. Between 1967 and 2003, the most significant change was the decision in 1982 to open the Public Accounts Committee to the public thus reversing the 1967 practice to hold PAC in camera.

COMMITTEE OF THE WHOLE

In addition to the Public Accounts Committee, the Legislative Assembly of Saskatchewan typically has operated two committees of the whole House—the Committee of the Whole and the Committee of Finance. While all members of the assembly are members of these committees, they operate less formally:

When the Assembly resolves itself into one of the committees of the whole, the Speaker leaves the Chamber, the mace is lowered to a position beneath the table, and the Chair presides over the committee from a seat at the table. While most of the Assembly's rules of procedure are observed in the committee of the whole, there are a few notable exceptions. Motions need not be seconded and there is no limit to the number of times a Member may speak. This flexibility allows for the exchange of questions and answers during the review of legislation or budget estimates. As well, Members are free to speak from any desk in the Chamber. The only restriction is that practice dictates that substantive motions may not be moved in any committee of the whole when Bills or budgetary estimates are under consideration.[14]

Before the recent changes to the committee structure, the primary function of the Committee of the Whole was to consider and debate legislation clause by clause, while the principle function of the Committee of Finance was to consider budgetary estimates. Together the consideration of legislation and the examination of estimates were, and are, one of the most time-consuming tasks of past and present legislative committees. The consideration of estimates refers to the annual review of a ministry's budget estimates by the legislature following the introduction of a government's budget. Legislature must debate and approve the budgetary estimates of each department before the money in a government's budget may be released (with the exception of the interim period between the start of the fiscal year and the passing of the budget). Along with the consideration of legislation, the Legislative Assembly's examination of the budget on a department-by-department basis is among its most important undertakings, as the collection and expenditure of revenues is the basis of power in a government.

The history of the public servants' role in the Committee of the Whole and the Committee of Finance is not as well documented as that of the Public Accounts Committee, but for many years the role of public servants appears to have remained unchanged. Senior government officials were permitted to attend committee meetings in order to assist the minister, provided that they were first introduced to the committee. It is important to note that while the officials could be present to provide assistance, senior officials could not speak to the committee—that role was strictly for the minister.

2003 CHANGES

Following a review of its rules and procedures which was initiated in 2000, the Saskatchewan Legislative Assembly adopted a new committee structure beginning in 2003.[15] The changes to the committee system were initiated with the intent of "creating procedures that would increase the importance of committees, enhance the role of private members, create more effective ways of dealing with public policy issues and increase public participation in the parliamentary process."[16]

A standing committee is a permanent committee established according to the permanent Rules of the Legislative Assembly. Under the new committee structure, there are three categories of standing committees—Policy Field, House and Scrutiny.[17] Within the Policy Field category, there are four Policy Field committees: the Standing Committee on Crown and Central Agencies; the Standing Committee on the Economy; the Standing Committee on Human Services; and the Standing Committee on Intergovernmental Affairs and Justice.

The Policy Field committees (PFC) are responsible for reviewing legislation, ministry estimates, annual reports, regulations and bylaws. Although the PFCs may be active in all of these areas, their responsibilities to review legislation and estimates are given priority.[18] The committees may also hold public hearings to aid them in their deliberations that would allow them to "investigate and report on important public policy issues."[19]

The second category of committee within the new structure is called the House Committee. This committee includes the Standing Committee on House Services, which "has a general oversight role for all the standing and special committees with respect to membership, the allocation of ministries, agencies and Crown Corporations to the various policy field committees;" the Standing Committee on Privileges whose mandate is "to examine and report on serious issues of privilege as referred to it by the Assembly;" and the Standing Committee on Private Bills, which was created to "consider and report on petitions for Private Bills and to undertake the clause-by-clause consideration of this category of Bill."[20]

The third and final category of committee is the Scrutiny Committee, which in Saskatchewan is called the Standing Committee on Public Accounts. This committee:

> monitor[s] the fiscal management and administration of the whole government… . The principal function of this committee is to scrutinize the past year's government expenditures through a detailed review of the Public Accounts and the Provincial Auditor's reports. In practice, examination of the reports of the Provincial Auditor is the main focus of the committee's review. These reports are permanently referred to the public accounts committee as soon as they are tabled in the Assembly or filed with the Clerk when the Assembly is adjourned or prorogued. The committee reviews each chapter by receiving a briefing from a representative of the Provincial Auditor's office and by questioning officials from the department or agency under review. The committee then determines whether it agrees or disagrees with the recommendation of the provincial auditor, or whether it wishes to adopt a recommendation proposed by a committee member.[21]

Under the new structure, all committees have seven members with the exception of the Standing Committee on House Services which has eight. In addition, member representation on the committees reflects the representation in the House (ie. a majority in the Legislative Assembly provides for a majority in a committee). As for the chair of the committees:

> At the committee's first meeting, the "organization meeting," the first item of business is the election of a Chair and Deputy Chair. Members of the Committee are nominated for these positions and are elected on motion by a majority decision of the committee Members… . The rules generally direct that a government Member shall serve as Chair and an opposition Member as Deputy Chair on all standing committees, except those committees where the Speaker is the permanent Chair … and the Standing Committee on Public Accounts. By tradition, the Chair of the Public Accounts Committee is a Member of the opposition.[22]

In addition to the structural changes made to the legislative committees, the 2003 modifications introduced the televising of all committee meetings. Far from being in-camera sessions, which was the practice of the Public Accounts Committee from 1967 to 1982, all committees would now hold their meetings on camera.

IMPLICATIONS OF COMMITTEE CHANGES

After having reviewed the functioning of the committees in the previous section of this paper, it is now possible to conduct at least a partial evaluation of what the changes have meant, in general, for accountability and for public servants in particular in their efforts to provide information to the people of Saskatchewan through the legislative committees.

While the report of the Special Committee described its intentions for the reformed committee structure, it was silent on what implications the changes might have for the public servants who appear before the committees as witnesses and advisers to ministers. As the Special Committee on Rules and Procedures—that group of government and opposition MLAs which stewarded the reforms—met largely in camera, it is difficult to assess the extent to which such implications may have been considered in the debates and discussions that led to the eventual reforms. For the same reason, it is difficult to evaluate the rationale for any of the changes, whether it be the creation of the Policy Field committees and their ability to hold public hearings, the televising of those committees along with the Public Accounts Committee or the change to enable and/or require non-elected officials to appear as witnesses in the Policy Field committees during ministry estimates and reviews of legislation. This closed-door approach differs from the one employed in the last major reform of the legislative committees, which was described earlier in this paper: the 1964 review was informed by a thorough consultation with experts and a detailed description of the proposed changes and their rationale which was made public.

Given the Special Committee's emphasis on elevating the importance of committee work and committee members in the legislative process,[23] it could be presumed that the Special Committee did not undertake a fulsome debate on the implications of the changes for public servants. If that debate did occur, it might have considered a range of issues including: 1) the challenges that might arise in keeping the respective roles of elected and non-elected officials clear in the context of having ministry officials answer committee questions directly; and 2) whether the televising of committee proceedings might have an enduring effect on the quality of the committees' examinations.

While there are a number of differences between the old and new committee structures, the two most significant differences for public servants are that the committees are now televised and that public servants are now compelled to speak as witnesses on record. As discussed previously in this paper, in the PAC, senior officials have been the primary witnesses since 1967. The most recent changes to legislative committees in Saskatchewan have done nothing to change that. In essence, the work of the PAC is retrospective and limited to scrutinizing the accounts of a ministry or agency. When forward-looking discussions do occur, they are generally in the context of what plans are needed to remedy a problem described by the provincial auditor in his or her reports. As such, although public servants are expected to provide thorough accounts of past expenditures in their ministries, they are rarely tempted to engage in big-picture policy debates. It is a relatively straightforward task to delineate between the role of the elected official and that of the senior official. Simply put, the former asks the questions and the latter answers—both of which are given within the confines of the scrutiny of a ministry's accounts.

The work of the Policy Field committees (PFCs) is fundamentally different from PAC in that the matters considered by the PFCs tend to be prospective in nature, such as proposed legislation or expenditures. As such, their work is prone to higher level, and more partisan, policy debate.

Before the creation of PFCs, the Committee of Finance was responsible for considering budget estimates and the Committee of the Whole was charged with examining legislation. For instance, during previous examinations of a ministry's estimates, questions were posed to the minister and the minister would respond, often after consultation—which was sometimes extensive—with the appropriate public servant. Although they were present and engaged in the process, public servants provided private counsel only to the minister. The minister assumed the sole responsibility for giving an answer on the record. Consequently, the minister exercised a wide discretion as to how to frame the answer to a given question. Such an answer could be strictly factual in nature, it could be intended to advance a particular policy position or it might be highly political and partisan.

Generally, the interplay between minister and public servant in both of these committees corresponded well with accepted notions of the role of the minister as compared to the role of the public servant. As the political head of a ministry, it is a minister's responsibility to set a policy direction that is consistent with the Cabinet's overall agenda to guide the work of the ministry. In addition, it is the minister's job to evaluate the political environment and assess the political implications of a particular course of action. A deputy minister is not expected to do the work of a minister, but she or he is expected to provide policy advice and implementation plans that are sensitive to the political realities facing a government.

In addition to bringing a sense of the public or political realities to the policy development process, it is the minister's responsibility to publicly promote the government's overall agenda and a ministry's particular initiatives within that overall agenda. While it may be appropriate for a deputy minister or ministry official to speak to the public or media about the technical or administrative aspects of a particular issue, such as the details of how a particular program works or a matter such as the composition or length of a health care wait list, it is the minister's job to justify a particular action, or in some cases inaction, to the public. Just as a ministry official is expected not to enter the public/political debate on contentious issues, so too must he or she avoid taking public credit for popular initiatives, as this is the sole domain of the elected official.

According to Alex Smith in a 2006 paper he wrote for the Canadian Parliament:

> One of the deputy minister's fundamental responsibilities is to support the minister's accountability to Parliament. Deputy ministers and other ministry officials appear before parliamentary committees on behalf of their minister by answering questions and providing information, but they explain rather

> than defend or debate policies. Public servants do not have a
> public voice, or identity, distinct from their minister; they are
> anonymous.[24]

This conception of the role of the deputy minister has been supported in the
Saskatchewan context in recent history and has been stated on the record in
public accounts in at least three instances—in 1971, 1976 and 1979:

> Mr. Chairman: [C]ivil servants should not be expected to dis-
> cuss policy. [1971]
>
> Mr. Chairman: 3. That the permanent heads and deputy
> Ministers rather than Cabinet Ministers be witnesses before
> the Committee. The intent of the Committee was to examine
> not the policy of why the expenditures were made, but
> whether the expenditures were made properly with adequate
> legislative authority. The examination of the permanent heads
> recognized the permanent head's authority and responsibility
> for the expenditures of their departments. [1976]
>
> Mr. Barnhart: [T]hey do not ask the permanent heads, should
> the department have established that program. That sort of
> question would be left to the House. The permanent head
> would be within his rights, according to the practices of this
> committee to say, I feel this is a policy decision and my minis-
> ter should answer that. [1979][25]

In general, the minister's job is public, political and policy-based, while the
deputy minister and ministry are concerned with administrative activities,
such as program design and delivery and the generation of policy options
consistent with the minister's and Cabinet's direction. The Minister's job is to
provide direction to the ministry and evaluate the proposals and alternatives
generated, not join with the ministry in developing policy alternatives.

The concept of ministerial responsibility is key to understanding the role of
the minister. Based on the Westminster System, ministerial responsibility
refers to the practice in governments where a cabinet minister bears the ultimate responsibility for the actions of his or her ministry, even if the responsible minister had no knowledge of the actions to which he or she is being held
accountable. The intent of ministerial responsibility is to hold elected officials
responsible for all government decisions. As many commentators have noted,
the notion of ministerial responsibility has evolved: public servants are
increasingly being made to answer directly for their actions in instances where
the minister could not reasonably have been aware of the actions of a public
servant or where statutory responsibility has been directly assigned to an official. Although ministerial responsibility is often associated with calls for a
minister to resign, it is more common that a minister has to *answer* for actions
taken within a ministry's administration for which he or she may or may not
have had knowledge.

According to Aucoin and Jarvis (2005), ministerial responsibility has three components:

> First, the minister is the chief executive of a department, the person in charge of the officials, the one with the statutory authority to take action so that the purposes of the law are realized. Second, the minister has been assigned the duties or obligations that are also set forth in statutes. And, third, the minister must provide an account and may be held to account for his or her actions, or the actions of officials, whether or not the minister had knowledge of these actions. In short, the term responsible encompasses three dimensions of ministerial responsibility: authority, responsibility and accountability.[26]

Ministers can and do delegate their authority to public servants for the purpose of administering government business. While a minister's authorities and responsibilities may be delegated, his or her accountability to the legislature is not transferable.[27]

Consequently, pubic servants are not expected to be "held to account" for the actions or directions of a government; rather, their role is to provide factual information. In the case of committee appearances, Aucoin and Jarvis advocate that:

> [P]ublic servants must always answer with only factual information concerning the conduct of departmental business. They are not to provide a defense or justification of government policy, programs or ministerial actions. In other words they are to answer but not to give an "account" because they do not possess the authority on their own.[28]

The previous committee structure in Saskatchewan lent itself to a straightforward demarcation of the appropriate roles for ministers and officials. During the committee's review of budget estimates, officials simply did not speak on the record; rather, they provided factual and detailed program and budget information in keeping with their administrative responsibilities and in confidence to their ministers. Ministers were then free to interpret that information as they saw fit and provide the answer that they deemed to be most appropriate or advantageous. In the event that a public servant exceeded his or her responsibility to provide factual, administrative information and strayed into policy or partisan-level debates, such an action would be masked by the fact that he or she never stated a position on the record, as it was always the minister's role to do so. In the new committee structure, ministers still retain the discretion to answer a question or not, but public servants must also exercise discretion because unlike the previous Committee of Finance or Committee of the Whole, public servants' testimony may be given during a highly partisan debate.

If the job of public servants has become more complicated by virtue of their role as witnesses in the Policy Field committees, the consequences of missteps have increased also because the committees are now televised. Although the Special Committee did not provide a rationale for why committee debates should be televised, it may have thought that televising debates would increase the profile and importance of the committee work and increase accountability. Similar arguments were articulated in advance of the publicly debated decision to televise the proceedings of the House of Commons in Britain in 1988.[29] Barnet and Gaber (1992) contend that the televising of committees in Britain was done with the intention of increasing the influence of Parliament vis-à-vis the executive and that doing so would make the committees more efficient: "[B]y subjecting the activities of select committees to public gaze, more effort is expended by witnesses, experts and MPs themselves in ensuring that their job is done – and therefore seen to be done—properly."[30] Whether this will be the case in Saskatchewan is too early to tell. It is also too soon to determine if there will be any negative, unintended consequences of televising committee proceedings, such as the tendency toward showmanship that accompanies television and that is all too evident in the most popular televised legislative proceeding—question period. Another consequence of televising committee proceedings, which may or may not have been intended, is the endangerment of the anonymous status of the public servant which, for better or worse, has been a defining feature of the Westminster model and key to understanding the role of the public servant in contrast to that of the minister.

At the least, the larger role for public servants in the new Policy Field committees requires a clearly defined understanding of the role of the public servant vis-à-vis the minister or elected official. To date, in the Saskatchewan experience, the public service as had little involvement in the discussion and formulation of the committee changes. If it is important to increase both the level and quality of accountability in government and if one accepts ministerial responsibility as a key feature of our system of accountability, then, by extension, it is important to properly understand the role of the minister and the role of the public servant, especially in the context of legislative committees which are central in enabling the Legislative Assembly to hold governments to account.

As such, it would have been advisable both to engage the public service in a dialogue concerning the changes and entertain a public discussion on the rationale for the changes. As this did not occur, a strong argument can be made now for taking the time within the public service to gain a full understanding of the committee changes and their implications for public servants, especially with respect to having a clear understanding of the role of public servants vis-à-vis elected officials and how that role should be reflected in the appearance of public servants before the Policy Field committees. The beginning of a new government's mandate is the most opportune time to examine issues of accountability and to clearly articulate the expectations of public servants and elected officials alike.

In his review of the Federal Accountability Act (FAA) and Action Plan (FAAP), Peter Aucoin describes a compelling reason to correctly identify the respective roles and responsibilities of ministers and senior officials. Aucoin argues that the root cause of the recent sponsorship scandal was not "a lack of knowledge as to what was occurring in the bowels of the bureaucracy … [r]ather, it was that both ministers and senior officials did not fulfill their responsibilities."[31] By implication, the absence of a discussion and opinion on the proper roles of ministers and senior officials may contribute not only to an ineffective consideration of matters brought before legislative committees, but, more seriously, to a diminution of the project of increasing accountabilities within government generally.

Another matter to be considered in light of the fact that public servants can testify now before legislative committees is whether this change may unintentionally reduce the profile and by implication diminish the importance of the minister within government. This possibility should be considered within the context of two other forces that affect the role of the minister. The first force is government's tendency in the modern era to centralize power and decision-making within the Prime Minister's Office (PMO) at the federal level or the Executive Council at the provincial level. The case has been made that at the federal level in Canada?since Trudeau, and especially under the Harper Conservatives?power and decision-making have coalesced around the PMO. In a recent article in the *Globe and Mail*, Donald Savoie refers to this as "court government":

> Inside government, prime ministers and their courtiers, perhaps to get things done, have concentrated effective power in their own hands. By "court government," I mean that effective power now rests with the prime minister and a small group of carefully selected courtiers. I also mean that there has been a shift from formal decision-making processes in cabinet and in the civil service, to informal processes involving only a handful of key actors.[32]

The second force affecting the power of the minister is the heightened influence of senior public servants within increasingly large and complex public agencies. Simply put, as public institutions get larger, the ability of a minister to fully understand let alone exert influence over those institutions shrinks. If the exercise of power in a government is a fixed-sum game and if the powers of the PMO/Executive Council and senior bureaucrat have increased, it stands to reason that the ability of the minister and the legislature or parliament, including the committees, to influence decisions has decreased.

If this is the case, this shift in power raises an important question for the government of Saskatchewan: Will the renovations to the committee system conceived in 2000, and now fully implemented, have the effect of making ministers and private members more influential and consequently more accountable?

In its observation on the Public Accounts Committee, which could be extended to all committee work, the 1964 Special Committee on Public Accounts Procedures of the Saskatchewan Legislative Assembly summarized perhaps the most important feature of an effective legislative committee:

> When a public accounts committee is effective, it is a commit-
> tee of the legislature rather than a committee of parties. In the
> public accounts committee party discipline is relaxed, and the
> members of the committee—government or opposition—have
> the free opportunity to investigate the transactions of the gov-
> ernment systematically, thoroughly and with the expert assis-
> tance of a legislative auditor. Without this opportunity for
> non-partisan investigation, a public accounts committee can-
> not make the necessary examination, and there is no assurance
> that the ground rules of parliamentary finance are being
> observed.[33]

Set as it was for the Public Accounts Committee, this statement provides a compelling standard for legislative committees in general, as does the report in which it was contained. Both provide a compelling standard for the careful and thoughtful review of the purpose of legislative committees and the intent of changes. The Saskatchewan Legislative Assembly would do well to recon-sider changes to its committees, following the standard established in 1964.

In retrospect, the important issue is the considerations that are absent from public discussion in the Saskatchewan context, which raises many important questions. What did legislators hope to achieve in their renovation of legisla-tive committees? What are the implications for and expectations of public ser-vants and, perhaps most importantly, is the doctrine of ministerial responsi-bility central to the functioning of the committees? If so, is that doctrine under-stood by the actors? Is it in need of modernization, and what does an adher-ence to the doctrine mean for the assignment of accountability between min-isters and senior public servants?

The Saskatchewan Legislative Assembly should reconsider the changes it made to the committee structure, and it should include in its deliberations a full discussion of the nature of ministerial responsibility and the role of the public servant. As Donald Savoie (2008) describes in his recent book on the state of accountability in Canada and Britain:

> [I]t is now important to define and locate which powers and
> responsibilities should fall to elected politicians and which to
> civil servants, and how they should be held to account, in
> order to give citizens a chance of knowing where power and
> influence are located and to have a sense that someone in gov-
> ernment can be held accountable.[34]

NOTES

The author wishes to thank Rob Cunningham for his assistance with this article.

1. Saskatchewan. *Report of the Special Committee on Public Accounts Procedures* (Regina: Legislative Assembly, 1964), 26.

2. Ibid., 26.

3. Ibid., 27.

4. Ibid., 5.

5. Ibid., 5.

6. Ibid., 29.

7. Ibid., 10.

8. Ibid., 11.

9. Ibid., 32.

10. Ibid., 34.

11. Ibid., 34-5.

12. Ibid., 36.

13. Ibid., 36.

14. Saskatchewan, *Guide to Committees* (Regina: Legislative Assembly, 2007), March. <http://www.legassembly.sk.ca/Committees/Main%20and%20Common%20Pages/ General%20Outline%20of%20Committees.htm#CommitteesoftheWholeHouse> (accessed on January 16, 2009).

15. Saskatchewan, "An Overview of Standing and Special Committees" in *Reference Materials for Standing and Special Committees* (Regina: Legislative Assembly, 2007), 1.

16. Saskatchewan, *Special Committee on Rules and Procedures, 2nd Report* (Regina: Legislative Assembly, 2001), 1.

17. Saskatchewan. "An Overview of Standing and Special Committees," 2.

18. Ibid., 8.

19. Ibid., 7.

20. Ibid., 8–9.

21. Ibid., 9–10.

22. Ibid., 12.

23. Ibid., 2.

24. Alex Smith, *The Accountability of Deputy Ministers Before Parliament* (Ottawa: Library of Parliament, 2006), 3.

25. Saskatchewan, *Committee Clerk Re: Public Accounts Committee Terms of Reference* (Memo to the Members of the Public Accounts Committee from Craig James) (Regina: Legislative Assembly, 1984), 1–2.

26. Peter Aucoin and Mark D. Jarvis, *Modernizing Government Accountability: A Framework for Reform* (Canada: School of Public Service: 2005), 14.

27. Ibid., 15.

28. Ibid., 15.

29. Steven Barnett and Ivor Gaber. "Committees on Camera: MPs and Lobby Views on the Effects of Televising Commons Select Committees," *Parliamentary Affairs: A Journal of Comparative Politics* 45, no. 3 (1992): 409.

30. Ibid., 418.

31. Peter Aucoin, "After the Federal Accountability Act: Is the Accountability Problem in the Government of Canada Fixed?," *FMI Journal* 18, no. 2 (2007): 12.

32. Donald Savoie, "The Broken Chain of Answerability," *The Globe and Mail*, May 16, 2008.

33. Saskatchewan, *Report of the Special Committee on Public Accounts Procedures* (Regina: Legislative Assembly, 1964), 11.

34. Donald Savoie, *Court Government and the Collapse of Accountability in Canada and the United Kingdom* (Toronto: University of Toronto Press, 2008), 293.

THE ELECTORAL PROCESS

The 2007 Saskatchewan Election: Watershed or Way Station?

Howard Leeson

> "I made a commitment that our party, that our team of women and men that were candidates across the province, would make this election about new ideas for the province," Brad Wall, November 8, 2007[1]

The election of 2007 in Saskatchewan was largely about change. In one sense it was about whether or not to change the governing party in the province, but it was also about how to manage change resulting from the sudden upsurge in the economy of the province. For the first time since the 1970s the province was booming, people were returning by the hundreds, and the future looked extremely bright. Responding to this good fortune the New Democratic Party (NDP) emphasized experience, reliability, and trust. The message was simple. Don't take a chance on upsetting the new prosperity by putting in an untried and untested group from the opposition. By contrast the Saskatchewan Party portrayed itself as a party of new ideas, the party best able to capture the new economic momentum of the province. As we know from the results, the voters of Saskatchewan were in the mood for change. They elected the Saskatchewan Party to office with over 50% of the vote and a solid majority of seats.[2]

Given the manner in which elections have been characterized in the past by scholars how important was this election? Was it, as Premier Brad Wall said, a decisive change, or was it just another change in officeholders, presaging business as usual? Put another way, was this one of the watershed elections in the province, signalling a new direction for politics and the parties, or, was it one more election confirming the already existing direction set in previous important watershed elections such as in 1944 and 1982. Finally, if this election signals a decisive watershed in the political life of the province, what implications are there for the way we study politics in Saskatchewan?

In order to try and answer these questions this article will do two things. First, it will examine the policy positions of the two major parties, the Saskatchewan Party and the NDP, during the four years prior to the election of 2007, with the specific purpose of ascertaining whether or not there was significant policy convergence between the two parties in Saskatchewan. Second, it will review the policy platforms of both parties during the election campaign and comment on the similarities and differences between them.

HISTORICAL CONTEXT

The adoption of a federal system in Canada in 1867, and the subsequent creation of 10 provinces, virtually ensured the creation of 10 unique provincial
political systems as well. The differences and similarities between and
amongst them provide a fruitful field of study for political scientists, histori-
ans, and casual observers. As you might expect, the extent to which
Saskatchewan is different from other provinces relates to its history, environment, institutional development, economy, and settlement patterns, to name
just a few of the variables involved. Of course, Saskatchewan shares much in
common with the other western Canadian provinces that developed at
approximately the same time. Authors like W.L. Morton, who studied the
Progressive Party in Canada, elaborated on the role of economic dependency
in Western Canada as one of the most important variables affecting the party
system.[3] Others, like Douglas Owram, in his landmark work *The Promise of
Eden*, have detailed the sources and reproduction of western Canadian alienation in the decades after the settler communities were created.[4]

   While there is little doubt that similarities exist between the western
provinces, especially between the Prairie Provinces, there are also substantial
differences. The distribution of natural resources like oil and natural gas
among Alberta, Saskatchewan, and Manitoba, the concentration of potash and
uranium in Saskatchewan, and the variations in the agricultural industry are
just a few of the differences in the economies of the provinces. There was also
a distinct difference in the settlement patterns of Manitoba and Saskatchewan
on the one hand and Alberta on the other. There is now a vast population difference between Alberta and the other two. Finally, most would agree that
each of the three provinces has developed a unique political system. As John
Richards and Larry Pratt concluded in their book, *Prairie Capitalism: Power and
Influence in the New West*, "in the final analysis it has been the ideas of politicians and the actions of governments that mattered most of all."[5] Nowhere is
this more important than in the province of Saskatchewan.

THE PARTY SYSTEM IN SASKATCHEWAN

When he published his book on prairie liberalism in 1974, David Smith began
by saying, "The tap root of Saskatchewan politics has been the Liberal Party."[6]
Shortly after the publication of his work, the Liberal Party in the province
began to fail. For 30 years it has struggled to regain its former status, flower-
ing only once in the election of 1995 when it became the official opposition
under Lynda Haverstock. In 2007, it dropped to its second-lowest level in public support ever, at just over 9% of the vote. However, Dr. Smith's observation
is still relevant today. The Liberal Party of Saskatchewan is the only party to
be continuously present in every election since 1905. It has governed the
province for 41 of 103 years.

   In duration the Liberal record is exceeded only by the CCF/NDP which
has governed the province for a total of 47 years since 1944. Between them the
Liberals and NDP account for 88 of the 103 years that the province has been in
existence. More importantly, they also provided a focus for one of the most

important ideological divides in the province. After its formation in 1933, and the adoption of the Regina Manifesto, the CCF established itself as the left of centre party in the political system, while the Liberal Party occupied the right of center position. As a result, for half a century elections were characterized by most scholars and observers as bitter ideological contests between the left and the right. This "bipolar" model of Saskatchewan politics has dominated academic discourse on the party system. Writing about the Saskatchewan Party in the last edition of *Saskatchewan Politics* Kevin Wishlow described it in the following way:

> The [bipolar] model has an established history of acceptance among political observers going back to the end of World War II. It has been acceptable to describe the provinces party system as being polarized along clearly defined ideological lines—between socialism and unfettered capitalism. John C. Courtney and David E. Smith generally subscribe to this paradigm. However, the pair carefully describes the system as a division of "moderate democratic socialism versus a peculiar prairie variety of liberalism." Courtney and Smith are also careful to point out that there are no absolutes. Despite an overriding tendency toward ideological polarization within the party system, the CCF/NDP and its right-wing competitor have generally been considered resistant to radicalism. Even within the broader framework of the polarization paradigm there has been the acknowledgment by some analysts that brokerage politics has not eluded the Saskatchewan party system. In essence, the political competition has reflected the emergence of two major populist parties-one on the left, the other on the right [7]

Wishlow also notes that in the bipolar paradigm, core support for these parties is characterized as firmly divided. Left of center support has remained attached to the NDP, while right-wing support has alternated between the Liberals in the 1960s and the Progressive Conservatives in the 1980s. After the 1991 election, and the discrediting of the Progressive Conservative Party, right-wing voters looked poised to reassemble under the Liberal Party. This did not happen, in part because the Liberal Party was unable to rally behind its leader Lynda Haverstock. Thus, a number of Liberals and Conservatives came together after 1997 in order to form the Saskatchewan Party, which successfully supplanted the Liberals as the Official Opposition in the legislature.[8] Nevertheless, according to most academics, the traditional bipolar explanation of Saskatchewan politics remained valid. The fact that both the Progressive Conservative Party and the Liberal Party of Saskatchewan had been superseded by a new party confirmed in their mind the theory that right-wing voters in the province were willing to coalesce around whichever party could defeat the NDP. In other words, class politics was alive and well, and the bi-polar approach intact.

However, in his article Wishlow questioned the validity of this interpretation, and the bipolar model, especially after the election of 1999. In particular
he contended that with the formation of the coalition government between the
NDP and the Liberals in 1999, "Ideological distinctions between the competing parties were clearly diminishing."[9] He went on to say:

> The NDP/Liberal coalition had stolen some aspects of the
> Saskatchewan Party's policy agenda, leaving the opposition to
> criticize the government's integrity and management style.
> The onus was on the Hermanson team to demonstrate the
> government wasn't doing what it promised. Ideological dis-
> tinctions between the competing parties were clearly dimin-
> ishing. Given these developments the traditional bipolar
> explanation of the province's party system weakens, demand-
> ing the consideration of an alternative paradigm.[10]

He also made the argument that class is no longer the most significant
determinant of partisan support in the province. He attributed this to the fact
that throughout the Western industrialized world there has been a rise of neo-
liberal regimes which "has been marked by a transformation of the role of the
individual to the state—citizenship has been replaced by consumership."[11] He
argued that there had been considerable change in the working class, especially in its relationship to the state, using healthcare as an example:

> Citizens might view accessible and affordable health care as
> important. But they are no longer convinced that the state
> should hold the monopoly on delivering those services. As
> long as citizens receive adequate redress for their taxes paid,
> they remain happy. Instead of looking to the state as the means
> to offset the vagaries of the market, the working class is now
> receptive to employing market solutions to meet social needs.[12]

He concluded that where there are no longer fundamental ideological divisions in the population the party system cannot remain polarized between
right and left. Thus, the parties are drawn to a brokerage system which
emphasizes matters such as ethnic and regional concerns. "The difference
between Saskatchewan's two major parties, in the end, is less a matter of ideology than of who speaks for whom."[13]

A particular interest for this article was the prognostication by Wishlow
that the Saskatchewan Party would increasingly behave as a brokerage party,
broadening its appeal amongst voters, in particular urban voters. In order to
do so, it would move toward the center of the ideological spectrum on questions that differentiated it from the NDP. The Wishlow approach was extremely well argued and appears quite prescient given the campaign of 2003 and the
platform of the Saskatchewan Party in the election of 2007.

However, many are unwilling to concede that the bipolar model has lost
currency. Writing in the *Canadian Political Science Review*, Dr. David McGrane
concedes that there has been some policy convergence between the two

parties, but argues that the NDP under the leadership of Lorne Calvert actually moved to the left after 2003:

> After the 2003 election, the Calvert government followed what may be characterized as a slightly left-wing version of third way social democracy compared to the Romanow government. The Calvert government's slight move to the left was much more apparent in its social policy than in its economic policy.[14]

In his article in this volume McGrane maintains that analysis and extends it to conclude that the Saskatchewan Party has moved decisively to the left on important issues.

THE URBAN RURAL SPLIT AND BIPOLARISM

Despite differences about the bi-polar model, most authors understand that both approaches require adjustment to accommodate the urban-rural dimension of party support. Since 1982 the NDP has had difficulty winning seats in rural Saskatchewan. Conversely, since its creation in 1997, the Saskatchewan Party has been unable to maintain a significant presence in urban Saskatchewan. Both parties have considerable voter support in most ridings, but barring a major swing such as occurred in 1991, both lack the momentum in these ridings to win. Although the Saskatchewan Party made some inroads in the election of 2007, it should be noted that even with over 50% of the vote the Saskatchewan Party left the NDP with most of the seats in the urban centres.

Historically, this is a major change from the period between 1944 and 1982 when the CCF/NDP was able to dominate much of rural Saskatchewan. The 1982 election, and the massive win by the Progressive Conservative Party, radically altered the electoral landscape in the province. Seats like Canora and Pelly in east central Saskatchewan, which had been steadfast in their support for the CCF/NDP for decades and used to be part of what was called "Red Square," suddenly switched to the Progressive Conservative Party. More importantly, in subsequent elections those seats tended to stay with the party in opposition to the NDP. By contrast, seats in urban Saskatchewan, some of which had been beyond the reach of the NDP for decades, suddenly became safe seats for them. For example, an upper income seat like Regina South, which had clearly voted along class lines in the past, turned out large majorities for the NDP in the elections after 1991. This new dimension was most evident in the elections of 1999 and 2003. Given the balance of population in the province, this dichotomy translated into narrow majorities in the legislature.[15]

Thus, it is fair to say that the election of 1982 could be compared to the election of 1944 in importance. Both reflected a substantial change in the province's electoral and political system, a change that was rooted in important economic and social changes. In particular, in rural Saskatchewan, the small farms of the pre-World War II period had been replaced by larger farms.

The resulting depopulation diminished the importance of agriculture and rural voters and their problems. More importantly for the NDP, the decline of small farms meant the decline of their electoral base. Larger farmers tend to act more like entrepreneurs and businessmen, and to vote accordingly. Serious downturns in agricultural income tended to exacerbate this decline. Finally, specific actions of the early 1990s by the Romanow government, the cancelling of the GRIP, an agricultural support program, closing or converting over 50 rural hospitals, as well as reducing educational, highway, and other services in response to the debt crisis, solidified the electoral urban-rural divide. Wishlow describes this as a regionalization of electoral support:

> It is my argument that the Saskatchewan Party behaved in the 1999 provincial election much the same as Reform—as a region—based brokerage party. The rural voters, experiencing a complex barrage of setbacks to their local economies, had come to view the Saskatchewan Party and its leader, Elwin Hermansen—himself a farmer—as the most representative of their interests. The NDP by contrast has come to be viewed by rural voters as the party of the more prosperous cities, representing big government with close ties to the big labour and corporate interests of the heartland.[16]

Interestingly, Wishlow also argued that many of the interests of labour and capital are largely synonymous in urban Saskatchewan, concluding that those interests are qualitatively different from the interests of rural Saskatchewan. Ironically, this sets up a bipolar analysis, albeit different from the bipolar analysis normally associated with Saskatchewan. However, Wishlow also concludes that this urban-rural divide will eventually disappear:

> The difference between Saskatchewan's two major parties, in the end, is less a matter of ideology than of who speaks for whom. The Saskatchewan Party as it exists now remains a regional party built on the momentum of rural discontent ... but gaining ... power ultimately demands developing a platform that transcends rural and urban differences — something of which the Saskatchewan Party's leadership is acutely aware. That platform and model can be found in Alberta. There, Conservative Premier Ralph Klein rose to power by appealing to rural discontent and then went on to stay by appealing to Alberta's liberal middle ground.[17]

He goes on to conclude that if the Saskatchewan Party does this, it could become the dominant party in Saskatchewan.

Two things are interesting about this view. First, it asserts that the urban-rural dimension of Saskatchewan politics is transitory. Second, unarticulated is the assumption that urban voters will once again begin to divide along class lines. As we know from the election of 2007 this has occurred. That is, the inner-city lower income seats of the two cities remained the hands of the NDP. Upper income suburban seats were won by the Saskatchewan Party.[18]

In a recent speech another political scientist at the University of Regina, Dr. Ken Rasmussen, Director of the Johnson-Shoyama Graduate School of Public Policy, provides a modified view of this approach. He dismisses the so-called urban rural divide: "To begin with, the November 2007 election was not one that pitted traditional, deeply religious, conservative rural Saskatchewan voters against a modern urban, secular class in the cities."[19] He describes this as a false dichotomy.

> What we do have is a voting preference which sees the NDP support concentrated in the cities and the Saskatchewan Party support concentrated in rural areas and smaller municipalities but these voting preferences are more about strategic issues than a wide chasm of value differences.
>
> The fact that the Saskatchewan Party does better in rural areas and the NDP does better in the cities is a dilemma for both parties.
>
> The swing voters that both are desperate to attract [reside] in the vast and expanding suburbs, and as I shall note further, it is this group of unattached votes that all political parties must appeal to which is leading to the suburbanization of political parties and public policy in Saskatchewan.[20]

Rasmussen goes on to assert that despite "differences in strategic political calculation," as between the urban and rural communities, they are essentially "morally tolerant, personally optimistic and generous of heart and perhaps boringly middle-class." His thesis is that the political parties actually recognize this convergence of views and cast their political platforms in what he calls "middle-class or suburban, themes."[21]

It is an interesting analysis, though it lacks an empirical base. He concludes by rejecting the older bipolar thesis about Saskatchewan politics:

> While there is still something vaguely called right and left, they are pale imitations of themselves. The right has given up on social conservatism which has been a huge failure and has achieved none of its major policy objectives and has been abandoned by all parties of the right, and the left has given up on their version of Keynesian welfare economics, economic redistribution and visions of social justice.[22]

He goes on to contend that the major public policy problems in Saskatchewan, such as aging population, labour shortages, climate change, growing disparities between the aboriginal population of the rest of the province, lack of immigration, and others, are not amenable to the solutions proposed by the "old ideologies of the left and the right." He describes these as the "so-called wicked problems," which "have no easy or obvious ready-made solutions and make politicians very nervous."[23]

Both Wishlow and Rasmussen, albeit for some different reasons, come to the conclusion that a brokerage system of party politics has come into existence in Saskatchewan. Both attribute this to changes in the economic and social structure of Saskatchewan, including most importantly, the disappearance of the small rural producers, and the increasing urbanization of the province. Both recognize that the aboriginal communities, urban and rural, stand outside the analysis in many respects, and need to be incorporated in a different paradigm, although they both conclude that the two major parties in the province will seek to incorporate aboriginal representation issues as if they were another interest group in the society.

THE ROLE OF POLITICS IN PARTY CHANGE IN SASKATCHEWAN

Until now our analysis has treated politics as largely the dependent variable in a larger social process. What of the observation by John Richards and Larry Pratt that "the ideas of politicians and the actions of government ... mattered most"?[24] Most who write about Saskatchewan politics understand that the decisions of governments and parties matter. However, there is a tendency to view social and economic change as the independent variable in the process of political change.[25]

Such is not the view of this article. Rather, most of us now understand that political outcomes involve a sophisticated interchange between social, economic, and political variables. Therefore, the shape of the party system in Saskatchewan is at least in part a result of the decisions taken by those involved in the parties themselves. For example, the election platform of the NDP in 1982, and the failure of the party leadership to realize the depth of unease about economic matters in the population of the province, certainly exacerbated the defeat of the party in rural areas. The massive election victory by the NDP in 1991 owes as much to the budgetary decisions taken by the Devine government during his term in office, as it does to broader social and economic changes that were taking place at the time. Finally, the actual individuals involved, especially at the leadership level, often have a decisive impact on the shape of political events. This was certainly true inside the Liberal Party between 1995 and 1997, when a number of the MLAs decided to remove Lynda Haverstock from her post as leader.

In attempting to place the election of 2007 into some context, it is therefore necessary to understand the role played by the parties and their leaders. In particular, we need to pay attention to the interaction between those individuals and groups both before and during the election itself. As we know from the election of 2003, campaigns can matter.

PRELIMINARY CONCLUSIONS

What can we conclude at this point from our discussion? First, at the systemic level, we can accept the fact that there have been fundamental changes in the economic structure in Saskatchewan since World War II. In particular, these changes have accelerated in the last three decades. We know also that these economic changes have had a profound effect on the social structure of Saskatchewan. The most obvious impact in this regard has been the dramatic urbanization in the province, with the consequent disappearance of many small rural communities and farms. As well, with the growth of resource extraction industries like oil, natural gas, coal, potash, and uranium, the employment structure of the province has also changed dramatically. Finally, Saskatchewan has also struggled to accommodate changes in educational opportunities, transportation and communication, gender roles, as well as other changes experienced by most jurisdictions in Canada and around the world. All of these changes have shaped the context and outcome of political activity in Saskatchewan.

Second, these changes have not altered every aspect of politics in the province. For example, we have noted that there is now an urban-rural dimension to support for the two major parties in the province. This is a significant change in the last 25 years. However, some things have remained the same. For example, unlike some other provinces, Saskatchewan has maintained a largely two-party system, with the NDP remaining as one constant for the last 70 years.

Third, at present there is no agreement on whether or not we should abandon earlier models of analysis in favour of a new paradigm which more adequately explains the current party and political system in the province. More specifically, there is no agreement that the major parties permanently abandoned earlier ideological positions in favour of something that could be characterized as more centrist brokerage positions in the political spectrum.

It is this latter question which is of most interest to us in this article. An examination of the political context leading up to the 2007 election and of the platforms of the two major parties during the election itself might provide more evidence for a definitive conclusion. At the very least it might allow us to examine what, if any, ideological differences remain between the two major parties and point us in the direction of one conclusion or the other.

PREVIOUS ELECTIONS

The elections of 1999 and 2003 are critical to an understanding of the election of 2007. The election of 1999 produced a minority government, and eventually a coalition government between the Liberal and the New Democratic parties in the province. It also produced a change in leadership in the NDP.

As noted in the previous edition of *Saskatchewan Politics* the Romanow years had decisively changed politics in the province:

> These three forces—fiscal constrictions, party leadership, and gradual change in the NDP—all acted in the period up to 2001 to move political debate inside the NDP away from the "norm" of the previous decades, and to produce a political system less sharply defined by ideological differences.[26]

The new Calvert government that came into office in 2001 was severely constrained by several important forces. First, the new premier had inherited a coalition government. It was inherently unstable. Second, he did not carry the same moral authority with the coalition that Mr. Romanow had enjoyed. Lorne Calvert was untried, untested, and had emerged from a hard-fought leadership contest with some political damage. Third, public opinion polls, and general opinion during this period of time, indicated that the new premier would have a hard time putting the NDP back in office for a fourth time. In short, most political observers at the time thought that the new Saskatchewan Party would win the next election handily.

In the run-up to the 2003 election it appeared that the Saskatchewan Party led by Mr. Hermanson would indeed form the next government. However, as we know from the results, the election campaign itself mattered greatly. During the campaign Mr. Hermanson made several strategic blunders, allowing the NDP to cast doubt upon his intentions should he take office. This was particularly true about his intentions toward Crown corporations in the province. The result was a decisive win by the NDP in terms of popular vote. However, because of the distribution of these votes, it resulted in a narrow win in terms of seats in the House. The NDP had 30 seats, and the Saskatchewan Party had 28. This narrow victory meant that the government had virtually no room for manoeuvre in the House, and could not afford the defection or loss of even one MLA. Unfortunately for Premier Calvert, his Deputy Premier fell ill to cancer almost immediately after the election, meaning that the House was virtually tied after the election of a Speaker.

It was hardly a stable situation, and would prove to affect every decision made by the government during its next four years in office. Indeed, no one actually thought the government would survive in the House for the entire term.

This lack of manoeuvrability was compounded in 2004 by a short downturn in the fiscal situation for the government. Instead of being able to act immediately upon promised property tax cuts and other portions of the platform, the government was forced to raise taxes in the short term and put off other promises to later in the term. As a result, the NDP was thoroughly denounced by not only the opposition Saskatchewan Party, but by most of the media outlets in the province as well. It was not an easy time for the NDP.

In the short term, the NDP was aided by the fact that the opposition Saskatchewan Party was in complete disarray after the election. Expectations had been high, and when the party lost the election it became evident that someone would have to bear the blame. As is most often the case, blame settled upon the party leader, Elwin Hermanson. He announced his resignation in early 2004, and the party concentrated upon finding a successor. That successor was Mr. Brad Wall, a former executive assistant in the government of Grant Devine. After the fall of the government in 1991 Mr. Wall had gone to work in the private sector in Swift Current, Saskatchewan, starting his own business. He was elected to the legislature for the first time in 1999. He was reelected in 2003. In March of 2004 he was elected party leader.

It was immediately apparent that there would be a sharp contrast between

Mr. Wall and his predecessor, Mr. Hermanson. Under Brad Wall, the party became less ideological, and more electorally driven. During his first year he undertook the task of reorienting party policy on a number of key issues. This included privatization of Crown corporations, acceptance of publicly funded health care as the cornerstone of health care delivery in the province, as well as the adoption of a number of policy positions more attuned to urban Saskatchewan. In short, Wall was determined remake the image of a Saskatchewan Party that had been characterized as a rural, socially conservative, and small town.

The first three years after the election of 2003 were, as mentioned above, problematic for the NDP. The agricultural economy was stalled over low prices, job creation continued to remain stagnant, and the party suffered from constant media attack about its credibility. By contrast, after 2004 the Saskatchewan Party enjoyed increasing public acceptance. The new leader was telegenic, dynamic, young, and was given credit for revitalizing the party after the election defeat of 2003. Thus, the constant theme of the Saskatchewan Party became the need for change. They constantly referred to the "tired old NDP" at every turn.

CONVERGING POLICY AGENDAS

In several key policy areas, the NDP and the Saskatchewan Party converged during the years of the Romanow and Calvert administrations.[27] This was particularly evident in the area of taxation and economic policy. Over several budgets, the NDP reduced business taxes significantly, and most importantly, reduced royalties on key natural resources to the point that they were similar to royalty rates in neighbouring provinces like Alberta. It signalled a major departure from the approach taken by the previous NDP administration under Allan Blakeney. During the Blakeney years the public sector played a role in economic development, especially in the areas of oil and potash, where the government used crown corporations like the Potash Corporation of Saskatchewan and SaskOil as major vehicles of development. By 2007, it was clear that the NDP was content to rely upon the private sector for development in the resource sector. This meant that taxation and royalties had to be competitive with other regimes, not only in Canada, but around the world. Indeed, the NDP was not content simply to enact these policies as an electoral strategy but actually featured them in their campaign literature.[28] This convergence left the Saskatchewan Party with fewer avenues of political attack during the year leading up to the election. In particular, it removed one of the major differences between the two parties, the use of tax cuts as a mechanism to spur economic development.

On matters of social policy, environmental policy, and policy toward aboriginal peoples, there was less convergence than on economic policy during the same time period. In particular, the introduction of a universal drug plan during the last year of the Calvert administration differentiated the two parties decisively in the area of health care. The Saskatchewan Party remained committed to targeted and means tested plans, while the NDP was willing to expand its universal program to encompass everyone. In most other areas however, the Calvert administration remained committed to more targeted programs. The major difference between the Calvert and Romanow administrations lay not in a return to "more socialist" policies but rather in the total resources dedicated to social policy.

Early after the 2003 election Premier Calvert signalled that his administration would place greater emphasis on environmental policy. In part, this came as a result of increasing social awareness of matters like global warming and its impact on the whole planet. However, Premier Calvert was also deeply committed personally to placing environmental concerns and considerations high on the policy agenda for his government.[29] He was also deeply committed to matters of social and economic justice involving aboriginal peoples. This was not a departure from the Romanow administration, but rather a continuing emphasis.

Of course, the word convergence implies movement between two objects toward each other. In this case the Saskatchewan Party changed a number of key policies as well to move it closer to the NDP. In particular, as already outlined above, the party changed its attitude toward crown corporations, emphasizing that no privatizations of major crowns would take place during its administration. The Saskatchewan Party also emphasized that it would maintain the health care system as a publicly funded single-payer system, and promised no wholesale changes such as the introduction of deterrent fees or private health-care facilities. In addition, the Saskatchewan Party adopted an environmental approach which was a very close to that of the NDP.

THE PRE-ELECTION PERIOD

As both parties entered 2007, however, a dramatic change in the economy became apparent. Suddenly, job creation began to boom, real estate prices rose dramatically, people began to return to Saskatchewan from Alberta and other parts of the country, and in general it became apparent that the economy was into a dramatic expansion phase. Throughout 2007, agricultural prices for various agricultural commodities like wheat, flax, and oilseeds doubled and sometimes tripled. Oil prices began to move ahead decisively, along with potash and uranium prices. The relative economic stagnation of the previous few years was quickly transformed into an economic boom.

As a result, both parties entered the legislative session in the spring of 2007 with different "game plans." For the NDP, it was time to point out that the policies of the past four years had begun to bear fruit, and that the province had finally turned around convincingly. In the legislature Premier Calvert said:

> Now, Mr. Speaker, it's fair to say that this budget comes at a
> time of unprecedented economic strength in our province.
> This budget, Mr. Speaker, is sustained by the strength and the

> prosperity of the economy that we have built in Saskatchewan
> in the past five years[30]

He also stressed the difference between his party and the Saskatchewan Party, concluding that the NDP was much more inclusive:

> It is a budget which says economic prosperity should be
> shared among the many not just the few, that economic pros-
> perity should seek to build equality and community. These are
> not the values of the Saskatchewan Party.[31]

As a result, the NDP began to use some of the new fiscal capacity to put in place programs that had not been fiscally feasible even two years before. This included a new drug plan for seniors, medical care help for the working poor, and an increase in social assistance payments to name a few. In the words of Premier Calvert, it was a time to ensure that the new prosperity meant that "no one is left behind."

By contrast, Brad Wall emphasized how little had been accomplished, and how long the government had been in office, drawing the conclusion that the government was "tired and old":

> But this isn't a vibrant, energetic NDP Party. This is a four-
> term, tired, old government that I believe, Mr. Speaker, has
> among the worst records in the history of Canadian politics for
> hiding the facts, for not telling the truth, Mr. Speaker, to the
> people of this province. And they will not trust this govern-
> ment not now and not when that election is called, Mr.
> Speaker.[32]

He also attempted to portray the NDP government as "reckless spenders," in an attempt to defend against NDP charges linking the Saskatchewan Party to the previous Devine government:

> Mr. Speaker, even the Minister of Finance can't get his own
> story straight as to whether this is a deficit or not a deficit. …
> You know, he's on the public record. And he should know, Mr.
> Speaker, that the people of the province will be reminded of
> his own candour. I think the Minister of Finance had an
> absolute moment of honesty and candour, and he did the right
> thing. Don Newman asked the right question, and the
> Minister of Finance said, it is a deficit. The Minister of Finance
> said, it is a deficit, Mr. Speaker. And just in case the Premier
> hasn't heard—because I sit beside the member for Canora, Mr.
> Speaker—the Minister of Finance said, it is a deficit, Mr.
> Speaker.[33]

In addition to these main themes, the Saskatchewan Party pressed the govern-ment on a number of so-called "scandals." Chief amongst them was the matter of Murdoch Carriere. Mr. Carriere, a senior employee of the government, had been fired for misconduct. However, the process of firing was not handled properly, and Mr. Carriere sued for wrongful dismissal. The government settled with him. The Saskatchewan Party continually referred to this matter:

> Mr. Wall:—Thank you, Mr. Speaker. Mr. Speaker, this tired, old NDP government has lost, completely lost its sense of right and wrong. Last week this Premier and this NDP government awarded 275,000 taxpayer dollars to a man who was fired for harassment and convicted of assault. Mr. Speaker, this decision was and remains obviously wrong. It was wrong to the people of Martensville who handed the NDP its worst loss in 63 years. It's wrong to the taxpayers of this province. It's wrong to everyone in Saskatchewan, most assuredly wrong to the nine women who are subject to the harassment. Mr. Speaker, it's wrong to everyone in Saskatchewan except for this NDP government. Mr. Speaker, will the Premier stand in his place today and explain this outrageous decision? Why did the NDP government provide $275,000 in a payoff to a man who was fired for harassment and convicted of assault?[34]

The combination of "time for a change" as well as alleged misconduct and incompetence seemed quite effective for the opposition. Polls released during the spring session of 2007 indicated an overwhelming lead for the Saskatchewan Party.[35] Such a huge lead created a dilemma, however. Although time for a change remained a potent line of attack, other avenues of attack on employment, economic activity, and budgetary expenditures, were beginning to ring false when compared to what was actually happening in the society. The worry, therefore, was that "time for a change" would not be sufficient when the election was called.

By the end of the session it was quite clear that both parties had positioned themselves for the election if it was called in the spring or in the fall.

As we know, it was October before Premier Calvert actually called the election for early November. During August and September, the NDP began a series of ads designed to remind the voting public that Mr. Wall could be tied directly to Mr. Hermanson and to the Devine government. In particular the ads, which showed a sheep's face slowly becoming a wolf, were designed to reinforce any doubt about the intentions of the Saskatchewan Party toward provincial institutions like the Crown corporations. This technique had been successful during the campaign of 2003, and the NDP hoped it would be successful again. The Saskatchewan Party countered by ridiculing such attempts and by strengthening their platform in areas where it was most assailable. By the time the election was called, both parties had staked out solid "electoral ground" and saw no need to make dramatic changes. In particular Premier Calvert, although behind in the polls, felt comfortable enough to call the election for November, even though he could have waited a year longer had he wanted to.

ELECTION PLATFORMS OF 2007—CONVERGENCE OR DIVERGENCE?

During the spring of 2007, the Saskatchewan Party had launched an advertising campaign. In August of 2007, the NDP began to advertise in advance of the election call. Once the election was called, both parties published extensive documents outlining their campaign promises to the voters. These documents provide an excellent opportunity to compare the ideological and public policy choices of the two parties. As well, they should provide some evidence about the general thesis of Rasmussen and Wishlow that there has been significant ideological and policy convergence between the two major political parties in Saskatchewan.

BROAD THEMES

As we will see from our detailed examination of these documents, they are remarkably similar. However, there are some broad themes embedded in the documents that also reflect the general ideological approach of each party toward the electoral contest. Each of the parties attempted to convey a sense of momentum and change to the electorate. Each of the parties concentrated in the future. The Saskatchewan Party document was entitled "Securing the Future: New Ideas for Saskatchewan." The NDP document was entitled "Moving Forward Together. Making Life Better for Saskatchewan Families." Both parties thought it critical to emphasize their ability to generate a positive future for the people of the province.

The Saskatchewan Party coupled together two general themes. The first involved an attempt to portray the government as the "The Tired Old NDP." The second theme involved in portraying themselves as a fresh new team with new ideas for the people of Saskatchewan. The phrase which wrapped all of this together was, "Time for a change." For their part, the NDP attempted to capitalize on the obvious change in economic circumstances in the province by characterizing themselves as the only trustworthy steward of the new-found economic opportunities. As well, they sought to differentiate themselves from their opposition by emphasizing their commitment to greater equality amongst individuals and groups within the province. This was captured in the phrase "No One Left Behind." A broad theme of equality was something not unfamiliar to the platforms of the CCF/NDP during the previous several decades.

It is also interesting to note some other general similarities. For example, both documents started with policies about young people, attempting to tap into the general perception that the province should concentrate on the future of young people. The issue of health care is second for the Saskatchewan Party, an obvious move to defend against a possible attack by the NDP. By contrast, the NDP document moved from young people to pocketbook issues. On pocketbook issues there were very few differences between the parties. Both parties concentrated on the environment and have a "green section" that is extensive and detailed. Both parties managed to cover all of the major issues covered by their competitor.

SPECIFIC CAMPAIGN PROMISES[36]

The party platforms are too lengthy to review in detail in a short paper. However, a comparison of two or three issues provides evidence for the similarity of the documents.

HEALTH CARE

On the issue of health care, both parties had detailed proposals on matters like surgical wait times, recruitment of nurses, the drug plan, and the provision of new health facilities in the future. There were some differences. Most notably, the NDP proposed to expand the prescription drug program to a universal program that would cover everyone in the province, capping drug costs at $15 per prescription for everyone. By contrast, the Saskatchewan Party promised to keep the existing seniors' drug program, which was universal, but to make it income-tested. On the matter of the recruitment of health-care professionals the Saskatchewan Party included specific targets, especially for registered nurses. The NDP platform chose instead to build on a $500 million investment to train and recruit and retain more doctors, nurses, technologists and other health care workers. On the matter of health care facilities, the NDP was quite specific, promising to complete the Academic Health Services Center in Saskatoon and a new maternal and children's hospital as well. The Saskatchewan Party countered with a 10-year plan for health-care equipment and infrastructure.

The major difference between the two parties in this area involved the promise by the NDP to provide a universal drug plan for everyone, as contrasted with the Saskatchewan Party which proposed an income tested plan for seniors and for children aged 14 and under. This is one of the few areas where there continued to be a significant ideological division between the two parties.

FAMILIES, TAXES, AND PUBLIC FINANCE

Interestingly, neither party proposed large tax cuts, although both parties promised to reduce education property taxes. This undoubtedly occurred because of the substantial personal income and corporate income tax reductions by the NDP during the previous two years. Instead, the two parties concentrated on other issues such as providing funding to postsecondary educational institutions. The NDP also promised to put "more money in your pocket" by increasing the minimum wage to $9.25, capping utility fees, and expanding housing choices for Saskatchewan families. The Saskatchewan Party concentrated on funding for postsecondary institutions, funding for cities and municipalities for infrastructure projects, and providing better support for agricultural and farm families. There were few major differences between the parties in this area.

YOUNG PEOPLE

As mentioned above, both parties focused upon young people. Each tried to put forward platforms which would attempt to make Saskatchewan a more desirable place for young people to stay in, or if they had left Saskatchewan, to return to it. The centerpiece of the Saskatchewan Party platform involved tax rebates of up to $20,000 for each graduate who stayed in Saskatchewan seven years after graduating. As well, they promised to provide a $10,000 tax-free exemption each year for five years for young entrepreneurs and self-employed young people under the age of 30. It also promised to keep postsecondary education affordable by increasing post-secondary funding by 28%, and creating a Saskatchewan Scholarship Fund. The NDP promised to cut university tuition by $1000, to provide 10,000 new training spaces, and to provide $100,000 in income provincial tax-free for postsecondary graduates who stayed were moved into sketch one for five years. Although differing in specifics, the two parties generally focused on the same issues, and provided similar solutions.

THE ENVIRONMENT
Once again both parties emphasized the need to "go green" in the future. There are some differences in approach, but they generally agreed on matters such as greenhouse gas emissions, support for energy conservation, and support for bio-fuel initiatives in the province. Indeed, promises by the two parties on greenhouse gas emissions are identical in goal and in wording.[37] Of course, there are some differences in the platforms, and the parties differed on whether or not they were both equally committed to a green future.

CROWN CORPORATIONS
The election outcome of 2003 ensured that the Saskatchewan Party would pay particular attention to the matter of Crown corporations. The commitment by the Saskatchewan Party in particular was explicit and unambiguous. In 2004 the Saskatchewan Party had voted in the legislature to support the Crown Corporations Public Ownership Act, which essentially guaranteed that the Crowns would remain publicly owned. In their platform document the Saskatchewan Party said, "The Saskatchewan Party government will keep our crowns publicly owned and ensure that Saskatchewan people continue to enjoy high quality utility services at the lowest cost."[38] As you might expect, the document was critical of the fact that the NDP had allowed the Crowns to invest outside of Saskatchewan. The Saskatchewan Party committed itself to strengthening Crown investment in local communities and postsecondary institutions in Saskatchewan. By contrast the NDP, which had little to prove on this issue, simply reiterated that they would keep Crown corporations publicly owned and continue to use them to ensure that the people of Saskatchewan paid the lowest utility rates in Canada.

OTHER ISSUES
There were some other minor differences between the platforms on some specific issues. For example, the Saskatchewan Party emphasized a more accountable government, promising fixed election dates, banning pre-election urban advertising, and ensuring that government would not grow faster than the

population. By contrast, the NDP emphasized democratic renewal, promising to constitute a citizens assembly on democratic reform if re-elected.

CONCLUSIONS ABOUT THE TWO PLATFORMS

After reviewing the two platforms, we can only conclude that there are significant similarities between the two documents. First, they both emphasize the same issues. One could argue that this is in part an expected outcome since political parties tend to focus on the issues of the day. However, the fact that both parties clustered about the environment, young people, healthcare, reform of government, and economic growth, indicates that both felt that these were policy areas that needed to be emphasized or defended. Both were comfortable with platforms that dealt similarly with the same issues.

Second, the policy prescriptions in many of the areas are also very similar. Indeed, in one instance of environmental policy, the two platforms are entirely interchangeable.

Third, with the exception of the universal drug plan proposals by the NDP, there is little of the major ideological clash that one might have seen between the left and right parties in Saskatchewan 30 or 40 years ago.

Finally, there are of course some differences in emphasis, particularly in the broad themes. The Saskatchewan Party document emphasizes "time for a change," while the NDP document emphasizes trust and experience. Overall, however, one cannot help but be impressed by the similarities in the two documents.

GENERAL CONCLUSIONS

Let us return now to our general questions. The first question involved the importance of the election in 2007. Specifically, was it a watershed election which signalled a new direction for politics in the province? Superficially, one could make a good case that this election is a watershed. For example, the fact that the Saskatchewan Party, a new party in the system, was elected to office less than a decade after its creation is an important event. That importance is enhanced given the fact that it has largely supplanted the Liberal Party, and decisively suppressed the Progressive Conservative Party in the province. For the first time since 1982 the opponents of the NDP aggregated their support behind a single party and won the election. As well, the Saskatchewan Party appears to have moved ideologically quite far toward the centre of the political spectrum. By guaranteeing the existence of the major Crown corporations in the province, and by accepting a single payer, publicly financed and operated health care system, the Saskatchewan Party would appear to have moved rather decisively left. For its part of the NDP seems also to have moved to the ideological right on a number of important policy matters. Most importantly, it appears to have accepted the proposition that the private sector will be the engine of economic growth in the province, and therefore moved to the right on important matters of taxation, royalties, and regulation. Shortly put, the evidence conclusively suggests that there has been considerable policy convergence between the two major parties.

All of the above, and other arguments, could be marshalled to support the proposition that this is a watershed election. However, there are counter arguments. For example, it could be argued that the election itself was simply a continuation of a process that actually has its roots much further back, at least to 1991. Wishlow and others have made this point. While the governing party changed in 2007, one could argue that general policy movement has proceeded smoothly toward the right during the whole period since 1991. It could also be argued that the 2007 election does not demonstrate any significant disruptions to the support bases of either major party. The NDP continues to have the most seats in the cities, and the Saskatchewan Party continues to have almost all of the seats in rural Saskatchewan. The urban-rural dimensions of the electoral system remained largely in place. Contrast this with the election in 1944, or the election in 1982, where one of the parties decisively expanded its support base in the system. Finally, no major issue of an ideological, social, or economic nature dominated the election campaign. Put another way, there was no galvanizing issue which forced a decisive policy split between the two parties.

After considering the various arguments, in my opinion, the 2007 election was not a watershed election. It did not change the electoral or political system in a fundamental way.

What of our second question, the implications of this election for the way we study politics and the province? More succinctly, is the bipolar model still useful for our study of the parties and the party system in Saskatchewan, or has it been replaced by something we might call the convergence model? Here, I believe the evidence is less clear. There is little doubt that the Saskatchewan Party and the NDP now agree on a number of important ideological and policy matters. This does not mean that some of these positions are their preferred policy outcomes. For example, it is clear that most of the members of the Saskatchewan Party would prefer that most Crown corporations in Saskatchewan be privatized. They fundamentally believe that the private sector could do a better job. However, they were convinced that they could not win office, at least in 2007, by putting forward that policy position. As well, it is probably true to say that they would prefer a much greater involvement of the private sector in some areas of health-care and the provision of health-care services. Once again, however, they were persuaded that this position was electorally unpopular, and that it had to be modified. Finally, in some areas, such as on labour issues, the Saskatchewan Party maintained its ideological position, preferring to suffer any electoral consequences that resulted from the loss of trade union votes.

For its part, the NDP and its members would probably prefer a much greater involvement a public enterprise in the economy of the province. However, they were persuaded during the period in 1991 to 2007 that the province did not have the resources needed to re-nationalize industries in the natural resource sector, or to expand Crown enterprises in any significant way.

Nevertheless, the party continued to maintain a strong defense of the role of public enterprise, albeit now truncated, in the life of the people of the province. In the area of health care, Premier Calvert was willing to go somewhat further than Premier Romanow, and brought back a universal drug care program, and proposed to expand that universal program if re-elected. Finally, on the matter of taxation, there is now little difference between the two parties. Once again, however, it would appear that the NDP has been forced unwillingly toward some taxation changes, such as substantial changes to the business tax, for electoral reasons. In other words, like the Saskatchewan Party on Crown corporations, the NDP was forced to adopt changes to business taxes for electoral reasons.

The above would seem to reinforce the view of David McGrane, who concludes in his article that the NDP remains at its core a party dedicated to economic equality, but willing to pursue that goal through the use of private sector means. In other words, despite policy convergence on some issues, he believes that there are still decisive ideological differences between the NDP and the Saskatchewan Party, and by implication, that the bi-polar model is still useful for our analysis of the political system in the province.

For his part, Raymond Blake, writing about the Saskatchewan Party in this volume, believes that there has been a general decline in ideology between and among all political parties in Canada. He believes, as he says in his article, that Saskatchewan has followed this trend. He views the election and subsequent political behaviour by the Wall government, as clear evidence of that trend. In essence, he agrees with the position put forward by Wishlow in the first edition of this book. Much of the evidence in this article would seem to support his view.

There can be little doubt about the convergence of the two election platforms, or the policy positions espoused by the two parties prior to the election. Whether or not these are the preferred ideological positions of the parties is of little relevance, they are the policy positions that they have promised to put into effect if elected, and presumably, will be politically punished for abandoning should they choose not to do so. Therefore, the fact that some, or even a majority of members of either party, would want a different policy position on a particular issue is, as noted above, of little relevance.

Should we conclude, therefore, that convergence has taken place, the two parties are attempting to aggregate many of the same voters, and they have, as Blake puts it, become "pragmatic parties," rendering the old bi-polar model of analysis redundant? For my part, I am reluctant to do so. Clearly there are fewer ideological differences between the two parties than there were even 20 years ago. As well, there is little doubt that the ideological center of politics has moved decisively to the right in most liberal democracies during the last three decades. However, there are still sufficient differences of an ideological nature between the two parties to warrant caution in our conclusion. As well, it would appear that the support bases of each party remain relatively class-based. Specifically, when we look at the socioeconomic makeup of the constituencies won by each party, in urban areas the NDP remains dominant in constituencies that have a lower socioeconomic status, while the Saskatchewan Party was successful in constituencies that rank higher on the socioeconomic index. This evidence should cause us to be cautious in our conclusions.

The process of convergence is underway, but not yet complete, and as we know from the economic turmoil at the end of 2008, the direction and ideological center of politics can change rather quickly. However, it is unlikely that we will ever return to a time when the two major parties in this province will be as dramatically different as the Liberals and the CCF were in 1944. Fortunately or unfortunately, Saskatchewan looks more and more like other political jurisdictions in Canada.

NOTES

1. Brad Wall, *Saskatoon StarPhoenix*, November 8, 2007, A1

2. For the exact number of seats and votes please see Appendix A

3. W.L. Morton, *The Progressive Party in Canada* (Toronto: the University of Toronto Press, 1967).

4. Douglas Owram, *The Promise of Eden* (Toronto: the University of Toronto Press, 1980).

5. John Richards and Larry Pratt, *Prairie Capitalism: Power and Influence in the New West* (Toronto: McClelland and Stewart Ltd., 1979).

6. David E. Smith, *Prairie Liberalism: The Liberal Party in Saskatchewan 1905–71* (Toronto: The University of Toronto Press, 1975).

7. Kevin Wishlow, "Rethinking the Polarization Thesis: the Formation and Growth of the Saskatchewan Party, 1997–2001," in Howard Leeson (ed.), *Saskatchewan Politics: Into the Twenty-first Century* (Regina: Canadian Plains Research Center, 2001), 176.

8. For a discussion of this see Linda Haverstock, "The Saskatchewan Liberal Party" in Howard Leeson (ed.), *Saskatchewan Politics: Into the Twenty-first Century* (Regina: Canadian Plains Research Center, 2001), 199.

9. Wishlow, "Rethinking the Polarization Thesis," 178.

10. Ibid.

11. Ibid.

12. Ibid., 179

13. Ibid. 197.

14. David McGrane, "The 2007 Provincial Election in Saskatchewan" *Canadian Political Science Review* 2, no. 1 (March 2008): 2

15. This was particularly evident in the elections of 1999 and 2003.

16. Wishlow, "Rethinking the Polarization Thesis," 180.

17. Ibid., 197.

18. For example, seats like Regina South, and Regina Qu'Appelle were won by the Saskatchewan Party.

19. Dr. Ken Rasmussen, "Suburban Province," a speech delivered on April 15, 2007 at the Hotel Saskatchewan in Regina.

20. Ibid.

21. Ibid.

22. Ibid

23. Ibid.

24. See footnote 5.

25. In this category are people like Seymour Lipset and others. However, as you might expect, their views are not holistic in this matter. For an interesting discussion of this see "Agrarian Socialism or Agrarian Capitalism " in David E. Smith, *Lipsett's Agrarian Socialism: A Re-examination* (Regina: Saskatchewan Institute of Public Policy/Canadian Plains Research Center, 2007).

26. Howard Leeson, "The Rich Soil of Saskatchewan Politics," in Howard Leeson (ed.), *Saskatchewan Politics: Into the Twenty-first Century* (Regina: Canadian Plains Research Center, 2001), 9

27. For a longer discussion about policy convergence during the Romanow years see the articles by Kevin Wishlow, and Michael Rushton in the first edition of *Saskatchewan Politics*. For a detailed discussion of more recent policy convergence see the articles by Blake and McGrane in this volume.

28. On page 29 of the NDP campaign platform, bullet number 3 says, "complete the most aggressive business tax cuts in Saskatchewan history."

29. The Prebble article in this volume provides a detailed description of these policy initiatives.

30. *Hansard*, Saskatchewan, April 2, 2007, 1137.

31. Ibid. 1138.

32. Ibid. 1133.

33. Ibid., 1134.

34. Ibid., March 7, 2007, 728.

35 McGrane, "The 2007 Provincial Election in Saskatchewan," 2.

36. Everything in this section has been taken from the campaign documents published by both parties on their website during the election campaign.

37. These details can be found on page 38 of the Saskatchewan Party platform, and on page 26 of the NDP platform.

POLITICAL PARTIES
IN THE PROVINCE

Which Third Way? A Comparison of the Romanow and Calvert NDP Governments from 1991 to 2007

David McGrane

After the legendary Saskatchewan Cooperative Commonwealth Federation (CCF) government of T.C. Douglas and Woodrow Lloyd, the Saskatchewan New Democratic Party (NDP) government that was in power from 1991 to 2007 is the second-longest serving social democratic government in Canadian history. The most recent Saskatchewan NDP government, under the leadership of Roy Romanow and Lorne Calvert, has evidently played an important role in shaping the history of Saskatchewan and is an excellent example of the transformation of social democratic ideology that has taken place in Canada and around the world. Given the recent defeat of the Saskatchewan NDP in the fall 2007 provincial election, it is an opportune time to explore the ideology of the NDP government during the 1990s and 2000s: to analyze its overall structure, examine how it fits with global trends in social democracy, and contemplate its future trajectory.

The history of the CCF-NDP in Saskatchewan before 1990 has been written about extensively.[1] Further, there have been several articles and books which have analyzed the Romanow government from a critical, sympathetic, or neutral standpoint.[2] However, researchers have yet to analyze the Calvert government and no research has attempted to compare the Romanow government to the Calvert government. To fill this gap in the literature on the Saskatchewan NDP, this chapter examines ideological differences in the public policy of the Romanow and Calvert governments. After presenting a definition of the "Third Way" based on the work of Anthony Giddens, this chapter argues that the Calvert government represented a slightly more left-wing version of Third Way social democracy compared to the Romanow government. The Calvert government's minor move to the left was more apparent in its social policy than in its economic policy, which basically just extended the policies adopted by the Romanow administration. The Calvert government's expansive social policy can be explained by the absence of a deficit, a resource-based economic boom which drastically increased government revenues, a reinvestment in social programs by the federal government, and a change of leadership within the Saskatchewan NDP. However, certain structural limitations related to the emergence of globalization and the need for Saskatchewan to remain competitive with other jurisdictions prohibited the

Calvert government from following a substantially different set of economic policies than the Romanow government. The chapter ends with a discussion of the legacy of the Romanow and Calvert governments and the future of the NDP in Saskatchewan.

TRADITIONAL SOCIAL DEMOCRACY VERSUS THE THIRD WAY

Following a number of speeches by Tony Blair and Gerhard Schroeder, the term "Third Way" emerged to describe European social democracy's transformation into a more liberal, moderate ideological stance in the 1990s as compared to the ideology of traditional social democracy that was developed in the century between 1890 and 1990.[3] In Saskatchewan, many commentators noted a similar ideological shift to the right by the Romanow government in comparison to the traditional social democracy of previous Saskatchewan CCF-NDP governments under the leadership of T.C. Douglas, Woodrow Lloyd, and Allan Blakeney.[4] While the term 'Third Way' was rarely used by Saskatchewan NDP politicians in the 1990s and early 2000s to describe the shift within the party's ideology, it is the best theoretical apparatus available to conceptualize the transformation of the Saskatchewan NDP's ideology during the Romanow and Calvert governments.

While recognizing that there are many definitions of the Third Way and its relationship to traditional social democracy,[5] Anthony Giddens' work provides the most appropriate model for the argument presented in this paper.[6] For Giddens, the Third Way is not the wide boulevard between capitalism and communism but the considerably narrower path between the radical neo-liberalism of the 1980s and traditional social democracy. Conceptually, Gidden sees the Third Way as a variant of social democracy that nevertheless displays a number of key differences from the ideology of traditional social democracy. First, the Third Way employs a shallow notion of equality as the allocation of government benefits based on merit or need in contrast to traditional social democracy's deeper notion of equality which guarantees benefits to all regardless of merit or need as an essential component of citizenship. For instance, traditional social democracy would provide family allowance to all families regardless of income in order to create equality, whereas the Third Way would try to promote greater equality through targeting a skills training allowance to low-income single mothers who have shown the 'merit' to want to improve themselves through education. Second, the Third Way sees the free market as a mechanism which ensures autonomy and freedom through consumer choice and generates wealth for all of society. Thus, to encourage private investment, the free market needs to be supported by state action, such as tax incentives, and a regulatory environment that is competitive with other jurisdictions. On the other hand, traditional social democracy believes that the free market needs to be restrained through expanding public ownership to produce a redistribution of society's wealth. Third, the Third Way is critical of solutions that depend too heavily on the state and recognizes that the state has the potential to be overly-bureaucratic and inefficient. Conversely, traditional social democracy holds that the state should play a preponderant role in all spheres of society and displays no fears concerning an overbearing bureaucracy or the inefficiency of government. Finally, citing the example of the Blair government, Giddens contends that the Third Way involves partnerships between the state and public sector to provide public services and streamlines public ownership, whereas the large expansion of nationalization and exclusively government-administered social programs are a critical part of traditional social democracy.

Giddens also argues that there are a number of significant differences between the Third Way and neo-liberalism. Whereas the Third Way supports the notion that the state should play a role in reducing economic inequality through an effective welfare state, neo-liberalism is indifferent to inequality and holds that the state should not assume responsibility for the social consequences of market outcomes. The Third Way advocates strategic intervention in the economy through the maintenance of Crown Corporations and direct subsidies and targeted tax incentives to business. On the other hand, neo-liberalism believes in the wholesale privatization of publicly-owned corporations and the removal of as much state intervention in the economy as is feasible.

As opposed to the Third Way's advocacy of a strategic role for the state in the economy through public ownership and direct subsidies to business, neo-liberalism believes in the wholesale privatization of publicly-owned corporations and the removal of as much state intervention in the economy as possible. Finally, Giddens claims that neo-liberalism links the dominance of unfettered market forces to the defence of traditional institutions such as the nuclear family, whereas the Third Way is supportive of policies that encourage the insertion of women into the labour market.

THE THIRD WAY OF THE ROMANOW AND CALVERT GOVERNMENTS

This section will examine the policies of the Romanow government (from November 1991 to January 2001) and the Calvert government (from February 2001 to November 2007) under the two general themes of economic policy and social policy. This section will attempt to demonstrate how these governments were generally representative of Giddens' definition of the Third Way and illustrate the subtle ideological differences between the two administrations.

Rather than using public ownership to create jobs and stimulate economic growth like previous CCF-NDP governments in Saskatchewan, the Romanow and Calvert governments strove to make Saskatchewan's investment climate more competitive in order to attract external private investment to fuel job creation. While the Romanow government initially increased income taxes and capital taxes on large corporations, it simultaneously implemented several "targeted business tax cuts," such as the tax credits for manufacturers, the film industry, and research and development activities, as well as removed the provincial sales tax (PST) on aviation fuel, mining equipment, and 1-800 telephone lines.[7] In addition, the Romanow government lowered royalty rates for natural resources to spur increases in investment and extraction and reduced the tax rate for small businesses. The Calvert government followed the Romanow government's lead by enriching several targeted tax incentives, further reducing royalties, decreasing small business taxes, and bringing in broad-based tax cuts for large corporations in its 2006–07 budget.[8]

The Romanow government moved aggressively to reduce the "regulatory burden" on business by streamlining licensing procedures, condensing the procedures to start a new business, and creating a sunset clause that eliminated all business regulation after 10 years unless it had been reviewed and restored in advance by cabinet.[9] Due to the extensive action by the Romanow government, the Calvert government had less to do in this area. Nonetheless, it did reduce regulatory pressures further in the film sector and removed restrictions on the ownership of farmland by non-Saskatchewan residents.[10] Both the Romanow and Calvert governments moved to create a more skilled workforce by providing subsidies for employers to train people for new jobs, by subsidizing post-secondary graduates' wages for the first two years in targeted companies in growth areas of the economy, by providing quick response training to meet immediate industry needs, and by allocating funding for human resource planning for specific sectors. The Romanow and Calvert governments were also active in the commercialization of university research by providing increased funding to build strategic partnerships between universities and the province's businesses.[11]

Neither the Romanow nor the Calvert government provided significant support to Saskatchewan's co-operatives. The Romanow government passed legislation to allow Credit Unions to enter new lines of business and approved the New Generation Co-operatives Act, which created a legal framework for a new type of agricultural co-operative that required a high level of equity investment from its members and allowed investment from non-members, while retaining the principle of one member, one vote.[12] For its part, the Calvert government established a fund in partnership with several large Credit Unions to invest in small and medium-sized businesses, particularly those in rural Saskatchewan.[13]

In terms of taxation, the Romanow government introduced a 10% "Deficit Reduction Surtax" on all taxpayers which hit high-income earners rather hard since 10% of the total tax bill of a high-income earner is substantially more than 10% of the total tax bill of a low-income earner.[14] At the same time, it increased corporate taxes and raised consumption taxes, such as the sales, gas, and tobacco taxes. After the deficit was eliminated in 1995, the Romanow government began to reduce taxes. It lowered the PST from 9% to 6% and introduced a large package of personal income tax cuts in its 2000-01 Budget. The 2000–01 multi-year personal income tax reform eliminated the Basic Saskatchewan Tax, Flat Tax, Deficit Reduction Surtax, Low Income Reduction Surtax and High Income Surtax (introduced by the NDP in 1976) in favour of a simple and progressive three-bracket structure which reduced personal income tax rates for all taxpayers.[15] At the same time, the Romanow government introduced universal child and senior tax credits as well as a PST tax credit for low-income earners, while expanding the number of goods and services to which the PST applied. Finally, the government reduced property and fuel taxes for farmers and committed to the indexation of the provincial income tax brackets and personal tax credits to avoid the impact of tax reductions being eroded through inflationary pressures. According to the Romanow government's calculations, the tax savings flowing from its tax reforms in the 2000–01 budget would be greatest for low-income earners as a percentage of their overall tax bill, but in absolute monetary terms, the savings evidently would be greater for high-income earners.[16]

The Calvert government's taxation policies varied little from those of the Romanow government. For the most part, the Calvert government simply implemented the tax reforms announced in the 2000–01 budget. Besides the business tax cuts discussed above, the additional tax reforms by the Calvert government included raising the PST to 7% in 2004 only to reduce it back to 5% before the 2007 provincial election, increasing property tax relief for both homeowners and farmers, and following the federal government's move to permit income splitting for seniors. Building on the small Post-Secondary Graduate Tax Credit introduced by the Romanow government in 2000, the Calvert government incrementally moved to ensuring that post-secondary graduates would not pay provincial income tax on the first $20,000 of their income for five years following graduation as a mechanism to entice young people to stay in Saskatchewan and attract young skilled workers from outside the province.[17]

The Romanow and Calvert governments had very similar policies on agriculture and free trade. Both governments were strident in their support for the Canadian Wheat Board and called on the federal government to provide more funding to farm income support and to act decisively in international forums to reduce American and European farm subsidies.[18] Both governments emphasized the need for diversification and the importance of adding value to Saskatchewan's raw agricultural products by providing grants to meat-packing operations and other projects which processed Saskatchewan crops before their exportation.[19] They supported free trade as beneficial for Saskatchewan but declared that health, education, culture, and social programs should be exempt from any free trade agreement.[20]

It would be inaccurate to state that the economic policy of the Calvert and Romanow governments was exactly the same. There were several areas where variations existed, such as Crown Corporations, labour policy, immigration, subsidies to business, and promotion of the green economy; however, the differences in these areas were very slight and nuanced.

The Romanow and Calvert governments did not attempt to return to the Blakeney era by re-nationalizing the province's resource extraction Crown Corporations that had been sold off by the Progressive Conservative government during the 1980s. Indeed, the Romanow and Calvert governments completed the privatization of these natural resource Crown Corporations by selling the government's remaining shares in these companies at a considerable profit. On the other hand, they were very insistent that the province's four major Crown utilities (electricity, car insurance, telephone, and natural gas distribution) should remain publicly owned because the utilities were financially viable, guaranteed head offices in the province, ensured reasonable rates, provided a return on public investment in the form of dividends, and advanced social and economic objectives.[21] At the same time, both governments decided that Crown Corporations should behave more like private sector businesses in order to be responsive to shifting market conditions and succeed in an era of increased global competition and deregulation. As such, the Romanow and Calvert governments moved assertively to expand these Crown Corporations' lines of business within the province and to have them compete with other companies in order to provide their goods and services worldwide.

The Calvert government was more aggressive than the Romanow government in keeping utility rates low and using Crown Corporations to promote specific public policy goals. The Romanow government limited the cross-subsidization of utility rates whereby higher commercial rates were used to create lower residential rates, allowed the human resources policies of the Crown utilities to deviate from those of the rest of the public sector, and removed ministers from the boards of Crown utilities to reduce the perception of political interference and increase the corporation's ability to react quickly to market forces.[22] On the other hand, the Calvert government put ministers back on Crown boards, provided a series of rebates to consumers to insure that Saskatchewan residents had the "lowest-cost bundle of basic utility services in Canada," and instituted programs by which Crown Corporations encouraged environmentally friendly consumer behaviour, hired and trained young First Nations people, and provided free internet service in downtown areas as a tool of economic development.[23]

In terms of labour legislation, the Romanow and Calvert governments attempted to cultivate a consensus between unions and employers to keep the province's investment climate competitive. While both governments made several improvements to labour standards that were applauded by the province's labour unions, they also backed down on the implementation of regulations requiring that employers offer additional or new hours to part-time workers based on their length of service.[24] Perhaps, compared to the Romanow government, the Calvert government did pursue a labour policy that was slightly more favourable to unions as evidenced by its institution of a new statutory holiday in February, significant increases to the minimum wage, and refraining from legislating employees back to work.

Besides the Calvert government's willingness to use Crown Corporations for public policy objectives and its mild assertiveness on labour policy, there were only three other areas of economic policy in which the Calvert government differed from the Romanow government. First, the Romanow government did not actively develop an immigration policy, whereas the Calvert government put in place various programs aimed at increasing Saskatchewan's intake of immigrants and improving integration services for immigrants once they arrived in the province.[25] Second, while the Romanow government relied heavily on tax incentives to promote economic growth, the Calvert government was much more willing to provide direct cash grants to retain and attract business to Saskatchewan.[26] Finally, instead of creating over-arching environmental legislation for its industries, the Romanow govern-ment negotiated bi-lateral agreements with several of Saskatchewan's largest businesses to improve their environmental practices so as not to endanger the province's competitiveness.[27] While the Calvert government undoubtedly agreed that the objectives of economic development and environmental pro-tection should be balanced, it was more aggressive in promoting the green economy than the Romanow government. The Calvert government increased Saskatchewan's supply of wind power, put in place a plan aimed at having 10% of Saskatchewan farmers involved in organic production by 2015, and imposed regulations requiring that automotive gasoline contain 7.5% ethanol.[28]

The more clear-cut ideological differences between the Romanow and Calvert governments were in social policy. As shown in Table 1, the Romanow government initially cut funding to health and education and then made some minor re-investments. While medicare in Saskatchewan remained a publicly administered system whose essential services were free to all residents, the Romanow government's funding cuts meant the de-listing of optometric and

Table 1: Saskatchewan Expenditures in Constant 1995 Dollars (In Millions)										
Year	Total Expenditures	Health	Education	Social Services	High-ways	Agri-culture	Justice	Interest on Debt	Other	Deficit/ Surplus
Romanow										
1992–93	5090	1586	926	434	168	269	174	757	775	-607
1993–94	5067	1498	884	514	184	333	169	894	592	-277
1994–95	5096	1533	902	526	177	304	172	881	601	128
1995–96	5046	1533	857	528	167	219	183	837	722	18
1996–97	4935	1557	857	508	165	316	177	769	586	393
1997–98	4924	1611	892	514	204	195	189	724	596	34
1998–99	5244	1669	939	535	218	309	208	700	666	25
1999–2000	5297	1794	946	529	216	309	209	639	655	76
2000–01	4690	1851	990	516	244	197	207	593	94	51
Calvert										
2001–02	4978	1913	982	504	269	348	206	536	219	1
2002–03	4916	1998	926	518	251	265	157	521	280	1
2003–04	5162	2106	1052	507	245	278	162	504	308	1
2004–05	5263	2264	1061	492	208	319	165	472	282	312
2005–06	5746	2409	1186	508	212	340	175	438	479	322
2006–07	6084	2528	1316	561	242	291	187	425	533	231
2007–08	6223	2690	1319	483	273	232	194	422	609	204
Sources: Saskatchewan Public Accounts, 1992–2008.										

chiropractic services, the doubling of deductibles for the Prescription Drug Plan, the institution of fees for eye exams and air ambulance service, the closure of rural hospitals, and the expansion of home care. The Romanow government's funding cuts to the education system were mostly carried out through increasing class sizes, raising tuition, reducing administration costs, and limiting the building of new infrastructure. When the Romanow government did begin to re-invest in health care during its second term, it augmented funding to shorten wait lists, improve access to cancer treatment, enhance women's health programs, and provide incentives for physicians to locate in rural areas.[29] Most of the Romanow government's re-investment in education went towards building new infrastructure and increasing student loans and grants to promote access for low-income students to post-secondary education.

In contrast to the Romanow government, the Calvert government aggressively increased funding for health and education. The boost in funding to health care allowed the Calvert government to introduce a number of initiatives such as new investment in infrastructure, the further reduction of wait times, funding to train and recruit more nurses and doctors, a telephone health service, increased responsibilities for nurses, and the Health Quality Council.[30] Late in its second term, the Calvert government introduced two new health programs that were "universal" in the sense that they were targeted in terms of age and not income. First, the government began to provide insulin pumps for children under age 18. More significantly, the government created a program to guarantee that all senior citizens would pay no more than $15 per drug prescription.[31] In the area of education, the Calvert government provided funding to increase the use of information technology, create more training spaces, implement literacy programs, and introduce the *SchoolPLUS* program to develop a variety of additional health and social services within schools.[32] In addition to increasing student debt relief and creating more student summer jobs, the Calvert government also froze tuition during its last three years in power.

The Romanow government decreased funding for housing programs from 1992 to 1997 in an effort to eliminate its deficit.[33] However, during the final years of its mandate, the Romanow government created a number of housing programs targeted to remote communities in the province's North, seniors, growing rural communities, and inner-city neighbourhoods.[34] The Calvert government greatly expanded on these housing initiatives. Under its *HomeFirst* strategy, the Calvert government created a myriad of affordable housing projects for the same groups that the Romanow government had targeted and expanded housing assistance beyond the targeted groups that the Romanow government had identified. For instance, the Calvert government created the Saskatchewan Rental Housing Supplement for all low-income earners regardless of their location and raised the maximum allowable income limit to qualify for housing assistance in order to provide aid to "moderate-income families."[35] After adjustment for inflation, the Calvert government was spending 32% more on housing during its final year in power than the amount spent by the Romanow government during its last year in power.[36]

During its first term in government, the Romanow government ended the Conservatives' workfare programs, made a one-time increase to basic social assistance rates, and introduced the *Saskatchewan Action Plan for Children*. The *Action Plan* evolved into a large number of small, targeted programs for children and families, many of which were run in co-operation with local groups.[37] In its second term of government, the Romanow government undertook a major redesign of the province's social assistance system called *Building Independence*. The central idea behind *Building Independence* was to remove disincentives to work for social assistance recipients and to provide improved financial support for working poor families to ensure that they did not fall into a cycle of dependence on social assistance. This strategy included an employment supplement which ensured that social assistance recipients who found work would see a substantial increase in their overall income rather than a decrease equal to that of their employment earnings. The strategy also provided working poor families with the same health benefits that social assistance recipients receive, a training allowance for social assistance recipients to pursue post-secondary education, and a voluntary program which offered a personalized package of counselling services, education, training, and work experience opportunities to youth ages 18 to 21 who were on social assistance or whose parents were on social assistance.[38]

The Calvert government increased the benefits in the *Building Independence* program and expanded them to include a greater number of working poor. Additionally, the Calvert government created low-cost bus passes for social assistance recipients, introduced a dental care program for students in schools in low-income areas, and made a large number of increases to basic social assistance rates.[39] Unlike the benefits attached to *Building Independence*, these social assistance rate increases were not contingent upon recipients finding work and were available to recipients who were permanently unemployable due to disability.

Despite the overall austerity of the Romanow government's 1992 budget, it did increase operating grants to licensed child care centres by 21%, which was the first increase since 1986–87.[40] However, the Romanow government dismissed calls from the province's women's groups for the establishment of universal, free, and public daycare. Instead, under the *Action Plan for Children*, the government targeted its improvements in child care to low-income and "at-risk" children and created pre-kindergarten programs for three- and four-year-olds in low-income neighbourhoods.[41]

In contrast to the Romanow government, the Calvert government was much more active in the area of child care and early childhood development. Recognizing the limited number of regulated child care spaces in Saskatchewan, the Calvert government increased the number of licensed child care spaces by 21% over its six years in power as compared to the Romanow government which increased licensed child spaces by only 9% over its 10 years in office.[42] The Calvert government also implemented the innovative *KidsFirst* strategy to provide extensive support services for babies and very young children from vulnerable families and embarked on a major expansion of the number of pre-kindergarten programs in low-income areas.[43] With a pledge of increased financial support from the federal Liberal government in 2005, the Calvert government began to make plans for a universal pre-kindergarten program for all four-year-olds in the province.[44] However, the new Conservative federal government eliminated funding for the Liberals' child care agreements with the provinces, and the Calvert government abandoned its plans for a universal pre-kindergarten program.

Unlike other areas of their social policy where there were importance differences, the Romanow and Calvert governments did not have significantly divergent First Nations or women's policies. The Romanow government ensured that nearly half of its appointments to government boards were women, legislated pay equity within the public sector, and implemented programs to train women in skilled trades, prevent sexual harassment, and protect women who were victims of spousal violence.[45] The Calvert government followed up on the Romanow government's women's policy by increasing the length of unpaid parental leave and allowing pharmacists to prescribe the morning-after-pill. The Calvert government also introduced an action plan on women in 2003 out of which some modest initiatives flowed, such as increasing the number of women health care providers in rural areas.[46] However, the Calvert government was criticized by women's groups for reducing the size of the Status of Women's office and shifting it into the Department of Labour.[47]

In terms of First Nations policy, both the Romanow and Calvert governments were most active in the areas of justice, economic development, skills training, and labour force integration. The Romanow government developed the *Saskatchewan Aboriginal Justice* strategy in 1993 which implemented community-based and restorative justice services for Aboriginals, and the Calvert government spent $48 million to extend similar services in response to the First Nations and Métis Justice Reform Commission in 2005.[48] Both governments supported the creation of a number of new First Nations educational institutions and sought to promote training and employment through partnership agreements in which employers voluntarily increased the representation of First Nations in their workforce. Calvert's minister of Indian Affairs argued that "we could have imposed quotas through legislation but felt that wasn't the way to achieve the objective that we wanted to achieve.... . What, in fact, has worked better is to create awareness in the workforce about what our representative workforce really looks like."[49] The Romanow and Calvert governments also financed a variety of joint ventures between Métis and First Nations groups and private sector companies, and allowed the opening of several First Nations casinos.[50]

GIDDENS AND THE THIRD WAY IN SASKATCHEWAN

It is clear from the above description that the ideology of the Calvert and Romanow governments is generally representative of Giddens' definition of Third Way social democracy. Both governments enacted economic policies that sought to support wealth creation in the free market through the promotion of a competitive economic environment to attract private investment. The eschewing of policies such as the nationalization of natural resources in favour of reducing regulation, lowering royalties, and commercializing university research illustrates that the Romanow and Calvert governments were critical of solutions that depended too heavily on state action and preferred solutions which emphasized private sector growth. In terms of social policy, the vast majority of new social programs created by the Romanow and Calvert governments were targeted to citizens based on their need (income or geographical location) and merit (willingness to find employment or begin educational programming). Only in the final years of the Calvert government were two significant, non-targeted social initiatives introduced: the tuition freeze and the seniors drug plan. The expansion of social policies under the Calvert government, two of which were universal in character, illustrates that the Calvert government developed a slightly more left-wing version of Third Way social democracy than the Romanow government.

The only significant difference between Giddens' definition of the Third Way and the actions of the Romanow and Calvert governments was that public-private partnerships were not a large part of the NDP's ideology. While Giddens points to several private-public partnerships that were created by the Blair government in Great Britain as exemplary of Third Way governance, the Saskatchewan NDP only created two small private-public partnerships in the tourism and exportation sectors.[51] There are two reasons for the Saskatchewan NDP's lack of enthusiasm for private-public partnerships. First, by the 1990s and 2000s, the concepts of a publicly administered health care system and government-owned utilities were deeply engrained in the political culture of Saskatchewan and were considered an important touchstone of Saskatchewan identity.[52] Second, the privatization of health care and Crown Corporations was used as a "wedge" issue by the NDP in electoral competition with the Saskatchewan Party. Since the NDP constantly raised the spectre of the Saskatchewan Party privatizing medicare or Crown Corporations, it was difficult for the NDP to embark on any type of initiative that would remotely resemble the privatization of either the welfare state or public utilities.

EXPLAINING THE DIFFERENCES AND SIMILARITIES
BETWEEN THE ROMANOW AND CALVERT GOVERNMENTS

There were four primary factors which explain the subtle ideological differences between the Romanow and Calvert governments. First, the most obvious factor in explaining the Calvert government's more expansive social policies was the absence of a large deficit and debt. While the Romanow government was forced to reduce social spending to deal with the massive deficit and debt that it had inherited from the Devine Conservatives, the Calvert government was able to expand social programs because it was left with a robust financial situation that included no deficit and a relatively low debt-to-GDP ratio.[53]

Second, as shown in Table 2, while the Romanow government saw its transfer payments from the federal government fall drastically after the 1995

Year	Total Revenue	Individual Income Tax	Corporate Taxes	Sales Tax	Fuel Tax	Tobacco Tax	Resource Revenue	Crowns Dividends	Federal Transfers	Other
Table 2: Saskatchewan Revenues in Constant 1995 Dollars (In Millions)										
Romanow										
1992–93	4483	1101	228	552	310	118	405	137	1290	341
1993–94	4789	1092	323	682	351	113	463	171	1277	317
1994–95	5225	1057	357	728	331	115	717	294	1297	329
1995–96	5063	1096	452	768	336	114	664	344	934	354
1996–97	5330	1237	458	814	354	108	879	412	736	333
1997–98	4958	1275	465	723	361	118	750	401	531	329
1998–99	5269	1362	406	698	347	115	585	518	904	334
1999–00	5373	1327	523	606	325	121	865	147	1108	351
2000–01	6026	1120	602	657	308	109	1154	941	778	357
Calvert										
2001–02	5272	1041	442	670	307	104	786	488	1076	358
2002–03	5508	1219	475	694	282	135	1061	590	682	369
2003–04	5491	1042	570	715	298	147	955	514	864	384
2004–05	6361	1085	521	804	295	153	1203	558	1360	381
2005–06	6663	1166	739	896	303	138	1386	494	1019	523
2006–07	6824	1317	842	852	302	150	1337	463	1096	456
2007–08	7053	1472	785	725	298	138	1507	473	1260	395
Sources: Saskatchewan Public Accounts, 1992–2008.										

federal budget, the Calvert government benefitted from the federal re-investment in social programs that took place after the federal government eliminated its deficit and began to lower its debt. Even with the reduction in the province's equalization payments in the early 2000s, the Calvert government's increased spending in the areas of health, housing, and child care was aided by infusions of federal cash that generally had been unavailable during Romanow's time in power.

Third, the revenue generated from positive economic growth during the Romanow government was mostly put towards deficit reduction during its first term and basic re-investment in social programs during its second term.[54] Although the economy performed poorly during the Calvert government's first couple of years in power, the government was well positioned to take advantage of the economic boom that occurred in Saskatchewan during its final term.[55] In particular, soaring world demand combined with the NDP's policy of using low royalties to attract investment led to a significant increase in activity in Saskatchewan's natural resource sector during the later years of the Calvert government. As depicted in Table 2, the Calvert government benefitted from this resource-based economic boom through increased corporate taxes, sales taxes, and resource revenues, which were considerably higher than those of the Romanow government. The Calvert government was able to use this new-found wealth to increase its spending on social programs.

Finally, it is important to take into account agency when discussing the ideological differences between the Romanow and Calvert governments. Calvert was considered one of the left-wing members of the Romanow cabinet, and his victory in the leadership contest in 2001 should be seen as the articulation of a desire within the NDP to go in a more left-wing direction. Indeed, Calvert ran on a platform to return the NDP to its social democratic roots, and one of the surprises of the leadership race was the strong third-place showing by Nettie Wiebe whose platform stressed very left-wing social and economic policies and resistance to neo-liberal globalization.[56] Once Calvert was in power, many of the high-ranking, right-wing cabinet ministers from the Romanow era, such as Janice MacKinnon and Dwain Lingenfelter, retired and were replaced by ministers that held views closer to Calvert's left-wing version of the Third Way, such as Pat Atkinson, Peter Prebble, Harry Van Mulligen, and Joanne Crofford. Undoubtedly, the change in the NDP leadership and the desire by the party's grassroots to pursue a more aggressive left-wing agenda played an important role in the adoption of expansive social policies by the Calvert government. As Janice McKinnon reveals in her memoirs, the left-wing agents within the Calvert government successfully pushed for a greater portion of revenues to be spent on social policy objectives instead of debt reduction.[57] Indeed, an ideological choice was made by the Calvert government to drastically slow the pace of debt reduction in favour of increasing social spending. The total provincial debt under the Calvert government did fall by 7%, but total expenditures increased by 35%.[58]

It should be noted that the same structural constraints which drove the Romanow government's economic policies were still very active during Calvert's time in power. The emergence of globalization led to drastically increased exports and imports in Saskatchewan during the 1990s and the early 2000s.[59] Simultaneously, free trade agreements, primarily Chapter 11 of NAFTA, restricted the expansion of public ownership.[60] When the re-nationalization of resource extraction was no longer an option, the Saskatchewan NDP government had little choice but to perpetuate the growth of the provincial economy based on the export of oil, potash, uranium, and agricultural products through stimulating the private sector. Once the government committed to export-led growth through the private sector, the mobility of investment resulting from the fall of trade barriers necessitated that the Romanow and Calvert governments pay close attention to providing competitive advantages in order to attract investment to the province.

As such, the Calvert and Romanow governments were compelled to train a skilled workforce, keep business tax rates competitive, limit regulation, and encourage the commercialization of university research to attract mobile private investment to the province. Despite its more left-wing disposition, the Calvert government decided to fully implement the personal income tax cuts proposed by the Romanow government and introduce deep business tax cuts. The Calvert and Romanow governments felt that it was necessary to keep

personal income tax rates for high-income earners low in order to attract
skilled workers from other jurisdictions. Citing pressures from tax cuts in
Alberta and Ontario, the Romanow and Calvert governments reduced
Saskatchewan's top marginal tax rate from 19.9% to 15%, which they claimed
made it the third lowest in Canada.[61]

Therefore, due to structural limitations imposed by globalization, it is clear
that the agents of the Calvert government were very restricted in their ability
to create economic policies that drastically varied from those of the Romanow
government. Perhaps the lesson is that social democratic governments are
more constrained by globalization in the innovation of their economic policy
than in expansion of their social policy. In terms of economic policies, social
democratic governments are forced to follow policies that prioritize economic competitiveness relative to other jurisdictions in order to get their slice of
global trade and investment. However, in regard to social policies, social
democrats can implement relatively generous policies with little fear of negative consequences for their economy's competitiveness as long as those social
policies are not financed through excessively high taxation rates.

CONCLUSION

The Romanow and Calvert governments have had an important effect on the
politics of Saskatchewan. Throughout the history of Saskatchewan politics, a
perfectly viable conservative position has always been that government
should be shrunk and that Crown Corporations should be privatized. This
was the position of all the non-CCF-NDP premiers since 1934: James G.
Gardiner, William Patterson, Ross Thatcher, and Grant Devine. However, in
their quest to be elected, the Saskatchewan Party was forced to move to the
left into what was traditionally considered NDP territory. Under the leadership of Brad Wall, the Saskatchewan Party supported the NDP's Crown
Corporations Public Ownership Act despite opposition from the province's
major business groups.[62] The Act requires a thorough study of any proposed
privatization to be tabled in the Legislative Assembly and stipulates that the
sale of a Crown Corporation would be effective only after a general election.
Further, during the 2007 election campaign, the Saskatchewan Party promised
that it would not privatize any Crown Corporations and that it would provide
"all citizens with access to a comprehensive, publicly funded, and publicly
administered health care system that ensures high quality, timely health services are universally available and accessible throughout the province."[63] In an
effort to combat a NDP promise to expand the seniors drug plan to all citizens
during the 2007 provincial election, the Saskatchewan Party even committed
to expanding the drug plan to children under 14, while limiting it to seniors
with incomes under $65,000.

The privatization of Crown Corporations and medicare has now become
the third rail of Saskatchewan politics. Under the leadership of Roy Romanow
and Lorne Calvert, the Saskatchewan NDP in the 1990s and 2000s seems to
have succeeded in firmly entrenching social democratic values of government

ownership of major public utilities and the expansion of public health care into the political culture of Saskatchewan to a greater extent than ever before. In doing so, the greatest legacy of the NDP's time in power during the 1990s and 2000s is to have made it exceedingly difficult for the Saskatchewan Party government or other future right-wing governments to follow their natural ideological inclinations to reduce the size of government and privatize Crown Corporations.

Considering that the NDP was in power for 16 years from 1991 to 2007, it is clear that the Third Way social democracy of the Romanow and Calvert governments was electorally successful. The key to the NDP's popularity was that it was able to offer voters a package which combined fiscal prudence, competitive economic policies, and generous social policies. After its defeat, the inevitable question for the NDP will be if its ideology is in need of renewal?

As is argued in this paper, the Calvert government did a better job than the Romanow government of balancing the demands to remain economically competitive in an era of globalization with the social democratic objective of growing economic equality through altruistic social policies. In order to get back into power, the Saskatchewan NDP should follow the basic ideological recipe created by the Calvert government: develop economic policies focused on maintaining competitiveness with other jurisdictions and stimulating private investment coupled with generous social policies that share the wealth created by private sector-led economic growth. This ideological direction can be summarized by Blair and Schroeder's phrase: "We support a market economy, not a market society."[64]

In terms of economic policies, the NDP should start by assuring voters that it would maintain the competitive tax structure that it created in terms of personal income taxes, business taxes, and resource royalties. However, a recent report by the Organization for Economic Co-operation and Development (OECD) has illustrated how income tax cuts in Canada have generally benefited the rich.[65] If the NDP were to propose further tax reductions, they should be structured to ensure that low-income earners would receive greater benefits than high-income earners. For instance, future reductions to personal income tax rates could be configured as follows: a 3% reduction for low-income earners, a 2% reduction for middle-income earners, and a 1% reduction for high-income earners.

However, beyond just ensuring a competitive tax structure, governments should be ready to positively intervene in the economy to address structural problems which could endanger economic growth. The NDP should propose aggressive policies focusing on providing skills training, increasing immigration, and integrating Aboriginal people into the workforce in order to meet the growing labour shortage of both skilled and unskilled workers in Saskatchewan. The NDP must also stress that it would use a combination of tax incentives and direct grants to attract new investment, research, and development to the province. The clear message the NDP must send to voters is that its activist economic strategies are a better way to manage and sustain economic growth than the *laissez faire* approach of the Saskatchewan Party.

To regain its dominance in urban Saskatchewan, the NDP must find social policies to attract the young voters, suburban voters, and women voters who had previously voted for the NDP but moved to the Saskatchewan Party during the 2007 election.[66] Young voters and suburban voters could be attracted by promises to combat climate change and create a province-wide curb-side recycling program. In addition, a commitment to implement a universal pre-kindergarten program for all of the province's four-year-olds may be popular with women. Further, the NDP should propose an activist policy in terms of providing affordable housing and should promise a large transfer of funds to municipalities to deal with infrastructure pressures and to reduce property taxes, which could shore up the core NDP vote in inner cities and increase the NDP's suburban vote. The NDP could also attract more female voters by nominating more female candidates or electing a female leader who could become the first woman to be premier of Saskatchewan. The NDP should also continue to take a hard line with the federal government over equalization and other issues so that it can be seen as defending Saskatchewan's interests in contrast to Wall's close cozy relationship with Stephen Harper.

Finally, the NDP's greatest challenge is to find policies and leaders that appeal to rural Saskatchewan. With grain prices so high, Saskatchewan farmers do not seem to have much use for statist policies. Nonetheless, policies to provide grants to encourage organic farming and the value-added processing of agricultural products, as well as an aggressive strategy to reduce transportation and input costs, could attract some farm voters. Voters in small rural communities and cities may be more susceptible to the NDP's message than farmers. They could be attracted by promises of programs to beautify the downtowns of small towns, to build local infrastructure, and to provide grants for businesses to locate in communities with populations under 30,000. The idea would be to attract and maintain a new population to these rural communities as they become important service centres for the agriculture and resource industries as well as vibrant bedroom communities for people commuting to larger urban centres.

In conclusion, with a strong contingent of 20 opposition MLAs, the Saskatchewan NDP remains a viable electoral vehicle for regaining power and eventually implementing Third Way social democratic policies once in government. While the NDP needs to make slight alterations in its ideology, it should concentrate equally on cultivating a new generation of leaders and on finding ways of presenting policies that engage and excite the general public. Undoubtedly, the content of its new policies is vital to the NDP's success, but it is just as important to present these policies in way which grabs the attention of the people of Saskatchewan and articulates a clear and inspiring vision of the future of Saskatchewan as the province advances into the 21st century.

NOTES

1. See Seymour Lipset, *Agrarian Socialism: CCF in Saskatchewan*, 2nd ed. (Garden City: Anchor Books, 1968); A.W. Johnson, *Dream No Little Dreams: A Biography of the Douglas*

Government of Saskatchewan, 1944–1961 (Toronto: Institute of Public Administration of Canada and the University of Toronto Press, 2004); Dennis Gruending, *Promises to Keep: A Political Biography of Allan Blakeney* (Saskatoon: Western Producer Prairie Books, 1990); Eleanor Glor, *Policy Innovation in the Saskatchewan Public Sector, 1971–1982* (North York: Captus Press, 1997); Jim Harding (ed.), *Social Policy and Social Justice: The NDP Government in Saskatchewan During the Blakeney Years* (Waterloo: Wilfrid Laurier University Press, 1995).

2. For a left-wing critique of the Romanow government, see Lorne Brown, Joesph Roberts and Jack Warnock, *Saskatchewan Politics from Left to Right '44 to '99* (Regina: Hinterland Publications, 1999); John Warnock, *Saskatchewan: The Roots of Discontent and Protest* (Montreal: Black Rose Books, 2004); John Warnock, "The CCF-NDP in Saskatchewan: From Populist Social Democracy to Neoliberalism," in William Carroll and R.S. Ratner (eds.), *Challenges and Perils: Social Democracy in Neoliberal Times* (Black Point: Fernwood Books, 2005), 82–104; John Conway, *The West: The History of a Region in Confederation*, 3rd ed. (Toronto: James Lormier and Company, 2005). A more sympathetic treatment of the Romanow government can be found in Janice MacKinnon, *Minding the Public Purse: The Fiscal Crisis, Political Trade-offs and Canada's Future* (Montreal: McGill-Queen's Press, 2003) and Gregory Marchildon, "Roy Romanow," in Gordon Barnhart (ed.), *Saskatchewan Premiers of the Twentieth Century* (Regina: Canadian Plains Research Center, 2004), 353–94. Finally, a quite neutral treatment of the Romanow government may be found in Jocelyn Praud and Sarah McQuarrie, "The Saskatchewan NDP from the Regina Manifesto to the Romanow Years," in *Saskatchewan Politics into the Twenty-First Century* (Regina: Canadian Plains Research Center, 2001), 143–68.

3. See Tony Blair and Gerhard Schroeder, "Europe: The Third Way," < http://www.psinfo.net/dossiers/gauche/3voie/blairvo.html> (accessed on February 3, 2009).

4. Warnock, "The CCF-NDP in Saskatchewan: From Populist Social Democracy to Neoliberalism," 82–104, and Praud and McQuarrie, "The Saskatchewan NDP," in Leeson (ed.), *Saskatchewan Politics: Into the Twenty-First Century*, 55–165.

5. For a discussion of the extensive European literature concerning the definition of the Third Way, see Armando Barrientos and Martin Powell, "The Route Map of the Third Way," in Sarah Hale, Will Leggett, and Luke Martell (eds.), *The Third Way and Beyond: Criticisms, Futures and Alternatives* (Manchester: Manchester University Press, 2004), 9–26.

6. See Anthony Giddens, *The Third Way: The Renewal of Social Democracy* (Cambridge: Polity Press, 1998).

7. Government of Saskatchewan, *1993 Budget Speech*, Delivered by Janice MacKinnon (Regina: Queen's Printer, 1993), 6 and Government of Saskatchewan, *1995 Budget Speech*, Delivered by Janice MacKinnon (Regina: Queen's Printer, 1995), 5, 8.

8. See Government of Saskatchewan, *2006–2007 Budget Speech*, Delivered by Andrew Thomson (Regina: Queen's Printer, 2006).

9. Government of Saskatchewan, "Speech from the Throne," in *Saskatchewan Legislative Debates and Proceedings, Twenty Third Legislature—First Session* (Regina: Queen's Printer February 29, 1996), 2; Government of Saskatchewan, *1996 Budget Speech*, Delivered by Janice MacKinnon (Regina: Queen's Printer, 1996), 6 and Government of Saskatchewan, *1998 Budget Speech*, Delivered by Eric Cline (Regina: Queen's Printer, 1998), 6.

10. Saskatchewan Department of Culture, Youth and Recreation News Release, "Province Cuts Red Tape for Film Industry," July 18, 2002 and Murray Mandryk,

"Farm Land Law To Be Proclaimed by Jan. 1," *Regina Leader-Post*, December 11, 2002, B2.

11. Saskatchewan Department of Economic Development, *Research and Technology Commercialization Strategy and Action Plan* (Regina: Saskatchewan Economic Development, June 1994) and Government of Saskatchewan, *2004–2005 Budget Speech*, Delivered by Harry Van Mulligan (Regina: Queen's Printer, 2004), 18.

12. See Chad Haaf and Brenda Stefanson, *New Generation Co-operatives and the Law in Saskatchewan* (Saskatoon: Centre for the Study of Co-operatives, 2001).

13. Angela Hall, "$100M Apex Fund Created," *Regina Leader-Post*, February 15, 2007, B3.

14. Government of Saskatchewan, *1992 Budget Speech*, Delivered by Ed Tchorzewski (Regina: Queen's Printer,1992) 10–11.

15. The new bracket system worked as follows: 11% on the first $30,000, 13% on the next $30,000, and 15% on all income above $60,000. This system replaced the previous complex system whereby a Saskatchewan resident's income taxes were calculated as a percentage of the Basic Federal Tax combined with a variety of increases or decreases based on one's income.

16. For example, as a result of the reform, the government estimated that a two-income family making $35,000 would have their overall tax bill decreased by $622 or 28.5%, while a two-income family making $100,000 would have their overall tax bill decreased by $2500 or 20.4%. See Taxation and Intergovernmental Affairs Branch, Saskatchewan Department of Finance, *A Plan for Growth and Opportunity: Personal Tax Reform in Saskatchewan* (Regina: Saskatchewan Department of Finance, March 29, 2000), 9.

17. Government of Saskatchewan, *2007–2008 Budget Speech*.

18. Saskatchewan New Democratic Party, *The Saskatchewan Way: It's Working* (Regina: Saskatchewan New Democratic Party, 1995), 6–7 and Michelle Lang, "West Unanimous in $1.3 Billion Aid Call," *Regina Leader-Post*, May 11, 2002, A1.

19. Saskatchewan Agriculture and Food News Release, "Agri-Food Equity Fund Invests in Big Quill Resources Incorporated," May 12, 1999 and Murray Lyons, "$110M Pork Plant Planned," *Regina Leader-Post*, July 8, 2005, B4.

20. Regina Coalition Against the MAI Press Release, "Saskatchewan government's rejection of MAI a good first step, say the Regina and Saskatoon Coalitions of Against the MAI and the Council of Canadians-Saskatoon Chapter," February 19, 1998 and Saskatchewan Department of Intergovernmental and Aboriginal Affairs News Release, "Saskatchewan to weigh merits of FTAA," April 20, 2001.

21. Government of Saskatchewan, *Saskatchewan's Crown Corporations: A New Era* (Regina: Queen's Printer, 1997) and Saskatchewan New Democratic Party, *2003 Election Platform: Building the Future for Saskatchewan Families* (Regina: Saskatchewan New Democratic Party, 2003), 12–13.

22. All Crown utilities reduced cross-subsidization in the late 1990s. See SaskPower News Release, "SaskPower posts successful year," April 24, 1996; Saskatchewan Government Insurance News Release, "SGI Proposes Rate Adjustment," August 10, 2000; and Sasktel, *1997 Sasktel Annual Report* (Regina: Sasktel, 1997), 24.

23. James Wood, "Wiggling Out of Bundle Trouble," *Regina Leader-Post*, November 18, 2004, A1 and Crown Investment Corporation, *2005 Annual Report* (Regina: Crown Investments Corporation, 2005).

24. Joesph Garcea, "Saskatchewan," in *1995 Canadian Annual Review of Politics and Public Affairs* (Toronto: University of Toronto, 1996), 193 and Neil Scott, "NDP Scuttles 'Job-killer' Law: Labour Fumes at 'Capitulation' to Business Lobby," *Regina Leader-Post*, February 19, 2005, A1.

25. See Government of Saskatchewan, *Open up Saskatchewan : A Report on International Immigration and Inter-Provincial In-Migration Initiatives to Increase the Population of the Province of Saskatchewan* (Regina: Queen's Printer, September, 2003).

26. Examples here would include cash grants to the Prince Albert Pulp Mill, Mind's Eye Productions, Pastryworld Enterprises, and ethanol plants in Belle Plaine, Tisdale, and Yorkton.

27. Examples are bilateral agreements on environmental practices with IPSCO (steel), Kalium (potash), Saskferco (fertilizer), and Moose Jaw Asphalt (asphalt).

28. Angela Hall, "Ethanol Plant 'Full Steam Ahead' for September Start," *Regina Leader-Post*, April 25, 2005, B4 and Saskatchewan Department of Regional and Economic Development News Release, "Premier Receives Organic Report," September 26, 2007.

29. Government of Saskatchewan, *1999 Budget Speech*, Delivered by Eric Cline (Regina: Queen's Printer, 1999), 13.

30. See Government of Saskatchewan, *Action Plan for Health Care* (Regina: Queen's Printer, December 2001).

31. See Saskatchewan Government, *2007–2008 Budget Speech*.

32. For more information on the Calvert government's SchoolPLUS program, see its website at <http://www.learning.gov.sk.ca/schoolplus>.

33. Statistics Canada, "Federal and Provincial General Government Revenue and Expenditure, for Fiscal Year Ending March 31," CANSIM II table 3850002.

34. See Government of Saskatchewan, *Investing in People and Communities: A Housing Policy Framework for Saskatchewan People* (Regina: Queen's Printer, 1997).

35. Tim Switzer, "Supplement Intended To Boost Quality of Life," *Regina Leader-Post*, March 23, 2005, B4.

36. In constant 2007 dollars, the Calvert government spent $255 million on housing in 2007 compared to $174 million that the Romanow government spent in 2001. Statistics Canada, "Federal and Provincial General Government Revenue and Expenditure, for Fiscal Year Ending March 31," CANSIM II table 3850002.

37. An inventory of the large number of initiatives begun under the *Saskatchewan Action Plan for Children* can be found in Government of Saskatchewan, *Our Children, Our Future: Saskatchewan's Action Plan for Children—Four Years Later* (Regina: Queen's Printer, 1997) and Government of Saskatchewan, *Saskatchewan's Action Plan for Children: 1998/99 New Initiatives* (Regina: Queen's Printer, 1998).

38. Government of Saskatchewan, "Speech from the Throne," in *Saskatchewan Legislative Debates and Proceedings, Third Session—Twenty Third Legislature* (Regina: Queen's Printer, March 9, 1998), 4.

39. Government of Saskatchewan, *2006–2007 Budget Speech*, Delivered by Andrew Thomson (Regina: Queen's Printer, 2006), 9 and Department of Community Resources News Release, "Government Investments Reduces Poverty," April 24, 2007.

40. Louise Carbert, in Jane Arscott and Linda Trimble (eds.), "Governing on 'The Correct, The Compassionate, The Saskatchewan Side of the Border'," *In the Presence of Women: Representation in Canadian Governments* (Toronto: Harcourt-Brace Canada,

1997), 168 and Government of Saskatchewan, 1992 Budget Speech, Delivered by Ed Tchorzewski, (Regina: Queen's Printer, 1992), 16–17.

41. For instance, daycare subsidies were increased for teen parents in low-income neighbourhoods.

42. Childcare Resource and Research Unit, "Child care Space Statistics 2007," <http://www.childcarecanada.org/pubs/other/spaces/ccspacestatistics07.pdf> page 15 (accessed on February 2, 2009).

43. Janet French, "Calvert announces child-care funding," *Regina Leader-Post*, September 29, 2007, A5.

44. Department of Learning News Release, "Saskatchewan Still Needs Early Learning and Childcare System," April 24, 2006.

45. See David McGrane, "A Mixed Record: Gender and Saskatchewan Social Democracy," *Journal of Canadian Studies* 42, no. 1, (Winter 2008): 192–98.

46. See Saskatchewan Department of Labour News Release, "Progress on Addressing Women's Equality Issues," April 24, 2005.

47. Adrienne Bangsund, "Shakeup Causes Some Concerns for Women: Sekhar," *Regina Leader-Post*, April 3, 2002, A5.

48. See Government of Saskatchewan, *Creating a Healthy, Just, Prosperous and Safe Saskatchewan: A Response to the Commission on First Nations and Metis Peoples and Justice Reform* (Regina: Queen's Printer, May 2005).

49. Kerry Benjoe, "Sask. Signs Job Deal for First Nations," *Regina-Leader Post*, June 12, 2007, A6.

50. For example, see Saskatchewan Economic and Co-operative Development News Releases, "New Forestry Partnership in Zenon Park," April 30, 1999; "New Forestry Partnership in Northeast Saskatchewan," May 7, 1999; and "New Forestry Partnership in La Ronge," May 10, 1999.

51. The Saskatchewan Tourism Authority and Saskatchewan Trade and Export Partnership were private-public partnerships where the government provided funding and the overall mandate, while boards of directors composed of members of the private sector made strategic decisions.

52. See Nelson Wiseman, "Social Democracy in a Neo-Conservative Age: The Politics of Manitoba and Saskatchewan," in H. Telford and H. Lazar (eds.), *Canada: The State of the Federation, 2001* (Montreal: McGill-Queen's Press, 2002), 217–40.

53. If we exclude Crown Corporation debt, the Romanow government saw its debt-to-GDP ratio rise as high as 40.5%, while the Calvert government inherited a debt-to-GDP ratio of 23%. Government of Saskatchewan, *Financial Highlights of 2001–02 Budget* (Regina: Queen's Printer, March 30, 2001).

54. Besides 1992 and 1999, Saskatchewan's real GDP grew between 2% and 4% in each year of Romanow's government. See Saskatchewan Bureau of Statistics, "Real GDP—Chained 2002," <http://www.stats.gov.sk.ca/database/pea_search.php> (accessed on February 2, 2009).

55. Ibid. After two years of stagnant growth in 2001 and 2002, Saskatchewan's real GDP grew by 4.5% in 2003, 3.3% in 2004, 4.7% in 2005, and 3.4% in 2007. The exception to this growth was a downturn to 0.1% real GDP growth in 2006.

56. For a discussion of the 2001 NDP leadership race, see Praud and McQuarrie, "The Saskatchewan NDP," 164–67.

57. MacKinnon, *Minding the Public Purse*, 281–82.

58. See Table 2 for increases in spending under the Calvert government. For decreases in the Calvert government total debt see Government of Saskatchewan, *Budget 2002–2003: Meeting the Challenge for Saskatchewan People* (Regina: Queen's Printer, 2002), 42 and *Budget 2008–2009: Ready for Growth* (Regina: Queen's Printer, 2008), 57.

59. Total exports of goods and services from Saskatchewan to other countries increased by 18% from 1980 to 1990 and by 48% from 1990 to 2000, with the strongest growth taking place in lumber, oil, uranium, potash, manufactured goods, and services. In 2000 to 2006, exports remained at this high level and even increased by another 5%. See Saskatchewan Bureau of Statistics, "Total Exports to Canada and Abroad—Chained 2002," http://www.stats.gov.sk.ca/database/pea_search.php, February 2, 2009.

60. See Stephen Clarkson and Roopa Rangaswami, "Canada and continental integration under NAFTA," in *Canadian Politics*, 4th Ed., James Bickerton and Alain-G. Gagnon (eds.), (Peterborough: Broadview Press, 2004), 389–402.

61. Department of Finance News Release, "More Personal Income Tax Reductions," January 2, 2003 and Saskatchewan Department of Finance, *A Plan for Growth and Opportunity: Personal Tax Reform in Saskatchewan* (Regina: Saskatchewan Department of Finance, March 29, 2000), 14.

62. James Wood, "Business Groups Pan New Privatization Law," *Regina Leader-Post*, December 2, 2004, B3.

63. Saskatchewan Party, *Securing the Future: New Ideas for Saskatchewan* (Regina: Saskatchewan Party, 2007), 8.

64. Blair and Schroeder, "Europe: The Third Way," 1.

65. See OECD, *Taxing Wages 2006/2007: 2007 Edition* (OECD: OECD, 2007).

66. A comparison of polling done in Saskatoon during the 2003 and 2007 elections confirms that the NDP lost its significant advantage in terms of women and young voters while it is clear that the urban seats lost in the 2007 election were disproportionately in suburban areas. See Western Opinion Research, "Saskatchewan Election Survey for The Canadian Broadcasting Corporation, October 27, 2003," <http://www.cbc.ca/saskvotes2003/images/CBCResults Summaryv5.pdf> (accessed on April 15, 2008) and Insightrix, "November 5th, 2007: Poll shows Slight Lead for the Saskatchewan Party in Saskatoon," /0bd335b98b6fbe086f1135a6244a81d9.pdf> (accessed April 18, 2008).

The Saskatchewan Party and the Politics of Branding

Raymond B. Blake

The founding of the Saskatchewan Party in 1998 continued western Canada's long tradition of creating new political parties. This tradition has been manifested at the national level in the Progressive Party of the 1920s, the Co-operative Commonwealth Federation of the 1930s, and the Reform Party in the 1980s. At a provincial level, notably examples include the creation of the United Farmers in 1919 and its winning a majority government in Alberta two years later, Social Credit in Alberta in 1935, and the election of the CCF in Saskatchewan in 1944. These parties began as protest movements when influential and powerful groups in society came to believe that the traditional parties no longer effectively represented their interests.

Within the past decade or so, Saskatchewan has been the only province other than Quebec that has seen the emergence of a new political party that threatened the dominance of more established ones. In 2007, the Action Démocratique du Quebec (ADQ), a party that combines fiscal and social conservatism, nationalism and populism, nearly unseated the Liberal government in Quebec. In that same year, the Saskatchewan Party, another right of centre party, defeated the NDP government less than a decade after the creation of the new party.

Saskatchewan has long been viewed as having a more polarized political environment than any other province in Canada. Its political parties supposedly espouse either a right or left wing ideology.[1] This polarization has often been presented as an epic struggle between socialism and left wing democracy, as represented by the CCF/NDP and a variety of right wing challengers in various guises, ranging from the Thatcher Liberals in the 1960s to the Devine Conservatives in the 1980s and, more recently, the Saskatchewan Party. However, it should be noted that even during the CCF party's first term as North America's first socialist government, Premier T.C. Douglas and his party moderated many of its more radical policies to win support from the growing urban middle class.[2] Similarly, when Ross Thatcher defeated the NDP in 1964, his Liberal government largely left most state enterprises intact, even though Thatcher had vociferously attacked public enterprise and state capitalism while in opposition. The market-oriented Grant Devine Conservatives intervened in the economy, and Roy Romanow's NDP privatized some of the

Crowns, reduced social spending and continued the brand of fiscal conservatism well-accepted in Saskatchewan. The NDP continued its swing to the right under Lorne Calvert with his program of debt reductions and balanced budgets, tax cuts, and smaller government, as the traditional redistributive and interventionist platform of the NDP lost popularity amongst voters when the province teetered on the brink of financial collapse.[3] Saskatchewan politics in the last half-century has seen a coalescence of political views where flexibility has become the guiding ideology. Some have argued that political parties have largely become undifferentiated as they have positioned themselves to create coalitions to appeal to as many voters as possible.[4] Still, the myth of a polarized politics persists in spite of the reality of the nature of politics in the province.

Saskatchewan is not alone because political parties at both the provincial and federal level in Canada are increasingly undifferentiated when it comes to political ideology. Harold Clarke has long argued that political parties in Canada have essentially become brokers of political interests (i.e. brokerage parties) and have largely avoided hard positions on a variety of issues. Parties have become ideologically flexible to attract a broad coalition of support from citizens in an attempt to win power.[5] If political parties are, in fact, increasingly similar and are largely undifferentiated one from the other, and they all act as brokers, then what explains the rejection of one party over another and, in the case of Saskatchewan, the rise of a new political party in the Saskatchewan Party?[6]

The success of the Saskatchewan Party was the result of three interconnected and almost parallel processes: the nature of recent party politics in Saskatchewan, particularly the demise of the Haverstock Liberals in the mid-1990s; the discontent sweeping rural Saskatchewan that began in the 1990s; and then the optimism that accompanied the resource boom and the rise in commodity prices that began in 2003.[7] Maurice Pinard has argued that third (or new) political parties cannot arise without one-party dominance.[8] Clearly, in Saskatchewan the NDP had established itself as the natural governing party and, in Pinard's model, new parties emerge only in the presence of serious strain in society which leads to dissatisfaction with the dominant governing party. When this occurs, voters will not turn to weak traditional opposition parties since they are perceived not to be viable alternatives. While languishing in the political wilderness those traditional parties (such as the Liberals and Conservatives in Saskatchewan) lose all legitimacy.

In the case of Saskatchewan, this meant that neither the Liberals, which had not been competitive in the four decades since the 1967 provincial election, nor the Progressive Conservatives were considered viable alternatives when voters became disenchanted with the NDP. Even though the Liberals had elected 10 MLAs in the 1995 general election, the party was marred by internal dissension and ineptitude and never exuded any confidence among voters that it could form a government to replace the NDP.[9] The Progressive Conservative Party, which had been tarnished by the conviction of 12 of its members of the legislature for fraud and breach of trust for misuse of government allowances after the 1991 election, saw its support slip in each subsequent election; it, too, was not seen as a credible alternative to the governing NDP. The Conservatives saw both their share of the popular vote and the number elected to the Legislature drop precipitously in the 1995 general election.

The political reality was that, as separate parties, neither the Liberals nor Conservatives would be able to unseat the NDP any time soon. Pinard maintains that if the traditional and existing parties are seen as ineffective, or simply as "losers," then the discontented will not rally around the traditional parties, and for tactical and ideological reasons will not attempt to take over the existing opposition parties. "Rather than try to subdue and rejuvenate such a machine," Pinard argues, "the new leaders prefer to create an altogether new organization under the charismatic enthusiasm of a popular leader... From then on the new party is no longer a weak party to start with, and its supporters, by turning to it, are not choosing an altogether weaker alternative."[10] In the 1995 election, 53% of voters had cast their ballot for a party other than the NDP but still it was re-elected easily with 42 of the 58 seats.

The second process was what Pinard has called "the serious strain" in society. In the mid-1990s, rural Saskatchewan was seething with discontent. There were real concerns over crumbling roads and a decaying rural infrastructure, school and hospital closures, rail line abandonment and the closure of grain elevators, the centralization of utility (telephone, power) offices, and the RCMP out of small communities, and diminished employment opportunities that added to their anxiety and sense of abandonment.[11] Many rural areas came to believe governments did not care about them, as the Romanow government reduced municipal spending and closed hospitals. The Reform Party capitalized on this disaffection in the 1993 federal election when it elected four MPs, but neither the provincial Liberals nor the Progressive Conservatives were able to translate this disaffection into sufficient seats in the provincial legislature to defeat the NDP. Leeson has noted that rural depopulation throughout the 1990s accomplished what Lipset and others had predicted. In the wave of farm consolidations, the old CCF generation moved to the towns and was replaced by young farmers who were not imbued with the social democratic political populism of their parents. Instead, they saw a new and diminished role for the state, and favoured the private-sector over the co-operative. They were socially conservative and as participants in agribusiness (rather than family farms) no longer saw the urban labour movement as their allies; the labour movement and the professional classes, including the civil service, were considered as part of the problem among those struggling in the rural hinterland.[12] The newly created Saskatchewan Party capitalized on this discontent in 1999 when it won every seat in rural Saskatchewan.

Much of the decade of the 1990s had not been kind to Saskatchewan. The province had to deal with a declining population, especially in rural areas, a struggling agriculture sector, a difficult fiscal reality, and a growing urban-rural split. When the first edition of this book appeared in 2001, Leeson described the turmoil caused by these issues as contributing to the change that was sweeping the province. The past seven years has, indeed, witnessed considerable change, and the Saskatchewan Party benefited, first, from the upheaval and uncertainty in rural Saskatchewan and, later, the wave of optimism that rolled into the province around 2003. Initially, the party had been unable to break the hold of the NDP on the urban constituencies, as the NDP had been successful in convincing its core constituencies that the situation would be grave for the urban middle class if the Saskatchewan Party were to secure the reigns of power. However, by 2006, optimism had displaced fear as the new reality for the province. Gone were the notions expressed by novelist and essayist Sharon Butala in her "Time, Space and Light: Discovering the Saskatchewan Soul" where she described "Saskatchewan [as] only a holding area where one waited impatiently till one was old enough to leave in order to enter the excitement of the real world."[13] Today, Joni Mitchell's words from 1990—"I get a rush when I go to Saskatchewan"[14]— better captures the exuberance and excitement of the province. These sentiments are shared by Craig Wright, the chief economist at the Royal Bank, who described Saskatchewan as the new "It" province—a view echoed recently by the *Globe and Mail*.[15]

Saskatchewan is the new Alberta, and it has suddenly become the economic miracle of Canada. The boom in potash, uranium, oil and gas, and agriculture have been reflected in the move from "have-not" to "have" status within the Canadian federation, and in the rapid increase of more than 50% in real estates prices in both Regina and Saskatoon over the past two years. In April 2008, for instance, energy companies paid $266 million for new exploration rights, eclipsing the previous annual record of $250 million that was set in the previous year. Bill Boyd, the province's energy minister, told the *Globe and Mail*, "This level of interest is unprecedented and speaks to the optimism about the economic prospects of both our province and our No. 1 industry."[16] In such a period of sanguinity, there was little interest in pessimism and cynicism. The Saskatchewan Party, which had initially benefited enormously from the discontent and pessimism of the late 1990s, also captialized on the reversal of both economic fortunes and the mood throughout the province.

The Saskatchewan Party could do this largely because it had branded itself as a party of the centre following the 2003 general election.[17] Fear, for the moment, had been cast aside, and all but the most pessimistic embraced the new optimism. The NDP was simply not able to ride the wave of optimism that the province was experiencing; its emphasis on the province's mistreatment by Ottawa over equalization, its campaigns to repatriate citizens because of cheap housing prices in the province, and its warning of impending disaster if voters elected a Saskatchewan Party government had little appeal when, finally, the province was prospering and the future was promising. The NDP failed to link itself to the sense of optimism. This period of optimism and excitement was, too, a period of upheaval—and even "the serious strain" in Pinard's analysis—and the Saskatchewan Party was able to take advantage of it just as it had in the period of discontent and pessimism in rural areas nearly a decade earlier.

SASKATCHEWAN PARTY: THE MARCH TO POWER

The creation of the Saskatchewan Party by the Liberal and Conservatives MLAs was an elite movement, orchestrated by party stalwarts to transform two rump political parties into a new political party that would, first, attract the fiscally and socially conservative elements and, second, tap into the agrarian protests and the changing view of the role of the state and, third, create a viable alternative to the ruling NDP. Moreover, Liberal MLAs feared that the Reform Party of Canada, which had swept across the West in the 1993 federal election, would establish a provincial wing in the province.[18] Four Liberals—Ken Krawetz, Bob Bjornerud, Rod Gantefoer and June Draude—left the Liberal Party that was then mired in controversy and discord to join with the Conservatives and three federal Reformers to create the Saskatchewan Party. Former Liberal leadership candidate Tom Hengen and other prominent Liberals endorsed the new party.

The Saskatchewan Party was born out of a sense of frustration among the opposition elements in provincial politics as well as the frustration and anger sweeping rural Saskatchewan. The difficulties experienced in agricultural communities, combined with reductions in provincial services, sent the message to rural Saskatchewan that it was unimportant, a theme that held considerable resonance in the West and had played a key role in the formation of earlier protest parties such as the Progressive Party in the 1920s. With the demise of the Progressive Conservatives in the 1991 election, both the PCs and the Liberals had become little more than fringe parties. The NDP, under charismatic and charming Roy Romanow, had re-established the old party of Tommy Douglas as the natural governing party. By the 1950s, the Co-operative Commonwealth Federation (CCF), and its successor the New Democratic Party (NDP), had become the pragmatic party of the centre in Saskatchewan, governing for nearly 50 of the past 64 years, and it shifted to the left or right as the electoral conditions warranted. The party did well when it had a clear vision and was able to articulate that vision to the electorate. When the NDP returned to power in 1991, it clearly tapped into the popular sentiment of the necessity of eliminating the deficit and placing the economy on a sound foundation. Romanow's government was clearly right-of-centre in its philosophy. In fact, the most important issue for both the Conservatives and the NDP in the 1991 election had been the deficit; the two parties differed primarily over the source of the province's financial woes.

When the opposition parties joined to create the Saskatchewan Party, the new party struggled with the lingering image that it was merely the disgraced Conservative Party under a new name. This mattered greatly because the Conservative brand in Saskatchewan had been severely tainted. When prominent members of the Conservative Party, such as Dan D'Autremont and Bill Boyd, became key players in the Saskatchewan Party many wondered what was particularly new about the "new" party. Moreover, many of the caucus office staff from the Conservative Party simply moved to the Saskatchewan Party office which only served to further blur the lines between the old Conservative Party and the new Saskatchewan Party. A weekend before the

Saskatchewan Party founding convention, the Conservatives had met to suspend the PC Party for at least two provincial elections, ostensibly because the party supporters had found a new home in the Saskatchewan Party. Wayne Elhard, who was the first Saskatchewan Party member elected to the legislature and is now the Minister of Highways and Infrastructure, recalls that throughout rural/southwest Saskatchewan there was a sense that the new party could succeed where the Liberals and Conservatives had not.[19] Because of this, many of those in the Conservative constituency associations shifted to the Saskatchewan Party and became that party's earliest members.

Premier Roy Romanow immediately seized on the connections between the Conservatives and the Saskatchewan Party. He then set the stage for what would be the NDP's major strategy in attacking the Saskatchewan Party for the next decade: describe the party as being simply Conservatives in disguise and warn voters that the party could not be trusted. "We can be proud that our party was created in the bright sunlight, in the daylight of hope and optimism by men and women of vision and character and pride and passion," Romanow said. "What a contrast," he continued, speaking to a NDP Convention, "the Saskatchewan Party, cobbled together by a handful of opposition politicians secretly scheming in the dead of night." He went on describe the party as "dim bulbs" who would lead the province back to the dark days of huge debts and right-wing policies, and frequently referred to the Saskatchewan Party as "Saskatories."[20] Romanow also dismissed the selection of the name that the dissident Liberals and Conservatives had chosen. "The so-called Saskatchewan Party, [there is] no such thing," he told the NDP convention several weeks after the creation of the Saskatchewan Party. "There already is a Saskatchewan Party. There has been for over 50 years and it's us… It's the CCF, it is the NDP. We're the Saskatchewan Party."[21]

Although the Saskatchewan Party had been created by political elites, it strived to present a populist image. This was most evident in its approach in selecting its first leader. All members of the party could vote in the selection process and not just representatives sent to a leadership convention. Elwin Hermanson, the former Reform MP for Kindersley-Lloydminister from 1993–97 who had helped to bring provincial Tories and Liberals together a year earlier, emerged as the leader. It was clear that Hermanson saw the new party as providing a viable alternative to the governing NDP. He told the press when he announced his intention to run for the party leadership that "A vacuum seeks to be filled. I want to help fill the political vacuum in Saskatchewan for the good of the province."[22] Hermanson later remarked to Lawrence Martin that "we didn't debate for months and years whether we would create a new party in the public forum [but] it was an idea whose time has come."[23] Hermanson believed that one way of removing some of the stigma of the disgraced Conservatives and dysfunctional Liberals was to select a leader not associated with either party.

The NDP criticized the Saskatchewan Party for "poking their fingers in the eye of democracy" because the party was created without consulting the voters who had elected the PC and Liberal candidates who crossed the floor to create a new party. Romanow had promised a Respect for Constituents Act that would have prevented elected MLAs from switching parties without consulting their constituents, but he never delivered on his promise (perhaps because he had two ministers in his Cabinet who had been elected as Liberals), even though polls found that nearly 80% of voters believed that elected members should first subject themselves to a by-election before switching parties. What Romanow and his political advisors hoped to do was simply to cast a pall of distrust over the Saskatchewan Party, and it seemed to be working. By the time of the 1999 general election campaign, 51% of those polled said that the Saskatchewan Party could not be trusted largely because of its association with the Conservatives and because many of its members had betrayed the voter's trust when they switched parties.[24]

Although the Saskatchewan Party was an unknown entity on the political landscape of the province and it spoke the language of the new right with its emphasis on limits to state involvement in the economy, a reduction in taxation, and greater self-reliance among citizens, it did not stray too far from the political philosophy articulated by the governing NDP. As Ken Rasmussen has argued, the NDP government under Romanow "signaled the end of Saskatchewan's tradition of activist, entrepreneurial government" as the focus shifted to "[fiscal] restraint and market-centred development."[25] Still, the Saskatchewan Party was a new player and its policy platform and rhetoric worried many in the province. It called for major tax cuts, including a 2% reduction in the provincial sales tax and 20% cut in basic personal incomes taxes, and promised to make government deficits unlawful. These policies, by the late 1990s, were reflected in the platforms of all parties, but it was other issues such as plans to abolish no-fault insurance, impose PST on off-reserve purchasing for Status Indians, privatize Crown corporations when it was in the public interest, allow private surgical clinics, make able-bodied welfare recipients perform community service or attend job-training programs, send young offenders to boot-camp, increase support to families, and eliminate preferential recruitment practices in the civil service that worried many voters and opened the party to easy attack from the NDP.

In the 1999 general election, the Saskatchewan Party, which had campaigned primarily on fiscal responsibility as had the NDP, won 25 seats in a campaign that saw the NDP reduced to a minority position in the legislature with 29 seats. With 39.6% of the popular vote, the Saskatchewan Party surpassed the NDP with 38.7% of the popular vote. While the Saskatchewan Party did not win any seats in either Regina or Saskatoon, it finished second in 24 urban constituencies, and won 37% of the popular vote in Moose Jaw, 29% in Saskatoon, 26% in Regina, and 23% in Prince Albert.[26] It was clear the party had to broaden its appeal in urban areas, and that became the primary focus for the Party.

At the Saskatchewan Party's 2000 annual convention, Hermanson acknowledged that the urban areas were the only area of growth as the party held every seat in rural Saskatchewan. Don McMorris, Indian Head MLA and co-chair of the convention, told reporters that the party would have to address

issues "from more of an urban basis."[27] McMorris agreed image was an issue
for the Saskatchewan Party. "I think some people perceive us as strictly a
farm party and maybe we have to deal with some of the issues a little bit differently."[28] This was critical for a party that saw itself as a government in waiting, but the party leadership believed that opening up the convention to a serious policy debate on any of the potentially controversial issues when it was
just a handful of seats from a majority might be akin to political suicide.
Abortion was one of these issues and the party's stand on certain Aboriginal
issues was another. Saskatchewan's pro-life community had hoped that it
could achieve its goals within the Saskatchewan Party. The same was true of
those who believed that the system favoured Aboriginal peoples when it came
to issues of taxation. In a convention session called "Winning in the Cities,"
the party hoped to present a more moderate image and it believed the best
means of achieving that goal was not to allow debate on any of its controversial policies. As a result, the convention tabled three controversial policies
dealing with Aboriginal issues and defeated a fourth; it also rejected a resolution calling for the provincial government to cease paying for abortions.[29]
While the party talked about the need for a moderate platform that might
appeal to urban voters and had rejected social conservative policies at its convention, to most voters in urban areas the party had not changed very much.

One area that would prove to be the Achilles heel for the party, especially
among unionized and professional workers in the urban areas (many of
whom were employed in the public and Crown sectors), was its position on
privatization of the province's Crown corporations. This issue was not an easy
one for the Party to deal with, as it continued to maintain that whether or not
to sell the province's Crown corporations was a practical rather than ideological policy. Initially, the Party had insisted that it would liquidate the non-util-
ity Crown holdings when market conditions were favourable and use the proceeds to pay down the provincial debt. It had promised a referendum on any
specific proposal to sell any of the Crown utilities, but at its 2001 annual convention it dropped all references to a referendum. Instead, it promised privatization only if it could be demonstrated that government ownership was no
longer in the best interests of taxpayers. If any of the utility companies were
privatized, however, the Saskatchewan Party promised it would be done
through an initial public share offering for residents of Saskatchewan and the
profits would go to debt reduction. The policy was meant to soften the party's
position on the crowns, but it did not help change the party's image, even if
there were persistent rumors during 2001 that the NDP government had considered privatizing either SaskTel or SaskEnergy in the mid-1990s.[30]

By 2002, the Saskatchewan Party was clearly anxious for another election,
confident that it would win the contest. Many in the party knew that it was
not ready to govern in 1999, but in the ensuing three years it had learned a
great deal about policy and what it would take to run a province. It believed
that its policies were sound, and Hermanson set policy issues aside and
attempted to broaden the base of his party as he reached out to the Liberals
which he saw a major obstacle as the two parties were surely to split the vote

in many urban areas. "There is a role for them in a Saskatchewan Party government," Hermanson said,[31] as his overtures to the Liberals showed his interest in building a broader coalition rather than in staking out an ideological position for the party.

When the election was held in November 2003, the Saskatchewan Party campaigned on a platform of decreased government involvement in the economy and tax reductions. Although its share of the popular vote drop by nearly 2%, it increased its seat count to 28; but it was still not enough to defeat the NDP. "The results were a real disappointment and a great surprise," Wayne Elhard recalls.[32] Going into the campaign, the party had fully expected that it would win, given that it had a significant lead in the polls and a strong political organization that it had built since the last election. The 1999 campaign had been about legitimizing the Saskatchewan Party, but the 2003 campaign had been about winning.

In a highly polarized campaign in 2003 where the issue of Crown corporations and health care waiting lists dominated, the Liberal Party failed to win a single seat; and even though the Saskatchewan Party increased its seat total to 28, it failed to achieve the victory that so many within the party believed was imminent. The NDP, under new leader Lorne Calvert, increased both in seat numbers and the popular vote and retained its hold on power. During the campaign, when voters were asked who they did not want to see as premier—the way the question was framed was itself an indication of the cynicism towards all politicians—nearly 50% chose Hermanson compared to 30% for Calvert.[33] Moreover, Hermanson played into the hands of NDP campaign organizers when he said, as soon as the campaign began, that while the Saskatchewan Party had no plans to sell the province's four major Crowns, he would consider offers on them if he thought it would benefit the province. That equivocation, together with his promise of boot camps for young offenders, work for welfare, tax cuts for corporations and more business-friendly labour laws, sealed the fate of his campaign in a province where the NDP can traditionally count on between 35% and 38% of the electorate. Many other voters, including the elderly, were small "c" conservatives wary of change.[34] The nastiness of the political discourse in the province and, indeed, of the whole campaign was evident when an internal NDP cartoon was leaked showing Hermanson as a Nazi herding NDP sympathizers into boxcars, giving the impression that under the Saskatchewan Party there would be a purge of the civil service and that he was an uncaring dictator. All of this was designed to cast the Saskatchewan Party as untrustworthy and an entity to be feared—a theme that Romanow had seized upon shortly after the creation of the Saskatchewan Party.

Clearly, the Saskatchewan Party could not win with Hermanson as leader, and he resigned shortly after the election. With Hermanson's resignation the party began a branding process tied to strong, dynamic leadership and moderation that was designed to capture that 10 to 15% of the electorate that shifts its vote during most elections.[35] This branding process was an attempt to reposition the party within the political landscape of the province from that of opposition to power[36]; unlike the Bloc Quebecois and the federal NDP, for instance, which are generally satisfied with their roles as perpetual opposition parties, the Saskatchewan Party was dissatisfied with its opposition role. It believed that it could win if the party could appeal to the moderates, the independents, and those who were not stalwart supporters of the NDP. In fact, rumors that the Saskatchewan Party would fold if not elected soon were rampant in party ranks.

The first step in that process began with a new leader. Brad Wall was unchallenged for the leadership of the party. Wall, who was first elected to the legislature in 1999, had worked previously as a ministerial assistant in the government of Grant Devine, was considered more moderate than Hermanson. Wall insisted that he took a "pragmatic" approach and promised a sweeping review of the party's policies. He wanted to change the perception of the party and appeal to the mainstream and not the edges of the polity. He understood the need to brand the party as centrist and shed any right-wing image it might have. Shortly after he became leader, Wall admitted in *Signal: The Newsletter of the Saskatchewan Party* that change was necessary: "Our party members have developed a strong policy framework over the past seven years, but obviously, there were a few areas that Saskatchewan voters weren't quite comfortable with in the last provincial election." A wide-ranging policy review was initiated under the guidance of Wayne Elhard and three other MLAs. "The goal of this policy review," Wall said, "is to have our members involved in a process that will build on our strengths, address our weaknesses, and create a policy framework that will help us to fight and win the next election."[37]

The policy review was to be a "populist" undertaking whereby party members in every riding association considered a wide range of issues that would then be debated at a policy convention scheduled for February 2005. Moreover, the party held meetings with citizens in cities and towns across the province, and consulted more than 50 individuals outside the party, including academics, professionals, and business people. The party continued to hope that it might appeal to Liberal voters as well. Wall also realized that the party's presentation of its policy had to be controlled and that the image of the party could not be defined by the NDP as had often been the case under Hermanson.[38] It is not at all clear that that the Saskatchewan Party even had a clear policy agenda under Hermanson, but when Wall became leader whatever cause or agenda the party might have had was dropped in favour of a new brand that promoted good, sound, trustworthy government. The most important goal for the party became how it could construct a brand that voters found appealing. In this process party philosophy and ideology often become submerged in the ultimate goal of building an electable party.

The second stage of the branding process for the Saskatchewan Party occurred at the party's 2005 annual convention in Regina when it completed its makeover in an attempt to move itself closer to the seat of power. Hermanson had said before the convention that: "The party since its inception has tried not to be dogmatic or … ideological. I just think the more history we have, the easier it is to convey that message. New parties are slightly frightening to the voters."[39] Even so, the party had been seen by many as a rural-based right-wing party, and Wall used the policy review and the convention to change that image. "We are re-founding the policy of the party," Wall said as the convention began, and he promised to replace about 147 resolutions in an attempt to re-brand the party.[40] It was also an admission that the party with its right-wing image was hard to elect in the urban areas. Wall's goal was simple: make the Saskatchewan Party more appealing to urban voters. He told the Convention that "We want to present a well-rounded alternative [to the NDP, and] I'm trying to ensure that this party is reflective of where the people of this province are."[41] But could be convince his party to follow? Had the party faithful come to realize, like Wall had, that the party was unelectable in Saskatchewan without presenting a different image. The Saskatchewan Party had rocketed onto the political landscape in 1999 when it forced the NDP into a minority government, but it had failed to grasp the ultimate prize when its campaign in 2003 floundered on the issue of public ownership of the province's Crowns.

The Saskatchewan Party followed its new leader and adopted 141 of the 145 resolutions debated at the convention in the hopes that those changes would lead the party to victory in the next election. Much has been made of the fact that the debate at the convention occurred behind "closed doors" and away from the television cameras, but Wall and party leaders clearly did not want those who had joined the party in hopes of fulfilling their personal or narrowly focused agendas to get on their hobbyhorses and argue, for instance, against the health care system covering the cost of abortion. Such images would not only provide the NDP with further ammunition to argue that nothing had changed in the party, it would also interfere with the branding process that Wall understood was necessary to make the party electable.[42]

The convention approved several changes in policy that were clearly in keeping with Wall's design to re-brand the party. First, there would be no room for misunderstanding on the issue of the Crown corporations. The convention understood clearly that Hermanson's ambiguous comments during the 2003 campaign that while the party had *no intention* of selling the Crowns, it *might consider* doing so if the province stood to benefit handsomely from any privatization initiatives. Such fine distinctions lead only to misunderstanding in an election campaign, and although the convention delegates did not remove the issue of privatization from its policy book, it was understood, nonetheless, that there would be no immediate rush to privatization under a Saskatchewan Party government. Second, Enterprise Saskatchewan—an agency promoted as a partnership between government and business leaders that would promote the province and guide the government's economic strategy—was moved to the centre of the party platform. Wall wanted to make it a centerpiece of the party's strategy. The party promised to include organized labour, Aboriginal representatives, the business community and youth within Enterprise Saskatchewan in an effort to make the party more appealing to a greater number of voters. The economic strategy implied that the major Crowns would not be sold and that the party was willing to work with labour and Aboriginal leaders as well as the business community.[43]

The third element of the branding process came in the Party's approach to social policy. It dropped any discussion not to cover abortions under the province's health insurance and its opposition to equity hiring programs. It replaced a resolution calling for harsher sentences and the creation of boot camps for young offenders with a youth justice board to advise government on how best to handle crime among young people. It also called for increased food allowances for people on social assistance, increased support for people with disabilities, and tax credits for people caring for elderly parents or relatives. It also attempted to broaden its appeal to Aboriginal peoples by promising to include in the province's curriculum the history and content of First Nations' treaties, and it promised greater consultation with First Nations on any legislation that affect their jurisdiction. Wall talked to the convention about diversity in the party and the need to appeal to a broader-cross section of voters.[44] Wall became an important part of the branding process—as a voice of moderation. He became the "brand personality" of a restylized Saskatchewan Party that worked to reposition itself within the political space in the province. He succeeded in moving the Saskatchewan Party out of the traditional space to the right of the NDP and situated his party in the centre with some social policies to the left of the NDP.

A fourth element important to the branding process was an internal reorganization of the party. It was clear that the party had to appeal to a younger age group and revise some of its policies to target, particularly, women and urban supporters. However, these objectives could only be met if the party organization was improved. After Wall became leader, Bob Mason, a Regina-area businessman, was hired as the executive director, and under his direction the party implemented a series of reforms ranging from election planning to finances to research and polling. All of these were designed to prepare the party for the 2007 election and to present to the electorate a new image for the Saskatchewan Party. The new visual identity, for instance, that replaced the old stylized letter "S" (which resembled a serpent) emblazoned on an outline map of the province was replaced by a simple, yet effective logo. The new visual identity was designed by a professional firm and adopted only after it was market-tested in a way that many commercial logos are. How the Saskatchewan Party organization changed after the 2003 election will make an interest case-study of how political parties manage change.[45]

As the Saskatchewan Party attempted to brand itself as a party of the political centre, it demonstrated that it was essentially an elite-based brokerage party like most other Canadian political parties, even if party membership grew rapidly under Wall's leadership.[46] It was not a movement nor was it a grassroots party nor was it a party driven by a particular ideology unless one would consider their mantra that the NDP government was mismanaging health care and the economy and that it was anti-capitalist and pro-labour a political philosophy. Clearly, the Saskatchewan Party under Wall had the party members focus on what he considered pragmatic and what was necessary to win.

With the policy review completed, Wall and the Saskatchewan Party were confident the branding process was well underway. For Wall, it was not about ideological positions as he continued to insist that there is no right and left in politics.[47] In fact, it was the NDP and the media that harped on the lack of policy debate at the 2006 and 2007 Saskatchewan Party conventions as if public policy is made at party conventions. It is not, usually.[48] As Ken Rasmussen, the director of the Johnson-Shoyama School of Public Policy at the University of Regina, told the *StarPhoenix* following the 2007 Saskatchewan Party convention, "Political parties are really no longer real incubators of public policy [...] Basically parties these days are about two things—selecting a leader and helping organize for an election campaign." Wall admitted as much when he attempted to defend the lack of policy debate within his party. He told the press, "Some people might find ... a convention that lacked policy a little drier than others. Others frankly, and many, I would suggest, who are involved in politics ... they are interested in winning the election, they are interested in strategies, in planning for the upcoming election." The 2007 convention focused on election preparedness and how to win an election. For the time being, at least, there was no attempt to modify the party's policies further after the 2005 policy convention.[49]

In the months leading up to the 2007 election, the Saskatchewan Party was able to capitalize on several miscues from the NDP government. One of the most damaging episodes for the NDP was the adverse publicity it received over its handling of the Murdoch Carriere case. Carriere, a former bureaucrat with the province's department of the environment, had been fired in 2003 over harassment allegations. He launched a law suit against the government for its handling of the affair, and, when the government reached a $275,000 out-of-court settlement with Carriere, the Saskatchewan Party launched a major advertising campaign, charging the Calvert government with rewarding harassment in the work place with tax dollars.[50] During the lengthy media coverage of the Carriere affair that was kept alive in part with the Saskatchewan Party's mailings to 350,000 homes in the province, opinions polls showed Saskatchewan Party support surging above 50% among voters.[51]

The Saskatchewan Party also benefited from the NDP's advertising in Alberta and its public feud with the Harper government in Ottawa. The NDP rented billboards in Calgary inviting ex-pats to return home to Saskatchewan and benefit from affordable housing and shorter commute times. However, the Saskatchewan Party alleged that the NDP failed to understand that inexpensive real estate prices can be seen as a symptom of economic failure, not success. Wall certainly kept this in mind when he traveled to Calgary. His message to Albertans emphasized the opportunities in Saskatchewan without begging people to return. Wall talked about how he planned to create an economically competitive Saskatchewan and how Saskatchewan offered great opportunities; his was an attempt to brand Saskatchewan as a land of opportunity that would be open for business with the proper investment climate and not as a place with low housing prices and all the negative images that often conjures up. An important part of political branding is about appealing to people's dreams and selling hope to people.[52] "We've been branded over the decades as the place to be from … as a place that's not too accepting of free enterprise, private investment," Wall told the *Western Standard*. "We can't change that brand with more billboards around Calgary or more TV ads in Saskatchewan."[53] The difference in the messages was immense.

The Saskatchewan Party also benefited from Calvert's equalization quarrel with Ottawa, even though it, too, adopted a similar policy. Saskatchewan was Canada's second largest producer of oil with more than 423,000 barrels per day; it benefited immensely from the huge surge in oil prices and was among the fastest growing economies in Canada. Premier Calvert failed to convince voters that the province had been victimized by a cruel and uncaring prime minister because Ottawa had reneged on the changes Stephen Harper had promised in the equalization formula that denied Saskatchewan some $800 million in transfer payments. Attacking Ottawa might have worked for Danny Williams in Newfoundland and Labrador but it did not pay dividends for Calvert. Calvert's very public quarrel with Ottawa, demanding millions in transfer payments came at the same time that the province implemented major cuts to business taxes and reduced the PST from 7% to 5%. Moreover, in 2006, the NDP had cut the corporate tax rate from 17% to 12% and eliminated the corporation capital tax.[54] The NDP government continued through its feud with Ottawa to present an image of a province that was struggling economically despite the optimism and excitement that had enveloped much of it.[55]

As the province waited for Premier Calvert to call an election throughout 2007, the Saskatchewan Party was careful not to jeopardize the lead it had in the public opinion polls. Not only had it changed its party policy on the contentious issue of the Crown Corporations, it supported the NDP legislation banning privatization in the 2004 Crown Corporations Public Ownership Act which passed unanimously in the legislature. In mid-2007, with a 25-point lead in the polls, the Saskatchewan Party in rejecting the Trade, Investment and Labour Mobility Agreement (TILMA) that had been signed in 2006 between the governments of Alberta and British Columbia before the NDP government took a public position on the Agreement. TILMA allowed for freer trade, investment and labour mobility between the two provinces and created the second-largest economic region in Canada. Businesses and workers in both provinces were given access to a larger range of opportunities in the energy and transportation sectors, and the agreement simplified business registration and government procurement within the economic zone.[56] While the policy seemed to be one that the Saskatchewan Party might have supported, Wall made it clear that under a Saskatchewan Party government the province would not be joining TILMA, even though a year earlier Wall had called upon the government to consider the Agreement.

Despite the re-branding of the Saskatchewan Party that had occurred since the 2003 election, it was clear that the NDP would, nonetheless, resort to the tactics that had worked so well for them in previous campaigns. In September 2007, just weeks before the election was called, the NDP attempted to plant the seeds of fear once more: it launched a series of television ads and created a website that portrayed the Saskatchewan Party as wolves in sheep's clothing. The message was clear: a Saskatchewan Party government, the NDP warned, meant the end of public ownership of the provincial utilities and the end of publicly funded health care.[57] Deputy Premier Clay Serby told *Macleans* that "Mr. Wall is a pretty good-looking guy. This [the ad] is about a guy who looks like he's friendly and warm and cuddly but the reality is he's not even close to that image. That's how sheep get enticed by friendly wolves."[58] Some of the NDP government's major supporters, including the province's major unions such as the Canadian Union of Public Employees (CUPE) and the Communications, Energy and Paperworkers Union, rolled out similar messages. Both unions launched campaigns, attacking the Saskatchewan Party as untrustworthy. A CUPE pamphlet, distributed to its 26,000 members in Saskatchewan, for instance, warned that "Brad Wall doesn't want you to have three weeks of vacation each year," and "The Saskatchewan Party doesn't want you to enjoy Family Day [a February holiday recently introduced by the NDP government].[59] The Saskatchewan Party countered those attack ads not simply with the message that the party was "not so scary," but presenting Wall in a positive image. The ads ridiculed the NDP's message and had Wall telling voters "They might say anything, like winters will be longer if you elect Brad Wall or maybe that I'm a secret Calgary Stampeders' fan."[60] The counter-messaging worked, especially as Wall appeared in television ads relaxing with his family and exemplifying a personality that was casual and informal; it was anything but scary. In fact, Wall appeared "cool" in the ads which contrasted sharply with the image of Premier Calvert in the media.

The final step in the branding process came when the Saskatchewan Party released its election platform on October 19, 2007. The document was a clear indication of the party's flexible and pragmatic approach to policy as it sought to avoid an ideologically driven right-wing image; the policy platform portrayed the party as a centrist broker, keen to appeal to the broad array of interests in the province, and as a rational actor in the political process where the ultimate goal is winning. In fact, the Saskatchewan Party platform was not radically different from that offered by the governing NDP; the essential difference was that the Saskatchewan Party promised to deliver the mix of policies better than the governing party.

The Saskatchewan Party's major promise was sound fiscal management and a moderate approach to governing. It guaranteed to require the government to balance budgets annually rather than the NDP policy to balance over the four-year cycle of a government. The populist and conservative side of its platform was limited to a promise to increase the size of the civil service only as the population grew, to increase the number of police officers and hire more correction workers to eliminate drugs and gangs in jails. The party also promised to change Saskatchewan's labour laws to facilitate investment in the province. The platform called for a balance between tax and debt reduction and investment in such areas as health and infrastructure; it promised to cut property taxes. It also promised fixed election dates. The party reiterated its policy on the Crowns, pledging that the Crowns would continue to be publicly owned: "Under no circumstances would a Saskatchewan Party government sell Crowns," Wall said emphatically. "The position of the Saskatchewan Party is clear … [we] have committed that Crowns will remain publicly owned under a Saskatchewan Party government."[61]

Another aspect of the branding process was to demonstrate the social conscience of the party. At a campaign stop at the Saskatoon and District Food Bank, Wall outlined a number of his party's social policies. This included an additional $2 million over four years for children's lunch programs in community schools, an increase in funding for sexual assault centres and transition houses for victims of domestic violence, and a promise to fund the Saskatchewan Association of Sexual Assault Services umbrella organization. In the branding process, community-based organizations assumed an added importance. As part of the party commitment to long-term funding for community-based organizations (CBOs), Wall had earlier promised to increase funding by $20 million to CBOs to assist in life skills and development and employment training for persons at risk. He also promised to hold a summit of community-based organizations to help determine the future direction of social policy in Saskatchewan. These programs were designed to foster attachment to the market economy. The party also reiterated its support for a publicly funded, publicly administered health care in accordance with The Canada Health Act.

The strategy was obvious: play to the centre. The election was no duel of ideologies, prompting Lorne Gunter to write in the *Edmonton Journal* following the election that this was not the Brad Wall that he had met three years earlier at a fund-raising dinner in Calgary. He wrote that Wall was "a politician who had intellectualized the philosophy" of personal responsibility, individual liberty and free-market economics. His conservative principles were cut from the same cloth as those of Ronald Reagan and Margaret Thatcher, and he had wowed the Calgary audience with his ideology that understood the economic benefits that flowed from major tax cuts, a reduction in the size of government, and a market-driven economy.[62] Instead, Wall embraced a platform that would win him the election: "We want to provide people with an option in this election and that option has to be a complete option. We want to provide an option that's offering the best economic plan for the province, a long-term plan for infrastructure, fiscal responsibility with debt reduction, social policies that we know will work … it's important for us to have a complete plan, a complete vision for the government."[63]

Throughout the campaign, the Saskatchewan Party's image was tightly controlled by the party leadership and it centred on Wall as leader which is quite consistent with both a brokerage form of politics and the branding of political parties. In fact, Wall dismissed as "hypothetical musings" comments made by long time Saskatchewan Party MLA Cannington Constituency, Dan D'Autremont that a Saskatchewan Party government might consider privatization of minor Crowns; the branding of political parties requires strong party discipline because without it, the message and the brand becomes blurred to voters.[64] While the Saskatchewan Party did not promise the electorate to be a party of great change, Wall's focus throughout the campaign was to rebrand Saskatchewan as a leader in the "New West" and promised to build pride in the province.

Still, the NDP hammered away at the issue of trust throughout the campaign, but the rebranded Saskatchewan Party gained from the NDP's negative campaign. Pat Atkinson, the deputy-premier and a long-time NDP cabinet minister, set the tenor of the NDP campaign when she said "I know these people and what they actually do when they get inside the legislature are two different things entirely. We believe you cannot trust the Saskatchewan Party."[65] Premier Calvert took advantage of Hallowe'en to warn voters that the ghost and goblins prowling the streets should not be their real concern; it was the scary spectre of the Saskatchewan Party that they would have to contend with for years if they won the election. He warned that the Saskatchewan's Party's privatization agenda would lead to huge jobs losses throughout the province. "Show Saskatchewan people what's behind the mask," he demanded of Wall.[66] Another NDP advertisement attempted to scare voters by comparing Wall to Grant Devine and warned voters that a vote for the Saskatchewan Party meant the end of publicly funded health care and the end of the Crown utilities. The final days of the campaign saw the NDP use a series of Monty Python-inspired ads linking Wall to Grant Devine.

The voters were not swayed by the NDP rhetoric, and they gave the rebranded Saskatchewan Party an overwhelming victory. The party garnered 51% of the popular vote and 37 seats to the NDP's 21. The NDP's share of the popular vote was one of the lowest ever for the party at 37% (down more than 7% from the previous election). The Liberals also saw their share of the popular vote drop from 13% to 9%. The Saskatchewan Party increased its share of the vote in urban areas to 40% from 29% in 2003, and was able to take three seats from the NDP in Regina and two in Saskatoon.[67] The rural-urban split that had marked the 1999 and the 2003 elections had largely disappeared.

THE SASKATCHEWAN PARTY AS GOVERNMENT

What could Saskatchewan expect from Brad Wall and a Saskatchewan Party government. In an earlier analysis of the Saskatchewan Party, Kevin Wishlow had suggested that a Saskatchewan government under Hermanson wanted to implement a policy platform similar to that orchestrated by the Ralph Klein Conservatives in Alberta.[68] That would not be Wall's approach. In fact, as Alberta Premier Ed Stelmach increased the resource royalty agreement and, in some ways, moved Alberta away from the conservative approach of Klein and towards a traditional Saskatchewan approach, Premier Calvert had moved Saskatchewan—economically and fiscally, at least—in the conservative direction of Alberta with major cuts to both sales and corporate income taxes and a huge reduction in its royalty regime. These measure made doing business more attractive in Saskatchewan than Alberta; the NDP had earlier made major reductions in personal income taxes. The NDP had already moved Saskatchewan to the right, and had in some respects remade Saskatchewan in the image articulated by Wall and the Saskatchewan Party. It might have been a way for the NDP government to fend off the Saskatchewan Party, but the NDP's move to the right was another indication of the undifferentiated nature of political parties in Saskatchewan and, indeed, Canadian politics in recent years. The NDP governments under both Romanow and Calvert had implemented many of the economic and fiscal policies that the Saskatchewan Party would have enacted if these policies were not already in place.

The Saskatchewan Party government asked all departments to find ways to reduce spending growth, as all governments now do when they assume office. It also followed through on its election promise to end direct government investment when it cancelled a memorandum of agreement between Domtar and the NDP government that saw the province inject funds to reopen the Prince Albert Pulp Mill.[69] The Speech from the Throne and the Saskatchewan Party government's first budget were in many ways anti-climactic as they were essentially a carbon copy of the Saskatchewan Party election platform. The first Saskatchewan Party budget was not a slash and burn effort. Quite the opposite really, as government spending increased by 10%, surpassing that of the previous NDP budget that had increased expenditure by 9%. The government moved quickly to implement The Saskatchewan Growth and Financial Security Act which requires annual balanced budgets, fixed election dates, and sets out a formula for using half of any budgetary surplus to paying down the debt and half for promoting economic growth; this was very similar to the NDP's Fiscal Stabilization Fund. Finance Minister Rod Gantefoer acknowledged that the approach did not signify any substantial difference from the previous government, but insisted that the practical reality of a resource economy such as Saskatchewan's with its volatile revenue stream made such a fund necessary.[70] It created Enterprise Saskatchewan, a public-private partnership, to lead economic growth. It introduced new labour laws to keep the province competitive with other jurisdictions, but it also approved the increases to the minimum wage legislation that the NDP had legislated (which business organizations had opposed). The budget was, in many respects, an infrastructure budget that saw nearly $1 billion dollars directed to hospital repairs, schools and post-secondary institutions, highways and other capital projects. It also put more money into child care, prescription drugs, policing, tax credits for caregivers, child protection plans, and basic education programs for Aboriginal peoples, but it made the Saskatchewan drug plan for seniors an income based plan (rather than a universal program). It pledged money for municipalities and post-secondary education institutions. It introduced plans to keep graduates in the provinces through tuition rebates of up to $20,000 over seven years if students remained in the province, and plans to reduce the education portion of property taxes. It addressed the shortage of nurses, doctors and other health professionals and promised a review of the health care system. It also continued the freeze on university tuition, and put $250 million on the provincial debt. The NDP finance critic even said he would have to agree that was "an almost-NDP budget."[71]

It is too early in the government's mandate to draw any conclusions about the long term approach that Premier Wall and his party will follow in the remainder of their term before the next election already set for November 6, 2011, but it has delivered on nearly half of its campaign promises. What is clear, however, is that Wall created a new brand for the Saskatchewan Party and under his leadership the Party became a flexible, pragmatic and less partisan party. Moreover, Wall does not seem intent on leading a policy revolution in Saskatchewan, but he seems determined to create a realignment in provincial politics. He clearly wants to break the long-standing dominance of the New Democrats; he believes that a pragmatic and practical approach to policy development and governing with moderation as the fulcrum of party he can with two or three election victories make the Saskatchewan Party the new "government party."

Wall's first pronouncements in office have continued that process of brokering the various social and economic interests, though there have been a few bumps along the way. First, Wall and his advisors dismissed more than 200 civil servants, including some in provincial agencies, boards, and commissions, which smacked of old-style politics. Most new governments do this early in their first mandate and in doing so the Saskatchewan Party did what has been commonplace in Saskatchewan. Second, the government cut funding for the Station 20 West project in Saskatoon that provided a variety of services for low-income people, and eliminated the Saskatchewan Workers' Benefit Program which helped low income workers pay for prescription drugs, eye exams and some chiropractic services and had been introduced just before the 2007 election by the NDP government. It also eliminated funding for dental sealments for inner city kids.[72] The new government disbanded the Saskatchewan Council on Disability Issues in favour of more consultation with groups representing people with disabilities and introduced new labour laws.[73] Wall has not reached out to placate labour, perhaps because organized labour has traditionally been a strong supporter of the NDP and it remains a bitter opponent of the Saskatchewan Party. Moreover, having labour as a foe is one way that the Saskatchewan Party might win public support on a variety of public policy issues. To date, Wall has not introduced any policies that will bring down the government but too many such miscues might help undo the new brand that Wall has so successfully created for the Saskatchewan Party.

CONCLUSION

In Saskatchewan where many commentators continued to see politics as polarized and driven largely by ideology applying the idea of branding is challenging, and clearly more research is required on this topic. Although there has been a growing interest in applying the concepts of branding and brand management to political parties in the United States and Britain, it is perhaps time to consider how political parties in Canada have adopted the principles of brand management here. What has become clear is that the role of ideology, especially in fiscal and social policy, has obviously declined in the past two decades in Canadian politics. Saskatchewan had been no exception to that trend.

The Saskatchewan Party was able to defeat the governing NDP and form the government of Saskatchewan in 2007 largely because it was able to convince voters that it, too, could be a main stream party of the centre. To create a party with a decent chance of winning, the Saskatchewan Party moved to the centre of the political spectrum, and in the process it expunged much of the right-wing image that it espoused in its early years under Elwin Hermanson and the right-wing ideology that the NDP had successfully convinced the electorate ran rampant within the Saskatchewan Party. The Saskatchewan Party was able to accomplish this goal by rebranding itself as a pragmatic party that would practice a form of brokerage politics under its new leader Brad Wall. Under Wall, the party became a disciplined machine where the message was tightly controlled and the task at hand was winning. The rebranding of the Saskatchewan Party was complete when it won the 2007 election, but the challenge for the party will be to build brand loyalty among much of the urban electorate that had distrusted the party for much of the time since it was created without alienating its original base in rural Saskatchewan.

NOTES

I wish to thank Janice Stokes and Wayne Elhard for reading a draft of this paper and offering their comments and suggestions.

1. See R.K. Carty and David Stewart, "Parties and Party Systems," in Christopher Dunn (ed.), *Provinces: Canadian Provincial Politics* (Peterborough: Broadview Press, 1996), 84–85; and Ken Rasmussen, "Saskatchewan: From Entrepreneurial State to Embedded State," in Keith Brownsey and Michael Howlett (eds.), *The Provincial State in Canada: Politics in the Provinces and Territories* (Peterborough: Broadview Press, 2001), 258–59.

2. On this point, see John Richards and Larry Pratt, *Prairie Capitalism: Power and Influence in the New West* (Toronto: McClelland & Stewart, 1979), and Rasmussen, "Saskatchewan: From Entrepreneurial State to Embedded State," 241–77. By 1956, the CCF had become a party of moderation, when it adopted the *Winnipeg Declaration* that dropped all reference to eradicating capitalism, a goal that had been so important in the earlier *Regina Manifesto*, and promised instead a social democratic mixed economy.

3. John C. Courtney and David E. Smith, "Saskatchewan: Parties in a Politically Competitive Province," in Martin Robin (ed.), *Canadian Provincial Politics* (Scarborough: Prentice-Hall, 1972), 314. See also Jocelyne Praud and Sarah McQuarrie, "The Saskatchewan CCF-NDP from the *Regina Manifesto* to the Romanow Years," in Howard Leeson (ed.), *Saskatchewan Politics: Into the Twenty-first Century* (Regina: Canadian Plains Research Center, 2001): 143–67. Almost 40 years ago John Courtney and David Smith noted of Saskatchewan politics, "it is, of course, one thing to be progressive and leftist on the hustings: it is quite another matter to be so when elected to power." The same holds true for the traditional right—there is often a difference between what is said on the hustings and what become policy once a party finds itself occupying the seat of government.

4. In an earlier edition of this book, Kevin Wishlow argued that the ideological differences between Saskatchewan's major parties have narrowed and contended that it was time to reconsider the polarization thesis. See Kevin Wishlow, "Rethinking the Polarization Thesis: The Formation and Growth of the Saskatchewan Party, 1997–2001," in Leeson, *Saskatchewan Politics*, 169–97.

5. Harold Clarke, Jane Jenson, Lawrence LeDuc, and Jon Pammett (eds.), *Absent Mandate: Electoral Politics in an Era of Restructuring* (Toronto: Gage Publishing, 1996).

6. The rise of the Saskatchewan Party equaled that of the Saskatchewan CCF in the 1940s and was in some ways similar to it. In 1932, the United Farmers of Canada, Saskatchewan Section, had joined with the Independent Labour Party to create the Farmer-Labour Party, which managed to elect five candidates in the 1934 election. T.C. Douglas was one of the unsuccessful candidates, even though he had established a branch of the Independent Labour Party in Weyburn. After the election, the Farmer-Labour Party joined forces with the newly formed national CCF to create the Saskatchewan wing of the party, and M.J. Coldwell, the leader of the Farmer-Labour Party, became the leader of the CCF. Like the CCF, the Saskatchewan Party was born of a coalition and, it, too, tapped into federal politics to find its first leader.

7. Ryan Macdonald, *Not Dutch Disease, It's China Syndrome*. Statistics Canada, 2007. Also available at http://www.statcan.ca/english/research/11-624-MIE/11-624-MIE2007017.pdf.

8. Maurice Pinard, "Third Parties in Canada Revisited: A Rejoinder and Elaboration of the Theory of One-Party Dominance," *Canadian Journal of Political Science* 6, no. 3 (September 1973): 439–60.

9. For a discussion of the Saskatchewan Liberal Party, see Lynda Haverstock, "The Saskatchewan Liberal Party," in Leeson, *Saskatchewan Politics*, 199–250.

10. Pinard, "Third Parties in Canada Revisited," 439–60.

11. On this point, see Rasmussen, "Saskatchewan: From Entrepreneurial State to Embedded State," 241–77; Don McMorris, the minister of health who was first elected as a Saskatchewan Party MLA in 1999, claims that hospital closures were an important issue in southern and southeastern Saskatchewan. Personal interview with Don McMorris, Regina, May 26, 2008.

12. Howard A. Leeson, "The Rich Soil of Saskatchewan Politics," in Leeson, *Saskatchewan Politics*, 7.

13. Sharon Butala, "Time, Space and Light: Discovering the Saskatchewan Soul," in Douglas Fetherling (ed.), *Best Canadian Essays 1989* (Saskatoon: Fifth House, 1989).

14. Quoted by Stephen Ward, *The Winnipeg Free Press*, September 11, 1990.

15. RBC News, "Saskatchewan—The New Provincial Growth Leader," April 3, 2008 (http://www.rbc.com/newsroom/pdf/20080403economic-sk.pdf); and *Globe and Mail*, April 12, 2008.

16. See, David Ebner, "The New "It" Province," *Globe and Mail*, April 12, 2008.

17. On the subject of how political parties are increasingly becoming consumer driven in the ascent of consumerism and how the role of ideology has declined, see Peter Reeves, Leslie de Chernatony and Marylyn Carrigan, "Building a Political Brand: Ideology or Voter-Driven Strategy," *The Journal of Brand Management* 13, no. 6 (July 2006): 418–28. A brief overview of the necessity of branding can be seen in Peter van Ham, "The Rise of the Brand State: The Postmodern Politics of Image and Reputation," *Foreign Affairs* 80, no. 5 (September/October 2001) 2–6.

18. Mark Wyatt, "Sask. Reformers Split on Forming Provincial Party," *StarPhoenix*, September 4, 1997; and Lynda Haverstock, "The Saskatchewan Liberal Party," in Leeson, *Saskatchewan Politics*, 240–41.

19. Interview with Wayne Elhard, Regina, May 15, 2008.

20. "Sask. Party Title Belongs to NDP: Premier," *StarPhoenix*, November 24 1997.

21. Ibid.

22. Mark Wyatt, "Former Reformer Campaigning for Leadership of Sask. Party," *StarPhoenix*, February 11, 1998.

23. Lawrence Martin, "Sask. Right Shows Strength," *Edmonton Journal*, July 1, 2001.

24. Randy Burton, "Sask. Party Origins Still a Sticking Point With Premier, NDP," *StarPhoenix*, 31 August 1999. Still, 49% of those polled also said that the Liberal and Conservatives members acted properly by providing a viable alternative to the NDP.

25. Rasmussen, "Saskatchewan: From Entrepreneurial State to Embedded State," 252.

26. Randy Burton, "Sask. Party Must Broaden Appeal," *StarPhoenix*, November 2, 1999.

27. Quoted in James Parker, "Saskatchewan Party looking for ways to gain urban seats," *Leader-Post*, November 1, 2000.

28. McMorris interview.

29. "Saskatchewan Party Steers Away from Controversial Resolutions," *Canadian Press NewsWire*, November 5, 2000.

30. James Parker, "Crowns' Fate Under Sask. Party Debated," *StarPhoenix*, July 27, 2001, and Centre for Policy Alternatives, *Saskatchewan Notes* 2, no. 2 (February 2003): 4.

31. Kevin O'Connor, "Sask. Party Focuses on Next Election: Convention Debates Only One Resolution," *StarPhoenix*, November 18, 2002.

32. Interview with Wayne Elhard, Regina, May 15, 2008.

33. Bill Doskoch, "Fear and Trust: How the NDP Emerged Victorious" CBC News Online, November 6, 2003 (http://www.cbc.ca/saskvotes2003/features/feature11.html).

34. Those sentiments were expressed by John Courtney, a political studies professor at the University of Saskatchewan, to James Parker, "Hermanson Must Quit," *StarPhoenix*, November 7, 2003.

35. On this point, see Jon White, "New Labour: A Study of the Creation, Development and Demise of a Political Brand," *Journal of Political Marketing* 1, nos. 2/3 (2002): 45–52. White examines the recent history of the British Labour Party and how it rebranded itself as "New Labour" after a long time in the political wilderness and swept to power under Tony Blair. He explores how the party began a process to branding as a means of establishing party values and winning political support. It is, however, not my intention here to explore in any great detail the ways in which the Saskatchewan Party successfully managed the branding process but simply to introduce the subject in hopes that others will investigate this subject and examine how it was developed and used to generate political support. I use the word "brand" in this essay to describe voters' ideas about a particular political party; like branded products, political brands also depend on trust and customer satisfaction. See also, Bruce I. Newman, *Handbook of Political Marketing* (Thousand Oaks, CA: Sage Publications, 1999), and Nicholas J. O'Shaughnessy and Stephan C.M. Henneberg (eds.), *The Idea of Political Marketing* (Praeger Publishers, 2002).

36. The argument has been made that the public sector has consciously used the branding process by borrowing from advertisers to shape public impressions of governments. See, for example, Jonathan Rose, *Making Pictures in Our Heads, Government Advertising in Canada* (New York: Praeger Press, 2000).

37. *Signal: The Newsletter of the Saskatchewan Party* 3, no. 1 (November 2004): 1.

38. Wayne Elhard insists that "We needed to define who we are, not let other people define us." Elhard interview.

39. James Wood, "Will Sask. Party's Policy Review Win It Votes?," *Leader-Post*, November 12, 2004.

40. James Wood, "Sask. Party Retools Policies," *StarPhoenix*, February 7, 2005.

41. Tim Cook, "Sask. Official Opposition Presents Its Policy Makeover at Regina Convention," *Canadian Press Newswire*, February 5, 2005.

42. Tim Cook, "Sask. Official Opposition Members Sign Off New Policy at Regina Convention," Canadian Press Newswire, February 6, 2005.

43. Wood, "Will Sask. Party's Policy Review Win It Votes?"

44. James Wood, "Sask. Party Retools Policies," *StarPhoenix*, February 7, 2005.

45. Personal interview with Bob Mason, Regina, May 27, 2008.

46. McMorris interview.

47. Wood, "Sask. Party Retools Policies."

48. On the role of party organizations and policy development, see William Cross, *Political Parties* (Vancouver, University of British Columbia Press, 2004), especially Chapter 3, "Policy Study and Development." Cross argues that party organizations have never been particularly active in policy development as leaders have usually controlled party policy.

49. James Wood, "Sask. Party Convention for Preparation, not Policy," *StarPhoenix*, February 10, 2007.

50. Angela Hall, "Sask. Party Calls Carriere Mailer a Success," *Leader-Post*, April 20, 2007.

51. Murray Mandryk, "Sask. Voters Fail To See Scary Sde of Wall," *StarPhoenix*, November 8, 2007.

52. On this point, see Bruce I. Newman, "Branding and Political Marketing in the United States," in Andreas Strebinger, Wolfgang Mayerhofer and Helmut Kurz (eds.), *Werbe-undMarkenforschung Meilensteine—State of the Art—Perspektiven* (Gabler, 2006): 197–212. http://www.springerlink.com/content/v37755/front-matter.pdf.

53. Cyril Doll, "The Life of the Sask. Party," *Western Standard*, April 9, 2007.

54. Ibid. At the same time, the province promised $60 million as an investment fund for small and medium-sized businesses, and injected $3.5 million in to Moose Jaw Pork Packers (which incidently the Saskatchewan Party supported).

55. On this point, see Todd Hirsh, "Saskatchewan Should Pick Its Friends Carefully," *Policy Options/Options politique* (May 2007): 10. http://www.irpp.org/po/archive/may07/hirsch.pdf.

56. Angela Hall, "Sask. Party Rejects TILMA," *Leader-Post*, June 29, 2007. See also, http://www.tilma.ca which was accessed April 17, 2008.

57. Jennifer Graham, "Sask. Party Launches Sdvertisements To Show Voters It's 'not so Scary'," *Canadian Press Newswire*, September 4, 2007.

58. Quoted in *Maclean's*, September 24, 2007.

59. Angela Hall, "Sask Party Blasts Union Pamphlet," *StarPhoenix*, October 6, 2007.

60. Graham, "Sask. Party Launches Advertisements To Show Voters It's 'Not So Scary'."

61. Angela Hall, "Campaign Platform Released," *Leader-Post*, October 20, 2007.

62. Lorne Gunter, "Wall Talked the Talk, Didn't Walk the Walk," *Edmonton Journal*, November 9, 2007.

63. James Wood, "Wall Using Social Policy To Soften Image," *Leader-Post*, October 26, 2007.

64. "Saskatchewan Party Denies Privatization Plans," CBC News, August 24, 2007. http://www.cbc.ca/canada/saskatchewan/story/2007/08/24/private-health.html.

65. Angela Hall, "Campaign Platform Released," *Leader-Post*, October 20, 2007.

66. Angela Hall, "Calvert Raises Fears Over Privatization," and Murray Mandryk, "Optimism Abounds: Analysis, Opinion and Expert Insight," *Leader-Post*, November 1, 2007.

67. Margaret Woods, *Canadian Parliamentary Review* 30 (Winter 2007): 64, and Anne Kyle, "Sask, Party Moves Into NDP's Traditional Turf," *Leader-Post*, November 8, 2007.

68. Wishlow, "Rethinking the Polarization Thesis," 169.

69. James Wood, "Sask. Party Kills Mill Deal," *Leader-Post*, December 1, 2007.

70. James Wood, "New Act Called for Annual Balanced Budget," *Leader-Post*, December 14, 2007.

71. Randy Burton, "Billion-dollar spending spree," *StarPhoenix*, March 20, 2008.

72. http://www.cbc.ca/canada/saskatchewan/story/2008/04/23/workers-benefits.html.

73. James Wood, "Sask. Party Scraps Disability Council," *Leader-Post*, January 31, 2008.

Saskatchewan's Political Party Systems and the Development of Third Party Politics

Kevin O'Fee

This paper provides an historical overview of the Saskatchewan party system. It illustrates the rise and fall of each party, and how the environment in which they operate has changed over time. It shows that the province has operated with a number of distinct political party systems. By system, we mean the relationship between and among political parties as they compete for voter support and government power.[1] This has had a bearing on the fortune of third parties who have found themselves in political systems that did not foster their longevity. In relatively few instances in Saskatchewan's political history did the rise of alternatives to a two-party formation result in a sustainable multi-party competitive system. Invariably where new alternatives to dominant parties emerged they were either unable to sustain themselves as a viable electoral alternative or came to supplant one of the traditional two dominant parties.

Five political party systems can be identified: a one-party dominant system (1905–34); an emergent multi-party formative system (1934–38), a traditional two-party system (1944–75), a transitional two-and-a-half-party system (1975–2003), and finally, a return to what is currently once again a two-party system.

ONE-PARTY DOMINANT SYSTEM

Figure 1 shows how the Liberals and Conservatives, under the banner of the Provincial Rights Party,[2] dominated the early provincial electoral landscape. In the province's first four elections the Liberals and the Provincial Rights Party combined garnered no less than 90% of the popular vote. Despite the two-party configuration, the Saskatchewan legislature was dominated by the Liberal Party which formed government uninterrupted in the first quarter century under Premiers Walter Scott (1905–16), William Martin (1916–22), Charles A. Dunning (1922–26) and James G. Gardiner (1926–29). A string of consecutive Liberal governments was broken only briefly by the one-term Conservative government formed by J.T.M Anderson (1929–34). The success of the Liberals in Saskatchewan for much of this period can be attributed to the close ties the party and its leadership maintained with that of the Saskatchewan Grain Growers' Association (SGGA).[3]

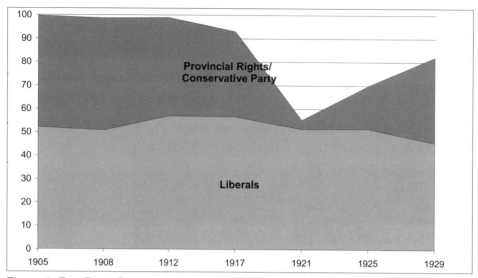

Figure 1: Two-Party System: 1905 to 1929 (Source: Elections Saskatchewan).

EMERGENT MULTI-PARTY SYSTEM

Percolating under this two party arrangement, were the specific class interests of urban labour and the agrarian community. Throughout the 1920s and 1930s, a range of alternatives to the main parties emerged reflecting a mix of agrarian and labour class interests. The Progressive Party with its agrarian-based attacks on the traditional parties and party-led governments provided the first real test of Canada's national two party system. Federally, it was able to acquire more seats in the House of Commons than the Conservatives in the 1921 federal election, although it eschewed official opposition status. At the provincial level, this same anti-partisanship emerged as the Progressives fielded candidates in the provincial election of 1921. This was the first occasion in which a "third party" alternative challenged the two-party dominance of the Liberals and Conservatives. By the election of 1925, the Progressives supplanted the Conservatives, finishing second to the Liberals under Charles Dunning.

After 1929 the dramatic change in the economic fortunes of the province contributed to undermining the political support that the traditional parties had enjoyed. Beginning with the elections of 1934 and 1938, large numbers of voters supported parties that were relatively new on the provincial scene. In the 1934 election, 24% of the votes went to a newly formed coalition grouping, the Farmer-Labour Party. By the 1938 election, this emerging coalition of farmer and labour interests had coalesced into the CCF which received 19% of the votes while another 16 % voted for another populist entity the Social Credit Party. Increasingly, voters within the province began a tradition in which they supported provincial or regionally identifiable political movements not directly tied to federal parties. These parties were more inclined to express the sentiments of their provincial supporters and the social and economic realities of their constituents than were the two traditional parties, which were seen as subordinate to the federal Liberal and Conservative

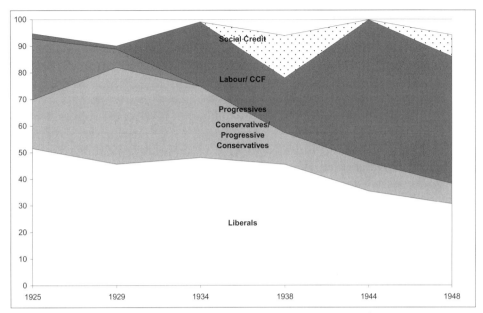

Figure 2: Emergent Multi-Party System (Source: Elections Saskatchewan).

parties. While the Liberal party would continue to have relevance, this period marked the beginning of a long hibernation for the Conservative Party and its successor the Progressive Conservatives (PC).

TWO-PARTY SYSTEM

With the election of 1944, the province once again returned to a virtual two-party system. However, the new dominant party winning elections in 1944, 1948, 1952, 1956 and 1960 was the CCF, with the Liberal Party now cast as the perennial opposition. As shown in Figure 3, the CCF and Liberal parties

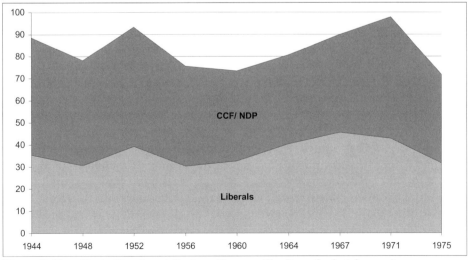

Figure 3: Two-Party Dominant System (Source: Elections Saskatchewan).

captured no less than 70% of the popular vote during this time, effectively crowding out third-party alternatives.

For some, this period marks the beginning of a trend toward polarization in Saskatchewan's electoral politics.[4] Certainly, given the strong leftist language of the Regina Manifesto and the campaigns of 1934 and 1938 the CCF clearly positioned itself in opposition to the liberal-capitalist model of the Liberals, who found themselves largely obliged to take on the role of defenders of free enterprise. However, increasingly the CCF moderated some of its more radical positions in order to make a credible attempt to appeal more broadly to Saskatchewan voters. Nevertheless, throughout the period the labour and farm vote coalesced around the CCF while business and urban interests coalesced around the Liberal Party, effectively limiting the room for third-party alternatives.

TWO-AND-A-HALF-PARTY SYSTEM

A number of factors emerged by the mid-1970s to cause a realignment of electoral politics in the province. Perhaps the most significant factor was the federal Liberal Party and the Trudeau government. During the last few years of the provincial Liberal government of Ross Thatcher relations with the federal government became strained. Later, federal policies, most notably abandoning the "Crow Rate" on grain transportation, disputes with Saskatchewan over resource rents in the province, and the National Energy Policy, all conspired to undermine the credibility of the provincial Liberals. Deep divisions emerged between the federal and provincial wings, contributing to the weakening of its organization.[5]

Into this vacuum emerged a resurgent Progressive Conservative Party, capitalizing on a wave of neo-conservative politics both nationally and internationally. It positioned itself further to the right of the provincial Liberal Party, capturing the imagination of an increasingly disaffected rural population, as well as that of the province's more conservative urban electorate. In the election of 1975, this shift of support away from the Liberal Party to the PC Party had became evident when the PC Party polled just 4% below that of the Liberals, a huge increase from just 2% in the previous election. They had emerged as a significant challenger to the Liberals, and replaced them in opposition by the election of 1978.

In the crushing electoral defeat of the NDP in 1982, whether it was a coalescing of the right, or the coalescing of anti-government sentiment, the PCs siphoned off Liberal support entirely, reducing the party to less than 5% of the popular vote. The third-party PCs had in the course of the elections of 1975, 1978 and 1982 emerged as the clear alternative to what had effectively been the province's governing party over the course of the previous 30 years. In the process, the Liberal Party of Saskatchewan, for the first time in the province's history, was no longer a major player in the province's political life.

By 1991, the collapse of the PCs in scandal provided a momentary revival for the Liberals. They elected only one member in 1991, but in 1995 the

Liberals, with 11 members, became the emerging alternative to the governing NDP. Despite the subsequent collapse and eventual dissolution of the PCs, the resurgent Liberal Party was roiled by internal discord. This led the remnants of the now discredited PC Party and the more conservative elements within the Liberal caucus to come together to form the Saskatchewan Party before the election in 1999. In that election the newly formed Saskatchewan Party surged in the polls, narrowly missing forming government in its first electoral contest. The NDP was forced to govern in coalition by bringing two Liberal MLAs into Cabinet. In what became an ill-fated move this formal coalition with the NDP further alienated many Liberal supporters, consolidating the Saskatchewan Party as the clear alternative.

THE RETURN TO TWO-PARTY DOMINANCE

Entering the election of 2003, the Saskatchewan Party, under its leader Elwin Hermanson, seemed poised to end the reign of the 12-year-old NDP government, led now by Lorne Calvert who had replaced Roy Romanow as party leader in 2001. In the 1999 election, the Saskatchewan Party had narrowly missed toppling the incumbent NDP. Despite being considered a "government-in-waiting" the Saskatchewan Party spent much of the 2003 campaign on the defensive. It had publicly promised a review of the province's Crown corporations, which led to speculation about wholesale privatization. The NDP seized upon the issue of privatization and gained momentum by polarizing the campaign as a choice between the social democratic tradition of the CCF-NDP and the Saskatchewan Party's neo-conservative "hidden agenda" of privatization. The Liberals, whom some speculated were poised to maintain their status as "king makers" in a tight election campaign, found themselves largely on the outside of the campaign's main issues. The new Liberal leader, David Karwacki, attempted to address the main elements of the campaign and give the party relevance in the debate. However, the NDP successfully made the election a clear choice between itself and the Saskatchewan Party, and the Liberal's were unable to gain traction. Not only did the Liberal's fail to hold the balance of power in the ensuing NDP victory, as they had in 1999, they were completely shut-out in the provincial legislature. From a high of 35% of the popular vote in the 1995 election, the Liberals declined to just over 20% in 1999 and fell further for the third consecutive election to just 14% by 2003.

The trend toward a traditional two-party dominant system continued in the election of 2007. Following the disastrous campaign of the previous election, after the resignation of party leader Elwin Hermanson, the Saskatchewan Party appointed the youthful Brad Wall as leader in an effort to attract a younger and more urban electorate. They also began a process of moderating their policies both in recognition of the endurance of the province's social democratic traditions and to avoid a repeat of the 2003 campaign. For example, as an important indication of the revamped platform, the Saskatchewan Party supported the NDP government's Crown Corporations Public Ownership Act in the legislature.

At the outset of the 2007 campaign the Saskatchewan Party pre-empted many of the attacks aimed against them by clearly setting out its intention to protect the Crown Corporations and to leave the public health care system untouched. Thus, when the NDP used the unveiling of the Saskatchewan Party's proposal for "Enterprise Saskatchewan," an appointed body with an as yet unspecified agenda for guiding the province's economic development, to suggest once again the presence of secret neo-conservative agenda. The attempt failed to stick as it had in 2003. Instead, the campaign focused on policy issues, particularly plans for expanding the provincial drug plan, incentives directed at post-secondary students, and property tax reform.[6]

Unlike the previous election in which the Liberal Party went into the election with momentum and the potential to hold the balance of power in the event of a minority election, this time they began the campaign needing to capture the imagination of the electorate without the benefit of a physical presence in the previous legislature. An indication of the state of the Liberal Party's fortunes prior to the election was illustrated by David Karwacki's inability to win a seat in consecutive by-elections in 2006 and 2007. Heading into the election, therefore, the party had little opportunity to present itself as an alternative and relied heavily on its performance in the campaign to generate momentum. Despite this the Liberals were the last of the main parties to release their platform on October 26, 2007, several days after both the Saskatchewan Party and the NDP. The platform itself focused heavily on a proposal to phase out residential education property taxes with greater reliance on the provincial treasury and initiatives to improve government accountability and transparency.

None of the major initiatives in the Liberal Party platform inspired Saskatchewan voters, nor did it elicit a response from either the Saskatchewan Party or the NDP. The Liberal Party's efforts to make the election a three-party race failed. As with the rise of the Progressive Conservatives in the mid-1970s, and despite a momentary resurgence in the mid-1990s, the rise of the Saskatchewan Party as a clear alternative to the NDP siphoned off support for the Liberal Party. Liberal leader Dave Karwacki, in the aftermath of the election, acknowledged this polarization: "I think that people are not voting for ideas right now in Saskatchewan, they're voting to keep the Sask [sic] Party out, or to keep the NDP out."[7] Once again, the Liberals failed to elect a single member to the Saskatchewan legislature and the party's share of the popular vote dwindled to below 10%.

In the 2007 provincial election, a total of seven registered parties competed. Only four of which ran full slates of candidates: the Saskatchewan Party, the NDP, the Liberal Party and the Green Party of Saskatchewan. The others, including the PCs, the Marijuana Party and Western Independence Party captured less than 1% of the popular vote combined and did not run full slates of candidates.

The Green Party of Saskatchewan was initially founded in 1998 as the New Green Alliance (NGA). Like its national counterpart, the NGA represented environmentalists, but also included social justice activists disillusioned with the NDP under Premier Roy Romanow. Unlike many Green Parties in Canada, the NGA was decidedly left wing, favouring, for example, progressive taxation, workers' rights and the elimination of poverty.

The Green Party of Saskatchewan, with a modest gain of 2%, had the largest gain in popular support of any third party between the elections of 2003 and 2007. While less than meteoric, the result clearly emboldened the emerging Greens who shortly after the 2007 provincial election served notice that they envisioned a merger with the struggling Liberal Party of Saskatchewan. The response from the Liberals' interim leader at the time, Frank Proto (David Karwacki having resigned following the Liberals collapse), was that similar proposals for formal mergers had been floated on a number of occasions, including with both the NDP and Saskatchewan Party at various times.[8] Nothing further has come of this initiative. Clearly, the Liberal Party was not interested in a merger. Since 2007, the Liberals have fallen even further. They failed to field a candidate in the last provincial by-election in Cumberland and the race to succeed David Karwacki did not garner much interest. Ryan Bater was chosen as party leader by acclamation.

CONCLUSION

Saskatchewan has operated with a number of party systems since joining Confederation. This includes an early formative system in which a single party dominated within a functioning two-party alternating system that reflected the nation's national two-party system of Liberals versus Conservatives. It was replaced by an emergent multi-party system that reflected the changing demographics of the province. The system was transformed by the election in 1944 and the consolidation of the left under the CCF. Since then, three different parties that have served those on the political right in the province at different times, including the Liberals in the 1960s, the Progressive Conservatives in the 1980s, and the Saskatchewan Party since 1999. Despite periods of instability, the system has always returned to a largely two-party system.

In conjunction with this ideological consolidation, the political profile of the province's electorate has also become largely divided on a rural/urban basis, with the two main opposing political parties reflecting the social and political outlooks of urban and rural Saskatchewan. Yet, over the course of the past 60 years, voting behavior in urban and rural constituencies has sometimes shifted between these two parties, suggesting that political behavior within the political system is not entirely ideological, but also based on other considerations.

It is clear from our short survey that the Saskatchewan system has not been a multiparty system. Given a choice between a multiparty system and a two-party system, voters have tended to support a two-party system. The reasons for this preference are not entirely clear. At times, it has reflected a profound ideological split in the electorate. At other times, it has reflected the urban rural divide. In general, however, the electorate in the province seems to be more comfortable with a system in which there are two major parties.

The only anomaly is that the Liberal Party, which has continued in existence in the province throughout its electoral history. We must conclude that this is reflective not only of the fact that the Liberal Party has a vigorous national counterpart, but also that the party has a long and honourable history in the province. As for the other minor parties, it is unclear whether they will remain viable in the system, or replace one of the two major parties. The only thing that is clear is that minor parties in the Saskatchewan political system will continue to have only a small influence on the politics of the province.

NOTES

1. James Bickerton, Alain Gagnon and Patrick Smith in *Ties that Bind: Parties and Voters in Canada* (Don Mills, ON: Oxford University Press, 1999.)

2. Frederick Haultain so objected to the powers granted to the newly formed province, that he protested against the Conservative federal government by changing the provincial Conservatives to the Provincial Rights Party.

3. Evelyn Eager, *Saskatchewan Government* (Saskatoon: Western Producer Prairie Books, 1980).

4. John C. Courtney and David E. Smith, "Saskatchewan: Parties in a Politically Competitive Province," in Martin Robin (ed.), *Canadian Provincial Politics* (Scarborough, ON: Prentice-Hall, 1972), 314; R.K. Carty and David Stewart, "Parties and Party Systems," in Christopher Dunn (ed.), *Provinces: Canadian Provincial Politics* (Peterborough, ON: Broadview Press, 1996), 84.

5. Linda Haverstock, "The Saskatchewan Liberal Party," in Howard Leeson (ed.), *Saskatchewan Politics: Into the Twenty-First Century* (Regina: Canadian Plains Research Center, 2001), 213.

6. David McGrane, "The 2007 Provincial Election in Saskatchewan," *Canadian Political Science Review* 2, no.1 (March–April 2008): 64–78.

7. *Saskatoon StarPhoenix*, Thursday, November 8, 2007.

8. Murray Mandryk, *Regina Leader-Post*, Wednesday, April 23, 2008.

FIRST NATIONS
AND ABORIGINAL POLITICS

Saskatchewan First Nations Politics: Organization, Institutions and Governance

Bonita Beatty

INTRODUCTION

Politics is part of humanity and can be found at even the most basic level with children playing in a sandbox. It is about getting along. A useful definition suggests that politics is "all activity that impinges upon binding decisions about who gets what, when and how, and that brings together contending interests and differences for the supposed advantage of society."[1] It is essentially some structural or organized means for settling conflicts and balancing power relations. Saskatchewan First Nation politics is generally about how First Nations organize or structure themselves to make collective decisions and to balance competing interests and differences, both internally and externally.

This chapter traces the past and contemporary development of Saskatchewan First Nation politics. It asks questions such as: What is First Nation politics? What are the various levels of political organization and how do they work? What is the Federation of Saskatchewan Indian Nations (FSIN) and how does it work? How are different and often competing interests balanced in First Nation politics on issues such as women's rights, urban issues, representation and relationships with other governments? Throughout the discussions, we trace the common political threads that have united the individual First Nation Bands in Saskatchewan under the Federation of Saskatchewan Indian Nations. Foremost are the protection and fulfillment of inherent rights and international Treaties that are understood as being spiritual and living covenants between the First Nations and the Crown. First Nation Treaty sovereignty underlies the Treaties and is seen as something that has never been extinguished nor can be because it lies within a spiritual framework set by the Sovereign Creator to ensure the protection and future of First Nations peoples.

TERMS: FIRST NATION, INDIAN, BANDS

The term "First Nation" is a used throughout this chapter to refer to registered or Status Indians because of the political issues of legal representation in First Nations politics. It does not necessarily reflect the traditional family and kinship lines of personal identification that people might use in their respective customs and practices. Most families are a blend of Status, non-Status, Métis and non-Aboriginal people, but political representation is separated along legal status lines. For example, the Federation of Saskatchewan Indian Nations represents the 74 First Nation (Bands) who represent registered Status members. At the national level, the term "Aboriginal" is a constitutional pan-Canadian term referring to Indian, Métis and Inuit peoples as a whole. Unlike the everyday use of the term "Native," the term "Aboriginal" has more specific legal and political connotations. Politically, the First Nation (Indian), Métis and Inuit have separate histories and political organizations and only come together on matters of national and constitutional concern. "Indigenous" is another panoramic term usually used in an international context to refer to Native people in general.

The term First Nation has roots in early First Nation political activism to correct public rhetoric about the "two founding nations," by reminding Canadian governments that First Nations were the original "unique and distinct" sovereign nations.[2] They were never lost, therefore could not be "found," neither could they be ignored as if they did not exist. By signing Treaties on a "nation-to-nation" basis with the British Crown as set out in the 1763 Royal Proclamation, First Nations were also "founding nations" because their Treaties paved the way for the development of Canada.3 The term "First Nation" gained popular usage in the 1980s as a clearer alternative to the colonial usage of "Indian."[4]

Today, while it may be politically correct to use the term "First Nation" in everyday language, the federal Indian Act legislation still defines legal Indian status and the jurisdiction of Indian governments operating on Indian lands. The First Nation individuals are referred to in the legislation as "Indians," First Nation governments as "Bands," and Indian lands as "reserves."[5] A *Band* is "a body of Indians for whose collective use and benefit lands have set apart or money is held by the Crown, or declared to be a Band for purposes of the Indian Act"; a *reserve* is "a tract of land, the legal title to which is vested in Her Majesty, that has been set apart by Her Majesty for the use and benefit of a band."[6]

While Saskatchewan First Nations may identify themselves around family and traditional kinship lines, the governments do not.[7] A legal "Indian" is "a person who pursuant to the Indian Act criteria is registered as an Indian or is entitled to be registered as an Indian."[8] Non-Status Indians are those Indians that do not fit the Indian Act criteria because they or their parents and grandparents before them lost their Indian status through any of the various discriminatory provisions of the Indian Act. While some of the discriminatory injustices were rectified by the 1985 amendment to the Indian Act through the passing of Bill C-31, which brought the Act into line with the Charter of Rights and Freedoms,[9] there is still much fear that future generations of First Nations will continue to lose Indian status because of the Act's restrictive criteria. This 1876 federal legislation, which essentially consolidated all pre-Confederation laws, regulations and policies concerning "Indians," governs to this day, establishing criteria around individual "legal" status and collective "Band" status.[10] Notwithstanding, the legal criteria and its often-ensuing divisive and confusing effects, First Nations struggle to maintain their traditional family systems[11] and prefer to identify themselves as "members of specific First Nations"[12] with clear notions of who they are as a People. For example, Peter Ballantyne Cree Nation members are the "Assin'skowitiniwak" or "people of the rocky area,"[13] while the Saulteaux call themselves the "Anishnabe" or "the First People that came down from the Creator."[14]

SASKATCHEWAN FIRST NATIONS

Saskatchewan First Nation politics has always been activist-oriented, raising many First Nations leaders to popular profile and influence in Canadian politics. In the 1880s, prior to the emerging development of Saskatchewan as a province, Plains Chiefs such as Poundmaker, Big Bear, and Piapot,[15] and others—including past northern Chiefs James Roberts, Amos Charles, Peter Ballantyne and John Iron[16]—strove for political sovereignty and for the survival of their own people amidst great famine, sickness and political change. After World War II, emerging generations with family names like Tootoosis, Spence, Cuthand, Dreaver, Dieter, Ahenakew, Venne, Cook, Bird, among many, continued the political struggle through organized political institutions and an extensive array of political, social and economic arrangements with all levels of government.

At a national level, all groups of Indigenous ancestry are recognized in the Canadian Constitution as "Aboriginal Peoples" of Canada. They include the "Indian, Métis and Inuit."[17] According to the 2006 Census, the Aboriginal population[18] of Canada surpassed the one million mark with the largest distribution living in the Territories and the Prairie Provinces. While 22 non-enumerated reserves did not participate for various reasons, trends still reflect a changing national profile. Representing nearly 4% of the total population of Canada, the Aboriginal population is young (over half under 25 years of age), 54% live in urban areas, 29% speak an Aboriginal language, and are about four times as likely to live in crowded and poor housing.

Saskatchewan First Nations are diverse, consisting of five linguistic groups situated throughout the various regions of the province, including the Plains Cree, Nakota/Assiniboine, Dakota, Lakota and Saulteaux in the south and central areas, and to the north, the Woodland Cree, Swampy Cree and Dene people. The total Registered Indian population of Saskatchewan First Nations as of December 31, 2007 was 125,666.[19] In Saskatchewan, out of a provincial population of 953,850, with 141,890 (14.9%) self-identifying as Aboriginals, the majority (91,400 or 64%) of the Aboriginal people are First Nations (Status Indians) or about 10% of the provincial population.[20] The provincial First Nation profile is similar to the national profile, with an increasing young and more urban population. However, the Saskatchewan figures still show a fairly stable on-reserve population trend at 47,765 or 52% living on reserves, which is a small 9% increase since the 2001 Census. Prince Albert showed the highest self-identified First Nation grouping at 17.94 % with Saskatoon at

5.37% and Regina at 5.17%. Poor housing conditions, especially on reserves, remain a problem. With a fast growing population trend, associated issues and new developments, Saskatchewan First Nation politics in Saskatchewan has become an even more significant factor in the political and economic fabric of Saskatchewan.

THE FIRST NATION POLITICAL LANDSCAPE

From the early days of contact and subsequent British and Canadian colonization, First Nations have been immersed in an ongoing struggle to protect their inherent political sovereignty and control over their lives and lands against government laws and policies. The First Nation political landscape is complex, consisting of their relationships and experiences with state pre-Confederation and post-Confederation treaties, legislation, policies and bureaucratic administration. First Nations in Saskatchewan have a legacy of strong political governance systems in their own respective communities, which have evolved over the years into equally complex institutions of local, regional, provincial, national and international organizations. There are over 70 First Nation Bands in Saskatchewan with 62 affiliated to one of the eight regionally-based Tribal Councils.[21]

The common political perspective providing the unifying foundation for First Nation's politics today is the permanent or continuing treaty relationship with the British Crown or what is now Canada. First Nations believe that treaties embody the sacred doctrines of "wahkohtowin" (all are relations) and "miyo-wecehtowin" (good relations), which are considered essential for harmonious First Nation-State relations.[22] Treaties cover all of Saskatchewan and First Nations perceive these boundaries to be as real as boundaries between provinces. Out of 11 Numbered Treaties in Canada; five were made in Saskatchewan—4, 5, 6, 8, and 10 (T2 on southeast edge)—from 1871 to 1921 with the Plains, Swampy and Woodland Cree, Saulteaux, Assiniboine and Dene people.[23]

Saskatchewan Treaties are part of the Robinson Treaties of the 1950s, named after Commissioner William Robinson, who was tasked to negotiate surrenders of Aboriginal title to lands in parts of Ontario and much of the prairie West. The basic legal recipe was to have the treaties negotiated by Commissioners of the Crown promising First Nations such things as annuities, education, hunting and fishing rights, and reserves in exchange for land surrenders of vast territories.[24] In turn, the federal government gained access to First Nation lands and the means to develop their national settlement policies and agricultural and resource developments. Since then, Treaty interpretation and implementation has been battered about for over a century by a myriad of peripheral federal policies and legislative initiatives, with little resolution. The constitutional changes in 1982 provided a step forward with provisions enshrining existing Aboriginal and Treaty Rights,[25] but beyond policy recognition, governments continue to deny that substantive inherent and treaty rights exist in areas such as health and education, among others.

In addition to Treaties, government actions, policies and administration—

whether by omission or commission—relating to the interpretation of the Constitution, the Indian Act and other legislation, and Supreme Court decisions, often generate much of the action-reaction activities in First Nation-State politics. Since 2000, First Nations have reaped many benefits from the political work of their forefathers and past leadership. Aboriginal and Treaty Rights are now recognized in the Constitution. Some amendments have been made to the Indian Act. New land claims agreements have been made, including the 1992 Treaty Land Entitlement Agreement in Saskatchewan. There has been much community and economic development in First Nation communities, with most Bands taking over much of their public services such as education and health, as well as developing their own businesses. Yet, in spite of these positive developments, First Nations still struggle: to meet the basic health and socio-economic needs of their communities; to keep pace with a larger competitive and changing world of information technology; and with escalating social and environmental pressures and a complex web of government service systems. For example, delivering public services at the reserve levels is not a simple matter. It can often raise what should be routine administrative issues to the level of national political and human rights profiles, largely due to unresolved jurisdictions creating constitutional gray areas of responsibility as to who ultimately pays for the services. At any one time a First Nations child with serious illnesses can be caught between jurisdictions and endure needless suffering as a result, as was the case of Jordan, a First Nations child from Norway House, Manitoba.[26] Jordan was born with complex medical problems (needed a ventilator, could not walk, talk, or even cry) and spent over two years in a Winnipeg hospital because federal and provincial officials could not agree on who would pay for his homecare needs on the reserve. Jordan passed away having never been able to go home.

This particular case reached national profile with national advocacy campaigns calling on all governments to adopt a "child first" principle in resolving jurisdictional conflicts involving First Nations children. In December 2007, a private members bill to adopt what is now called "Jordan's Principle" was tabled in Parliament.[27] Jordan's Principle states that First Nations children will be provided with immediate medical and health services at the point of their need with the first contact agency paying the costs without delay or disruption. Once the needs of the child are dealt with first, the paying government agency can then settle the matters of jurisdiction through jurisdictional dispute mechanisms. First Nations across Canada and Saskatchewan have taken on this principle advocating a "child first" approach to First Nations health and children's care services, but federal and most provincial governments, including Saskatchewan, have yet to move beyond a moral prerogative.[28]

LEVELS OF POLITICAL ORGANIZATION AND INSTITUTIONS
First Nation politics in Saskatchewan can be conceptualized for explanatory purposes as a continuum of evolving levels of political representation and governance. First Nation government is fundamentally Chief and Council

Band government, although Bands may be involved in various regional, provincial, national and international organizations and networks. Political governance in a very broad sense illustrates the process of decision-making in a government system. While First Nation governments are autonomous, their decisions are also influenced by the variety of political structures and relationships that they had and continue to have with each other and with the State through treaties and other historical arrangements. The levels of First Nation political governance in Saskatchewan can be illustrated as such:

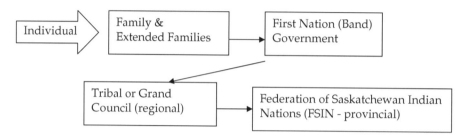

FIRST NATION (BAND) LEVEL

The basic government unit of First Nation political organization in Saskatchewan is the Band,[29] with an elected Chief and Council. Historically, political organization was a spiritually based, family kinship system where leaders emerged and maintained their leadership status by virtue of demonstrating superior personal skills and good character. While First Nations have different linguistic, territorial and cultural histories, they share a common conceptualization of a holistic way of life, where everything is interconnected and controlled by a benevolent Creator. Reciprocity or sharing was a spiritual principle characteristic of most traditional societies covering every aspect of life. Scholars suggest that "people shared food; there were no rich and poor. They made decisions collectively; some people were more influential than others, but there were no powerful chiefs. Foraging peoples worked hard, but contrary to popular stereotypes, life was not a grim battle for survival."[30] Elders today explain that it was the Creator that placed them on this land from time immemorial and they consider treaties to be "Kihci-asotamatowin"— sacred promises to one another—that cannot be changed or altered. In the words of Elder Jimmy Myo: "The Creator sets out the laws that govern our relationship ... all the ways by which to understand who is God and what He is, and how He created the universe and how we came from our Creator through a circle of life, and how we return there again."[31]

The spiritual foundation of treaties continues to influence First Nations even though so many changes have occurred through time. The 1876 Indian Act replaced traditional governance with the elected Chief and Council system, although First Nations assert that their power primarily flows from the Creator and Band Custom. The Minister of Indian Affairs and Northern Development is charged with the administration of the Indian Act that sets, among other things, the legislative powers and authority of the Chief and

Council governments.[32] The Minister's power comes from section 91(24) of the Canadian Constitution that gave the federal government, rather than the province, exclusive jurisdiction over "Indians and lands reserved for Indians."[33] The Indian Act refers to First Nation governments as "Bands."[34] For example, in the case of the Peter Ballantyne Cree Nation, the terms Peter Ballantyne "Cree Nation" and Peter Ballantyne "Band" are often used synonymously. However, "Cree Nation" is preferred because it better reflects the inherent nation-to-nation relationship recognized in the treaties, which have international standing, rather than the more subordinate legislated position reflected in the Indian Act.[35]

HOW FIRST NATION GOVERNMENTS WORK AT THE BAND LEVEL

While First Nations assert and continue to work towards the recognition of inherent jurisdiction over treaty lands and all aspects of their own affairs, the Indian Act sets out the governing jurisdiction of Chiefs and Councils on reserves.[36] The only legislatively recognized governments are First Nation (Band) governments, and while their powers are wide-ranging, they are also "limited only to those activities that are outlined in the Act, particularly in Sections 81 and 83."[37] These activities include control over such things as: elections, membership, bylaws (not inconsistent with the Act or other federal regulations) relating to health, traffic regulation, law and order, roads and other public works, zoning, sports activities, trespass, licensing for businesses, etc.[38] Ultimately, the Minister of Indian Affairs has final authority relating to Band government within the Indian Act. Notwithstanding these, and other, policy limitations, First Nations have progressively developed their own institutions and governing systems in response to their changing environments.

Most First Nations have their own Band Custom elections and election codes and if they do not, they follow the election provisions of the Indian Act that prescribes elections every two years. In either case, independent electoral officers, usually supported by some form of Elder appeal committees, manage the elections. Chiefs and Councils are elected by the one-person, one-vote majority representative system.[39] All Band members are eligible to vote, and with growing off-reserve populations, and the implications of the Corbiere decision,[40] most First Nations in Saskatchewan allow urban members to vote—some allow them to run for Chief and Council, which is a changing trend considering that First Nations leaders are generally expected to be residents of the reserve.

A myriad of duties and responsibilities face Chiefs and Councils, ranging from dealing with personal complaints to attending multiple meetings and overseeing the processes and delivery of public services, such as health, education, public works, water delivery, environment, and other aspects of local government. While most First Nations are engaged in similar activities, their methods of governance vary depending on their location, size, and developmental status. First Nation governance follows a portfolio system of distributing duties and responsibilities not unlike the way Cabinet Ministers are assigned portfolios by the Premier or Prime Minister. Most Chiefs assign portfolios to

Councilors and usually take on their own as well. Some also appoint Vice-Chiefs from among the Councilors. Councilors can be assigned one or more portfolios to oversee areas such as health and education. The primary functions of Portfolio Councilors are usually limited to broader governance activities involving bylaws, policy making and political advocacy, rather than the day-to-day management of the programs and services that are the responsibility of Band administrations and the various sectors of First Nation civil service.

First Nation administrations each have their own unique organization structures, but generally are no different in overall functions from other public sector organizations. They have a CEO or Band Administrator that oversees the implementation of Chief and Council decisions with reporting responsibilities to the Chief and Council. First Nation public administrations can vary from having centralized management systems divided into various departments for each area, such as economic development and housing, to having more decentralized versions with separate agencies managing the bigger areas, such as education and health. More often, it is a blend of both systems—a mix of departments and affiliated agencies—but all having delegated responsibilities from Chief and Council, with the requisite reporting requirements back to them.

Decision-making at the Chief and Council level is done through Band Council Resolutions (BCRs) that are recorded in the minutes of the Chief and Council meetings, usually chaired by the Chief.[41] Depending on the size and complexity of the Band's governance system, procedures for getting a decision on any item can range from something as simple as a manager taking a request to the Chief or Councilor to put something on the agenda at the Chief and Council meeting or it can involve a complex vetting process that may take weeks to reach the Chief and Council table.

Political accountability is both formal and informal. Chiefs and Councils report to their membership annually at a special assembly or community meeting where financial and program reports are presented. Public meetings are also held on a regular basis throughout the year to report to the membership. Informal processes are the day-to-day interactions between the leadership and their membership, and these appeals for help can range from visiting sick relatives in the hospital to trying to get a house. Leaders are frequently stymied from being able to adequately respond to community requests due to issues of underfunding, technical capacity, and other factors out of their control. These situations can trigger requests to their political affiliations with Tribal Councils and the FSIN to help support and advocate with them at the larger political levels.

REGIONAL/DISTRICT OR TRIBAL/GRAND COUNCIL LEVEL

There are over 10 tribal or regional councils in Saskatchewan along with unaffiliated or independent Bands in the regions. Tribal Councils or Grand Councils, as many are commonly known, are regional political and administrative organizations whose memberships consist of district Chief representatives from the various Bands. Tribal Councils function as a regional political voice for the member First Nation Bands in common matters relating to the entrenchment and protection of inherent rights and treaties, as well as providing them with technical and other types of support for self-government developments, community programs and services, and other common interests. The Prince Albert Grand Council (PAGC), for example, celebrated its 30th anniversary in 2007. In 1977, 12 First Nations located in central and northern Saskatchewan set up the district political organization,[42] which today represents one of the largest Tribal Councils in Saskatchewan, representing over 32,000 people.[43]

Unlike First Nation Bands who have legislated government authority under the Indian Act, Tribal Councils are regional political organizations and do not have legislative authority over the member Chiefs and Bands. Only member Chiefs and Councilors, and/or their designated representatives attending the annual conventions get to vote for the leadership and executive of the Tribal or Grand Council organizations, not individual Band members. This is a convention style political system of selecting executive leadership similar to the one used by political parties when they select their party leadership and executive. Only party members attending party nomination conventions get to vote.[44] The notion of having only Chiefs and Councils, and/or their designates, voting at the Tribal Council assemblies is a result of a variety of factors, including the recognition of the legislated government status of Bands, the legal incorporation requirements, the preservation of the political autonomy and power of the member Band governments and the ensuing tribal council accountability to them. The most important facet of Tribal Council governance is to support their member First Nation Bands.

HOW TRIBAL /GRAND COUNCILS WORK AT THE REGIONAL LEVELS

Tribal or Grand Councils get their delegated political authority from their member First Nations (Bands) and vary in size and structure. For example, the Meadow Lake Tribal Council (MLTC), the Prince Albert Grand Council (PAGC), the Saskatoon Tribal Council (STC) and File Hills Qu'Appelle Tribal Council (FHQ) are among the largest groupings in the province.[45] While Tribal/Grand Councils have their own distinct organization structures and practices, most generally manage along the lines of corporate organizations with ruling Boards of Directors (Chiefs) setting overall policies and strategic direction, with elected Executives (Tribal/Grand Chief, Vice-Chiefs) overseeing implementation and administration activities of the organizations. Portfolio systems are used to assign areas of responsibilities to the Executive members and their political accountability to the member Chiefs are structured through various reporting procedures and annual assemblies. For example, in the case of the Meadow Lake Tribal Council, the Tribal Chief and the two Vice-Chiefs are "responsible for sustaining the political efforts of the Meadow Lake First Nations to expand the development of their communities."[46]

The member Chiefs govern the Tribal/Grand Councils and elect the Tribal/Grand Council Executive, usually consisting of a Tribal/Grand Council Chief and one or more Vice-Chiefs. The work of the Executive involves broader policymaking and ensuring effective administration rather than the day-to-day administration or operational functions that are carried out by the Chief Executive Officer (CEO) and other members of the civil service. In most First Nations, Elders are integrated into the various governance structures in advisory and spiritual guidance capacities. For example, Meadow Lake Tribal Council has an Elder's Advisory Council consisting of two Elders from each of the nine member communities and they meet on a regular basis to advance traditional knowledge and guidance to the various issues facing their communities. Similarly, the File Hills Qu'Appelle Tribal Council has a Senate Council.[47] Women's Commissions are also becoming a common feature of First Nation governance. For example, the Prince Albert Grand Council formed a Women's Commission in 1990 and formally established it in the PAGC governance structure through its Convention Act in 1993, with the mandate "by the Council of Chiefs to promote and protect the rights of women, Elders and youth."[48] Situating urban offices and service centres in major cities to provide help to urban First Nations is another emerging development, as in the case of the File Hills Qu'Appelle Tribal Council in Regina.

Decision-making is often more structured along policy and administrative lines in Tribal Councils than First Nation (Band) administrations, with the exception of the larger multi-community First Nations, like the La Ronge and Peter Ballantyne Cree Nation, who operate more like regional councils. The tendency seems to be that the bigger the area served, the more structure is required and the less contact there is with individuals. While Tribal/Grand Councils have varying governance structures, they all have annual assemblies where the member Chiefs makes major decisions through Tribal/Grand Council resolutions (TCRs). These resolutions do not come to the annual assemblies unless they have been vetted through certain procedural processes and requirements set out in the regulations governing Tribal/Grand Council assemblies. In the day-to-day decisions, the Portfolio system of Executive Chiefs and the administrations with their various departments and affiliated institutions provide the daily services and programs.

Some examples of the work done by Tribal/Grand Councils involve issues relating to the residential school settlement agreement, matrimonial real property issues on reserve, duty to consult requirements of governments on matters affecting First Nations, and economic development initiatives. Tribal/Grand Councils are also linked to the FSIN through representation in its governance and institutional structures, thus ensuring First Nations (Bands) representation at all levels of the political spectrum.

PROVINCIAL LEVEL: FSIN AND HISTORY

The provincial First Nations organization, The Federation of Saskatchewan Indian Nations (FSIN), was set up in 1958, and today consists of a membership of 74 First Nation Bands, as represented by elected Chiefs and Councilors/Headmen.[49] In 2006, FSIN celebrated its 60th anniversary, a leading achievement among First Nation political organizations in Canada.

Much of this can be attributed to the strong foundations set by the First Nation political activists from the early War eras, including veterans, social activists, and political leaders.

Veterans became especially important public voices for political change. Estimates from various source records suggest that about 1,000 Aboriginal people enlisted in the war effort with 900 returning home.[50] Although most veterans did not benefit from the immediate post-war economy and were not particularly politically active,[51] their credibility in voluntarily fighting for Canada improved public opinion towards First Nations and it helped build broad political support for the advancement of Indian rights.[52] As the veterans became more economically mobile by the 1950s, they also became more politically active in fighting the federal bureaucracy for better living conditions on the reserves which were experiencing rapid population increases. While socio-economic pressures forced many people to move to urban areas to seek employment, some veterans were able to find jobs in their communities; some had their own businesses, and some attained management positions in government and the private sector.[53]

FSIN was formally organized as a province-wide First Nations political organization in 1958 under the leadership of the late John Tootoosis from the Poundmaker Reserve, a descendant of the famous Plains Chief Poundmaker who helped negotiate the early treaties. Prior to that, there had been other political organizations situated largely in the southern areas of the province as a response against the collective poverty and negative treatment at the hands of government officials. The larger organizations—the Saskatchewan Treaty Protection Association (1930) situated in the Fort Qu'Appelle area under the leadership of Andrew Gordon and John Gambler, and the Association of Saskatchewan Indians led by Joe Dreaver (1943), and the League of Indians of Western Canada led by John Tootoosis and Joe Taylor—eventually amalgamated in 1946 to form the Union of Saskatchewan Indians (USI) and, in 1957, the USI became the Federation of Saskatchewan Indians (FSI) with John Tootoosis as its first president, from 1958–67.[54] As the organization grew and times changed, the FSI reorganized in 1982 to become what is now the Federation of Saskatchewan Indian Nations (FSIN).

Tootoosis attributed the uniting of the various organizations to a collective agreement by the leaders because they found that they were stronger as a united group. Over 100 Chiefs and Councilors from across the province attended the founding unification conference in 1946. He recalls:

> they could not accomplish anything because they were few in numbers… On the 24th of February, 1946, we had a big meeting at Barry Hotel in Saskatoon and the three organizations amalgamated, under the name of the Union of Saskatchewan Indians. We continued to hold meetings and the delegates came at their own expense or were supported by their own people… There were two or three bands not represented at the 1958 Conference. It was time to strengthen unity. I asked that

we be given a new name. They agreed and we called it, "The
Federation of Saskatchewan Indians."[55]

The federal department of Indian Affairs did not support the early politi-
cal efforts of the First Nations. During the 1930s, organizing efforts by a
Mohawk veteran to organize a national political organization to fight for
Indian rights had been stymied by regulations, making it an offence to raise
money for Indian organizations.[56] It was not until 1944 that national First
Nation political organizations emerged with the North American Indian
Brotherhood, becoming the National Indian Brotherhood in 1968, and the
Assembly of First Nations (AFN) today.[57]

Much of the political organizing in the western provinces was done independently without government aid and it was only in 1946 when the USI was
formed in Saskatchewan that First Nations were given financial support, not
by the federal government, but by the provincial Premier, Tommy Douglas,
who supported the amalgamation efforts of the First Nation organizations.[58]
One explanation is that Tommy Douglas and his Co-operative Commonwealth
Federation (CCF) government wanted to work through a single organization to
handle First Nation grievances and concerns and also to legitimize provincial
concerns regarding the administration of First Nation Affairs.[59] Some First
Nations felt that Premier Douglas "was, as in the past, an easy man for Indians
to approach,"[60] and he was "concerned about (their) plight."[61] Whatever the
motive, the financial support helped with the unification process that was
already happening over common treaty right issues such as post-war reforms
for better schools, more local control, better health and social services, veteran's
benefits and the debate around the franchise. First Nations were not allowed to
vote in provincial or federal elections until 1960 and while some First Nations
saw the right to vote as a right; others suspected that it would take away their
treaty rights and federal status and assimilate them into provincial jurisdiction.
Some believed that the provincial government was trying to assimilate and
control them through the new association and that it was a "product of white
people meddling in Indian matters."[62]

FSIN adapted to many changes and continues to be rooted in treaty nationalism to the present day, although, in the late 1950s, other organizations, more
service-oriented than political, also emerged in the cities in response to the
poor living standards facing urban Aboriginal people.[63] While its longevity
can be attributed to many things, one of the influencing aspects was leadership. FSIN leaders have largely consisted of veterans, community leaders,
educated professionals, and business people, all having strong treaty ideologies, proven leadership skills in their own reserves and effective political networks.[64] For example, the current FSIN Chief, Lawrence Joseph (2006–09), is
from the Big River First Nation and a former Vice-Chief of FSIN with extensive administrative experience in the federal civil service.

AFFILIATIONS

The FSIN is affiliated at a national level with the Assembly of First Nations
(AFN), which is the political organization representing the political voice of

First Nations across the country. First Nation Chiefs from across the country meet every year at the AFN annual assembly to decide on "national policy and direction through resolution."[65] At an international level, First Nations are linked to the World Council of Indigenous Peoples (WCIP) through the Assembly of First Nations.[66] The AFN was established in 1982, but its roots as a national organization extend back to the end of World War I when the Mohawk war veteran, Lieutenant Frederick Loft, after seeing the poverty and poor conditions that First Nations were living under, went to England to lobby the British Parliament and the King of England for help. Upon their advice to set up a stronger political voice, the First Nation League of Canada was organized in 1919 with its goal of protecting the rights of First Nations. The first Chief of FSIN, the late senator John Tootoosis, became involved in the organization in 1921, but the organization could not sustain a national presence and was replaced by a series of organizations until 1982, when the AFN was set up.[67]

The first AFN Chief was Dr. David Ahenakew, followed by a series of successors, including other Saskatchewan leaders, such as the late Walter Dieter and Noel Starblanket, to the current Chief from Manitoba, Phil Fontaine.[68] The AFN changed with time and events, including the growth in both First Nations government and provincial First Nation organizations, such as the FSIN, and desiring a more representative and accountable national organization geared to protecting inherent and treaty rights.[69] It was important that the national organization protect the bilateral nation-to-nation or sovereign relationship in the treaties between First Nations (Bands) and the Crown/Canada. The AFN structure became an organization of First Nation Chiefs rather than just representatives from the provincial regions as a means of respecting each First Nation's sovereignty.[70] The AFN is currently governed by a Charter outlining details of guiding principles and organization, one of which is the clear mandate that the AFN remain at all times "an instrument to advance the aspirations of First Nations and shall not become greater in strength, power, resources or jurisdiction, than the First Nations for which it was established to serve."[71] In 2003, the AFN restructured to include three other advisory groups representing elders, women and youth to participate in the annual Chiefs' Assembly. This was done to better reflect and respond to the changing First Nation demographics across the country.

FSIN MANDATE AND GOVERNANCE

The political evolution and mandate of FSIN was, and continues to be, based on the promotion, protection and implementation of treaties and Treaty Rights. Treaties are considered both sacred and practical, although for some scholars this might infer colonization.[72] The goals and objectives of the FSIN include:

> The protection of Treaties and Treaty Rights, the fostering of progress in economic, educational and social endeavors of First Nation people, co-operation with civil and religious authorities, constructive criticism and thorough discussion on

all matters, the adherence to democratic procedure, and the promotion of respect and tolerance for all people.[73]

The governance capacity and political growth of the FSIN has evolved significantly since 1960 with the addition of educational and other corporate institutions.[74] In 1982, the FSIN changed its governance structure from a non-profit organization to a First Nation Legislative Assembly model consisting of a federation of First Nation Bands. It was the first of its kind in Canada. It had outgrown its non-profit organization structure to become a political legislative government model befitting what Saskatchewan Chiefs called a "true federation of nations."[75]

FSIN GOVERNANCE STRUCTURE: FSIN CONVENTION ACT 1985

The 1985 FSIN Convention Act establishes the structure, rules and purposes of the Federation. It came by way of a resolution passed and signed at a Chiefs assembly approving the restructuring of FSIN as a political legislative entity consisting of First Nation governments and treaty-based institutions shaped by First Nation laws. All FSIN-affiliated institutions also report to the Chiefs in Assembly. The Chiefs essentially control and enforce the executive and administrative functions of FSIN through various reporting mechanisms throughout the year and at legislative assemblies. The Convention Act specifies three assemblies per year—fall, winter and spring. Special assemblies may also be called when required. Major decisions having potential implications for all First Nations, such as, for example, creating First Nation childcare standards, are vetted through extensive processes before being introduced as resolutions at the legislative assemblies. The Chiefs in assembly have the authority to initiate and approve First Nation laws, ordinances, statutes, regulations and codes, and to determine the structure and authority of the FSIN Executive among other governing responsibilities. The governing and organization structures of FSIN, as set out in the Convention Act, consist of[76]:

- Chiefs-in-Assembly: Legislative Assembly.

- Senate: A cultural and spiritual body providing guidance and advocacy to FSIN and its related institutions on all treaty and related issues. Has powers to monitor and investigate issues deemed as a potential threat to FSIN integrity and Treaty Trust Relations with the Federal Crown.

- Elders Council: Advises and guides FSIN governance on First Nation spiritual, cultural and traditional values and customs.

- Executive: Consists of the FSIN Chief—currently Chief Lawrence Joseph—and four (4) Vice-Chiefs.[77] Elected for three-year terms as per the FSIN Election Act and assigned authorities and responsibilities (portfolios, committees) as set out by resolution of Chiefs in assembly.

• Executive Council: Consists of FSIN Executive and Tribal/Grand/Agency Council representatives who monitor and provide policy support relating to strategic directions and Convention Act principles.

• Indian Government Commission. Oversees compliance of all FSIN Commissions and related entities to Inherent and Treaty Rights; governance processes and policy reviews.

• Others include an Auditor General, Treasury Board: Enforcement of independent auditing functions and management of FSIN financial and administrative functions, respectively.

• Major Commissions and Secretariats include: Lands and Resources, Economic and Community Development, Education and Training, Health and Social Development, Women and Justice. Commissions (Chiefs) offer political and strategic policy direction and support over their assigned areas. Secretariats are overseen by FSIN Executive Chiefs assigned Secretariat portfolios with staff providing administrative functions implementing the strategic directions of the Commission Chiefs.

• Also includes institutions, committees, secretariats and other entities, as may be determined necessary. Among others, includes sport, culture, youth & recreation; urban development; Women's Council, Treaty Governance Office.

• Saskatchewan Veterans Association: Responsible for all matters relating to First Nation War Veterans and their beneficiaries.

• Affiliated Institutions: These include the Saskatchewan Indian Cultural College (SICC), Saskatchewan Indian Institute of Technology (SIIT), First Nations University of Canada, Saskatchewan Indian Gaming Authority (SIGA), First Nations Bank of Canada, Saskatchewan Indian Equity Foundation (SIEF), among others.

Commissions serve important functions within the FSIN in relation to strategic policy setting, advocacy and support in the major portfolio areas. The goal is for the betterment of First Nations people through First Nation control, jurisdiction and implementation of Treaty Rights in all areas. Commissions provide strategic focus on Treaty Rights as well as ensuring accountability and equity throughout the whole FSIN system. Representation of the various interests is accommodated throughout the system through strategic policy directions in all FSIN Commissions and Secretariats, and depending on available resources and political will, the establishment of special Commissions, such as the Women's and Elder's Commissions. Senators also play important roles in supporting the various Commissions and Secretariats on a number of issues such as Justice Reforms and Treaty Governance.

The Saskatchewan First Nations Women's Commission, consisting of FSIN women Chiefs, plays an important function advocating on issues at the FSIN Legislative Assemblies and other public arenas affecting children, youth, women and families: family violence, addictions, mental health, sexual abuse, etc. For instance, the tragic freezing deaths of the two children at the Yellow Quill First Nation in January 2008, and the increasing numbers of youth suicides were among issues raised by the Women's Commission Chair, Chief Marie-Anne DayWalker-Pelletier, at the February 2008 FSIN Assembly. In a media interview that followed, she stated: "We need training for people to provide the education and safe environments—healthy environments—and wellness to our young people, our mothers and our fathers and our children... We have to start talking about these things instead of hiding from them. When you're silent about the issues you can't do anything about them."[78]

The Saskatchewan Indian Education Commission is one of the older Commissions set up under the auspices of the 1985 Saskatchewan Indian Education Act, to ensure recognition of the treaty right to education and to speak as a "common voice on matters of mutual interest."[79] Early successes included the establishment of First Nations-controlled post-secondary institutions offering certificates, diplomas and degrees in a variety of disciplines such as Indian Studies, Indian Languages, Indian Education, Indian Administration and Indian Social Work. In 1976, the FSIN signed an agreement with the University of Regina, setting up the Saskatchewan Indian Federated College, the forerunner to the current First Nations University of Canada. The college grew quickly from seven students in 1976 to 1200 students in 1994, and over 200 faculty and staff.[80] Today, the First Nations University of Canada operates campuses in Regina, Saskatoon and Prince Albert. Among other developments, the economic development area has also progressed in facilitating First Nation developments and training opportunities. One of the more successful ventures was the creation of the Saskatchewan First Nation Gaming Authority (SIGA). After ten years of operation, SIGA casinos had earned over $130 million and profits of close to $49 million in the 2006–07 fiscal year.[81] Over 25% of its net profits were used for helping First Nation community developments and it employed over 1,500 people, with over 70% being First Nation.

FSIN DECISION-MAKING
The Chief of Staff, who is responsible for the overall operations and staff of FSIN, implements FSIN decision-making processes and decisions made by the Legislative Assembly and Executive. The potential process triggers are many, but usually issues are first raised to the Secretariats or any of the Executive. This is followed by a policy analysis and review and, depending on the issue, briefing notes are then presented to the Commission Chiefs at their regular meeting—motions adopted by Commission are forwarded to the clerk of the

Legislative Assembly. If the issue has financial implications, it is routed to the
Treasury Board for review and approval, but if does not, it goes onward; a
draft resolution is submitted to the Joint Executive Council and the Indian
Government Commission. It then goes to the Senate for review and approval,
and then it is introduced at the Legislative Assembly during the Executive
Reports and the resolution is discussed and voted upon. Since the Legislative
Assembly meets at least three times a year, sometimes more, the extensive
process can delay decision-making, but it also ensures that only important
issues get discussed at the Chiefs assemblies.

BALANCING INTERESTS

While the FSIN is the political voice of its member First Nations, it has no
political authority over them and is accountable to them. Notwithstanding the
fiscal and reporting constraints of funding agreements, the primary work of
the FSIN and its affiliates covers a broad range of political advocacy, coordination and policy activities at the provincial and national levels in all matters
of treaty importance. It also provides technical and other support, as required,
to individuals, First Nations and Tribal Councils. An example of the kind of
high level advocacy work done by the FSIN was the successful lobby of British
Parliamentarians by FSIN Chiefs and others, in the early 1980s, that led to
First Nations being included in the repatriation talks and the recognition and
affirmation of Aboriginal and Treaty rights in the 1982 Canadian
Constitution.[82] Until then, First Nations had been excluded from taking part in
the constitutional talks although they were also "founding nations" of
Canada.[83]

The Treaty Land Entitlement Framework Agreement in 1992 is another
good illustration of the coordination, policy and advocacy work that the FSIN
does in dealing with and balancing very complex interests relating to politically sensitive treaty issues such as the settlement of outstanding land entitlements. The federal government set out two claims processes, one for
Comprehensive Claims where there are no treaties (James Bay, Nishga) and
Specific Claims, where there are treaties. In Saskatchewan, treaties covered all
lands and the Specific Claims process was followed to try to restore reserve
lands that had been lost or taken away from Bands by the government or its
agents. The identification of outstanding claims involved extensive co-ordination and research. Eventually, along with the First Nations, the Office of the
Treaty Commissioner, and the federal/provincial governments, the FSIN was
instrumental in achieving some redress through a "Saskatchewan Formula"
that provided over 1.5 million acres owed to 27 entitlement First Nations
(Bands) under treaty.[84] The Framework Agreement was the first step towards
a long process that shifted implementation to the signatory entitlement Bands
to negotiate their own Band Specific Agreements, Band Trust Agreements, and
to have both approved through a complex ratification vote by their respective
memberships.

LOOKING FORWARD

A paradox of opportunities and challenges face First Nations and other citizens of Saskatchewan. The growing, young First Nation populations remain a largely untapped labour and intellectual resource due to a variety of issues involving access, permanence and promotion. Barriers to employment and employability can also mask elements of personal prejudice against Aboriginal people as in the case of some workplace relations, attitudes and behaviors.[85] Poor socio-economic conditions as well as limited employment and educational opportunities are primary push factors from the reserves to the cities. At the same time, there has been a plethora of emerging First Nation developments and institutions, both on and off reserve, that are creating new economic and social opportunities. Although politicians and the work of political organizations may sometimes be seen by some as "rhetoric and promised actions that never get translated into real benefits for the people at the local level,"[86] there is visible development with most First Nations managing and controlling their own public services and many are engaging in a variety of economic ventures with both the corporate and public sectors.[87]

Compared to reserve developments, urban services are less developed, although some First Nation Bands have set up urban offices for their members and some Tribal Councils located in the bigger cities provide off-reserve services to the First Nations in their region. Urban development, as far as business or commercial development is concerned, is progressing faster than the public service sector (health, housing, employment agencies). This was in part due to the nature of the Land Entitlement Agreements that allowed for commercial but not residential developments in the cities and towns. As well, service funding agreements with First Nation Bands restrict coverage to on-reserve public services. It is evident from all this is that First Nations politics are not isolated political efforts. Much emphasis is placed on meaningful partnerships that are practical and effective with regards to organization and economies of scale.

All developments have their challenges and strengths, and the FSIN and its affiliates are no exception. Some of these challenges are often played in the media. These include: struggles facing the First Nation University of Canada with its governance and administration issues; the FSIN with its debt reduction challenges; and social and addiction problems, including gambling, in First Nation communities. While actions of individuals may certainly play a part in political dilemmas, the larger environment that helped shape the situation is often less visible. For example, First Nations are not on level playing field with other provincial and federal governments as far as having appropriate resources and personnel, yet they are often judged by the same standards. Capacity issues in many areas, including the management of communications, can be limited from having to balance multiple demands on financial and human resources. Nonetheless, First Nations political history has proven that they have and will continue to work out their own solutions, and will work with other partners as well who are willing to work towards the collective good.

The common political threads weaving throughout the whole network of political organization from the First Nation (Band) to the AFN level are based on protecting First Nation inherent rights and treaties. Treaties were, and continue to be, the distinguishing feature of "political accommodation"[88] and the basis of the relationship between First Nations and the Canadian government. In Saskatchewan, First Nation political organizations—Tribal/Grand Councils, FSIN and AFN—exist to protect and support the inherent rights, treaties and self-government developments of First Nation (Band) governments. Failures by government to fulfill treaty promises and concurrent problems with both federal and provincial jurisdiction and policies relating to First Nations remain major pillars spearheading First Nation politics in Saskatchewan.

For First Nations and Saskatchewan politics, the idea of looking forward may well be encapsulated in the words of the late Elder, former Councilor of the Canoe Lake First Nation, and FSIN Senator, Jonas Lariviere, from Canoe Lake, who at over 100 years old, reflectively said:

> To be in tune with one's self is important today; one must value his life and to be kind and not be pressured towards negative actions. Using your mind wisely is the way of thinking that is needed today. Young people must become a praying people to be able to ask for help when they are in need. Gathering food and other things is not as important as being a prayerful being.[89]

NOTES

1. Robert J. Jackson and Doreen Jackson, *Politics in Canada: Culture, Institutions, Behaviour and Public Policy, Sixth Edition* (Toronto: Pearson, Prentice Hall, 2006), 8.

2. James S. Frideres and Rene R. Gadacz, *Aboriginal Peoples in Canada* (Toronto: Pearson, Prentice Hall, 2008), 22–23.

3. Harold Cardinal and Walter Hildebrandt, *Treaty Elders of Saskatchewan: Our Dream is That Our Peoples Will One Day Be Clearly Recognized as Nations* (Calgary: University of Calgary Press, 2000).

4. In the 1982 Canadian Constitution, "Aboriginal Peoples of Canada" included the Indian, Métis and Inuit. First Nations are Indian but not Metis or Inuit. Many First Nations still use Indian interchangeably since it is still a prevalent legal term.

5. Some contemporary First Nation land claim agreements in Canada may no longer be under the Indian Act legislation, but in Saskatchewan, the Indian Act is still operational.

6. The Minister of Indian Affairs and Northern Development. First Nations and Northern Statistics Section Strategic Research and Analysis Directorate Strategic Policy and Research Branch Department of Indian Affairs and Northern Development. *Registered Indian Population By Sex and Residence 2007* (Ottawa: Minister of Public Works and Government Services Canada, 2008), v.

7. Bonita Beatty, "Pimacesowin (To Make Your Own Way): First Nation Governance" (PhD dissertation, University of Alberta, 2006), 99.

8. Shin Imai and Donna Hawley, *The 1996 Annotated Indian Act* (Scarborough, ON: Carswell Thomson Professional Publishing, 1995). A definition of "Indian" appears on p. 4.

9. www.johnco.com/nativel/bill_c31.html

10. Imai and Hawley, *The 1996 Annotated Indian Act*. A definition of "Band" appears on p. 3.

11. Elder Alfred Billette from the Buffalo River Denesuline Nation describes government assimilation policies as "playing havoc on their families" in Cardinal and Hilderbrandt, *Treaty Elders of Saskatchewan*, 21.

12. Cardinal Harold, *The Unjust Society: With a New Introduction by the Author* (Vancouver/Toronto: Douglas and McIntyre, 1999), xii.

13. www.peterballantyne.ca

14. Elder Danny Musqua in Harold and Hilderbrandt, *Treaty Elders of Saskatchewan*, 40

15. Christian Thompson (ed.), *Saskatchewan First Nations: Lives Past and Present* (Regina: Canadian Plains Research Center, 2004,) xiv. There are so many more that it would take a book itself to do justice to the many unsung and sung First Nations leaders.

16. www.LLrib.ca/history.php; and http://www.otc.ca//learning_Resources/Historical_biographies/treaty-10/John _Iron/. There is also good history in Donald B. Ward, *The People: A Historical Guide to the First Nations of Alberta, Saskatchewan and Manitoba* (Calgary: Fifth House Ltd., 1995).

17. Section 35(2) of the Constitution Act, 1982. http://laws.justice.gc.ca/en/const/annex_e.html#II

18. Aboriginals refer to the Indian, Métis, Inuit and Non-Status Indians. The 2006 Census refers to 1,172,790 self-identified Aboriginals. http://www12.statcan.ca/english/census06/analysis/aboriginal/index.cfm

19. SRAD, SPR Branch, *Registered First Nation Population by Sex and Residence, 2007* (March 2008): ix.

20. "Saskatchewan Aboriginal Peoples." 2006 Census of Canada. January 15, 2008. www.stats.gov.sk.ca

21. http://www.ainc-inac.gc.ca/sk/fnmap_e.html. These are 2004 figures. FSIN identifies 74 First Nations.

22. Cardinal and Hilderbrandt, *Treaty Elders of Saskatchewan*, 15.

23. Office of the Treaty Commissioner: http://www.otc.ca/abouttreaties.htm

24. John J. Borrows and Leonard I. Rotman, *Aboriginal Legal Issues: Cases, Materials & Commentary: Volume 1* (Markham, ON: LexisNexis Canada Inc., 2003), 121.

25. Section 35(1) of The Constitution Act 1982 recognizes and affirms the "existing Aboriginal and Treaty Rights" of Canada's Aboriginal Peoples. Aboriginal Rights are based on customary laws and traditions and are not dependent on Treaty or other legislative instrument.

26. www.manyhandsonedream.ca/english/advocacycampaign.html; and http://www.givemeaning.com/project/jordan

27. http://www.ndp.ca/page/5318

28. FSIN passed a resolution supporting Jordan's Principle on October 25, 2007: http://www.fsin.com/mediarelease/2007/healthnatchilddaynewsreleasefinal.pdf

29. The word "Band: when it refers to the Chief and Council, is capitalized.

30. Eleanor Leacock and Richard Lee (eds.), *Politics and History in Band Societies* (New York: Cambridge University Press: 1982), 8, 9.

31. Cardinal and Hildebrandt, *Treaty Elders of Saskatchewan*, 30. Quoting respected

elder, FSIN senator and University of Saskatchewan honorary Degree recipient 2006, Dr. Jimmy Myo.

32. The Indian Act does not apply, or has limited application, to some First Nations, such as the James Bay Cree and Northern Quebec Inuit, because of their new Land Claims Agreements.

33. Frank Cassidy and Robert L. Bish, *Indian Government: Its Meaning in Practice* (Lantzville, BC: Oolichan Books, 1989), 5. This special or nation-to-nation relationship between First Nations and Britain/Canada is rooted in the Royal Proclamation of 1763.

34. Most Bands have one reserve community, but some have more than one community and are called multi-community Bands. Example: Peter Ballantyne Cree Nation has eight communities and Lac La Ronge Indian Band has seven.

35. The administration of the Indian Act is done by the Minister of Indian Affairs and Northern Development.

36. See note 32.

37. Cassidy and Bish, *Indian Government: Its Meaning in Practice*, 41.

38. *Consolidated Native Law Statutes, Regulations and Treaties 1994* (Scarborough, ON: Carswell Thomson Professional Publishing, 1993).

39. Representative democracies (Canada) prescribe competitive elections and elected leadership.

40. *Corbiere* 1999 was a Supreme Court of Canada decision brought about by a Charter of Rights challenge that forced changes to the voting rules under the Indian Act permitting off-reserve members to vote in Band elections. See First Nation websites for elections—roughly estimated that over 50 First Nations are under Band custom election systems in Saskatchewan.

41. BCRs are recognized by the Department of Indian Affairs as formal Chief and Council decisions with the authority to trigger governmental action.

42. It was first called the Prince Albert District Chiefs, then Prince Albert Tribal Council, and now PAGC.

43. PAGC 2006 Population totals 32,881: http://www.pagc.sk.ca/submenu/annual report/pagc_annualreport07.pdf

44. This is slowly changing to one-person-one vote in some provinces, but not in Saskatchewan.

45. Check their websites for details.

46. http:www.mltc.net/

47. http://www.fhqtc.com/programs.php

48. See http://www.pagc.sk.ca/submenu/annualreport/pagc_annreport07.pdf

49. For details, see FSIN website. http://www.fsin.com/aboutfsin/membersoffsin. html

50. Robert A. Innes, "The Socio-Political Influence of the Second World War Saskatchewan Aboriginal Veterans, 1945–1960 (Masters thesis, University of Saskatchewan, 2000), 19.

51. Ibid. Innes describes 1945–50 as a time of "passive participation" by veterans in the political arenas. Few reasons cited included lack of work experience, racism, and problems of readjusting to civilian life. First Nation veterans were denied benefits given to other veterans.

52. Ibid., 16.

53. http://esask.uregina.ca/entry/aboriginal_veterans.html

54. For more details see: "FSIN History by John Tootoosis" www.sicc.sk.ca/heritage/ethnography/fsin/fsin_history_it.html

55. Ibid., 4, 5; www.sicc.sk.ca/heritage/ethnography/fsin/fsin_history_it.html

56. Jean Goodwill and Norma Sluman, *John Tootoosis* (Winnipeg: Pemmican Publications Inc., 1982), 148–49. This was in reference to Frederick Loft, a lieutenant during World War I, who had organized a short-lived national organization called the League of Indians in Ontario (1919) and had inspired much of the earlier First Nation political organizing efforts in Saskatchewan.

57. The AFN is a national political organization representing First Nations consisting of those identified as Bands under the Indian Act. Membership is by Bands as represented by Chiefs. At the AFN annual assemblies, each of the 630 First Nation Chiefs from across the country have seats and voting rights.

58. Goodwill and Sluman, *John Tootoosis*, 187.

59. F. Laurie Barron, *Walking in Indian Moccasins: The Native Policies of Tommy Douglas and the CCF* (Vancouver: UBC Press, 1997), 64.

60. Goodwill and Sluman, *John Tootoosis*, 202. In June 1960, the Provincial Elections Act enabled Saskatchewan First Nations to vote. In July 1960, changes to the provincial Liquor Act allowed First Nations to drink alcohol off reserve.

61. Federation of Saskatchewan Indian Nations, *Federation of Saskatchewan Indian Nations Annual Report 2006* (Saskatoon: FSIN, 2006), 106.

62. Barron, *Walking in Indian Moccasins*, 74.

63. Canadian Native Society of Regina led by Veteran Walter Balhead in mid-1950s; Indian and Métis Friendship Centre in Saskatoon led by Walter Deiter in 1958.

64. See FSIN website for a description of past leaders. http://www.fsin.com/about fsin/pastfsinleaders.html

65. Frideres and Gadacz, *Aboriginal Peoples in Canada*, 333.

66. The WCIP has First Nation political roots in Canada. George Manuel, a Shushwap First Nation from British Columbia, schooled in early First Nation national politics, was instrumental in organizing the first international conference on Indigenous peoples which led to the development of WCIP in 1975. See details in http://www.cwis.org/fwdp/International/wcipinfo.txt

67. See the AFN website. http://www.afn.ca/article.asp?id=59. Following World War II, the NAIB; 1961-NIC; 1968-NIB; 1982-now, AFN.

68. See details. http://www.afn.ca/article.asp?id=51

69. See http://www.sicc.sk.ca/saskindian/a91/sum08.htm

70. Frideres and Gadacz, *Aboriginal Peoples in Canada*, 331–34.

71. See http://www.afn.ca/article.asp?id=57.

72. Métis scholar, the late Dr. Howard Adams, provocatively suggested that treaties represented 'cruel thefts of Aboriginal rights" and that "when Indians hold that treaties as sacred testaments, the process of colonization is complete." See Howard Adams, *Prison of Grass: Canada from a Native Point of View* (Toronto: General Publishing, 1975), 72, 73.

73. See FSIN website. http://www.fsin.com/aboutfsin/index.html

74. Examples include the Saskatchewan Indian Cultural Centre, The First Nations

University of Canada, The Saskatchewan Indian Equity Foundation, and the Saskatchewan Indian Institute of Technologies.

75. FSIN, *Federation of Saskatchewan Indian Nations Annual Report 2006*, 107.

76. See Appendix 1 for the FSIN Legislative Assembly and organizational structure; see FSIN web citations: http://www.fsin.com/legislativeassembly/index.html and http://www.fsin.com/aboutfsin/organizationalchart.html

77. See FSIN website. http://www.fsin.com/executive/index.html

78. http://www.canada.com/saskatoonstarphoenix/news/story.html?id=4b4a1ecd-fd3b-404c-9017-07413a168bab&k=16544

79. Federation of Saskatchewan Indian Nations, *Inherent Right of Self-Government: Self-rule in Education* (Saskatoon: Federation of Saskatchewan Indian Nations, Office of Education, 1994), preamble of political principles developed by the Education Commission.

80. Saskatchewan Indian Federated College, *Facility Proposal, March 1994* (Regina: SIFC, 1994), Introduction.

81. http://www.fsin.com/saskindian/editions/SKIndian_MayJuneEdition_2007_web.pdf

82. FSIN, *Federation of Saskatchewan Indian Nations Annual Report 2006*, 9; also see, http://www.sicc.sk.ca/saskIndian/a82apr04.htm

83. See AFN website. http://www.afn.ca/article.asp?id=59

84. Federation of Saskatchewan Indian Nations, *The History of Treaty Land Entitlement in Saskatchewan* (brochure) (Saskatoon: FSIN, 1992).

85. Adams, *Prison of Grass*, 146.

86. Ibid.

87. See websites of First Nations, Tribal Councils and FSIN.

88. Sebastian Grammon, "Aboriginal Treaties and Canadian Law," in Isaac Thomas (ed.), *Readings in Aboriginal Studies: Volume 5: Aboriginal People and Canadian Law* (Brandon, MB: BearPaw Publishing, 1996), 152.

89. http://www.horizonzero.ca/elderspeak/stories/wisdom.html

APPENDIX 1

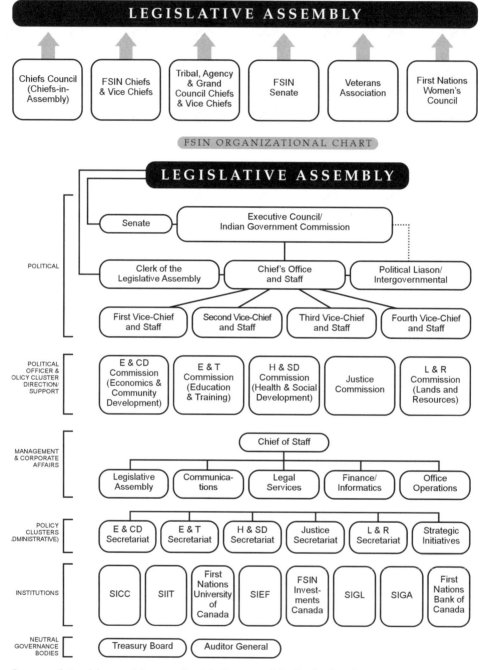

Sources: http://www.fsin.com/legislativeassembly/index.html;
http://www.fsin.com/about_fsin/organizational_chart.html

We Are All Treaty People

David Arnot

When my ancestors came to an area in Canada's North-West Territories that would later become Saskatchewan, they were exercising their treaty right to enter the region. This also applies to your ancestors if they came here from other parts of the world. As descendants of those settlers, you and I have benefited by inheriting their negotiated treaty right to enter the land. And with that right we have inherited certain treaty obligations. Perhaps you are an immigrant to Canada who lives in Saskatchewan. Did you realize that when you moved here you were exercising a treaty right and that you also have treaty obligations? You may be a First Nations person, a descendant of the people who occupied this place from time immemorial and who, in the late 19th century and the beginning of the 20th century, made treaties with representatives of the Crown, the so-called Numbered Treaties, which permitted outsiders to share this land with them. As a First Nations Canadian, you have inherited certain rights and obligations from those treaties and this makes you a treaty person. We are all bound by those treaties and always will be. We are all treaty people.

THE HOPE OF TREATY RENEWAL

While I was Treaty Commissioner for Saskatchewan from 1997 to 2007, I usually dealt with complex matters. Yet, when I talked to people, the question often asked was simple: "Is there hope?" They wanted to know if there was hope for a better relationship between Canada and First Nations. They also wanted to know if there was hope for greater self-sufficiency in First Nations communities and if First Nations could share Canada's prosperity, peace and harmony.

With my experience as Treaty Commissioner I could say there was hope and that it lay in the efforts undertaken by the heirs of the original parties to the treaties—Canada and the Federation of Saskatchewan Indian Nations— who were talking about the social, political and economic relationship outlined in our treaties.

We have seen important changes in the way Canada and First Nations work together. The parties have taken an historic step by seriously discussing their common understanding of their treaty relationship and their common vision of the future. They have gone back to the source of that relationship— the Numbered Treaties—and discussed them from all perspectives, while examining their spiritual, legal, economic, social and political foundations.

When I told people there was hope in the treaties, I was often asked, "What place do treaties that were signed in the 19th century have in the present reality of the 21st century?" After I began working with the treaties, I soon discovered that they have a crucial, although sometimes misunderstood, role in our province. Simply put, a treaty is an agreement between two groups of people to do things for each other in respectful ways, and the Numbered Treaties express what the Crown agreed to do in exchange for access to the land each treaty embraces.

THE DEFINITION OF "TREATY"

What does the word "treaty" mean? How can treaties signed a century or more ago continue to impose obligations or confer rights today? One definition of "treaty" is that it is a contract. We all know what a contract is: I agree to build a house for you and you agree to pay me a negotiated sum of money. However, that's as far as it goes. If the house doesn't collapse within a year and your cheque is good, the contract will be fulfilled and has no lasting effect. In no event could it be invoked after 100 or so years have gone by.

Another definition of "treaty" is that it is a formal contract or agreement negotiated between countries, sovereigns or other political entities. While this brings us closer to what actually occurred between First Nations and the Crown, the definition leaves much to be desired. Treaties of this nature are either utilitarian or determine the destiny of a state defeated in war. Examples of the first sort are the North American Free Trade Agreement and the Nuclear Non-Proliferation Treaty. They remain in force only as long as the parties to them feel they are being served by their provisions. As for treaties made following a war, or peace treaties, one that readily comes to mind is the 1919 Treaty of Versailles, which addressed the fate of Germany after its defeat in World War I. However, the Treaty of Versailles was written by the victors— France, Britain, Italy and the United States—without participation of the German government. The Germans were forced to accept it or face Allied occupation. This was not a treaty as defined above, but a diktat. And as later events demonstrated, it had only temporary effect.

The Numbered Treaties are unique because they elude conventional definitions and notions. They are not contracts because they are not limited by time—they endure in perpetuity. They may be viewed as utilitarian because both parties stood to benefit from them; however, unlike conventional treaties of this kind, the Numbered Treaties cannot be abrogated by either party for any reason. Furthermore, so-called peace treaties have nothing in common with our Numbered Treaties because there was no war between First Nations and the Crown, and neither party negotiated from a position of advantage or vulnerability. Canada's treaties have been described by our courts as *sui generis* or unique.

THE BASIS OF TREATIES

There was a simple basis for the treaties. First Nations possessed territory the Crown wanted settled with European farmers, and because First Nations realized they could benefit from European technology, they were willing to accept these farmers if certain conditions were met. The various economic benefits offered during negotiations satisfied First Nations representatives and persuaded them to sign the treaties that allowed European settlement. However, not all of these perceived benefits were documented; an omission perhaps not considered significant at the time because First Nations chiefs and headmen were unable to read and write.

More important than what was actually said or written, the treaties embody a spirit of reciprocity that both sides understood during their discussions. Moreover, the treaties were less about barter and more about accommodation and trust—a harmonious sharing of a vast and bountiful land. First Nations were promised perpetual and unconditional use of their realm if they chose to continue their hunter-gatherer traditions, or they could adopt agriculture like the settlers and receive the required tutoring and resources. While there is no evidence that Crown negotiators were guilty of sharp practice, this spirit of reciprocity seems to have been soon forgotten by the ministers of the Crown. It endures in the consciousness of First Nations.

THE TREATIES AS COVENANTS

Because the conventional characterizations of "treaty" seem inadequate for what was agreed between First Nations and the Crown, I prefer to use "covenant" and identify treaty implementation as fulfilling the covenant. The word has biblical origins and religious communities use it to describe the bond between God and humanity. In common law a covenant is distinguished from an ordinary contract by a seal, which symbolizes an unusual solemnity in the promises made. It is notable that at the conclusion of each treaty negotiation all parties shared a pipe. To First Nations the pipe ceremony had the same significance that the seal had for Europeans. The presence of missionaries lent more solemnity to these occasions. The Crown relied on missionaries to persuade First Nations leaders to accept treaties, and missionaries sat with the Crown's party during negotiations. The practice confirmed the Crown's solemn perspective on the treaties.

Historically, a covenant described a formal promise made under oath or an agreement that would survive forever. Religious ceremonies can forge a covenant between two parties and God. With their binding nature of obligations and promises, those covenants may be compared to the Numbered Treaties, especially if God is put in the picture. As Treaty 4 Saulteaux Elder Danny Musqua said: "We made a covenant with Her Majesty's government, and a covenant is not just a relationship between people, it's a relationship between three parties, you (the Crown) and me (First Nations) and the Creator." Words such as "covenant," "relationship" and "partnership" reveal how First Nations view the treaties and express their hope that they will be eventually fulfilled. There is no doubt that First Nations hold the treaties and the treaty relationship as sacred covenants.

THE HISTORY OF TREATIES IN CANADA

The history of Crown-First Nations treaties is unique. After the conquest of New France in 1763 it was necessary for Britain to win the trust of its new colony's occupants—the First Nations. Therefore, a Royal Proclamation published over the name of George III prohibited individuals from purchasing land from First Nations. The proclamation stipulated that First Nations land could only be voluntarily ceded to the Crown in a public assembly. This set a precedent in British law that made mutual agreement or treaty the basis for acquiring access to First Nations land. In regions without a legislature, as was the case with British North America at the time, a Royal Proclamation had the force of a statute.

The Proclamation is viewed by many First Nations as their Magna Carta for inherent rights: it protected First Nations lands and recognized First Nations peoples as nations. It established that a treaty with the Crown was the sole means by which the British could acquire land and excluded private interests from such transactions. This legal framework was followed in western Canada with the Numbered Treaties.

Treaty making was nothing new for the Crown or for First Nations. The British had long employed treaties when acquiring new territories, thereby creating military and economic allies, as well as peaceful relations with other nations. First Nations also had a long tradition of forging new relations through treaty. And both sides believed the treaties between them were meant to secure an eternal relationship. During Treaty 6 negotiations at Fort Carlton, August 18, 1876, Alexander Morris, Canada's treaty commissioner, said: "What I trust and hope we will do is not for today or tomorrow only; what I will promise, and what I believe and hope you will take, is to last as long as that sun shines and yonder river flows." These words reflect the world view of First Nations; however, they were spoken by Morris to convey the idea that treaties were not simple land sales, but a means to providing a bridge to future political, economic and social relations between First Nations and settlers. Throughout the 19th century and into the 20th century, the Crown made some 67 treaties with First Nations, in most cases, to gain access to their land.

A CHALLENGE FOR A NEW NATION

In Western Canada relations between First Nations and Europeans developed as the fur trade expanded. The Hudson's Bay Company, established by charter in 1670, played a principal role. Agents for the company developed alliances with First Nations and adopted their protocols. In 1870, three years after Confederation, Canada purchased Rupert's Land, later designated as the North-West Territories, from the Hudson's Bay Company for 300,000 British pounds. It should not surprise the reader that the sale angered First Nations leaders. How, they wondered, had this property changed hands without their assent? And why didn't they collect the money? Conflict was the outcome. Government surveyors were stopped and non-First Nations turned away, preventing settlement. Peace and security were in peril. Meanwhile, the expanding United States of America was eyeing the territory hungrily. This newly acquired land, which would later become the Prairie Provinces, presented a challenge to the Canadian government. To forestall US annexation, sovereignty had to be asserted promptly by way of settlement with Europeans and construction of a transcontinental railway; and to do either required access to the region.

In its westward extension, the US government waged wars with indigenous occupants of unsettled territory. However, these wars were costly and almost bankrupted Washington. Of this the Canadian government was aware, so it chose a peaceful approach—making treaty. Because of their rapidly changing economic circumstances, First Nations were amenable. Commercial harvesting of buffalo and other wildlife was impacting their livelihood and threatening the way they lived. Fur prices were in decline. Their health suffered from European diseases for which they had no immunity. First Nations were seeking the means and mechanisms to enter the new economy. They realized that for any chance of a successful future they had to work with the newcomers and learn their ways; they had to gain new skills, such as farming. But they wanted to make an economic transition without the assimilation of their culture. A treaty relationship, they believed, was a path to economic advancement while affording protection of their interests and their way of life. And like the Canadian government, they, too, wanted peace above all.

Throughout treaty negotiations, First Nations leaders emphasized their need for education. They viewed agriculture as the means to sustaining future generations. Oral tradition indicates they were willing to share their land in return for the Queen's benevolence and protection. However, Canada needed unfettered control to bolster its sovereignty and facilitate settlement. The treaties were a centrepiece of Sir John A. Macdonald's National Policy.

As early as 1857, Chief Peguis expressed concern about the impact of settlement. He wrote to the Aborigines Protection Society in England that before whites "take possession of our lands we wish that a fair and mutually advantageous treaty be entered into with my tribe."

The principle of mutual advantage was put forward by Chief Mawedopenais during the 1873 negotiations for Treaty 3, covering part of present-day Manitoba and Ontario:

> All this is our property where you have come. … This is what
> we think, that the Great Spirit has planted us on this ground
> where we are, as you were where you came from. … Our

hands are poor but our heads are rich, and it is riches that we
ask so that we may be able to support our families as long as
the sun rises and the water runs.

… The sound of the rustling of the gold is under my feet where I
stand; we have a rich country; it is the Great Spirit who gave us
this; where we stand upon is the Indians' property, and
belongs to them.

Commissioner Morris urged chiefs and headmen to think of the future: "I only
ask you to think of yourselves, and your families, and for your children and
children's children."

SASKATCHEWAN'S UNFULFILLED TREATIES

Prairie Treaties 4, 5 and 6 were negotiated successively in 1874, 1875 and 1876.
The Canadian government viewed these three treaties as crucial because they
would permit settlement along the Saskatchewan River and its tributaries.
Northern Treaties 8 and 10 were negotiated in 1899 and 1906. The discovery of
gold in the Yukon and the ensuing expansion of exploration and mining was
the precipitating feature in Canada's move for treaty making in the Treaty 8
territory. The government wanted Treaty 10 because the new province of
Saskatchewan exceeded the boundaries of the former treaties. Northern First
Nations, apprehensive that their way of life would be threatened and their
livelihood impaired, were told they would be as free to hunt and fish after
signing the treaty as they would be if there had been no treaty; there would be
no interference in these activities, they were promised.

Unfortunately, these promises, along with others made to First Nations
during treaty negotiations, were not honoured. This is Canada's national
shame. First Nations were promised sharing and fairness. They were told that
if settlers were allowed onto their land, all people would benefit. Not only
would First Nations survive, they would prosper, and the benefits created by
the coming together of two ways of life would be shared. This simply did not
happen and the failure of Canada to keep these promises has left profound
scars.

The European settlers formed communities and enjoyed land ownership
and religious freedom, practices usually denied in their homelands. Ironically,
in this New World these basic human rights were denied to First Nations. The
good treaty intentions of the Crown were disregarded and new strategies
enforced pursuant to a paternalistic federal Indian Act. Assimilation, a policy
doomed to fail both First Nations and other Canadians, became Ottawa's
ambition. This policy prohibited First Nations spiritual rituals and inspired
the iniquitous residential schools that fractured their families.

While settlers enjoyed unimagined economic freedom, any First Nations member
attempting to farm required a permit from an Indian agent to buy, sell or lease land,
livestock, implements and produce. Profits were kept and administered by the agents.
Until it was removed from the Indian Act in 1951, a pass system restricted First

Nations to their reserves. Anyone wanting to leave had to get a pass from the Indian agent. A First Nations person absent without a pass was classified as a criminal. Before that same year, First Nations people could not hire a lawyer to bring claims against the Crown. They were given the right to vote in 1960.

THE CONSEQUENCES OF REPRESSION

Repression, economic marginalization and attempted compulsory assimilation have had significant consequences. First Nations are an important segment of Saskatchewan, but bear the results of generations of mistreatment— pathetic economic prospects, social isolation, cultural impairment and bad health. The majority of the First Nations population today is young and prolific relative to other Saskatchewan citizens. They want to reach a basic level of education the rest of us take for granted, while holding onto heritage languages and cultures, absorbing the teachings of their Elders, creating practical governance, achieving economic independence and becoming healthy, not only individually, but as families and communities. They want to end violence and incarceration. They want self-esteem and respect, both from their fellow First Nations citizens and the rest of Saskatchewan's people.

The province has recently acquired greater prosperity and confidence than its inhabitants could ever imagine, but First Nations living conditions in Saskatchewan, as in other parts of Canada, remain in Majority World circumstances. It is clear that these conditions are not the fault of First Nations; nor are they accidents of history. They are, for the most part, the consequence of consistent refusal by federal officials in the early days to honour treaty promises and of official imposition of misguided policies devised at the highest levels of government.

Demography determines destiny. It is imperative that all governments— federal, provincial and First Nations—ensure that Saskatchewan's large cohort of First Nations students receive education equivalent to what their ancestors were promised in the 19th century, so they can participate effectively in the economy of the 21st century. This is fundamental to a prosperous future in Saskatchewan. All parties share in the blame for the failures of the past.

We must move beyond blame to develop strategic policies and programs to remedy this unconscionable situation. While contemporary governments have recognized this problem, they have continuously failed to commit the necessary resources to create the required education outcomes.

THE TREATIES AND THE CONSTITUTION

Throughout most of the 20th century, as the plight of First Nations gradually deteriorated, the treaties that were supposed to help them slid into disrepute and were all but forgotten. "By the late 1960s, Aboriginal claims were not even recognized by the federal government as having any legal status," the Supreme Court of Canada observed in its 1990 landmark judgment in *Sparrow v. The Queen.* The case was a turning point for the neglected treaties and would not have been possible had it not been for Section 35 of the Constitution Act 1982, which embedded recognition of First Nations treaty rights in Canada's new constitution. The Supreme Court's reliance on Section 35, in this and other cases in the 1990s, forced lower courts to pay heed to the Constitution Act when hearing First Nations cases.

Then, in 1998, the Canadian government, in its communiqué *Gathering Strength*—a response to the report of the Royal Commission on Aboriginal Peoples—acknowledged significantly:

> • That treaties between the Crown and First Nations are the basic building blocks in the creation of our country; and

> • That a vision for the future should build on the recognition of the rights of Aboriginal peoples and on the treaty relationship.

THE OFFICE OF THE TREATY COMMISSIONER

By this time, the Office of the Treaty Commissioner (OTC) had been established in Saskatchewan by an Order of the Governor in Council, effective January 1, 1997. The office was conceived by the treaty parties to act as a neutral body while filling two roles:

> 1. Advance the treaty process; and

> 2. Use public education to enhance greater understanding and harmony.

The method was designated the "made in Saskatchewan approach" to treaty resolution because both Canada and the Federation of Saskatchewan Indian Nations (FSIN) voluntarily dedicated themselves to dialogue rather than litigation. Both the FSIN and Canada saw the Exploratory Treaty Table as an impartial forum where treaties could be explored; others saw it as a model for Canada.

To advance the treaty process, the OTC oversaw discussions at the Exploratory Treaty Table meant to build consensus between the FSIN, the Government of Canada and the Government of Saskatchewan. The goal was to determine the original spirit and intent of the treaties and their meaning in today's context. The parties agreed that the treaties are not confined to the written text and that they cannot be fully understood without consulting both oral and written First Nations history. They also agreed on the importance of the honour of the Crown, which can be interpreted as the capacity of Canadians to exemplify the highest moral standard.

It was the first time since the treaties were concluded that the parties discussed them. As facilitator, I strived to be independent and impartial. The FSIN, as the representative of the First Nations signatories, stressed it was necessary for it to convey how it envisioned the treaty relationship, how it understood treaty history, how it viewed the purpose of treaty making, and how it interpreted the objectives of the signing parties. The FSIN relied on Elders' oral history for an overview of treaty making in terms of original intentions, understandings and commitments. The FSIN expressed the view that its forebears made treaties with the Crown to secure a good future for their descendants, but that they also intended to go on governing themselves, using laws handed down by the Creator. They also expected to earn their living and provide for their material and spiritual needs; and they imagined they would live in brotherhood and peace with the settlers.

TREATIES IN THE COURT OF PUBLIC OPINION

In addition to advancing the treaty process, the OTC's mandate was to develop better harmony between First Nations and others by creating greater public awareness of treaty issues. No matter how successful treaty negotiations are, the results could be meaningless unless they receive widespread support from Saskatchewan citizens. The OTC built its public education program on the premise that knowledge is a foundation for mutual respect. Our goal was to create awareness and understanding about treaties through public education. When I recall my school days in this province, I find it strange how we had to study foreign treaties, such as Versailles, while treaties affecting Saskatchewan were not on the curriculum. So we took the view that a good place to start is in the schools. In 2002, the OTC and the teachers of Saskatchewan produced the teachers' resource kit *Teaching Treaties in the Classroom*, which was distributed to all provincial schools, including those on First Nations, for grades seven to twelve. The 4,000 teachers who were trained to teach treaties constitute an army of change agents in the province. Their ranks are increased each year as young people graduate from high school with a better understanding of our history. I feel that if students are taught about treaties in a balanced and neutral manner it will ultimately go a long way toward building peace and harmony among the people of Saskatchewan. Research shows that exposure to treaty information leads to better understanding of the treaty relationship.

As well as the teachers' resource kit, the OTC produced other books, texts and videos on treaties. It created a speakers bureau with 40 volunteers, many of them First Nations, to talk about the treaties and the treaty relationship to students and other groups. More than 60,000 people have heard them. The OTC established the Treaty Learning Network, made up of 26 Elders and 111 teachers trained in treaty education, which has been supported by Saskatchewan Learning, the school divisions and First Nations schools.

FIRST STEPS IN UNDERSTANDING

The meaning of the treaties in today's context is not confined to their written text. To understand their spirit and intent and capture their original context and meaning we must look to First Nations oral history. To do this, the OTC commissioned two research projects. The first was conducted by the late

Harold Cardinal and Walter Hildebrandt, who focused on the oral history of
First Nations Elders in Saskatchewan. The Elders were asked to help answer
the question "What was the motivation, intention and expectation for First
Nations when they entered into the treaties?" The answer is contained in the
book *Treaty Elders of Saskatchewan: Our Dream is That Our Peoples Will One Day
Be Clearly Recognized as Nations*, published by the University of Calgary Press
in 2000. To find the answer the researchers met with some 160 Elders during
20 days of discussion in more than nine communities throughout
Saskatchewan. Much of the information obtained had never been shared with
non-Aboriginal people. The First Nations Elders discussed nine fundamental
principles that guide First Nations culture, worldview and treaty making
foundations. I believe that this book represents a milestone achievement
because it allows the non-Aboriginal world to understand the First Nations
perspective and world view for the first time. This Elders' recording of the
First Nations cultural foundations is a critical contribution, which will serve
all Canadians far into the future.

The second research project was conducted by Professor Jim Miller of the
University of Saskatchewan, Professor Frank Tough of the University of
Alberta and Professor Arthur Ray of the University of British Columbia. Their
work, *Bounty and Benevolence: A History of Saskatchewan Treaties* was published
by McGill-Queen's University Press, also in 2000. We asked them to explore
the same question, "What was the motivation, intention and expectation of the
Government of Canada when it entered into the Numbered Treaties?" They
responded with a compelling in-depth history of the Saskatchewan treaties,
captured for the first time. This work corroborates First Nations belief that the
treaties were principally about a relationship between peoples. This book
makes it easy to understand why the First Nations expected that the treaty
relationship between themselves and the Government of Canada would be
similar to the one they enjoyed with the Hudson's Bay Company. *Bounty and
Benevolence* makes it clear First Nations expected the treaty relationship with
the government to be reciprocal and based on mutual respect. This book
demonstrates that both sides were motivated by good intentions.
Unfortunately, those good intentions and expectations have not been realized.

These two major research projects were fundamental to the discussions at
the Exploratory Treaty Table, the development of the Statement of Treaty
Issues and the public education materials generated by the OTC.

TREATIES AS A BRIDGE TO THE FUTURE

After 18 months of discussion, the OTC produced *Treaties as a Bridge to the
Future*, a document identifying understandings reached by the parties. They
agreed upon these principles:

> • Treaties created a fundamental political relationship
> between Treaty First Nations and the Crown. Treaties gave
> shape to this relationship, establishing obligations and
> expectations on both sides.

• The treaties are solemn agreements. That acknowledgement is a fundamental treaty principle.

• The treaty relationship was founded on the ideas of mutual respect and mutual benefit. Both treaty partners hoped to gain something from the treaties. They wanted to share the land peacefully and respect each other's ways of living.

• Treaty making reflected the principles of the honour of the Crown and the honour of Treaty First Nations in maintaining the treaty relationship. The parties expect to resolve their differences through discussion in the treaty relationship.

• Canada and Treaty First Nations can make agreements whereby Treaty First Nations exercise governance and jurisdiction over their lands and people.

• The participation of the Government of Saskatchewan is needed to reach agreements on First Nations governance and jurisdiction issues.

The parties reached these understandings for three principal reasons:

1. When work began, they were encouraged to consider their interests, both short and long term, and to set aside treaty positions while focusing on shared understanding of the meaning of the treaty relationship.

2. First Nations Elders provided wisdom, guidance and prayers which contributed to the success of these initial discussions.

3. The parties embraced the following principles in Exploratory Treaty Table discussions:

  • Mutual recognition, respect, reciprocity and responsibility.

  • Respect for ethical and honourable conduct.

  • Approaching the Treaty Table as partners.

  • Respect for each other and the OTC.

  • Candour and good faith in oral and written submissions to the OTC.

  • Sharing information and expertise without undue restrictions.

  • Importance of flexibility and need to avoid legal disputes.

  • First Nations have distinct perspectives, rooted in culture and embodied in language.

• Elders are keepers and transmitters of oral histories and must play an integral role.

• Knowledge transmitted orally by First Nations must be accepted as a valuable resource along with documents and other evidence.

This approach to treaty implementation is also flexible. The original 1996 mandate for the OTC identified seven areas for discussion, but allowed parties to add other issues. Accordingly, in 1999 the Elders insisted, and the parties agreed, that lands and resources be included. And in the same year, the Indian Affairs Minister and the chief of the FSIN asked the OTC to add discussions between the Government of Canada and the Dakota and Lakota First Nations in Saskatchewan regarding a treaty adhesion. Four Dakota and Lakota First Nations with reserve lands inside the boundaries of Treaty 4 and Treaty 6 have never negotiated or adhered to any treaty with the Crown.

Treaty adhesions are as important as the treaties themselves. First Nations who sign adhesions incur the same rights and obligations as the original treaty parties. Adhesions were signed throughout treaty areas for many years by bands not present at the original negotiations.

THE NEED FOR CONSTRUCTIVE, RESPECTFUL DIALOGUE

In Canada, we have seen primarily three ways by which First Nations issues have been approached: confrontation, litigation or co-operation. The outcomes of confrontation, whether the standoff at Oka, the violence at Ipperwash, the blockades in British Columbia and Ontario, or the lobster dispute in New Brunswick, are well-known. There are no winners.

We all know the cost and outcomes of legal action where litigants can spend many years in courtroom disputes that result in little satisfaction for either party.

We need to work together. We need to promote co-operation and recognize our common interests. My experience at the OTC leads me to firmly believe that the treaty parties need a political forum, chaired by an independent, arms-length, neutral facilitator who can host discussions and commission research. Only in such a forum will the way be found to implement the treaties in the modern context. The required dialogue must be based on solid information, stripped of myth, rhetoric, misconception and misunderstanding. Such a forum could foster better understanding between the parties and lead to constructive solutions, to the benefit of all parties to the treaties.

LEGISLATURE CENTENARY HONOURS FIRST NATIONS

When the Saskatchewan Legislature commemorated its centenary on March 29, 2006, the participation of First Nations representatives made the celebration a historically significant event. During a day of solemnity and ceremony, a fully beaded moose hide runner for the Speaker's table and a

beaver pelt pillow for the Speaker's Mace were presented by the province's
First Nations. The runner beadwork depicts the sun, grass and river,
representing the covenant between the Crown and First Nations with the
Creator as witness.

Lieutenant-Governor Lynda Haverstock, in accepting the gift, said: "As we
begin our second century as a province we are reminded of our past, of the
noble intentions of our ancestors who chose co-operation over conflict. They
were people of sacrifice and of vision, and it is thanks to them that our present and future are so full of promise."

In my remarks, I noted the ceremony recognized that the treaty relationship binds us all together as we live on the land of Saskatchewan. I acknowledged that Treaties 2, 4, 5, 6, 8 and 10 cover every square metre of our province
with a promise that goes with that sacred blanket. The promise is that we will
work together for mutual benefit out of mutual respect and live in harmony.
The treaties are sacred covenants that blanket our province. Our shared
history has many difficulties, I said. First Nations have suffered because the
treaties were not implemented according to the spirit and intent of the treaties.
We must take a shared responsibility to move forward, to ensure that First
Nations have an equal opportunity to succeed, to use our common values and
to build a positive future based on the treaty relationship.

The ceremony was designed to honour the First Nations contribution to
Saskatchewan, to honour the treaties and to honour the treaty relationship.
The day began with Elders conducting a pipe ceremony in the Legislative
Chamber; it was the first time pipes were raised there. The Red Dog Singers
from Star Blanket First Nation heralded a grand entry led by Harvey
Thunderchild carrying the Eagle Staff of the FSIN and the Sergeant-at-Arms
carrying the Mace. Behind them were Lieutenant-Governor Lynda
Haverstock, Chief Alphonse Bird of the FSIN, myself as Treaty Commissioner,
Speaker Myron Kowalsky, Premier Lorne Calvert, Opposition Leader Brad
Wall, Elders, veterans, chiefs, FSIN vice-chiefs and all members of the
Legislative Assembly.

At the close of the event, Speaker Kowalsky said:

> This was a perfect day to honour the First Nations treaty rela-
> tionship in Saskatchewan. It was exactly 100 years ago today
> that we marked the beginning of the Saskatchewan
> Legislature. One hundred years ago there was little interaction
> between First Nations and this Legislative Assembly; much
> has changed. We are into an era of interdependence, not isola-
> tion. Our future lies in partnerships. It is my hope that today's
> ceremony will be marked as a day of relationship renewal and
> respect.

TREATY IMPLEMENTATION

Canada and the FSIN asked the OTC in July 2005 to produce a report that
answers the question: How do you implement the treaties in a modern

context? By asking this question, Canada was admitting that the treaties had not been properly implemented. The resulting report, *Treaty Implementation: Fulfilling the Covenant*, was published in February 2007 (distributed by Purich Publishing). In it, the OTC concludes that treaty implementation has not occurred although there has been some recent progress; moreover, an examination of the history of the last 100 or more years reveals implementation has been overtly stymied. The report examines the importance of treaty implementation to Saskatchewan's economy and finds it to be critical. Furthermore, an analysis of the legal record on First Nations claims shows the courts have consistently ruled in their favour and against government. The report contends that the performance of Canada, FSIN and Saskatchewan in treaty implementation is poorly organized and unfocused. I suggest in the report a change in political commitment is needed to ensure implementation. Finally, the report provides a strategic plan to move the implementation agenda ahead.

We asked: What is treaty implementation? We answered: It is fulfilling the covenant made when treaties were signed. What was that covenant? It was the promise to reconcile differences between First Nations and the Queen through a treaty relationship made before the Creator in the name of the Queen and in the name of First Nations.

There are four pillars to reconciliation:

> 1. Political. Reconciling two sovereignties is not something new to either Canadians or First Nations; it is the basis of federalism. This reconciliation has not been achieved, but it must be to fulfill the covenant and the treaty relationship.

> 2. Legal. Reconciling two legal systems would define First Nations rights in the Canadian context.

> 3. Socioeconomic. First Nations expected the treaties would reconcile their traditional economy with the economy of the settlers. More must be done on this for full treaty implementation.

> 4. Spiritual. By entering into treaties, First Nations and the Queen promised to respect each other's culture, spirituality and way of life, and to live in harmony.

In contradiction to the promise and intent of the treaties, First Nations have been excluded from the new society, the report finds. Only through legal pressure based on its 1982 Constitution has Canada abandoned policies of assimilation in favour of treaty implementation. However, despite this new attitude, neither party is adequately prepared to even address the issues.

THE FOUNDATION FOR HARMONY

When you distill the treaties to their core value they offer a blueprint for harmony. Treaty implementation is about justice in the truest sense of the word. The treaties were designed to answer two salient questions:

1. How are we going to live together in harmony?

2. How are First Nations going to make the transition to the new economy?

The principles that underlie the treaty relationship are the basis for that blueprint. It is a model for justice that is as good today as the day the treaties were made.

What we desperately need in Saskatchewan is harmony; the harmony that a proper implementation of the treaty relationship offers. Before we can achieve harmony we need to have respect between the treaty parties. Before we can achieve respect we need to have understanding. Before we can achieve understanding we need knowledge. Knowledge comes from education. Education is the foundation for harmony.

Through education it is possible to understand First Nations grievances concerning the lack of treaty implementation. These grievances must be understood and acknowledged before we can bridge to the future. Constructive solutions cannot be built on shame, blame and guilt. They must be built on the solid treaty principles of mutual benefit and mutual respect.

Just as Alexander Morris had hope, I also have hope. I have hope for a better partnership, a better relationship between all treaty Canadians. I have hope that the First Nations will share in the prosperity, peace and harmony that is the very essence of life in Canada.

I hope that the treaty relationship will find its rightful place in the Canadian state. I hope that the covenants made in the treaties will be implemented according to the spirit and intent of the original treaty parties.

Saskatchewan Métis Governance Priorities: Nationhood and Cultural Identity

Marilyn Poitras

> We urge federal, provincial and territorial governments to proceed rapidly with nation recognition so that Métis nation(s) can negotiate treaties or accords in the same manner as other Aboriginal peoples. These would specify the powers of their governments, the extent of their land base, the compensation owing to them for past injustices, their Aboriginal rights (such as the right to hunt, fish and trap on Crown land in all seasons), and the nature of their fiscal arrangements with other governments. These negotiations will be neither quick nor easy—all the more reason why they should begin now.
>
> — Royal Commission on Aboriginal People 1996

Twelve years after the most comprehensive study on the position of Aboriginal people in Canada, Métis people are still looking for the door to the room where a discussion on Métis Nationhood will take place. Almost 140 years after Riel's provisional government created a list of rights for the Métis, which included land, language and political recognition, they are still chased across the prairie, more elusive than the buffalo ever were. Over the generations, the Métis in Saskatchewan have organized and reorganized in an effort to participate finally as equals among nations in Canada, and the rebirthing of a structure to represent and to serve the Métis continues today.

The question of how the Métis government moves forward in Saskatchewan is on the minds of those who have participated in the many Métis government incarnations over the years, and also on the minds of many people who are just curious about Métis politics. With some progress having been made in the elections process, there is currently room to move ahead on other governance fronts, and to make positive change in areas which have been neglected due to the vast amount of time and energy that has gone into the election issue. Elections were never the only issue facing the Métis in Saskatchewan, but because they affected everything they took centre stage. The election issue affected literally every aspect of Métis governance from accountability to capacity, to funding, to programs and services, and, ultimately, to transparency. The issues faced by Métis people organizing politically are further complicated by the current level of financial dependency on federal and provincial governments. One of the most obvious repercussions of the Saskatchewan Métis election crisis that demonstrated governmental dependency was the fact that funding from both levels of government was inaccessible to the MNS during the struggle for a transparent election process. This essentially halted many services across the province, causing problems in remote and rural areas in particular.

HISTORY OF THE SASKATCHEWAN MÉTIS POLITICAL PROCESS

The development of Métis political structures is as diverse as the Métis culture. These structures have changed and evolved to where, in Saskatchewan, we have a provincial organization funded by federal and provincial agreements through non-profit corporate-like structures. The original Métis political structures started within matrilocal communities and Buffalo Hunt Councils. Traditional Buffalo Hunt Councils used the gifts and strengths of an individual during the hunt in a manner that was consistent with success of a hunt. Therefore, leadership was not only shared, it even rotated within the day or the hunt. The leader for the day could have appointed others in the evening or over certain parts of the hunt, thus constantly grooming other leaders in the process. The Council was made up of family heads where decisions were made and leaders selected for hunts and for daily living within the Métis settlements. Old and young spent time together and women not only had roles, they were regarded as important, respected leaders as well.

On the prairies, when the focus for the Métis moved from economic survival based on the fur trade to political survival within the evolving new world of the late 1800s, a different kind of leadership was fashioned and the now famous Riel Rebellion set the stage for future relations between the Métis, the Indians and the federal government—a legacy that lasts today. The new government of Riel's time was a provisional government in response to the settlement of the West, the loss of land and resources through the sale of the land by the Hudson Bay Company, and the need to unite as a Nation through common cultural practices, language and religion. At that time—the late 1860s—this democratic-like structure was designed to meet the Dominion government head on and allow the Métis to develop a land base, protect their language, and to participate within the larger, Dominion government.

When the Hudson Bay Company sold land to the Dominion of Canada that was actually Aboriginal land or land under Indian title—land which the Hudson Bay Company had never bought, fought for, or owned—that was when the Métis could see the writing on the wall in terms of their own political future. Treaties were negotiated—some of which included Métis—and the crude idea of scrip for Métis as a means of extinguishing their claims to their land was hanging in the balance. At that time, everyone, all races, fought for a legitimate connection to land, through spirit, through existence, or through a paper conquest. Settlement was on its way, and everyone knew what was at stake: the land. The Métis unrest arose out of this climate of settlement and treaty making in which the Métis felt their way of life, of self-determination, of economic self-reliance, and of living with the land was threatened. The

"Métis issue" in the West had to be settled and this was the role that the Rebellion of 1885 was intended to serve. The Métis National Committee, which eventually became Riel's provisional government, never did take a seat in the House of Commons as it had demanded. However, political status, representation, language and land remain today the issues that consume the Métis and remain unresolved.

After the Rebellion and the huge losses for the Métis, many dispersed to deal with the aftermath, both political and personal, and to get on with life and family. With the disappearance of the Buffalo Hunt Councils, various Métis governance structures arose from the ashes in an effort to find a structure that would embody Métis Nationhood. Organizations and societies erupted from the numerous Métis communities, which included not only established villages and rural communities, but also, road allowance people, folks living in the bush and urbanized Métis. In Saskatchewan, northern Métis people were represented by the Métis Association of Saskatchewan that was founded in the 1960s. In the southern part of Saskatchewan, the Métis were represented by the Saskatchewan Métis Society founded in 1941. Métis alliances eventually resulted in the Métis Society of Saskatchewan—the MSS—that now represents Métis people throughout the province. For a time in the mid- to late 1900s, Métis people in the province were loosely organized with people deemed to be Non-Status Indians (through the loss of status via enfranchisement, marrying outside the Nation or simply being missed on the list when enumeration was completed) to push common political objectives. Both groups were represented by the Association of Métis and Non-Status Indians of Saskatchewan, which was created in the mid-1970s and which again split into two separate organizations in 1988 to leave each group in a better political position to negotiate self-government. The internal politics were such that a new organization had to be born if advancement was to be achieved; thus, the birth of the Métis Nation-Saskatchewan.

Today, the Métis Nation-Saskatchewan has an executive with a President, a Vice-President, a Secretary and a Treasurer, along with twelve Regional Directors. Within each region, there are smaller, local units of government, each with an elected executive. This provincial structure fits, along with the other Métis provincial structures, into the organization that represents the Métis at a national level—the Métis National Council.

LEADERSHIP AND LEGITIMACY

Early in 2000, Métis people in Saskatchewan began to turn away from many Métis governmental processes, from elections to programs and service delivery, which they felt were not reliable. They turned to the federal and provincial governments to ask for, even demand, assistance in establishing an independent election process. In 2007, the federal and provincial governments agreed, along with the Métis National Council, that an election with reliable results was necessary. Just prior to that time, both federal and provincial funding to the Métis Nation-Saskatchewan (MNS) had been cut off. This resulted

from the fact that a governing body had declared itself the Métis elected government despite one report, which held that the election that had placed them
in power was faulty. Two further election reports reflected concerns over
internal corruption issues within the MNS itself and identified many issues
that needed to be addressed in order for the Nation to right itself. Most programs and services for the Métis slowed to a near halt. Despite estimates indicating that there were between 40,000 and 80,000 Métis in the province, the
Métis voting population was slowly diminishing. The fund created after the
Powley decision for recognition of Métis hunting rights, and available through
the federal government, was accessible by other Métis governments at that
time, but could not be accessed by the MNS because of the election issue.
Finally, people were tired of the fighting over the election issue.

In 2008, an election was held after a special general assembly of the MNS
agreed to have the election run outside the parameters of the Métis Nations
Saskatchewan Constitution. What this essentially meant was that the election
could be held outside the powers of the MNS Senate, whose jurisdiction in
elections covers running the office, selecting the Chief Electoral Officer, as well
as appeals. Ultimately, the election was a double-edged sword. Although it
allowed for fairly elected leadership to emerge, it also left Métis nationhood
and cultural identity an open question.

Now that the election is over, with some 5,000 voters having participated,
and with the appeals processes now complete, people are waiting to see where
the new government of the Métis Nation in Saskatchewan will focus its attention. Will this new government continue to focus on issues that have plagued
the Métis since before the Rebellion and look for legitimacy within the
Canadian political processes? What of a land base, or lack of a land base? Will
there be pressure brought to bear on other levels of government to recognize
the need for the Métis to participate in the development, or stewardship of
natural resources? What will be the interplay between the provincial and the
national Métis governments, particularly in light of the fact that the national
Métis organization has had its own growing pains in terms of representation
and legitimacy? Will internal government structures be revamped to move
away from a non-profit corporations model and move toward a structure that
is more in keeping with Métis nationhood? Will the Locals—originally formed
of family heads who held decision-making authority—regain authority and
be held accountable or will they remain reduced to delivering services and
programs? Rather than constantly looking for nationhood, can the MNS actually be the embodiment of a nation?

The Métis in Saskatchewan are at an important crossroads. Is the Nation
important enough, strong enough to evolve into a Nation that holds value for
all of the Métis in Saskatchewan? The reality is that the Métis population is
very diverse. Out of this diversity come regional issues. There are long-standing north and south demands for attention and recognition within the MNS.
There are large rural pockets of Métis here and there throughout the province
at the same time as there are large urban Métis populations. Some are bonded
by culture, others are bonded by politics, but few are bonded by both. Many

Métis people are not participating in any cultural or political arenas. Many have taken a place within the larger provincial and federal political, socio-economic reality, or are integrated enough that the importance of the role of an MNS, for them as individuals, is questionable. More and more, Métis people are looking for a culture devoid of the political virus that has tainted the Métis self-image in Saskatchewan. In order for the MNS to regain its strength, the diverse Métis population will need to see something within the nation that reflects their values and their current reality. This new government will need to take what works, what is good and healthy, and install within it a Nation which is connected to its origins and, more importantly, reflective of its current cultural reality.

Métis people are ready for leadership that listens, inspires and evolves. Métis people are ready for leadership that is advised by Elders, includes youth, and motivates people to participate. They are ready for a leadership that claims its members because they belong to the community. Whether they are rural or urban, from the North or the South, Métis people are looking for a role within their community that is meaningful and carries on throughout the term of a government. Métis people are ready to be united as a Nation. Thus, the notion that democracy is limited to the act of casting a ballot must be shed.

AN AGENDA PENNED BY THE MÉTIS

All governments function best when operating under their own agenda, and when the governance process reflects the people and the culture that the government represents. This applies to Indigenous governments throughout the world and will apply equally to the Métis in Saskatchewan. How Indigenous governments function in practice, in theory or in community, varies across the country. As the federal and provincial governments continue to view their relationships with Indigenous governments through the lens of dependence and problems, the act of setting a separate, independent agenda proves to be a difficult undertaking for a Métis government. Focusing attention and dollars on Indigenous people only in a social services format to deal with things which are real enough—housing problems, employments problems, social welfare problems, etc.—sets the agenda of Indigenous governments by highlighting dependency and creating a to-do list that is attached to the social service dollars. As a result, there is a constant struggle by Indigenous governments to be recognized as a legitimate voice rather than just a delivery mechanism for social service programs. By defining the relationship between external governments and Indigenous people—in this case, Métis—in terms of dollars and cents spent, the dependant/problematic model of interactions with Indigenous people and external governments is constantly perpetuated. The reality is that the federal government determines the priority of issues for Indigenous governments to a great extent through social service program delivery measures, including funding arrangements.

The federal and provincial government focus on programs and services, and away from community strength, has always refocused Métis politicians toward program delivery. Once funding for service was received regularly under the Association of Métis and Non-Status Indians of Saskatchewan (AMNSIS), it became the major political focus. Today, this still holds true. This is the reality in which the Métis government has carried out decision-making in the past and against which it will have to make its decisions to move forward now. Even with fairly elected leadership, when health dollars are dangled like candy, and when the funds available through the "success" of the *Powley* decision are doled out to the Métis governments who work within the federal agenda, can the MNS be considered an independent nation?

Consultation and rights-based litigation are simply the latest distractions taking attention away from any other set of Indigenous government priorities. Developing as a Nation will not be easy in the face of the preset agendas of others and of age-old government policies, and in the climate represented by the current federal government's refusal to sign onto the Declaration of Indigenous Rights at the international level.

Meanwhile, the actual needs of the people within the Métis community are ongoing. These may or may not match the issues determined by external government agendas and financial arrangements. Many individuals in the Métis community are transient, many have little or no employment, and many deal with the lasting effects of having children removed from families to educate or protect them. Many Métis kids are in need of athletic, academic or cultural education to ensure they have access to the choices available to members of the non-Indigenous society: a need which is only exacerbated by the current demographic boom and all that it entails. In addition, many Métis have turned away from the political warfare, and the larger issues of sovereignty and land rights, to deal with the basic daily need to eat, have shelter, raise children, and simply survive. Those people who had to turn to their own devices to continue with the fundamentals of life, in spite of the political reality, are slow to return to participating within the Métis political process.

IDENTITY: WHO DEFINES WHO IS MÉTIS?
Métis reality is compounded by the ultimate question of who is or is not a member within the Métis community. Identity. Is the purpose of identification as a Métis, to have access to the funding, housing, and educational programs currently available as a result of various government programs, being offered within a community? This has been the agenda of the federal government from the beginning of colonization. Or is identification of the members of a Nation something more; something based on belonging, on *wahkohtawin*— living in a way which bonds people as an identifiable group with common values, language and culture—which establishes that group as distinct? If it is the latter, will there be a Métis leadership able to set its own identity agenda, one that advances the Métis people, rather than simply reacting and responding to the federal or provincial agenda?

To be sure, identity is not static. Like culture, it is alive, organic, and it is the life force of a Nation. Identity haunts all Indigenous communities because it is another area encroached upon by non-Indigenous governments. This is revealed by court decisions, like *Re: Eskimo* and *Powley*, as well as by federal legislation, like the Indian Act. Métis know who they are, where they were raised and who their kinfolk are. However, an agenda which includes chasing government funding and looking to non-Indigenous courts to define the basis of Métis rights and identity blurs the lines between culture and rights. When Métis become involved in a process like litigation, or are ruled by documents such as federal or provincial legislation, the cost is the loss of the ability of the Nation to define for itself who its members are.

Indeed, it is true that many people in the later part of the 1900s commonly bounced back and forth between the classifications of Non-Status and Métis. It was a known practice and was accepted. Today, with the intervention of legislation regarding re-instatement of Indian Status, this has stopped. The future is open as to who will once again be part of either community.

"Aboriginality" within the Canadian Constitution is at once the Métis' strongest and weakest link. The constitutional label, "Aboriginal," sets Métis people apart—along with other Indigenous peoples—within Canada, as those who were here within a predetermined time frame and who hold some type of legal rights the courts define as Aboriginal rights, perhaps even Aboriginal title. At the same time the term "Aboriginal" homogenizes all the Indigenous Nations within Canada, and determines legally that all individuals who are Aboriginal will fall into one of three groupings: Indian, Inuit or Métis. Thus, direction is sought through litigation to determine who has Aboriginal rights, what those rights are, and how the governments need to interact with Aboriginal people to give effect to those rights. By doing this, the courts end up making declarations about various Indigenous peoples' identity, rights and roles within Canada. Ultimately, this will impact on governance, on how funding is transferred/accessed, and on culture. This is the current backdrop against which the newly elected Métis government must operate.

This question of where the Métis fit within that constitutional structure, whether it is a box that is empty, or one that is full and which merely needs to have its contents defined, remains open. The truth of the matter is that Canadian history is full of examples in which governments and governmental institutions, such as courts—institutions that are external to Indigenous people—define who Indigenous people are. These examples, which include the Indian registry, Bill C-31, and the modifications to the Indian Act to slowly eliminate "Status" Indians, do not bode well for the Métis. Stuck between a rock and a hard place, the Métis look to the non-Indigenous courts for parameters setting out their rights, recognitions of rights, and inclusion in predetermined rights, just like other Indigenous people in many countries. In Canada, it has become the rights game and, as stated earlier, it has a cost far more than the time and money that it takes to play. It has contributed to the erosion of Métis rights and identity.

The Métis National Council definition of Métis, which has been adopted by the Métis nationally, reads as follows:

> Métis means a person who self-identifies as Métis, is of historic Métis Nation (the Aboriginal people then known as Métis or Half-Breeds who resided in Historic Métis Nation Homeland—the area of land in west central North America used and occupied as the traditional territory of the Métis or Half-Breeds as they were then known) Ancestry, is distinct (for cultural and nationhood purposes) from other Aboriginal Peoples and is accepted by the Métis Nation (the Aboriginal people descended from the Historic Métis Nation, which is now comprised of all Métis Nation citizens and is one of the "aboriginal peoples of Canada" within s.35 of the Constitution Act of 1982).

Within this definition, several points seem to be key. One key point is the separation of the Métis from the Indians and the Inuit. Or is it? The Métis are a distinct society with distinct customs and culture, descended from First Nations or Indians, which affords the Métis constitutional recognition as one of Canada's Aboriginal peoples. This seems straightforward enough, until it is applied to the actual living situations of real people. There are many people who would fall into the Métis definition but for the fact that their ancestors signed a treaty, and are now "Indians" registered with the federal government. Historically, people who had lost Indian status due to their mothers "marrying out" were considered Métis or Non-Status for some purposes. However, many regained status after the *Lovelace* decision, and following the amendments to the Indian Act, a new Aboriginal grouping was created: Bill C-31, which has become the label for people who regained their status. Section 6 of the Indian Act, as amended after the *Lovelace* decision, essentially created a way for the federal government to maintain control of Indian status, i.e. band membership, and we see a scheme by which there will be, once again, a loss of status for children if a First Nations person has a child with a non-First Nation person. Although that kind of parentage represented the beginnings of the Métis, that is not who is, or who is considered to be, Métis today because of the way history has evolved. Métis culture is a key component to the identification question. And even after the development of the Métis culture and identity—when Métis and Non-Status Indians joined forces for political purposes—it was easy to identify as either Métis, or Non-Status, because both were part of the same political organization, benefitting from the same social programs, and identifying as kin. Following the trend of defining "Indian" by the government, and further interpretation of that definition by the courts, may provide a reason for caution for the Métis. However, to wait and see what the government or courts will do with a legal definition of Métis once again removes control over identity and membership from the Métis. Furthermore, because culture is alive, and organic, we see from the evolution of the Métis Nation to date that it is not likely that newborn children of a First Nations person and a Non-Indigenous person will ever be Métis. The identity issue continues.

Nations set their own agendas. Because the Métis once had a process to select leaders in a way that recognized the strengths of individual candidates for leadership positions, as well as one that encouraged shared responsibility and groomed youth for leadership, we know that there are other ways to lead. That is what Nations do: they select leaders by way of their own processes and they define membership based on a celebration of their own cultural identity and solid traditions. A Nations decides who *belongs* based on community values, participation, and cultural practices among its membership. However, it is precisely this human and interpersonal, or relational, aspect of the identity or the lived experience that is excluded in the legal definition. This problem of defining identity for the Métis Nation is shown in the growing divide between the grassroots of the Métis Nation, and people who are using "Aboriginality" as a political positioning tool.

Currently, there is a connection between the legal definition of Métis and financial opportunity for the Métis government as well as for individuals. This is separate from Métis Nationhood where identity would focus on cultural identity. Cultural identity, as a vision, has disappeared as financing for programs and services has emerged as the priority for all governments. With all energy focused on accessing federal dollars for flavour-of-the-month programs and services that put Métis government and institutions in the position of administrators for the federal and provincial government, meaningful Métis participation in a larger national and international context falls by the wayside. It is clear that, right now, identity for Métis does focus on accessing financing. This does not encourage growth within the Nation or participation of its membership. It does not inspire youth to be part of the creation of the government or even promote their natural participation in the practice and creation of Métis culture since these items are simply not lucrative. Furthermore, through this limited financial filter, Métis distinctiveness is lost. Among the losses are: the practice of Métis traditional gatherings, which maintain lines of communication within the community; spirituality; and the strength of the Métis language. The traditional education methods and practices in hunting, trapping, gathering, birthing and child rearing are also devalued. Missing is the understanding of the essential nature of men's roles within matrilocal communities, and the importance of the connection between Elders and youth.

The pragmatics of identity go further than the legal definitions for the purposes of counting half-breeds. To look at identity in terms of what right, program or service one may or may not have access to, has Indigenous people in Canada self-colonizing. The government needs to count people and separate some off for funding but is that the basis for an identity? The very fact that Métis are "distinct"—which is actually part of the definition of Métis—seems to be becoming less and less important. Thus, if the identity question is not answered by the Métis in a way that reflects the values of the community as a whole, and if Métis do not leave the groove in the road carved by non-indigenous governments and stop the nearly exclusive pursuit of a financial agenda, then to be Métis, half-breed or Non-Status has no pride or purpose separate from the federal or provincial governments, and it becomes the perpetuation of a racial oppression agenda.

Within the geographical borders of Saskatchewan, there is diversity that must also be recognized. There are Métis who are connected to the Cree, some who are Ojibwa, while others are Dene, or Lakota and so forth. Who the Métis are is a decision that should be reached through a conversation of the collective. An understanding of who is Métis, in some instances, has become watered down, and people who are in fact Métis, become *persona non grata* even within our own Nation. Bound by the financial definition, we live in a time where we are overlooking our own children, grandchildren and our nieces and nephews. All of this might even be acceptable if it is the Métis collective who decide that that is the way it is—the way it should be. However, it is not acceptable when such decisions are made by the federal or provincial government, or a lone half-breed and his or her posse, focusing on the idea that there is only one pie—the Aboriginal rights and title pie—and the first to the table gets the rations.

THE FUTURE

Although no one has a crystal ball, we can certainly learn from the lessons of the past. Jurisprudence has emerged on Aboriginal title and rights, which has a focus on time lines and proof of cultural practices, and as a result a clear direction of limited recognition of rights for ceremony, subsistence or survival for a limited group of the Métis population. Is every Aboriginal rights case going to impact on all of the constitutional groupings and expand or reduce the available claims? Will a legal win for the Métis apply equally to the Indians and the Inuit? If so, should there be communication and a strong relationship politically, culturally, and spiritually with the other Indigenous Nations within the country to push a predetermined Indigenous agenda through the litigation process?

The demands placed on the Métis Nation-Saskatchewan by the Métis people are high. They realize that too much has been put on hold for too long. Dancing to the tune of the federal or provincial government is always going to be a challenge with limited benefits in the movement toward true nationhood. Setting and following its own agenda, defining who the Métis are, and being a Nation should be the focus of the MNS. However, setting the priorities around those goals and not falling prey to financial trappings will be very difficult. The way governance has been undertaken in the past will not die easily. The Métis Constitution and legislation are in desperate need of revision due to: the overuse of amendments; the lack of clearly defined roles for elected and non-elected positions; contention regarding the role of the Senate; and problems arising from general ambiguities and inconsistencies. Revision will ultimately create a foundational document which must reflect Métis values and hold a Métis vision if it is to be a successful, solid foundation. Leadership, credibility, trust, and a self-sustainable political body are all on the table and delivering these things is a tall order for any government.

Being a nation is no small task. Few successful examples of Indigenous Nations within other countries exist to serve as a model for the Métis, so they will have to create it from scratch. It will not be the first time the Métis break new trail; in fact, it is part of the Métis genetic make-up to do so. The people need a successful nation to unite within the province and, ultimately, to work with other Métis and Indigenous nations within Canada. Implementation of nationhood must come from the ground up, through the community. Métis must change the language of governance and not only claim nationhood but be a nation. The relationship with other governments must grow. Fences must be mended internally and externally, and the dependency role must be shed. Métis people must demand a role within the governmental process. They must act to support responsible, respectable leadership, identify the gaps in the current government processes, and propose solutions for change. They must be open to, and even insist on, the creation of new avenues of nationhood, and actively participate within the nation in areas where they believe that they have something to contribute. The Métis cannot use a traditional model that relies on the strength and participation of family heads, of revolving leadership and of reliance on capable individuals, if people are not participating and showing what their strengths are.

Government language must also change. Monetary transfers should be seen for what they are: rent, or the cost of living in Canada for non-Indigenous people. They are a legitimately owed debt to Métis or other Indigenous Nations to compensate for loss of land and resources, and for harms done to individuals, families or communities by dispossession and racism. Although monetary transfers are necessary to support and ensure a better future for the Métis people within the story of Canada—as the story is lived today—it cannot be at the cost of nationhood and identity. The dynamics will change when we are working together against common enemies like poverty, unemployment and racism. In that climate, all of the priorities of all the governments will be able to shift; inter-dependence, rather than dominance, will be possible. This kind of relationship will allow the Métis Nation-Saskatchewan to respond and work, within a Métis-defined agenda, with passion, dignity, strength—and be a strong basis in a strong Métis culture.

MUNICIPAL POLITICS
AND GOVERNMENT

Municipal Restructuring in Saskatchewan 1905–2005: A Case of Institutional Inertia and Immunity

Joseph Garcea

INTRODUCTION

One of the most interesting and important legacies of municipal governance in Saskatchewan is the paucity of either any substantial restructuring of the boundaries of municipalities or any changes to the basic types of municipal governments after the system was established in the early 1900s. This is particularly true of the municipal system in the southern half of the province that consists of over 800 municipalities and, to a lesser extent, of the northern municipal system that consists of approximately two dozen municipalities, most of which are very small even by Saskatchewan standards.

The paucity of restructuring to the municipal system in Saskatchewan stands in stark contrast not only to the structural reforms to the municipal systems in some of the other provinces in Canada but also to the restructuring of the other two major systems of local governance within Saskatchewan, namely education and health. As this analysis reveals, the paucity of restructuring of Saskatchewan's municipal systems has persisted despite both a plethora of proposals produced during the past century by various task forces and committees, and a few notable efforts by provincial governments to implement policies designed to achieve such restructuring on a voluntary basis.

The objective of this chapter is to provide the following: an overview of the proposals, policies and politics of municipal restructuring in southern Saskatchewan from 1905 to 2005; an explanation of what accounts for the paucity of municipal restructuring during the past century; and some prognostications on restructuring in the future. In explaining the paucity of restructuring, this chapter devotes attention to what is termed "institutional inertia" and "institutional immunity" and the factors that account for them. Whereas institutional inertia refers to the lack of any notable impetus or imperative on the part of municipal officials or the people they represent to restructure the system, institutional immunity refers to their ability to prevent the implementation of any externally initiated restructuring initiatives.

The chapter concludes that restructuring in the form of amalgamation of existing local municipalities is unlikely to occur in the near future because of the persistence of such inertia and immunity that is likely to be perpetuated by a mix of parochialism, political power and political imperatives. A more likely restructuring scenario is the retention of the existing local authorities and the reconfiguration of the boundaries and functions of some existing regional authorities. However, even for this reconfiguration scenario to materialize adequate and appropriate incentives for key stakeholders in the municipal sector will be required.

FIRST ERA OF MUNICIPAL RESTRUCTURING IN SOUTHERN SASKATCHEWAN: 1905–44

A full appreciation of the restructuring of the municipal system in southern Saskatchewan since 1905 requires an understanding of the fledgling municipal system that had been established prior to that date. The structuring of the municipal system started in 1883 with the Municipal Ordinance, enacted by the North-West Territories Council, which permitted the creation of municipalities on a voluntary basis through petitions by individual communities. Another major step in the structuring of the municipal system was taken in the mid- to late-1870s with the creation of local improvement districts, fire districts, and statute labour districts, all of which eventually were converted to local improvement districts by the Local Improvement Ordinance of 1898. In 1904 the smallest local improvement districts were abolished to ensure that all of them were of a minimum size of 108 square miles and three to six townships.[1]

ROYAL COMMISSION ON MUNICIPAL ORGANIZATION (1907)

The structuring, and in some cases the restructuring, of the fledgling municipal system continued after the establishment of Saskatchewan as a province in 1905. This was part of the efforts of Premier Walter Scott's government to design and establish the various governance institutions at the provincial and local levels. In 1906 it assigned the task of making recommendations regarding the design of the municipal system to the Royal Commission on Municipal Organization. In its report submitted in 1907, the Commission recommended the creation of a municipal system for the southern half of the province consisting of cities, towns, villages and rural municipalities. The Commission also recommended that the rural municipalities were to be uniform in size and shape.[2]

The provincial government accepted those recommendations and prepared the requisite legislation for the creation of the new system. Between 1908 and 1909 it enacted separate acts for cities, towns and villages, and rural municipalities. The statutes for villages, towns, and cities affirmed the incorporation of existing municipalities and also provided the basis for the incorporation of other new urban communities.

The legislation for rural municipalities authorized the government to convert local improvement districts (LIDs) to larger rural municipalities (RMs) based either on a vote by members living within the proposed municipal boundaries or by ministerial order. The government established a conversion plan that gave residents of the LICs until the end of 1912 to vote for the conversion. The proposed conversion was strongly resisted by many rural residents who were concerned about the property tax regime that would be implemented by new municipal councils using their broader taxing authority. However, despite such resistance, approximately 75% of the 361 LIDs voted for the proposed conversion. The remaining 25% that had not voted in favour of such a conversion by the end of 1912 were converted by ministerial order.[3]

After 1912 the provincial government transformed almost all LIDs to RMs. It did so without providing residents with the opportunity to express their preferences through a plebiscite or referendum.[4] This would be the last time for the next 100 years that the provincial government was able to achieve, either on a mandatory or a voluntary basis, a substantial structural reform to the municipal system in the southern half of the province.

Following the establishment of the province, the provincial government was able to implement the new rural municipal system in southern Saskatchewan with relative ease for two reasons. First, despite their concerns regarding the imposition of a property tax regime, ratepayers were unable to mount a coherent and coordinated opposition on their own. Second, the existing fledgling municipal associations did not mount a strong united opposition to the reconfiguration of the municipal system. Evidently, the reason for this is that for the majority of SARM members at that time, the prospect of increasing the governance status and powers of municipal governance institutions and officials trumped any concerns that many ratepayers had expressed regarding any property tax regime that would be implemented by the newly established rural municipal governments.[5] Indeed, instead of mounting a strong resistance to the restructuring, the Saskatchewan Local Districts Association (SLDA), which had been established in 1905, focused on changing its name to make it consonant with the nomenclature of the new municipalities to become the Saskatchewan Association of Rural Municipalities (SARM) in 1911.[6]

Similar considerations were also evident among ratepayers and municipal officials of the various urban areas that were being incorporated as municipalities pursuant to the villages, towns, and cities acts of 1908. The executive of the Union of Saskatchewan Municipalities (USM), which had its founding convention in 1906 and would eventually become the Saskatchewan Urban Municipalities Association (SUMA), perceived the reform as a positive step in the institutionalization of municipal governance.

The restructuring that occurred between 1908 and 1914 had a profound effect on the configuration of the municipal system in the southern half of the province. Before that restructuring it consisted of 503 local governance units. This included 361 governance units in rural areas (i.e., 359 local improvement districts, 2 RMs) and 144 governance units in urban areas (i.e., 4 cities, 43 towns, and 97 villages). In the subsequent six years the number and types of urban municipalities remained relatively constant, but there was a dramatic shift in the types and number of rural governance units. By 1912 there were 172 RMs and 97 LIDS for a total of 269 rural governance units, and by 1914 the number of RMs jumped to 295 as a result of the provincially mandated conversion of LIDs to RMs.

During the subsequent 35 years the number of rural municipal units changed very little, but the number of urban municipalities proliferated. Thus, by 1948 the number of rural local government entities had decreased to 282 (269 RMs and only 13 LIDs) as a result of the dissolution of some RMs facing financial difficulties and their integration with neighbouring RMs in the 1940s, but the number of urban municipal government entities had increased to 486 (8 cities, 98 towns, and 380 villages). Those numbers did not change much in the subsequent half century. In 2005 there were 975 municipalities and quasi-municipalities. Of these, 486 were in the urban sector (13 cities, 145 towns, 289 villages, and 39 resort villages); 465 in the rural sector (296 rural municipalities and 169 organized hamlets); and 24 in the northern sector (2 northern towns, 13 northern villages, and 9 northern hamlets).

PATRICK AND PILKINGTON REPORT (1921)

After that initial structuring of the system, no restructuring occurred during the subsequent three decades. Nevertheless, during that time several reports were produced that advocated some restructuring. All of those reports, except one, were produced by commissions established either by the provincial or federal governments to examine various aspects of the provincial and municipal governance and financial systems in Saskatchewan. The exception was the first of these reports that was produced independently by Thomas Alfred Patrick, a former politician in the Legislative Assembly of the North-West Territories who was very influential in the establishment of the existing provincial boundaries, and F.J. Pilkington, the City Clerk for Yorkton. In the report published in 1921, less than a decade after the municipal system had been established, they argued that Saskatchewan should adopt a county system. The proposed county system would consist of larger units that would essentially integrate all governance and the provision of some services under the auspices of a county council and various special purpose authorities. They suggested that the county should be governed by a county-council with the assistance of either appointed or elected boards responsible for secondary education and health, and some other appointed officials responsible for elementary schools, roads, and engineering.[7] They argued that a county system would result in improved governance and service provision capacity, more equitable taxation between urban and rural taxpayers, increased potential to minimize the incidence of "free-rider" behaviour on the part of rural residents who relied on services provided by urban municipalities, and increased local authority and autonomy vis-à-vis the provincial government. The publication of a synopsis of that report in the *Western Municipal News* in 1921 placed the county system option on the policy agenda for the next four decades and provided the rationale for establishing it not only in Saskatchewan but also in the neighbouring western provinces.[8] However, as discussed in a subsequent section of this chapter, in Saskatchewan it was not until the end of those four decades that legislation would be enacted to permit neighbouring communities to create counties on a voluntary basis.

The impetus for the production of subsequent reports that addressed municipal restructuring was provided by the challenges, indeed the crises, created by the Great Depression and World War II. Those historic events prompted the appointment of a series of commissions of inquiries mandated to produce reports that focused either in whole or in part on the nature and scope of the problems within the municipal sector and the reforms needed to address them. Three such reports were produced from 1936 to 1943. Two were commissioned by the provincial Liberal government of Premier William John Patterson, and the other by the federal Liberal government of Primer Minister William Lyon Mackenzie King.

COMMISSION OF INQUIRY INTO PROVINCIAL AND MUNICIPAL TAXATION (1936)

The first of those reports was produced in 1936 by the Commission of Inquiry into Provincial and Municipal Taxation appointed by Premier Patterson's provincial government. In addition to recommendations regarding the need to reform the basis of taxation, the property tax assessment system, and the tax collection system, the Commission made three key recommendations pertaining to municipal restructuring. The first was either for the conversion of all local improvement districts to rural municipalities or for their integration into existing rural municipalities. The second recommendation was to amalgamate rural municipalities as a means to increase their size and efficiency and to decrease the cost of rural government. The third recommendation was that any such restructuring "should be made only on the majority vote of taxpayers resident within the areas affected, and conditioned upon a satisfactory solution of the municipal indebtedness within these areas."[9] The call for a voluntary approach to restructuring articulated in this report would become a major rallying cry for the municipal sector in subsequent decades.

ROYAL COMMISSION ON DOMINION-PROVINCIAL RELATIONS (1940)

The municipal restructuring issue in Saskatchewan and other provinces was also broached by the Royal Commission on Dominion-Provincial Relations established by the federal government in consultation with the provinces. This was part of the undertaking by the federal government to seek a realignment of the functional and financial frameworks between the various orders of government. The Royal Commission provided one of the most cogent explanations of the problems posed by the existing structure of the municipal system and the means by which to address those problems. It noted that particularly in the Prairie Provinces "many local government units are no longer the appropriate areas for governmental purposes of any description."[10] The Royal Commission noted that this was equally true of urban and rural municipalities. In the case of urban municipalities, it suggested that efficiency cannot be achieved "when five or ten separate governments operate in a single integrated urban area among people who are economically interdependent; nor can the maximum economic welfare of the whole be expected if there are a number of widely varying tax-rates, standards of education and health measures and the like."[11] In the case of rural municipalities, it argued that the boundaries should be altered because the shift in transportation from horses to motor cars had effectively extended the boundaries of the communities both for governance and various types of service provision, including social services for the destitute, beyond what they had been during the previous decades.

SASKATCHEWAN URBAN ASSESSMENT COMMITTEE (1943)

In 1943, another report that recommended municipal restructuring was produced by a committee established by the provincial Liberal government.[12] The report, produced by the Saskatchewan Urban Assessment Committee, called for a "general rearrangement of the boundaries of municipal and other units."[13] It added that it was "high time that the attention of the Government and of municipal associations should be directed to the possibility of improving local government in the province through a reorganization of municipal units."[14] It then explained that the restructuring was necessary due to demographic, economic and service changes. In its words:

> At the time the municipal system was established it seems likely that an excellent piece of work was done in the fixing of municipal boundaries but most people agree that these boundaries are in too many cases most inconvenient today. Changes in the economy of the province, the uneven growth of urban units and changes in the type of services rendered to the community have all played their part bringing about maladjustment so that at the present time not only are many municipalities and school districts quite unable to finance the performance of their obligations but in general the municipal institutions are not adapted to the ends to be served.[15]

SASKATCHEWAN RECONSTRUCTION COUNCIL (1944)

The last report that touched on municipal restructuring prior to the end of World War II was produced by an advisory body established by Premier Patterson's Liberal government. Between 1943 and 1944 the Saskatchewan Reconstruction Council was mandated to determine what had to be done to redevelop the infrastructure, service provision and governance capacity in Saskatchewan's communities. The Council noted that some representatives of rural municipalities had indicated that RMs were too small to look after roads and other local and regional infrastructure and services, and that their revenues were too unstable.[16] To deal with these problems the Council recommended amalgamating RMs to create larger units. It argued that this would make it possible for them to generate the revenues for roads, schools and hospitals, and that for this reason the proposals to change boundaries were deemed to be "worthy of careful considerations."[17] With that in mind the Council recommended that a committee chaired by a person appointed by the provincial government, a specialist in municipal administration and several other members be established to examine issues and options related to the adjustment of municipal boundaries. As discussed below, in 1945 this recommendation led Premier Tommy Douglas' Co-operative Commonwealth (CCF) government to appoint the Committee to Investigate the Reorganization of Rural Municipal Boundaries.

While the aforementioned reports were being produced between 1930 and 1945, officials of rural municipalities generally opposed any restructuring to the municipal system. When they were asked to express their views either through a survey, as happened in 1932, or through a convention resolution, as happened in 1943, the vast majority indicated they were opposed. One of the factors that prompted such opposition during the Depression and World War II was a concern among officials from municipalities with relatively strong finances that they would be amalgamated with municipalities with relatively weak finances.[18] Another factor, and one closely related to the first, that was undoubtedly significant in precluding such restructuring during this particular era was what might be termed the pervasive sense of loss created by the economic and military crises. Successive provincial governments were undoubtedly very reluctant to add to that sense of loss to communities by restructuring municipal governments in a way that would have resulted in some of them losing their municipal governments.[19] A third factor was undoubtedly the provincial government's paucity of organizational and financial capacity to mount a restructuring initiative while dealing with the challenges posed by the economic and military crises. It must be noted, however, that while those factors created obstacles to restructuring, they were not insurmountable. This is evident in the fact that between 1940 and 1944 the Alberta government, which faced many of those same obstacles, was able to consolidate 140 municipal districts into 40 larger units.

SECOND ERA OF MUNICIPAL RESTRUCTURING IN SOUTHERN SASKATCHEWAN: 1945–63

The second era of municipal restructuring corresponded to the 19 years that the CCF was in power. This era is renowned for the wide range of governance and policy reform agendas and actual innovative reforms. One of the major items on the CCF government's policy reform agenda throughout that era was municipal restructuring. The reason that it was on its agenda is that the CCF provincial government, led by Premier Tommy Douglas from 1944 to 1961 and by Woodrow S. Lloyd from the latter part of 1961 to 1963, felt that the municipal system was experiencing serious governance and service provision capacity problems that had to be addressed for the benefit of municipal governments, their communities and ratepayers, and the province as a whole.[20] Toward that end, the CCF government commissioned several reports that made important observations and recommendations on the need for and nature of municipal restructuring. However, during this era none of the restructuring reforms proposed in those reports was implemented. The only significant step taken in that direction was the enactment of a statutory framework for voluntary restructuring by the CCF government during its last term in power. That framework, however, did not yield any restructuring.

COMMITTEE TO INVESTIGATE THE REORGANIZATION OF RURAL MUNICIPAL BOUNDARIES (1946)

The CCF government started its protracted effort to restructure the municipal system the year after it came to power. In 1945 it acted on the recommendation of the Reconstruction Council and appointed the Committee to Investigate the Reorganization of Rural Municipal Boundaries. The Committee consisted of two professors from the University of Saskatchewan's College of Agriculture; two representatives of the two municipalities associations; the secretary of the Saskatchewan chapter of the United Farmers of Canada; and three technical advisors.[21] The chair was Hadley Van Vliet, who was one of the two professors appointed to the Committee.

The Committee conducted public hearings, received briefs from various associations including SARM, compiled a substantial amount of information on various issues and options related to municipal governance, and conducted research on Alberta's restructuring between 1940 and 1944 that led to the consolidation of 140 municipal districts into 40 larger municipal units. Despite all the preparatory work that it had done, and the release of a preliminary report, for reasons which are not altogether clear that Committee did not produce a final report. In that preliminary report it pointed to the changes that were occurring to the political economy, the governance processes and provision of services in the province. The Committee argued that in light of those changes there was a need for greater coordination of governance and service provision functions on a larger geographic scale. That report contributed substantially to the emerging rationale for the creation of multi-functional municipal and county governments, and adjustments to the alignment of functions and finances between the provincial and municipal governments.[22]

As the government was setting out to establish this committee and encourage participation in its work both by municipal officials and their ratepayers, the Minister for Municipal Affairs, J.H. Brockelbank, had to begin that task of reassuring the municipal associations that it would lead to positive outcomes. At SARM's 1945 convention, for example, he noted that any resulting reorganization would be beneficial for enhancing their capacity to perform their governance and service provision functions and would not result either in the loss of local autonomy or local government.[23]

At the same time that the Committee to Investigate the Reorganizations of Rural Municipal Boundaries was doing its work, SARM established a two-person committee to examine the merits of Alberta's larger municipal units that had been established in the previous five years. In its report submitted in 1945, SARM's committee reported that its investigation revealed that properly managed larger units could increase efficiency and effectiveness in road construction and maintenance, but that claims of improved efficiency in general operating costs were not evident. It also noted that although strong feelings either for or against the larger units were not expressed by Alberta municipal officials and ratepayers, their impression was that residents were most satisfied with the smaller versions of the larger units.[24] Based on that information, SARM delegates at the 1945 annual convention adopted a resolution, which had already been adopted by the SARM executive earlier that year, to delay any reorganization of the municipal system until the provincial government had appointed a committee to investigate the matter very carefully as proposed in the *Report of the Reconstruction Council*.[25] The provincial government heeded that resolution and appointed such a committee three years later.

COMMITTEE ON PROVINCIAL-MUNICIPAL RELATIONS (1950)

The Committee, appointed in 1948, consisted of three notable members. Two of the members were prominent academics from the University of Saskatchewan who had been involved in preparing the provincial government's case to the Royal Commission on Dominion-Provincial Relations. One was G.E. Britnell, an expert on inter-governmental finances and head of the Department of Economic and Political Science, and the other was F.C. Cronkite, a former President of SUMA and Dean of the Law School. The other member was Louis Jacobs, an expert in municipal finance who had served both as Director of Municipal Auditing and Accounting and as a member of the Saskatchewan Assessment Commission.[26]

The Committee provided a detailed analysis of the evolution of the system of municipal governance and the challenges it was facing in the immediate post-World War II period. Although restructuring was not necessarily a core element of its mandate, it felt compelled to make some observations and recommendations on this issue. The Committee's key observation was that to ensure that municipal governments had the autonomy and capacity to perform their core functions it was necessary to establish larger municipal units. It added that the "fear that any reasonable increase in the size of Saskatchewan's rural governing units may take government away from the people is not well founded."[27] It added that the same was true of the fear that municipal governments would become mere administrative and collection agencies for the provincial government, and indicated that this was much less likely to happen if the municipalities were "enlarged to the point where they can assume a large responsibility."[28] The Committee noted that although it was not part of its mandate to recommend how or to what extent reorganization should be carried out, felt compelled to make two important and interrelated suggestions. The first of these was that the provincial government's department responsible for the municipal system should establish a research unit to examine the alteration of municipal boundaries. The other recommendation was that, in restructuring the municipal sector, attention should also be devoted to the boundaries of education and health districts, and that for this purpose special attention should be given to the proposed experiment with the county system in Alberta.[29]

ROYAL COMMISSION ON AGRICULTURE AND RURAL LIFE (1955)

During the CCF era the strongest case for restructuring the municipal system was made by the Royal Commission on Agriculture and Rural Life in its historic report released in 1955. In its letter of transmittal for that report, the

Commission noted that municipal restructuring was imperative. In its words: "the recommended changes in local government are among the most fundamental adjustments now required for the future welfare of rural life in Saskatchewan. This is because few other adjustments are related to so many aspects of rural development and will have such a profound influence on the provision of modern rural services to the farm people of the province."[30] The Commission concluded that, given changing demographic and economic conditions, restructuring comparable to what had already occurred in the health and education sectors was imperative, otherwise many municipalities would find it increasingly difficult to perform their core functions.[31] It was this imperative to reconcile or rationalize the boundaries of the municipal, education and health systems that provided the impetus for municipal restructuring at this particular juncture in history. The Commission felt that the time had come to deal with reorganization. Its statement on this matter was influenced by one the technical reports that it had commissioned, which noted that despite the series of reports that had called for restructuring, "the fundamental question of reorganization of the rural municipalities has never been seriously faced."[32]

The Commission recommended the establishment of either a modified or a full county system for rural municipalities. In effect, it was recommending the implementation of Alberta's municipal counties and districts system that had already been established a few years earlier. The units envisioned by the Commission were approximately four to five times larger than the existing RMs.[33] It also recommended a process for achieving the proposed reorganization. The first step was for the provincial government to launch extensive community consultations on the proposed reorganization with positive leadership provided by all political parties, SARM, the Rural Municipal Secretary-Treasurers' Association, The Saskatchewan School Trustees Association, The Saskatchewan Teachers' Federation, and various farm organizations. The second step was for a conference of provincial organizations to review the proposed reorganization and to advise the provincial government on their implementation. The third step was for the provincial government to establish a Local Government Boundaries Committee consisting of members from organizations directly concerned with municipal reorganization to advise the provincial government on boundaries for the proposed reorganization. The final step was for the provincial government to implement either a modified or full county system throughout the province.[34]

In the two years after the Commission submitted its report, Premier Douglas and his Minister of Education echoed its views regarding the need for municipal reorganization and the reconciliation of municipal boundaries with those of the education sector at the annual conventions of various local government associations. The importance of rationalization among those policy sectors was underscored by the Premier and the Minister of Education.[35] At SUMA's 1956 convention the Premier noted that "reorganization of the multiple local authorities is a prerequisite for a sound local system in Saskatchewan"[36] because, as he noted at SARM's 1957 convention, small units did not have sufficient capacity to perform their core governance, service provision and taxation functions that were equitable both for municipalities and their ratepayers. In his address he articulated his government's position on the restructuring issue as follows:

> The government is prepared to lead but it will not drive. All local government bodies are creatures of the province but no legislature in its right mind would try to make changes unless the people concerned thought them both necessary and desirable. We will go as far and as fast as local government wants, but some day people will have to wrestle with this problem and the choice is whether to tackle it now or pass it on to posterity. […] You have the opportunity to make this a historic convention at which you set up a committee to map out a program to strengthen democracy in Saskatchewan.[37]

The only organization of local authorities that expressed outright support for the creation of counties at that time was the School Trustees Association. The two municipal associations had to be persuaded even to support the formation of the Local Government Continuing Committee to examine the options for restructuring the local government sector. The most strident opposition to the proposed changes came from elected and appointed officials from rural municipalities who felt that they were the ones that were likely to be most directly affected by the proposed restructuring agenda.[38]

LOCAL GOVERNMENT CONTINUING COMMITTEE (1961)

Five years later the recommendations of the Royal Commission were echoed in the report of the Local Government Continuing Committee established by the CCF government in 1958. The Committee consisted of senior cabinet ministers, representatives from the urban, rural, school and hospital associations and more than three dozen researchers, consultants, and staff members. The Committee provided a very detailed analysis of the evolution of the municipal system, the problems it faced and the means by which to deal with those problems. It concluded its report with a clarion call for not only restructuring the municipal system, but for a more general reorganization of local governments in Saskatchewan to enhance their capacity and autonomy in performing their functions.[39] More specifically, it recommended the creation of counties consisting of a single county council for each of them that would deal with municipal and educational matters. The Committee also considered the merits of some other models for reorganization, including a modified county system with coterminous boundaries, but separate councils, for municipal and school governance. In an effort to rationalize the local government sector beyond the municipal and education sectors, the Committee also recommended the establishment of geographically large regional councils responsible for providing health and social services that would cover an area of two or more counties.

Before producing its final report, the Committee conducted an extensive round of public consultations that involved public meetings in 72 communities across the province attended by nearly 17,000 people. At those meetings the

Committee outlined its proposal for reorganization and showed the maps of the proposed boundaries. During those local meetings the most common response on a questionnaire regarding various options was that restructuring was "not necessary."[40] In light of that response, it is not surprising that the Committee recommended that there should not be a plebiscite or referendum. In effect it treated the response on that questionnaire as a poll and realized that chances were very slim that a plebiscite or referendum would result in a mandate from the people for reorganization.[41]

The issue of restructuring was also voted on by delegates at the SARM and SUMA annual conventions. The SARM convention of 1959 adopted Resolution Number 18 not to include any existing RM in any proposed larger municipal unit or county.[42] At the 1961 SARM convention, the 1,456 representatives of rural municipalities voted overwhelmingly against the restructuring proposed by the Committee, but indicated that they were willing to approve a process for allowing pilot projects to proceed if supported by a plebiscite of ratepayers of the municipalities that would be involved.[43] SARM's position was based on an informal plebiscite that the executive asked RMs to conduct prior to the 1961 convention on the Committee's reorganization proposal. Approximately 200 RMs held such plebiscites. Of the 65,000 residents who expressed their preference on the Committee's plan, 57,840 opposed it and only 7,288 supported it. SARM's position was also supported by the Rural Municipal Administrators Association (RMAA). By contrast, the majority of delegates at SUMA's 1961 convention indicated that they were willing to support the Committee's restructuring model in principle. However, like their SARM counterparts, they preferred that its implementation would be subjected to the will of the majority of local ratepayers as expressed in a plebiscite.[44]

In its brief to the provincial government, approved by its members at the 1961 convention, SARM's executive made two key recommendations. The first was that restructuring pilot projects should be permitted in areas where local municipal councils requested them. The second was that a special committee should be set up involving representatives of the provincial government, SARM, small urban municipalities, and the Saskatchewan School Trustees Association (SSTA) to discuss issues and options related to processes and potential restructuring models. The provincial government agreed with the proposal for a special committee and on October 1, 1961, it established the Local Government Advisory Council. At the same time it broadened the mandate of the existing Municipal Advisory Commission to include defining boundaries for local governance.

On January 15, 1962, the provincial government promised that residents would be given the opportunity to express their views on any proposed restructuring. However, in keeping with the recommendation of the Local Government Continuing Committee, it did not promise that it would provide them with an opportunity to express their views through a plebiscite or referendum. At that time the provincial government also promised SARM that it would be given a chance to review the draft legislation for restructuring before it was enacted.[45]

THE MUNICIPAL UNIT AND COUNTY ACT (1963)

In the spring of 1962 the CCF provincial government, led by Premier Woodrow Lloyd, who succeeded Premier Douglas, introduced the Municipal Unit and County Act. The two major provisions in the Act were those outlining the governance model that would be used for restructuring purposes, and the mode of implementation of that model. In the case of the governance model, it permitted the creation of either municipal districts or counties covering areas comparable in size to those in Alberta, which were approximately five to seven times larger than the average rural municipality in Saskatchewan. Whereas counties would consist of a single governing authority responsible both for the municipal and education functions, municipal districts would consist of separate governing authorities for municipal and education functions, but both would operate within coterminous boundaries. In the case of the mode of implementation, the statute contained a framework for voluntary restructuring. The inclusion of the provision regarding voluntary restructuring indicates that Premier Lloyd's CCF government had listened and responded to the preference of the majority of those who attended the Committee's public hearings, those who participated in the plebiscites held by RMs, and the majority of the delegates at the SARM and SUMA conventions. In April 1962, the Minister for Municipal Affairs provided assurances in the provincial legislature that the government had rejected the Continuing Committee's recommendation that restructuring should be undertaken without local or regional plebiscites or referenda, and chose to allow "people of each area to decide whether their local government should be reorganized or not."[46]

Undoubtedly, the decision by Premier Lloyd and his government to be responsive to those preferences was rooted both in political and policy rationality triggered by the Medicare debate. By the spring of 1962 the CCF government had already used up much of its political capital in dealing with the strong opposition to its Medicare legislation that had been introduced on October 31, 1961, just seven days prior to the shift in the premiership from Douglas to Lloyd. The Medicare debate was far from being over, however, as the government moved toward the enactment and implementation of that particular statute, which had initially been set for the spring of 1962 but had to be postponed until July 1, 1962.[47] By the time that the political battle on Medicare was over the government had not only incurred the defection of one of its caucus members to the Liberal Party, but also had to endure a 23-day strike by 90% of the doctors in the province that started the very day the Act went into effect. In that political climate, the first objective of Premier Lloyd and his Cabinet was undoubtedly to ensure that both the Medicare statute and the government would survive the strong opposition that they were facing. The government was hardly in a position to open itself up on another political battle front with the municipal sector by introducing a statute mandating municipal restructuring by provincial fiat. Indeed, given the political battle in which it was embroiled on the Medicare front, it is quite surprising that it decided to introduce legislation for municipal restructuring, even if it was on a voluntary basis.

The statutory provisions for restructuring on a voluntary basis contained in the Municipal Unit and County Act enacted in 1963 was not enough to appease SARM on the proposed legislation. The restructuring debate continued to rage throughout 1962 and 1963, largely because SARM wanted some additional concessions. One such concession was regarding who should be allowed to vote in any plebiscite on reorganization. Whereas the government's draft legislation allowed all eligible residents to vote in a municipal area on any proposal to establish a larger municipal district or country, SARM argued that since reorganization would have implications for taxation, only "burgesses and wives" should be given the right to vote.[48] A second concession sought by SARM was that the county system would not be implemented either on a mandatory or even a voluntary basis because its preference was that municipalities should not have to deal with the education function. The other key concession that it sought was that any new boundaries for larger municipal districts would be drawn by the Municipal Advisory Commission, rather than the provincial government, before being submitted to a vote of the burgesses in each of the proposed larger municipal districts.[49] The government was willing to be flexible on some of those demands, but it did not accede to SARM's demand to eliminate any provisions for the establishment of counties in the province. One possible reason for this may well be that it had been able to obtain SUMA's support to include provisions regarding that particular type of local authority in the statutory framework.

Although the Municipal Unit and County Act remained on the books from 1963 until June 1, 1984, when it was eventually repealed, no counties or municipal districts were created pursuant to it. In fact, the only notable restructuring initiatives during that time were undertaken pursuant to the existing Rural Municipality Act. This included the amalgamation of two sets of RMs—one occurred in 1968 with the amalgamation of two neighbouring RMs (i.e., Royal Canadian and Mantario) to form the RM of Chesterfield, and one occurred in 1969 with the amalgamation of three small neighbouring RMs (i.e., Cory, Warman and Park) to create the RM of Corman Park. Those amalgamations occurred on a voluntary basis through an agreement involving the RM councils.[50] Although the Municipal Unit and County Act did not have any effect on amalgamations, it had an important residual political effect. The strong opposition that it generated just before the CCF lost power during the first quinquennium of the 1960s affected the way in which subsequent provincial governments generally approached and managed various attempts at restructuring in subsequent decades.

THIRD ERA OF MUNICIPAL RESTRUCTURING IN SOUTHERN SASKATCHEWAN: 1964–90
Although the period from 1964 to 1990 was in no way comparable to the previous period in terms of proposals, policies and politics related to municipal restructuring, that issue received some attention by SARM, the provincial government, and four reports commissioned by the provincial government. Those reports explored various aspects of planning and development as well as municipal finances in the province.

In the aftermath of the enactment of the Municipal Unit and County Act, SARM and the provincial government considered whether there was any will for voluntary amalgamation. The topic was broached at the SARM conventions of 1967 and 1968 by its president, E. Murphy. At the 1967 convention he noted that the tax assessments of 37% of rural municipalities was less than $2 million and suggested that one option for dealing with the financial challenges was to consider amalgamation to create larger municipal districts to deal exclusively with municipal functions, rather than counties which would have also required them to deal with the education function.[51] At that convention he also reminded delegates that Premier Ross Thatcher had offered to establish some restructuring pilot projects to create larger municipal districts if SARM and the municipalities that would be involved submitted a proposal. His address to the 1968 convention was equally direct on the financial challenges faced by some municipalities and the need for them to consider amalgamation. He suggested that in the case of "small, low assessed municipalities we are trying to feed a dying horse or temporarily keep in existence a system of local municipal administration that is less able to take care of itself as time progresses."[52] He added that rural municipalities should take control of their affairs and then asked delegates to consider the merits of larger municipal districts at least as pilot projects that had been proposed by the provincial government. Following a brief discussion of the matter, the convention delegates adopted a resolution that authorized the SARM executive "to become active in the area of rural municipal amalgamation" as had been proposed by their president.[53] At the 1969 convention the president reported that only two RMs had amalgamated to form the new RM of Chesterfield (Royal Canadian and Mantario). He added that Premier Thatcher's government was becoming impatient with the limited progress in municipal restructuring and that they had to become more proactive on this matter "otherwise the initiative may be taken out of their hands and they will be obliged to live by the decisions made by others."[54] Despite the effort by SARM's president to rally the membership to support amalgamation, only one other notable amalgamation occurred before the 1971 provincial election. Regardless of its views on the inadequacy of progress in restructuring, the Thatcher government did not address the matter in any substantial manner before its loss in the 1971 election to the NDP led by Allan Blakeney.

RURAL DEVELOPMENT ADVISORY GROUP (1976)

The restructuring issue abated for the first quinquennium of the 1970s. However, by the mid-to late-1970s it re-emerged, albeit in a more muted form, after the provincial government appointed the Rural Development Advisory Group. In its report, released in November 1976, the Advisory group noted that without restructuring some rural and urban municipalities would find it increasingly difficult to perform their functions. Its three major recommendations were: the amalgamation of villages with less than 100 people into the surrounding RMs; the amalgamation of rural municipalities using the principle of contemporary "trading areas" to provide a larger property assessment tax base for municipal councils; and the commissioning of a study by the provincial government for the purpose of producing a restructuring plan. The Advisory Group indicated that it believed that changes could be carried out through negotiations between the provincial government and municipal governments, but noted that the "ultimate responsibility for local government, its role, structure and welfare rests with the province."[55]

After receiving that report, the Minister of Municipal Affairs, Gordon MacMurchy, invited the municipal governments and their associations to submit their views on the recommendations. SARM's president, Charles Mitchell, indicated that although the report provided the right assessment of the situation it was unlikely that many municipal officials would support any of the changes proposed. Nevertheless, in his presidential address for SARM's 1977 annual convention, he encouraged SARM members to consider the merits of restructuring and noted that, given the limited taxation base of some municipalities and the escalating costs for services, amalgamation was inevitable. His presidential address, which had been discussed and approved by the entire executive, proved controversial before he even delivered it. So controversial in fact that he and others believed that it contributed to his failed re-election bid at that convention.[56] Evidently, his address was accidentally distributed to some delegates the night before he was to deliver it orally and early the next morning copies had to be distributed to others who wanted to read it before he delivered it orally. After some intense debate the convention delegates adopted a resolution directing the executive to produce a study of rural municipalities that they deemed appropriate on the restructuring issue to be submitted to all rural municipalities prior to the 1978 annual convention. Pursuant to that resolution a survey of municipal councils was conducted. The survey revealed the following: only approximately 12% indicated a willingness to explore the potential for amalgamation with neighbouring municipalities; 93% indicated that larger municipal units would not improve municipal governance; and more than 75% felt that larger provincial government grants would solve their problems.[57] In 1978, the provincial government acted on the preference of municipal councils for larger provincial grants by implementing Canada's first provincial-municipal revenue sharing plan. Regardless of any other effects, that financing program pushed the restructuring issue far down the policy agendas of the provincial and municipal governments until the mid-1980s.

During the second quinquennium of the 1980s the restructuring issue re-emerged as a result of reports produced by several committees established by Premier Grant Devine's Conservative government. Those reports advocated inter-municipal cooperation, the rationalization of boundaries of municipal governments as well as those of other local and regional authorities, and financial frameworks and incentives that would facilitate and sustain the implementation of the proposed reforms.

SPECIAL TASK FORCE ON RURAL DEVELOPMENT (1985)

The first of these reports was produced by the Special Task Force on Rural Development. The Task Force noted that a debate still prevailed in the province between those who believed and those who did not believe that municipal restructuring resulting in fewer and larger municipalities would contribute to improved municipal governance and to improved rural development. Rather than take sides in that debate, the Task Force argued that "a strong case could be made for enhanced inter-municipal cooperation" along with the establishment of some additional institutions in "rural Saskatchewan to supplement—not supplant—existing local government efforts in the area of economic development."[58] The Task Force suggested that for that purpose the provincial government should provide increased financial assistance targeted at participating rural and small urban municipalities that cooperated to establish what it termed "area development corporations." It concluded its recommendations with a call for prudence and participatory decision-making. In its words, "any action to deal with this sensitive issue must be both cautious and open, and be carried out with a high degree of participation from and cooperation with the organizations directly concerned."[59]

LOCAL GOVERNMENT FINANCE COMMISSION (1984–86)

The second report was produced by the Local Government Finance Commission, which had been established by the Devine government in 1984. Although the Commission focused primarily on municipal finances, it postulated its report with some observations regarding the adverse effects that the structural features of the municipal system had on some financial matters, and concluded that it "would be highly appropriate for the provincial government to initiate a review of the structure of local government."[60] By the time that the Commission included that recommendation in its final report, the representatives from SARM and SUMA had both withdrawn from the Commission due to disagreements on various taxation issues.[61] The recommendation of the Commission was not acted upon by the Devine government largely because it recognized that it would likely be met with strong resistance by the municipal associations, especially given that their representatives had withdrawn from the Commission before that recommendation was included in the report.

CONSENSUS SASKATCHEWAN COMMITTEE (1990)

The third report was produced by the Consensus Saskatchewan committee, which was established by the Devine government in the late 1980s to examine the need for and nature of reforms in various policy sectors to foster economic and community development in the province. The Committee consisted of a wide cross-section of representatives from various economic and social sectors and communities. The Committee asserted that if some communities are to survive and thrive in the 21st century, changes were necessary in community, governance, and service delivery structures. Rather than addressing the issue of restructuring as a matter limited only to the adjustment of municipal boundaries, it advocated adjustments to the boundaries of an array of local and regional authorities as well as provincial electoral constituencies. The Committee noted that none of the following had common boundaries:

> 538 [urban] municipalities, 298 rural municipalities, 116 union
> hospital districts, 45 home care districts, 13 provincial

community health care regions, 8 provincial mental health care regions, 108 ambulance districts, 6 provincial social services regions, 115 school divisions, 11 regional colleges and a host of other service delivery areas.[62]

To minimize such fragmentation it recommended common regional boundaries for education, health, social programs, protective services, cultural and recreation services, government services, emergency measures, ambulance services, transportation systems, communication systems, and environmental management. The Committee also advocated a general governance framework for each region that consisted of "a regional council mandated to ensure coordination of services, sharing of resources, and the elimination of duplication."[63]

On the matter of the process by which the common boundaries should be achieved, the Committee suggested that it was imperative that the provincial government "take the initiative to effect the rationalization of local governments and provide leadership in establishing efficient, practical and rational common boundaries."[64] However, it added that the implementation of local government rationalization should be a co-operative and non-partisan process involving the provincial and local governments, the urban and rural associations and the general public. Finally, the Committee indicated that the introduction of regionalization and rationalization of boundaries had to be complemented by flexible taxation powers that would make it possible to generate more revenue at the local level and reduce dependency on provincial financial transfers.

As discussed in the next section of this chapter, these recommendations regarding the process for restructuring and increasing the fiscal capacity of larger municipalities would be echoed in the report of the Task Force on Municipal Legislative Renewal precisely 10 years later.

FOURTH ERA OF MUNICIPAL RESTRUCTURING IN SOUTHERN SASKATCHEWAN: 1991–2005
The issue of municipal restructuring again received substantial attention from 1991 to 2005. Upon assuming the reins of power in 1991, Premier Roy Romanow's provincial government decided to explore whether any restructuring was required in the three major local governance sectors (i.e., municipal, health, and education). For that purpose it established a separate reform process for each sector. All three processes produced proposals for restructuring, but ultimately only the health and education processes resulted in any substantial restructuring as the largest regional districts in history were established across the province for both of those sectors.

The municipal restructuring reform processes during this era had three relatively distinct periods in which proposals and policies for restructuring were developed. The first period, which lasted from 1991 to 1996, focused on the development of financial and statutory frameworks to facilitate inter-municipal cooperation. The second period, which lasted from 1997 to 2000, focused on options for restructuring through a combination of policy parameters established by the provincial government and provincial-municipal consultations. The third period, which lasted from 2001 to 2005, focused primarily on developing a statutory framework for voluntary restructuring by municipal councils.

MUNICIPAL RESTRUCTURING AGENDA: 1991–96

During the period from 1991 to 1996 there was a concerted effort to act on the recommendations that had been made by various advisory committee reports in the previous two decades, including the 1991 report of the Consensus Saskatchewan committee for initiating and institutionalizing inter-municipal cooperation as a means to achieve greater efficiencies, effectiveness, and equity in the municipal sector.[65] Significant initiatives in this respect included the decision of the provincial government to establish the advisory committee on Inter-Community Cooperation and Quality of Life (ICCQL), SUMA's Task Force on Urban Governance Renewal (TFUGR), the provincial government's Bill 33 (The Municipal Services Districts Act), and the tripartite Memorandum of Understanding between the provincial government, SARM and SUMA. These initiatives are discussed in turn below.

ADVISORY COMMITTEE ON INTER-COMMUNITY COOPERATION AND QUALITY OF LIFE (1994)

The ICCQL Committee was appointed by the Romanow government in 1993. Its mandate was to consider how to foster inter-community or inter-municipal cooperation, as had been advocated in the report of the "Consensus Saskatchewan" committee that, to reiterate, had been commissioned by the previous provincial government. The ICCQL Advisory Committee that consisted of representatives of the provincial government, SARM and SUMA.

The Advisory Committee proposed a framework for improved governance in the municipal sector that included the following elements: a comprehensive strategic plan for the municipal sector; an appropriate statutory and regulatory framework that would empower municipal governments in managing change; a revamped financial framework that would provide incentives for inter-municipal cooperation and structural reforms; extensive consultations with the key stakeholders and the public on directions for reform; and a coherent strategy for restructuring the municipal system. It underscored the importance of restructuring as a means to ensure sustainability of communities and services as follows: "Restructuring of service delivery [...], new organizational frameworks or models, rationalization of municipal boundaries, reversion of villages to hamlet status, and consolidation of local government boards and authorities are all issues that need to be considered. There must be a clear recognition that not all communities will be sustainable. Sustaining access to services is more important than sustaining communities and access to services should be the focus of a restructuring strategy."[66] Despite the importance that it attached to restructuring, the Advisory Committee stated that it was not prepared to recommend the provincial imposition of an overall structure of governance or service delivery, but preferred an approach for renewal based on "consultation and gentle encouragement through permissive legislation."[67]

That was essentially the approach that was used in establishing the Regional Economic Development Authorities (REDAs). Those special purpose bodies were developed in the 1990s to supplant the Rural Development Corporations (RDCs) that had been created by the Progressive Conservative government in 1986. The main difference between them was that the REDAs were designed to operate on a larger geographical basis than the RDCs.[68] The provincial government's decision to create REDAs was heavily influenced by a need stimulate economic development in the province by any means possible to help it deal with one of the most serious fiscal crisis in recent decades.

SUMA'S TASK FORCE ON URBAN GOVERNANCE RENEWAL (1995)

Many of the recommendations made by the ICCQL Advisory Committee were echoed shortly thereafter in the work of the Task Force on Urban Government Renewal (TFUGR), which was established by SUMA. The impetus for TFUGR and its report was provided by a resolution passed at SUMA's 1993 annual convention to develop a comprehensive set of proposals that would be brought back to the membership in 1995. In addition to SUMA members and staff, TFUGR included representatives of SARM, the Saskatchewan Association of Northern Municipalities (SANC) and the provincial government. TFUGR was funded through the provincial Inter-Community Co-operation program and a special levy on SUMA members. TFUGR made several recommendations related to restructuring, including the following: that inter-municipal cooperation on a regional basis should be promoted as an option for dealing with the service capacity issues faced by many municipalities; that the provincial government establish some financial incentives programs to encourage municipalities to undertake inter-municipal cooperation; that municipalities develop broader and formal inter-municipal agreements; and that efforts be made to facilitate not only the voluntary creation of service districts, but possibly also amalgamations where needed and desired.[69] However, TFUGR cautioned that although there was strong support among municipal governments for formalizing agreements on inter-municipal cooperation and eliminating obstacles to such cooperation and the consolidation of municipalities, there was substantially less support for moving prematurely toward the creation of regional service districts or municipal amalgamation either on a mandatory or even a voluntary basis.[70]

The major reform initiatives that resulted from the aforementioned reports for fostering and facilitating inter-municipal cooperation and voluntary amalgamation included two small restructuring incentive programs funded by the provincial government and the draft legislation to foster inter-municipal cooperation (i.e., the Service District Act, Bill 33). The first of the restructuring incentive programs was the Inter-municipal Cooperation Program (ICCP) introduced shortly after the ICCQL Advisory Committee submitted its report to the Minister in the fall of 1993. Under the ICCP the provincial government made grants available to urban municipalities to encourage them to develop projects with any other municipality (including rural municipalities), local authority, or service agency to enhance the quality and effectiveness of shared service delivery. Another related initiative introduced in 1996 was the Municipal Restructuring Assistance Program which provided neighbouring municipalities $7,500 to explore the possibility of amalgamation. The program was terminated within two years largely as a result of the remarkably limited demand. While some have suggested that the low demand was in part due to the relatively small amount of the grant, others have mused that even substantially higher sums would not have increased the demand due to the reticence to engage in inter-municipal cooperation and the strong antipathy to amalgamation.

MUNICIPAL SERVICE DISTRICTS ACT (1996)

After two years of limited experimentation with the modestly funded programs for inter-municipal cooperation and amalgamation the provincial government decided to take another step forward in fostering inter-municipal cooperation by establishing a statutory framework that facilitated the creation of service districts and service district boards. Toward that end it produced some draft legislation that it hoped would assist municipalities in initiating and institutionalizing such cooperation. Thus, on December 1, 1995, just seven months after the election that gave it a second term in office with a large majority, Premier Roy Romanow's government presented SARM and SUMA with draft legislation for creating municipal service districts. The draft legislation was submitted for first reading in the provincial legislature on March 19, 1996, as Bill 33 (An Act Respecting Service Districts).

The purpose of Bill 33 was to provide municipal governments with the statutory authority to create service district boards on a voluntary, piecemeal and ad-hoc basis. Such boards were to be composed of councillors from member municipalities chosen by their respective councils, and they were to be responsible for planning and delivering any one or more of an array of basic municipal and emergency services. Individual municipalities were to have extensive freedom not only to opt-in or opt-out of a service district, but also to opt-in or opt-out of any service that they provided. Member municipalities were to have extensive control over the type of services that district boards could offer and their general management of those services. Finances for such boards were to be drawn from a variety of sources including provincial grants, service fees, and funds requisitioned from member municipalities.[71] The district services boards envisioned in Bill 33 were modelled primarily on British Columbia's regional districts and, to some extent, also Alberta's regional services commissions.[72] Moreover, the approach for the creation of such districts was comparable to the so-called "gentle imposition" approach that had been used in creating British Columbia's regional districts.[73]

To the surprise of the provincial government, Bill 33 was met with substantial opposition from elected and appointed municipal officials. The provincial government had hoped that the inclusion of the provisions that maximized the scope of voluntary initiative and institutionalization on the part of such officials and their communities would preclude any opposition from them to that legislation. There were several reasons that it did not have the effect that the government had hoped. The most significant reason is that many municipal officials perceived the legislation as the proverbial 'thin edge of the wedge' designed to introduce a statutory framework that the provincial government could eventually use to compel municipal governments to establish district services boards in one of two ways.[74] One way was through the provincial government's "power of the pen" that would result in amendments to that legislation for the purpose of replacing the provisions for locally-driven, voluntary action with some for provincially-driven, mandatory action in the creation of such boards. Another way was through the "power of the purse," by establishing municipal financial frameworks that would constrain municipalities to establish district service boards to maximize their financial capacity to provide certain services.[75]

The second major reason that municipal officials opposed the creation of District Service Boards was a concern that it would lead to a "hollowing out of the municipal state," not only through the possibility that a long list of service functions could be devolved to such district services boards, but also through the potential loss of existing municipal staff to them. The third major reason, and one that made it possible for them to engender antipathy toward the legislation among their ratepayers, was their belief that in all likelihood service provision by larger regional service district boards would be more costly for ratepayers. Neither those arguments nor their effects were new. As had happened with various other proposals for any form of restructuring in previous decades, the articulation of those arguments engendered substantial opposition primarily among elected and appointed municipal officials, as well as some of their ratepayers who were aware of it, to the type of restructuring that was envisioned in Bill 33.

The lead role in opposing Bill 33 was taken by SARM's leadership and membership who were very strongly opposed to it from the start. By contrast, SUMA's leadership and membership initially seemed more inclined to support it largely because a survey that had been conducted as part of the TFUGR initiative indicated that 92% of respondents favoured more inter-municipal cooperation, and 65% of those felt that a high priority should be given to developing more formal regional co-ordination mechanisms.[76] Despite that initial support for Bill 33, within a very short time SUMA's leadership decided to side with its SARM counterparts on the issue for two reasons. First, some informal surveys of its membership conducted after the draft legislation was produced indicated that many shared some of the same concerns as their SARM counterparts on the potential problems with Bill 33 and the creation of service districts.[77] Second, SUMA's leadership wanted to maintain a constructive working partnership with SARM. For this purpose it decided to join SARM in asking the provincial government to withdraw Bill 33. This was a gesture of solidarity designed to strengthen the working relationship between the two associations.

In providing a rationale for its position, SUMA indicated that Bill 33 only addressed a very small part of the large number of issues that had to be dealt with on the municipal reform agenda, and that everything should be addressed as part of a comprehensive reform initiative in the near future.[78]

The municipal associations and their members were not the only ones opposed to Bill 33. Their cause was quickly taken up by both of the opposition parties represented in the provincial legislature. Spokespersons for both the Official Opposition, which was the Liberal Party at the time, and the Progressive Conservative Party, criticized Bill 33 on several occasions. In doing so they echoed arguments that had been made by the municipal associations on whether there was a real need for such legislation for purposes of inter-municipal cooperation, or whether the provincial government was enacting it as a first step toward either supplanting municipal governments with the proposed district boards or full-fledged mandated amalgamation.[79] The criticism of Bill 33 by the opposition parties occurred during two successive question periods in May of 1996, just a few days before the provincial government, SARM, and SUMA signed the *Memorandum of Understanding (MOU)* related to Bill 33 and agreed on the next steps in the reform process which are discussed below.[80] Their questions in the legislature at that particular time stemmed from a statement that the Minister of Municipal Government had made a few days earlier to the effect that the government planned to give third reading to Bill 33 before the legislative session ended in the next few weeks, but not proclaim it unless it was deemed necessary to do so in implementing a 9-1-1 service as part of its emergency services system.[81] When asked about this in the legislature, the Minister confirmed that the government intended to pass Bill 33 but not proclaim it unless it was necessary to do so.[82]

Some criticism of Bill 33 also came from some editorial boards and columnists. Some of them agreed with the municipal associations that, at best, Bill 33 would not make a difference, and at worst it would actually be counterproductive because, if service district boards were created, they would constitute another level of government with operating costs that would offset, and possibly even surpass, any economies of scale that could be achieved in the consolidation of service delivery.[83] Although many media commentators generally echoed the position of many members of municipal associations and municipal councils regarding the potential problems of Bill 33, they did not all share the position of those municipal officials regarding either what type of consolidation should occur or how it should be accomplished. To the chagrin of many members of municipal associations and municipal councils, some of the editorials and commentaries advocated amalgamation of municipal units on a mandatory basis.[84]

Faced with such opposition from various sources, the provincial government decided to withdraw Bill 33 approximately two months after introducing it. Its decision was based on its programmatic and political interests. In terms of its programmatic interests, the provincial government realized that, given the opposition to it by the municipal associations, it was unlikely to be utilized sufficiently, if at all, for creating service districts. In terms of its political interests, the provincial government concluded that the imposition of Bill 33 over the opposition of the municipal associations and both opposition parties was potentially problematic in maintaining the support of some voters whose votes would be needed to win seats in the next election. This concern regarding electoral support was based on indications from the municipal associations and the opposition parties that they were prepared to undertake various initiatives to oppose it at the second and third reading stages and even thereafter. The results of the provincial election seven months earlier in which some of its prominent front-bench members and backbenchers lost their seats due in part to the controversial mandated creation of the regional health districts two years earlier certainly contributed to its decision.

THE TRIPARTITE MEMORANDUM OF UNDERSTANDING (1996)

Bill 33 was withdrawn pursuant to the provisions in the *MOU* signed by the Premier and the presidents of SARM and SUMA on May 30, 1996. The *MOU*, produced after a month of negotiations, committed the signatories to develop an "action plan" for a series of reform initiatives designed to enhance the governance capacity and efficacy of municipalities into the next century. The *MOU* identified several key initiatives that were to be undertaken in preparing the action plan. This included reviews of, and recommendations for, reforms to five components of the municipal system: inter-municipal cooperation in service delivery; provincial and municipal responsibilities in service delivery; systems of municipal structures and governance; cost and expenditure patterns of municipalities; and municipal statutes and regulations. The *MOU* project management plan released in January 1997 indicated that in preparing those five reviews attention would be devoted to issues and options based on agreed principles and criteria, and that those issues and options would be the focus of trilateral negotiations that were to take place prior to July 31, 1997.[85]

Within one year after it was initiated, the *MOU* process started to stall and eventually came to a grinding halt due to two major factors. The first factor was the failure of the municipal associations to live up to their commitments in producing the requisite background studies as outlined in the project management plan. The second factor was the disputes between the provincial government and the municipal associations regarding a proposed reduction to the revenue sharing pools over and above the reductions that had been included in the previous budget, and to the proposed level of revenue-sharing.[86] Given the challenges they faced in coordinating the review of the municipal system on a trilateral basis, representatives of the provincial government, SARM and SUMA agreed that the review should be undertaken by a task force appointed and funded by the provincial government.

MUNICIPAL RESTRUCTURING AGENDA 1998–2000
TASK FORCE ON MUNICIPAL LEGISLATIVE RENEWAL (1998–2000)

In 1998, pursuant to the aforementioned agreement, the provincial government established the Task Force on Municipal Legislative Renewal, which was given a very broad mandate that, in effect, required it to deal with the various elements of the unfinished review and renewal agenda of the *MOU* process. More specifically, it was mandated to:

- Consider the role and responsibilities of municipal government in Saskatchewan in the next decade;

- Confirm, or set new directions for the evolution and development of municipal governance;

- Define and clarify the relationship between provincial and municipal governments; and

- Make recommendations for municipal renewal.[87]

During the first year of its mandate, the Task Force tried to put the restructuring issue at the bottom of the review and renewal agenda and focused on issues and options related to the functions, finances and jurisdictional authority of municipal governments. Ultimately, however, it came to the conclusion that all four of those elements had to be considered together to maximize the efficacy of any reforms to the municipal system. Furthermore, initially the Task Force explored the prospects for examining whether inter-municipal cooperation would suffice to deal with some of the problems caused by the structural features of a highly fragmented municipal system. Only when it became evident that this was highly unlikely, did the Task Force start to shift its focus from the inter-municipal cooperation option to the amalgamation option. It did so with considerable reticence and consternation because it was fully cognizant that amalgamation was a not only a controversial subject, but for many in the municipal sector it was also a taboo subject that should not be on the reform agenda.

Following a series of public consultations in the spring of 1999, the Task Force produced its interim report containing several recommendations related to the following four key aspects of municipal restructuring— the number, size, and types of municipalities and the approaches to restructuring. Regarding the number of municipalities, the Task Force recommended that it be reduced from approximately 1000 municipalities and quasi-municipalities to fewer than 125. Regarding the size of municipalities, the Task Force recommended reliance on the principle that the geographic size of municipalities should correspond to economic and social regional districts and that it should provide municipalities with the requisite resources, capacity and sustainability to perform their functions. Toward that end, the Task Force recommended that special attention should be given to four key bases needed to provide the requisite resources and capacity—the economic base, the assessment base, the population base, and the land base. Regarding the types of municipalities, the Task Force recommended the creation of two types of one-tier, rather than two-tier, regional municipalities. The first type was "Metropolitan Municipal Districts" that would consist of the larger cities and the surrounding communities, and the second type was "Regional Municipal Districts" that would consist of other urban centres and the surrounding rural areas. Its decision to recommend one-tier regional municipalities was in response to the prevailing view expressed by many participants in the first round of consultations that a two-tier system would be more cumbersome and costly.

The Task Force also made two key recommendations regarding the approaches to renewal. The first was that in matters related to municipal restructuring a "directed consultative approach" should be undertaken, and that in all other matters a "negotiated approach" should be undertaken. The phrase "directed consultative approach" was intended to convey the notion that to achieve restructuring it was necessary to create an optimal mix of some direction, guidance and incentives by the provincial government, and extensive provincial-municipal and inter-municipal consultations. The Task Force was convinced by arguments made by some participants in the first round of community consultations who had indicated that history suggested that neither substantial restructuring nor even inter-municipal cooperation was likely to occur without some direction, guidance and support from the provincial government.

Despite the fact that the Task Force never stated how much direction should be provided by the province, the words "directed consultative approach" were interpreted to mean "forced amalgamation" by some key stakeholders in the municipal sector and most notably by leaders and members of SARM and RMAA. Thereafter, the recommendations for the creation of one-tier regional municipalities using the 'directed consultative approach' became one of the most controversial issues in the municipal sector since the 1950s and early 1960s during the highly protracted and controversial reform process that led to the enactment of the Municipal Unit and County Act, 1962.

Shortly after releasing the interim report, the Task Force held the second round of public consultations to provide groups and individuals with an opportunity to express their opinions on its preliminary recommendations. Unlike each session of the first round of public consultations which was generally attended by approximately one to three dozen people, each session of the second round public consultations was attended by several hundred people for a total of more than 5,000 people. The vast majority of the participants had been mobilized by the special efforts of elected and appointed municipal officials to pack the meetings with persons opposed to what they had depicted as "forced amalgamation." The singular and central theme in the vast majority of briefs and oral presentations was captured in the campaign buttons that read "Say No to Forced Amalgamation." That was also the central theme in a petition developed and circulated by SARM and RMAA officials who were able to collect a few thousand signatures from other municipal officials and ratepayers in their respective municipalities.

After completing the highly controversial public hearings, the Task Force focused on producing the final report that provided a relatively comprehensive and multi-faceted framework for municipal renewal. In that report the Task Force continued to argue that reforms to the municipal system had to include some restructuring. In the introduction to that report, it noted that successful reforms required "an appropriate balance between local and regional municipal governance" and that the challenge would be to "find both the appropriate forms and the appropriate balance between the two for different purposes, in different places, at different points in time."[88]

In providing some direction for restructuring, the Task Force decided that rather than proffering a singular statutory and organizational model or approach, it would highlight a wide range of statutory and organizational frameworks and approaches used in various jurisdictions in Canada. Moreover, The Task Force emphasized that the objective of its final report was not to produce the "blueprints" for renewal, but to provide "building blocks" that could be used in constructing such blueprints. It added that the responsibility for producing such "blueprints' rested with the local and provincial governments and the communities they serve using various decision-making processes.[89]

With that in mind, the Task Force decided to provide an overview of alternative models that existed for restructuring, including many that were used in other provinces. The three major sections of the final report devoted to restructuring dealt with various models for establishing municipal classification systems, municipal restructuring processes, and regional governance systems. The section on municipal classification systems focused on different types or categories of municipalities and the incorporation criteria for the various types. The section on municipal processes focused on the modes and means by which to restructure, with special attention to the processes for incorporation, reversion, dissolution, annexation, and amalgamation. The section on regional governance profiled models for establishing a statutory framework for municipal regional governance systems in the province. In doing so, it highlighted models for developing four key frameworks for regional governance: the structural frameworks (i.e., boundaries), the organizational frameworks (i.e., governance and management systems), the functional frameworks, and the financial frameworks.

MUNICIPAL-PROVINCIAL ROUNDTABLE REPORT OF 2000

Within five days after the Task Force had completed its public hearings on the interim report and as it commenced writing the final report, the Premier and the presidents of the two associations of municipalities (SUMA and SARM) had concluded a preliminary round of negotiations on how to proceed with municipal reform. At that time they agreed to reconvene the tripartite Municipal-Provincial Roundtable that had been established in conjunction with the *MOU* in 1996 and 1997. This time, however, the Roundtable would also be mandated to focus on producing a framework to eliminate any obstacles to voluntary restructuring.

Between May and December 2000 members of the Roundtable met to discuss some important issues and options related to developing a statutory framework for facilitating municipal restructuring on a voluntary basis. After some preliminary meetings, they agreed that the first order of business would be the issue of the approach to municipal restructuring. Several months later they produced a report that merely focused on eliminating any impediment to restructuring on a voluntary basis.[90] Evidently, efforts on the part of provincial representatives to consider other important issues such as precise models of restructuring as well as functions and finances of restructured municipalities were resisted and ultimately rejected by representatives of the municipal associations. Eventually, however, they reached an agreement on expanding the authority and autonomy of municipal councils. Agreement on those two matters helped to demonstrate that they were making some progress in moving forward with the municipal reform agenda, something which was of political importance for all involved. Their agreement on those two matters led to a set of amendments, which are discussed below, to the municipal statutes in the spring session of the legislature in 2001. However, they were unable to reach agreement on any other major initiative for municipal reform. This included the important issues of a realignment of core functions between the provincial and municipal governments, and either financial transfers from the provincial government to the municipal governments or increased tax room for municipalities to the property tax base by reducing the dependency of school authorities on that particular base.

MUNICIPAL RESTRUCTURING AGENDA 2001–05
From 2000 to 2005 the focus of the provincial government and the municipal associations was on producing a new statutory framework that included provisions for the restructuring of municipalities. Whereas the focus during the first year was on including the appropriate amendments to the existing municipal acts for urban and rural municipalities, the subsequent four years were devoted to the enactment of a new statute for cities and another for all other types of urban and rural municipalities in southern Saskatchewan.

STATUTORY REFORMS OF 2001
On May 4, 2001, approximately one year after the Municipal-Provincial Roundtable was convened, the provincial government introduced some amendments for the Rural Municipality Act, 1989 and some for the Urban Municipality Act, 1984. Those amendments were designed to remove barriers to voluntary amalgamation, boundary alterations, and other forms of restructuring.[91] This was in keeping with the spirit of the Roundtable agreement to maximize local initiative in structural reforms. Under the resulting statutory framework municipalities were authorized to enter into restructuring agreements and determine the terms and conditions under which to restructure. Those amendments placed the onus and authority on municipal governments, rather than the provincial minister or cabinet, to initiate and establish an operational framework for various types of restructuring. The minister's power was limited largely to reviewing, adjusting, and approving or rejecting the proposed restructuring.

REFORMS TO RURAL MUNICIPALITY ACT (2001)

The amendments in the Rural Municipalities Act, 2001 were essentially devoted to facilitating restructuring agreements among municipalities that wanted to amalgamate or restructure in other ways.[92] Four major provisions contained in that Act were related to restructuring. The first provision outlined the requirement for any two or more municipalities that wanted to form either a new rural municipality or a municipal district to enter into a restructuring agreement. The designation of the resulting municipality as a "municipal district" was largely a symbolic matter of importance to urban municipal councillors and their ratepayers who wanted to make it clear that they were forming a new municipality through a partnership and that they were not being "swallowed up" by the rural municipality. Such an agreement had to include the following: an indication regarding whether the participating councils wanted to form a rural municipality or a municipal district; the composition of the new council; and the terms and conditions by which a restructuring agreement could be amended by the council of a new rural municipality or municipal district. The participating councils were also authorized, but not mandated, to include by mutual consent some other provisions in such agreements related to a range of transitional, financial and organizational issues, including the manner with which to deal with the following matters: the disposition of any assets, their respective liabilities, the imposition of any special levies, the allocation of conditional and unconditional grants owed to any of them at the time of restructuring, and the location of the municipal office of the new rural municipality or municipal district. The second provision was a requirement for the participating councils to apply to the minister in writing and, when doing so, providing the minister with the restructuring agreement. The third provision was a requirement for the minister to review the application and issue an order for incorporating the new rural municipality or municipal district if the restructuring agreement complied with all statutory requirements. The fourth provision in that statute authorized the council of any rural municipality or municipal district created pursuant to the new statutory framework to enact a bylaw declaring that any provision of the Urban Municipality Act, 1984 applied to any area within its jurisdiction. This provision was intended to make it possible for restructured municipalities to deal with any matters related to urban areas within their boundaries that were not covered under the Rural Municipality Act, 2001.

REFORMS TO URBAN MUNICIPALITY ACT (2001)

The statutory framework for restructuring outlined in the Urban Municipality Amendment Act, 2001 was very similar to and consonant with the one contained in the Rural Municipality Amendment Act, 2001. The consonance was important because both statutes permitted restructuring involving urban and rural municipalities. The Urban Municipality Amendment Act, 2001, contained five key provisions for restructuring.

First, the council of either an urban municipality or of any other type of municipality that wanted to apply for an alteration to boundaries or for amalgamation or restructuring was required to publish a notice of its intentions. Such a notice was to include a map of the affected area, an explanation of the reasons for the proposal, and a statement that any person could file a written objection to the proposal with the clerk of the municipality that proposed the restructuring. Moreover, a copy of such a notice and all the related material was also to be provided to each ratepayer, municipal council, and school division board in the area of the proposed alteration, amalgamation or restructuring.

Second, if any such objection was filed with the clerk of the municipality that proposed the restructuring, the municipal council was required to call a public meeting. Any such meeting was also to be publicized in a newspaper and by notifying ratepayers, municipal councils and school boards in the area of the proposed alteration, amalgamation or restructuring. Any such meeting would be conducted by the council that initiated the proposed restructuring to hear any person who wanted to make a representation.

Third, the council of an urban municipality had the option of entering into a restructuring agreement with one or more urban or rural municipalities before applying to the minister for the amalgamation or restructuring. The stipulations regarding the contents of such an agreement were identical to those contained in the provisions regarding the restructuring agreements contained in the Rural Municipality Amendment Act, 2001.

Fourth, after having dealt with the aforementioned requirements of the notification and the meeting, the council was required to submit a formal written application either for an alteration of boundaries, amalgamation or other restructuring. In the case of an alteration to boundaries, the application would be submitted either to the minister if supportive resolutions of all other municipalities affected by the proposal had been obtained, or to the Saskatchewan Municipal Board if such resolutions had not been obtained. However, in the case of an application for amalgamation or other type of restructuring, such an application and the requisite documentation were to be submitted only to the minister. Nevertheless, the minister was authorized to ask the Saskatchewan Municipal Board to review any such application. After reviewing the application, either the minister or the Saskatchewan Municipal Board, depending on which of them was dealing with it, could approve or reject it. Moreover, if they approved such applications they were authorized to include any special terms and conditions they considered appropriate either for the processes leading to the modified system or for the actual operation of that system.

In the four years that the provisions contained in the Rural Municipality Amendment Act, 2001, and the Urban Municipality Amendment Act, 2001, were in force they were never used for any substantial restructuring. Over the subsequent four years, those provisions were supplanted by comparable provisions that were included both in the Cities Act, 2002, which went into effect on January 1, 2003, and the Municipalities Act, 2005, which went into effect on January 1, 2006. Both of those statutes were modelled on new generation statutes that were designed to provide greater clarity on the functions of municipalities and greater authority and autonomy for municipalities in performing them.

THE CITIES ACT, 2002

In the Cities Act, 2002 five key provisions were included regarding the alteration of boundaries and amalgamation. First, any council wishing to pursue a restructuring initiative is required to issue a public notice and also notify either in person or by mail all ratepayers, councils of other municipalities, and boards of all school divisions that will be affected by the proposed alteration, amalgamation, or restructuring. Any such notification must include a map of the area affected by the proposed restructuring, a brief explanation of the reason for the proposed restructuring, and a note that any person may file a written objection to the proposed restructuring in the office of the city clerk. Second, if any such objection is filed, the council is required to call a public meeting where ratepayers and residents may make representations relevant to the proposed alteration, amalgamation or restructuring. Third, in the case of an alteration to boundaries, the council must apply either to the minister if it has been able to obtain complementary resolutions for restructuring from other municipalities involved, or to the Saskatchewan Municipal Board if such resolutions have not been obtained. Fourth, either the minister or the SMB may approve or reject an application for an alteration to the boundaries. When approving an application they may impose any terms and conditions that are deemed appropriate. Fifth, in the absence of an application for an alteration to a city's boundaries the Minister is authorized to mandate an alternation (e.g., annexation) after consulting with the councils of the affected municipalities. However, the minister is not authorized to initiate an amalgamation of two or more municipalities. Although the initiation of amalgamations is a municipal council prerogative, the Minister has the authority not only to approve an amalgamation application of a city with other municipalities, but also to include any terms and conditions that the minister or cabinet deem appropriate for that purpose.

THE MUNICIPALITIES ACT (2005)

The 2005 Municipalities Act contains several provisions that either require or allow essentially the same processes for various types of municipal restructuring contained in the 2001 amendments and in the Cities Act, 2002. First, the councils of any two or more municipalities may apply to the minister to restructure. Second, prior to submitting any such application to the minister, the municipalities may enter into a voluntary restructuring agreement. Such a restructuring agreement must contain the same information outlined in the other three statutes enacted during that quinquennium. Third, pursuant to Article 54(1) the voters of any municipality may petition to require their council to apply to restructure the municipality, and if the majority of those voting support the proposed restructuring, the council is required to apply for restructuring without any unreasonable delay. This particular provision contrasts both with the amendments of 2001 that only authorized municipal councils to initiate amalgamations, and the Cities Act, 2002 that only authorized municipal councils and the minister to initiate boundary changes. Fourth, the voters of a municipality are also authorized to initiate a petition requiring

their councils to hold a plebiscite or referendum on any restructuring proposal. Fifth, pursuant to Article 58(1) municipal councils are also authorized to
initiate such plebiscites and referenda on their own, and the minister is
authorized to mandate them to do so when it is deemed necessary. Sixth, the
minister is authorized to refer any matter in dispute between municipalities
on an application to the Saskatchewan Municipal Board. Seventh, any councils involved are required to submit their restructuring application to the
Saskatchewan Municipal Board if they are unable to obtain a certified resolution in support of the application from the council of every other municipality affected by the application. Eighth, the minister is responsible for approving any such applications and for ordering the proposed restructuring. Finally,
pursuant to Article 61(1) the minister may issue orders for restructuring initiatives, regardless of which legitimate entity initiates them, which are designed
to:

> a) establish an organized hamlet, alter the boundaries of an
> organized hamlet or change the status of an organized hamlet;
>
> b) incorporate a municipality;
>
> c) restructure municipalities by:
>
>> i) altering the boundaries of two or more municipalities;
>>
>> ii) merging the whole or any part of two or more municipal-
>> ities;
>>
>> iii) providing for the inclusion of a municipality in any other
>> municipality; or
>>
>> iv) incorporating new municipalities; or
>
> d) change the status of a municipality.

Finally, unlike the previous statutory frameworks enacted for restructuring
in the previous five years, the 2005 Municipalities Act did not contain the
word amalgamation. This is so, despite the fact that the amalgamation of
municipalities is clearly what is envisioned in words such as "merging the
whole or part of two or more municipalities" and "providing for the inclusion
of a municipality in any other municipality." Ostensibly, the omission of the
word amalgamation was more a case of tightening up the language in the
statute, rather than attempting to give the impression that amalgamations
were not covered by this particular statute.

In summary, the foregoing overview of the fourth era of reforms lasting
from 1991 to 2005 reveals that the only accomplishments in municipal restructuring were the production of reports, a more detailed and clearer statutory
framework for voluntary restructuring, a few very minor consolidations of
municipalities, and two minor amalgamations of rural municipalities. Thus,
100 years after the municipal system was established, its basic structural form
remains essentially the same but the number of municipalities has increased

substantially over that time. In 2006, the official number of municipalities in the province was 802, including 296 rural municipalities, 346 villages, 147 towns and 13 cities.[93] If the quasi-municipalities, known as organized hamlets, are included the number of total municipal units was approximately 950.

CONCLUSIONS

The objective in this concluding section is threefold: to provide a brief summary of the findings regarding the restructuring proposals, policies and politics in the municipal sector between 1905 and 2005; to explain the determinants of the paucity of municipal restructuring during the past century; and to provide some prognostications on restructuring in the future.

FINDINGS ON PROPOSALS, POLICIES, AND POLITICS OF RESTRUCTURING

The overview reveals that during the past century there has been a plethora of proposals for restructuring the municipal system. Those proposals have been articulated primarily in a series of reports commissioned by the province during the past century, as well as one report produced independently by two former municipal officials in the 1920s, one produced by the federally appointed Royal Commission on Federal-Provincial Relations in 1940, and one produced by SUMA in the 1990s.

The overview also reveals that, despite all of those proposals, only two notable policy frameworks for restructuring were entrenched in legislation after the original municipal legislation was adopted. Both of those policy frameworks were designed to facilitate restructuring on a voluntary basis. The first was the Municipal Unit and County Act enacted in the early 1960s by the CCF government, and the second were the provisions for restructuring included during the first five years of the 21st century in the Cities Act and the Municipalities Act. Neither of those statutory frameworks for restructuring on a voluntary basis produced any substantial restructuring. Indeed, the only substantial restructuring in the municipal sector was mandated. This occurred from 1908 to 1914 when the provincial government mandated the conversion of LIDs to RMs. Although many ratepayers were opposed to that particular mandated conversion because they were concerned that it could result in more and higher taxes, the existing municipal associations did not mount any major opposition to the conversion because they saw it as a valuable means of empowering local governance.

The overview also reveals several notable features of the politics of restructuring. One feature is that such politics have been very intense and have had to be approached and managed very carefully by successive provincial governments and municipal associations. The reason for this is that provincial and municipal leaders realized that restructuring proposals and initiatives have important political implications for all of them. A second feature is that opposition parties have generally opted to stake out the politically safe ground by supporting restructuring only on a voluntary basis. A third feature is that the politics have generally pitted the provincial government primarily against either one or both of the two major municipal associations (i.e., SARM and SUMA).

A fourth feature is that, on balance, SARM's leadership has been more resistant to exploring some restructuring proposals than SUMA's leadership. Part of the reason for this is that the focus of restructuring has often been more on the rural sector than on the urban sector. Moreover, even when the focus has been on the urban sector, it has been primarily on the smallest units within that sector, rather than the larger ones. However, in fairness to SARM's leadership, it must be noted that there have been times, particularly during the 1960s and 1970s, when some of its presidents and other senior officers implored their members to consider some form of restructuring at least on a limited and experimental basis.

A fifth feature, and closely related to the fourth, is that the degree of solidarity between those two major municipal associations (i.e., SARM and SUMA) in rejecting restructuring proposals and blocking provincially initiated restructuring initiatives has fluctuated over time. Part of the reason for this is that there have been some differences between them on some proposed restructuring initiatives. Despite those differences, however, invariably the SUMA leadership has never completely abandoned the SARM leadership whenever the latter has made demands for concessions or accommodations in relation to any proposed restructuring. Indeed, generally, the two municipal associations have demonstrated a relatively high degree of solidarity in resisting or blocking various restructuring proposals.

FINDINGS ON DETERMINANTS OF PAUCITY OF RESTRUCTURING

The overview has also revealed that the paucity of restructuring after 1914 is attributable to "institutional inertia" and "institutional immunity" as conceptualized at the start of this chapter.

The inertia has been evident in the fact that only on a few occasions have municipal officials broached the subject on their own, or even took the initiative to explore whether some restructuring to the municipal systems undertaken in other provinces were appropriate for Saskatchewan. Moreover, the leaders of municipal associations have never initiated a major restructuring initiative. The inertia has resulted from a widespread belief over time among the majority of municipal leaders that the existing structure of the system was not the cause of any problems in municipal governance, and that restructuring was not the solution to those problems. Indeed, the consensus among the leadership over time has been that the existing system performed the core functions relatively well and that structural reforms were not needed. In their view the source of any existing problem lay beyond the structural features of the system and that is where reforms must focus. The fact that they managed to convince a substantial proportion of ratepayers that structural reforms were not needed contributed to the inertia. Another major factor that has contributed to the inertia has also been the pecuniary interests of municipal officials and ratepayers. Whereas municipal officials worry about losing whatever power they wield and remuneration they receive under the existing framework, ratepayers worry about losing whatever power and control they have had over municipal officials to provide them with the services they need at the tax rates that they prefer. Pecuniary interests have also been a factor among leaders of municipal associations, the majority of whom feared that that broaching or exploring the restructuring issue would likely subject them to criticism, ostracism, and the loss of their leadership position.

The immunity has resulted from the municipal sector's organizational capacity and political power. That capacity and power stemmed from the extensive human and financial resources that have always existed in the municipal sector due to the extensive network of municipalities and the corresponding large number of elected and appointed officials. The resources have been concentrated primarily in the two associations of municipalities (SARM and SUMA) and, to some extent, also in the associations of municipal administrators (RMAA and UMAAS). In addition to the resources that they have at their disposal, their organizational capacity and political power stems from two interrelated factors. The first of these is the leadership roles of elected and appointed officials within their respective communities. Those roles make it possible for them to influence the views and positions of residents in their communities both on the need for restructuring and any particular proposals for restructuring. This has never been difficult because from the time the municipal system was first established, localism has generally trumped regionalism in discourses regarding the structure of the municipal system, and the idea of voluntary restructuring has trumped the idea of mandatory restructuring in discourses regarding the process that should be used in restructuring.

Another significant factor that boosted the political power of those organizations and ultimately the immunity of the municipal sector to restructuring has been the conventions of the two major municipal associations (SARM and SUMA). Those conventions, which traditionally have been held on an annual or semi-annual basis and have been attended by an average of approximately 1,000 to 2,000 delegates in recent decades, have created important forums for municipal officials to mount campaigns against any restructuring contemplated or proposed by provincial governments and any of the task forces or committees that they appointed. Those forums have been important for two major reasons. First, invariably they are among the largest political and policy events in the province each year that receive extensive media attention, especially when controversial issues arise. Second, a tradition has developed for the premiers and members of their cabinets to participate in what are known as the "cabinet bear pit sessions" to deal with questions on issues of importance to the municipal associations and their members. Those conventions and "cabinet bear pit sessions" have augmented the political power of those associations in pressuring provincial governments to be responsive to their preferences on important issues such as restructuring.

One other observation is in order regarding the immunity of the municipal sector to restructuring, especially in light of the loss of that immunity by the educational and health sectors in recent decades. The factors noted above regarding the immunity of the municipal sector are all significant, but some of them were also evident in the other sectors. Thus, it may well be that a major factor that cannot be underestimated in terms of the ability of the municipal sector to retain its immunity has been that the provincial government decided to use its organizational and political resources to restructure those other two sectors first. Their decision to focus on those sectors was that they had much more immediate and direct cost implications for the provincial government because of the funding arrangements.

PROGNOSTICATIONS REGARDING RESTRUCTURING IN THE FUTURE

There is nothing to suggest that any substantial restructuring will occur within the municipal sector either on a voluntary or on a mandatory basisin the near future. One important reason for this is that the majority of existing and emerging elected and appointed provincial and municipal officials understand that the pursuit of substantial restructuring in this particular sector continues to be a politically risky endeavour. This is especially true of any restructuring that would involve the amalgamation of existing local municipalities. For this reason, a more likely scenario for reforms aimed at achieving regional municipal governance will originate from outside the municipal sector per se. More specifically, it is likely to originate from within the economic development sector. The recent reconfiguration of the Regional Economic Development Authorities to form larger Enterprise Regions may well be the first step in that direction.[94] Additional steps could include: the transformation of the Enterprise Regions from single-function authorities to multi-function authorities by expanding their functions to include some of those that are currently performed by municipal governments and some of those that are currently performed by other regional authorities (e.g. watershed authorities, transportation authorities). If the functional load of the Enterprise Regions is expanded in this way, it would entail a shift from the current local governance system to the regional governance system that was envisioned in the Service Districts Act produced by NDP government in the mid-1990s.

Finally, it should be noted that for any restructuring to occur, much more attention will have to be devoted to the nature of the incentive structures than has been the case at any time during the past century. As noted in a recent analysis of the municipal system: "There will always be evolution in the municipal governance system, and it may even reach a 'tipping point' of more sudden transformation, if it is not prematurely pushed into an imposed structure. [Yet, to date] … too little attention has been paid to creating incentives for change."[95] This will have to include not only financial incentives to municipal governments and ratepayers, but also incentives related both to the authority and autonomy of municipal governments and the status and compensation of municipal officials. Such incentives are absolutely imperative for trumping the "institutional inertia" and "institutional immunity" that have stood in the way of any restructuring within the municipal sector. For such incentives to work they will have to be substantial. In short, any provincial government wanting to achieve substantial restructuring in the municipal sector will have to figure out how provide substantial financial and non-financial incentives not only for municipal governments but also for rate-payers.

NOTES

1. Fiona Colligan-Yano and Mervyn Norton, *The Urban Age: Building a Place for Urban Government in Saskatchewan* (Regina: Century Archive Publishing, 1996), 1–5.

2. Saskatchewan, *Report of the Royal Commission on Municipal Organization* (Regina: King's Printer, 1907).

3. Saskatchewan, *Report of the Committee on Provincial-Municipal Relations Saskatchewan 1950* (Regina: King's Printer, 1951), 15.

4. Donald J.H. Higgins, *Local and Urban Politics in Canada* (Toronto: Gage Educational Publishing Company, 1986), 53.

5. Ibid., 11–12.

6. Jenni Mortin, *The Building of a Province: The Saskatchewan Association of Rural Municipalities* (Regina: PrintWest, 1995), 4.

7. Thomas Alfred Patrick, *The County System for Saskatchewan, An Urgently Needed Reform: Arguments and Data in Support of It* (Yorkton: The Enterprise Publishing Co. 1921), 3–18.

8. T.A. Patrick and F.J. Pilkington, "The County System for Saskatchewan, An Urgently Needed Reform," *Western Municipal News* (July 1921): 183–91.

9. Saskatchewan. *Report of the Commission of Inquiry into Provincial and Municipal Taxation to the Government of the Province of Saskatchewan* (Regina: Kings Printer, 1936), 177.

10. Canada, *Report of the Royal Commission on Dominion-Provincial Relations: Book 2: Recommendations* (Ottawa: King's Printer, 1940), 139.

11. Ibid.

12. Rod Bantjes, *Improved Earth: Prairie Space as Modern Artefact, 1869–1944* (Toronto: University of Toronto Press, 2005), 65–91; and Rod Bantjes, "Modernism and the Machine Farmer," *Journal of Historical Sociology* 13, no. 2 (June 2000): 121.

13. Saskatchewan *Report of the Saskatchewan Urban Assessment Committee to the Minister of Municipal Affairs, Regina, Sk.* (Regina: King's Printer, 1943), 68.

14. Ibid.

15. Ibid.

16. Saskatchewan, *Report of the Saskatchewan Reconstruction Council* (Regina: Thos H. McConica, King's Printer, 1944), 83.

17. Ibid.

18. C.G. Bryden, "Saskatchewan Association of Rural Municipalities: Report of Executive Committee to March Convention," *Western Municipal News* (June 1945): 153.

19. Saskatchewan, Royal Commission on Agriculture and Rural Life, *History of Rural Local Government in Saskatchewan: A Technical Reference Document to the Commission's Official Report on "Rural Roads and Local Government"* (Regina: Queen's Printer, 1955), 136, 146–47.

20. Colligan-Yano and Norton, *The Urban Age*, 77–95 and 110–11; Mortin, *The Building of a Province*, 51–56.

21. Saskatchewan, Royal Commission on Agriculture and Rural Life, *History of Rural Local Government in Saskatchewan: A Technical Reference Document to the Commission's Official Report on "Rural Roads and Local Government,"* 224–26; and Edward W. Weidner, "Foreign Government and Politics: Some Comparative Experience in Adjusting Local Units and Areas," *The American Political Science Review* 42, no.4 (August 1948): 730–45.

22. Saskatchewan, *Preliminary Draft Report of the Committee to Investigate the Reorganization of Rural Municipal Boundaries* (Regina: King's Printer 1946), 2; and Saskatchewan, Royal Commission on Agriculture and Rural Life, *History of Rural Local Government in Saskatchewan: A Technical Reference Document to the Commission's Official Report on "Rural Roads and Local Government,"* 225–26.

23. J.H. Brocklebank, "Saskatchewan Association of Rural Municipalities: Address of Hon. J.H. Brocklebank to March Convention," *Western Municipal News* (May 1945): 124–25.

24. Mortin, *The Building of a Province*, 40.

25. Ibid., 41.

26. See L.F. McIntosh, Minister of Municipal Affairs, "Foreword" in the *Report of the Committee on Provincial-Municipal Relations Saskatchewan 1950* (Regina: Thos H. McConica King's Printer, 1951).

27. Saskatchewan, *Report of the Committee on Provincial-Municipal Relations. Saskatchewan* (Regina: Thos H. McConica King's Printer, 1951), 25.

28. Ibid.

29. Ibid., 26.

30. Saskatchewan, Royal Commission on Agriculture and Rural Life, "Letter of Transmittal," in *Final Report Volume 1*: vii.

31. Ibid., 251–53 and 262–64.

32. Saskatchewan, Royal Commission on Agriculture and Rural Life, *History of Rural Local Government in Saskatchewan: A Technical Reference Document to the Commission's Official Report on "Rural Roads and Local Government,"* 253.

33. Colligan-Yano and Norton, *The Urban Age*, 110.

34. Saskatchewan, Royal Commission on Agriculture and Rural Life, *Rural Roads and Local Government*, Report No. 4 Volume 1, 268–71.

35. "Municipal Reorganization in Saskatchewan," *Western Municipal News* (May 1957): 151; and "Words and Wisdom," *Western Municipal News* (July 1957): 236.

36. Colligan-Yano and Norton, *The Urban Age*, 110.

37. Premier T.C. Douglas, "Words and Wisdom," *Western Municipal News* (July 1957): 236.

38. This point is noted in a document on the Rural Municipal Administration Association website at http://www.rmaa.ca/.

39. Saskatchewan, Local Government Continuing Committee, *A Technical Document to the Report on Local Government in Saskatchewan* (Regina: Queen's Printer, 1961), 61–107.

40. Colligan-Yano and Norton, *The Urban Age*, 111.

41. Ibid.

42. SARM, "Saskatchewan Association of Rural Municipalities: Resolutions Passed at the 1959 Convention," *Western Municipal News* (September 1959): 273.

43. Mortin, *The Building of a Province*, 53.

44. Colligan-Yano and Norton, *The Urban Age*, 111.

45. Ibid., 52.

46. Hon E.I. Wood, Saskatchewan Minister of Municipal Affairs, *Legislative Assembly of Saskatchewan Debates and Proceedings* (April 1962): 6.

47. Mortin, *The Building of a Province*, 51–53; and Hon. E.I. Wood, "Vote Promised On County System," *Western Municipal News* (March 1962): 8–11; and J.G. Hamilton, President S.A.R.M, "Mind Unchanged," *Western Municipal News* (March 1962): 12–13; and Hon. E.I. Wood, "Minister's Address," Western Municipal News (April 1962): 4–8; and J.G. Hamilton, President S.A.R.M, "Address To the Fifty-Seventh Annual Convention," *Western Municipal News* (April 1962): 9–10; and S.A.R.M, "S.A.R.M Executive Report," *Western Municipal News* (April 1962): 12–13; and Dr. M. Brownstone, Deputy Minister of Municipal Affairs, "Deputy Minister Address," *Western Municipal News* (April 1962): 14–16; and Hon. E.I. Woods, "Hon. E.I. Wood's Address To Convention," *Western Municipal News* (June 1962): 15–19.

48. SARM, "President J.G. Hamilton's Address to the Fifty-Seventh Annual Convention," *Western Municipal News* (April 1962): 9–10.

49. "Municipal Districts for Saskatchewan Approved by Convention," *Western Municipal News* (May 1963): 18.

50. Mortin, The Building of a Province, 55; and Colligan-Yano and Norton, *The Urban Age*, 112.

51. Mortin, *The Building of a Province*, 56.

52. Ibid., 56.

53. Ibid.

54. Ibid.

55. Saskatchewan, *Report of the Rural Development Advisory Group* (Regina: Queen's Printer, 1976), 91–95.

56. Mortin, *The Building of a Province*, 63.

57. Ibid.

58. Saskatchewan, *Strategy for the Development of Rural Saskatchewan (Special Task Force Report) (1985)*, 134.

59. Ibid.

60. Saskatchewan, *Overview of the Final Report of the Local Government Finance Commission (1986)*, 96.

61. Colligan-Yano and Norton, *The Urban Age*, 123; and Mortin, *The Building a Province*, 66–67.

62. Saskatchewan, Consensus Saskatchewan Committee, *Leading the Way: a Blueprint for Saskatchewan (1990)*, 53.

63. Ibid., 53–54.

64. Ibid.

65. See the following reports: Government of Saskatchewan, A Government of Saskatchewan Special Task Force Report, *Strategy for the Development of Rural Saskatchewan (1985)*; Saskatchewan, Local Government Finance Commission, *Final Report (1986)*; SUMA, SARM, SSTA, Vision 2000, *Financing Local Governments and Economic Development in the Year 2000* (Symposium Report, 1991); Saskatchewan Municipal Government, *Advisory Committee Report on Inter-Community Cooperation and Community Quality of Life, (1993)*; Saskatchewan Municipal Government, *Review of*

Emergency and Protective Services (1995); and Saskatchewan Urban Municipalities Association, *Task Force on Urban Government Renewal, Recommendations. The ABC's of Renewal, 1995.*

66. *Saskatchewan, Advisory Committee Report on Inter-Community Co-operation and Community Quality of Life, 1994*, 18.

67. Ibid., viii.

68. Neville Fernandes, *Saskatchewan's Regional Economic Development Authorities: A Background Document* (Community University Institute for Social Research, 2003); Andrew Conte, "Saskatchewan's REDA's: Bottom-up Economic Development," *Government Finance Review* 12 (August 1996): 4; and Kiley Frantik, "Regional Economic Development Authorities in Saskatchewan" (MA thesis, Department of Political Studies, University of Saskatchewan, 2007).

69. See SUMA Task Force on Urban Government Renewal in SUMA's *Annual Convention Handbook 1997*, 16; and SUMA Task Force on Urban Government Renewal, *Recommendations, The ABC's of Renewal, January 1995.*

70. SUMA Task Force on Urban Government Renewal, *The ABC's of Renewal, January 1995*, 98.

71. See Saskatchewan, *An Act Respecting Service Districts (Bill 33)*, 1996.

72. For an excellent overview of the organization, functions, and finances of British Columbia's Regional Districts and Alberta's Regional Services Commissions see Saskatchewan Municipal Government, "Examples of Intermunicipal Approaches in Other Provinces," in Saskatchewan Municipal Government, *Advisory Committee Report on Inter-Community Co-operation and Community Quality of Life, 1995*, Appendix E.

73. Paul Tennant and David Zirnhelt, "Metropolitan Government in Vancouver: The Strategy of Gentle Imposition," *Canadian Public Administration* 16 (Spring 1973): 124–38.

74. Mark Wyatt, "Co-operation Sought: Gov't Wants Municipalities to Merge," *Leader-Post*, April 18, 1996.

75. Murray Mandryk, "Gov't May Tie Money to Municipal Amalgamation," *StarPhoenix*, April 16, 1996.

76. See SUMA, Task Force on Urban Government Renewal, *Renewal in Motion*, 19.

77. See SUMA, "A Hitchhiker's Guide to Bill 33" in Special Insert with *Urban Voice* (Spring 1996).

78. See SUMA president's comments in Mark Wyatt, "Municipal Streamlining Not Subject to Quick Remedy," *StarPhoenix*, April 27, 1996.

79. Saskatchewan, *Saskatchewan Legislative Proceedings and Debates* (March 20, 1996): 392–93.

80. Murray Mandryk, "Bill 'Misunderstood': Legislation has Municipalities Worried," *Leader-Post*, May 27, 1996.

81. Murray Mandryk, "Bill 'Misunderstood'," and Murray Mandryk, "Teichrob Says Bill Benign," *StarPhoenix*, May 27, 1996. See also Mark Wyatt, "Romanow Still Pondering Fate of Municipal Bill," *StarPhoenix*, May 30, 1996.

82. Saskatchewan, *Legislative Assembly of Saskatchewan Debates and Proceedings* (May 27, 1996): 1853–54; ibid. (May 28, 1996), 1908–10.

83. See "Push Harder To Meld RMs," *StarPhoenix*, January 10, 1996; Kevin Hursh, "For Real Savings, Merge Tiny Villages, RMs," *StarPhoenix*, January 17, 1996; and "Legislation Points RMs in Right Direction," *Leader-Post* March 22, 1996.

84. See "Push Harder To Meld RMs," and "RMs: Making a Case That Bigger is Better," *Leader-Post*, January 11, 1996; "Legislation points RMs in Right Direction," and "RMs Already Cooperating," *StarPhoenix*, April 22, 1996.

85. See Saskatchewan, *Memorandum of Understanding Project Management Plan*, 8.

86. See SUMA, "Province Takes Health Levies Out of Municipal Revenue Sharing," Press Release, September 26,1996; Murray Westby, SUMA President, "SUMAReplies to Romanow," Letter to the Editor, *Leader-Post*, November 30, 1996; and "Health Levies Cured with Municipal money," *Urban Voice* 1, no. 6 (October, 1996).

87. Saskatchewan, Order in Council 507/1998, August 13, 1998.

88. Saskatchewan, *Task Force on Municipal Legislative Renewal* (Government of Saskatchewan), 9.

89. Ibid., 2.

90. Saskatchewan, Municipal-Provincial Roundtable, *Impediments to Voluntary Restructuring: A Review of the Legislative and Financial Impediments to Voluntary Municipal Restructuring in Saskatchewan* (June 12, 2000): 11.

91. Saskatchewan, Minister of Municipal Relations. News Release: May 4, 2001; *Saskatchewan Legislative Assembly of Saskatchewan Debates and Proceedings* (May 14, 2001): 1108–19.

92. Saskatchewan, An Act to Amend The Rural Municipality Act, 1989 and to make consequential amendments to certain other Acts and to repeal certain Regulations, Saskatchewan Statues, Chapter 38, 2001.

93. Government of Saskatchewan, Bureau of Statistics, Department of Finance. *Saskatchewan Fact Sheet 2007*. http://www.stats.gov.sk.ca/docs/factsheet07.pdf

94. *Annual Report 2007–2008*.

95. Colligan-Yano and Norton, *The Urban Age*, 110.

FEDERAL-PROVINCIAL
RELATIONS

Saskatchewan and Canadian Federalism
David E. Smith

INTRODUCTION

Saskatchewan has been described in many ways: as a backwater, hinterland, and (until very recently) a have-not province. With fewer than one million residents, and governed usually by a political party never in power in Ottawa, what political capital does such a jurisdiction possess when it comes to the conduct of federal-provincial relations? At first glance, the answer would seem to be "very little." Yet, as this chapter will argue, Saskatchewan has exerted an influence on the conduct and character of Canadian federalism far in excess of its size and wealth. Indeed, the effect has been almost in inverse proportion to those traditional measures of influence. This chapter argues that the explanation for Saskatchewan's weight in the federation lies not in such quantifiable factors as its contribution to the Canadian economy, but in less concrete phenomena, such as political leadership, administrative acumen, and ideological commitment and resourcefulness.

FEDERAL THEORY AND CANADA

In his 2000 MacGregor Lecture on Canadian federalism, political scientist Richard Simeon lamented the state of federal studies in Canada. In light of his own contribution to the field, Simeon's critique commands attention. At its heart is a plea to fellow scholars to turn from what he calls "present minded-ness" and to engage with theory.[1] The Quebec (or unity) question has dominated academic attention for 40 years, to the exclusion of grappling with other issues and to the detriment of understanding the complex forces that mould Canadian federalism. Two examples prove his point: the Canadian Charter of Rights and Freedoms and the evolving status of the First Nations have each generated their own extensive scholarship, some of which touches on the conduct of federalism, but neither subject can be said to have been incorporated into a theory of Canadian federalism. Commentary on the Meech Lake and Charlottetown constitutional agreements of the 1990s is no exception, since these comments usually describe the terms or processes that, in each instance, became the principal reasons for rejecting the proposal.

Part of the continuing reason for the neglect is, as Simeon suggests, the spectre of Quebec nationalism and the threat of separation. But there is another—generic—explanation, and it lies in the genesis of Canadian federalism itself: Canada's terms of union embrace no recognizable federal theory. Representational federalism in the United States (the modern world's federal prototype), achieved through layered institutions of President, Senate and House of Representatives (each with its own "term"), held no appeal for Canadians. Nor was there a consensus among drafters of what became the British North America Act, 1867 (renamed in 1982 the Constitution Act, 1867), as there had been among the delegates at Philadelphia, that underlying the new constitution lay a principle—resistance to concentrated power. Quite the contrary, for Canadian colonists the objective was to transfer as much power from London as was possible into their own hands.

But in whose hands? At its simplest, a federal, as opposed to a unitary, system is about divided jurisdiction, a fact the Confederation debates,later court decisions and academic commentary acknowledge. Yet, in and of itself, division is only a mechanism devoid of purpose. Nor is meaning to be found in the anodyne claim that federalism reconciles the competing desires of unity and diversity. The conundrum of Confederation deepens when the debates of the 1860s and the resulting legislation are examined. Two operating conceptions of federalism are embedded in Canada's terms of union and provide the source for two broad and conflicting streams of interpretation that flow through the decades into modern Canadian politics.

The first might be called the federal paramountcy stream. This operating conception sees the federal government as the paramount power in Canada with the provinces occupying a second, inferior level of government. In this conception, only the federal government is charged with acting in the national interest, and this national interest by definition is expected to trump regional or provincial interests. John A. Macdonald, along with many—likely most—of his successors, certainly assumed this view. Moreover, the formal distribution of powers in the constitution speaks to this view—from the provisions concerning disallowance and reservation to that of appointment for senators, senior judges and lieutenant governors—and to Macdonald's desire to be only one step away from a legislative union rather than a true "confederation."

In the 20th century, the most prominent exponent of the federal paramountcy stream was Pierre Trudeau, although Mackenzie King and Jean Chrétien were close competitors. Each placed great emphasis on the federal Parliament and the legislative instruments at its disposal. Each advocated in favour of greater federal leadership and a federal role in almost all policy areas. More than any other prime minister, however, Trudeau elaborated what might be called a "theory" of paramountcy. Still, it needs to be said that in this enterprise he was not alone. One of the chief intellectual precursors of this position was F.R. Scott, one of Trudeau's professors at McGill, who had great influence on the thinking of the Cooperative Commonwealth Federation (CCF), thereby buttressing the belief in the efficacy of a strong federal government by generations of CCF and, later, New Democratic Party (NDP) leaders. As well, Scott was a critic of the Judicial Committee of the Privy Council whose opinions he believed leaned in the direction of empowering the provinces, and, in consequence, supported the Supreme Court of Canada as the final court of appeal. By contrast, since 1949, the Supreme Court of Canada has acted with restraint in defining the reach of federal power despite those justices, such as Bora Laskin, who were sympathetic to this conception.

In contrast to federal paramountcy, the second, "confederal," stream assumes that both orders (not levels) of government are equal and sovereign in their own constitutional spheres. In addition, the responsibilities for both orders of government, as spelled out in the constitution, should be regarded as separate watertight compartments, with neither order of government infringing or interfering in any way with the authority of the responsible order of government. Clearly, this is what a majority of the Quebec fathers of confederation wanted, joined in part by some of their colleagues from the Atlantic colonies. Early on, and perhaps not very surprisingly, the premiers of Ontario and Quebec were advocates of a confederal conception. All Quebec premiers have adhered to types of confederal orthodoxy including the notion (the compact theory) that the provinces created the federation and therefore have the right to exit the federation. The judgments of the Privy Council not only reflected a confederal view of the Canadian federation but also gave life to the provincial powers found in Section 92. of the Constitution Act, 1867. This view places emphasis on the provincial governments, their leading role in the design, administration and delivery of most government programs that Canadians actually receive, and argues forcibly in favour of greater decentralization. The Conservative government, formed in 2006 and led by Stephen Harper, has proved to be a strong proponent of this view, pledging to "introduce legislation to place formal limits on the use of the federal spending power for new shared-cost programs in areas of exclusive provincial jurisdiction."[2]

Purpose—to build railways, improve trade or resolve political deadlock—not principle guided action in British North America. Yet, without a theory to start with, none could develop. Thus, long before the threat of Quebec nationalism to Canadian unity, a basis for agreement did not exist on the level of provincial consent—one, some, or all provinces—required for constitutional amendment, or on the terms for a new province's admission to the Union. Rather, these and other foundational issues were matters for political negotiation, first between Westminster and the original colonial delegates, then between Ottawa and leaders of the remaining British North American colonies, and, still later, between Ottawa and the provinces, including on occasion the First Nations.

Federalism without a unifying theory is not a sign of inferiority, although commentaries on the subject written by non-Canadians might lead to that conclusion. The dean of federal studies in the post-war world, when federal government proliferated in the newly-independent countries of Asia and Africa, was K.C. Wheare, Australian-born but Oxford-based. Unlike the United States, Australia and Switzerland, the other countries examined in his classic work *Federal Government*, Canada, he concluded, did not meet his essential federal criteria.[3] Its governments were not coordinate and independent; rather, the paramountcy of the central government made the provinces, in law, dependent. He allowed that in practice, however, Canada had long functioned as a system of divided jurisdiction because the central government exercised self-restraint in the use of its power.

William Livingston, an American, later shifted the emphasis from constitutions to societies and what he called their instrumentalities, that is, those processes and institutions, such as courts and upper chambers, which are put in place to protect the diversities that give rise to federal government in the first instance.[4] Canada fares better under this analysis than at Wheare's hands, for the country's historic particularisms of law, language and religion receive guarantees under the 1867 constitution Still, the latent strength of the central government remains a threat to the stability of the federation. Like Wheare, Livingston's work pre-dated the Canadian Charter of Rights and Freedoms, and as a result, he was spared the task of reconciling the diversities of Canada's societal federalism on the one hand and the uniformity of values represented by the Charter on the other.

A third, but by no means last, example of Canada's perceived weakness as a full-fledged federation can be found in Australia's Federation Debates of the 1890s, which preceded the creation of that country's Commonwealth. There invidious comparisons abound between the American and Canadian federal systems. Those powers of the central government that Wheare later found so dubious, the Australian delegates used as grounds for rejecting the Canadian model despite other strong constitutional similarities between the then Dominions. Canada's federal arrangement was too political, too lacking in principle.

A century later that judgment echoes in the position advanced by proponents of the Triple-E Senate: the Canadian federation, they say, privileges the centre at the expense of the provinces. More than that, the provinces are unequal in the federation. This runs counter to the central assumption of Triple-E theory that all units in a true federation must be the same in powers and rights. This is why Triple-E advocates have repeatedly drawn comparisons between equal representation of states in the Senates of the United States and Australia and the unequal representation of provinces in the Senate of Canada. Other critics have used different vocabulary, complaining that Canada is deficient in institutions to promote intra-state federalism, as, for example, performed by the upper house of the German Parliament, the *Bundesrat*, whose members are drawn from the governments of the *lander*, or states, but the conclusion is the same—Canada is incomplete as a federation.[5]

Although troublesome for federal theory, the absence in Canada of a house of the provinces analogous to the United States Senate has a practical explanation. First, participants in the Confederation debates in the Province of Canada in 1865—to a man—attributed the cause of the American Civil War to the sovereignty the Constitution of 1787 conferred on the states. Whatever supporters of a confederal view of Canadian federalism might say later, at the important moment of decision on their future, the colonists of British North America drew back from emulating the American scheme. A clear division of jurisdiction with federal paramountcy would protect the new Dominion from internal disruption. Subsequently, some commentators described this view as naïve; yet, it is understandable in the comparative context in which they were working.

There is a second reason why the Canadian Senate was not constructed as later federalists would have liked. Canada was a double federation of cultures (English and French) and of provinces. It was not possible then (or now) to adopt the integrative mechanism of equal state representation in one part of the national legislature. Instead, in its place was the compromise to create equal senatorial regions, with some regions encompassing only one province (Ontario and Quebec) and others comprised of several provinces. The Senate of Canada exists to protect sectional minorities distributed among the individual provinces.

Finally, but most important for an understanding of later political developments, in the British imperial world of the last four decades of the 19th century, Parliament was supreme in practice and in mind. And that meant the lower house, the Commons, to whom the government was increasingly accountable as the franchise was progressively expanded to include almost all adult males. There are numerous references in the Confederation debates to parallels between the new Senate (as it was to become) and the House of Lords. In the legislative process the Senate, like the Lords, would be a revising chamber, one of second thought. The most significant factor of the Lords, however, was that it was in eclipse as a decision-making body, a condition which was increasingly evident in the period after the passage in 1832 at Westminster of the Reform Bill, which broadened the franchise for the first time.

Unlike the United States, and Australia afterward, there was no need to construct an institution at the centre through which interests of the states would be injected into national policy. Clarity of jurisdiction and federal paramountcy would be protection enough, along with—and this is where Canadian federalism was different—the incorporation in law of Canada's particularisms of language, religion and law. Unlike those Anglo-American federations, where the states and the federation are co-terminus, either territorially, as in the case of Australia ("a continent for country") or constitutionally, as in the United States, where according to Peter Onuf, the original colonies re-wrote their constitutions following the Philadelphia Convention and whose statehood was legitimized through "mutual recognition" by other states in Congress,[6] Canada's experience was distinct. After 1867, it was an empire within an empire expanding from four to 10 provinces through a series of political negotiations. If Canada was ever incomplete, its incompleteness lies in this historical fact: at the beginning, the country was neither territorially nor constitutionally whole. The roots of regionalism run deep as a consequence.

A NEW THEORY: INTERLOCKING EXECUTIVE FEDERALISM

Particularism and regionalism mark Canadian politics at every stage of its evolution. At each one of these stages, the advocates for their recognition are politicians—federal leaders on one side and colonial or provincial or, sometimes today, First Nations on the other. Here is the origin for some of the distinctive features of Canadian federalism: the asymmetrical relationship that exists between the centre and the different provinces (for example, retention by Parliament of the prairie provinces' natural resources and then, after prolonged negotiations and a host of inquiries, their transfer in 1930); the different conditions for entry for a province into the Union, as seen in a range of financial and representational terms, depending upon the respective needs and skills of the negotiators; the constitutional provision for denominational schools in some but not all provinces; or the continuing compromises of the representation-by-population principle following each decennial redistribution, one consequence of which is an ever expanding House of Commons. (In 2007, the Harper Government proposed to give new Commons seats to Alberta, British Columbia and Ontario to take account of population growth. However, Ontario would be treated differently from the other two provinces and would, as a result, remain "under-represented." Since under existing guarantees no province may have its Commons seats reduced, the only way to recognize growth is to add seats to the total number.)

Compare these practices to the undeviating formula for admission to statehood in the United States, found in the North-West Ordinance passed in 1787 before the signing of the Constitution, which pledges republican governments and constitutions to be erected out of that vast territory; or to the mathematical calculations, rigidly followed, in the allocation of seats in the House of Representatives; or to the strict separation of church and state, insofar as education is concerned. Yet, neither paramountcy nor confederal conceptions of federalism—nor, for that matter, the much-studied opinions of the Judicial Committee of the Privy Council which conferred on the provinces greater jurisdiction than Macdonald, Cartier or Brown would have wished—explain what happened. Had either of the original conceptions triumphed, there would be no asymmetry. It is the lack of sameness, the absence of uniform treatment, which is so striking about Canadian federalism, and which makes federal-provincial agreements so difficult and unpredictable.

This not to say agreement is impossible; clearly, that is not the case. Still, the mosaic of Canadian federalism makes explaining agreements difficult. Textbook definitions of federalism, with their static concerns for boundaries and their assumptions of equality, are unhelpful to the task. Nor are the familiar labels in Canadian literature on the subject—administrative, cooperative, or flexible—of assistance. They may explain how decisions are made, or how policy flowing from those decisions is implemented, but they fail to reveal why agreement happens in the first place. Something is missing. Federalism cannot function without some interposition occurring between the orders of government.

The concept of executive federalism, with its focus on first ministers, directs attention to where it is needed—on the individuals who are responsible for reaching agreements. That is, it acknowledges the primacy of political negotiation. Yet, it is deficient in explaining why events happen. More particularly, it fails to account for the course of federal-provincial relations over the past six decades. In its place, a new thesis is needed to explain modern

Canadian federalism. If a label is required to describe this approach, then the phrase "interlocking executive federalism" is one possibility. The advantage of the adverb lies in its emphasis on connection rather than on coordination.

As the title of this chapter indicates, this is a study from the vantage of one province, Saskatchewan. The chronology is simple enough: it coincides with the hegemony of the CCF, later the NDP, which (as of 2007) had formed the government of the province for 47 of the past 63 years. But there is more. It is well known that the CCF was a party with an ideology, and publicly funded health care was its best-known accomplishment. T.C. Douglas, the first CCF premier, introduced the scheme in stages in Saskatchewan with similar schemes introduced nationally some time later. In 2007, medicare is deemed by a majority of Canadians as the most important public policy to them and as a policy that helps unite Canadians. For all that, Douglas did not introduce public health into federal-provincial discussions. The government of Mackenzie King included a public health insurance scheme in its Green Book proposals for discussion at the Reconstruction Conference of federal and provincial leaders called in 1945—the details of this initiative may be found elsewhere.[7] The reason for mentioning the King government's proposal is to draw attention to the federal-provincial linkage provided by shared ideas. Here is an example of interlocking executive federalism, and it is cited now to underline the nature of the tie—theory, be it economic, social or cultural.

Arguably, because Canadian federalism from its start was atheoretical, Canadian writers have paid little attention to theories of any kind insofar as they might influence the developments and practice of federalism. Nonetheless, they should, and it is important to state the reason why. Absent that awareness in the context of this study, the course of Saskatchewan politics and the position its governments adopted in intergovernmental relations remains a closed book. Under the CCF/NDP, Saskatchewan was anything but provincial in its receptivity to theory. If, as this chapter maintains, Saskatchewan played a role in federal-provincial relations far in excess of any objective measure—population or resources, for example—of its importance in national affairs; if, more colloquially, Saskatchewan punched above its weight, then it did so because of theories.

Some were Canadian: Eric Kierans on crown corporations, David Lewis on labour legislation and F.R. Scott on the need for a strong central government; some were American: the Wagner Act (1935), which recognizes the right of workers to form and join trade unions, is the model for collective bargaining in Saskatchewan; and some were British: the Fabians, Maynard Keynes on economics and Sir William Beveridge's report on social insurance (1942). Here is a sample of non-elected and non-Saskatchewan influences. But the province provided its own influences, among them the political economy theorists of the Department of Economics and Political Science at the University of Saskatchewan, for instance, Mabel Timlin, Vernon Fowke and George Britnell.[8] The authors of Saskatchewan's mammoth brief to the Rowell Sirois Commission (the Royal Commission on Dominion-Provincial Relations), George Britnell and F.C. Cronkite, Dean of Law, University of Saskatchewan, argued for compensatory treatment from Ottawa on theoretical grounds echoed in a letter by the minister responsible, Attorney General T.C. Davis: "I am engaged in preparing this brief for the Rowell Royal Commission and I have in mind so drafting it that it can become more or less a political Bill of Rights in Saskatchewan."[9]

This is not new information. Rather, what requires emphasis is that many of the same ideas, same values, and same beliefs were reciprocated by Ottawa. There is no doubt that in his sympathy for social programs in the 1940s, Mackenzie King was motivated in part by the CCF's potential electoral threat. It was equally true, however, that he had promoted some of the same sentiments in *Industry and Humanity*, the book he had written at the end of the First World War. Left-leaning Liberals in the governments of Louis St. Laurent and Lester Pearson, and men like Paul Martin Sr. and Allan MacEachen, echoed these views and, in the mid-1970s, influenced the direction of government policy. Ideas enter the discussion by another less familiar route: whether on the left or right, members of the Liberal Party saw themselves as the builders of Canada through the vehicle of a strong national government. A strong national government, this time to advance social programs, was a goal shared by the Saskatchewan CCF and its intellectual progenitors. In addition, both the CCF and Liberal governments after the war saw themselves as modernizers and innovators in government, an impulse that assumed concrete form in the radical transformation of their respective bureaucratic practices and institutions. The dissemination of the Saskatchewan CCF model (as well as some of its personnel) to other provinces in the 1960s when they were out of power in Regina is well-documented.[10]

The concept of interlocking executive federalism directs attention to this common perspective, one that lasted for some decades, at least until new ideas about the role of government in society and the economy changed in response, first, to the transformation in attitudes carried through by Margaret Thatcher and Ronald Reagan and, second, to renewed emphasis on federal paramountcy under Pierre Trudeau. Saskatchewan's understanding of its place in the federation and of federalism itself changed as a result.

From Saskatchewan's perspective, the economic and political orthodoxy of the post-war period—strong institutions and strong national purpose—disappeared in the 1970s. Shared-cost financing had provided the glue, allowing the province to experiment with its own hospitalization and medicare programs and, in doing so, promote its policy priorities and influence the thinking of Canadians generally. Conversely, shared-cost financing offered the federal government entry into fields otherwise jurisdictionally clouded. The significant aspect of post-war federal-provincial relations lay not in the triumph of paramountcy or confederal conceptions of federalism, but in the moulding of a shared conception of Canada in the third-quarter of the 20th century. The details of shared-cost financing are never unimportant, although for the thesis of this chapter they are of secondary concern. Rather, the purpose of this chapter is to demonstrate that shared-cost financing coupled with a commitment to universal social programs transformed how Canadians and Saskatchewanians view their country and the role of government. It is no exaggeration to say that modern intergovernmental relations and the bureaucracy that sustains them have their genesis in the mutual understandings of this period.

Arguably, all of these assumptions changed in the 1970s. The ascendancy of free-market thinking in place of interventionist government challenged CCF/NDP beliefs and practices and, at the same time, threatened Saskatchewan's influence in the Canadian federation. Interest group politics in place of universal programs were ideologically repugnant to the CCF/NDP. However, the implications of this shift in values went further. In any competition among interests, Saskatchewan's economy based on agriculture and natural resources was vulnerable. It was during this decade and in its battle with Ottawa over control of natural resources that the waning of the province's influence in the federation became apparent.

The 1970s marked a transformation of Canadian politics for reasons closer to home. In 1968, Pierre Trudeau had succeeded Lester Pearson as Liberal Party leader and prime minister. Unlike his recent predecessors in office, Trudeau's interest in national programs seldom deviated from Quebec and the question of Canadian unity. The victory of the Parti Québécois in 1976 concentrated his government's attention on Quebec at the very time attitudes favorable toward an interventionist role for government in the economy and society were weakening. Debate, and more especially proposals in the 1980s and 1990s to assure Quebec's place in Canada, confounded Saskatchewan's understanding of federalism. Perplexing too was the transformation in positions on this matter adopted by the federal NDP following the retirement in 1979 of T.C. Douglas, who had become leader of the party in 1961. The new central Canadian leadership of the NDP (formed nearly two decades earlier when the national CCF joined with organized labour) appeared less interested in promoting a national government committed to national programs than it did in courting Quebec voters.

A broad centrist party like the Liberal Party of Canada, embracing a spectrum of opinion on economic and social issues, provided the basis for cooperation with the Saskatchewan CCF and the NDP. Following the latter's lead Ottawa found that it could strengthen national objectives in social programs delivered by the provinces. In the decades when it was in power after the Second World War, the CCF in Saskatchewan and the central government worked together to create, in effect, a bureaucratic coalition to implement the programs they supported. Yet, it was the very breadth of opinion within the federal Liberals that made political coalition in national politics impossible. In the minority governments of the 1960s and the one led by Pierre Trudeau after the election of 1972, there was every reason to contemplate formal coalition. Nothing came of the possibility, while, ironically, the bureaucratic coalition came under strain as Trudeau embarked upon a new, "systems approach" to policy formulation.

Unease in the West at the transformation underway in Ottawa during the 1970s mounted as the federal government displayed a predisposition to deal unilaterally with the threat posed by Quebec nationalism. Paramountcy redux described the actions of the Trudeau Government after 1980, whether in the matter of patriating the Constitution and introducing the Charter of Rights and Freedoms, or in imposing the National Energy Policy, or in abolishing the Crow's Nest rates (the farmers' Magna Carta). A transformation in Canadian politics and Canadian federalism had begun. The Charter, proposals for mega-constitutional reform (followed by failure), and a Quebec referendum on secession presented a new order of federal-provincial relations quite different from anything familiar to T.C. Douglas And yet, Saskatchewan continued to play a major role. The goal now was less about furthering social programs than demonstrating that interlocking executive federalism worked. The argument Saskatchewan advanced in its factum before the Supreme Court of Canada in the Quebec secession reference was two-fold: in Confederation there is a federal principle and a national principle. Only when both are honoured can Canadian federalism prosper. Accepting this argument, the Court rejected unilateralism on all sides. Instead, it affirmed the Saskatchewan proposition—the obligation of all parties to negotiate constitutional change.[11] More than affirmed, the Court quoted from the Saskatchewan brief.

To understand how Saskatchewan came to adopt this view of Canadian federalism and its role in the federation, it is necessary to provide some historical context. To this end, the discussion that follows describes Saskatchewan, first, under the CCF and, then, projects that examination back even further, to the province's politics before the CCF.

SASKATCHEWAN AND THE CCF

The subject of this chapter is Saskatchewan in Canadian federalism; the period under review, 1944 to the present. The reason for choosing a single province is defensible because Canadian federalism is governmental federalism. Other factors help explain events, but governments determine their outcome. The use of the plural is important, for Saskatchewan's relationship with the central government, both as ally and as opponent over the last half century, is crucial to understanding the course of modern Canadian politics. Traditional federal theory, such as offered by K.C. Wheare, fails to explain the influence of a province like Saskatchewan during much of this period, nor does it offer grounds for explaining the waning of that influence evident during the last two decades.

Saskatchewan is a small province, and is becoming smaller. Between 1921 and 1951, it was the third-most-populous province in Canada. Since then, its population growth has shrunk as a result of out-migration; the 2001 census revealed a total figure only 46,000 greater than the population peak reached in 1936. (The resource boom of the first decade of the 21st century brought a reversal in this demographic trend, but the change is so recent as not to alter the argument presented here). For a long time Saskatchewan's economy, based on grain, was the country's economy. That too has altered, precipitously in national terms and significantly within the province. These quantifiable indices of decline coincided with the period under review when, it will be argued, Saskatchewan exerted exceptional qualitative influence in the Canadian federation. By inference, the resource available to its government was political not economic capital.

The thematic unity of the era emerges from a study of that capital and its use. Success is obviously part of the story—medicare, Section 92A of the Constitution Act with its guarantee of provincial control of natural resources, and more—but so too is failure. Electoral failure, beginning with the CCF's federal electoral reverse in 1945, confined social policy initiatives to where they were most passionately held (in the Saskatchewan CCF under the leadership of T.C. Douglas) and most capable of implementation (under the newly-emerging expert bureaucracy). But there was policy failure, too, particularly on the part of the federal Liberal government under Mackenzie King; at the 1945 Reconstruction Conference, the Liberals could not rally provincial support for their Green Book proposals on social policy, which included national medicare. The effect here was to throw initiative back to the provinces, if they were willing to accept it, which in the case of Saskatchewan they were. The events of 1945 set Canadian federalism on a path blazed by the provinces, one from which it has seldom deviated in succeeding decades.

In its evocation of continuity that last sentence alludes to a feature of Canadian politics too often accepted without comment or ignored altogether. Parties hold power for long periods in Canada. In the 63 years this chapter takes for its focus, the CCF/NDP held office in Saskatchewan for 47; in Ottawa, the Liberals held office for almost the same length of time. Governments and their leaders are long-lived too: T.C. Douglas was premier for 18 years; Pierre Trudeau was prime minister for 15. As a consequence, and excluding the few months Joe Clark, John Turner and Kim Campbell held office, between 1944 and 2007 there have been eight prime ministers (King, St. Laurent, Diefenbaker, Trudeau, Mulroney, Chrétien, Martin and Harper) and six premiers (Douglas, Lloyd, Thatcher, Blakeney, Romanow and Calvert); five of the first group and five of the second have come from one party.[12] A limited number of politicians interacting over long periods of time may strengthen a province in Canadian federalism because the channel of federal-provincial contact becomes a series of individual bilateral relationships. However, more is needed to effect influence; personal skills and commonality of interests between the province and Ottawa are necessary but not sufficient conditions to assure this result. In the case of Saskatchewan there was an additional factor—a passion and a program that propelled the CCF/NDP in its relations with the federal government.

Critics of prime ministerial government and, more recently, of first ministers conferences say they contribute to what is now called a democratic deficit. The public and its representatives in the legislature have a minimal role to play in the formation of public policy. Echoing theorists like Wheare on federalism, critics say power is concentrated not dispersed. There is room to question the validity of that indictment as applied to Canadian federalism, and the doubt persists when the subject is joined to parliamentary government.[13] For the focus of federalism in Canada is just that: government-in-Parliament or the legislature. Certainly this is the case of Saskatchewan under the CCF, and later the NDP. It helps explain why a party, which as a government was the first in the Commonwealth to introduce a Bill of Rights (1947) should after so long in power oppose the introduction of the Charter in 1981. In other words, the party of T.C. Douglas, Woodrow Lloyd and Allan Blakeney believed in the efficacy of legislatures to speak on behalf of the people and in so doing affirm the validity of public policy placed before them by the executive. Elections not legislatures were the place for democratic sanction to be expressed.

The Saskatchewan CCF was the first provincial government, and only a year or so behind Ottawa, to establish the machinery of the modern executive, that is, the planning, advisory and budgetary agencies in company with a cabinet secretariat, to assist in the formulation of policy. Even before it came to power, the party had set its policy priorities in preparation for the explosion in legislative activity that would follow electoral victory. One might say that the Regina Manifesto of 1932 had set the direction and indicated the pace the party as government would follow. While it is true that provisions with regard to land ownership deemed extreme by opponents and electorally damaging by CCF leaders themselves were altered before 1940, the significance of the Manifesto did not change. It gave the party a purpose, a plan and a project, which together set out a public agenda that is visible decades later in the politics of the province and in its relations with the federal government.

Programmatic parties have goals and, to advance those goals, a timetable. The timetable might have to be adjusted to accommodate the unexpected, and policies (such as medicare) might have to be delayed, but they could not be forgotten or ignored. The public knew, party and caucus members knew, as the title of Allan Blakeney's biography says, there were "promises to keep."[14] That phrase is more than political rhetoric; it signifies the sense of urgency to create administrative and economic capacity to realize social policy objectives. And it signifies the perspective the CCF and NDP brought to federal-provincial negotiations.

Provincial but not federal Liberals (with one notable exception) criticized the new, executive-centered bodies as establishing a non-constitutional wing of the executive, one that they said undermined responsible, representative government. The notable exception was James G. Gardiner, the former Saskatchewan premier in 1926–30 and 1935–36, and after 1936 the federal minister of Agriculture and chief Liberal on the prairies.[15] In the context of federal-provincial relations, Gardiner's presence in the federal cabinet at the same time that the Saskatchewan CCF was furthering its socialist agenda through cooperation with Ottawa offered an example of competing (though nonetheless government-centred) approaches to federal-provincial relations. The charge that Gardiner and his Saskatchewan brethren laid was this: administrative innovation of the kind the CCF introduced in Saskatchewan lengthens time horizons beyond the electoral cycle. Government of the magnitude envisioned by the CCF would escape control of the electorate. The irony was that government of this magnitude was made possible in the post-war era by the expansion of shared-cost programs negotiated with Ottawa.

Still, enormously complex programs like health care could not be realized within one electoral cycle. This did not mean that the CCF could ignore elections and talk about some indeterminate future. On the contrary, program planning had to be coordinated with appeals to the people. For example, the introduction of the provincial hospitalization scheme, a major step on the road to medicare, had to be set in place before the first election following the 1944 victory. That was the promise in 1944, and by 1947 a Saskatchewan Hospital Services Plan had come into operation. The details of its creation are beyond the present discussion. What is relevant is that in the 1948 election the CCF lost votes and some seats, but there was no question that the results endorsed the CCF and its policies, which in the context of the government's priorities meant an endorsement of medical care. And with this result, "there was no turning back" until medicare was achieved.[16]

In the eyes of CCF and NDP leaders, election outcomes following electoral campaigns and legislative debate legitimized policies, such as in 1948 after the introduction of the hospitalization plan, or in 1960 before the introduction of medicare, or in 1995 during the fight to reduce the provincial deficit. Planning and shared-cost programs might lengthen time horizons beyond the electoral cycle, but they did not release the government from being held accountable by the electorate. Contrary to criticism heard from all sides today—that party discipline is part of the so-called democratic deficit since legislators bend with the whip and not the people—the CCF/NDP saw party discipline as assuring accountability. Only with the legislative troops behind ministers promoting policy endorsed in an election could voters be assured that government would deliver on its promises.

Measured by voter turnout, or by the percentage of total vote won by the two leading parties, Saskatchewan was for a long time the country's most electorally competitive province. It would be surprising if that distinction did not enter into the discussion of the province's relationship with the federal government, especially since discipline reinforced ideology. When Douglas, Blakeney or Romanow advanced a position or resisted a proposal in federal-provincial meetings, they knew, and others knew, they spoke on behalf of organized opinion. Of course, there might be disagreement within the ranks—the CCF/NDP was a movement, but it was not monolithic—however unity of the collectivity mattered. W.R. Bennett of British Columbia, or Ernest Manning of Alberta, or Joey Smallwood of Newfoundland might take their respective parties for granted at home and in negotiations with Ottawa; the CCF/NDP leaders in Saskatchewan never did. They could not afford to do so, for even if the possibility of the rejection of a policy by party members at annual conventions, for instance, was slight, the possibility nonetheless existed. More than that, the need to defend and explain policy to the rank and file, when combined with the vigorous electoral traditions of the province and when placed in the context of a non-conformist religious culture that placed a premium on advocacy and commitment, honed skills essential to promoting Saskatchewan's case whether for economic improvement or social betterment.

Thus, added to the CCF's burgeoning bureaucracy of advisors, planners and experts supporting the premier in daily and federal-provincial dealings, there was a phalanx of partisan supporters (some elected, but most rank and file) whose encouragement must be acknowledged and whose potential for opposition could never be ignored.

If, as one Canadian political scientist has said, K.C. Wheare's definition of federalism is "anachronistic"—and it is, because it makes federalism seem static and confrontational, the political science equivalent of the western front in the First World War —executive federalism depicted in cabalistic overtones is equally flawed.[17] Dissent behind closed doors by a dozen or so men might literally be true; metaphorically, the description does not convey the Saskatchewan experience, where the bond between premier and province as provided through party remained sound.

Whether Saskatchewan's experience is a representative or unique illustration of Canadian federalism at work cannot be determined in a chapter with a single-province focus. What can confidently be said is that the structure of that relationship may best be described as one between governments. In this respect, the relationship was not unique; in the post-war world, intergovernmental relations became the vehicle for the conduct of federal-provincial business. From the point of view of the CCF, this was a welcome development. Partisan considerations and calculations, which once pervaded Ottawa's ties with the provinces, gave way to diplomacy. Provinces were treated more equally than they had been in the past, when the governments of only some shared partisan affiliation with the government in Ottawa. Although not totally discarded, party currency suffered marked devaluation. Party's decline and policy's rise favoured the CCF/NDP, as the following discussion of Saskatchewan-federal government relations during the province's first four decades makes clear.

SASKATCHEWAN BEFORE THE CCF

"Classic" might be considered an exhausted adjective; still, as an indication of Saskatchewan's place in Canadian federalism in the first four decades of the 20th century, it is hard to improve upon. The literature on political parties in federations ascribes to them an especially important function as agencies of integration. Triple-E proponents often celebrate the integrative capacity of the United States Senate whose members are drawn equally from each state. They seldom mention one of the most influential factors of American politics, which is the dominance in electoral politics, nationally and in the States, by two (the same two) parties. Party allegiance accounts for far less in the United States than in parliamentary systems, but it counts for far more than people outside the United States think it does. In short, parties can be major unifiers in federal systems, a function they once played in Canada and at which the Saskatchewan Liberals excelled. For all but five years after the province's creation in 1905 and the CCF's coming to power in 1944, the Liberals governed. During this period inter-governmental relations took place under the guise of intra-party relations.

A substantial literature exists that describes intra-party federalism. The federal Liberal cabinet was composed of ministers with governmental responsibilities but also with organizational duties on behalf of the party in their respective provinces. In his book, *The Government Party*, Reginald Whitaker described this arrangement as ministerialism.[18] Hierarchical and integrative, the party was the conduit between Ottawa and the provinces for support (up) and rewards (down). The federal and provincial party organizations were one, with a Liberal being a Liberal regardless of issue or jurisdiction. Nowhere in the country did this telescopic arrangement work as smoothly as it did in Saskatchewan.

The Saskatchewan Liberals survived the rupture of Union Government in 1917, and unlike the Manitoba and Alberta Liberals, they tamed the farmers' revolt in the early 1920s. They even weathered the Depression, returning to power in 1934 after their singular defeat in 1929 at the hands of combined Conservatives and Progressives, who had profited from an anti-Liberal campaign organized by the recently-arrived Ku Klux Klan. To the east in Manitoba, there was coalition; to the west in Alberta, the United Farmers followed by Social Credit. After 1944 the issues might have changed and the language might have moderated, but the pivotal role of the province in Canadian politics so evident in later CCF/NDP rhetoric remained rooted in the past. Looking east and west in 1936, T.C. Davis saw "two freak Governments." In this situation, Davis told Gardiner, "the province of Saskatchewan is the sheet anchor for sanity in Western Canada, and, therefore, the sheet anchor of Canada as a whole."[19]

CCF/NDP politicians believed that in federal-provincial relations their task was to effect policy; Liberal politicians assigned themselves a different role—to keep the federal party in office. Both interpretations had this in common—a strong federal orientation. Much separates the Liberals and the CCF/NDP, although almost all originates in the fact that the CCF/NDP had an ideology and the Liberals did not. The point of the distinction is not the content of the ideology but that its presence in one party and absence in the other affected how those parties approached the task of governing. Because of their ideology, CCF/NDP policies framed political debate (and still do). The Liberals did not have an ideology; instead, they took positions. Compared to, say, the Quebec Liberals of the pre-war era, they saw themselves as progressive. They supported local initiatives (for instance, early health care measures), and they encouraged cooperatives (in grain handling, insurance, creameries and much else). But they opposed government ownership so passionately, in fact, that this became, in effect, their impoverished ideology. During the Liberal period, political debate centred mostly on growth and expansion. It is difficult to discover policy issues, in part, because the Liberals faced weak legislative opposition.

The provincial Liberals held a vision of electoral success and, as often as not, of federal Liberal victories. It would be wrong to infer from this comment that the CCF/NDP did not care about elections. All their leaders after 1944 cared intensely about party and legislative organization. It was this political sensibility combined with his ideals that made Douglas such a formidable campaigner. Yet, in the CCF/NDP order of things, electoral success served a higher purpose. All Saskatchewan Liberals (until Ross Thatcher in the 1960s) believed in the necessity and virtue of the federal Liberal cause. Here was partisan loyalty to be sure, but underlying it was a more fundamental commitment: Saskatchewan Liberals believed that not only were they building a province after 1905 but they were building a country. The celebrations of 1905 communicate clearly the sense that provincial autonomy in Alberta and Saskatchewan represented the rounding-out of Confederation, the fulfillment of the transcontinental dream of Canada's architects.

Yet, autonomy then did not mean what it seemed to say. Saskatchewan, politically, was anything but autonomous. Instead, federal politics were superimposed on local politics, which before 1905 had been formally non-partisan.[20] Until 1944, the Saskatchewan Liberal party served the federal cause: the first four premiers (Walter Scott, William Martin, Charles Dunning and James G. Gardiner) sat in Parliament either before or after their time in office; Gardiner made Prince Albert the only safe seat Mackenzie King ever held, one he represented in the House of Commons as prime minister between 1926 and 1945; and Gardiner also worked as tirelessly, but with moderate success, to secure seats for the federal Liberals in the neighbouring prairie provinces. He was, in Whitaker's language, the archetypal ministerialist melding the fortunes and resources of federal and provincial Liberals. It was a sign of his and the province's eclipse under a new prime minister, Louis St. Laurent, that Gardiner failed to secure approval for the construction of the much-studied South Saskatchewan River dam, which now bears his name but was approved by St. Laurent's successor, John Diefenbaker, another Prince Albert prime minister.

In the minds of Liberal leaders before the CCF, the role of the party was to integrate the province politically and in every other respect with Canada. The metaphors that apply to these years are not the familiar ones of federalist literature—boundaries and pendulum—rather, they are of interposition. To return to an earlier observation, the prairie provinces (Saskatchewan, Alberta, and Manitoba) were created to make Canada whole. And there were many parts to fit together. Saskatchewan settlers, whose numbers tripled between 1905 and 1921, built a grain industry to serve the national economy, as well as provide for their own livelihood. Saskatchewan settlers, almost half of whom were characterized in these years as the "non-English," had to be, as it was also said, "Canadianized." Controversies over language, that is, languages other than English, especially in the schools, were common. The schools issue itself—in their acts of creation Parliament gave Saskatchewan and Alberta denominational (separate) schools—proved contentious, feeding anti-foreign and anti-Catholic sentiment and providing a base for the KKK.

Federal Liberals saw, and depicted, themselves as the tolerant party of Canadian politics. Saskatchewan Liberals adopted the same stance, seeking to make the "non-English" part of the Liberal electoral base and professing multiculturalism long before the term had been coined. Until the harsh winds of depression and drought purged provincial politics of religion and language, these national issues made a strong claim on the province. The 1930s said goodbye to all this. The natural resources of the prairie provinces, which had been retained (discriminatorily so, the provinces said) by Parliament "for the purposes of the Dominion," were transferred in 1930. Yet, the economic catastrophes of that decade followed by the demands of war denied the expected benefits from the transfer. With "nearly 50 per cent of the total rural population in receipt of government assistance" in the 1930s, Saskatchewan continued to look to Ottawa only now for economic assistance.[21] In 1939 and in response to Gardiner's goading, the government introduced the Prairie Farm Assistance Act with assistance payments based on need, the principle of economic redistribution appeared for the first time in Canadian public policy.

Rural Saskatchewan (then and now) is an enormous area whose settlement pattern resulted in hundreds of communities and thousands of miles of roads and railways. (Saskatchewan still has more miles of roads than any other province.) The story of Saskatchewan for the last quarter century and the explanation for the rise of the Saskatchewan party (the CCF/NDP's most potent opponent to date) rests in the decline of these communities, the deterioration of local infrastructure and the depopulation of the countryside. Rural Saskatchewan in the decade before 1944 is the setting for Seymour Martin Lipset's account of the farmers' political mobilization.[22] Community organizations in the form of cooperatives, elevators, credit unions, and school and rural municipality boards flourished. Here is where agrarian socialism was born, much to the outrage of the Liberals. The CCF, with the help of drought, pestilence and war, partisanized Saskatchewan community organizations, a tactic, the Liberals said, that demonstrated the CCF's disrespect for boundaries. In a more current language, the CCF "politicized" civil society. CCFers might demur and say the Liberals bought votes wherever patronage allowed them to do so. The justice of these charges and counter-charges is outside the focus of this discussion. Still, the boundaries question warrants acknowledgment, for to the extent that it is true it helps explain further the assurance the CCF brought to its dealings with the federal government. It spoke for *the* community. One could go further and say, although it would be difficult to prove, that the coming of the CCF following a decade of economic devastation destroyed any memory of the past before these events. Saskatchewan's collective identity today begins with the Douglas Government.

The continuity between pre- and post-1944 politics in Saskatchewan lay in the predisposition of the Liberals and CCF to adopt a national perspective in their dealings with Ottawa. A distinctive feature of Canadian politics and Canadian federalism is the prevalence of third parties ever since the Progressives burst upon the scene winning 65 seats in the 1921 federal election, more than any subsequent challenger to the country's "old" parties. The CCF is often grouped with the so-called protest movements of western Canada. There is some justification for doing so in light of the overwhelming rejection of the Liberal party in the provincial election of 1944 (the CCF won 47 of 52 seats), and in the federal election the following year when the CCF took 18 of Saskatchewan's 21 seats. Still, the CCF was not a party like the others. It was not mainstream, although it set out to realign Canadian politics in a manner similar to British politics, nor was it protest in the sense that it represented rejection of the status quo only. Certainly, in its own mind, it was never a "third" party.

What set the CCF apart was its organic or communitarian view of society. In their more desperate moments, the Liberals claimed to see in this view the specter of totalitarian rule. Extreme rhetoric won few votes; if anything, it helped isolate the Liberals. Yet the focus of their attack was right: their collectivity—one might say—lay at the heart of CCF values. The CCF did not introduce public health measures to Saskatchewan—the Liberals could point to legislation of 1916 establishing the first municipal doctors scheme in North America.[23] What the CCF did was make social and health schemes, and any other such measure, universal. The CCF thought in universalistic terms.

It is worth remembering this attitude for the light it throws on the Saskatchewan CCF's relations with Ottawa. K.C. Wheare might talk of federalism's coordinate and independent spheres, but that legal dichotomy is unsatisfactory in explaining how a federal system actually works. Society does not fit or, better still, cannot be distributed into neat jurisdictional compartments. Much of the story of Saskatchewan in Canadian federalism after 1944 concerns questions of social programs and national standards. Significantly, medicare, a Saskatchewan CCF-creation before it was "nationalized," is now identified with Canada's sense of nationhood. If the thesis of this chapter—that Saskatchewan has played an extraordinarily influential role in the development of modern Canadian federalism—is defensible, then a fundamental element of the explanation lies in the transposition of the CCF's collective or communitarian view of society into federal-provincial politics.

As already noted, the failure of the Reconstruction Conference in 1945 and rejection of the Green Book proposals by some provinces meant there would be no Beveridge-like transformation to Canada's social programs. Instead, there would be incremental change following long federal-provincial negotiations, with many occasions to debate the respective roles of the provincial and federal government. Who, for instance, defines national goals? Do the provinces have a part to play in determining that definition? Initiative passed to the provinces; in Saskatchewan's case in the 1940s that meant to a very poor province. Social goals required provincial economic resources (at least until federal shared-cost programs came into operation), and thus practical need as much as ideological desire drove Saskatchewan then, and later, into experimenting with provincial crown corporations.

Whatever the utility of federal theory to explaining Canadian practice, there is one irreducible feature of federalism—territory. Or so it would seem. At their birth, socialist parties, the CCF in Canada or the Labor Party in Australia, were not strong proponents of federalism, for the reason that divided jurisdiction impedes the realization of social policies. Yet in Canada federalism made the CCF the force it became. The Douglas and Blakeney governments, especially, gave new meaning to the argument that the parts of a federation can become social laboratories. The CCF experience in Saskatchewan was figuratively (and sometimes literally) grounded in the province's resources. A half century later, new technologies, new economies and new values cast doubt on whether territorially-based federalism is sustainable.

The election returns show that agrarian socialism has become urban social democracy. During the past two decades, and for the first time in its history, Saskatchewan's governing parties have secured legislative majorities either from rural or urban constituencies but not from both. Rural Saskatchewan, from which the CCF emerged, now opposes policies put in place to protect the farmers. The mechanization of agriculture, consolidation of farms and migration of population have undermined any sense of rural unity. Where once there was one Saskatchewan dependent upon a grain economy, now there are several Saskatchewans: urban, suburban and rural, farm and non-farm, and (not mentioned until now) Aboriginal and non-Aboriginal. The economic and social transformation of Saskatchewan extends to its relations with the federal government in a number of ways beginning, most seriously, with the reality that its government no longer speaks for one community.

But if Saskatchewan's voice is less distinct, its audience is also less attentive. The Second World War had primed the King government to be receptive to Keynesian economic and Beveridge social theories. These were theories the CCF liked. The War had accustomed the federal Liberals to think big and plan for the future. Here, too, was another reason for Regina to cooperate with Ottawa. Even when Ottawa disagreed with the Saskatchewan position it listened, as during the constitutional discussions of the early 1980s. Pierre Trudeau wanted to patriate the constitution with an entrenched Charter of rights. After the National Energy Policy, Saskatchewan (and Alberta) wanted natural resources constitutionally guaranteed and a Charter with limits. In the end, both governments got what they sought. The Saskatchewan view of federalism, a compound of what it described in its factum to the Supreme Court of Canada at the time of the Quebec secession reference as the nation and the federal principles, advocated respect for the multiple loyalties embraced by Canadian federalism. This approach, along with a very large Aboriginal population, helps explain Saskatchewan's continuing leadership in one area of federal-provincial relations: the place of Aboriginal people in Canada.

Still, the tide of interventionist government had begun to ebb before two new forces. Rights and globalization challenged the (now) NDP in Saskatchewan in a particularly acute way: the first contradicted the communitarian values so long promoted, and the second undermined the territorial autonomy that federalism offered an activist, socialist regime. Neither the Charter nor globalization showed respect for boundaries, be they political, jurisdictional or economic. Federalism is about rootedness and rights, and globalization about transcendency. More than that, rights and globalization foster suspicion of the state, the actor under which the CCF/NDP had defined Saskatchewan at home and in the nation for more than half a century.

The recent past is no guide to Saskatchewan's future in Canadian federalism, nor can federal theory be expected to provide assistance. In the 1960s, continentalism was the scourge and the federal Liberals, led by Lester Pearson, a frail and undependable reed of a government to combat the threat. That was the opinion of George Grant in his much-cited book *Lament for a Nation*.[24] Four decades later, globalization is the challenge and Canada's distinctiveness, even its unity, is said to rest on national medicare, a program introduced by Pearson in the 1960s and in fulfilment of the vision of the CCF.

CONCLUSION

Both as a field in a discipline and as a dimension to Canadian politics, federalism suffers from rigidity. Theories of federalism abound, but every federal system in practice becomes a special case of, or exception to, the general theory. Thus, Canada, seen through the lens of K.C. Wheare, is a federation with a difference. Similarly, despite all the concern expressed in Canada about asymmetry, when it comes to Ottawa's relations with different provinces, each relationship is distinct, and has been from the beginning. It is one of the great errors of Canadian federalism to impose unity and conformity where there is none.

Executive federalism is a useful concept in the study of Canadian politics. It is also a malleable concept; that is, it may apply to situations where the relationship between the centre and a province is conflictual, or it may apply to others where the atmosphere is one of cooperation. It is this latter *modus vivendi*, which this chapter labels interlocking executive federalism, and that for much of its history has characterized Saskatchewan's relationship with the federal government. Different circumstances in different eras since the achievement of provincial autonomy explain the evolution of this set of attitudes. Absent from that explanation is either the distribution of powers set down in the Constitution Act, 1867 or the structure and operation of the institutions of government found at the centre of the federation.

NOTES

1. Richard Simeon, *Political Science and Federalism: Seven Decades of Scholarly Engagement*, 2000 Kenneth R. MacGregor Lecture (Kingston: Institute of Intergovernmental Relations, 2002), 1.

2. Canada, Speech from the Throne, *A Strong Federation: Strengthening the Federation and Our Democratic Institutions*, October 16, 2007. <http://www.sft-ddt.gc.ca/eng/media.asp?id=1369.

3. K.C. Wheare, *Federal Government* (Toronto: Oxford University Press, 1953).

4. William S. Livingston, *Federalism and Constitutional Change* (London: Oxford University Press, 1956).

5. See, for example, Donald V. Smiley and Ronald L. Watts, "Intrastate Federalism in Canada," vol. 39, *Royal Commission on the Economic Union and Development Prospects for Canada* (Toronto: University of Toronto Press, 1985).

6. Peter S. Onuf, *The Origins of the Federal Republic: Jurisdictional Controversies in the United States, 1775–1787* (Philadelphia: University of Pennsylvania Press, 1983), 147.

7. Malcolm G. Taylor, *Health Insurance and Canadian Public Policy: The Seven Decisions*

That Created the Canadian Health Insurance System (Montreal: McGill-Queen's University Press, 1978), ch. 1, "The 1945 Health Insurance Proposals: Policymaking for Post-war Canada."

8. Shirley Spafford, *"No Ordinary Academics": Economics and Political Science at the University of Saskatchewan, 1910–1960* (Toronto: University of Toronto Press, 2000).

9. Saskatchewan Archives Board, Papers of James G. Gardiner, T.C. Davis to Gardiner, September 13, 1937, 41320-2.

10. Margaret Conrad, "'Saskatchewan is a Maritime Province Too': Rethinking Canadian Regionalism in the Twenty-First Century." Address, University of Saskatchewan, October 4, 2004, 6–7. <http://atlanticportal.hil.unb.ca:8000/archive/00000048/01/Conrad_Saskatchewan.pdf>

11. Reference re Secession of Quebec, [1998] 2 S.C.R. 217, para. 88.

12. In November 2007, Brad Wall led the Saskatchewan Party, formed in 1998 by disaffected Progressive Conservatives and Liberals, to power. The Saskatchewan Party is the first non-NDP government to govern the province since 1991.

13. For an elaboration of the argument, see David E. Smith, *The People's House of Commons: Theories of Democracy in Contention* (Toronto: University of Toronto Press, 2007).

14. Dennis Gruending, *Promises to Keep: A Political Biography of Allan Blakeney* (Saskatoon: Western Producer Prairie Books, 1990).

15. The principal works on the Liberal party in Saskatchewan are: Norman Ward and David Smith, *James G. Gardiner: Relentless Liberal* (Toronto: University of Toronto Press, 1990) and David E. Smith, *Prairie Liberalism: The Liberal Party in Saskatchewan, 1905–71* (Toronto: University of Toronto Press, 1975).

16. See note 7: Taylor, *Health Insurance and Canadian Public Policy*, 103.

17. Hamish Telford, "The Federal Spending Power in Canada: Nation-Building or Nation-Destroying?," *Publius* 33, no. 1 (Winter 2003): 31.

18. Reginald Whitaker, *The Government Party: Organizing and Financing the Liberal Party of Canada, 1930–58* (Toronto: University of Toronto Press, 1977), 184.

19. SAB, Gardiner Papers, Davis to Gardiner, August 28, 1936, 41271-4.

20. Lewis H. Thomas, *The Struggle for Responsible Government in the North-West Territories, 1870–97* (Toronto: University of Toronto Press, 1956).

21. Saskatchewan. A Submission by the Government of Saskatchewan to the Royal Commission on Dominion-Provincial Relations (Canada 1937), prepared under the direction of Hon. T.C. Davis, K.C., Attorney General for Saskatchewan, 1937, Part VI "The Economy of Saskatchewan on Trial 1929–1937," in David E. Smith (ed.), *Building a Province: A History of Saskatchewan in Documents* (Saskatoon: Fifth House Publishers, 1992), 239.

22. S.M. Lipset, *Agrarian Socialism: The Cooperative Commonwealth Federation in Saskatchewan* (Berkeley: University of California Press, 1950). For a re-assessment of the thesis of that book, see David E. Smith (ed.), *Lipset's Agrarian Socialism: A Re-examination* (Regina: Canadian Plains Research Center, 2007).

22. C. Stuart Houston, *Steps On The Road to Medicare: Why Saskatchewan Led the Way* (Montreal: McGill-Queen's University Press, 2002), ch. 3, "Municipal Doctors and Municipal Hospitals."

24. George Grant, *Lament for a Nation: The Defeat of Canadian Nationalism* (Toronto: McClelland and Stewart, 1965).

POLITICAL ISSUES:
SOME OF THE GREAT DEBATES

Managing Prosperity:
Saskatchewan's Fiscal and Economic Challenges

Gary Tompkins

INTRODUCTION

In April 1982, the Conservatives led by Grant Devine swept into office based in part on a pledge to redirect government fiscal policy to provide benefits to middle and upper income residents of Saskatchewan. The Conservatives had seized upon a perception that the Blakeney NDP governments had used the relative prosperity of the 1970s to improve social programs for lower income groups and increase the size of civil service (including Crown Corporations), but had ignored the plight of middle and upper income groups who were faced with losing their homes as a result of 20% and higher mortgage interest rates. The benefits of the oil, gas and commodity booms in the 1970s were to be shared more universally within the province, starting with two key campaign promises—the elimination of the gas tax and mortgage interest relief for homeowners.

Unfortunately, the Conservatives took power at almost the precise moment when the commodity price boom was ending. Upon reviewing the financial situation, the Conservative finance minister concluded that the province could not afford the elimination of the gas tax, but his concern was trumped by political considerations.[1]

From 1982 to 1991, the Saskatchewan government embarked on a deficit spending program. By the second term of the Devine Conservatives, the fiscal crisis was apparent and some program cuts and tax increases were introduced. At the beginning of the Romanow NDP government in 1991, the measures taken by the Conservatives were clearly exposed as inadequate and the NDP government implemented a fiscal austerity program that included expenditure restraint and tax increases that targeted the structural deficit in the province's finances. The measures included deferring new capital projects, limiting increases in salaries of the civil service and government-funded employers to 0%, 0%, and 1% over three years, cuts in program spending and reductions to third-party grants. New tax measures included increasing the provincial sales tax from 7% to 8%, the introduction of a 10% income surtax, increasing the corporate capital surcharge from 2% to 3% and the corporate income tax rate from 16% to 17%, as well as increasing the taxes on gasoline and tobacco. In 1993, the province was in a fiscal crisis, having great difficulty selling its BBB-rated bonds on international financial markets.

Since the turn of the millennium, there has been a complete turnaround in the provincial economy and the government's fiscal situation, creating considerable optimism for the near future. For example, a July 2008 forecast by the Conference Board of Canada[2] predicts that GDP growth in 2008 will be 14.3%, the highest of all provinces and slightly less than three times the Canadian growth rate. A new commodities boom has seen significant increases in the prices of the province's export commodities and the resulting government revenues have allowed the Calvert NDP government and now the Saskatchewan Party government to reverse some of the measures that were taken during the fiscal crisis and to restructure the program infrastructure and tax system. While the recent global credit crisis has reduced the short-term optimism, the most recent Conference Board forecast still anticipates positive GDP growth in Saskatchewan, even with forecast recessions in both Canada and the United States. While the size and duration of the economic slowdown that is being triggered by the credit crisis are difficult to predict, as well as its possible impact on the provincial economy, it is reasonable to believe that the fiscal climate in Saskatchewan has improved to the point that the provincial government is now more focused on managing and sustaining prosperity rather than avoiding fiscal collapse.

This chapter will present the various fiscal policy options for Saskatchewan and assess the changes that have been made to date in response to the improved economic circumstances. In the next section, a brief fiscal history is presented that describes and assesses the policy responses to both the fiscal crisis and relative prosperity of the past five years. The following section describes the fiscal challenges the province faces and suggests which should have higher priority in the near future. The last section presents conclusions.

THE SASKATCHEWAN FISCAL CLIMATE: 1982–83 TO 2003–04

THE DEVINE YEARS: 1982–91

The election of the Devine Conservative Party in April 1982 was in part a reaction to the perception that the Blakeney government was either unwilling or unable to distribute the fruits of the 1970s commodities boom to anyone other than civil servants, Crown corporation employees, third party grant recipients and individual beneficiaries of government programs. Interest rates and inflation had risen to unprecedented heights in the early 1980s, placing considerable economic pressure on the middle class. The Devine fiscal plan was predicated on a sustained economic expansion, but by the time it was implemented the increases in commodity prices had ended.

The previous history of Saskatchewan governments was characterized by fiscal conservatism, at least in the short term. The boom of the 1970s allowed the government to increase its role in the economy through the creation of new Crown corporations, as well as the expansion of the role of existing

Table 1. Selected Commodity Prices, 1981–86

	Potash ($US/tonne)	Oil ($US/bbl)	Spring Wheat ($CDN/tonne)	Fall Wheat ($CDN/tonne)
1981	120.00	35.75	189.00	181.00
1986	60.00	14.44	105.00	92.00

Sources: Saskatchewan Agriculture and Food, Statistics Canada, Natural Resources Canada.

Table 2. Government of Saskatchewan Fiscal Position, 1981–82 to 1985–86 (Millions of Dollars)

GRF Fiscal Year	1981–82	1982–83	1983–84	1984–85	1985–86
GRF Revenue					
Own-source	2,134.5	2,282.8	2,181.7	2,325.3	2,406.0
Federal Transfers	529.2	408.3	551.8	590.3	643.0
Total Revenue	2,663.7	2,691.1	2,733.5	2,915.6	3,049.1
Operating Spending	2,481.2	2,876.6	3,008.4	3,192.9	3,437.6
Interest	43.3	41.7	56.5	102.5	190.3
Total Spending	2,524.5	2,918.3	3,064.9	3,295.4	3,627.9
Pre-transfer Balance	139.2	(227.2)	(331.4)	(379.8)	(578.9)
GRF Surplus/(Deficit)	139.2	(227.2)	(331.4)	(379.8)	(578.9)
GRF Debt (as at March 31)					
Government Debt	191.5	323.4	842.2	1,270.6	1,622.3
Crown Corporation Debt	3,338.1	4,318.1	4,680.5	5,269.8	6,861.8
Total Debt	3,529.6	4,641.5	5,522.7	6,540.4	8,484.1

Table 3. Government of Saskatchewan Fiscal Position, 1986–87 to 1990–91 (Millions of Dollars)

GRF Fiscal Year	1986–87	1987–88	1988–89	1989–90	1990–91
GRF Revenue					
Own-source	2,011.6	2,381.6	2,628.1	2,927.4	3,169.0
Federal Transfers	789.0	914.2	1,067.0	1,231.0	1,489.1
Total Revenue	2,880.5	3,295.8	3,695.1	4,158.4	4,658.2
Operating Spending	3,840.1	3,556.2	3,699.5	4,013.2	4,544.1
Interest	192.6	282.0	320.0	523.0	474.5
Total Spending	4,032.7	3,883.2	4,019.5	4,536.2	5,018.6
GRF Surplus/(Deficit)	(1,232.1)	(542.4)	(324.4)	(377.7)	(360.4)
GRF Debt (as at March 31)					
Government Debt	2,881.9	3,744.7	4,464.8	5,334.8	5,821.1
Crown Corporation Debt	7,057.7	6,908.2	6960.3	7,361.1	7,439.5
Total Debt	9,939.6	10,652.9	11,425.1	12,696.1	13,260.6

Crowns. In addition, program expenditures were increased with the addition of new programs, especially in health. At the end of fiscal 1981–82, the government's books were in order. The General Revenue Fund debt stood at $191.5 million, only 7.5% of annual spending. Crown corporation debt was $3.3

billion and the total government debt represented about 23% of provincial GDP. Provincial bonds were given a AA+ credit rating.

However, it could be argued (with hindsight) that the NDP established a spending program infrastructure that was unsustainable. In spite of high prices for its export commodities, the government had been running on an approximate budget balance. Therefore, the tax/spending package given to Saskatchewan taxpayers could only be continued if commodity prices were sustained at late 1970s levels and even if that were so, any new spending or tax reduction initiatives would need to come from either increases in other taxes or lower spending from established programs.

However, this was not the program that elected the Devine Conservatives. The mortgage protection program and the elimination of the gas tax went ahead without the necessary compensating adjustments. In addition, the economic and fiscal environment had changed dramatically for the worse at the time of the election and there were increasing demands for additional spending to protect the farm sector. Over the first term of the Devine government, annual general revenue fund deficits rose from $227.2 million in 1982–83 to $578.9 million in 1985–86.

There were two unfortunate lessons that were drawn from the experience from the first term of the Devine government. The first was that there was little public concern over the deficits and considerable public support for universal government programs, rather than income-targeted spending support. Second, one bit of good fiscal news for the Saskatchewan government was the experience with the bold and popular mortgage protection program. Guaranteeing 13.5% mortgage rates would have been a prohibitively expensive program had interest rates remained in the 18–22% range for any significant length of time. Fortunately, interest rates fell dramatically over the first two years of the program and the final cost was significantly lower than it could have been.

The 1986 election saw both the Conservatives and NDP offer enhanced housing programs that would lower the mortgage rate threshold to 9.75% (Conservative) or 7% (NDP), with both parties offering subsidies and low interest loans for home renovations. That election returned the Conservatives to power, albeit with a substantially reduced majority and fewer total votes than the NDP. Notably, the Saskatchewan Liberal Party, campaigning on a platform of fiscal prudence, elected only one member.

The pre-election budget forecast for 1986–87 was $459.1 million. However, the continuing poor economic performance of the Saskatchewan economy resulted in a record $1.232 billion deficit (which included some investment write-offs), representing over 30% of total government spending. A number of program spending restraint programs were introduced during this period. The gas tax was reinstated. Initially, tax rebates were available to provincial residents, but these were quickly eliminated. The provincial sales tax was increased from 5% to 7%. Personal income, corporate income, and tobacco taxes were increased. The Saskatchewan Flat Tax, a flat tax of 2% of earned income, and a 2% output tax on large resource companies were introduced. In spite of these tax increases and spending restraint, deficits persisted, leading to increased debt, increased interest payments and increased pressure on the provincial government balance sheet.

While the level of the GRF deficits fell over the remaining years of Devine's second term, there was still a consistent record of deficit budgets. These occurred in spite of the use of financial management techniques designed to reduce the size of the GRF deficit by transferring the deficit to "off-budget" government corporations, changing how Crown corporations budgeted for capital equipment, financing programs thorough tax expenditures rather than direct spending (such as the Saskatchewan investment tax credit) and other measures. The Provincial Auditor said the following in his 1991 report: "The financial statements do not include all organizations owned or controlled by the government. ... If appropriate accounting principles were followed, the financial statements would be materially different."[3]

On October 2, 1991, the Conservatives were resoundingly defeated by the Romanow-led NDP. While many NDP supporters anticipated a return to increased program spending, the NDP inherited a total provincial debt of over $14 billion, which was reduced to $13.26 billion as a result of NDP measures taken early in their term of office. Any hope of restoring spending programs would be predicated on either a quick return of higher commodity prices, a lowering of interest rates or increased federal transfers. None of these events took place and so the Romanow government was forced to implement a harsh regime of spending cuts and tax increases.

ROMANOW/CALVERT NDP: 1991–2002
In the first year of the NDP government, having inherited much of the tax and expenditure regime of the previous administration, the GRF deficit ballooned to $824 million. It was clear that the combined federal and provincial debt represented not only a significant limitation on the ability of governments to meet public expectations of the level of programs and services that could be provided at reasonable tax levels, but that the country and the provinces were in danger of having to adjust their fiscal regimes to satisfy bond rating agencies, rather than the needs of their constituents. In 1991, Saskatchewan bonds were rated A- (with negative implications) by Standard & Poors, A2 by Moody's and BBB (high) by DBRS. In 1992, S&P dropped their rating to BBB+ and Moody's rating was reduced to A3. In 1993, DBRS dropped the rating of Saskatchewan bonds to BBB, which implied that most domestic lenders (such as pension funds) could not purchase Saskatchewan bonds. Other rating agencies rated Saskatchewan bonds at A2 or A3 but indicated that Saskatchewan was on a credit watch.

The NDP government responded to the fiscal crisis by taking measures that alienated a significant number of its traditional supporters. Among the first steps taken by the new government was the creation the Saskatchewan Financial Review Commission (the Gass Commission) to analyze the province's fiscal situation. The May 1992 budget provided limited tax relief in the form of small strategic rate cuts, targeted at encouraging investment and economic activity. The disastrous mega-projects of the 1980s were addressed through negotiation of the financial arrangements with particular focus on reducing the level of loan guarantees that had been pledged by the Devine government. Taxes on small businesses were decreased along with a reduction in oil royalty rates. The first NDP budget reduced spending by 3.7%, through measures such as merging or eliminating government departments, reducing grants to third parties and closing or converting 52 hospitals. In spite of these measures, the provincial government continued to run deficits and the accumulated Saskatchewan government debt reached a record $14.797 billion in March 1993.

The Saskatchewan government's fiscal response to the debt crisis was described by DBRS as the toughest provincial budget ever delivered, but the forecast impact on government debt was small relative to its size. The fiscal strategy could be described as introducing fiscal discipline to achieve some debt reduction while waiting for the provincial economy to grow to reduce the ratio of debt to GDP. Tables 4 and 5 show how the economy recovered over the period 1993–97. While the government was able to run budget surpluses and reduce the debt by about 22%, the economic growth experienced by the province led to a significant decrease in the ratio of debt to provincial GDP, which is the widely accepted measure of the burden of debt on an economy.

Table 4. Economic Indicators, Saskatchewan, 1994–2000							
	1994	1995	1996	1997	1998	1999	2000
Real GDP (annual % change)	3.7	1.9	3.2	5.7	3.7	0.1	2.9
Ratio Sask/Can GDP per capita	.94	.93	.95	.97	.98	.93	.92
Mineral Sales ($ millions)	4,167	4,600	5,599	5,701	4,776	6,116	8,611
Total Personal Income	18,603	19,925	21,120	20,675	21,563	22,404	23,115
Source: Saskatchewan Bureau of Statistics, *Saskatchewan Economics Review, 2002.*							

During the period 1993–94 to present, the government also began to reverse some of the tax measures that were taken during the 1980s. The deficit surtax (10% on the personal income tax) was eliminated, along with the Saskatchewan Flat Tax.

The first major fiscal policy initiative of the NDP government was focused on taxation. The Saskatchewan government appointed two commissions to consider Saskatchewan's competitive position with respect to personal and corporate income taxes. Both were given narrow mandates, comparing Saskatchewan taxes to other provinces and taking the view that tax rates were a significant factor determining Saskatchewan's ability to attract and retain high income earners and private investment. The recommendations of the commissions were predictable and the 2000 budget announced personal income tax rates cuts of about 33% that were phased in over a period of four years. This was followed by a phased in program of reductions of the sales tax and a reduction in corporate income and capital taxes.

Government spending increased rapidly over the period 2000–01 to 2006–07, but grew at or below the growth in GDP. There was little in the form

Table 5. Government of Saskatchewan Financial Statistics, 1993–94 to 1999–2000 (Millions of Dollars)

GRF Fiscal Year	1993–94	1994–95	1995–96	1996–97	1997–98	1998–99	1999–00	2000–01
GRF Revenue								
Own-source	3,431.6	3,928.4	4,156.9	4,742.7	4,609.3	4,641.6	4,648.1	5,881.4
Federal Transfers	1,248.2	1,297.0	974.9	760.5	553.1	961.3	1,208.8	872.2
Total Revenue	4,679.7	5,225.4	5,131.8	5,503.2	5,162.5	5,602.9	5,856.9	6,753.6
GRF Spending								
Health	1,464.3	1,533.9	1,554.8	1,608.0	1,677.2	1,774.6	1,955.7	2,075.7
Education	864.5	902.3	869.0	886.2	929.8	998.5	1,031.8	1,110.0
Social Services	502.7	526.7	535.6	525.4	536.0	569.2	577.9	578.6
Other	1,246.9	1,252.5	1,305.0	1,282.6	1,229.7	1,488.0	1,511.9	1,492.6
Operating Spending	4,078.3	4,215.4	4,264.4	4,302.1	4,372.7	4,830.3	5,077.4	5,256.8
Interest	873.2	881.6	849.0	794.2	754.6	744.7	696.1	664.1
Total Spending	4,951.5	5,097.0	5,113.4	5,096.3	5,127.3	5,575.0	5,773.5	5,920.9
GRF Surplus/(Deficit)	(271.8)	128.4	18.4	407.0	35.2	27.9	83.5	57.7
GRF Debt (as at March 31)								
Government Debt	9,250.2	8,891.3	9,126.8	8,577.9	8,279.5	8,029.8	7,830.5	7,676.4
Crown Corporation Debt	5,653.0	5,282.5	5,059.6	4,284.7	3,770.3	3,479.3	3,389.8	3,520.1
Total Debt	14,903.2	14,173.8	14,186.4	12,862.6	12,049.8	11,509.1	11,220.3	11,196.5

Source: Saskatchewan Finance.

Table 6. Saskatchewan Government Finances, 2000–01 to 2006–07 (Millions of Dollars)

GRF Fiscal Year	2000–01	2001–02	2002–03	2003–04	2004–05	2005–06	2006–07
GRF Revenue							
Own-source	5,881.4	4,822.0	5,655.9	5,525.4	6,125.5	6,952.2	7,254.2
Federal Transfers	872.2	1,237.1	800.8	1,033.0	1,666.3	1,265.4	1,388.8
Total Revenue	6,753.6	6,059.1	6,456.7	6,558.4	7,791.8	8,217.6	8,643.0
Operating Spending	5,256.8	5,721.2	5,762.5	6,165.7	6,447.9	7,133.4	7,706.9
Interest	664.1	616.8	611.4	602.7	578.8	544.7	538.3
Total Spending	5,920.9	6,338.0	6,373.8	6,768.4	7,026.7	7,678.1	8,245.3
Pre-transfer Balance	832.7	(278.9)	82.9	(210.0)	765.1	539.5	397.8
GRF Debt (as at March 31)							
Government Debt	7,676.4	7,785.3	7,974.7	8,139.3	7,600.5	7,242.4	7,278.4
Crown Corporation Debt	3,520.1	3,645.6	3,657.6	3,618.0	3,584.4	3,631.9	3,558.0
Total Debt	11,196.5	11,430.9	11,632.3	11,757.3	11,184.9	10,874.3	10,836.4

Note: 2000–01 revenues include a one-time transfer from Saskatchewan Liquor and Gaming retained earnings, of which $775 million was transferred to the Fiscal Stabilization Fund.
Source: Saskatchewan Finance.

of new programs and the government did not move to re-introduce programs that were cut during the fiscal crisis. In spite of a commission recommending a significant increase in provincial government funding of K–12 education, the government only implemented modest increases to their contributions to local school boards. At the end of the 2006–07 fiscal year, the provincial government had reduced the total provincial debt to $10.84 billion, yielding a debt to GDP ratio of 0.26, compared with the 1994 ratio of 0.62.

FUTURE CHALLENGES IN AN ERA OF ECONOMIC GROWTH

While the experience of the early 1980s should leave people leery of predicting strong economic growth into the future, recent long-term economic trends suggest that the province is well placed to enjoy a reasonably long period of sustained economic growth. Economic development in Asia has led to strong growth in commodity prices, especially with respect to energy and agriculture. Prior to the recent global credit crisis, the June 2008 Conference Board of Canada forecast predicted that the growth in nominal GDP in Saskatchewan would exceed 10% on average over the next three years, well ahead of the Canadian average of 5.3%. While recent events serve to illustrate that forecasting Saskatchewan's economy is a difficult task given its reliance on export markets and growing conditions, it is likely (but by no means certain) that the government should expect a continued strengthening in its fiscal capacity over the next few years. While the recent downturn in the world economy resulting from the global credit crisis has dimmed optimism to some degree, recent announcements of tax cuts in Saskatchewan while other provinces contemplate deficit budgets and spending cuts demonstrate the relatively strong fiscal position enjoyed by the provincial government.

As indicated above, there was little in the way of innovative policy initiatives by the Calvert NDP government, other than managing the spending expectations of traditional NDP supporters and cutting taxes. (The pre-election budget did contain a prescription price cap for seniors) The election of the Saskatchewan Party (comprised largely of former Conservative Party members) may seem ominously like a repetition of 1982. It will be their responsibility to address long-term priorities for the province with respect to the role of the public sector, the introduction and maintenance of important economic and social support programs, and how government can address longer term issues facing the province.

There is an immediate-term need to address some of the legacy of two decades of expenditure restraint. Numerous program areas, municipal governments and school boards have operated under severe funding restraints for a long period. To their credit, provincial governments avoided significant one-time cuts to most large programs and restraints were generally in the form of freezing the level of support or limiting increases to rates below inflation. However, given the length of time of general restraint programs, there have been inevitable implications for the public sector, such as increased reliance on property taxes to fund school boards and local governments, and non-competitive salaries for some groups of civil servants and employees of organizations that rely on provincial government support. Recent contract settlements for teachers and nurses have in part reflected this problem. There also needs to be a review of social safety net programs to ensure that they maintain a reasonable level of support for recipients, especially considering the recent increases in housing prices and rental rates that accompanied the recent growth in the economy.

In the next section of the paper, I identify three major policy areas that, in my opinion, represent important areas that require government attention.

The first policy area is the Saskatchewan tax system, particularly with respect to resource royalties, income taxation of low-income households, corporate taxation and the sales and property taxes. While there has been some action with respect to the reduction or elimination of the more egregious forms of taxation (e.g. the Saskatchewan Flat Tax and corporate capital taxes), there are many potential changes that could be done to improve the fairness, efficiency and effectiveness of the tax system. Changes in the tax system could also serve to distribute more evenly the benefits of the Saskatchewan economic expansion.

The second is the future role of Crown corporations in the province. Much has changed since the creation of the Crowns and it is time for government to review the role of the Crowns and to define what part they will play in the province's future.

The third and, in my opinion the most important for the future of the province, is that the province needs to prepare for the changes that will be caused by the province's demographics. The province's population is aging and not only is the cohort size of young adults shrinking, but the Aboriginal share of that cohort will be increasing rapidly. These trends will change the province profoundly and have the potential of severely restricting Saskatchewan's economic potential unless the issues raised are effectively addressed, especially with respect to increasing the participation of the Aboriginal population in the economy.

THE SASKATCHEWAN TAX SYSTEM

The fiscal recovery of the government has allowed it to deal with what it considered to be the most immediate problem—that high tax rates were scaring off investment and people, thus preventing the province from achieving its full economic potential. As discussed above, the first and most dominant policy change that occurred when the fiscal climate improved was a significant reduction in personal income taxes, corporate income and capital taxes and the sales tax. Surprisingly, relatively little of the increase in fiscal room was directed towards issues that had received plenty of public attention—the reliance on the property tax to fund K–12 education, as well as municipal government revenue sharing.

The Boughen Commission (2004) delivered a comprehensive report that demonstrated that the province relies excessively on property taxes to fund K–12 education. Among its findings were that Saskatchewan was by far the leading province in terms of using the property tax to fund K–12 education. The property tax covered about 70% of those expenses in Saskatchewan while the next highest province (Manitoba) was about 40%. Some provinces did not use the property tax at all for this purpose. The tax has been criticized on a number of grounds, including its progressivity, vagaries in its administration, and the high burden it places on farmers. As a result, until the fiscal crises of the 1980s, the trend in Canada had been for provinces to reduce or eliminate their use of that tax by increasing funding to school boards and municipalities. Evidently, this issue was not a high priority item, as the Calvert NDP government chose to reduce personal income taxes rather than using the funds to increase transfers to school boards and municipalities and thereby reduce property taxes.

Another facet of our tax system is the low income level at which income taxes are payable. The most recent tax changes announced in the provincial throne speech addressed this issue by substantially increasing personal and child tax credits. Until recently, the province's income tax system merely reflected the federal system by using a tax on tax method to calculate Saskatchewan taxes. Over time, the Saskatchewan income tax has diverted from the federal system by using its own income brackets, personal exemptions and tax rates so that it is now possible for Saskatchewan to contribute to changing the system to improve fairness for people earning low levels of income.

The problem has arisen as a result of two changes to the federal income tax system that occurred in the 1980s—the change from deductions to non-refundable tax credits which made all income taxable and the less than full indexation of tax brackets and tax credits. Until the recent changes, the income threshold above which Saskatchewan income taxes were payable for a single individual was $9,400, well under the various definitions of the poverty line. The recently announced changes increased the threshold to $13,700. It would not be difficult to defend the normative proposition that households who live below the poverty line should not pay income taxes. The Saskatchewan Flat Tax, which levied a flat 2% rate on all income with no deductions or tax credits, is a particularly good example of a tax that unfairly burdens the very poor. The elimination of that tax and the recent increases in personal tax exemptions addressed a significant portion of this problem, but there is some distance to go to ensure that people who have trouble paying for food and shelter do not have to pay income taxes.

Another potential area for investigation would be an assessment of the personal and corporate income tax reforms that were implemented after 2000. Not only were personal income taxes lowered by about one third, the changes significantly flattened the tax rate structure to three brackets, with marginal tax rates of 11%, 13% and 15%. The rationale for this was that high tax rates were scaring off high-income earners. Lowering corporate income and capital taxes was to encourage investment in the province. While it is likely that the changes had some of the impacts that were promised, there should be an assessment of the impact of the changes in tax rates and structure to assess whether they delivered the anticipated results.

Another issue that should be addressed is the method and level of taxation of non-renewable natural resources in Saskatchewan. There has been a lively debate in the province with some suggesting that the current taxation structure does not capture for taxpayers a fair share of the value of the resources extracted. Using ratios such as tax revenues as a share of gross revenues, or as a share of resource company profits, a number of authors have suggested that the government could increase its tax revenues in excess of a billion dollars if a more aggressive tax system was in place. The issue is complex. Economic theory suggests that governments can extract economic rent (the difference between price and extraction costs) without affecting the level of activity in the resource industry. As resource prices rise, economic rents are affected in two ways—the economic rent associated with developed facilities will increase and new extraction sites will be developed, ones that were not economically feasible at lower resource prices and therefore will generate less economic rent. As a result, the percentage share of tax revenues may increase or decrease, depending on which effect is larger.

There are other complicating factors in assessing the effectiveness of a resource taxation regime. The impact on exploration activity, interaction of resource royalties with other forms of industry taxation (exploration leases, capital taxes, profit taxes) and other factors would need to be considered in a careful assessment of the efficiency and effectiveness of our tax system. However, the estimated revenues losses developed through the simple ratio calculations—comparing, for example, tax shares of total revenues during the Blakeney government with the current shares—suggest there is a potential issue here and Saskatchewan's system of resource taxation should be carefully reviewed.

Another aspect of the Saskatchewan government increasing its reliance on resource revenues relative to traditional sources of revenues (sales and income taxes) is that future revenues are likely to be subject to greater fluctuations than in the past. While, this should not pose a problem over a reasonable length of time, the current fixation of many Canadian governments on maintaining either a balanced or surplus budget on an annual basis should be re-examined. Transparency of government activity is an important contribution to our ability to conduct democratic oversight on elected officials. When faced with a demand for balanced budgets, governments have responded either with spending decisions that appear to be largely motivated by the need to spend money before fiscal year-end and/or artificial accounting mechanisms to hide surpluses or deficits. As indicated above, the Conservative governments in the 1980s resorted to various accounting measures to effectively hide some part of the general revenue fund deficit. In recent times, successive governments have used the Fiscal Stabilization Fund (later renamed the Growth and Financial Security Fund) to accomplish the same task. While the Summary Financial Statements sort through the numbers, there are still problems in the way the provincial government reports its budget decisions to the public, such as the treatment of some capital/infrastructure costs as expenses.

If increased reliance on revenues from non-renewable resources decreases the stability and predictability of revenues, we must expect larger changes in the year-to-year fiscal status, including deficits during "bad" years, as normal. It will be difficult to transfer larger and larger deficits and surpluses to off-side "funds" while claiming to have balanced the general revenue fund. Since one of the most important decisions of any government is to determine the relative stable spending commitments that can be sustained from a highly variable stream, the government's policies and actions on this issue should be readily transparent to taxpayers and voters.

CROWN CORPORATIONS

Crown corporations are policy instruments that provide a mechanism to achieve policy goals other than taxation, subsidy and regulation. For example, a government faced with an industry that would normally be monopolized may wish to respond by price regulation or by running the industry as a state-operated enterprise (SOE). One potential advantage of SOEs is that the state can achieve its goals directly, rather than indirectly through regulation. The rationale for their existence is therefore a situation where private markets would not produce efficiently and where a SOE is the most effective form of achieving the state's goals.

While a complete assessment of the positive and negative aspects of the use of Crown corporations is beyond the scope of this paper, changing technology may obviate the need for the SOE, either by eliminating the problem that was addressed or creating a more effective means of addressing the issue. The role of Saskatchewan's Crown corporations should be subject to ongoing assessment and review. Unfortunately, political discussion over what, if any, changes to make to the way the Crowns participate in Saskatchewan has to date been characterized by ideological concerns regarding the relative productivity of the private vs. public sectors or the alleged reduction of service arising from the pursuit of profit or the potential transfer of direct and indirect jobs out of the province rather than a practical discussion of the appropriate role of the Crowns.

The recent announcement by the Wall government of a "Saskatchewan First" policy, where Crowns can no longer invest outside the province is a case in point. According to the government, the experience of out-of-province investing has been negative thereby justifying the change. However, it is likely that a more careful review would have identified a limited set of criteria under which an investment may be undertaken. An example might be a joint venture that uses expertise developed within a Crown corporation (e.g. developing rural electricity distribution networks).

It may be appropriate to not use the Crowns as venture capital corporations with shareholders who were compelled to invest (taxpayers). Unfortunately, the nature of the public debate that has taken place has not been helpful in exchanging views on this issue and provides little guidance to government in developing policy involving the Crowns.

ECONOMIC ENGAGEMENT OF FIRST NATIONS PEOPLES

There have been many studies documenting the "baby boom" that has experienced the Saskatchewan First Nations. A recent Statistics Canada study forecast that the Aboriginal population in Saskatchewan will grow from 155,000 in 2006 to 203,000 in 2017. Incredibly, the projection suggests that 60% of that population will be 30 years of age or younger. Projecting trends even further suggests that our population will be 40% aboriginal by 2025. If the current socio-economic status of Aboriginal populations continues to 2025, the province does not have a bright future. Table 7 provides some data on employment rates to illustrate this and what is particularly disturbing is that the problem seems to be getting worse.

Table 7. Employment Rates by Aboriginal Status, Off-Reserve Only Population 15 and older, April 2004–March 2005

	Manitoba	Saskatchewan	Alberta	British Columbia
Non-Aboriginal	66%	66%	70%	61%
Métis	66%	58%	66%	63%
First Nations	49%	42%	57%	50%

Employment Rates (%) Persons Aged 25–54, 1981 and 2001

	Aboriginal		Non-Aboriginal	
	1981	2001	1981	2001
Regina	58.7	55.4	80.6	86.4
Saskatoon	48.2	53.9	78.3	84.6
Winnipeg	52.7	65.3	79.8	84.7

Source: Statistics Canada.

Addressing this problem will not be an easy task, but it essential that the province take immediate steps to enhance the engagement of First Nations people in the Saskatchewan economy. Fortunately, there is evidence that improving literacy skills and formal levels of educational attainment will significantly improve the socio-economic position of Aboriginal peoples.

Table 8. Proportion of Population by Highest Level of Schooling, 2001

	Registered Indian		Other Aboriginal		Others	
	25–44	45–64	25–44	45–64	25–44	45–64
Less than Grade 9	13.8	38.8	7.5	23.4	3.8	16.1
Secondary school	36.9	24.6	40.9	33.5	32.0	33.6
Trades or non-university	34.8	26.1	37.9	28.5	34.8	27.6
University level	14.5	10.4	13.8	14.6	29.4	22.7

Source: Statistics Canada.

The disparity in terms of completed programs is even larger, indicating that Aboriginal students have much more difficulty completing programs than non-Aboriginal students.

Current data suggests that education is a very effective way to achieve significant reductions in these labour market disparities. The difference in labour force participation between Registered Indians and non-Aboriginal males ages 25–44 falls from almost 30% (63.8% vs. 34.0%) for educational attainment if less than grade 9 to -0.5% (92.4% vs. 92.7%) for those with university degrees.

Achieving success in improving socio-economic outcomes for Aboriginal people is dependent on our finding ways to engage them in education, training and employment in a way that they find appropriate. Present trends suggest that Saskatchewan's efforts in this area have not been sufficient to accommodate the increased numbers of young Aboriginal people.

This is likely an ideal time to take action, with the Saskatchewan government enjoying unprecedented fiscal room and a looming wave of retirements and labour shortages in the province in the near future. Increased economic activity in the resource sector also suggests that there will be increased economic opportunity in the north, mitigating the issue of a geographical mismatch between jobs and Aboriginal people.

CONCLUSIONS

This paper presented a brief history of the evolution of the Saskatchewan provincial government's fiscal position. While the problems and issues that must be faced in the future are formidable, they are certainly easier to manage than the fiscal crisis that was addressed by the Romanow government in the early 1990s. There are a number of important lessons that may be derived from our recent history.

The first is that projecting positive economic conditions into the indefinite future is a risky proposition. As we have seen in late 2008, resource and commodity prices can be extremely volatile and we can reasonably expect poor economic conditions for the province in the near future and periods of economic decline further ahead. Apart from the general revenue fund debt, we face other unfunded liabilities going into the future, namely the need to invest in education and training, particularly for the Aboriginal population, and the effect on the cost of programs such as health care as the number of seniors increase.

Further, the long term sustainability of the provincial tax system and program spending may be threatened by our dependence on resource revenues, given that these are non-renewable resources and that there is a perceived need to reduce the use of fossil fuels for environmental reasons. Future Saskatchewan governments will face a formidable challenge to ascertain what level of program spending may be supported by volatile and time-limited tax sources. An informed debate on this issue would be facilitated by transparency in government accounting of surpluses and deficits.

A second is that the development of an unsustainable level of debt was a process that most people in the province still remember. One of the factors that led to the political demands for universal benefit programs in the 1980s was the belief that the benefits of the economic growth of the 1970s were not widely shared. Middle class voters, facing punishing mortgage rates and feeling left out of the boom times, demanded entitlement programs that were not targeted to the needy. It will be important that government ensures that the benefits of profitable resource companies and surging government revenues be distributed widely. The recent increases in personal tax exemptions represent a way of accomplishing that goal.

Finally, the period of the fiscal crisis taught us that if a government is determined to engage the electorate in a policy discussion about serious problems, such a discussion can take place and the electorate will support difficult decisions. The Romanow government was able to move public discussion beyond ideological and urban/rural divides by being transparent regarding the scope of the fiscal crisis and why painful measures were necessary. Influencing and engaging public discourse on important issues is certainly not as critical today as it was in the early 1990s, but it would help that current government policies deal with positive economic times and new fiscal challenges in an effective manner.

SELECTED REFERENCES

Hale, Geoffrey. 2000. "The Tax on Income and the Growing Decentralization of Canada's Personal Income Tax System," in Harvey Lazar (ed.), *Canada: The State of the Federation 1999/2000*. Montreal and Kingston: McGill-Queen's University Press

Hansen, Phillip. 2003. *Taxing Illusions Taxation, Democracy and Embedded Political Theory*. Halifax: Fernwood Publishing.

MacKinnon, Janice. 2003. *Minding the Public Purse: The Fiscal Crisis, Political Trade-offs and Canada's Future*. Montreal: McGill-Queen's University Press.

Perry, David. 1997. *Financing the Canadian Federation, 1867 to 1995: Setting the Stage for Change*. Toronto: Canadian Tax Foundation, 1997.

Saskatchewan Business Tax Review Committee. 2005. *Report of the Saskatchewan Business Tax Review Committee*. Regina: Government of Saskatchewan, 2005.

Saskatchewan Financial Management Review Commission. 1992. *Report of the Saskatchewan Financial Review Commission*. Regina: Government of Saskatchewan, 2005.

Saskatchewan Personal Income Tax Review Committee. 1999. *Final Report and Recommendations*. Regina Government of Saskatchewan, 1999.

NOTES

1. Janice MacKinnon, *Minding the Public Purse: The Fiscal Crisis, Political Trade-offs and Canada's Future* (Montreal: McGill-Queen's University Press), 20.

2. The Conference Board of Canada, *Provincial Outlook Executive Summary Summer 2008* (Ottawa: Conference Board of Canada, 2008).

3. Provincial Auditor of Saskatchewan, Auditor's Report, 17 July 17, 1991, quoted in *Report of the Saskatchewan Financial Review Commission* (Regina: Government of Saskatchewan, 1992), 17.

The Fyke in the Road: Health Reform in Saskatchewan from Romanow to Calvert and Beyond

Tom McIntosh and Gregory P. Marchildon

INTRODUCTION

As the birthplace of medicare in Canada, Saskatchewan is not a province like all the others when it comes to health care. Ultimately, it was Saskatchewan's model of universal, single-payer hospital and medical care insurance that became the Canadian model, despite the strong preference of provinces such as Alberta, British Columbia, Manitoba and Ontario for a means-based, multi-payer system delivered through private health insurers. Yet, a vocal minority has, since medicare's inception, argued for a greater role for private insurance and private, for-profit delivery within the Canadian health care system. A 2005 decision by the Supreme Court of Canada (*Chaoulli v. Quebec (Attorney General)*) may have opened the doors to just such an eventuality by ruling that Quebec's ban on private insurance violated the Quebec Charter of Rights. While the decision's impact on medicare continues to be debated, it has served to polarize viewpoints, even further, as to the role of the state in health care in general and the funding and administration of public health care in particular.[1]

While the future of the Canadian model of medicare will likely be determined outside the province, Saskatchewan's historical role almost guarantees that the province will continue to have considerable influence. For this reason, the health reforms initiated by the Romanow and Calvert New Democratic Party (NDP) administrations, as the successors of the original Co-operative Commonwealth Federation (CCF) government that implemented hospitalization in 1947 and medical care insurance in 1962, or the reaction to those reforms by the Saskatchewan Party government first elected in 2007, will have an impact well beyond Saskatchewan.

If hospital and medical insurance were medicare's first phase, then its second was to be a reorganization of health and human services to focus on the social and economic causes of ill-health and the prevention of disease.[2] Roy Romanow in particular tried to push medicare beyond its first phase. His government attempted to remove financial and other barriers to reform so that a reorganized delivery system could put wellness and prevention rather than illness care at the centre of the system. This was an agenda he carried into his work as Head of the Commission on the Future of Health Care in Canada after retiring as Premier of Saskatchewan.[3]

The election of 2007 brought an end to the Romanow-Calvert era in Saskatchewan, and it is as yet unclear how this will change the province's approach to health care. As a new government based on a philosophy and political background opposed to the collectivist ideology of the CCF-NDP, the Saskatchewan Party government under Premier Brad Wall will be carefully watched within and outside the province to see if it is prepared to break with the Canadian model of medicare in any of its essential attributes.

HEALTH REFORM IN THE ROMANOW ERA

THE POLITICAL AND POLICY ENVIRONMENT

The changes to health care brought about in Saskatchewan during the Romanow years were significant and, for the most part, lasting. But while Saskatchewan has probably gone further than most Canadian provinces in achieving its health reform goals, economics, politics, ideology as well as the self-interest of key actors in the system necessitated compromises that slowed, diverted and blunted some of the more ambitious elements of the agenda.

The early years of the Romanow government were marked by fiscal restraint and the contraction of publicly provided health and social services, as the province teetered near bankruptcy brought about by years of over-spending by the previous Conservative administration under Grant Devine. As the province began to achieve a greater level of fiscal security, the Romanow government undertook to reshape the governance and financing of the provincial health care system under the rubric of a "wellness agenda" aimed at refocusing health care away from its preoccupation with doctor and hospital services and toward preventative and population health services.[4]

Yet, the successful implementations of the reforms planned under the Romanow government, which were introduced by the government earlier in its time in office, were often undercut by the political fallout of the restraint measures. In particular, the closure or conversion of 50 small rural hospitals as part of the province's rationalization of acute care delivery in Saskatchewan gave rise to a public perception that the "wellness agenda" was, in fact, merely a code for neo-liberal fiscal restraint that undermined Tommy Douglas' vision of accessible, publicly funded care.[5] Politically and ideologically, this was a difficult position for the social democratic successor of the government that had originated medicare.

However, the Romanow government had the advantage of facing a weak and divided opposition in the provincial legislature throughout much of its tenure, especially during the early years. The Conservative Party won only 10 of the province's 66 seats in 1991 and the Liberals only one. It was not until the 1999 election, with the creation of the new Saskatchewan Party, that Romanow faced a unified opposition in the legislature. In 1999, the Liberals managed to elect only four members (later reduced to three in a by-election loss to the Saskatchewan Party), the Saskatchewan Party 25 and the NDP 29. Facing a minority government, Romanow negotiated a coalition agreement with the

Liberals that saw two of the Liberals appointed to Cabinet and the third take the Speaker's chair.

Thus, from 1991 until 1999, Romanow, much like federal Liberal Leader Jean Chrétien during the same period, had comfortable majorities in the legislature coupled with a weak, divided opposition unable to mount effective campaigns against the changes the NDP planned. Even after winning only a minority government in 1999, Romanow's coalition agreement allowed the government to operate as a *de facto* majority NDP government, especially after the expulsion of the Liberal MLAs from their own party.

The government's relations with key stakeholders in the health care system are also important to understanding how the reform initiatives during both the Romanow and Calvert governments played out. Because of the financial power of the health sector as well as the historic challenge of recruiting and retaining health care workers in the province, government-stakeholder relations in the health sector in Saskatchewan are a complicated balancing act between interest-promotion and turf-protection on the one hand and a desire to avoid mutually destructive behaviour on the other. For example, the Saskatchewan Medical Association (SMA) rarely engages in the kind of open hostility towards government that marks physician-government relations in other provinces, for fear of both undermining public confidence in the system and alienating its own membership. Similarly, the health care unions, notably the Saskatchewan Union of Nurses (SUN), had traditionally staked out positions much in line with the goals of the Romanow reforms and, like other labour organizations, had been official supporters of the provincial NDP. At the same time, a series of health worker strikes in the mid- to late-1990s significantly damaged the NDP government's relationships with SUN and other unions, which remain strained to this day.

As important as these factors are, though, there is also a prevailing culture within the stakeholder organizations that reduces the possibility of open conflict with the government. The legacy of Saskatchewan as the "birthplace of medicare" looms large in the province. In the aftermath of the 1962 doctors' strike, despite the bitterness the strike engendered, the SMA eventually took on the mantle of one of Medicare's chief architects and has been a consistent defender of its principles and its preservation inside the province and within the medical community nationally. Similarly, virtually all of the major players within the system see themselves, at some level, as participating in the project initiated by Tommy Douglas and the CCF in the 1940s. Though this does not eliminate the traditional sources of tension between the government and the stakeholder community (or between stakeholders themselves), it does serve to encourage negotiation, consultation and compromise.

THE ROAD TO WELLNESS: REGIONALIZATION AND PRIMARY HEALTH CARE

Between 1992 and 1994, the Romanow government would embark on an ambitious package of reforms aimed, first, at restructuring the governance of the provincial health care system and, second, at reorienting the organization, funding, coordination and delivery of primary care and acute care services.[6]

The government undertook restructuring with the express intent of integrating and rationalizing the delivery of health services in an effort to shift the
system's focus to the delivery of primary health care (much of it to be delivered outside of traditional health care institutions). With the changes came a
new driving philosophy for health care: that of health promotion and disease
prevention, or "wellness."

The reorganization of the health system in Saskatchewan was to be two-
fold: first to restructure the system into health districts[7] and then to focus the
system on *primary health care* which has a broader focus than traditional primary care. Primary health care can be defined as an "approach to health and
a spectrum of services beyond the traditional health care system" that
"includes all services that play a part in health, such as income, housing, education, and environment," while primary care is the subset of activities "within primary health care that focuses on health care services, including health
promotion, illness and injury prevention, and the diagnosis and treatment of
illness and injury."[8]

The assumption underpinning this two-stage approach was that the existing governance structure was a barrier to primary health care reform. The
government believed that it needed to remove those elements of the system
that it felt would be resistant to change. Individual hospital boards in particular were expected to resist a change in which they might no longer be at the
centre of the provincial health care system. By eliminating individual hospital
boards and replacing them with district boards with clear mandates to integrate and coordinate services across a broader geographic region, it was
expected that the government would then be able to move forward on implementing a more fundamental reorientation of the system. However, as became
apparent, the second half of the plan—the wide-scale implementation of new
primary health care or "wellness" models and the heightened emphasis on
prevention and health promotion—had limited implementation. A series of
decisions, some related to the restructuring of the health system and some
related to the financial crisis in the province, created a widespread public perception that the government's commitment to wellness was, in fact, a code for
government cutbacks and retrenchment of services. This negative perception
limited the extent of the second phase of reform.

The government defended the closure of a small number of hospitals and
the conversion of a much larger number to community "wellness centres" on
the basis of these facilities' inability to provide quality acute and emergency
care. As Deputy Minister of Health during these years, Duane Adams recognized that the closures and conversions were as much about efficiency and
cost-savings as about the quality of care—it was the black horse of health
reform, with regionalization being the white horse.[9] This public identification
of hospital closures as health reform may well have hindered the government's ability to effectively implement some of the subsequent decisions that
were an integral part of the reform agenda. Despite this, the Romanow government did manage to change some elements of the funding of the system by
moving to a system of "population needs-based funding" for health districts.

Under this new financing formula, districts would be funded relative to the health care needs of the population they served. Districts with higher proportions of individuals with higher health care needs (e.g. the elderly, Aboriginals, children) would receive proportionately more money per capita to design and deliver services that would meet and alleviate those needs.

The government also attempted to change the way doctors were paid within the system but with only limited success. The predominant system of paying for each service provided by a physician (referred to as "fee-for-service") encourages doctors to maximize the volume of services provided rather than the quality of those services: the more patients a doctor sees and the more tests are performed, the greater the physician's income. Rather, the government attempted to negotiate alternative payment plans for physicians that would reward them for focusing on the quality of the services they provided. One strategy was to offer physicians a global amount of money to provide care for a "roster" of patients; thereby, a doctor would receive a set amount per patient (adjusted for age and health status) regardless of whether any particular patient visited the physician during that year. This allowed physicians to provide more in-depth care to sicker patients without losing income in the process. While there are an increasing number of physicians on so-called alternative payment schemes (and a growing interest amongst younger physicians to participate), the old fee-for-service model remains the predominant form of remuneration in the province.

LIMITING ACCESS TO PRIVATE-FOR-PROFIT CARE

The ambitious nature of the "wellness agenda" reforms put forward by Romanow took a significant toll on the government and its political support. The upheaval produced by the creation of the health districts and the attempts to push the system toward a new emphasis on prevention and primary health care and away from hospital-based, physician-centric acute care generated anxiety on the part of the public and some stakeholders as well as some hostility towards the NDP government. Regionalization of the system, linked as it was in the public's mind with hospital closures and fiscal restraint, may have also eroded the government's credibility as a defender of medicare, a credibility it would soon reassert in its handling of private clinics.

In 1996, the Romanow government passed the Health Facilities Licensing Act (HFLA) in order to clarify the legal status of any privately operated facility that might be opened in the province. The legislation did not make it illegal to operate private-for-profit clinics; rather, it created a process for their accreditation and regulation, thereby filling a policy and regulatory void. In effect, the HFLA only allowed private clinics if they could: 1) prove the need for such a facility in the proposed location to the Minister of Health; 2) meet the regulatory standards set by the Saskatchewan College of Physicians and Surgeons; and 3) prove they were prepared to rely entirely on private payment for the services they provide.[10] In other words, the province imposed the same rule on facilities that existed for physicians who must opt-out of medicare completely if they want to receive patients on a private basis. This rule prevented private clinics from using medicare patients to help underwrite their private business or from charging medicare patients extra fees for so-called "Cadillac services," which are deemed to be superior to those offered in publicly administered facilities. Given the difficulty of establishing a private clientele in the small provincial market without significant public subsidy, this law made the development of private clinics—such as those in Alberta and British Columbia—unlikely.

While privately unhappy with the legislation, the Saskatchewan Medical Association (SMA) chose not to make its displeasure public. At the same time, knowing that at least some elements within the SMA would be opposed to the legislation, the government consulted with the SMA and made some minor changes to the legislation prior to its introduction. Despite touching on a hot-button issue, the debate in the Saskatchewan Legislature was short, with little to no criticism by the Liberal and Conservative opposition parties. For the NDP government, however, the HFLA reflected their commitment to a publicly administered, single-tier system with access determined on need rather than ability to pay. Developments outside the province had also put pressure on the Romanow government. Private cataract clinics were opening in Alberta at this time, and there were rumours of similar clinics being proposed in Saskatoon. The recent adoption of the North America Free Trade Agreement (NAFTA) had also sparked significant concern, especially on the political left, that expanded free trade could threaten Canada's social safety net if it allowed private enterprise to gain a foothold in the Canadian health care sector. In this view, then, the HFLA served to close the door to such operations by making them legal but unlikely to be profitable.

Viewed within the context of the Romanow government's overall health reform agenda—the regionalization, the "wellness" agenda, and the restructuring of public facilities—the HFLA is consistent with the government's stated objectives of modernizing medicare. While critics would argue that the HFLA in fact froze in place an out-dated vision of health care delivery (one that needed to be reformed with a greater reliance on private payment), the legislation served to fill a regulatory gap that had been unanticipated decades earlier and did so in a manner consistent with the stated vision of the province's political leaders. At the same time, the legislation came at a time when the NDP's status as a defender of medicare had suffered after the closure and conversion of rural hospitals; it was an important reassertion of the government's commitment to publicly funded and administered health care.[11]

THE FYKE IN THE ROAD

THE POLITICS OF CANADIAN HEALTH CARE IN THE 1990S
The political backlash caused by the budget cuts to health care from 1992 until 1995 dogged the Romanow government well into the late 1990s. The cabinet had become so exhausted by the constant criticism that it injected a further $50 million during the budget finalization process in order to prevent the health

districts from closing more rural hospitals in 1996. Although the districts were simply trying to live within the budgets allocated to them by the Department of Health, the government reversed some of these difficult decisions in an effort to avoid further public criticism. Not only did the tactic not work but the government ended up damaging its relationship with the boards and management of the districts and undermining the incentives for districts to make difficult decisions in the future.

Internally, the reforms combined with the budget cuts had exhausted many of the leading reformers within the Department of Health itself. The political leader of the reforms, Health Minister Louise Simard, left government to return to the practice of law in 1995. Her deputy, Duane Adams, exited the department after suffering a heart attack in 1997. Facing a regular barrage of public, media and opposition attacks for problems associated with wait lists and professional shortages, the department focused on fixing more pressing, short-term problems than on long-term reform.

At the same time, Roy Romanow became increasingly concerned by what he saw in the rest of the country.[12] His anxiety was shared by many in his government and his political party. In 1994, the Parti Quebecois had been elected, and Premier Jacques Parizeau immediately began to plan for a referendum on separation. In the federal budget of 1995, the Chrétien government, under Finance Minister Paul Martin, introduced the Canada Health and Social Transfer (CHST), cutting federal transfers for health care, social services and education to the provinces after a program review which reduced the federal role. Tom Courchene referred to the 1995 Martin budget as "a devolution of power to markets (privatization, deregulation, contracting out, etc.) and a decentralization to lower levels of government."[13] Romanow immediately attacked the Martin budget as un-Canadian.

Using the federal cuts as a pretext, Alberta Premier Ralph Klein professed his dissatisfaction with the Canadian model of medicare and his desire to experiment with more private funding and private delivery. He was supported in his sentiments by the newly elected Conservative government in Ontario. In their mutual opposition to the federal government and the principle of using the spending power to enforce federal conditions including the principles of the Canada Health Act, Alberta and Ontario were joined by the separatist government of Quebec. Although he was also upset by the transfer cuts, Romanow opposed all three governments in terms of their desire for greater decentralization and their view that the Canada Health Act was a relic of a bygone era.

By 1999, the war of words between the provinces and Ottawa was reaching a crescendo. Ontario was awaiting the final report of its Health Services Restructuring Commission, and provinces such as Alberta and Quebec were announcing the formation of their arm's-length task forces on the future direction of health care. Fearing disparate recommendations, some of which would be hostile to the Canada Health Act and the Canadian model of medicare, Romanow asked Prime Minister Chrétien to consider establishing a federal royal commission in order to insert some national leadership into the debate on the future direction of medicare.[14] When Chrétien refused, Romanow decided he had to establish a Saskatchewan task force both as a way to obtain advice on the next phase of reform but also to influence the larger debate on the future of medicare in Canada.

SASKATCHEWAN'S COMMISSION ON MEDICARE

From Romanow's perspective, the country had come to a major fork in the road in terms of public health care. Either the provinces, supported by the judicious use of the federal spending power, would reshape and renovate public health care to suit the new needs of the 21st century on Medicare's foundation of equitable access, or the provinces, without input from Ottawa, would each go their own way without the "impediment" of any national principles, with some choosing to rollback medicare in favour of private funding and for-profit delivery. Although he was already considering in his own mind the possibility of retiring, spurred on by his party's near election loss just months before, Romanow had no intention of dropping this critical piece of unfinished business.[15] He wanted to ensure that Saskatchewan would once again play a leadership role in medicare, this time by preserving the moral foundation of medicare for all Canadians. Whoever might succeed him as leader of the provincial NDP would have the strongest possible policy basis from which to struggle against the rising tide of anti-medicare sentiment. For this, Romanow asked Ken Fyke to be the sole head of a task force that would recommend future directions within months of his appointment on June 14, 2000.

The mandate of Fyke's Commission on Medicare was to: 1) identify the key health and health care challenges facing Saskatchewan residents; 2) recommend an action plan to improve the delivery of health services throughout the province; and 3) investigate and make recommendations to ensure the long-term sustainability of provincial medicare. Significantly, the Order-in-Council appointing the Commission was explicit concerning the values which Fyke was to apply in interpreting his mandate. These included the assumption that the "people and the Government of Saskatchewan share a profound commitment to a publicly funded, publicly administered health system," one that also:

- Embodies the principles of The Canada Health Act: Universality, Portability, Accessibility, Comprehensiveness and Public Administration;

- Promotes the collective good and overall health and well being of the population;

- Provides a high standard of quality in the services provided;

- Treats people in a caring and compassionate manner;

- Clearly defines accountability and responsibility;

- Distributes costs in a way that is fair and equitable;

- Ensures access to services based on health need and not on the ability to pay; and

- Uses public resources effectively.[16]

Three months later, on September 25, 2000, Roy Romanow announced his intention to resign as Leader of the provincial NDP. In a speech broadcast throughout the province, Romanow traced his original motivation to enter politics to the great medicare debate and the Doctors' Strike of 1962 when he became "passionately committed to the principle of making health care accessible on the basis of need, rather than income." Expressing his pride in his government's "efforts to secure the future of Medicare," he explained that his decision to create the Fyke Commission was to help "propose new ideas" based on principles consistent with medicare to challenge those ideas constructed on values inimical to universality and solidarity.[17]

With over 35 years of experience, Ken Fyke was one of the most experienced health administrators in the country as well as a committed defender of the principles of medicare sympathetic to the values and assumptions underpinning his mandate.[18] In addition to stints as a deputy minister of health in Saskatchewan and British Columbia, Fyke also had experience as a chief executive office of a hospital system in Victoria and, subsequently, as the first chief executive officer of the Capital Health Region in Victoria. He had also been a member of the British Columbia Royal Commission on Health Care and Costs (the Seaton Commission) in 1990–91.[19] Fyke was also a committed defender of the principles of medicare and, therefore, sympathized with the values and assumptions underpinning his mandate.

THE FYKE RECOMMENDATIONS

On February 8, 2001, Lorne Calvert succeeded Romanow as Premier of Saskatchewan. Two months later, almost to the day, Fyke delivered his report, *Caring for Medicare*, to the Calvert government and the general public. While acknowledging that regionalization had achieved one major goal—that of integrating and coordinating a number of previously disparate services from hospital and long-term institutional care to home and community care—the report concluded that "some of the enormously ambitious goals set in the early 1990s" had not be achieved. Moreover, Fyke argued that the emphasis of the Department of Health and the health districts on the volume of services and providers—from the number of hospital beds and physician interventions to the number of health providers—was unhelpful. Instead, he urged the government and districts to focus on quality including decreasing medical errors and increasing value for money in terms of efficiency and health outcomes.

Arguing that the provincial health system was "under measured and under managed," Fyke recommended the implementation of a thorough system of quality indicators as well as performance measurement that would shift the focus to the "quality and efficiency problems that are the true enemies of sustainability."[20] In terms of quality, Fyke recommended the establishment of an arm's-length "Quality Council" that would be responsible for developing

quality benchmarks for the provincial system. This new organization would
also raise the bar for improving health care quality by working with the
Department of Health and the health districts to establish best practices.
Given the existence of lower health status indicators as well as poorer health
care access in northern Saskatchewan, Fyke recommended the development
of a "Northern Health Strategy" to begin reducing such health and access disparities. In terms of wait lists, Fyke recommended the development of publicly disseminated performance indicator reports.

Citing problems with quality in Saskatchewan's smaller hospitals, the Fyke
Commission recommended the closure or conversion of the smaller hospitals
remaining in the province and the designation of ten to 14 regional hospitals
with a minimum breadth and depth of services in addition to the main terti-
ary hospitals in Regina, Saskatoon and Prince Albert. To achieve a higher
degree of efficiency and quality among the districts, Fyke recommended that
the 32 districts (33 if one includes the far northern district of Athabasca which
is funded and administered in concert with the federal government and the
Dene First Nations living in the region) be collapsed down to nine to 11 larger health regions and that their relationship to the provincial government be
clarified. He also urged the Department of Health to plan and manage health
human resources on a provincial basis.

From a larger perspective, Fyke concluded that primary health services,
rather than hospital-based care, should be at the centre of Saskatchewan's 21st
century public health care system. In the future, it would make more sense for
the province to invest an increasing share of public funding in top-notch,
upstream services emphasizing illness prevention and health promotion, in
addition to early detection of sickness, than in sophisticated medical technologies and downstream acute treatments. Viewing the solo physician practice as
unsustainable in Saskatchewan from both a clinical and cost perspective, Fyke
recommended the establishment of interdisciplinary teams involving nurses,
pharmacists, physiotherapists and other professionals, in addition to family
physicians, to provide these upstream services. He pointed to the participants
in the public consultations who agreed that the predominant fee-for-service
system for physicians was a barrier that prevented more innovative approaches to delivering higher quality primary health care.

THE CALVERT GOVERNMENT'S RESPONSE

In December 2001, the provincial government issued its action plan to meet
the challenges outlined in the Fyke Report. Accepting the analysis that a large
number of relatively small, rural health districts could never achieve critical
mass in terms of facility infrastructure and managerial capacity, the government replaced the 32 districts with 12 consolidated health regions and regional health authority (RHA) boards slated to begin operating by 2003.[21] Partly in
response to the outcry in rural Saskatchewan against further hospital closures,
the government did not close or consolidate the hospitals in the province in
the manner suggested by Fyke, although it did reorganize hospitals into categories providing different levels of acute care.[22]

Accepting Fyke's argument on the centrality of improving quality to the future sustainability of public health care, the government established the Health Quality Council in 2002. The first agency of its type in Canada (but much imitated since), the Council's mandate was to initiate major quality improvement initiatives in terms of access, effectiveness, efficiency, equity, timeliness, patient-centredness and patient safety. Working with the Department of Health, RHAs and health providers, the Health Quality Council is required to advise the Minister of Health concerning best practices and the performance of the health system. The Council went beyond reporting on and promoting quality. It initiated (and participated directly in) individual quality improvement projects in priority areas such as asthma care, drug management among seniors, post-heart attack care, skin and wound care, emergency department care and breast cancer care.[23]

In terms of primary health care reform, the province chose a more gradual approach of encouraging primary care physicians to join interdisciplinary primary care teams and accept alternative remuneration rather than fee-for-service payment. In addition, the Department of Health initiated a number of pilot, primary health care team projects in the province to determine their strengths and weaknesses. Yet, despite the attention paid to the issue by governments and policy analysts, primary health care reform proceeds, in Saskatchewan and elsewhere, at a gradual pace. Moving physicians away from fee-for-service payments and the creation of interdisciplinary teams challenge the position of the dominant health professions (i.e. doctors and nurses) within the health system hierarchy. Despite whatever rhetorical support these professions provide for such changes, they have been slow to truly cede their central role in the system.[24]

There is an irony in the primary health care debate that is often ignored by policy analysts and health system researchers. While the public consistently voices support for the idea of multi-disciplinary teams of service providers and a larger focus on prevention and public health,[25] primary health care reform is rarely their most immediate concern when it comes to health care. Instead, their concern is focused on their inability to find a family physician, shortages of health professionals in their communities, lack of access to specialists, and long wait times for advanced diagnostic tests, such as MRIs, and elective surgery.

CRISIS OF CONFIDENCE: WAITING FOR CARE IN SASKATCHEWAN

Two factors pushed the issue of wait times to the forefront of the government's health care agenda in the 1990s. The first was the increased media attention given to individual cases of provincial residents either waiting for elective surgery of various types (usually joint replacements of hips or knees) or having to travel out of the province (often to the United States) to receive surgery at public expense. The second factor was the media attention given to an annual study from the right-of-centre Fraser Institute called *Waiting Your Turn: Hospital Waiting Lists in Canada*, that consistently showed Saskatchewan has having amongst the longest wait times in the country. By the late 1990s, the wait list issue had become as politically threatening to the NDP government as hospital closures in the early 1990s.

The government responded by creating a centralized, mandatory surgical registry employing standardized assessment tools to both consolidate and manage access to surgical and diagnostic services across the province through the Saskatchewan Surgical Care Network (SSCN). An advisory committee to Saskatchewan Health, SSCN was responsible for providing advice to Saskatchewan Health on three points: 1) the planning and management of surgical services in Saskatchewan; 2) the development of standards and monitoring performance; and 3) the communication of surgical access issues to the public and health providers. Through this initiative, the NDP government tried to obtain comparable surgical data among centres, reduce wait times and achieve a transparent process that would allow the public to see exactly how long they could expect to wait for a given procedure, thereby increasing the perception of the fairness of the public system.

Prior to the development of the SSCN, two reports were important in focusing public and government attention on the issue of wait lists: the annual Fraser Institute report and the 1998 Health Canada report *Waiting Lists and Waiting Times for Health Care in Canada.*[26] Despite widespread criticism from policy-makers and academics about the Fraser Institute's methodology,[27] the work of the free-market think tank was particularly damaging to the Government of Saskatchewan. The province was singled out for having the longest wait times and longest wait lists in the country, while the Health Canada report showed that wait lists were being poorly managed in all provinces including Saskatchewan. Indeed, following the 1999 Health Canada report, the Romanow government commissioned the Task Team on Surgical Waiting Lists to "describe a fair and transparent system for scheduling elective surgical procedures" and to "recommend the steps necessary to implement the waiting list system across the province."[28] Saskatchewan also joined the Western Canada Waiting List Project (WCWL), a consortium of governments, regional health authorities and researchers charged with developing better tools to manage wait lists and reduce wait times.

Immediately following the Task Team's report in March 1999, the Romanow government announced a $12 million wait list initiative. The fund transferred money to the health districts in Regina and Saskatoon (Prince Albert and Moose Jaw being added later) in the hope that increased capacity would lead to shorter surgical waiting lists. However, this first initiative fared poorly in part because the health districts used the money for purposes beyond purchasing more surgical time. A subsequent province-wide study entitled *Surgical Wait List Management: A Strategy for Saskatchewan*[29] was released in January 2002. Among the nine recommendations was the call for an electronic surgical registry in Saskatchewan, the development of priority criteria tools and the designation of a surgical services coordinator to allow for communication between the district, the patient and the physician. These ideas were eventually moulded into the Saskatchewan Surgical Care Network (SSCN).

It is interesting to note that although some actors within the health system were less than enthusiastic about the SSCN, there was little in the way of organized opposition from stakeholders, especially physicians. Despite the prospect that the SSCN would have some impact on how physicians and surgeons practiced medicine, the SMA remained officially neutral on its appropriateness, design and implementation processes.

THE FUTURE HEALTH REFORM AGENDA: CHALLENGES FOR THE WALL GOVERNMENT

The decisive defeat of the NDP by the Saskatchewan Party in the fall election of 2007 marked the end of the Romanow/Calvert era. At this point, it is difficult to know the shape or content of the new government's health policy agenda. The only health care issue that received much attention during the 2007 election campaign revolved around the expansion of the province's drug program for seniors and low-income families. The NDP promised to make the program universal for all provincial residents, while the Saskatchewan Party promised only to expand the drug program to all children in the province. Will the new government continue its predecessor's emphasis on quality measurement and improvement? Will it try again to restructure the governance of the health system by possibly reducing the number of regional health authorities? Will it pick up the pace of primary care reform? Or will it attempt to reverse some of the reforms initiated by the NDP in deference to its own free-market orientation by introducing increased reliance on private, for-profit delivery and private payment by individuals? For all its criticisms of the NDP's policy prescriptions, the Saskatchewan Party's election platform came down consistently in favour of promising to do more of the same, only faster and with better results.

What is clear, though, is that the reforms initiated by the Romanow and Calvert governments during their combined decade and a half in office were substantial but also incomplete. As was noted earlier, Saskatchewan has probably gone as far as any province (and further than many) in meeting the health reform agendas staked out by such national undertakings as the National Forum on Health (1994–97) and the Romanow Commission on the Future of Health Care in Canada (2001–02). More close to home, Saskatchewan has implemented many of the recommendations of its own Commission on Medicare, but there remains much to be done in terms of reform; challenges both old and new persist. These challenges are now the responsibility of a new government with a very different base of political support and a very different political outlook.

While the Saskatchewan Party government's position on health reform remains largely unknown (at the time of writing), it is safe to say that the Party will face three major challenges. The first challenge is workforce related, namely to plan for a sufficient supply of health providers, in particular to provide high quality and timely services in the province's vast rural and remote areas. The second is to continue to shift the emphasis from "downstream" illness care to upstream illness prevention and health promotion in order to improve the overall health of the Saskatchewan population and reduce health care costs. The third challenge is to address Aboriginal health and reduce the gap in health status between Aboriginal residents and the majority population.

Due to an aging population and the absence of large urban centres, there is a premium on health human resource planning (HHR) in Saskatchewan. In 2005, the Calvert government released the Health Workforce Action Plan. Developed with the significant collaboration of key stakeholders in the province,[30] the Action Plan is rooted in a fundamental belief that HHR planning, if it is to be successful, must plan across professions rather than for each profession in isolation. The Plan also assumes that it is preferable to plan for the system the province will need for the future rather than the system as it exists today. The Calvert government tried to meet short-term labour shortages by creating health workforce recruitment initiatives and retention programs, and improving working conditions. The Wall government entered into a partnership agreement with the Saskatchewan Union of Nurses (SUN) to hire hundreds of new registered nurses for the province, recruiting nurses from developing countries, and provided funding to increase the number of training seats in nursing programs. These initiatives may relieve the pressure on the existing system, but they also risk replicating the problems of the past by focusing on a single profession in a multi-professional system.

Over the last 15 years, much of the rationale for the regionalization and reorganization of the health care system in the province rested on the stated desire to move toward a model of primary health care rooted in health promotion, disease prevention and the reorganization of the way care is delivered by all health professions. According to this vision, the division between social and health services was at least blurred, if not erased, and the social and economic determinants of ill health (poverty, poor housing, lack of educational opportunities, etc.) were tackled with the same kinds of resources that are routinely given to treating specific illnesses. This focus on the causes of ill health would be coupled with a reorganization of health care services delivered by teams of health care providers. These teams would work collaboratively and in a less hierarchical fashion to deliver services in a manner where the patient, not the physician or the institution, was at the centre of the system. Again, the move toward a new model or models of primary health care delivery has been consistently stymied by opposition from and fighting between powerful interests within the provincial health care system.

Similar challenges are faced by every provincial government in the country, such as redefining the way in which health professionals deliver care to individuals, breaking down the barriers between professions and integrating new health professions into the existing system (e.g. nurse practitioners, physician assistants and mid-wives). There are existing models of new primary health care arrangements in every jurisdiction in Canada, but governments continue to struggle with finding ways to replicate those successful models in new places. The Saskatchewan Party, with its strong base in rural communities across the province, is perhaps better placed than the NDP to review with rural residents the ways in which high quality health services can be delivered in new ways that may not resemble the traditional model of a family physician as the key point of entry into the health system.

By any health indicator, Saskatchewan's First Nations and Métis peoples have benefited far less than the non-Aboriginal populations from the introduction of universal, publicly administered health care.[31] They live shorter lives, have higher incidences of chronic diseases and consume disproportionately more health care resources compared to the non-Aboriginal population in the province. Demographically, the Aboriginal population is growing faster than the non-Aboriginal population in Saskatchewan, and it is significantly younger than the non-Aboriginal population given its higher birth rate. At the same time, significant strides have been made in Aboriginal peoples taking greater control over both the delivery of health services and definition of their own health and health care needs. This is especially true in the northern half of the province where the Athabasca Health Authority operates as a partnership between the province, the federal government and the Northern Inter-Tribal Health Authority (NITHA). Less success has been seen in dealing with Aboriginal health issues in the other RHAs and those First Nations people living off-reserve.

The three issues noted in this paper as being of particular importance to the maintenance of Saskatchewan's health care system are not the only ones that will confront the new government. However, they are three that will likely provide the biggest challenges to the government because how the government approaches these issues will likely set the parameters of how they will be able to approach the other issues that arrive during their tenure. They are at the core of the system's future and, as such, they also present the government with its greatest opportunities to shape the health care system for the next generations of Saskatchewan residents.

NOTES

1. Gregory P. Marchildon, "Private Insurance for Medicare: Policy History and Trajectory in the Four Western Provinces," in C.M. Flood, K. Roach, and L. Sossin (eds.), *Access to Care, Access to Justice: The Legal Debate over Private Health Insurance in Canada* (Toronto: University of Toronto Press, 2005), 429–53; and Tom McIntosh, *Don't Panic: The Hitchhiker's Guide to Chaoulli, Wait Times and the Politics of Private Insurance* (Ottawa: CPRN, 2006).

2. Gregory P. Marchildon, "The Douglas Legacy and the Future of Medicare," in B. Campbell and G. Marchildon (eds.), *Medicare: Facts, Myths, Problems and Promise* (Toronto: James Lorimer, 2007), 36–41.

3. Roy Romanow, speech to the provincial NDP convention, November 16, 1996. Roy Romanow, "Canada's Shared Destiny and the Future of Medicare," in Campbell and Marchildon, *Medicare: Facts, Myths, Problems and Promise*, 351–66.

4. Louise Simard (Minister of Health), *A Saskatchewan Vision for Health: A Framework for Change* (Regina: Saskatchewan Health, 1992).

5. Amanda M. James, "Closing Rural Hospitals in Saskatchewan: On the Road to Wellness?" *Social Science & Medicine* 49, no. 8 (1999): 1021–34.

6. "Primary care" refers to the care individuals receive during their "first" contact with the health care system for a particular ailment, usually by their family physician. "Acute care" refers to care received, mostly, in hospitals—advanced diagnostics like MRI scans, visits with specialists, surgery, etc.

7. The creation of health districts not only built on but expanded the ideas first put forward by the Murray Commission's final report in 1990: Government of Saskatchewan, *Future Directions for Health Care in Saskatchewan* (Regina: Saskatchewan Commission on Health Care in Saskatchewan, 1990).

8. Health Canada, *About Primary Health Care* (2006) <http://www.hc-sc.gc.ca/hcs-sss/prim/about-apropos_e.html> (accessed January 16, 2009).

9. Duane Adams, "The White and the Black Horse Race: Saskatchewan Health Reform in the 1990s," in Howard Leeson (ed.), *Saskatchewan Politics: Into the Twenty-First Century* (Regina: Canadian Plains Research Center, 2001), 267–93.

10. Kay Wilson and Jennifer Howard, *Missing Links: The Effects of Health Care Privatization on Women in Manitoba and Saskatchewan* (Winnipeg: University of Winnipeg for the Prairie Women's Health Centre of Excellence, 2000), 4, 23.

11. Tom McIntosh and Michael Ducie, "Health Reform in the Romanow Era: From Restraint to Restructuring," in H. Lazar, P-G. Forest, and J. Lavis (eds.), *Comparative Provincial Health Care Reform* (Montreal and Kingston: McGill-Queen's University Press, forthcoming).

12. See Roy Romanow, "Canada's Shared Destiny and the Future of Medicare," in B. Campbell and G. Marchildon (eds.), *Medicare: Facts Myths, Problems and Promise* (Toronto: James Lorimer, 2007), 351–66.

13. Thomas J. Courchene, "Chaste and Chastened," in R.B. Blake, P. Bryden, and J.F. Strain (eds.), *The Welfare State in Canada: Past, Present and Future* (Concord, ON: Irwin, 1997), 14.

14. Roy Romanow, speech to the Public Policy Forum in Ottawa, ON, March 31, 2000.

15. Gregory P. Marchildon, "Roy Romanow," in G. Barnhart (ed.), *Saskatchewan Premiers of the Twentieth Century* (Regina: Canadian Plains Research Center, 2004), 353–94.

16. Kenneth J. Fyke, *Caring for Medicare: Sustaining a Quality System* (Regina: Government of Saskatchewan, 2001), Commission on Medicare terms of reference, 86.

17. Roy Romanow, text of news conference statement held at Legislative Building in Regina, SK, September 25, 2000.

18. Fyke, *Caring for Medicare*, 84.

19. Government of British Columbia, *Closer to Home: Report of the British Columbia Commission on Health Care and Costs* (Victoria, BC: British Columbia Commission on Health Care and Costs [P. Seaton, Chair], 1991).

20. Fyke, *Caring for Medicare*, as quoted in Gregory P. Marchildon and Kevin O'Fee, *Health Care in Saskatchewan: An Analytical Profile* (Regina: Canadian Plains Research Center/Saskatchewan Institute for Public Policy, 2007), 121.

21. Gregory P. Marchildon, "Regionalization and Health Services Restructuring in Saskatchewan," in C.M. Beach et al. (eds.), *Health Services Restructuring in Canada: New Evidence and New Directions* (Montreal and Kingston: McGill-Queen's University Press, 2006), 33–57.

22. Minister of Health, *Healthy People, A Healthy Province: The Action Plan for Saskatchewan Health Care* (Regina: Saskatchewan Health, 2001).

23. Benjamin T.B. Chan, Marlene Smadu, and J. Stewart McMillan, "Quality Councils as Catalysts and Leaders in Quality Improvement: The Experience of the Health Quality Council in Saskatchewan," *Healthcare Papers* 6, no. 3 (2006): 38–45.

24. Tom McIntosh and Michael Ducie, "Health Reform in the Romanow Era: From Restraint and Restructuring," in H. Lazar, P.G. Forest, and J. Lavis (eds.), *Comparative Provincial Health Care Reform* (Montreal and Kingston: McGill-Queen's University Press, forthcoming).

25. Canada. Commission on the Future of Health Care in Canada, *Building on Values: The Future of Health Care in Canada (Final Report)* (Ottawa: Commission on the Future of Health Care in Canada, 2002), 115–35.

26. Paul Macdonald et al., *Waiting Lists and Wait Times for Health Care in Canada: More Management?? More Money* (Summary Report) (Vancouver: University of British Columbia for the Centre for Health Services and Policy Research, 1998).

27. The Fraser Institute's wait times studies are based on a mail-out survey to physicians which results in an unrepresentative sample of the target population. Furthermore, although the surveys do provide standardized definitions of wait times, they rely on respondents' recall of incidents rather than on clinical data. Finally, the Fraser Institute has consistently refused calls for an independent peer-review of the studies' results prior to publication.

28. Pat Atkinson (Minister of Health), *Health Task Team Announced to Address Wait Lists* (December 2, 1998). Quoted in <www.gov.sk.ca/news?neswID=84d78fbf-cfe2-47ed-b664-7f96f57c812c>

29. Peter Glynn, Mark Taylor, and Alan Hudson, *Surgical Wait List Management: A Strategy for Saskatchewan* (Regina: Saskatchewan Health, 2002).

30. T. McIntosh and R. Torgerson, *Setting Priorities and Getting Direction: Consultation Conference Report* (Ottawa, ON: Canadian Policy Research Networks, 2006); and T. McIntosh, *Building on Common Ground: Report from the Saskatchewan HHR Consultation Conference, February 27 and 28, 2007* (Ottawa: Canadian Policy Research Networks, 2007).

31. Marchildon and O'Fee, *Health Care in Saskatchewan*, 12–15.

Post-Secondary Education in Saskatchewan

Andrea Rounce

INTRODUCTION

In 2008, post-secondary education has become important for both the Saskatchewan government and for Saskatchewan people. Deemed relatively unimportant during the 1990s when faced with health care needs and the fiscal instability of the province, post-secondary education—and access to education—became an important election plank in both the 1999 and 2003 elections, and again in the recent 2007 provincial election that saw the Saskatchewan Party become government. Increasing university tuition fees, increasing student debt (for approximately 50% of post-secondary graduates), continued differences in educational attainment, and increasing demand for post-secondary graduates in Saskatchewan's hot labour market have combined to make post-secondary education more important to the public.

This chapter will present an overview of the institutions and learners in the post-secondary education sector in Saskatchewan, highlighting participation in the province and pressures facing the post-secondary sector. Next, developments in financing and priorities within the post-secondary sector under the previous NDP governments will be addressed. Finally, the chapter will address the recent provincial election, in which post-secondary education was the first issue addressed by both the NDP and the Saskatchewan Party. All four parties active in the election—Saskatchewan Liberals and Saskatchewan Green Party included—proposed changes to the post-secondary system as part of their platforms. Additionally, the students' unions of both Saskatchewan universities—as well as the President of the University of Saskatchewan—spoke out in response to various platforms. The chapter will conclude with a discussion of what has already occurred and what may happen next in post-secondary education under the Saskatchewan Party-led government.

CONTEXT: POST-SECONDARY EDUCATION IN SASKATCHEWAN

Post-secondary education is a provincial responsibility. However, there is a great deal of federal money that comes into the system through transfers to individual students (through student financial assistance, scholarships, and bursaries), to individual and groups of researchers (through research funding), and through transfers to the province. Despite these financial contributions, the frameworks for institutional governance are created provincially.

Saskatchewan's post-secondary education sector contains both public and private institutions. Public institutions include the University of Saskatchewan and the University of Regina and their federated and affiliated colleges, including: St. Thomas Moore College (U of S); Campion and Luther Colleges (U of R); First Nations University of Canada and its three campuses (FNUC); the Institute Français which offers French language instruction at the University of Regina; the four campuses of the Saskatchewan Institute of Applied Science and Technology (SIAST); and the Regional Colleges (nine in total, including Lakeland College in Lloydminster).

The sector also includes private vocational schools; Bible colleges; Aboriginal-controlled institutions and programs, such as the Gabriel Dumont Institute of Native Studies and Applied Research—which operates as an affiliated college of both the U of R and the U of S—and the Saskatchewan Indian Institute of Technologies (SIIT); and the Saskatchewan Apprenticeship and Trade Certification Commission (SATCC).

In addition to the public/private institutional division, public institutions in the province have traditionally been divided into the training system and the universities. The training system—most recently defined by McArthur (2005)—comprises the Saskatchewan Institute of Applied Science and Technology (SIAST), the Saskatchewan Apprenticeship and Trade Certification Commission (SATCC), the Regional Colleges, Gabriel Dumont Institute (GDI), and the Saskatchewan Indian Institute of Technologies (SIIT).

Learners in Saskatchewan can access distance, mobile, on-site, and in-person programming leading to certificates, diplomas, degrees, and journeyperson credentials. Although it has become common to talk about the post-secondary institutions in the province making up a "system," in reality, the institutions play both competing and complimentary roles and experience different levels of cooperation among themselves. The development of Campus Saskatchewan and the Saskatchewan Council of Admissions and Transfer (SaskCAT) transfer system has helped reinforce the connections between the institutions.

POST-SECONDARY EDUCATION POLICY IN SASKATCHEWAN: 1991–2007

Government priorities regarding post-secondary education have changed throughout the 1991–2007 period. One way to assess this change is to observe the ways that the government has organized its management and financing of post-secondary education.

Under the governing New Democratic Party, the issues facing post-secondary education in Saskatchewan have evolved over time. Post-secondary education has shifted from its early 1990s status when it was an important contributor to the economy, but one that was not of primary importance when compared with health care or the fiscal health of the province. Between 1991 and 2007, the government commissioned a series of externally- and internally-led reviews of various issues in post-secondary education.

In early 1992, the government established the University Program Review Panel, chaired by Albert Johnson, to assess programs at Saskatchewan's universities and colleges. The Panel was to look at the needs of students, while assessing goals of accessibility, accountability, and financial viability. Known as the Johnson Report, the review panel's report focused on the strengths and weaknesses of individual departments in both universities and the need to streamline program delivery to make the best use of available funds, while emphasizing the importance of ensuring accessibility for Saskatchewan students (University Program Review Panel, 1993). However, by the end of 1992, in spite of these findings, funding for education—along with funding for everything else—was being cut to help fight the deficit.[1]

By 1993, taxes were being increased and universities saw their grants cut again by the provincial government. In the government's budget of March 18, 1993, universities faced a decrease in their operating grants for the following year (Government of Saskatchewan, 1993). The situation was worsened in the fall of that year when the federal government also announced cuts to transfer payments, decreasing the amount of funds the province could anticipate in support of social programs (Canada News Facts, 1993). The federal government also attempted to introduce a surcharge on federal student loans, which was removed due to overwhelming public protest. Discussions around creating income-contingent loan repayment programming were occurring at the federal level, but were not popular among post-secondary student representatives.

The climate of fiscal restraint within the province and federally required the Saskatchewan government to re-evaluate its educational priorities, and Saskatchewan Education, Training, and Employment identified several (including distance education, education and training for Aboriginal peoples, the integration of the post-secondary sector) for 1994 onward (Saskatchewan Education and Skills Training, 1994). Expansion of funding or the provision of additional funds would be tied to development in these areas.

The 1995 budget froze spending on education for 1995–96, but followed that with a 2% increase for the next year (Government of Saskatchewan, 1995). Premier Roy Romanow called an election for June 21, 1995, with the promise not to do anything "rash" if re-elected. The three main political parties—the Progressive Conservatives, Saskatchewan Liberals, and the New Democratic Party—focused mainly on taxation, health care, size of government, and gambling during the 1995 election. Post-secondary education was largely considered a non-issue throughout the election, except among students: student groups were among the more active interest groups during the 1995 election. The University of Regina Students' Union and the SIAST Wascana Campus formed the South Saskatchewan Coalition for Education, to promote educational issues in the campaign, which was active during the course of the election (McMurchy, 1995).

Re-elected with a sizable, though reduced, majority, the NDP government promised to reform training programs and overhaul education. The spring 1996 Budget contained additional spending for education (2%), but projected that funding would drop in 1998. Much of the discussion at the government level was about the correct portioning of the costs of post-secondary education: what portion should the government and individual students be held responsible for? In 1995–96, government funding accounted for approximately 64% of the universities' operating budgets, while individual students' fees accounted for 27% of the costs. By this time, tuition fees had increased by a total of 62% since 1991 (Finnie and Schwartz, 1996). In a February 1996 speech, Premier Romanow reiterated the province's concerns about planned cuts to federal transfer payments for health, education, and welfare (Canada News Facts, 1996).

The first few months of 1996 were active ones in the post-secondary education policy arena, with the appointment of Harold MacKay as the Minister's Special Representative on University Revitalization. Tasked with "initiat[ing] a dialogue between the universities with the objective of establishing a longer-term process or processes to achieve university revitalization" (MacKay, 1996: 1), MacKay worked with the universities to identify key issues in post-secondary education and barriers to further co-operation in the sector.

A major policy change in student financial assistance was implemented in March 1996, with the provincial government signing an exclusive five-year contract with the Royal Bank of Canada to transfer negotiation, financing, and repayment of provincial student loans authorized after August 1, 1996, from the province to the bank. This occurred almost one year after the federal government had undertaken the same policy shift. Students dealing with this next situation would be able to make use of existing programs to manage their debt, and the banks would be paid a premium by the government to manage these loans until 2001.

As part of its downloading of responsibility in traditionally provincial areas of jurisdiction, the federal government offered to transfer responsibility for training to the provinces. Saskatchewan took on full responsibility for training, signing a Labour Market Development Agreement (LMDA) with the federal government, and moving to develop and expand programming around training.

The budget of March 20, 1997, reduced the provincial sales tax by 2%, while maintaining spending on health care, education, and social programs (Government of Saskatchewan, 1997a). However, the public was not entirely satisfied about the way post-secondary education was being funded. A great deal of debate over the 'correct' cost-sharing arrangement between universities, students, and governments took place in the Provincial Legislature.

The government's April 1997 training system strategy, *Bridges to Employment*, emphasized the province's role in providing access to post-secondary training and employment opportunities in the wake of the federal withdrawal from these areas (Government of Saskatchewan, 1997b). Among the goals for this new strategy were: "to develop a skilled workforce relevant to Saskatchewan's labour market, to enhance access and support opportunities for all learners and to create a coherent, effective and sustainable delivery system" (Government of Saskatchewan, 1997b: 2). The "new" system would include the Regional Colleges, SIAST, and the Aboriginal training institutions.

Concerns about the cost of post-secondary education—and the effectiveness of the Saskatchewan student loan program to address the costs—led to a review of student financial assistance in 1996. Mandated to "recommend possible improvements to current student assistance programs, and to present innovative approaches to student assistance that the government will be able to advance in discussions with the federal government and the other provinces" (Student Assistance Task Group, 1996), the Student Assistance Task Group undertook consultations and a province-wide survey to help shape its recommendations. The Student Assistance Task Group Report, released in June 1997, identified key principles that would guide program changes, including accessibility, equity, shared responsibility, affordability, and accountability. The provincial government responded to the Report by adding informed decision-making (of students) and the importance of a federal role in financing post-secondary education and training to the list of principles that must guide future program changes.

By mid-1997, the Government of Saskatchewan had released a formal response to the Report of the Minister's Special Representative on University Revitalization (the MacKay Report), emphasizing that education costs should be shared in a "reasonable way" between the provincial and federal governments and students. However, the government also noted that this cost-sharing must be done carefully:

> While the government believes that it is in the public interest for individual students to pay a fair share of the cost of their university programs, the government also recognizes that it is important that the burden on students not become so onerous that accessibility is significantly impaired. (Saskatchewan Post-Secondary Education and Skills Training, 1997: 19)

The government also noted that it was in the public interest to ensure that universities kept their tuition fees in line with those at universities in neighbouring provinces, but that it could also be in the public interest for universities to charge higher fees for high-cost professional programs.

In 1998, as part of the ongoing process of post-secondary revitalization and in response to the MacKay Report, the government and the universities hired DesRosiers and Associates to conduct an examination of the ways in which the universities were being funded. Part of their mandate involved the examination of tuition fees. In one of the early installments of their reporting, the consultants recommended that the government should establish annually expectations for tuition fee revenue for the post-secondary system, and leave the universities free to set tuition fee levels as they saw fit (DesRosiers and Associates, 1998: 17).

Investing in education and training continued to be a priority for the government in 1999-2000. Innovation in research and development was highlighted in the budget delivered in March 1999, with new funding for the

University of Saskatchewan's synchrotron and the Petroleum Technology Research Centre at the University of Regina (Government of Saskatchewan, 1999: 5). Operating grants for SIAST, the Regional Colleges, and the universities were increased, and capital expenditures were committed for the universities, SIAST, and Regional College facilities.

As would continue to be the case for the rest of the NDP's tenure, concerns about access to skilled trades and health-related programming were addressed in the 1999–2000 budget, with additional funds for training doctors. Important changes were made to the province's student loan system as well. Additional non-repayable funds were created for students with children, and people repaying student loans would be able to deduct interest payments from their income taxes (Government of Saskatchewan, 1999: 9).

By 1999, tuition fees were also an issue on the government's radar screen. Government polling conducted in April 1999 found that a quarter of respondents identified "lowering tuition fees" as the most important action to be taken by government to improve post-secondary education (Anderson/Fast & Associates, 1999: 10). As the province moved closer to a fall election, issues regarding access and affordability in post-secondary education became more prevalent.

Post-secondary education funding—particularly student support and tuition fees—became an issue in the 1999 election. Among the main priorities for all three parties were: job creation, taxation, education, health care, rural issues, government spending, and crime levels. The NDP's platform focused on seven priorities: more jobs, lower taxes, better education, better health care, rural opportunity, balanced budgets and less debt, and less crime (Saskatchewan New Democratic Party, 1999). Perhaps responding to the most recent provincial polling done on tuition fees and access to post-secondary education, the New Democratic Party's platform also included free tuition for first-year university and college students (Saskatchewan New Democratic Party, 1999).

When asked about this proposed policy shift, Premier Romanow stated: "What we had to weigh is we wanted to get the kids into post-secondary education. The other part of the story is to make tuition fees reasonable… Offering free tuition for the first year at a university or college is just a first step" (Nikkel, 1999: 1). At various points in the campaign, Romanow also floated the idea that the tuition package could be expanded past the first year if there was public support for such an action. In addition, the NDP platform included plans to improve student financial assistance.

The Saskatchewan Party included post-secondary education as a pillar of its 1999 election platform, through its *Education for a New Millennium*. As well as tax cuts and increased spending on health care, highways, and agriculture, the Saskatchewan Party proposed to ensure greater co-operation between the two universities, work toward greater labour market responsiveness in the post-secondary sector, and review the student loan program (Saskatchewan Party, 1998).

The Liberal Party emphasized many of the same priorities, but included post-secondary education as one of their main issues. Their approach to student support was announced in April 1999, prior to the election campaign. They addressed the tuition fee issue in a similar way to the NDP—promising $1,000 in tuition credits to each first- and second-year student enrolled full-time in a Saskatchewan post-secondary institution. When releasing the party's platform, Liberal leader Jim Melenchuk explained:

> We reviewed these budgets... and decided that now ... when economic conditions are not good ... now is not the time to be adjusting programs that are helping our young people obtain the skills they need to build a future... Now is not the time to be making adjustments in post-secondary program budgets...now is the time to enhance these programs ... now is the time to find the funds from other budget areas ... so we can enhance these programs that help young people build futures... Today, thousands of young people are delaying entering post-secondary education programs at our universities and SIAST ... for financial reasons... In today's economic conditions it is especially difficult for first and second year students ... many are having problems earning and saving enough for tuition... Government can't entirely overcome this problem ... but we had better try to help ... because Saskatchewan's future depends on a well educated labour force... (Saskatchewan Liberal Party, 1999: 3).

The University of Regina and University of Saskatchewan Students' Unions created the "Vote Education Campaign" during the 1999 election, to "focus on making the presentation of our universities a priority during the provincial election" (University of Regina Students' Union and University of Saskatchewan Students' Union, 1999). As part of their campaign to mobilize public opinion, a goal of the students' campaign was to "encourage voters to ask questions of their local politicians, write letters to the editor, and discuss with their friends and co-workers the importance of maintaining public post-secondary institutions" (University of Regina Students' Union and University of Saskatchewan Students' Union, 1999).

The NDP was returned to government in a challenging situation: winning half of the seats in the legislature, the NDP negotiated a coalition agreement with the Saskatchewan Liberals to maintain a majority. Given that both of these parties had emphasized post-secondary education in their platforms, it seemed that post-secondary education should remain on the agenda of the new government. In fact, the focus on post-secondary education—particularly the link between education and the needs of the economy—did not diminish.

Shortly after the election, public consultations into post-secondary education accessibility were announced. The community-based consultations were to be jointly led by the Minister of Education, Jim Melenchuk, and the Minister of Post-Secondary Education and Skills Training, Glenn Hagel. Speaking to people in 15 communities across the province, the ministers concluded that it was necessary to: support the post-secondary institutions adequately; address the need to provide education within rural communities and provide for the cost of living of students living away from home; expand technology-enhanced learning; focus on disadvantaged students; and ensure that student assistance was targeted and could be used for people staying in the province (Saskatchewan Hansard, 2000: 830–31).

The focus on accessibility in post-secondary education was emphasized in the government's 2000–01 budget. In the budget speech, Finance Minister Eric Cline stated:

> A plan for growth and opportunity must focus on our young people—on ensuring that they have the skills they need to take our economy into the future. It must include a plan for education and training, because the new economy is a knowledge-based economy. (Government of Saskatchewan, 2000: 6)

Incremental funding—in areas identified in previous budget speeches—played an important part of the 2000-01 budget. Additional operating funds for universities, Regional Colleges, and SIAST; capital funds for post-secondary projects for the universities, SIAST, and Regional Colleges; and more funding for increased capacity in nurse education programs were highlighted. In addition, new funds were provided to support access to post-secondary education for people with disabilities and for people accessing programming through technology-enhanced learning (Government of Saskatchewan, 2000). Additionally, the budget announced additional funding for student financial assistance through the creation of a tax credit for post-secondary graduates working in Saskatchewan—proposed as a direct response to the minister-led public consultations on accessibility. Research and development—in part through the creation of an Innovation and Science Fund—was also framed as an important way to promote growth and opportunity.

Supports for Aboriginal learners were also addressed in the 2000 budget, including training supports; supports for the Saskatchewan Indian Federated College (now FNUC), Gabriel Dumont Institute, the Northern Teacher Education Program, and the Saskatchewan Urban Native Teacher Education Program; and other training-related programming (Government of Saskatchewan, 2000: 10).

An additional report from DesRosiers and Associates (2000) on the challenges of implementing the new funding formula for Saskatchewan universities was received in June 2000. It reiterated the consultants' earlier advice that the government set a minimum level of universities' funding that would be obtained through tuition fees:

> Although it is beyond our mandate to make a recommendation on this matter, we believe the government will eventually be forced to abandon its present policy of complete tuition fee autonomy in favour of something more constraining. (DesRosiers and Associates, 2000: 12)

As the consultants were concluding that the government may in fact have to move toward the regulation of tuition fees, it is important to note that university tuition fees in Saskatchewan had increased by over 100% between 1990 and 2000.

Building on the focus on post-secondary education of the previous few years, the budget of 2001–02 saw an increased emphasis on post-secondary education. The 2001–02 budget noted that: "Connecting our education system to the future will ensure that Saskatchewan people have access to the life-long learning and skills programs they, our economy and our society need" (Government of Saskatchewan, 2001: 4). This access would be supported through a new program of Centennial Scholarships, for merit-based undergraduate aid.

Additionally, physical access would be supported through the creation of Campus Saskatchewan—a partnership designed to provide services for online learners and more online courses, as well as streamline admissions and transfers between provincial institutions (Government of Saskatchewan, 2001: 5). Training capacity—often a public issue for the province—was increased through the universities and SIAST, and through the Aboriginal apprenticeship program (Government of Saskatchewan, 2001: 6). Supports for students through the student aid program and the tax system were designed to make these programs more reflective of the realities of post-secondary education financing.

Health and education were identified as the people's priorities in the 2002–03 provincial budget, although the government noted that economic prospects were reduced for that year (Government of Saskatchewan, 2002). The budget speech emphasized competitiveness—through support for research and development and retraining for skilled labour—along with an "emphasis on learning" that involved new capital funds for teaching, learning, and research infrastructure –including technology, such as, high speed internet for Regional Colleges (Government of Saskatchewan, 2002).

A continued focus on youth—particularly when it came to educating and retaining them—was clear in the 2003–04 budget. Capital spending for the universities continued, and additional funds were made available for students, in part, through an increase in the scholarship/bursary exemption for student loans (Government of Saskatchewan, 2003: 4). The need for education and training opportunities to reflect the demands of the province's labour market was reflected in the increase of spaces in nursing programming and in out-of-province programming for health-related occupations. Health-related training would also be supported through return-for-service, bursary, and expanded loan programming.

The November 5, 2003, Saskatchewan election saw the NDP being returned to government with a slight majority in the Legislative Assembly. As with the 1999 election, post-secondary education was included in the platforms of the participating parties—particularly, as linked to standard of living, quality of life, and the future for Saskatchewan people. The NDP focused on building the future for young people, which included educational and funding initiatives such as: expansion of interest-free status for students working in the province (one-year grace period); expansion of grant programs; a $1,000 tax credit for graduates employed in the province after graduation; and increasing funds for SIAST and Regional Colleges to support training initiatives (Makarenko, 2003; University of Saskatchewan On Campus News, 2003). Additionally, the NDP emphasized the need to reduce the cost of post-secondary education through increasing bursaries and reducing debt, in order to help increase the quality of life of families in the province (Makarenko 2003).

The Saskatchewan Party also included post-secondary education spending in their 2003 platform. Linked to growth in the province and in the tax base, the Saskatchewan Party proposed that this new growth would help ensure that students would have access to post-secondary education opportunities in order to be part of the knowledge-based economy (University of Saskatchewan On Campus News, 2003).

In its focus on graduate retention, the Saskatchewan Party promised to provide an annual $7,000 tax deduction for graduates for four years after graduation. Combined with their proposed increase in the personal exemption, this would establish the lowest income tax rates in Canada for this group of people. They also committed to increase funding to the universities, SIAST, and the Regional Colleges by 5% annually and in investing in the Health Sciences Facility at the University of Saskatchewan (Makarenko, 2003; University of Saskatchewan On Campus News, 2003). Additional commitments included the remodeling of the student loan program to support access for children of middle-income families and expanding on-line and Regional College programming to facilitate access for people throughout the province, workers, and people with disabilities (University of Saskatchewan On Campus News, 2003). The focus on health care—through the need for increased nurse training seats—was also part of the Saskatchewan Party platform.

The importance of post-secondary education for the economy was also emphasized by the Liberal Party, which ran on "strengthening the economy by creating careers, not jobs" (Makarenko, 2003: 7). This included maintaining access to post-secondary education and providing incentives for graduates to stay in the province once their programs were complete. Commitments involved the forgiveness of undergraduate student loans through a four-year tax credit tied to residency in the province, as well as a commitment to keep university tuition fees at no more than 30% of the institutional operating budget (University of Saskatchewan On Campus News, 2003).

The Liberals also proposed to work to improve the social and economic situation of First Nations and Métis people, including increasing funding for post-secondary education through demanding that the federal government lift the cap on post-secondary funding for First Nations people (Makarenko, 2003; University of Saskatchewan On Campus News, 2003). Finally, the Liberals emphasized the importance of graduate studies, the attraction and retention of post-secondary faculty, and research supports (University of Saskatchewan On Campus News, 2003).

The NDP, successful in the 2003 election, delivered the first budget of a fourth term in spring 2004. The pre-election—and election—focus on education and health continued, with the government recommitting to education and opportunities for young people (Government of Saskatchewan, 2004: 6). Funds targeting entrepreneurship for youth, additional student summer employment, and Aboriginal-focused training and employment were highlighted in the 2004-05 budget. In addition, funds for research and development, nursing education and medical training, and post-secondary graduates, through the Post-Secondary Graduate Tax Credit, were increased (Government of Saskatchewan, 2004). Funds for capital projects in the post-secondary sector were also included.

The focus on post-secondary education as an important support for economic development continued in the 2005-06 provincial budget. Human capital—the people of the province—played an important role in both capital/infrastructure and learner-focused spending. Capital spending for SIAST, the Regional Colleges, expansions, new projects, and maintenance at the two universities, played a prominent part in post-secondary education spending (Government of Saskatchewan, 2005: 14–15). In addition, funds for research and development were expanded. Additional funds to help train, recruit, and support health professionals were also included.

As in the previous budget, much of the focus for post-secondary education was on youth—and on universities. This was the first budget to introduce a tuition fee freeze for university undergraduates, supported by the Saskatchewan Centennial University Tuition Grant of $6.7 million. The government also introduced a formal review of accessibility in post-secondary education (including student financial assistance), to be conducted by the Department of Learning (Government of Saskatchewan, 2005: 24). The tuition grant supplemented the increase to the universities' operating funds.

Additional operating funds were also provided to SIAST, the Regional Colleges, and to the Saskatchewan Apprenticeship and Trade Certification Commission to increase training opportunities (Government of Saskatchewan, 2005). The continued focus on expansion of training seats was reflected in the commitment to expand the number of nursing seats available, through the Nursing Education Program of Saskatchewan and through the Northern Nursing Education Program (Government of Saskatchewan, 2005). Finally, the 2005–06 budget provided for an increase—to $675—in the Graduate Tax Credit for post-secondary graduates.

Government expenditures on post-secondary education in the 2006–07 remained a priority, particularly through its "investment in people to ensure that working families and young people can participate fully in the economic benefits of the province" (Government of Saskatchewan, 2006: 5). The trend to invest in the expansion of the training and education system continued, with the government providing additional funds to the post-secondary sector to support expansion. Student assistance was increased, with government emphasizing the need to ensure that people from outside urban centres—particularly those in rural and northern communities—were able to participate in post-secondary education. The Graduate Tax Credit was increased, and the tuition fee freeze for university undergraduate students was extended for an additional two years (Government of Saskatchewan, 2006).

A distinct change in the way government had funded the post-secondary system was part of the 2006–07 budget: the government provided funding for the Saskatchewan Indian Institute of Technologies, an Aboriginal-run institution previously receiving no provincial money (Government of Saskatchewan, 2006). A final emphasis on the need to expand access to the skilled trades was the creation of a tax credit for tools, which would include an entry credit for new apprentices and a credit for those changing tools throughout their careers.

The final budget of the NDP's fourth successive term in government included post-secondary education spending as a priority. Funds for expansion of the training sector, including skilled trades and health-related occupations, were highlighted (Government of Saskatchewan, 2007b). Affordability was addressed, with spending on scholarships, bursaries, and loans and the continuation of the fully-funded university tuition fee freeze. The Graduate Tax Exemption allowed graduates—from universities, technical schools, trade schools, and other programs—working in the province to access an exemption on the first $20,000 of their income for five years (Government of Saskatchewan, 2007b).

As well as government spending on transfers to institutions, individuals, and in capital investment, the years 2005 to 2007 included reviews of post-secondary education—one department-led, one external, and one MLA-led—designed to assess and address the educational needs of Saskatchewan people. The Department of Learning undertook a review of access and affordability in post-secondary education in 2005-06; the Training System Review Panel (chaired by Douglas McArthur) took place in 2005, and the Review of Post-Secondary Education Accessibility and Affordability (led by MLA Warren McCall) did its work in 2006–07.

The Training System Review was mandated to ensure that the training system could meet the current and future needs of Saskatchewan's economy (Government of Saskatchewan, 2005b). After consulting with hundreds of learners, institutions, industries, and the public, the Training System Review Panel emphasized the need for a flexible training system that could respond to the needs of both learners and industry in the context of a booming economy.

The final post-secondary review of the 1991–2007 period was led by Warren McCall, who, in 2006, began the task as the MLA for Regina North Central and ended in 2007 as the Minister of Advanced Education and Employment. Building on work done internally by the Department of Learning in 2005–06, this review focused on access and affordability in post-secondary education, and took a system-wide approach to the issues. Post-secondary education was considered to be any education undertaken after high school—whether completed or not. The review focused on public institutions, but private institutions were also included in the research and consultation process. The review concluded that there were issues facing Saskatchewan people in terms of access and affordability, and that a comprehensive package of policies could address those issues.

The report included a total of 51 recommendations, with 12 priority recommendations in the areas of reducing tuition fees, expanding training opportunities, increasing scholarships, improving access for Aboriginal learners, improving student financial assistance, enhancing student supports and learner mobility, and connecting education and employment (McCall, 2007). The final report was released just before the election was called, so post-secondary education played a prominent role in the early stages of the election.

POST-SECONDARY EDUCATION IN THE 2007 ELECTION CAMPAIGN

The three main political parties included extensive post-secondary education commitments in their 2007 election platforms. Post-secondary education funding played a prominent role in the issues that were at the forefront— retaining young people in the province, ensuring that Saskatchewan people had access to the training they needed to participate in the booming labour market, and supporting innovation in the province's economy.

SASKATCHEWAN PARTY PLATFORM

The Saskatchewan Party placed the retention of young people up-front in its *Securing the Future* platform, arguing that "retaining young people is critical to the long-term growth and prosperity of our province" (Saskatchewan Party, 2007: 5). They linked youth retention with post-secondary education, proposing a rebate in tuition fee costs for graduates who stayed in the province for seven years. Based on the costs of their programs—prorated according to the number of years spent in school—graduates would be eligible for rebates of up to $20,000 over seven years. The program excluded graduate and professional studies as well as graduates who came into or back to Saskatchewan, focusing solely on Saskatchewan people who stayed in the province for their first-stage education and then for their employment.

As part of their commitment to "keeping post-secondary education accessible and affordable," the Saskatchewan Party proposed to invest an additional $125 million in operating funding over four years for post-secondary institutions in the province (Saskatchewan Party, 2007: 6). Included in this commitment would be the creation of a Saskatchewan scholarship fund to "retain our best students" (Saskatchewan Party, 2007: 5), operating at $3 million per year to be matched by provincial post-secondary institutions.

The immediate needs of the labour market were also considered in the Saskatchewan Party's platform. They made a commitment to fast-track the Integrated Health Services Facility at the University of Saskatchewan, while "providing almost $40 million over four years to work towards the goal of creating 300 new Registered Nurse education seats" in Saskatchewan (Saskatchewan Party, 2007: 9). Bridging programs for licensed practical nurses wanting to become registered nurses were also proposed. In addition, new physician training seats and additional residency positions would add to the training "output" in the health services sector. Furthermore, the Saskatchewan Party promised funding of $1 million over four years to the Johnson-Shoyama

Graduate School of Public Policy for professional development opportunities for public servants (Saskatchewan Party, 2007: 42).

The Saskatchewan Party also made the link between post-secondary education and entrepreneurship by creating a tax credit of $10,000 per year for five years for people under 30 who own a business or are self-employed (Saskatchewan Party, 2007). They also proposed to work with various stakeholders to "enhance business literacy, entrepreneurial and career education in Saskatchewan schools" (Saskatchewan Party, 2007: 6). Along with provincial stakeholders, the Saskatchewan Party proposed to work with western provinces to "expand economic opportunity, improve the effectiveness of public services and enhance security for Saskatchewan people," including initiatives regarding post-secondary education (Saskatchewan Party, 2007: 21).

Finally, the Saskatchewan Party made the link between post-secondary education and "an innovative economy" (Saskatchewan Party, 2007: 20). Additional funds for research—and the commercialization of research—were promised, including an increase in the research and development tax credit; the creation of a Global Institute for Energy, the Environment and Natural Resources; and additional funds for the Petroleum Technology Research Centre and the International Test Centre for Carbon Dioxide Capture (University of Regina). Innovation Saskatchewan—a new body within Enterprise Saskatchewan—would "coordinate government support for research, development and the commercialization of innovation in six priority areas," including the life sciences, environmental technology, mining and energy, agriculture, synchrotron-related initiatives, and information technology (Saskatchewan Party, 2007: 20).

NEW DEMOCRATIC PARTY PLATFORM

The post-secondary education-related planks of the New Democratic Party (NDP) were very much rooted in the recommendations of the McCall Report, which had been released just prior to the election call. Although the McCall Report focused on a wide understanding of the post-secondary education system, the NDP focused in its platform on the importance of youth or young people as its first plank. "More opportunities for young people" included a $1,000 cut to tuition fees for university students, which would take Saskatchewan's undergraduate tuition rates to below the Canadian average. This cut would be followed by a limit on university tuition fee increases based on the increase in the Consumer Price Index, anticipated to be approximately 2.3% per year (New Democratic Party, 2007: 6).

Expanding the training system was also an important plank of the NDP platform, including the creation of 10,000 new training opportunities. These opportunities were proposed to address access issues outside major urban areas and within Aboriginal communities. First, expansion would take place within the Regional Colleges through an increase in course offerings. Second, Aboriginal people could access new opportunities within the Saskatchewan Indian Institute of Technologies (SIIT) and the Dumont Technical Institute

(DTI). Expanded training for health professionals was also targeted as a way to support recruitment and retention issues (New Democratic Party, 2007).

The NDP had created the Graduate Tax Exemption Program in 2007, which provided for $100,000 in tax-free income over five years for graduates from an accredited institution, inside or outside of Saskatchewan, who worked in Saskatchewan after graduation (New Democratic Party, 2007: 7). This program was available for most post-secondary graduates, including those in graduate or professional programs.

As the incumbent governing party, the NDP emphasized a series of post-secondary education accomplishments that had been achieved since the previous election. These accomplishments included the creation of 6,300 new training opportunities since 2003; the creation of free wireless internet on post-secondary campuses and in urban core areas; and investment in adult basic education and training for Aboriginal learners, as well as providing training on-reserve and providing mobile training for remote Aboriginal communities (New Democratic Party, 2007: 7).

This emphasis on what had been achieved was carried through to the platform discussion of employees in the health sector. The NDP reported creating new nursing seats (for registered nursing, psychiatric nursing, and licensed practical nursing), new medical seats, and new medical diagnostic seats, as well as strengthening bursary programs and recruitment grants (New Democratic Party, 2007: 18). A further plank in the platform was to provide on-going support to the Academic Health Sciences Centre (U of S), which would "help us compete for new medical specialists, support important health research and provide state-of-the-art learning facilities for our health science students" (New Democratic Party, 2007: 18). The Centre would also support the province's health research priority.

LIBERAL PARTY PLATFORM

The Saskatchewan Liberal Party's platform also addressed post-secondary education investment, highlighting the importance of affordable access to high-quality, post-secondary education for individual students. The Liberals focused on post-secondary education as "one of the keys to maintaining the prosperity brought about by the boom" (Saskatchewan Liberal Party, 2007: 13). Included in their plan was the need to change the student loan program to remove parental, spousal, and individual assets and income from the assessment process to allow students to borrow without having those assets act as penalties. Furthermore, they proposed introducing a housing tax credit, which would help students address rising housing costs, in conjunction with the proposed property tax rebate for renters. University affordability would be ensured by extending the existing tuition fee freeze.

The Liberals' focus on quality education was demonstrated through the proposed introduction of a $5 million undergraduate teaching fund for the universities that could be used for educational support and the recruitment of undergraduate professors (Saskatchewan Liberal Party, 2007: 14). The link

between investment in post-secondary, education-based research and economic security was also emphasized in the Liberals' plan—with a focus on
research for advancing energy security (Saskatchewan Liberal Party, 2007: 17).
Finally, the Liberals proposed to address the labour market demand for skilled
workers. First, they would create 6,000 new apprenticeship positions over four
years. Second, they proposed to support additional training for licensed practical nurses to become registered nurses and offset some of the unmet demand
in the provincial health care system.

GREEN PARTY PLATFORM
Although not a significant player in the election of 2007, the Green Party also
addressed post-secondary education funding in its platform. It committed to
"restore funding to post-secondary institutions, and reduce tuition for higher
education to levels of the past, the lowest in Canada" (Saskatchewan Green
Party, 2007).

THE PLATFORMS COMPARED AND CONTRASTED
While there were some similarities among the parties' platforms, there were
differences in approach. All three parties included proposals that were also
included in the McCall Report, addressing everything from affordable university education to concerns regarding student loans, housing, and access to
training programs. However, the differences were really a matter of focus and
degree—which students would be emphasized (youth, university, skilled
trades, in or out of Saskatchewan) and how would costs associated with post-
secondary education be addressed (increases to operating budgets, funds for
teaching, tuition management).

It is also important to note that both the NDP and the Saskatchewan Party
placed emphasis on youth and youth retention as associated with post-secondary education, and that these planks were released first in the election
cycle. The NDP's announcements regarding youth and post-secondary education closely followed the release of the McCall Report, while the Saskatchewan
Party also took the approach of releasing its plank regarding youth early on in
the process. Despite this early emphasis on post-secondary education, the
election itself largely focused on health care spending through the proposed
seniors' drug plan and on whether Saskatchewan Party leader Brad Wall really *was* a wolf in sheep's clothing. There were two major exceptions to this
trend, however, which corresponded with the Canadian Federation of
Students-Saskatchewan's release of their *Saskatchewan Post-Secondary
Education Report Card 2007* and University of Saskatchewan President Peter
MacKinnon's public comments on the relationship between government and
universities in terms of establishing tuition fee levels.

The Canadian Federation of Students-Saskatchewan's (CFS-SK) report
card was released on November 2, 2007—the week before the election.
Representing students at the University of Regina, University of
Saskatchewan, and the First Nations University of Canada, the CFS-Sk created
the report card to evaluate the platforms of the Liberals, the NDP and the

Saskatchewan Party, on the four major issues identified by the students: tuition fees, student debt, accessible housing, and Aboriginal access. In terms of tuition fees, the NDP were ranked first (A), followed by the Liberals (B) and the Saskatchewan Party (C+). On student debt, although all three parties were not ranked highly, the Saskatchewan Party ranked first (C+), followed by the NDP (C), and the Liberals (C-).

Accessible housing—particularly important for the Saskatoon-based students facing a less than 1% rental vacancy rate—saw the Liberals ranked first (C+), followed by the NDP (C), and then the Saskatchewan Party (D). Finally, in terms of Aboriginal access, the NDP came out ahead (C), followed by the Liberals (C-), and the Saskatchewan Party (F) which was criticized for having said nothing about access to post-secondary education for Aboriginal people.

The involvement of the University of Saskatchewan's President Peter MacKinnon in the post-secondary education discussion came on November 1, 2007, and focused on the relationship between government and the universities as autonomous entities. In an interview with CBC News, MacKinnon argued that government subsidies for tuition fees should take the form of direct transfers to students, rather than as government-imposed controls on the universities. Universities have the right—and the ability—to manage tuition fees themselves. In addition, "problems have arisen in other provinces where governments have tried to regulate tuitions, while promising to fill in with extra money for the universities" (CBC News, 2007).

After a tight election race with some interesting discussion about post-secondary education, the Saskatchewan Party came through with a majority of seats in the legislature—thus forming Saskatchewan's new government.

POST-SECONDARY EDUCATION UNDER THE SASKATCHEWAN PARTY GOVERNMENT
Post-election, one of the first actions indicating a new direction in post-secondary education policy was the amalgamation of the Department of Advanced Education and Employment and the Department of Labour, to form the Ministry of Advanced Education, Employment, and Labour. Led by Minister Rob Norris, the ministry has been largely focused on labour-related issues since taking office—particularly with the introduction of essential services legislation through Bill 5, The Public Services Essential Services Act. However, the government has also acknowledged the need to focus on increasing the number of people in the province and to provide access to literacy, basic skills training, and post-secondary education, while emphasizing the connections between the labour market and education.

Minister Norris's message regarding Budget 2008–09 was that:

> The Ministry will take action to support and train Saskatchewan people; collaborate with stakeholders to identify and address areas of labour market needs; and support key innovation projects at our universities. (Saskatchewan Ministry of Advanced Education, Employment and Labour, 2008: 1)

This action included extending the focus on training by providing additional funds for nursing and medical student seats; more funds to SIAST for health-related training seats, and more funding for Regional Colleges, including support for expansion of on-reserve Adult Basic Education. The government also continued the NDP's commitment to Aboriginal institutions, through its investment in SIIT for on-reserve Adult Basic Education and skills training. Capital funds for post-secondary institution were also included in the provincial budget, as were funds for immigrant-related training programs.

As part of its youth retention strategy, the government introduced the Graduate Retention Program, replacing the NDP's Graduate Tax Credit. Designed to provide "up to $20,000 in tax credits for post-secondary graduates over seven years," the Graduate Retention Program contains both similarities to and differences from the NDP's program. While the NDP tax credit included all post-secondary graduates from accredited programs working in Saskatchewan—including those completing graduate and professional programs and those coming in to the province to work post-graduation—this new program originally focused only on those receiving certificates, diplomas, or undergraduate degrees in the province and remaining after completion. However, after consultation with stakeholders, the government changed the program to include all post-secondary graduates from approved programs that come to work in the province as well—acknowledging the need to attract students from out of province. They also changed the credit to equal $50,000 of exempt income over five years.

The 2007–08 budget also included an extension of the university tuition fee freeze for undergraduate students for an additional year, with the promise that the government would consult with key stakeholders about tuition costs and affordability. Considering that the previous government undertook both an internal department-led consultation process and an extensive review involving both stakeholders and the public, it will be interesting to see how this process may differ—and what the results will be. Beginning with consultation is a positive move, but failing to acknowledge—and incorporate—previous work with stakeholders and the public can lead to consultation fatigue. Additional funds were also provided to SIAST, the Regional Colleges, and the Saskatchewan Apprenticeship and Trade Certification Commission to help keep tuition affordable (Saskatchewan Ministry of Advanced Education, Employment and Labour, 2008: 4). This reference to tuition fees for non-university institutions is an important acknowledgement of the role that fees can play in discouraging participation in post-secondary education. The tuition fee freeze was extended a further year in the 2008-09 budget, but concerns have been raised about whether that freeze will be extended an additional year, given the economic situation facing the province.

CONCLUSIONS
As seen in the developments under the NDP governments of the 1991–2007 period and in the 2007 election, post-secondary education has become an

important political issue. There are a number of explanations for this evolution of post-secondary education on the provincial agenda. During the 1990s, the need for fiscal restraint meant that the emphasis on post-secondary education was linked primarily to the development of the flagging economy, but with a secondary emphasis on education's role for the social development of the province. Despite the financial pressures facing the province, which included the federal government's cutting of transfer payments to support post-secondary education, the government continued to fund post-secondary education much more consistently than governments in other provinces. Social and economic investments—including post-secondary education— were clearly part of the NDP government's agenda throughout the 1990s.

There are other factors that have had an impact on the importance of post-secondary education for the province, particularly throughout the early part of this century. Demographic pressures related to the aging of the general public and the growth of a youthful Aboriginal population have had an influence on the focusing on post-secondary education. The apparent need to ensure an adequate supply of people to fill available jobs has been pressing. Furthermore, the need to ensure that people who have traditionally been underrepresented in the post-secondary education system and the labour market—particularly Aboriginal people—has become vital for the future health and success of Saskatchewan as a province.

Saskatchewan's overall educational attainment is low compared with the rest of Canada. As of the 2006 Census, just over half (54%) of Saskatchewan people aged 25 to 64 had a post-secondary credential—lower than all provinces and territories except for Nunavut and New Brunswick. Saskatchewan people have fewer university degrees (17%) than the national average (23%), and people with university degrees have traditionally been more mobile—leaving the province in higher numbers than those with other post-secondary qualifications (Statistics Canada, 2008). The proportion of Saskatchewan people with a trade certification is the highest west of Quebec (14%), but this is still not enough to fill the available positions in the current labour market.

Fundamentally, post-secondary education has become so important for government because of its importance for the labour market. However, that does not mean that governments—both NDP- and Saskatchewan Party-led— do not understand the importance of education for social, cultural, and health reasons. Higher levels of education among a population has been shown to lead to improved health status, stronger community involvement, more cultural activity, and to lessen state dependence—all of which indicate a stronger society. These social impacts should not be lost in the focus on the individual's role in the labour market.

In the first months of the Saskatchewan Party government, the focus on certain elements of post-secondary education has reflected those within the party's platform in the November 2007 election. There has been evidence of convergence between the approaches to post-secondary education taken by both the NDP and the Saskatchewan Party, which should not be surprising given the importance of the booming Saskatchewan economy. Growing the economy has been identified as a goal by both the former NDP government and the current Saskatchewan Party government. The need to ensure that Saskatchewan people—and those coming in to the province—have the skills and education to support that economy is an important practical consideration, independent of ideology.

From the respective party platforms in the election, it is clear that post-secondary education is of great importance to the province. Its link to the knowledge economy—and particularly the need for people with post-secondary education to fill the gaps in the economy—has been greatly emphasized. While parties acknowledge that post-secondary education is an important social good that contributes to the health of society, it seems to be fundamentally reduced to an economic good that is required to support the needs of Saskatchewan's mixed economy.

However, given the importance of post-secondary education for the future of the province—both for its social and economic health—there are many issues that will have to be addressed by the new government. First is the importance of access to post-secondary education for Aboriginal people. Although there are jurisdictional issues regarding who should take responsibility for supporting Aboriginal people in post-secondary education, it is clear that the boundaries between jurisdictions are shifting. For example, the province will have to address the federal government's unwillingness to increase the funds available for First Nations people through the Post-Secondary Student Support Program (PSSSP), while ensuring that there are enough provincial supports in place to "pick up the slack."

Second is the need to ensure that Saskatchewan has access to graduates from advanced degree and professional programs, as well as from undergraduate programs. Advanced degree and professional programs can contribute greatly to Saskatchewan's innovation in the future, and should not be left out of the government's plans to attract and retain people to help support economic, social, and cultural growth in the province.

Third is the issue facing the Government of Saskatchewan regarding the need to ensure that the needs of lifelong learners are met. While youth are an important part of the post-secondary picture, they are far from the only ones attending post-secondary institutions in the province. The focus on keeping "our skilled young people right here where they belong" fails to acknowledge that there are other people in the province who want—and need—to access post-secondary education (Saskatchewan Advanced Education, Employment and Labour, 2008: 4). Currently, a majority of post-secondary participants and graduates are women. While it is incredibly important to have more women participating in post-secondary education, the decline in the number of men participating may be in part related to the booming resource sector. These young men will likely need access to post-secondary education later on in their lives, and they are only one example of people participating in lifelong post-secondary education.

The Saskatchewan Party has been given the opportunity to take up where the NDP government left off in post-secondary education. The economic benefits of post-secondary education are being emphasized, and while the links between the labour market and education are important ones, they are not always so easily defined. Whatever the drivers, the key to post-secondary education policy success for this Saskatchewan Party-led government will be if barriers to post-secondary education—both financial and non-financial—are addressed and participation in lifelong education is possible for all Saskatchewan people. This participation will require a range of supports and opportunities, as well as government working in partnership with educational institutions, employers, individuals, and families, to build on what was put in place during the NDP years.

NOTES

1. On September 20, 1992, the Royal Bank had announced that Saskatchewan had Canada's highest level of debt per capita, amounting to $14,000 for every person in the province. Clearly the deficit/debt was in the public eye at the time.

REFERENCES

Anderson/Fast & Associates. 1999. *Government of Saskatchewan: Public Opinion Polling and Market Research from January 1, 1999 to March 31, 1999*. Regina, SK: Government of Saskatchewan.

Association of Universities and Colleges Canada. 2008. Statement: First Nations University of Canada's Probationary Status Lifted. Accessed at http:// www.aucc.ca/ publications/statements/2008/FNUC_statement_04_02_e.html on April 2, 2008.

Association of Universities and Colleges Canada. 2007. *Media Release: AUCC Board of Directors statement on First Nations University of Canada*. Accessed at http:// www.aucc.ca/publications/media/2007/first_nations_18_04_e.html on April 2, 2008.

Campus Saskatchewan. 2007. *About Us*. Accessed at http://campussask.ca/about/ on April 20, 2008.

Canada News Facts. 1993. *Federal Budget*. Toronto, ON: Stephen D. Pepper and Barrie Martland, 4833.

———. 1996. *Saskatchewan*. Toronto, ON: Stephen D. Pepper and Barrie Martland, 5266.

Canadian Federation of Students. 2007a. *Saskatchewan Post-Secondary Education Report Card 2007*. Accessed at www.voteeducation.ca on November 2, 2007.

———. 2007b. Students Grade Political Party Platforms on Post-Secondary Education. Accessed at http://www.voteeducation.ca/sk/read.php?id=44 on April 27, 2008.

CBC News. 2007. Politicians shouldn't meddle with tuition, U of S president says. Accessed at http://www.cbc.ca/canada/saskvotes2007/story/2007/11/01/ mackinnon-students.html on April 27, 2008.

DesRosiers, Edward and Associates. 2000. *Implementation of the Saskatchewan Universities Funding Mechanism: Issues and Recommendations*. West Hill, ON: Author.

DesRosiers, Edward and Associates in collaboration with Edward J. Monahan and Charles Pascal. 1998. *Saskatchewan Universities Funding Review Final Report.* Regina, SK: Saskatchewan Post-Secondary Education and Skills Training.

Finnie, Ross and Saul Schwartz. 1996. Student Loans in Canada: Past, Present, and Future. Toronto, ON: C.D. Howe Institute.

First Nations University of Canada. 2007. *About Our Board of Governors.* Accessed at http://www.firstnationsuniversity.ca/default.aspx?page=77 on April 27, 2008.

Gabriel Dumont Institute of Native Studies and Applied Research. n.d.a *About GDI.* Accessed at http://www.gdins.org/AboutGDI.shtml on April 2, 2008.

——. n.d.b GDI *Programs and Services: Dumont Technical Institute.* Accessed at http://www.gdins.org/DTI.shtml on April 2, 2008.

Government of Saskatchewan. 1992. *Rebuilding Saskatchewan Together: Budget Address May, 1992.* Regina, SK.

——. 1993. *Securing Our Future: Budget Address March, 1993.* Regina, SK.

——. 1994. *Delivering the Promise: Budget Address February, 1994.* Regina, SK.

——. 1995. *A New Day Dawning for Saskatchewan: Budget Address February, 1995.* Regina, SK.

——. 1996. *Preparing for the New Century: Budget Address March, 1996.* Regina, SK.

——. 1997a. *Investing in People: Budget Address March, 1997.* Regina, SK.

——. 1997b. *Saskatchewan Releases Provincial Training Strategy.* News Release: April 16, 1997. Accessed at http://www.gov.sk.ca/news?newsId=93ac4a23-aca2-4070-ba8e-03f429d8f2a2 on April 27, 2008.

——. 1998a. *Investing in People: Building on the Momentum. Budget Address March, 1998.* Regina, SK.

——. 1998b. *Response from the Minister of Post-Secondary Education and Skills Training To the Report of the Task Group on Student Assistance.* Accessed at www.aee.gov.sk.ca/admin/pdfs/stg/response.html on May 20, 2002.

——. 1999. *Moving Forward Together: Budget Address, March 1999.* Regina, SK.

——. 2000. *A Plan for Growth and Opportunity: Budget Address, March, 2000.* Regina, SK.

——. 2001. *2001–02 Budget: Connecting to the Future.* Regina, SK.

——. 2002. *Budget 2002–03: Meeting the Challenge for Saskatchewan People.* Regina, SK.

——. 2003. *2003–04 Saskatchewan Provincial Budget: Building for the Future. Budget Address.* Regina, SK.

——. 2004. *Province of Saskatchewan 2004–05 Budget Speech.* Regina, SK.

——. 2005a. *2005–2006 Saskatchewan Provincial Budget: Budget Address.* Regina, SK.

——. 2006b. *Saskatchewan's Training System Under Review.* Accessed at http://www.gov.sk.ca/news?newsId=d7e5e031-ae40-4e07-92a5-d41a8eeb4ab6 on April 28, 2008.

——. 2006. *2006–07 Budget Address.* Regina, SK.

——. 2007a. *Budget Address 2007–08.* Accessed at http://www.finance.gov.sk.ca/budget2007-08/speech/ on March 22, 2008.

——. 2007b. *Mandate Letter.* Accessed at http://www.gov.sk.ca/adx/aspx/adxGetMedia.aspx?DocID=1594,1579,617,534,20 6,Documents&MediaID=2181&Filename=MandateLetter-MinNorris.pdf on April 27, 2008.

Green Party of Saskatchewan. 2007. ELECT Ingrid Alesich Regina-Elphinstone Centre.

MacKay, Harold. 1996. *Report of the Minister's Special Representative on University Revitalization*. Regina, SK: Post-Secondary Education and Skills Training.

Makarenko, Jay. 2003. *2003 Saskatchewan General Election*. Mapleleafweb. Available at www.mapleleafweb.com.

McMurchy, Tyler. 1995. "Parties Bicker Over Plans for Education Funding." *The Carillon* (June 15), 10.

McCall, Warren. 2007. *Post-Secondary Education Accessibility and Affordability Review Final Report*. Regina, SK: Government of Saskatchewan.

Nikkel, Greg. 1999. "Premier Grilled on Free Tuition Program and Agriculture Crisis." *Weyburn Review*, 1.

Regional Colleges Act, The.

Saskatchewan Advanced Education and Employment. 2007. *2006–2007 Annual Report*. Accessed at http://www.aeel.gov.sk.ca/Default.aspx?DN=c3b63732-613f-49e6-bc07-534fd75f086f on April 2, 2008.

Saskatchewan Advanced Education, Employment and Labour. 2008. *Private Vocational Schools Administration & Policy Manual*. Regina, SK.

Saskatchewan Education and Skills Training. 1994. *Annual Report 1993–94*. Regina, SK.

Saskatchewan Hansard. 2000. *Committee of Finance: General Revenue Fund Post-Secondary Education and Skills Training Vote 37*. Regina, SK.

Saskatchewan Indian Institute of Technologies. 2008a. *About SIIT*. Accessed at http://www.siit.sk.ca/AboutSIIT.html on April 27, 2008.

——. 2008b. *Our History*. Accessed at http://www.siit.sk.ca/OurHistory.html on April 27, 2008.

Saskatchewan Institute of Applied Science and Technology Act, The.

Saskatchewan Institute of Applied Science and Technology. n.d. *Mission, Priorities, Vision and Values*. Accessed at http://www.siast.sk.ca/siast/aboutsiast/boardof directors/boardmpvv.htm on April 27, 2008.

Saskatchewan Institute of Applied Science and Technology. 2006. *Policy and Procedure Statement: G-1.7 Role of President/CEO*. Accessed at http://www.siast.sk.ca/policies/pdf-governance/governance-g1/g17.pdf on April 27, 2008.

Saskatchewan Institute of Applied Science and Technology. 2007. *Policy and Procedure Statement: G-1.1 Board Responsibilities*. Accessed at http://www.siast.sk.ca/policies/pdf-governance/governance-g1/g11.pdf on April 27, 2008.

Saskatchewan Liberal Party. 1999. *Priorities 1999—Speech Notes for Election Platform*.

——. 2007. *Building a Province for Tomorrow: Your Family. Your Community. Your Priorities*. Regina, SK.

Saskatchewan Ministry of Advanced Education, Employment and Labour. 2008. *Ready for Growth: Budget 2008–09*. Regina, SK.

Saskatchewan New Democratic Party. 1999. *Building a Bright Future Together The Saskatchewan Way*. Regina, SK.

——. 2007. *Moving Forward Together. Making Life Better for Saskatchewan Families*. Regina, SK.

Saskatchewan Party. 1998. *The Way Up Election '99 Platform*. Regina, SK.

——. 2007. *Securing the Future: New Ideas for Saskatchewan*. Regina, SK.

Saskatchewan Post-Secondary Education and Skills Training. 1996. *Public Interest and Revitalization of Saskatchewan's Universities*. Regina, SK.

Statistics Canada. 2008. *Educational Portrait of Canada, 2006 Census*. Catalogue no. 97-560-X. Ottawa, ON: Statistics Canada.

University of Regina. 2004. Senate. Accessed at http://www.uregina.ca/presoff/senate/index.shtml on April 28, 2008.

University of Regina Act.

University of Regina Students' Union and University of Saskatchewan Students' Union. 1999. *Vote Education Campaign*. Regina and Saskatoon: Authors.

University of Saskatchewan Act, 1995.

University of Saskatchewan. n.d. Introduction to Senate. Accessed at http://www.usask.ca/university_secretary/senate/index.php on April 28, 2008.

University of Saskatchewan On Campus News. 2003. "Saskatchewan Election 2003." *On Campus News* Volume 11, no. 6. Available at www.usask.ca/communications/ocn/03-oct-31/news13.shtml.

University Program Review Panel. 1993. *Looking at Saskatchewan Universities: Programs, Governance, and Goals*. Regina, SK: Saskatchewan Post-Secondary Education and Skills Training.

APPENDIX A: PROVINCIAL POST-SECONDARY INSTITUTIONS

UNIVERSITIES OF REGINA AND SASKATCHEWAN

The two universities were created through provincial legislation to be self-governing autonomous bodies: the University of Saskatchewan in 1905 and the University of Regina in 1974. They have complex governing structures, with an academic Senate—comprised of representatives of the administration, affiliated and federated colleges, faculty, staff, and the wider community—which makes decisions concerning all matters related to the academic life of the institution, such as, programming, new schools, and changes to departments (University of Saskatchewan n.d., University of Regina, 2004). Each university has a Council, elected from among its members, that has taken on a wide range of governance issues, from academics to budgeting and planning. Often the work taken on by Council will support the work done at the Senate and the Board of Governors. The Boards of Governors look after the financial, infrastructural, organizational, and human resources-related issues and obligations of the universities, as well as any issues that are referred to them by the Senate (University of Regina Act; University of Saskatchewan Act).

Each university has both federated and affiliated colleges. The University of Saskatchewan has one federated college, St. Thomas More College, and seven affiliated colleges: St. Andrew's College, the Lutheran Theological Seminary, Central Pentecostal College, St. Peter's College, the College of Emmanuel and St. Chad, Briercrest College, and the Gabriel Dumont Institute of Native Studies and Applied Research (GDI). The University of Regina has three federated colleges: Campion College, Luther College, and the First Nations University of Canada; one affiliate, the Gabriel Dumont Institute of Native Studies and Applied Research (GDI); and one associated college, Athol Murray College of Notre Dame.

Despite their autonomy, they remain accountable to the Minister responsible for post-secondary education. The nature of—and challenges associated with—the autonomy of the universities has been addressed a number of times between 1991 and 2007, including within the McKay Report (1995) and the DesRosiers reports (1998 and 2000). In its response to the McKay Report, the Government of Saskatchewan argued that "the reality as always is interdependence [between government and the universities] as well as independence, and the solution to problems is an appropriate balance between these two" (Saskatchewan Post-Secondary Education and Skills Training, 1996:7). The protection of academic freedom and the universities' rights to act autonomously are enshrined in legislation through the University of Regina Act and the University of Saskatchewan Act, but are also balanced in practice with the universities' "service to the state" or to the public good (Saskatchewan Post-Secondary Education and Skills Training, 1996: 7).

SASKATCHEWAN INSTITUTE OF APPLIED SCIENCE AND TECHNOLOGY (SIAST)

The Saskatchewan Institute of Applied Science and Technology (SIAST) was created through The Saskatchewan Institute of Applied Sciences and Technologies Act, 1986. Its mission is to "share knowledge, provide skills training and engage in applied research, meeting the needs of students, employers, and our communities" (SIAST n.d.). Governed by a board of directors which "provides direction to SIAST through governance policies which reflect the board's priorities and values, advance SIAST's strategic direction, and which are consistent with the Government of Saskatchewan's goals and objectives" (SIAST, 2007), SIAST's operations are led by a senior management team headed by the president/CEO (SIAST, 2006). As a key player in the provincial training system, SIAST's programming is designed to reflect the current and future needs of the province's labour market.

REGIONAL COLLEGES

The nine Regional Colleges provide a uniquely Saskatchewan approach to delivering post-secondary education. Located in nine regions of the province, the Regional Colleges are designed to bring education and training to people outside the two major urban centres in the province. While originally focused on Adult Basic Education and skills training, the Colleges broker with SIAST, the universities, and other institutions for their programming to provide access to some graduate-level education, diploma and certificate programming, and some programming transferable to university degrees. Administered through The Regional Colleges Act, the Colleges are each governed by a board of governors. The board manages the business and affairs of the college, providing accountability to the provincial government (Regional Colleges Act). The Principal or Chief Executive Office of each college oversees the day-to-day and long range operations of the college.

ABORIGINAL INSTITUTIONS: FIRST NATIONS UNIVERSITY OF CANADA

Saskatchewan's post-secondary education system contains a number of institutions created and governed by—and for—Aboriginal people. Many of these institutions were established to provide programming and services responsive to the needs of Aboriginal people and communities within the province. Thus, their governance structures have traditionally reflected their connectedness to Aboriginal peoples and their communities.

While the First Nations University of Canada acts as a federated college of the University of Regina, it is administratively and financially autonomous. The Act establishing the institution (formerly known as the Saskatchewan Indian Federated College) was passed by the Federation of Saskatchewan Indian Nations (FSIN) Legislative Assembly. FNUC is governed by a board of governors appointed by the Chiefs of Saskatchewan, through the Federation of Saskatchewan Indian Nations (FNUC, 2007). While the board is composed of members appointed by the provincial and federal governments and by

FSIN and its senate, along with others, the role of the board vis-à-vis the day-to-day administration of FNUC has not always been clear.

One of FNUC's most recent challenges occurred in 2007-08, when the composition of FNUC's governing board—and its impact on the autonomous governance of the institution—was challenged both by some of its faculty members and by the Association of Universities and Colleges Canada (AUCC)—the body representing 92 universities and university-level colleges in Canada (AUCC, 2007). In its press release announcing the lifting of FNUC's probationary status within the organization, AUCC emphasized that its:

> criteria for membership specifically call for an independent board of governors, or appropriate equivalent, that is committed to public accountability and functions in an open and transparent manner; has control over the institution's finances, administration and appointments; and includes appropriate representation from the institution's external stakeholders, as well as from its academic community. (http://www.aucc.ca/FNUC_statement_04_02_e.html)

While the AUCC publicly addressed its concerns about FNUC's governance, the Canadian Association of University Teachers (CAUT)—an umbrella organization representing faculty associations within Canada—moved to sanction FNUC at the end of 2008. Additionally, the government of Saskatchewan moved to support a strategic planning exercise for FNUC throughout the fall of 2008, in order to help address some of the institution's on-going financial and planning issues. Ensuring that the FNUC has the confidence of the AUCC, the CAUT—and of the academic community throughout the country—is necessary for the continuing success of the FNUC as an institution serving a vital component of Saskatchewan society.

SASKATCHEWAN INDIAN INSTITUTE OF TECHNOLOGIES (SIIT)

The Saskatchewan Indian Institute of Technologies (SIIT) originated through a partnership with SIAST in 1976 as the Saskatchewan Indian Community College, but became an autonomous institution through The Saskatchewan Indian Institute of Technologies Act, 2000 (SIIT, 2008b). As an educational institution of the Federation of Saskatchewan Indian Nations, its board of governors is made up of FSIN senators, Tribal Council appointees, and an FSIN executive member (SIIT, 2008a). Collaborating with other institutions in the Saskatchewan post-secondary sector, SIIT delivers diploma, certificate, and trades programming designed to meet the needs of its students. It has recently expanded its work into on-reserve delivery, particularly for Adult Basic Education programming.

GABRIEL DUMONT INSTITUTE OF NATIVE STUDIES AND APPLIED RESEARCH

The Métis Nation of Saskatchewan is also represented within the post-secondary education system. The Gabriel Dumont Institute of Native Studies and Applied Research, created as a non-profit corporation in 1980, is the "only fully accredited Métis Post-Secondary, Adult Basic Upgrading and Skills Training institution in Canada" (GDI, n.d.a). Although federated with SIAST and affiliated with the University of Regina and the University of Saskatchewan, as the educational arm of the Métis Nation-Saskatchewan, GDI develops and delivers programming that responds to needs identified by GDI's board of governors (GDI, n.d.a). In order to ensure regional representation, the board of governors is comprised of representatives from the twelve regions of the Métis Nation-Saskatchewan.

GDI's focus on the needs of Métis people and communities is reflected in the SUNTEP program, a four-year Bachelor of Education program offered in conjunction with the Ministry of Advanced Education, Employment and Labour, the University of Saskatchewan, and the University of Regina. Educational opportunities are also provided in partnership with the universities, SIAST, the Regional Colleges, and Métis Employment and Training of Saskatchewan Inc. (METSI). The Gabriel Dumont College also delivers the first two years of undergraduate study in Arts and Science in Saskatoon and Prince Albert through the University of Saskatchewan (GDI, n.d.a).

DUMONT TECHNICAL INSTITUTE

Created in 1991, the Dumont Technical Institute (DTI) was originally established as an institute of the Saskatchewan Institute of Applied Science and Technology (SIAST). Métis communities can access Adult Basic Education and skills-based programming through DTI (GDI, n.d.b), delivered in cooperation with partners such as Métis Employment and Training of Saskatchewan Inc. (METSI), SIAST, SIIT, and the Regional Colleges. DTI continues to be federated with SIAST (GDI, n.d.b), while operating as the technical training arm of GDI.

NORTEP/NORPAC

The importance of communities in the northern region of Saskatchewan is reflected through the establishment of the Northern Teacher Education Program (NORTEP) and the Northern Professional Access College (NORPAC), designed to facilitate access to teacher education and other programming in the North. Located in LaRonge, NORTEP and NORPAC are accredited by the University of Saskatchewan, the University of Regina, and the First Nations University of Canada. Their board of governors is composed of members from the Northern Lights School Division, Ile-à-la-Crosse School Division, the Prince Albert Grand Council, the Meadow Lake Tribal Council, Lac La Ronge Indian Band, and the Creighton School Division.

SASKATCHEWAN APPRENTICESHIP AND TRADE CERTIFICATION COMMISSION

Apprenticeship is "an agreement between an individual who wants to learn a

skill and an employer who needs a skilled worker" (SATCC, n.d. http://
www.saskapprenticeship.ca/modules.php?name=Sections&op=view
article&artid=2). As of early 2008, Saskatchewan recognizes approximately 50
trades and four sub-trades—37 of which are recognized across the country
and known as "Red Seal trades." Training is offered by SIAST, SIIT, Regional
Colleges, private vocational schools, SaskPower, the Saskatchewan Tourism
Education Council, and selected out-of-province colleges (SATCC, n.d.).

In Saskatchewan, apprenticeship is overseen and managed by the
Saskatchewan Apprenticeship and Trade Certification Commission, which is
an industry-led agency working to ensure apprenticeship training and certification meet the needs of both employees and employers (SATCC, n.d.). The
SATCC board of directors represents employers and employees within industry, and is appointed by the Government of Saskatchewan. The board reports
directly to the Minister responsible for The Apprenticeship and Trade
Certification Act, 1999.

CAMPUS SASKATCHEWAN

Support for technology-based program delivery and for access to post-secondary opportunities for everyone in the province led to the creation of
Campus Saskatchewan in 2002. A partnership between provincial post-secondary institutions and the government, Campus Saskatchewan provides
support for faculty and students working with technology-enhanced courses,
while supporting the development of new courses (Campus Saskatchewan,
2007). Campus Saskatchewan also provides access to the online Saskatchewan
Transfer Credit Guide, developed by the Saskatchewan Council for
Admissions and Transfer (SaskCAT).

PRIVATE VOCATIONAL SCHOOLS

Private vocational schools include "any organization in Saskatchewan offering adult vocational training of more than 30 hours in duration"
(Saskatchewan Ministry of Advanced Education, Employment and Labour,
2008: 10). They are classified into two categories: Category I schools offer
training to fee-paying students, while Category II schools provide training
that is contracted and paid for by a sponsor. Private vocational schools must
adhere to government regulations as outlined in The Private Vocational
Schools Regulation Act, 1995, and the Private Vocational Schools Regulations,
1995, in order to remain certified, and so that their students may access government student loan programs. Each individual private vocational school
has its own governance structure.

As of 2006–07, there were 33 Category I schools in the province, providing
training in business/computer skills, cosmetology/aesthetics, medical administrative assistance, massage therapy, graphic arts/animation, broadcasting,
heavy equipment operation, and hospitality (McCall, 2007).

POST-SECONDARY LEARNERS

Saskatchewan post-secondary institutions—as well as institutions in other provinces—have not traditionally counted their students in the same ways. Therefore, it can be challenging to state unequivocally, how many learners there are overall in the Saskatchewan post-secondary sector. For example, learners may be counted on a full-time-equivalent basis (thus several part-time students may be equivalent to one full-time student), by assessing how many courses they enroll in, or on a full-time/part-time basis.

Between 2000–01 and 2005–06, the number of people enrolled in degree, certificate/diploma, apprenticeship, and Adult Basic Education programming increased (Saskatchewan Advanced Education and Employment, 2007). In 2005–06, nearly 32,000 students were enrolled in degree programming; 6,500 in certificate and diploma programs; 7,200 were registered in apprenticeship training; and nearly 5,400 in Adult Basic Education (Saskatchewan Advanced Education and Employment, 2007).

In its 2008–09 budget, the Saskatchewan government has projected enrolment across the post-secondary sector by institutional type, rather than by credential of study. According to these projections, DTI will have 600 enrolments; SIIT, 1,800; SIAST, 13,000; Regional Colleges, 20,000; University of Regina (including federated, affiliated colleges including FNUC), 12,000; University of Saskatchewan (including federated and affiliated colleges), 20,000; and private vocational schools, 3,500 (Saskatchewan Advanced Education, Employment and Labour, 2008).

Participation in post-secondary education has been identified by Saskatchewan people as a priority. However, enrolment—particularly in the universities—has become an issue for Saskatchewan in the past few years. Both universities have experienced declines in enrolment since 2006, and have undertaken strategies both to recruit and retain students. In addition, the most recent census data from 2006 shows that just over half (54%) of Saskatchewan people aged 25 to 64 had completed a post-secondary credential—the lowest of all of the provinces and territories (Statistics Canada, 2008). However, this outcome is influenced by the net outflow of post-secondary graduates that Saskatchewan had experienced (Statistics Canada, 2008). This outflow was particularly prevalent among university graduates, but much less so among people with trade certification: Saskatchewan had the highest proportion of trades-trained people west of Quebec in 2006 (Statistics Canada, 2008: 29).

Although learners in the province come from diverse backgrounds, research shows that some people are more likely to participate in post-secondary education than others. People from higher family income brackets or with parents who have completed some post-secondary education, women, non-Aboriginal people, and people from larger urban centres are all more likely to participate in post-secondary education—particularly in university education.

The Political Challenge of Implementing Social Housing Policy in Saskatchewan

Ryan Walker

> "In the end, the debate over whether and how to address housing need and homelessness comes down to a set of ethical questions. Will those in a position to make the necessary decisions do so? This is a political problem. There is no scientific or objective way to arrive at an answer to a political problem. That said, the nature of the problem is now well understood. Moreover, the package of solutions is not complicated or even very expensive for a country with Canada's wealth."
>
> J. David Hulchanski, Endowed Chair in Housing Studies,
> University of Toronto, 2002

The Saskatchewan housing market has in the past several years consisted of high demand, limited supply—particularly in the "affordable housing" market—and rising prices to rent and purchase. Average resale value of homes in the province increased over 40% between 2006 and 2007, and in Saskatoon, that figure was close to 50%. Apartment vacancy rates in communities around the province have dipped to historic lows and rents have increased by 7–14% between 2006 and 2007. The Minister of Social Services, Donna Harpauer, has expressed the view that we are experiencing an affordable housing crisis. She appointed a Task Force on Housing Affordability in March 2008, co-chaired by Bob Pringle and Ted Merriman, former NDP and Saskatchewan Party MLAs respectively. They submitted their final report to the Minister in June of the same year, which included 36 recommendations to address the affordable housing challenges they learned about during consultations across the province.[1]

The Task Force co-chairs noted on the release of their report that the "study was four years overdue," placing blame for inaction in the policy field on the former NDP-led government.[2] They also made it clear that their work was undertaken with the explicit purpose of being "solution-based." There are at least two steps to creating solutions. The first is determining the nature of the problem and a course of action. This is mostly a technical exercise. The second is implementing that course of action. Implementation is mostly a political exercise. The nature of the housing affordability problem and the courses of action to deal with it are well documented and have been for several years in a rich housing policy literature. I am not convinced that the Task Force had much work to do in that regard. The second step is the real challenge facing

Saskatchewan. Perhaps in the process of consulting with citizens and stakeholders over a couple of months, the profile of housing issues facing
Saskatchewan people was raised and the Task Force made a major step forward in priming the government for implementing a course of action. Time
will tell.

This chapter focuses on social housing policy. This is the sector of housing
in Canada that requires significant and sustained government intervention to
correct market failures and to meet social policy objectives. An historic housing policy context will be presented in the next section to situate it within the
broader pursuit of social redistribution and citizenship in the Canadian welfare state. This will be followed by a discussion of housing as a precursor to
achieving policy outcomes in other sectors, like health, education and income
security. A theorization of why governments across Canada, including
Saskatchewan, have neglected this important policy field will be examined,
followed by a discussion of what good social housing policy would look like
if governments made a serious and sustained commitment to the sector. The
political challenges of implementing social housing policy in Saskatchewan
are discussed in the final section of the chapter with reference to actual and
proposed initiatives.

SOCIAL HOUSING POLICY IN CANADA

The Constitution Act of 1982 does not allocate responsibility for housing, thus
creating some ambiguity about which level of government is responsible for
upholding this basic human right.[3] However, by demonstration effect, the federal government became the leader in housing policy. By this I mean it
entrenched its responsibility by demonstrating capacity for leadership in articulating, administering and resourcing the policy field, especially after 1964
when it amended the National Housing Act (NHA) to launch a large-scale
public housing program with the goal of producing one million housing units
for low-income Canadians over a period of five years through its Central
Mortgage and Housing Corporation (re-named Canada Mortgage and
Housing Corporation in 1979) (CMHC).[4] Coupled with an urban renewal program, the public housing program created about 200,000 units over roughly 10
years, falling short of its more ambitious target.[5] The 1969 report of the Federal
Task Force on Housing and Urban Development, chaired by Paul Hellyer—
which was critical of the public housing and urban renewal approach to housing people with low incomes—and a series of subsequent amendments to the
NHA in 1973 firmly placed the federal government at the helm in pursuing
the realization of a social right to adequate and affordable housing for all
Canadians.

The 1973 amendments brought forth a number of new social housing programs, including the co-operative housing, non-profit housing, rent supplement, neighbourhood improvement and residential rehabilitation programs.
Three programs specifically aimed at providing social housing for Aboriginal
peoples were also created—the 1) on-reserve; 2) rural and Native; and 3)

urban Native housing programs. Incidentally, the rural and Native housing program by the CMHC was inspired by a demonstration program for assisted home ownership in the late 1960s in remote Métis communities in Saskatchewan.[6] The program diffused subsequently to Manitoba and grew eventually, through the CMHC, into a national program. The public, non-profit co-operative (some of the units) and rent supplement programs operated as assisted rental programs, where tenants would pay rents according to their income level, typically 25–30% of household income. In total, approximately 661,000 units of social housing were developed in Canada under these programs until new construction was discontinued after 1993.[7]

The *Briefing Notes for the Cabinet Committee on Social Policy: Housing Policy for the 1970's and NHA Amendments* reveal a great deal about the thinking and rationalization that went on in Cabinet during the debate leading up to the 1973 amendments to the NHA. They advise that many Canadians ultimately blame the federal government if they are unable to find adequate and affordable housing and that trying to shift responsibility for housing to provinces would be imprudent:

> The [federal] government could choose to try to shift this burden to the other levels. The present policy direction accepts a major portion of the responsibility – along with the tools to ensure that this responsibility is not beyond the government's capacity. Current political conditions make a direct shift of responsibility an unlikely proposition.[8]

The *Briefing Notes* also advise Cabinet that the proposed 1973 NHA amendments would represent "an activist Federal stance which may result in provincial criticism. There is evidence that such criticism will not find a great deal of public support if the proposals themselves are considered sound."[9]

The 1973 NHA amendments had the effect, intentional or unintentional, of stimulating provincial action in the housing sector, following the lead of the federal government.[10] Relating the impact of the 1973 "package" of amendments and the statement at that time by the federal government that adequate and affordable housing was a *social right* of every Canadian, the Canadian Council on Social Development stated that:

> There can be no doubt that the scope for social housing had been broadened by this package. The Amendments are sometimes seen as a federal acceptance of responsibility for housing and pursuance of an aggressive housing policy. It was at this time that Mr. Basford (Minister of Urban Affairs and responsible for CMHC) made his "social right" declaration:

> "It is the fundamental right of every Canadian to have access to good housing at a price he can afford. Housing is not simply an economic commodity that can be bought and sold according to the vagaries of the market, but a social right."[11]

In line with the social citizenship prescriptions of T.H. Marshall (1950), social housing policy was aimed at providing a basic minimum threshold below which no Canadian should fall.[12] The aim was not, however, a more equitable distribution of income per se. The view of the federal government on housing policy development remained that housing was a basic human need and that it would "provide the beginning point for the social and economic viability of Canadian households – or the beginning point for a whole train of problems."[13] This perspective on housing prevailed into the 1980s in the federal government and among Canadians. However, there were increasing efforts to spread and share the responsibility with provincial governments, which during the 1970s expanded their housing capacity considerably, and with the private (lending) and community sectors (managing delivery), easing in the mid-to-late 1980s into a gradual reduction of federal spending and involvement that would reach its peak in 1993.[14]

The provincial governments began playing an important role in delivering and managing social housing portfolios in the 1970s through provincial housing authorities, and cost-sharing 25–50% of the capital and operating costs for social housing with the federal CMHC. Some created their own social housing programs as well. The language of housing as a social right of citizenship was used by provincial housing ministers in the 1970s in unison with the federal minister. Since the late 1990s, provinces have also assumed administrative responsibility from the federal government of existing social housing portfolios.

In 1973, the Saskatchewan Housing Corporation Act was passed in the Legislature and, like other provinces across Canada, ushered in a much increased provincial role in social housing. While provinces were similar in how they delivered social housing given that sharing the cost and administration of federal programs was their largest function, each province also set its own strategic focus. In Saskatchewan, for example, direct intervention to provide senior citizens with affordable and adequate housing was the top priority. Of the roughly 15,000 social housing units in Saskatchewan, just over 10,000 of them are designated for senior citizens.[15] Seniors were seen to be among the least able to meet their needs in the private market and the most "deserving" of assistance. (I will return to this idea of "deserving" and "undeserving" later on.) It was not until the mid-1990s that families became a greater focus of social housing intervention in Saskatchewan. Provinces had lobbied the federal government from the 1960s through the 1990s for more control over program design and priority-setting in social housing, believing the federal government tried to impose a "one-size-fits-all" program structure across the country. Federal fiscal policy led to the discontinuation of new units under all the federal social housing programs (except on-reserve housing) after 1993 and the negotiation from 1996 onward of administrative shifts of the existing social housing portfolios (except First Nations on-reserve and some off-reserve, and federal co-operative housing) to their respective provincial administrations. Saskatchewan was the first to complete the process, resulting in the 1997 *Canada-Saskatchewan Social Housing Agreement*. That year, the

Saskatchewan Housing Corporation (SHC) drafted and had approved the strategic policy framework that would direct their new responsibilities in the sector entitled: *Investing in People and Communities: A Housing Policy Framework for Saskatchewan People*.

Saskatchewan political leaders, under an NDP-led government, did not want to assume responsibility for off-reserve First Nation or Métis housing administration under the 1997 social housing agreement, but compromised, taking only Métis housing and leaving off-reserve First Nation housing organisations under federal administration. The SHC subsequently entered into a self-government agreement with Métis urban housing providers, negotiated from 1998 to 2001 that has served both parties well since then.[16] Having separate Aboriginal housing programs off-reserve (i.e., urban Native and rural and Native housing programs) had never sat well with the Government of Saskatchewan, and only recently has separate housing programming for Aboriginal peoples become more acceptable in this province.

The provinces, it would seem, had achieved, to a greater degree, the control they had been asking for, although, without the level of continued federal financing they may have expected. The federal and provincial governments have done very little in the social housing sector since the early 1990s, and it hardly matters who administers the policy field when so little is being done. Canada today has the most market-based housing system of all western nations and is second only to the United States for having the smallest social housing sector of any Western nation.[17] Social housing remains a shared redistributive responsibility of both senior levels of government that requires federal leadership in the policy field overall, but with space for shared priority-setting with provinces. Despite its neglect by both levels of government over the past 15–20 years, social housing is a cornerstone of good social policy. The next section explains why.

HOUSING AND SOCIAL POLICY

While Canadian governments have not implemented social housing policy in a sustained and responsible manner, there is an abundance of scholarship on its importance. Housing, when it is secure, adequate and affordable, augments quality of life, giving households continuity, privacy, a domain of control, space for self-expression and for maintaining social networks.[18] It is the most important setting for the development of personal values and social reproduction and the physical space most intimately linked with one's sense of self.[19] A sense of *home*, which embodies all of these elements that go beyond shelter from the elements, is very important because of the extent to which people construct their lives and bracket their existential questions through homes that are stable, secure and personalized.[20] These are not just pleasant luxuries; they are fundamental to health and well-being. Adequate and affordable housing is also a right. *The Universal Declaration of Human Rights* (1948) and the *International Covenant on Economic, Social and Cultural Rights* (1976) articulate substantive rights to housing, including legal security of tenure, availability of

services, affordability, habitability, accessibility, location and cultural
adequacy.[21] It is important to bear in mind—yet too often overlooked—that in
the period since the end of World War II we agreed as Western capitalist
nations that we would not unduly hinder the accumulation of personal
wealth, but that we would embed our liberal economy within certain basic
minimum standards for all. One of those was the clear agreement that in
Western countries with collective wealth such as Canada has; we will take care
of a basic minimum entitlement of all to have a home that is affordable and
adequate.

It is common to break public policy debate into discrete sectors, like housing, health, education and so forth. Increasingly though, housing scholars are
bringing forth the important linkages between sectors, and it is clear why.
Housing is such a central part of people's ability to have a quality of life that
it is no wonder having or not having housing is linked to outcomes in health
and well-being, educational attainment, employment and feeling well-situat-
ed in a particular place. As Tom Carter and Chesya Polevychok have convincingly argued, housing policy is good social policy from at least two perspectives.[22] The first is that adequate and affordable housing is a necessary household good, in and of itself. The second is that it facilitates the success of initiatives taken in other policy sectors like health, education and income security.

Living in poor quality housing impacts physical and mental health. Poor
physical design, overcrowding, poor state of repair and residential mobility
for reasons not chosen by the household all have significant impacts on health
and well-being.[23] On a socio-economic level, the domestic environment at
home, monthly expenditure on housing and shelter-related costs, exercise of
control, and security of tenure are significant predictors of physical and mental health.[24] Anxiety and depression increase with housing instability or poor
quality housing. People who are actually homeless—a phenomenon directly
correlated with the discontinuation of federal social housing programs in the
1990s—experience the worst health consequences; mortality rates can be as
much as 10 times higher than people who are properly housed.[25] Because other
types of supports, such as for mental health, addiction, or physical health
issues, are mostly ineffective for homeless people, and given that being homeless causes such stress and exacerbation of health problems, it is as much as
five times more expensive to shelter (in emergency shelters) and treat homeless people than it would be to just house them properly.[26] In Canada, we have
in the past decade come to focus quite heavily on homelessness as a policy sector in itself, perhaps too easily forgetting that it is housing and homes that we
need to focus on. This probably will seem obvious to the reader, but it is surprising how homelessness and emergency shelters have overtaken housing
and homes as a policy focus in many circles, particularly under the past
Liberal-led federal governments.

The impact of poor housing circumstances on educational outcomes is significant. Children living in overcrowded housing have poorer educational
outcomes, and those who are poorly housed or homeless have more problems with anxiety, depression, behavioural problems and educational

achievement.[27] Researchers in the United States found that residential mobility as a child had a greater impact on high school graduation than poverty or welfare dependency.[28] This connects directly with the security of tenure, affordability and adequacy of housing. Low-income households living in adequate and affordable social housing that are paying rent geared to their income can put their children on a more level playing field as far as life chances are concerned than if they are required to move because of rising rents, inadequate housing or shifts to the less secure secondary rental housing market (i.e., rental units that were not built for the purpose of long-term rental arrangements, such as secondary suites, rented condos or detached houses) on account of condominium conversions.

High housing costs and insufficient income intersect to affect both the income security and social housing policy sectors. In Saskatchewan, as elsewhere, social assistance includes a shelter allowance meant to cover the rental cost of private market accommodation. Until very recently, in spite of the steady rise in rents over time, the shelter allowance portion of social assistance had not increased for over 15 years. A study conducted in Winnipeg examined how money spent on developing new social housing units in the inner city, where the majority of people on social assistance live, compared with total expenditure on the shelter portion of social assistance in the inner city.[29] The authors found that about $5 million was spent on new social housing units in 1999–2000 while in the same year roughly $50 million was spent on housing through social assistance, most of which flowed to landlords through private sector rental accommodation. The $50 million figure accounts for more than the shelter allowance portion of social assistance, and reflects instead the reality that most households are paying 50% or more of their total social assistance income on rent. Carter and Janzen also found that a 10% increase in the shelter component of social assistance would cost the provincial treasury an additional $20 million a year, but would still not address the gap between market rents and shelter allowance. Furthermore, in many cities, the adequacy and suitability of a significant portion of the market rental universe housing those on social assistance is poor. Adequacy and suitability can be assured and maintained in social housing portfolios and investing in new social housing units is good policy. It creates new permanent adequate and affordable rental stock and has the added effect of placing downward pressure on market rents given that it adds new supply to a rental universe that has been stagnant or in decline for many years. The disparity between investment in social housing units versus shelter allowances and social assistance in Winnipeg is an example of how lopsided and inefficient our approach to social housing policy has become.

WHY HAS SOCIAL HOUSING POLICY BEEN NEGLECTED?

Given that housing is good social policy in its own right and is a basis for success in other policy sectors, why have governments so badly neglected this policy field? As the Canadian welfare state has become more residual over past decades, housing has become one of the most neglected sectors.[30] Yet there is no shortage of evidence that the proportion of low-income households experiencing housing affordability problems has increased remarkably over time in Canada, most notably since the federal government discontinued building new stock under its non-profit and co-operative social housing programs in the 1990s.[31]

Housing scholars agree that the only real way to address the shortage of adequate and affordable housing for those who cannot satisfy their needs in the diminishing private rental market or the high-pitched home-ownership market is for the state to build it.[32] Experience since the 1970s shows that it is most effective for the state to meet its unit targets by providing adequate and dependable resources to community-based social housing organizations for building and operating units at below market rent to those who need assistance.

The way the state intervenes in the housing market has changed significantly from the 1970s to today. During the period where the federal government led the way in building a non-profit and co-operative social housing sector (i.e., 1970–93), the state was a leader in program planning, implementation and long-term funding. In the period from 1993 to 2001 the state stopped building new social housing. The consequences were noticeable soon afterward. In 1999—after a rapid rise of absolute homelessness since discontinuing its housing programs and inner city socio-economic deterioration—the federal government re-entered the non-market housing sector through a back door, targeting "homelessness" instead of "housing" and using Human Resources and Social Development Canada (HRSDC) instead of CMHC.[33] In 1999, the Supporting Communities Partnership Initiative (SCPI) was launched by HRSDC, providing one-time funding contributions to urban communities able to mount proposals demonstrating sustainability and partnerships to address homelessness.

In 2001, the federal government launched an Affordable Housing Initiative (AHI) through the CMHC, officially marking a small scale re-entry into low-cost housing, avoiding the term "social housing" which might be associated with past programs, social welfare and social citizenship rights. What is remarkable is not only the much reduced impact of new programming on meeting housing needs, but also the lack of a coherent goal. For example, one could not be certain of what was the purpose of the AHI. The previous non-profit and co-operative (social) housing programs were designed to move steadily toward realizing the right of affordable and adequate housing for all Canadians. The AHI was not accompanied by a goal, vision or measurable targets, or a commitment to leadership in the sector by the federal government. It was a five-year initiative in partnership with provinces that provided a lump-sum capital subsidy to assist initiatives underway or being started locally in communities across Canada. It produced very few new units of housing and the funding was generally insufficient to reduce rents low enough to serve those most in need of non-market housing.[34] The funding did not provide for a sustained subsidy to housing providers that would allow them to maintain rents at an affordable level over the medium- to long-term, and so did not address the need for "social" housing.

The move from large-scale, state-led, goal-oriented social programs, like housing, to programs like the AHI and SCPI (both one-time commitments of capital funding to assist with local initiatives started in the voluntary sector) has been theorized differently by a number of scholars. Bob Jessop argues that the state must now, in contemporary times, be understood in a strategic-relational context, as one actor among many.[35] He argues that there is an increasing reliance on networks, partnerships, and "reflexive self-organization" across public, private and voluntary sectors to achieve societal goals.[36] It follows that the state provides strategic contributions to relational production processes in local communities where it is often the voluntary sector partners that are responsible for program sustainability.

A second and somewhat compatible way of theorizing the shift away from state-led social programs concerned with providing a strong foundation for common citizenship is presented by Anthony Giddens and, in Canada, adapted by Jane Jenson and Denis Saint-Martin.[37] They argue that in response to neo-liberal critiques of the welfare state, social democratic governments have moved away from attending to social rights such as affordable and adequate housing for all citizens. Social *cohesion*, understood as the strength of social bonds in society, replaces social *rights* as the goal of policy- and decision-makers. A focus on keeping people engaged in active citizenship, producing their own welfare, is seen as a way to increase social cohesion. Giddens conceptualizes this turn as a new relationship between a "social investment state" and an "active civil society," where both state and civil society actors are said to be able to better adapt to shifting economic conditions and change priorities and policy directions quickly and strategically in response to market and social forces. Long-term funding commitments, such as those embedded in the discontinued social housing programs (annual building targets for new units and 35-year operating agreements), are not highly compatible with this model of social-democratic state. The framework of the AHI and SCPI are much more so.

These theories of state and civil society set the state afloat on a wave of inevitability driven by seemingly too powerful market and social "forces." Some authors have, appropriately, opted to envision the state as a *powerful* rather than a *passive* force and present a third conception of the state's role in stabilizing citizenship, addressing market inadequacies and enhancing quality of life. These theorists have argued that the dismantling of social welfare, such as the social housing programs in Canada, was not inevitable but was at best the result of poor political leadership in the face of financial downturns and governance crises. At worst, they continue, it was a conscious move at an historic point of "opportunity" to usher in an era of power consolidation among the élite class at the expense of gains made by the rest of society through a strong welfare state after World War II.[38]

Under neo-liberal welfare state retrenchment—that has led to the residual welfare state we have today—the focus on collective social rights of national political communities was replaced with the primacy of individual (including corporate) consumption rights substantiated in the marketplace. Personal "freedom" would be realized through the consumption of goods, services and private assets of personal choosing, with minimal state interference. The other side of this type of "freedom" is that individuals also bear responsibility for their own welfare—investing in their own education, housing, income security and health. Shortfalls in personal development are increasingly seen as the result of individual failings and a lack of "entrepreneurial virtues," not as a shortfall of our collective political community and its apparatus, the state.[39] This is particularly troubling when seen against the backdrop of the growing gap between the richest and the poorest in Canada, where it follows that we must either be witnessing a rapid rise of individual failing in Canadian society, or evidence that there is a need for a stronger state to correct market inadequacies.[40]

Where civil society actors represent collective interests in social welfare, the focus on entrepreneurial virtues has been regularized through a new governance regime based on competitive urban policy.[41] By controlling financial resources, policy/program parameters, and accountability frameworks, the state maintains its ability to govern Jessop's cross-sectoral, self-organized networks and reward collective attempts to produce social welfare in communities at its discretion. Similar to the type of individual "freedom" discussed above, the state is able to embed in collective civil society actors a culture of "enterprise and winning, at the expense of egalitarianism."[42] The rhetoric of flexibility and freedom is used to motivate a type of circumscribed "innovation," but only some of the collective actors who participate in the social welfare contest are rewarded with social investment from the state.[43]

Nation-state collectivism and solidarity, substantiated through welfare state programs and social rights, is giving away significant ground to the normalization of individual, family and organizational competition and individualized accountability for success and failure. The pillars of the welfare state eroding most quickly are those like social housing that are connected in the public view most perceptibly—although erroneously—to individual poor choices.[44] Social housing and (un)employment are perceived this way, more so, than say, health care and old age security which are viewed as more firmly outside of one's control.

Revisiting in this light the propensity of Saskatchewan housing policy, over most of the past several decades, to focus most centrally on seniors' housing, the reason seems clearer. Seniors are not perceived to be a group who owe economic hardship to individual poor choices, unlike single-mothers or the middle-aged, single, working poor who people may still believe owe their hardship to poor personal decisions. However, even the areas of welfare perceived to be outside of one's control (e.g., health, old age security) are becoming more individualized and competitive, if relatively less so. In this new framework of individual "freedom" and voluntary sector competition and accountability, the perception of personal freedom may indeed be outpacing people's substantive freedom to participate in the political, economic and civic lives of their communities. With adequate and affordable housing being such a necessary precursor to the success of other policy inter-ventions such as health, education and income security, what should we aspire to in social housing policy development?

WHAT WOULD GOOD SOCIAL HOUSING POLICY LOOK LIKE?

Even though Canadian governments have not implemented social housing policy in a responsible and sustained manner, there is no shortage of scholar-ship on what should be done. While the owner-occupied housing market functions more or less as it should, there has been supply-side failure in the rental market for decades. As the gap in income between the rich and poor widens in Canada there continues to be high demand for rental housing, par-ticularly at the "affordable" end of the scale. Yet the ability of lower income earners to pay the rent levels that would be required to make investment in new rental housing construction a comparatively profitable enterprise, rela-tive to other types of housing construction, is too low. This has only been com-pounded by the attractiveness of developing individually titled condomini-ums instead of rental apartment buildings. Instead of making a long-term investment in a multi-unit structure that would be paid off over an extended period of time, with interest rate and inflationary uncertainty, condominiums can be sold off immediately unit by unit, avoiding financial risk and selling to a sector of the market that can pay a higher price for housing.

The disposition toward building condominiums rather than rental apart-ments was strengthened in the past few decades by unfavourable tax struc-tures, such as for example, municipal property tax structures with higher rates for rental than owner-occupied properties. Rental property owners also find that tax deductions available to other small businesses do not apply to them. The capital cost allowance rates associated with building depreciation are also considered too low and owners of multiple properties cannot pool allowances between buildings.[45] These and other unfavourable tax provisions act as disin-centives to new investment in rental properties. Tax policy needs to be revised to provide incentives for developing rental apartments and maintaining the existing stock.

One of the fundamental roles of the state is to intervene when there is mar-ket failure, especially in areas of significant public interest like the housing sector. Canadian governments have hardly intervened. The language of mar-ket determination is strong. Decision-makers can still be heard clearly and often referring to a common myth that the "market will decide," or some derivative of this unsubstantiated idea. There was in the 1960s, and still is today, a need for sustained state intervention in housing to serve those that cannot make it in the private market. From the 1960s through early 1990s the governments of Canada played a role, although from the mid-1980s to 1993 there was a steady diminution of annual unit targets, from 25,000 units a year in 1983 to zero in 1993.[46] Governments have undertaken measures to placate demands for new social housing investment through small short-term invest-ments like the SCPI, AHI and housing trusts, but have mostly remained committed to "letting the market decide." Meanwhile, the marketplace has shown for several decades now that it has already decided not to invest in purpose-built affordable rental housing.[47]

In 2001–02, the federal government spent roughly one percent of its annual budget (or roughly $2 billion) on the operation and subsidization of all social housing in the country. The provincial governments also fund social housing, mostly through cost-sharing with the federal government. Housing experts have recommended that five types of programs be pursued to begin closing the gap in adequate and affordable housing between lower and higher income Canadians.[48] These programs would require the investment of another one percent of the federal budget which, given the importance of housing as a basis for good social policy across numerous sectors, does not seem to be an unreasonable sum. This One-Percent Solution, proposed by Michael Shapcott and David Hulchanski, would be broken up into the following program directions[49]:

> • Capital funding for the provision of 20,000–25,000 new social housing units per year, by new construction or acquisition and upgrade—the same rate of development as in the early-mid-1980s, when the systemic problem of homelessness was not present in Canada. A subsidy to reduce construction costs to a level that permits a sustainable cash flow from rental incomes is important, as well as a subsidy to keep rent-geared-to-income for those on low and often fixed incomes on account of other life circumstances (e.g., senior citizens, mental illness, long-term disability).

> • Rent supplements for 150,000–200,000 households. Rent supplements, under the NHA and provincial housing corporation acts, are legal relationships established between a crown housing agency and private sector landlords, where the landlord agrees to rent a certain unit(s) to low-income tenants, typically from a general social housing wait list. In return the government pays the landlord the difference between market rent and what the tenant is able to pay using a rent geared to 30 % of income guideline. Benefits to the tenant and government are that units are inspected regularly for state of repair and suitability for household size and type and that the landlord agrees to adhere to tenant protection laws. A benefit to the landlord is that they have a guaranteed supply of prospective tenants, which cuts down on time that a unit remains vacant on account of household turnover and re-advertisement, a reliable source of rent, and an agency link to call if tenants exhibit health symptoms that affect tenancy (such as mental illness).

> In British Columbia, the ministries responsible for housing and health have partnered to ensure that landlords have a

mental health expert on-call should unforeseen issues arise with tenants.[50] For landlords who house many low-income tenants with health issues, this can be an enormous incentive to participate in rent supplement arrangements. Some have argued that landlords may get marginally higher rents by steering clear of rent supplement arrangements, particularly in rental markets with low vacancy rates. At face value, this may seem logical, but evidence from Toronto has shown otherwise. In fact, when lost rental income from unit turnover and the value of having a reliable source of rent payments and support people a phone call away are accounted for, it is actually financially favourable for landlords to opt-in to the security of rent supplement arrangements.[51]

• Roughly 10,000 new units of supportive housing where support services for mental, intellectual and physical disabilities are linked to the units.

• Renewing and expanding the Residential Rehabilitation Assistance Program (RRAP) for rental, rooming house and home-owners, that is set to expire in 2009. The existing private market rental housing stock is aging and represents an enormous asset that needs to be upgraded and preserved. It is less costly to preserve the existing stock of rental housing and upgrade it than it is to let it deteriorate to the point where it is lost to demolition and try and replace the stock with new construction. The TD Bank Financial Group estimates that the cost of upgrading existing aged apartment units is 40–50% of what it costs to build new. An expanded RRAP, cost-shared with provinces, would be an efficient program for maintaining a stock of affordable and adequate rental stock. Assisting community-based organizations to acquire and renovate older apartment buildings could stretch funding for new social housing units almost twice as far as new construction, with ongoing subsidies then attached to buildings to ensure that rent remains geared to income. There is considerable capacity among community-based social housing organizations to undertake this function.[52]

• Funding for services and shelters for homeless people is the last area, although this is an interim measure. Recall that homelessness is a new problem in Canada, and we should focus on eliminating it, not servicing it. As an innovative and successful program in Toronto called *Streets to Homes* is teaching us, the first step to solving homelessness is putting a person into a permanent home, not a shelter.

All three levels of government need to coordinate their strategies for social housing. The provinces can cost-share programs with the federal government. Provinces have a particular responsibility for affordability tools linked to income security, such as shelter allowances and old-age and disability pensions, and ensuring that they are regularly adjusted for cost-of-living increases. Provincial housing corporations, like SHC, could take the lead in augmenting investment in a rent supplement program with private sector landlords.

There is some debate over whether "shelter allowances" or "rent supplements" are better tools for creating affordability in the private market. The TD Bank Financial Group favours shelter allowances, although not without pointing out its weaknesses. One of the benefits is that the shelter allowance is not linked to a specific housing unit and is thus portable, maximizing "choice." However, the "choices" tenants have are at the lower end of the private rental market, and are not always good as far as adequacy and suitability are concerned. On the other hand, the rent supplement option ensures that public funds go to landlords that maintain quality standards in the housing and adhere to tenant-landlord legislation. There is something disconcerting about sending large sums of public money through shelter allowance programs with no assurance that we are collectively funding the supply of adequate and suitable housing, or in other words, with no guarantees of landlord accountability for basic standards in return for public investment.

It is important to bear in mind, whether shelter allowances or rent supplements are the program of choice (or any combination of both), that the necessary complement to these demand-side measures is construction of new social and market rental supply. An effective way to keep rental rates down across the whole market is for the state to keep building rental housing.

A study of 90 large metropolitan areas in the United States found that in areas where the number of households receiving a shelter allowance was higher than the number of households living in social housing units, low-income households in the private market experienced larger increases in rent.[53] Across the 90 centres, an average increase in market rents of 16% was observed as a result of increasing household ability to pay. Landlords are able to increase rents and provide the same service when the ability to pay of low-income households rises. However, when new supply is added this upward pressure on rents is mitigated.

Provincial and municipal governments should lead in protecting existing purpose-built rental housing from conversion to condominiums when vacancy rates are low (e.g., below 3%), and in advancing efforts to upgrade purpose-built rental housing with the federal government. It is an efficient way to preserve public subsidy already put into the building of that housing decades ago, and to maximize efficiency in new public subsidy to create more affordable housing. Yet, as the Saskatoon experience has recently shown, municipalities are not always the best arbiter of public interest in affordable housing. The City of Saskatoon's current policy on condominium conversions shows a lack of consideration for tenant well-being, privileging instead the upward filtering of unearned windfalls to a small group of property investors, many of whom are from out of province, at the expense of lower income households.[54]

The City of Saskatoon also has a housing business plan directed at creating new affordable rental housing. However, it is disappointing that such an innovative plan is at least partially eclipsed by the impact of a poor condo conversion policy. The business plan, to the degree that it is successfully implemented, could still fall short of creating enough affordable new units to replace those lost through conversions. Most disappointing though is that many people who had lived for years in rental housing with secure tenure were pushed out of their homes. The conversion of around 10% or perhaps more—the number of units lost to conversion has been rising monthly—of the City's purpose-built rental stock while vacancy is below one percent has contributed to overall rent increases for all renters in the market as present scarcity is compounded by the further removal of units from the rental universe.

Municipalities can play a variety of roles, to the extent that they are enabled by provincial legislation, such as inclusionary zoning, density bonusing, direct funding contributions, property tax equalization between multi-unit residential and single-family dwellings, tax rebates, permitting cost rebates, to name some of the most common.

THE POLITICAL CHALLENGE OF IMPLEMENTING SOCIAL HOUSING POLICY IN SASKATCHEWAN

The federal and provincial governments in Canada have shared responsibility for social housing, but neither, with the exception of a 20-year period from the mid-1960s to mid-1980s, has committed to a course of sustained target-oriented development in the sector. This is notwithstanding the facts that having secure adequate and affordable housing is a basic human right, is within the bounds of financial rationality in a country as wealthy as Canada, and is a precursor to optimal outcomes for investments made in other policy sectors like health, education and income security. Saskatchewan needs a social housing strategy that is co-ordinated with federal and municipal strategies. We need a national housing policy that sets direction, targets and timeframes for provinces to endorse and cost-share and for municipalities to facilitate. What we have are disjointed initiatives that rarely make sense in the light of reasoned and effective strategies such as those outlined in this chapter.

The Federation of Canadian Municipalities released recommendations for a national action plan on housing and homelessness in January 2008.[55] While it is not a mandated function of municipalities to set direction for a national housing policy, they are certainly well aware of the situation on the ground as a result of sustained neglect in the sector by senior governments. The recommendations include targets for ending homelessness, expanding the stock of social housing, and preserving and rehabilitating existing social and private housing stock.

One of the struggles organizations like the FCM will have to face as it lobbies the federal government to extend and augment its housing programs beyond the upcoming March 2009 end dates is that senior governments have moved away from sustained investment over longer timeframes to meet specific targets. Recent programs like the Affordable Housing Initiative, Supporting Communities Partnership Initiative, and the affordable housing trusts do not set measurable targets for new units or make any commitments to outcomes for the sector. They also have short funding timeframes and pro- mote competition for scarce social resources rather than an egalitarian com- mitment to meeting basic social standards for all citizens. The FCM is asking for program commitments spanning 10 years, with periodic targets. This may be a difficult sell given what seems to be the new approach of government to spending on social housing. But perhaps the time will have come for a change.

Turning to Saskatchewan housing policy, the HomeFirst policy framework that currently guides social housing investment is also nearing the end of its five-year horizon. The government elected in 2007, led by the Saskatchewan Party, has a new Task Force report on housing affordability to consider, with 36 recommendations. There is a striking difference between HomeFirst—cre- ated by the former NDP-led government—and the recommendations of the Task Force, in that the former makes little mention of enabling and prioritiz- ing private sector solutions to affordable housing and the latter makes little mention of direct state responsibility for intervention. This is likely a product of party ideologies which set different orientations toward private sector ver- sus state-led programs for affordable and social housing. The former NDP-led government could have worked harder to incentivize the creation of rental housing within the private market. However, to their credit, the former NDP- led government set goals, targets and timelines to create social housing units, which is fundamentally important. And they did so in a budget year (2004) that was very tight, while Saskatchewan might still have been considered a "have-not" province.

While the former NDP-led government proceeded with a view that the state has responsibilities to correct market failures directly, the Saskatchewan Party-led government appears at this early stage in its mandate—through its Task Force recommendations and its initial response to them—to be keeping with an approach that minimizes the direct role of the state and instead tries to assist *all other parties* to improve housing circumstances. When direct invest- ment does occur by a government like the current one, it may be more likely to be focused on assisting individual households and landlords, rather than on building state housing units or on a direct relationship between the state and landlords (i.e., through investment in rent supplement units with private landlords). Reducing income taxes for low- to moderate-income earners—one of the recommendations of the Task Force—may on the surface seem like a good idea for putting more money into the hands of low-income people that could then be used to augment housing affordability and adequacy. But research shows that assistance through the tax system, particularly through higher personal exemptions, can be relatively ineffective and inefficient, leaving little new disposable income in the hands of individual low-income people.[56]

The Task Force report contains recommendations that, if implemented, might go some way toward assisting municipalities, the private sector, and citizens to create or access more affordable and adequate housing. However, it is weak on articulating provincial government responsibility. It sometimes reads like a list of suggestions for everyone else. But it is primarily a joint federal and provincial responsibility to redistribute income tax revenue to meet social goals such as adequate and affordable housing. The Task Force document is not a responsible document in this regard, and further, it lacks targets and timelines. The document, a product of compromise between a former Saskatchewan Party MLA and a former NDP MLA, reflects more of the Saskatchewan Party's approach than the 50% representation on the Task Force would suggest. When task forces produce reports, they wish their recommendations to be implemented, and there is a fair bit of work done before the document is released to ensure that it is roughly compatible with what the governing party could implement, given its ideological approach. Then, at the level of the Minister and Cabinet, recommendations are further vetted. In the end, I cannot predict how many recommendations from the Task Force on Housing Affordability will be implemented, but I am more interested in the recommendations that should have been in the report but were not, many of which were discussed in this chapter.

It is a shame that political ideology gets in the way of good policy because a sustainable strategy for meeting basic social housing needs requires both demand-side and supply-side, state-driven and market-enabling programs. In other words, it requires some of what both the former NDP-led and the current Saskatchewan Party-led governments have presented. The heavy focus on shelter allowance increases in the Task Force report and the subsequent response from government is part of the answer, but as discussed above, is not nearly a complete or even terribly efficient strategy. In keeping with the notion of "individual choice" so prevalent in contemporary social policy discourse, shelter allowances fit well. However, the right of individuals to "choose" is not entirely substantial because they have not got the purchasing power that truly allows for choice. They would be better off with basic assurances that come with residing in purpose-built social housing units with rents geared to income or proper rent supplement programs.

It is a political challenge to implement good social housing policy that uses a combination of strategies quite detached from ideological propensities and centred on reasonably long timeframes with well-reasoned and measurable unit targets. The algorithm for successful implementation has not in the past decade and a half been used, although it seemed to be well understood some decades ago. One of the key pieces that has changed in this time period is that governments have told us that we cannot afford to care for one another's welfare like we used to, and most Canadians seem to believe that. The spirit of social democracy needs to be revived—and that needs to be borne out of communities themselves—before many real changes will occur in the housing sector (and other social welfare sectors). Until then the debates will continue but people may not notice much real change in their housing circumstances.

NOTES

1. Task Force on Housing Affordability, *Affordable Housing: An Investment* (Regina: Government of Saskatchewan, 2008).

2. Ibid., 1.

3. T. Crook, "The Supply of Private Rented Housing in Canada," *Journal of Housing and the Built Environment* 13, no. 3 (1998): 327–52; S. Pomeroy, "A Canadian Perspective on Housing Policy," *Housing Policy Debate* 6 (1995): 619–53.

4. T. Carter and C. Polevychok, *Housing is Good Social Policy* (Ottawa: Canadian Policy Research Networks, 2004).

5. J.D. Hulchanski, *Housing Policy for Tomorrow's Cities* (Ottawa: Canadian Policy Research Networks, 2002).

6. R.M. Bone and M.B. Green, "Housing Assistance and Maintenance for the Métis in Northern Saskatchewan," *Canadian Public Policy* 9, no. 4 (1983): 476–86.

7. J.M. Wolfe, "Canadian Housing Policy in the Nineties," *Housing Studies* 13, no. 1 (1998): 121–33.

8. Central Mortgage and Housing Corporation, *Briefing Notes for the Cabinet Committee on Social Policy: Housing Policy for the 1970's and NHA Amendments* (Ottawa: Central Mortgage and Housing Corporation, 1972), 1.

9. Ibid., 9.

10. Canada Mortgage and Housing Corporation, *The Relationship between Social Policy and Housing Policy: A Federal Perspective* (Ottawa: Canada Mortgage and Housing Corporation, 1979).

11. Canadian Council on Social Development, *Social Housing Policy Review* (Ottawa: Canadian Council on Social Development, 1976), 13.

12. T.H. Marshall, *Citizenship and Social Class and Other Essays* (New York: Cambridge University Press, 1950).

13. Central Mortgage and Housing Corporation, *CMHC Priorities for Policy Development 1975–1978* (Ottawa: Central Mortgage and Housing Corporation, 1975), 1.

14. Canada Mortgage and Housing Corporation, *Social Housing Review: Background Document for Federal Consultations on Housing* (Ottawa: Canada Mortgage and Housing Corporation, 1984); AbT Associates of Canada, *Attitudes Toward Social Housing in Canada* (Ottawa: Canada Mortgage and Housing Corporation, 1981).

15. Task Force on Housing Affordability, *Affordable Housing: An Investment*.

16. R. Walker, *Social Housing and the Role of Aboriginal Organizations in Canadian Cities* (Montréal: Institute for Research on Public Policy, 2008).

17. Carter and Polevychok, *Housing is Good Social Policy*; Hulchanski, *Housing Policy for Tomorrow's Cities*.

18. C. Després, "The Meaning of Home: Literature Review and Directions for Future Research and Theoretical Debate," *Journal of Architectural and Planning Research* 8 (1991): 96–115; P. Saunders, "The Meaning of 'Home' in Contemporary English Culture," *Housing Studies* 4 (1989): 177–92; S. Smith, "The Essential Qualities of a Home," *Journal of Environmental Psychology* 14 (1994): 31–46.

19. R. Imrie, "Disability, Embodiment and the Meaning of the Home," *Housing Studies* 19 (2004): 745–63; R. Bratt, "Housing and Family Well-being," *Housing Studies* 17 (2002): 13–26.

20. J. Dunn, "Social Inequality, Population Health and Housing: Towards a Social

Geography of Health" (PhD dissertation in Geography, Simon Fraser University, 1998).

21. M. Shapcott, "The Right to Housing and the Right to the City," presentation at the Planners Network conference (Winnipeg, 2008).

22. Carter and Polevychok, *Housing is Good Social Policy*.

23. R. Kearns, C. Smith and M. Abbott, "Another Day in Paradise? Life on the Margins in Urban New Zealand," *Social Science and Medicine* 33 (1991): 369–79.

24. J. Dunn, "Housing and Health Inequalities: Review and Prospects for Research," *Housing Studies* 15 (2000): 341–66.

25. M. Guirguis-Younger, V. Runnels and T. Aubry, *A Study of the Deaths of Persons who are Homeless in Ottawa—A Social and Health Investigation* (Ottawa: Saint Paul University and the Centre for Research on Community Services, 2003).

26. I. De Jong, "Streets to Homes in Toronto," presentation to housing and homelessness stakeholders in Saskatoon (2008).

27. D. Lezubski, J. Silver and E. Black, "High and Rising: The Growth of Poverty in Winnipeg," in J. Silver (ed.), *Solutions that Work: Fighting Poverty in Winnipeg* (Winnipeg and Halifax: Canadian Centre for Policy Alternatives—Manitoba and Fernwood Publishing, 2000); E.J. Mueller and J.R. Tighe, "Making the Case for Affordable Housing: Connecting Housing with Health and Education Outcomes," *Journal of Planning Literature* 21, no. 4 (2007): 371–85; P. Mullins, J. Western and B. Broadbent, *The Links Between Housing and Nine Key Socio-Cultural Factors: A Review of the Evidence* (Brisbane: Australian Housing and Urban Research Institute, 2001).

28. Mueller and Tighe, "Making the Case for Affordable Housing."

29. T. Carter and T. Janzen, *The Welfare of Neighbourhoods: The Spatial Distribution of the Social Assistance Caseload and Housing Policy in Winnipeg* (Winnipeg: Institute of Urban Studies, 2004).

30. S. Pinch, *Worlds of Welfare: Understanding the Changing Geographies of Social Welfare Provision* (New York: Routledge, 1997).

31. E. Moore and A. Skaburskis, "Canada's Increasing Housing Affordability Burdens," *Housing Studies* 19, no. 3 (2004): 395–413.

32. Ibid.; R.A. Walks, "Homelessness, Housing Affordability, and the New Poverty," in T. Bunting and P. Filion (eds.), *Canadian Cities in Transition: Local Through Global Perspectives*, 3rd ed. (Toronto: Oxford University Press, 2006).

33. Toronto Mayor's Homelessness Action Task Force, *Taking Responsibility for Homelessness: An Action Plan for Toronto* (Toronto: City of Toronto, 1999); Inner City Housing Coalition, *Inner City Housing Policy Platform: Federal Election* (Winnipeg: Inner City Housing Coalition, 2000).

34. S. Pomeroy, *A New Beginning: The National Non-reserve Aboriginal Housing Strategy* (Ottawa: National Aboriginal Housing Association, 2004); M. Shapcott, "Building Relations with the New Federal Government," paper presented at the National Aboriginal Housing Association conference (Vancouver, 2006).

35. B. Jessop, *Good Governance and the Urban Question: On Managing the Contradictions of Neo-liberalism* (Lancaster: Lancaster University, 2000).

36. B. Jessop, "Bringing the State Back In (Yet Again): Reviews, Revisions, Rejections and Redirections," *International Review of Sociology* 11, no.2 (2001): 149–73.

37. A. Giddens, *The Third Way: The Renewal of Social Democracy* (Cambridge: Polity Press, 1998); J. Jenson and D. Saint-Martin, "New Routes to Social Cohesion?

Citizenship and the Social Investment State," *Canadian Journal of Sociology* 28, no.1 (2003): 77–99.

38. D. Harvey, *A Brief History of Neoliberalism* (Toronto: Oxford University Press, 2005); J. Ralston Saul, *The Collapse of Globalism and the Reinvention of the World* (Toronto: Penguin, 2005).

39. Harvey, *A Brief History of Neoliberalism*.

40. There are several published reports on the growing gap between rich and poor in Canadian society. For example, see D.A. Green and K. Milligan, *Canada's Rich and Poor: Moving in Opposite Directions* (Toronto: Canadian Centre for Policy Alternatives, 2007) and; A. Yalnizyan, *The Growing Gap: A Report on Growing Inequality Between the Rich and Poor in Canada* (Toronto: Centre for Social Justice, 1998).

41. A. Kearns and I. Turok, "Power, Responsibility, and Governance in Britain's New Urban Policy," *Journal of Urban Affairs* 22 (2000): 175–91.

42. Ibid. 176.

43. D. Burns, "Can Local Democracy Survive Governance?," *Urban Studies* 37 (2000): 963–73.

44. K.G. Banting, "Neoconservatism in an Open Economy: The Social Role of the Canadian State," *International Political Science Review* 13 (1992): 149–70.

45. TD Bank Financial Group, *Affordable Housing in Canada: In Search of a New Paradigm* (TD Economics Special Report, 2003).

46. Hulchanski, *Housing Policy for Tomorrow's Cities*.

47. TD Bank Financial Group, *Affordable Housing in Canada*.

48. Hulchanski, *Housing Policy for Tomorrow's Cities*.

49. Hulchanski, *Housing Policy for Tomorrow's Cities*; TD Bank Financial Group, *Affordable Housing in Canada*.

50. R. Walker and M. Seasons, "Planning Supported Housing: A New Orientation in Housing for People with Serious Mental Illness," *Journal of Planning Education and Research* 21, no. 3 (2002): 313–19.

51. De Jong, "Houses to Homes."

52. For some examples, see Walker, *Social Housing and the Role of Aboriginal Organizations in Canadian Cities*.

53. S. Susin, "Rent Vouchers and the Price of Low-income Housing," *Journal of Public Economics* 83 (2002): 109–52.

54. A. Skaburskis, *Analysis Prepared for Saskatoon City Councilor, Charlie Clark* (dated April 14, 2008)

55. Federation of Canadian Municipalities, *Sustaining the Momentum: Recommendations for a National Action Plan on Housing and Homelessness* (Ottawa: Federation of Canadian Municipalities, 2008).

56. V.L. Pearson, F.H. Cuddington and D. Thorn, *Final Report and Recommendations of the Committee on Improving Work Opportunities for Saskatchewan Residents* (Regina: Government of Saskatchewan, 2006).

Climate Change and Saskatchewan Public Policy

Peter Prebble

INTRODUCTION

The world faces a climate crisis which is certain to be a dominant issue in the 21st century. The international scientific community is warning human civilization that the release of human produced greenhouse gas emissions into the atmosphere must be sharply reduced or life on our planet will be unalterably damaged. The world is already experiencing the early consequences of climate change: more intense drought, more flooding and more severe storms, hurricanes and typhoons. A growing number of animal and plant species are in decline or are becoming extinct as a result of climate change. Many ocean coral reefs, a rich source of marine biodiversity and beauty, are dying. All of these problems will become much more severe if greenhouse gas emissions are not reduced quickly.

The escalating consumption of fossil fuels is the biggest single reason why greenhouse gas concentrations in the atmosphere are steadily increasing. Canada is a major emitter of greenhouse gases, for our population size, accounting for approximately 2.3% of global emissions.[1] Saskatchewan is an even larger per capita emitter, accounting for just over 10% of Canada's greenhouse gas emissions.[2] This means Saskatchewan, with only 1 million people in a world of 6.5 billion people, accounts for well over 0.2% of global greenhouse gas emissions.

Saskatchewan's greenhouse gas emissions burden can also be put into perspective by comparing our emissions with other countries in the world. If Saskatchewan was hypothetically to become a nation, we would have the second highest greenhouse gas emissions per capita of any other country on earth. Only Qatar, a Middle Eastern country with a population slightly less than Saskatchewan's, has higher per capita emissions. At approximately 72 tonnes of carbon dioxide equivalent emissions per capita, Saskatchewan's per capita emissions are almost double those of the third highest emitting nation on the globe and more than triple the average per capita emissions in the United States and the rest of Canada.[3] Within Canada, only Alberta, with its large oil sands production, has per capita emissions in a similar range to Saskatchewan.

There are legitimate reasons for Saskatchewan to have a higher than average emissions load. Our climate is colder than most parts of Canada and colder than the vast bulk of the world. We are a growing oil and gas producer. Many Saskatchewan industries are energy intensive. However, in light of the serious global consequences of climate change, the current level of greenhouse gas emissions in Saskatchewan is not possible to justify. Moreover, other industrialized countries with cold climates have shown that emissions can be sharply reduced. For example, the national greenhouse gas emissions of Sweden (66.9 million tonnes) with approximately 9 million people, are less than the greenhouse gas emissions of Saskatchewan (71.9 million tonnes) with approximately 1 million people.[4]

Our disproportionate share of global emissions places a special responsibility on the Government of Saskatchewan and the Government of Canada to provide leadership in reducing greenhouse gas emissions. It also suggests the need for communities across Saskatchewan to closely examine their emission sources and plan for reductions in the coming decade. A serious public discussion on how we can successfully reduce provincial greenhouse gas emissions in every sector of our economy is needed, combined with a comprehensive set of policy initiatives.

This chapter examines the climate crisis and the part Saskatchewan people can play in helping to resolve it through the actions of their provincial government. It looks at the risks climate change poses to the global community and to Saskatchewan. It reviews estimates on the economic cost of investing to prevent the worst consequences of climate change. The chapter then examines the political debate in Saskatchewan on climate change. It also examines recently announced public policy initiatives intended to reduce Saskatchewan emissions. Finally, it analyzes what kinds of provincial public policy initiatives are best employed for Saskatchewan to do its part in helping Canada meet its obligations under the Kyoto Protocol and under the post Kyoto framework agreed to at the December 2007 United Nations Climate Change Conference in Bali, Indonesia.

WHAT ARE GREENHOUSE GASES AND WHAT HUMAN ACTIVITIES PRODUCE THEM?

Greenhouse gases are a class of gases which trap heat near the surface of the earth. These gases all have the capacity to block long wavelengths of the sun's energy. At the levels they have been over the past several thousand years, greenhouse gases are a good thing. They have kept our planet warm and livable. However, the steady increase in human produced greenhouse gases over the past 60 years is threatening the relatively stable climatic conditions under which human civilization and today's plant and animal life has thrived. One simple warning sign is that the past decade has been the warmest since records were kept. The United Nations World Meteorological Organization reports that 2007 global average surface temperatures were 0.41°C above the 1961–90 annual average.[5]

There are 30 greenhouse gases in all. Each absorbs heat at different wavelengths. Six greenhouse gases are monitored by the international community under the Kyoto Protocol. They include carbon dioxide, methane, nitrous

oxide and the fluorinated gases (HFCs, PFCs and SF6). At present the fluorinated gases account for only 1.1% of total greenhouse gas emissions.[6] Thus,
from a public policy perspective, the three greenhouse gases that are the most
important to understand are carbon dioxide, nitrous oxide and methane. It is
the increase in human produced emissions of these three gases that is altering
the composition of the atmosphere and taking our climate into uncharted
territory.

Understanding the principal sources of human produced greenhouse gas
emissions is central to shaping public policy aimed at reducing those
emissions.

The most important of all greenhouse gases is carbon dioxide (CO_2), which
accounts for approximately 77% of total human produced greenhouse gas
emissions in the atmosphere.[7] Carbon dioxide plays a crucial role as a regula-
tor of climate on Earth. There is a direct correlation between carbon dioxide
levels in the atmosphere and temperatures on our planet. Over the past 10,000
years the concentration of carbon dioxide in the atmosphere has been in the
range of 280 parts per million (ppm). This has helped maintain the average
surface temperature of our planet at approximately 14°C. As well as existing
in nature, carbon dioxide has been produced every time coal, oil and natural
gas has been burned in power plants, automobiles, industrial facilities, cement
and steel production and other sources. The capacity of vegetation on the
earth to absorb carbon dioxide has also been damaged by extensive deforesta-
tion as a result of human activity. As a result, by the end of 2007 carbon dioxide levels in the atmosphere had risen from a pre-industrial level of 280ppm
to over 384ppm and are continuing to rise at over 2ppm per year. Average surface and ocean temperatures on Earth are rising as a result. Using ice core sam-
ples that allow scientists to measure carbon dioxide concentrations hundreds
of thousands of years ago, the scientific community is in agreement that carbon dioxide levels are higher than at any time in the past 650,000 years.[8]

Nitrous oxide is released when commercial nitrogen fertilizers are used or
fossil fuels are burned. Livestock manure management, domestic human
sewage and the production of nitric acid are other sources. Nitrous oxide is far
rarer than carbon dioxide, but is 310 times better at capturing heat. This makes
it a very powerful and troublesome greenhouse gas. Nitrous oxide concentrations in the atmosphere have increased from a pre-industrial level of 270 parts
per billion (ppb) to over 320ppb by the end of 2007.[9]

Methane is released at locations such as landfills, cattle feedlots and hog
barns with liquid manure. Methane losses occur during the production, processing and transmission of natural gas and from coal mining operations.
Methane is 212 times better at capturing heat than carbon dioxide (over a 100
year period), making it a potent greenhouse gas. Methane levels in the atmosphere have risen from a pre-industrial value of about 715ppb to over 1,780ppb
in 2007.[10]

Greenhouse gas emission data will sometimes refer only to carbon dioxide
concentrations in the atmosphere (384 ppm in 2007). The term CO_2 equivalent
(CO_2e) is used to refer to the concentration of carbon dioxide, nitrous oxide,

methane and other greenhouse gases in the atmosphere and takes account of the heat capturing potential of gases like methane and nitrous oxide This measure is described in parts per million. By early 2006 CO_2 equivalent levels were at 430ppm CO_2e and were rising by 2.3ppm per year.[11] The substantial increases in atmospheric concentrations of carbon dioxide and methane that took place in 2006 and 2007 put CO_2e at close to 435ppm by the end of 2007.[12]

From a public policy perspective, the scientific community is warning all citizens of the world that we must collectively stabilize greenhouse gases in the atmosphere at between 450 and 550ppm CO_2 equivalent.[13] They warn that going above 550ppm CO_2 equivalent will have very grave consequences for our planet. Moreover, there is a significant risk of serious damage to the natural world in the 450–550ppm range, as well. The higher the stabilization level, the higher average global temperatures will ultimately become.[14] To stabilize atmospheric concentrations will require human emissions to be reduced to the point where they are equal to the rate of absorption/removal by nature. In order to accomplish stabilization at 450 ppm, a global reduction of approximately 70% of all human produced greenhouse gas emissions (from 2005 levels) would be required by 2050.[15] To achieve stabilization at 500ppm would require a global reduction of 50% in emissions by 2050 and 75% in emissions by 2100. Moreover, significant global progress on these targets would need to be made over the next 10–20 years or else the stabilization target becomes very hard to achieve. Given the vast difference in per capita emissions between developed countries and the developing world, emission cuts would presumably need to be deepest in the wealthier countries. This has led some developed nations to set greenhouse gas reduction targets of 80% by 2050. The immense scope of the global challenge is underlined by the fact that all human produced greenhouse gas emissions, weighted by their global warming potential, grew by 70% worldwide in the period 1970 to 2004.[16]

One reason why such a deep and rapid reduction in emissions is required is that once released into the air, greenhouse gases accumulate. For example, one half of a pulse of carbon dioxide to the atmosphere is removed over a 30-year time period; a further 30% is removed within a few centuries and the other 20% will typically stay in the atmosphere for thousands of years.[17] Nitrous oxide typically remains in the atmosphere for about 150 years.[18] Methane on the other hand remains in the atmosphere for 8–9 years.[19] The fact that greenhouse gases accumulate in the atmosphere means that the more society delays reducing greenhouse gas emissions, the greater the emissions reductions will have to be in the decades ahead. A second point to keep in mind is that not only is our atmosphere fragile, but it is not as expansive as many citizens think. The breathable portion of the atmosphere extends only four kilometers above us. Since we rely on the atmosphere for our very existence on the planet, it is self evident that protecting it is in everyone's self interest.

WHAT ARE THE WORLDWIDE CONSEQUENCES FOR THE
EARTH AND FOR HUMAN CIVILIZATION OF RISING GREENHOUSE GAS EMISSIONS?

There is a high level of consensus in the scientific community on the broad consequences of climate change. This consensus is perhaps best reflected in the work of the United Nations Intergovernmental Panel on Climate Change (IPCC). This scientific team, convened by the United Nations, represents the research and considered judgment of hundreds of the world's best scientists. The Panel's reports are based on trying to reach a high level of agreement among scientists. Thus the Panel tends to be quite cautious in its projections. The credibility of the Panel was further enhanced in 2007 when it received the Nobel Peace Prize, which it shared with former U.S. Vice President Al Gore.

A second major piece of work which is highly useful to policy makers has been assembled by the Government of the United Kingdom and led by Sir Nicholas Stern, the former Chief Economist of the World Bank and head of the U.K. Government's Economic Service. It provided a comprehensive report to the British Prime Minister on the consequences of climate change, the economic costs associated with those consequences and the economic investment that is required to prevent the climate crisis from accelerating.

To fully explain the consequences of climate change, I have drawn on citations from both these highly respected reports.

SIGNIFICANT RISE IN TEMPERATURES ON EARTH

The average surface temperature of the Earth has already increased 0.7°C since 1900. Most of the increase has come in the past 50 years because of climate change. Temperatures are predicted to continue rising during the rest of this century.

The United Nations Intergovernmental Panel on Climate Change projects as their best estimate that the average surface temperature of the earth will rise between 1.8°C and 4°C by 2099.[20] It states that even midrange projections for average surface temperature increases are predicted to seriously disrupt ecosystems, water supplies and agricultural production.

Temperature increases are expected to be much higher near the North Pole than at the equator. For example, the scientists who prepared the Arctic Climate Impact Assessment (2004) predicted further warming in the Arctic of 4 to 7°C is likely by 2100.[21]

The U.K. review led by Nicholas Stern (Stern Review) warns that a doubling of pre-industrial greenhouse gases (ie: to approximately 550ppm CO_2 equivalent) is likely to cause a rise of between 2 to 5°C in global average temperatures. The U.K. review forecasts this level of greenhouse gases will probably be reached between 2030 and 2060 unless major action is taken to reduce emissions. It says: "A warming of 5°C on a global scale would be far outside the experience of human civilization and comparable to the difference between temperatures during the last ice age and today."[22]

SPECIES EXTINCTION ON A LARGE SCALE

The United Nations Intergovernmental Panel on Climate Change states:

"Approximately 20–30% of plant and animal species assessed so far are likely to be at increased risk of extinction if increases in global average temperature exceed 1.5 to 2.5°C."[23] The Stern Review says that at 2°C warming "around 15-40% of lands species could be facing extinction with most major species affected including 25–60% of mammals in South Africa and 15–25% of butterflies in Australia."[24]

Species extinction does not just occur from rising temperatures, but from the fact that when animals and plants move towards the poles to escape higher temperatures, their migration is often unsuccessful.

MORE INTENSE HURRICANES, FLOODS AND OTHER STORM DAMAGE

Climate change is resulting in storms and floods becoming more intense and therefore more damaging. As the atmosphere warms, air holds more moisture, which often results in heavier rainfalls and much more intense storm systems.

Global losses from weather related disasters have been steadily rising since the 1970s. In the decade of the 1970's losses totaled approximately $83 billion. By the 1990's they had risen to $440 billion. Developing nations have been hit particularly hard. The Stern Review reports that in recent years 96% of deaths from weather related disasters have occurred in developing countries.[25]

In the past three years the world has witnessed an unprecedented number of severe weather events. For example, in July 2005 Mumbai, India received 37 inches of rain in one day.[26] That same year the U.S. suffered its deadliest hurricane season, including Hurricane Katrina. In the past three years Japan has set a record for typhoons and Australia was hit with the strongest cyclone ever measured off its coast. For the first time Brazil was hit by a hurricane on its South Atlantic coast.[27]

The summer of 2007 saw the worst flooding in the history of record keeping in parts of England and southeast Asia. For example, torrential downpours in 32 counties of England in July 2007 broke records dating back to 1914 by more than 25mm.[28] That summer in south Asia more than 10 million people were left homeless by severe flooding.[29]

In June of 2008 thousands were forced to flee as flooding inundated Midwest U.S. states causing billions of dollars of property damage in cities and on farms. As the Governor of Iowa declared 83 of the state's 99 counties disaster areas, Brian Pierce, a meteorologist with the National Weather Service in Davenport, U.S.A. stated "We're in uncharted territory. This is an event beyond what anybody could imagine."[30]

These severe weather events taken together are evidence that the early consequences of climate change are starting to be felt.

Looking into the future, the *Stern Review* says:

> By increasing the amount of energy available to fuel storms, climate change is likely to increase the intensity of storms. Infrastructure damage costs will increase substantially from even small increases in sea temperatures because peak wind speeds of tropical storms are a strongly exponential function

of temperature … and damage costs typically scale as the cube
of wind speed or more.[31]

MELTING GLACIERS AND REDUCED WATER AVAILABILITY

Almost all of the mountain glaciers in the world are melting because of rising
surface temperatures on Earth. Hundreds of millions of people rely on glacier-
fed water to meet their basic needs.

In South America, for example, the *Stern Review* notes: "The area covered
by glaciers has been reduced by nearly one quarter in the past 30 years… . Up
to 50 million people in this region will be affected by loss of dry-season
water."[32]

The Himalayan Glaciers are the source of more than half the drinking
water for 40% of the globe's population. Seven Asian river systems originate
on the Tibetan Plateau. Virtually all glaciers in China are showing significant
melting. Former U.S. Vice President Al Gore points out that: "Within the next
half-century … 40% of the world's people may well face a very serious drinking water shortage, unless the world acts boldly and quickly to mitigate global warming."[33]

The Fourth Assessment Report of the Intergovernmental Panel on Climate
Change (2007) underlines the severe impacts of reduced water availability as
a result of climate change. In Africa the IPPC states: "By 2020 between 75 and
250 million people are projected to be exposed to increased water stress due to
climate change."[34] In Europe the IPCC concludes: "Mountainous areas will
face glacier retreat, reduced snow cover and winter tourism, and extensive
species losses (in some areas up to 60% under high emissions scenarios by
2080)."[35]

INCREASING DROUGHT AND A DECLINE IN FOOD PRODUCTION

Climate change is projected to trigger food shortages, particularly in the trop-
ics and subtropics where crops are now grown just under the maximum temperatures they can tolerate. For example, the wheat growing belt from
Pakistan to northern India, to Nepal and Bangladesh is expected to become
too hot and dry to properly grow wheat by 2050.[36]

The United Nations IPCC Panel states: "Agricultural production, including
access to food in many African countries and regions is projected to be severely compromised by climate variability and change. In some countries yields
from rain-fed agriculture could be reduced by up to 50% by 2020."[37]

The *Stern Review* concludes: "Declining crop yields are likely to leave hundreds of millions without the ability to produce or purchase sufficient food,
particularly in the poorest parts of the world."[38]

One example of how climate change has already curbed food production
and water availability is Africa's Lake Chad. Once the sixth largest lake in the
world (the size of Lake Erie), it has shrunk to one twentieth its size in a time
span of 40 years.[39]

SEA LEVEL RISE

Sea levels are rising globally at around 3mm per year and the rise is accelerating. Over 200 million people in the world live in coastal areas at less than one metre above present sea level.

Warmer temperatures cause seawater to expand and melting land-based glaciers are adding to the volume of water in the oceans. Of particular worry is that parts of Greenland and the Antarctic ice sheets will melt. In Greenland significant melting and an acceleration of ice flows is occurring near coastal areas.[40] In the Antarctic Peninsula, ice shelves have already started to collapse. For example, in February 2002 the Larsen B ice shelf—a 3,250 square kilometer ice shelf (720 billion tones of ice)—broke up in a matter of weeks.[41]

The *Stern Review* states: "If the Greenland or West Antarctic Ice Sheets began to melt irreversibly, the rate of sea level rise could more than double, committing the world to an eventual sea level rise of 5–12 meters over several centuries."[42]

The United Nations Intergovernmental Panel on Climate Change provides a more cautious perspective predicting sea levels will rise 0.28 meters to 0.43 meters in this century. The UN scientific team states "many millions more people are projected to be flooded every year due to sea level rise by the 2080's."[43]

Higher sea levels increase risk from storm surges. In Tuktoyaktuk, North West Territories, the surging Beaufort Sea is already eating away at the community's roads and runways and damaging town infrastructure.[44] In northeast Norfolk in Britain, the community of Happisburgh is facing serious coastal erosion and the crumbling cliffs are forcing some homeowners to abandon their houses entirely.[45] In Bangladesh storms and floods have pushed sea water far inland, contaminating paddy fields and water supplies of thousands of farmers. Thousands of "climate refugees" have already left the country. If sea levels rise by one meter, a quarter of Bangladesh would be submerged, forcing over 30 million people from their homes.[46] As sea levels continue to rise, 22 of the largest cities in the world are at risk of flooding from coastal storm surges. Many small island nations are also at risk. Small island nations report coastal erosion, severe hurricanes, flooding and salinization of water supplies as some of the key issues they are experiencing as a result of climate change.[47]

DESTRUCTION OF CORAL REEFS AROUND THE WORLD

Coral reefs are a precious source of beauty and biodiversity. As the atmosphere warms, so does the ocean, although there is a lag time of approximately 30 years. If ocean temperatures go above a given threshold, they result in coral reefs bleaching and turning white. If these elevated water temperatures continue for a couple of months, parts of the reef die.

The Great Barrier Reef in Australia has already suffered coral bleaching, as has the Belize Barrier Reef, a World Heritage Site. In the Indian Ocean, 50% of the corals in the western India rim died in 1998, a particularly warm year on the globe.[48]

David Vaughan, director of the Center for Coral Reef Research at Mote notes that: "We have lost 25 percent of the world's corals in the last 25 years." He expects another 25% will be lost in the next decade or two.[49]

The United Nations IPCC forecasts that "a significant loss of biodiversity is projected to occur by 2020 in some ecologically rich sites, including the Great Barrier Reef…"[50] The Great Barrier Reef is home to 1,500 species of fish, a third of the world's soft corals and 6 of the world's 7 marine turtle species.[51]

NEGATIVE HEALTH IMPACTS

The United Nations Intergovernmental Panel on Climate Change states: "Projected climate change-related exposures are likely to affect the health status of millions of people, particularly those with low adaptive capacity through increases in malnutrition and consequent disorders…; increased deaths, disease and injury due to heat waves, floods, storms, fires and droughts; the increased burden of diarrhoeal disease; the increased frequency of cardio-respiratory diseases due to higher concentrations of ground-level ozone related to climate change; and the altered spatial distribution of some infectious disease vectors.[52] The Stern Review concludes that: "Climate change will amplify health disparities between rich and poor parts of the world."[53]

Already climate change impacts are being felt on many fronts. The World Health Organization has estimated that "the effects of the climate change that has (already) occurred since the mid-1970's may have caused over 150,000 deaths in (the year) 2000." It also concluded that these impacts are likely to increase in the future. WHO emphasized that measurement of health effects from climate change "can only be very approximate" and that its quantitative assessment took into account "only a subset of the possible health impacts."[54]

The United Nations Development Programme has expressed concern that the impacts of climate change on human development have been under-estimated. In a November 27, 2007 news release it projected that a more than 2° average global temperature rise could result in an additional 600 million people suffering from malnutrition by 2080 due to the expansion of drought affected areas.[55]

In Canada heat waves are projected to become worse as a result of climate change, especially in southern Ontario and southern Quebec. The recent arrival of West Nile Virus in Saskatchewan illustrates how new health-related risks are spreading north as the climate changes. In 2007 there were over 1,400 reported West Nile cases in Saskatchewan alone.[56]

The number of persons in the world forced to migrate for environmental reasons is now estimated to be at least 20 million people.[57] These decisions to relocate are often traumatic for the individuals involved. Not all of this migration is related to climate change, but a large part of it is, as a growing number of people face famines, floods and droughts that are directly connected to the changing climate. The United Nations forecasts that the number of environmental refugees will grow sharply over the next half century.

A local example of those severely impacted is the people of the Sundarbans, which lie where the Ganges and Brahmaputra Rivers enter into the Bay of Bengal. As the Himalayan glaciers melt they are causing river levels to rise. Lohachara island in the Sundarbans went beneath the waves in 2006 leaving over 7,000 residents homeless. Ghoramara island has lost one third of its land mass in half a decade. Sagar island has become home to 20,000 refugees as a result of the rising tides.[58]

RECENT WARNING SIGNS

Since the data base used by the UN Intergovernmental Panel on Climate Change to reach the conclusions in its early 2007 reports was compiled, there have been additional warning signs that climate change is accelerating.

For example, in the summer of 2007 Arctic sea ice melted to an unprecedented degree, causing NASA scientists to sharply move up their predictions about how soon the Arctic would be ice free. Greenland's ice sheet melted an estimated 17 billion tonnes more than the previous high mark.[59] "The Arctic is screaming" Mark Serreze, senior scientist at the U.S. government's snow and ice data centre in Boulder, Colorado was quoted as saying to The Associated Press.[60] The increased melting means that there will be less ice to reflect sunlight and more open ocean water that absorbs the heat of the sun, thus further accelerating the melting of ice and the vulnerability of many species that depend on it. By some estimates, such as Louis Fortier, scientific director of the Canadian research network ArcticNet, there will be no sea ice left in the summer in the Arctic Ocean somewhere between 2010 and 2015.[61] These recent estimates are based on observations in the summer and fall of 2007. They differ significantly from the UN IPCC forecast in its report published early in 2007, which relied on data gathered in earlier years and stated: "Sea ice is projected to shrink in both the Arctic and Antarctic under all (emission) scenarios. In some projections, arctic late-summer sea ice disappears almost entirely by the latter part of the 21st century."[62]

A January 2008 study led by Timo Vesala at the University of Helsinki and encompassing more than 30 monitoring stations spread across northern regions, including Siberia, Canada, Alaska and Europe concluded, on the basis of more than two decades of data, that the ability of forests to soak up man-made carbon dioxide is weakening. Scientists had originally expected that as spring and autumn temperatures rise in northern latitudes, the longer growing season for plants would help more CO_2 to be absorbed, thus helping to somewhat mitigate greenhouse gas emissions. While there has indeed been more greening, the researchers who prepared the study concluded that the date in autumn at which forests switch from being a net sink for carbon to being a net source of carbon has actually gotten earlier.[63] The report's authors state this has the potential to result in a bigger warming effect.

In February 2008 an international team of scientists representing some of the world's most prestigious organizations warned that many regions of the world could reach a "point of no return" as a result of climate change. In addition to the complete melting of Arctic sea ice in summer months, they identified a 50% chance that the Greenland ice sheet will begin melting unstoppably. If temperature increases of 3–5°C occur, international scientists expressed concern about the fragility of the Amazon rainforests, where reduced rainfall could claim large areas of rainforest that will not re-establish itself. Other areas of extreme vulnerability at these temperatures include the northern Boreal forest, where large areas of forest could die off over the next half century and the Antarctic ice sheet which is vulnerable to melting. Also highly vulnerable to disruption are the Atlantic currents that power the Gulf Stream. The international scientists who prepared the forecasts expressed concern about the growing intensity of the El Nino climate system and the potential for collapse of the west African monsoon, both of which were included as potential tipping points in the future.[64]

The World Glacier Monitoring Service recently reported on the results of work by experts who have been monitoring 30 glaciers around the world for nearly three decades. Their most recent figures, for the year 2006, show the largest ever "net loss" of ice. Achim Steiner, head of the UN Environment Programme describes this as the "loudest and clearest" warning signal of global warming with huge implications including failing infrastructure, mass migration and even conflict.[65]

In April of 2008 Nicholas Stern, in an interview with the *Financial Times*, expressed concern that the damage risks facing the world are even larger than he had argued in his report to the U.K. government. Stern stated: "We underestimated the risks … we underestimated the damage associated with the temperature increases … and we underestimated the probability of temperature increases."[66]

Taken together, these recent forecasts suggest there is a growing urgency for provinces, states and countries to act decisively in reducing their greenhouse gas emissions as quickly as possible.

Saskatchewan, with its exceptionally high per capita emissions, has a special obligation to take concrete measures that will result in major reductions in the decade ahead.

IMPACTS OF CLIMATE CHANGE IN SASKATCHEWAN

Saskatchewan will not be exempt from the consequences of climate change. Projected impacts include more summer drought, with higher evaporation rates and lower soil moisture. It is also expected that Saskatchewan will face more severe weather events, including more intense precipitation events and more flooding. It is projected that as glaciers in the Rocky Mountains decline, there will be less water in the South Saskatchewan River during the later summer and early fall. Other expected changes include milder winters, a longer growing season and warmer, wetter winters and springs.[67]

To date Saskatchewan has not been hit with the severity of consequences that many other parts of the world have experienced. Nevertheless, Saskatchewan has experienced negative impacts of such a nature that they constitute warning signs that climate change is very likely an important causal factor. Most notable among these is an increase in the number of severe weather events striking Saskatchewan communities. For example, in 2005, 2006 and

2007, a record number of claims were paid out under Saskatchewan's Provincial Disaster Assistance Program.[68] Saskatchewan Government Insurance saw significantly increased damage claims from storms in 2005 and 2007.[69]

Many towns and villages in northeast Saskatchewan are beginning to reflect the global pattern of more intense flooding. Communities like Porcupine Plain and Arborfield faced exceptionally heavy flooding in 2005, 2006 and 2007, including many washed out bridges, widespread crop loss and serious infrastructure damage. More than 1,000 residents from Cumberland House had to be evacuated in 2005 when flooding threatened their community.[70] In 2007 the Fishing Lake and Waldsea Lake communities faced unprecedented flooding. A total of 520 cabins were damaged at Fishing Lake.[71] Rapidly rising flood waters forced 632 people to evacuate the Red Earth First Nation reserve in mid April 2007.[72]

While north east Saskatchewan faced serious flooding in 2005, 2006 and 2007, parts of southwest Saskatchewan faced serious drought in 2004, 2005 and 2006. Although events in any one year cannot be directly linked to climate change, the pattern of more intensive drought in some geographic areas, while adjacent areas experience more intensive flooding is an increasingly common occurrence around the world as the climate changes.[73]

One important institution that has been concerned about the prospect of more widespread drought on the prairies is The Prairie Adaptation Research Collaborative. It was created in the year 2000 as a joint climate change research initiative by the provincial governments in Manitoba, Saskatchewan and Alberta and the federal government in Ottawa. Its scientists predict the prairies will experience some of the largest temperature increases in Canada from climate change. The biggest expected impact is increased aridity.[74] The scientists predict more frequent extreme weather events, especially drought.

Scientists at the Prairie Adaptation Research Collaborative also point out that warmer, drier conditions are likely to mean more frequent and intense forest fires.[75] There is also the risk of more insect outbreaks. Major forest fires can be a significant threat to northern communities. For example, in June of 2006 a massive forest fire threatened the hamlets of Stony Rapids and Fond-du-Lac and forced the evacuation of over 800 people. By July 4, 2006 over 2,000 people north of La Ronge had been evacuated, a major disruption in the life of local residents. The pattern was repeated again in the summer of 2008. By July 4, 2008 more than 2,800 residents of northern Saskatchewan had been evacuated from their communities and the provincial total for forest fires in 2008 had risen to 464.[76]

An example of the increased risk of insect outbreak referred to by The Prairie Adaptation Research Collaborative is the threat of the mountain pine beetle spreading from British Columbia and Alberta into Saskatchewan's boreal forest. This has the potential to cause widespread damage to Saskatchewan's jack pine population. Such damage would quickly increase the fire risk in northern Saskatchewan communities adjacent to jack pine stands.[77]

An excellent analysis of projected climate change impacts in Canada was prepared by Natural Resources Canada in 2007 and is entitled *From Impacts to Adaptation: Canada in a Changing Climate 2007*. The Prairies section of that study, written by lead authors Dave Sauchyn and Suren Kulshreshtha provides a thorough analysis of predicted impacts on the Prairies that is very relevant for Saskatchewan residents. The climate change scenario maps for Saskatchewan in this report show median projections in the range of a 6°C increase in mean annual temperature by the 2080s.[78] Precipitation is expected to increase, particularly in the winter and spring. The authors conclude that "Temperature scenarios are similar for the forest and grassland regions, but increases in precipitation are larger for the northern forest."[79]

Sauchyn and Kulshreshtha note that to date prairie resource management practices and policies "reflect a perception of relatively abundant water supplies and ecological resources within a relatively stationary environment." They conclude: "Future water and ecosystem management will have to abandon the assumption of a stationary environment, given the longer perspective from climate models and paleoenvironmental data, and the projected shifts in climate variability, biodiversity, disturbance regimes and distribution of water resources and ecological services."[80] In their paper they discuss the prospect that the Prairies will face a higher probability of extreme conditions, including greater frequency of severe drought and of flooding.

Drawing on the experience of the Prairie droughts of 2001 and 2002, the authors note the severe repercussions of drought. For example, agricultural production on the Prairies dropped by $3.6 billion during the 2001 and 2002 drought years. Net farm income was negative in Saskatchewan in 2002. Severe wind erosion events occurred, despite the improvements in conservation tillage.[81] Drought creates financial stress for many families and communities. It also increases other risks such as a much greater potential for wildfires.

Flooding in Saskatchewan has not only been a major problem for smaller communities, but has also hit some cities hard. For example, many Saskatoon homes were flooded during 2005 and 2007 when the city was hit with some of the heaviest downpours it has ever experienced.[82] Sauchyn and Kulshreshtha predict that flood control could become a significant climate related concern for many prairie cities. The authors observe that "Many (city) neighborhoods are located in flood-prone areas and existing risk management approaches are often inadequate."[83]

Sauchyn's and Kulshreshtha's analysis discusses a wide range of impacts from climate change in this century. Not all are negative. For example, Saskatchewan agriculture could experience benefits from milder winters and a longer growing season. There may be fewer weather-related accidents and fatalities. Costs incurred for snow and ice removal could decline.

A number of fundamental changes to prairie ecosystems predicted by the authors should concern us all. Reductions in stream flow as a result of climate change are likely to worsen water quality. Aquatic ecosystems will be stressed by drier conditions and many aquatic species are at risk of extirpation. Migratory waterfowl populations are likely to be negatively impacted. Soil landscapes will be negatively impacted. Increases in aridity will likely result in more widespread wind erosion.[84] Sauchyn and Kulshreshtha note that the semiarid to subhumid mixed grassland ecoregion of the Prairies "is at risk of desertification."[85] This is an area that encompasses approximately 200,000 square kilometers.

Aboriginal communities in Saskatchewan are vulnerable to the risks of climate change. The authors report on observations by elders who have identified trends of concern including that extreme weather events, such as tornadoes and hailstorms are occurring more often in recent years. Elders have also observed "a general imbalance in nature, reflected in the condition of wildlife and inferred from abnormal wildlife behaviour" This includes changes in population ranges and migration patterns.[86] The study concludes that: "Impacts of climate change have implications for flora and fauna, and declines or annual uncertainties in the availability of moose, caribou, deer, fish and wild rice will increase dependence on imported foods, with both economic and health implications for (aboriginal) residents."[87]

Climate change in Saskatchewan also poses a great deal of uncertainty for forest based communities and for the future of our national parks. For example, Sauchyn and Kulshreshtha note: "In forest regions, there will be a general reduction in tree growth, regeneration failure in dry years and a gradual reduction in tree cover and expansion of grassland patches."[88] They go on to say: "Climate change will be significant in all of the prairie-parkland national parks… These parks can expect increases in forest fire frequency and intensity, increased forest disease outbreaks and insect infestations, and loss of boreal forest to grassland and temperate forest."[89]

The projected impacts discussed here have major implications for future public investment that will be required in order to adapt to climate change and mitigate its worst consequences. Examples of provincial government adaptation measures might include installation of infrastructure aimed at flood prevention or a larger staff contingent within government to assist communities in responding to disasters that are beyond their capacity to deal with. While not the focus of this paper, adaptation investments should become an important part of Saskatchewan budget planning in the future. This paper will now focus on the politics of climate change and the public policy that is required to prevent its worst consequences from occurring.

THE UNEQUAL IMPACT OF CLIMATE CHANGE CONSEQUENCES

What is striking about comparing the above mentioned global impacts of climate change with the Saskatchewan impacts is that the consequences, at least in the short run, are far more severe for many other parts of the world. This difference in impacts becomes even more dramatic when comparing the consequences for developed countries and developing countries. This is not to minimize impacts in developed countries, but rather to emphasize how very severe impacts are on many poorer nations where there is greater vulnerability and less adaptive capacity.

The United Nations Development Program estimated in November 2007 that one in 19 people in developing countries are vulnerable to climate shocks. UNDP stated: "The most vulnerable people contribute the least to global emissions and are paying a high price for the actions of others."[90] This message was reinforced by Dr. Margaret Chan, World Health Organization Director General in April 2008. She stated: "Although climate change is a global phenomenon, its consequences will not be evenly distributed… In short, climate change can affect problems that are already huge, largely concentrated in the developing world, and difficult to control."[91]

From the point of view of residents in parts of the world such as sub-Saharan Africa, Bangladesh or small island states that are threatened with massive flooding, climate change is not just an urgent issue, but rather is a matter of survival. It is an international emergency. This is certain to influence the politics of discussions at the United Nations in the decades ahead.

A second unequal impact is the implications that climate change has for economic development in the developing countries. Developing countries have every right to improve their standard of living. Yet if this is done using conventional fossil fuel applications, it will have devastating environmental consequences. Fortunately, many environmentally sustainable technologies exist that can be successfully applied to better the lives of persons living in developing countries. There is a huge moral responsibility on the industrialized countries to share those environmentally sustainable technologies at very low cost with the rest of the world.

THE ECONOMIC COST OF FIGHTING CLIMATE CHANGE

Only a sharp reduction in greenhouse gas emissions will mitigate the risks that climate change poses for the global community.

What is the economic cost associated with reducing greenhouse gas emissions significantly enough to avoid the worst consequences of climate change? How does this compare with the financial cost of doing nothing and suffering the economic damage caused by climate change?

Olav Kjorven, assistant secretary general and bureau director for development policy at the United Nations Development Program (UNDP) estimates costs at 1% to 2% of global GDP. In a 2007 statement UNDP estimated an annual expenditure of $86 billion is needed to address the required reductions in global emissions.[92]

Nicholas Stern, as former Chief Economist for the World Bank is also well placed to assess this. In his landmark 2006 report for the Government of the United Kingdom he concluded.

"Using the results from formal economic models, the Review estimates that if we don't act, the overall costs and risks of climate change will be equivalent to losing at least 5% of global GDP (Gross Domestic Product) each year, now and forever. If a wider range of risks and impacts is taken into account, the estimates of damage could rise to 20% of GDP or more. In contrast, the costs of action—reducing greenhouse gas emissions to avoid the worst impacts of climate change—can be limited to around 1% of global GDP each year. The investment that takes place in the next 10–20 years will have a profound effect on the climate in the second half of this century and in the next."[93]

Stern's 2006 cost estimates were based on preventing global carbon dioxide equivalent levels in the atmosphere rising above 550ppm (ppm).[94]

However, speaking in London in June 2008 at the launch of the Carbon Rating Agency, the world's first rating agency for carbon offsetting projects, Stern expressed concern that climate change is happening even faster than had been previously thought. Accordingly, he made the case that greenhouse gas emissions in the atmosphere need to be kept below 500ppm. This requires a greater level of expenditure. He estimated the global cost of accomplishing that at 2% of global Gross Domestic Product each year—double his previous estimate. He also warned that limiting costs to that amount required governments to act quickly. "All this depends on good policy and well functioning (carbon) markets" he said.[95]

A third cost estimate has been provided in a major July 2008 report by PricewaterhouseCoopers. The accountancy firm stated its cost projections are broadly in line with the June 2008 estimates of Nicholas Stern, although slightly higher. It estimated the ultimate cost of a 50% reduction in global carbon emissions by 2050 at approximately 3% of global economic growth. John Hawksworth, the Head of Macroeconomics at PriceWaterhouseCoopers stated "This is broadly equivalent to sacrificing around a year of global GDP growth between now and 2050."[96] Hawksworth's comments underline the fact that many expenditures to reduce greenhouse gas emissions can prove to be cost effective investments by providing returns in energy savings. PricewaterhouseCoopers proposed that G7 countries (G8 minus Russia) would need to cut their carbon emissions by 80% by 2050 to make their contribution to the 50% cut in global emissions.

THE KYOTO PROTOCOL

While there has been a growing consensus on the realities of climate change and the urgency of reducing greenhouse gas emissions in the scientific community, there has been much less agreement in political circles.

Deep political divisions were evident in North America from the outset in the debate over whether to adopt the Kyoto Protocol.

The Kyoto Protocol is a first step to reducing greenhouse gas emissions. It is the only international treaty the world has agreed upon to address climate change. It includes six greenhouse gases in its monitoring and regulatory framework, the three critical ones that we have been discussing in this chapter, which account for almost 99% of total emissions, and the fluorinated gases (HFC's, PFC's and SF6) which account for just over 1% of emissions.[97] All major developed countries except for Australia and the United States had ratified the Kyoto Protocol by the time it came into force on February 16, 2005.[98] (Shortly after the election of the Labour Party in 2007, Australia also ratified the Kyoto Protocol.[99])

In the United States the Kyoto Protocol had been supported by President

Bill Clinton and Vice President Al Gore. The Clinton administration signed the treaty, but had not yet ratified it at the time of the 2000 Presidential election. With the election win of George W. Bush over Al Gore, the United States position on Kyoto changed to one of strong opposition to the Kyoto Protocol. Republican opposition to the Kyoto Protocol at the national level in the United States has remained consistent throughout President Bush's time in office.

The Government of Canada ratified the Kyoto Protocol on December 17, 2002.[100] It was one of the last major decisions made by Liberal Prime Minister Jean Chretien. Upon ratification Canada promised the international community that it would reduce greenhouse gas emissions 6% below national 1990 levels by the period 2008–12.

There was strong opposition to Kyoto from many quarters including the federal Canadian Alliance Party under the leadership of Stephen Harper.[101] In Saskatchewan the Kyoto Protocol was strongly opposed by the Saskatchewan Party.

THE SASKATCHEWAN DEBATE OVER KYOTO

In December 2002 the Saskatchewan Legislature debated the Kyoto Protocol for several days. Saskatchewan Party Leader Elwin Hermanson made his opposition to the Kyoto Protocol clear from the outset. On December 10, 2002 Mr. Hermanson stated: "But the problem, Mr. Speaker, is that the Kyoto Protocol, the Kyoto accord, is a flawed agreement. It's an impossible agreement, Mr. Speaker… . It's very clear—Kyoto cannot work… The Premier of Ontario has spoken out against the Kyoto Protocol, and his province has taken a position against Kyoto because obviously the auto industry, which employs hundreds of thousands of people, is at risk if Kyoto is approved. But here in Saskatchewan, where industries like agriculture, our resource-based industries, are hanging in the balance, IPSCO is hanging in the balance, where is the Premier of Saskatchewan?"[102]

Brad Wall, MLA for Swift Current presented several petitions opposing the Kyoto Protocol in the Legislature. On December 11, 2002 he reiterated his opposition to the Kyoto Protocol as follows: "Combine that with what the Premier of the province of Saskatchewan said, which is that he likes Kyoto in principle and that he wouldn't join any sort of a court challenge put forward by the province of Alberta and then ask yourself, Mr. Speaker, why those businessmen and women in this province, in my hometown, with all of their employees, would have any faith at all that an NDP government was interested in their issue, was interested in defending them, that an NDP government was prepared to fight for them. Mr. Speaker, they don't believe it. That's why they signed the petition… . Well the Minister of the Environment says there are no mixed messages. Then why won't he and his colleagues stand up and send a united message that they oppose the ratification of Kyoto, Mr. Speaker? Why don't they support our amendment?"[103]

Several Saskatchewan Party Members of the Legislature questioned during the debate whether climate change is even occurring. For example, Lyle

Stewart, Saskatchewan Party MLA for Thunder Creek stated on December 10, 2002: "The most common greenhouse gases are carbon dioxide and methane. Both are naturally occurring in our atmosphere.... The issue is the concentrations of these gases beyond natural levels may cause global warming, not that the scientific community can even agree as to whether or not any global warming is occurring outside of normal cyclic temperature swings, or if so, if it is man made or caused by natural events."[104]

In contrast, the NDP government took a position of support for the targets and principles of the Kyoto Protocol, while criticizing the federal government's implementation plan and lack of consultation with provincial governments and industry. Under questioning by Lyle Stewart in the Assembly, Premier Calvert stated: "I repeat, this government from day one has accepted its responsibility to share in building a sane and clean environment for the future. We take that responsibility very seriously. Our battle is not with the principle of Kyoto. Our battle is with a federal Liberal government who has refused from day one to participate with the provinces of Canada, with industry of Canada, with the people of Canada in building a strong implementation plan."[105] The Calvert government introduced a motion that "recognize(d) that climate change is a critical issue facing, Saskatchewan, Canada and the world" and expressing support for "the 12 principles adopted by the provinces and territories as a basis for negotiating a national climate change plan with the Government of Canada to address the Kyoto Protocol target of reducing national greenhouse gas emissions to 6 per cent below 1990 levels by 2012."[106] The 12 conditions agreed to by the provinces and territories were outlined by Industry Minister Eldon Lautermilch in the Assembly and included the principle that "no region or jurisdiction shall be asked to bear an unreasonable share of the burden and no industry, sector, or region shall be treated unfairly."[107] This motion was adopted on December 11, 2007 with NDP government members supporting it and Saskatchewan Party members opposing it.[108]

ACTIONS TAKEN IN SASKATCHEWAN TO ADDRESS
GREENHOUSE GAS EMISSIONS SINCE THE SIGNING OF THE KYOTO PROTOCOL

In the ensuing years Premier Lorne Calvert's government took several steps intended to address climate change. Between 2002 and 2006 the provincial government, largely through SaskPower, developed 171.2 megawatts of wind power, or about 5% of SaskPower's total electrical capacity.[109] It used wind power, demand side management and an Environmentally Preferred Power Program to meet electrical load growth in the 2001–07 period. It established an active Office of Energy Conservation. It worked with municipal governments and school boards to make their facilities more energy efficient. It implemented a 7.5% ethanol blend for automotive gasoline sold in Saskatchewan. A provincial sales tax rebate was introduced to encourage the purchase of energy efficient appliances. Five million trees were planted in the Porcupine Provincial Forest as part of a carbon sequestration agreement between SaskPower and Saskatchewan Environment. In late 2003 the Province adopted a stringent energy efficiency code for public buildings, requiring that schools, hospitals, provincial government buildings and all other construction that was built with 30% or more provincial funds must be built to an energy efficiency standard 25% better than the Model National Energy Code for Buildings. The Province invested $5 million over a 5-year period in upgrading the energy efficiency of its seniors housing portfolio.[110] The Calvert government provided financial assistance to homeowners for energy efficiency upgrades in 2005 and maintained the program even when the federal government withdrew funding in 2006. Between November 2005 and February 2007 more than 6,000 homeowners received provincial grants averaging $773 and undertook work that reduced their emissions by an average of 3.66 tonnes annually.[111] Finally, in 2005 Premier Calvert set a goal of achieving one third of Saskatchewan's energy from renewable energy sources by the third decade of the century and leading Canada in energy conservation practices.[112]

Saskatchewan's energy conservation efforts were recognized by the Canadian Energy Efficiency Alliance, Canada's leading non-governmental, energy efficiency advocacy organization. In its National Report Card on Energy Efficiency Across Canada for the year 2005, it graded the Saskatchewan government's efforts at a B minus and noted "Saskatchewan made gains again this year. The turnaround in 4 years is impressive."[113]

However, throughout these years the Province lacked a comprehensive climate change strategy with well defined emission reduction targets. Nor was there the necessary partnership and funding from the Government of Canada. Without such a well defined provincial and national plan, provincial greenhouse gas emissions continued to increase, especially in the face of a booming oil and gas industry. The growth of the economy received more attention from elected MLAs and officials than did the matter of reducing greenhouse gas emissions. Public opinion polling also showed the development of the Saskatchewan economy ranked more highly than the environment, when it came to where the Saskatchewan government should devote its attention. Moreover, the lead provincial department on climate change was the Department of Industry and Resources, a group of officials far more focused on economic development than on environmental protection.

The last year of the NDP's tenure saw a major shift in direction with the provincial government adopting a much more aggressive climate change strategy and earmarking significant dollars for a reduction of greenhouse gas emissions. This change was primarily driven by the elected members of government. Premier Calvert made it one of his top priorities. The Premier announced a provincial government target of a 32% reduction in greenhouse gas emissions from 2004 levels by 2020, the equivalent of a 22 tonne reduction per person in Saskatchewan.[114] The Province also committed to an 80% reduction in 2004 levels of greenhouse gas emissions by 2050. To help achieve the goal, Premier Calvert sold the Provincial Government's share in the New Grade heavy oil upgrader in Regina and used the bulk of the money to establish a Green Future's Fund intended to advance implementation of Saskatchewan's Climate Change Plan. The Fund included $100 million for energy conservation and efficiency, and $75 million to help increase the use of renewable energy. An additional $125 million was dedicated to developing carbon capture and storage technologies and $20 million was allocated to help correct the serious problem of methane emissions in the oil, gas and agricultural sectors of the Saskatchewan economy.[115]

The first nine months of 2007 were marked by a wide variety of other initiatives aimed at promoting energy conservation, promoting renewable energy, cutting greenhouse gas emissions and increasing public awareness of climate change impacts. Premier Calvert extended a personal invitation to former Vice President Al Gore to come to Regina to give a public address on climate change. He also organized the Premier's Forum on Climate Change, a full day event intended to enhance public awareness and discuss potential solutions. In the spring of 2007 a farm energy audit program was launched. The NDP government also expanded the Residential Energy Conservation Program (Energuide for Houses) to include electricity conservation and domestic hot water measures. The maximum provincial grant under the program was increased from $2,000 to $5,000 per homeowner.[116] A $1,000 provincial incentive was established for homeowners who purchase super energy efficient new homes (Energy Star or R-2000) in Saskatchewan. A provincial grant of $1,000 was also established for those who install solar hot water technology.[117] At the instruction of Premier Calvert, SaskPower adopted net metering for small scale producers of green, low impact electricity, allowing customers to own a small scale renewable electricity source of up to 100 kw and sell surplus renewable electricity to the provincial grid at a rate identical to the retail price at which that customer buys electricity from the grid. This policy increased the financial benefits of installing renewable electricity generation systems. As a further incentive, the Province provided financial assistance for net metering customers to purchase and install solar photovoltaic systems, small wind power systems and other renewable energy technologies, covering up to 25% of costs, including the costs of a bi-directional meter and a grid integration study.[118] SaskPower was asked to pursue an electricity conservation program with Ministers announcing a target of 300 MW electricity saving by 2017 and expenditures of $2.4 million in 2007 and $7.1 million in 2008.[119] As a first step SaskPower proceeded with mass distribution of compact fluorescent light bulbs at high profile retail locations such as Home Depot. 15,000 free compact florescent light bulbs were distributed free of charge over the summer of 2007.

In 2007 the Calvert government also published a comprehensive plan for reducing greenhouse gas emissions. In addition to the above mentioned measures, the 2007 Saskatchewan Energy and Climate Change Plan covered a wide array of planned initiatives. Key elements included:

- Ensuring all of SaskPower's new and replacement electricity generation facilities would be either emission-free or fully offset by emission credits;

- Developing corridors in Saskatchewan in which E-85 fuel

blends would be available and establishing a 1.4 billion litre biofuels industry;

• Implementing a government vehicle purchase policy that required all government vehicles to be hybrid-electric, alternative or flex fuel, or within the top 20% efficiency in their class;

• Plans to establish agricultural soil sinks to remove over 25 million tonnes of carbon dioxide equivalent annually from the atmosphere by 2012;

• Reforestation of 20,000 hectares by 2017, storing the equivalent of 4.9 million tonnes of carbon dioxide equivalent in regenerated forest lands;

• A plan to work with SIAST and regional colleges to create training opportunities in energy efficiency retrofit, solar, wind and biomass applications;

• Plans to establish a standard at least 30% better than the Model National Energy Code for all new government buildings.[120]

In the last months of the Calvert government, Cabinet approved a new supply decision for electrical generation over the period 2010–14. This included several environmentally friendly initiatives, including another 100 megawatts of wind power by 2012, 50 megawatts of electrical generation using waste heat recovery at natural gas compressor stations by 2010, 20 megawatts of biomass produced electricity by 2010 and a solicitation of Environmentally Preferred Power Projects from the private sector.[121] The plan also included up to 400 MW of simple cycle natural gas fired generation.

The provincial government launched new programs for business and municipal government. It allocated $700,000 per year to help fund new solar water heating systems in business, industry, multiple unit residential buildings of over three stories, hospitals, schools and municipal facilities. A municipal energy efficiency initiative was launched providing $400,000 per year for municipal lighting upgrades, solar water heating for municipal swimming pools and energy efficiency upgrades to curling and skating rinks.[122]

Finally, the Calvert government announced in early September the establishment of a Climate Change Secretariat that would provide the leadership and focus required to meet Saskatchewan's greenhouse gas reduction targets.

The progress made during 2007 led the Canadian Energy Efficiency Alliance to increase the Saskatchewan government's grade to a B plus, when issuing its "National Energy Efficiency Report Card on Government Activities."[123]

The election of Premier Brad Wall on November 7, 2007 resulted in some immediate changes to public policies that impact on climate change. One of the new government's first steps was to cancel the vast bulk of funds dedicated to the $320 million Green Futures Fund.[124] It thus dismantled an essential financial mechanism for implementing public policies aimed at reducing Saskatchewan greenhouse gas emissions.

By February of 2008 Premier Wall's government had removed the *Saskatchewan Energy And Climate Change Plan 2007* from its government's website. At the time of writing, no clearly defined policy direction has replaced this plan.

In another symbolic measure of policy change, Premier Wall's government closed the provincial Office of Energy Conservation that had been started under Premier Calvert in 2002.[125]

The Saskatchewan Party government also scrapped the newly formed Climate Change Secretariat.[126]

At first, Premier Wall kept in place the former NDP government's target of stabilizing greenhouse gas emissions by 2010 and achieving a 32% reduction in 2004 Saskatchewan greenhouse gas emissions by 2020. However, at the time of writing, this target is very much in question. In October 2008 Environment Minister Hon. Nancy Heppner indicated the Saskatchewan Party government may drop the 32% provincial greenhouse gas reduction target in favour of federal targets (which at the time aimed for a 20% greenhouse gas reduction below 2006 levels by 2020).[127] Premier Wall indicated another option could be moving to a model similar to that of Alberta.[128] In both cases, Saskatchewan's reduction targets would become much less stringent.

Premier Brad Wall has indicated an interest in pursuing a nuclear power plant in Saskatchewan, an electricity generation option that had not been prioritized by the previous NDP government because of concerns with high construction costs, reactor decommissioning problems and the unresolved problem of disposing of high level radioactive waste. Premier Wall has advocated the idea of small scale nuclear reactors for electricity generation and has expressed interest in the possibility of applying nuclear energy in the oil sands.[129] The new Premier is also advocating a uranium enrichment plant, a facility that if built would consume an enormous amount of additional electricity.[130] Such plants are also controversial because they give the nations who possess them the technical capacity to enrich uranium for nuclear weapons purposes.

Saskatchewan Party government ministers have also signaled support for the nuclear power option. Hon. Ken Cheveldayoff, Crown Corporations Minister in the new Saskatchewan Party government stated five months after taking office: "Every couple of months SaskPower is getting increased requests from its customers for energy demands and it makes the case for a nuclear situation in the province that much stronger." He described the chances of a nuclear reactor in Saskatchewan as "enhanced."[131] Shortly thereafter, he and Energy and Resources Minister Bill Boyd publicly welcomed an expression of interest by the Ontario based company Bruce Power to look at Saskatchewan as a potential nuclear reactor site and signaled his government's desire to see the private sector develop a nuclear reactor in Saskatchewan. In response to questions about Bruce Power's interest, Minister Cheveldayoff said: "The model we would like to follow is to entertain ideas from the private

sector to bring their money, their capital, their knowledge to Saskatchewan...
We're more interested from SaskPower's point of view in being a power pur-
chaser so we can meet the demand gap that's being created here in
Saskatchewan ... we would say the expertise regarding nuclear power is with
the Bruce Power's and Cameco's of the world."[132] On June 17, 2008 Bruce
Power Chief Executive Officer Duncan Hawthorne announced a formal feasibility study into a nuclear power plant in Saskatchewan. He was joined at a
high profile news conference by Enterprise and Innovation Minister Hon. Lyle
Stewart and Crown Corporations Minister Hon. Ken Cheveldayoff, who characterized the nuclear energy route as an effective way to lower Saskatchewan
greenhouse gas emissions.133

While there have been important shifts in direction, there are also several
areas where the new Saskatchewan Party government is taking a direction
that is similar to the one the NDP had pursued. For example, Premier Wall has
indicated an ongoing commitment to pursue clean coal technology (carbon
capture and storage).[134] The NDP government had shown enthusiasm for a
SaskPower clean coal project, until a short time before the 2007 provincial election when it announced a delay in plans to proceed because of escalating projected construction costs. The Saskatchewan Party Government has shown
less hesitation to proceed despite the cost issues. On February 27, 2008
Saskatchewan Party Crown Corporations Minister Hon. Ken Cheveldayoff
announced plans to move forward with a $1.4 billion clean coal project that
involves the retrofit of one of SaskPower's coal fired generation units at
Boundary Dam.[135] In August 2008 SaskPower issued a Request for Proposals
for carbon capture technology at the Boundary Dam site.[136]

Premier Wall has maintained the net metering policy introduced by the
New Democrats and to date has maintained the grants available to homeowners and other small scale producers of renewable energy. The Premier has also
maintained support for biofuels and promised in the November 2007 general
election that in addition to the NDP mandate for an ethanol blend in gasoline,
he would introduce a mandate for biodiesel in all diesel sold in
Saskatchewan.[137] In April of 2008 Premier Wall's government announced a
new initiative to support drivers of low emission vehicles with a 20% rebate
on SGI insurance and registration fees for hybrid cars and super fuel efficient
vehicles. Approximately 3400 SGI customers are expected to receive rebates.[138]
In September 2008 Crown Investments Corporation Minister Ken
Cheveldayoff announced SaskPower would partner with Project Porchlight to
continue and expand the distribution of free compact florescent light bulbs
across Saskatchewan.[139] SaskPower has also continued the process of encouraging waste heat recovery projects at natural gas compressor stations.

On the matter of oil sands development, Premier Wall has clearly endorsed
the pursuit of oil sands development in northern Saskatchewan. The former
NDP government had allowed permits to be issued for oil sands exploration in
the northwest part of the province. One month after his election, on December
12, 2007 Premier Wall committed to encourage development of Saskatchewan's
oil sands resource.[140] Given Alberta's experience with oil sands development,

a large oil sands project in Saskatchewan would inevitably mean another
significant increase in Saskatchewan's greenhouse gas emissions.

Where Premier Wall appears to be going much further than the former NDP
administration is on his apparent willingness to relax environmental regulations on new oil sands investment. For example, in a keynote address to the
FirstEnergy East Coast Canadian Energy Conference in New York City he signaled a willingness to seek a Saskatchewan exemption from federal government
environmental regulations governing the oil sands. In that speech he said:

> The federal government will allow some grandfathering *up to
> 2012* for oils sands projects that are operating before then,
> before they really get onerous with regulations. It's a concern
> to us, as we do not yet have a commercial oil sands project in
> place in Saskatchewan. We want one, and frankly, that dead-
> line wouldn't work for us. So we're going to work very close-
> ly with the federal government—we've developed a bit of a
> positive relationship there—to ensure there are some
> Saskatchewan exemptions.[141]

In the autumn of 2008, when Prime Minister Harper proposed to ban the
export of raw oil sands bitumen to countries whose greenhouse gas emission
standards are below Canada's, Premier Wall vowed to oppose such a policy.[142]

THE BALI CLIMATE CHANGE CONFERENCE
AND A CONSENSUS ON STIFFER GHG REDUCTION TARGETS

Saskatchewan's and Canada's climate change policies will inevitably be influenced by negotiations in the international arena, especially negotiations
among the countries that are party to the Kyoto Protocol. For example, in
December 2007 the 38 developed countries who are party to the Kyoto
Protocol met in Bali, Indonesia and agreed to plan for reductions in greenhouse gases of 25% to 40% below 1990 levels. It was agreed the target date for
this reduction would be 2020.[143] The detailed planning is still to follow, but this
reduction range is far deeper than Canada's existing Kyoto obligation of a 6%
reduction from 1990 emission levels by 2008–12. In Bali, the Canadian government resisted the new targets, but soon found itself isolated.[144] These newly
agreed upon targets by Kyoto signatories will form the foundation for negotiating a post-Kyoto Protocol agreement.

For the year 2006 Canadian greenhouse gas emissions were 721 megatonnes
of carbon dioxide equivalent, 22% above Canada's 1990 levels (592 megatonnes). This level of emissions is 29.1% above what is required to comply with
the Kyoto target for 2008–12 (558.4 megatonnes).[145] In order to comply with
even the low end range of the Bali targets (ie: a 25% reduction below 1990 levels by 2020), the Government of Canada would need to work together with
provinces, municipalities and the private sector to roughly halve Canadian
emissions over the next 12 years.

Saskatchewan per capita emissions are already three times higher than average per capita emissions across Canada. In this context, there can be little doubt that if Saskatchewan wishes to do its share in achieving the Bali GHG reduction targets, it would need to set an even stiffer provincial target for emissions reductions. Instead of the Province signaling that Saskatchewan's 32% reduction target for 2020 might be weakened, the focus should be on strengthening it.

To date, there is no evidence that Prime Minister Harper intends to try to comply with either the Kyoto targets or the new Bali targets. The federal government continues to target a 20% reduction below 2006 levels by 2020.[146]

ACHIEVING A LARGE-SCALE REDUCTION
IN SASKATCHEWAN GREENHOUSE GAS EMISSIONS

What then is required by way of public policy in Saskatchewan to achieve at least a 32% reduction in 2004 GHG emissions by 2020? The financial incentive programs adopted in 2007 and 2008 are a useful start. Several of the other measures originally proposed in the 2007 Energy and Climate Change Plan also have merit. However, these initiatives would at best only get Saskatchewan part of the way there. The remainder of this chapter discusses public policies that have been advocated by the Mitigation Working Group (Working Group 3) of the Intergovernmental Panel on Climate Change. It also examines conservation and renewable energy policies that have been adopted in other parts of North America and Western Europe that could be applied in Saskatchewan.

Due to space constraints, the buildings sector and electricity sector are used as the primary examples of how large scale emissions reductions could be moved forward. These two sectors have been chosen because they touch the day to day lives of every Saskatchewan resident. Some illustrations in the transport sector are also provided.

The United Nations Intergovernmental Panel on Climate Change (IPCC) has examined key mitigation technologies and practices that are currently commercially available in each of the major sectors of the global economy. By way of example, the sector where global growth in greenhouse gases has been the most rapid is the energy supply sector (145% increase in GHG emissions from 1970–2004).[147] Technologies identified by the IPCC as commercially available to reduce emissions in the energy supply sector include: "improved supply and distribution efficiency; fuel switching from coal to gas; nuclear power; renewable heat and power (hydropower, solar, wind, geothermal and bioenergy); combined heat and power; (and) early applications of Carbon Capture and Storage (CCS)"[148]

Upon examination of these commercially available technologies, the IPCC concludes:

> It is often more cost-effective to invest in end-use energy efficiency improvement than in increasing energy supply to

satisfy demand for energy services... Renewable energy generally has a positive effect on energy supply, employment and
on air quality. Given costs relative to other supply options,
renewable electricity, which accounted for 18% of the electricity supply in 2005, can have a 30–35% share of the total electricity supply in 2030 at carbon prices up to 50U.S.$/tCO2-
eq... . Given costs relative to other supply options, nuclear
power, which accounted for 16% of the electricity supply in
2005, can have an 18% share of the total electricity supply in
2030 at carbon prices up to 50US$/tonCO2eq, but safety,
weapons proliferation and waste remain as constraints. CCS in
underground geological formations is a new technology with
the potential to make an important contribution to mitigation
by 2030. Technical, economic and regulatory developments
will affect the actual contribution.[149]

Finally, the IPCC expresses concern that "higher priced conventional oil
resources ... may be replaced by high carbon alternatives such as from oil
sands, oil shales, heavy oils and synthetic fuels from coal and gas, leading to
increasing GHG emissions unless production plants are equipped with CCS
(Carbon Capture and Storage)"[150]

These United Nations IPCC conclusions have important implications for
Western Canadian energy policy. They particularly point to the desirability of
a focus on energy efficiency and renewable electricity. They point to some of
the disadvantages and limitations of the nuclear power option. They express
particular concern regarding the prospect of more conventional oil sands
development because of the resulting increase in greenhouse gas emissions.

The IPCC lists the following commercially available GHG mitigation technologies for buildings: "Efficient lighting and daylighting; more efficient electrical appliances and heating and cooling devices; improved cook stoves,
improved insulation; passive and active solar design for heating and cooling;
alternative refrigeration fluids, recovery and recycle of fluorinated gases."[151]
The IPCC draws the following conclusions:

By 2030, about 30% of the projected GHG emissions in the
buildings sector can be avoided with net economic benefit.
Energy efficient buildings, while limiting the growth of CO_2
emissions, can also improve indoor and outdoor air quality,
improve social welfare and enhance energy security.
Opportunities for realizing GHG reductions in the buildings
sector exist worldwide. However, multiple barriers make it
difficult to realize this potential. These barriers include availability of technology, financing, poverty, higher costs of reliable information, limitations inherent in building designs and
an appropriate portfolio of policies and programs.[152]

What types of policies and instruments need to be applied by government in order to spur the application of commercially available mitigation technologies? The IPCC identifies eight. These include:

 • Integrating climate policies in broader development policies;

 • Use of regulations and standards;

 • Taxes and charges that set a price for carbon;

 • Tradable permits which establish a carbon price. The IPCC notes that "the volume of allowed emissions determines their environmental effectiveness";

 • Financial incentives (subsidies and tax credits) … used by governments to stimulate the development and diffusion of new technologies;

 • Voluntary agreements between industry and government;" to accelerate the use of best available technology, thereby reducing emissions;

 • Information instruments (eg: awareness campaigns) … promoting informed choices and possibly contributing to behavioural change;

 • R&D (research and development) can stimulate technological advances, reduce costs and enable progress towards stabilization.;"[153]

This IPCC framework provides a useful start when putting together a comprehensive climate change strategy for Saskatchewan. Analytical work can be approached on a sector by sector basis, taking account of commercially available mitigation technologies in each sector and assessing which policies/instruments could be most effectively used to advance them. The IPCC analysis can be supplemented by the recent experience of governments around the world in the practical application of policies that promote greenhouse gas mitigation.

It is clear from the IPCC analysis that energy efficiency and renewable energy applications have very large potential for reducing greenhouse gas emissions in both the electricity generation and buildings sector. I will therefore begin by looking at these opportunities and how they might be applied in Saskatchewan.

In examining these opportunities I have particularly focused on five of the eight IPCC policy instruments: use of regulations and standards, financial incentives, voluntary agreements, information instruments, and research and development. I have also added other instruments such as: use of legislation to remandate policy direction, government leadership by example, and the role of education and training.

By way of background, in 2004, electricity production accounted for approximately 24% of Saskatchewan's greenhouse gas emissions, while residential and commercial space and hot water heating accounted for 6% of total provincial emissions.[154]

USING LEGISLATION TO SET A NEW DIRECTION IN ENERGY AND CLIMATE CHANGE POLICY

Changes in the law can play an important role in setting new direction. Some jurisdictions, such as the state of California, are setting legal requirements for total state-wide greenhouse gas reductions that must be achieved. In the area of electricity generation, the European Union and more than 20 U.S. states have set requirements for how much electricity must be generated from renewable sources by a given date, most commonly 2020 or 2025.[155] Following these examples, the Saskatchewan Legislature could adopt its own province wide greenhouse gas reduction target in law and could require by law that SaskPower achieve a much higher percentage of its electricity from renewable energy sources by 2025.

Legislation could also be used to change the mission of Crown Corporations so that their operations become more focused on environmental sustainability. For example, the mandate of SaskPower could be changed so as to "give first priority to electricity conservation as a source of energy and second priority to the adoption of renewable sources of electricity generation." Other options would then only be considered when conservation and renewable energy sources had been fully explored. Legislation could either prohibit additional fossil fuel plants for electrical generation or could require that they be low emission facilities that must use demonstrated carbon capture and storage technologies.

THE IMPLEMENTATION OF BUILDING CODES FOR ENERGY EFFICIENCY

The implementation of common sense energy efficiency standards for new commercial and residential buildings are a good example of what the IPCC refers to as the application of "regulations or standards." These energy efficiency standards would become a basic feature of Saskatchewan's building code. Ontario has an energy efficiency code for homes and businesses. In the United States 46 of the 50 states have an energy efficiency code for new buildings. Energy efficiency standards for new building construction and for the renovation of existing buildings are common place throughout the European Union.[156] Saskatchewan has one of the coldest climates in the world and yet we have no standard governing the energy efficiency of our newly constructed commercial and residential buildings. As a starting point, we could move to adopt Ontario's standard. In the residential sector, for example, Ontario will require construction of new homes to an Energy Star standard by 2012.[157] In Saskatchewan, a move to Energy Star would represent a 30% improvement in energy efficiency over typical new home construction today.

In some jurisdictions in the world, a building code is used to not only achieve energy efficiency standards, but also to achieve the introduction of renewable energy systems, particularly solar hot water. In Rizhao, a city of 3 million people in northern China, the city government has mandated that all new buildings must include solar hot water. So remarkable has the installation of solar hot water systems been that over 90% of Rizhao households now use solar hot water.[158] In August 2000 the City of Barcelona in Spain adopted a Solar Thermal Ordinance. The ordinance now makes it compulsory for new buildings, renovated buildings and buildings changing their use to install solar hot water systems. At least 60% of running hot water in all these buildings must be met using solar energy.[159]

A COMPREHENSIVE ELECTRICITY CONSERVATION PROGRAM USING FINANCIAL INCENTIVES

Saskatchewan Power Corporation has never had a comprehensive electricity conservation program, although the early beginnings of one began to take shape in mid 2007 at the direction of Premier Lorne Calvert. At that time SPC set a target of 300 megawatts of electricity savings by 2017. To put this in context, Saskatchewan has total electrical generating capacity of approximately 3,600 megawatts. The current government Minister Responsible for SaskPower, Hon. Ken Cheveldayoff, has stated new load growth targets for SaskPower are estimated at an additional 800 megawatts by 2020. This forecast should be reexamined in light of the climate crisis.[160] SaskPower's target, if it chose to make large scale electricity conservation investments, could sharply reduce projected load growth. With a sufficient investment load growth could be reduced to zero.

Instead of planning to spend billions of dollars on new generating capacity to expand the electrical grid, SaskPower could instead be focusing on spending an equivalent amount of money on electricity conservation. One of dozens of examples of where efficiency gains can be achieved is lighting. SaskPower could distribute millions of high efficiency compact fluorescent bulbs and LED bulbs free of charge and make on-site visits to residential and small commercial customers to install them in locations that get high daily use. For commercial businesses, the program could include the installation of super T-8 fluorescent lighting. SaskPower could provide financial incentives to install lighting controls, such as occupancy sensors and timers to turn lights on only when needed. It could help businesses and public institutions replace incandescent exit sign lamps with LED lamps and metal halide lights with low wattage metal halide lights. It could work with municipalities to upgrade municipal lighting systems to very high efficiency levels with lighting design that orients light downwards instead of upwards to the sky. By employing such a strategy, SaskPower could help Saskatchewan customers cut their electricity consumption from lighting by 50%.

Attractive financial incentives (to shorten payback periods) could be implemented to encourage the mass replacement of dozens of inefficient technologies that consume electricity with super energy efficient ones. By way of example, this would mean incentive programs for high efficiency motors, energy efficient pumps, energy efficient elevators, energy efficient irrigation systems, energy efficient retrofits to refrigeration facilities, energy efficient compressed air equipment, energy efficient dust collection systems and advanced controls for heating, ventilation and air conditioning systems. Incentive programs would be geared to installing the most energy efficient technologies available in the marketplace.

SaskPower could establish a special service aimed at helping large industrial customers cut their electricity consumption and their greenhouse gas emissions. The electricity conservation needs of large industrial customers tend to be industry-specific and are best addressed through supplying expert advice from those already deeply knowledgeable about energy use and industrial processes in the business in question. Industrial energy audits could be encouraged and cost shared by SPC.

The opportunity available to SaskPower in this area is underlined by the difference in traditional spending on electricity conservation between Manitoba and Saskatchewan. While neighboring Manitoba Hydro has spent more than $30 million per year on electricity conservation, SaskPower has traditionally spent under $1 million.[161] (In response to direction from government in 2007, SPC has made plans to increase this spending to over $7 million in 2008.) Manitoba has a good electricity conservation program, but there are more aggressive programs to be found in North America.

In Vermont, for example, the non-profit organization Efficiency Vermont, takes full advantage of time sensitive decisions related to renovation, new construction and equipment replacement. It is available to provide the technical help and financial incentives to make sure those decisions are energy efficient ones. In cases of equipment breakdown and replacement, it is available to help on a same day basis. Efficiency Vermont works intensively up and down the electrical products supply chain to ensure that wholesalers and retailers are carrying the most energy efficient choices available. Vermont's electrical customers pay a charge of 4% on their electricity bills to pay for the programs Efficiency Vermont delivers. This ensures a regular source of funding to electricity conservation programs. In exchange, Efficiency Vermont saves Vermont taxpayers $1.70 for every $1 it receives.[162] Vermont's State Department of Public Services is responsible for verifying the electricity conservation and monetary savings being achieved.

If Saskatchewan is to reduce its use of coal fired electrical generation, we must make electricity conservation a cornerstone of energy policy.

ADOPTION OF RENEWABLE ELECTRICITY OPPORTUNITIES
Another option for Saskatchewan people is to use renewable sources of electricity to reduce our reliance on fossil fuels.

Saskatchewan's most promising and cost effective opportunity to expand safe, renewable supplies of electricity lies in large scale wind power. Saskatchewan is blessed with one of the very best wind regimes in North America, especially in the area from Saskatoon south to the U.S. border. In the period 2002–06 171.2 megawatts (MW) of wind power was installed in Saskatchewan. Wind power now accounts for 5% of installed capacity, but only about 3% of total electrical energy consumed.

Wind power is cost effective and cost competitive with natural gas generated electricity. The limitation of wind power is its intermittency and that is often used as an argument by Saskatchewan Power Corporation for restricting its deployment. However, the example of other countries that have advanced their wind power systems demonstrate that it is possible to implement much higher levels of wind power than have been accomplished to date in Saskatchewan. Denmark has installed over five thousand wind turbines and produces over 3100 MW of wind generated electricity, approximately half of which is used for domestic purposes and half of which is exported. Wind power accounts for over 18% of total electricity generated.[163] When the exports are deducted, Danish domestic electricity consumption from wind is several times that of Saskatchewan. Germany has installed 22,247 MW of wind power and now provides about 6.4% of its electricity from wind energy with plans to double production by 2020. In a country with a geographical size much smaller than Saskatchewan, the Germans have installed over 19,000 wind turbines.[164] Ireland obtained 5% of its total electricity from wind and small scale generation in 2006 and government policy aims to more than double this by 2010.[165]

In the United Kingdom, John Sutton, the business secretary of the national government proposed in December of 2007 the construction of 7,000 wind power turbines by 2020 and the creation of up to 33 gigawatts of offshore wind. The Vice President of the Royal Academy of Engineering in the UK has described the targets as "laudible" but "enormous" and has stated that wind power could only provide about 20% of the country's electricity in order to preserve electrical grid stability.[166] The Royal Academy's perspective provides valuable insight into how much wind power penetration is possible.

Finally, one of the most inspirational examples for wind power production and integration is Spain, a country that is also significant because it exports very little of its electricity production. By 2008 Spain had already achieved 21% of its total electricity production from wind power and had over 15,000 MW of wind generated electrical capacity.[167]

These examples demonstrate that Saskatchewan, with good planning, could readily increase wind power five fold to approximately 15% of today's electricity production by 2020. By western European standards, this is a cautious projection. This would see Saskatchewan wind power growing to an installed capacity of at least 850MW. Wind power in Saskatchewan would be backed up with hydro and with natural gas electrical generating stations. The combination of new wind power installations and backup sources would be used to facilitate a reduction in coal fired generation.

Key to the successful use of wind in our province is the creation of a more decentralized wind power network and accurate wind power forecasting. The Danes have established a very decentralized wind power network with turbines located near a large number of communities. This helps with integrating wind power into the grid because the wind is generally blowing in at least some of the turbine locations. Denmark has also developed a high level of expertise in forecasting wind speeds, which has allowed it to more effectively back up its wind power system with hydro from Norway.

Adequate backup sources of electricity are important to facilitating a large scale expansion of wind power in Saskatchewan. One option is the use natural gas electrical generating stations in Saskatchewan that are planned to operate in conjunction with wind turbines. Natural gas stations can be ramped up and down quickly to back up wind. A second option would be to improve transmission lines between Saskatchewan and Manitoba and import hydro electricity from Manitoba. Just like Norway's hydro backs up Denmark's wind power, Manitoba's hydro resource could back up an enhanced wind power network in Saskatchewan. Saskatchewan and Manitoba have already signed a co-operation agreement on electricity supply and planning and this agreement could provide a framework for larger hydro imports from Manitoba to compliment an expanded wind power network in Saskatchewan. An important advantage of the latter option is that there would be less greenhouse gas emissions associated with hydro imports than there would be with the operation of natural gas generation facilities.

A second renewable electricity option for Saskatchewan simply expands on the concept of importing hydro from Manitoba. Instead of only importing hydro to back up wind power in our province, Saskatchewan could also import hydro electricity from Manitoba as a source of base load power. If transmission grid networks were sufficiently upgraded, it would be practical for Saskatchewan to purchase enough electricity from Manitoba to close a coal fired generating station in Saskatchewan. This option has generally not been favoured by Saskatchewan governments because the jobs and revenue flows benefit Manitoba rather than Saskatchewan residents. However, given the urgency of the climate crisis, the relatively low cost of purchasing hydro from Manitoba and the need for Saskatchewan to phase out its coal fired electricity generation plants, hydro imports from Manitoba are well worth considering.

A third renewable electricity option in Saskatchewan is small scale hydro. There is potential for several small scale hydro projects with low environmental impacts in northern Saskatchewan. Small scale hydro resources in the north need to be developed in close partnership with First Nations and Metis communities. Saskatchewan could readily target 125MW of low impact, environmentally friendly hydro by 2020. To further this development, the Province could consider introducing a royalty holiday on environmentally friendly hydro production for 5–10 years.

A fourth renewable electricity option available to our province is biomass energy, particularly electricity that is produced using waste wood residue. Biomass for electricity generation is attractive because it is always available (no intermittency) and can be converted to electricity according to the provincial demand for electricity. There are practical opportunities for at least 100 MW of electrical generation by 2020 from biomass in Saskatchewan's forest fringe and northern communities.[168]

There are other important opportunities to implement renewable electricity sources in Saskatchewan, but they are more expensive at the present time. These include biogas applications, solar photovoltaic systems and small wind power systems.

There is potential for a few small biogas projects in Saskatchewan using manure from commercial hog and dairy operations and other agricultural wastes. These have the advantage of destroying pathogens in the livestock waste stream while capturing methane, a highly potent greenhouse gas. By mid 2008, 13 biogas plants were operating in Canada.[169] Biogas plants have been actively promoted by provincial governments such as Ontario and U.S. state governments such as Vermont.

Several European countries have promoted biomass electricity generation and have offered higher electricity revenues to companies that produce electricity from this renewable source. For example, in Germany more than 120 biomass plants and cogeneration plants that use wood as their fuel source were in operation by 2007. In Denmark, the national government has directed that biomass be used to replace fossil fuels at existing large electrical generation stations.[170]

Another emerging source of renewable electricity is solar photovoltaic systems and small wind power systems. On October 1, 2007 the Calvert government put in place a program for net metering, allowing small scale producers of electricity to sell their electricity to the grid at the same price they buy electricity from the grid. Financial assistance was also established to help with installation costs and grid integration studies. The primary users of net metering at this point are likely to be those who install solar photovoltaic and small wind power systems. The costs of a solar PV system for the average household are currently in the $25,000 range. However, the cost of solar photovoltaic installations has been declining steadily, and a significant drop is expected in the decade ahead. As prices decline, the installation of these systems will become more widespread in Saskatchewan. Solar PV systems work well in cold climates and with our excellent sunlight resource could become important in meeting our future electricity needs. Small wind power systems are less expensive than solar PV systems today, but have somewhat less potential for price decline in the future.

Many jurisdictions in the world have gone beyond a net metering system that simply credits renewable electricity producers at a price that is equivalent to the retail price for purchasing electricity. Countries like Germany and Spain and provinces like Ontario have gone to feed in tariffs that offer significantly higher prices for those who produce renewable electricity from sources such as wind power and solar photovoltaic systems.[171] As a result of this policy, Germany now has 300,000 separate solar installations in their country. In 2007 Ontario Power Authority signed 145 contracts for the construction of solar power systems, which if fully completed would yield another 250 megawatts of electricity.[172] The feed in tariff policies of some European countries are especially significant because they empower citizens who no longer need the permission of power utilities to produce renewable electricity. Small and medium size producers of renewable electricity have guaranteed access to the grid, guaranteed payment for their production and no cap on how much can be produced.[173]

One natural place to promote renewable electricity technologies such as small-scale solar and wind is on Saskatchewan schools, SIAST campuses and university campuses. At each site opportunities could be created for students to help install, monitor and learn about the technologies and their potential.

On post secondary campuses, more advanced research and application could be encouraged. The state of Hawaii has taken this approach with solar photovoltaic systems. Their electrical utilities have helped install solar photovoltaic panels on more than twenty five local schools.[174] This is an excellent example of both an educational initiative and an initiative that advances public awareness of GHG mitigation technologies.

The use of wind, solar and other renewable electricity sources that are now intermittent will have much greater potential in Saskatchewan as electricity storage systems become better developed. For example, in Canada, VRB Power Systems of Vancouver has developed "flow battery technology," an electrochemical energy storage system that acts like a reversible fuel cell, using the element Vanadium. This technology allows electricity to be recovered instantaneously and the battery can recharge as fast as it discharges. An Irish wind power company has entered into an agreement with VRB Power Systems to build wind energy storage capacity at the Sorne Hill wind farm in Ireland. An earlier version of wind smoothing technology like this is operating in Sapporo, Japan where storage capacity to supply up to 6MW of peak electricity has been built in conjunction with a wind farm.[175] Saskatchewan Power Corporation should make it a high priority to test flow battery technology at a wind power facility in Saskatchewan.

While the example discussed here involves large scale wind, the potential for storage applies to any intermittent, renewable source of electricity, turning it into an electricity source that is reliably available 24 hours a day. In addition to reversible flow battery technology, there are many other helpful electricity storage options including the use of flywheels, pumped hydro storage (water is pumped into a water reservoir and released when needed through a turbine) and compressed air storage (air is compressed in an underground cavern and made available when required through a gas turbine).[176]

ALTERNATIVE APPROACHES TO SPACE HEATING USING CONSERVATION, RENEWABLE ENERGY AND FUNDAMENTAL CHANGES TO THE WAY ENERGY SYSTEMS ARE ORGANIZED

In order to achieve large emission reductions, Saskatchewan will not only have to reduce its use of coal, but also its use of natural gas. There are excellent opportunities to replace the use of natural gas for space heating and hot water heating. These opportunities include energy conservation, the use of solar energy and the use of district heating systems that could draw on a variety of heat sources.

Energy conservation has already been widely demonstrated to reduce natural gas consumption in residential settings. Reductions of 40% are readily achievable. Saskatchewan has good provincial government programs to encourage and provide financial assistance for residential energy conservation in existing homes. These programs could now be expanded to the small business and large commercial buildings sector, where there are opportunities for substantial energy savings. Conservation measures that could be encouraged include the installation of high efficiency furnaces with high efficiency motors, the installation of condensing or near condensing boilers, the installation of attic, floor and wall insulation, and simple measures such as caulking, weather stripping, duct insulation, hot water heater blankets and low flow showerheads. Whenever doors and windows are replaced, it could be done with an energy efficient product. Often the biggest obstacle to doing this work is access to upfront capital. Thus, in addition to financial incentives, the Provincial Government could establish an Energy Conservation Loan Program that offers low interest rates to all those who make energy conservation investments. Energy savings on conservation investments are very predictable and could consistently be used to ensure loan repayment within 6–8 years. The success of such a program has been demonstrated in several locations across North America, including the state of Oregon and the City of Toronto.[177]

This last observation is key in terms of public policy development. There are hundreds of millions of dollars worth of cost effective energy conservation opportunities in the Saskatchewan economy. A large scale low interest loan program that aims to make these investments possible is fundamental to securing a greener and more prosperous future. The program could be entirely structured around investments that pay for themselves in a manageable time period, solely through the energy savings that are achieved.

In northern Saskatchewan where *many* buildings are heated with electricity rather than natural gas, there are even greater opportunities for cost savings and greenhouse gas savings. A large percentage of northerners have low incomes, so the north could be a natural place for SaskEnergy and SaskPower to pilot a direct installation program at no cost to local residents.

Another target group for direct installation of energy conservation technologies is senior citizens, whose incomes are usually fixed and who may not occupy their homes long enough to recapture the financial benefits of a large energy conservation investment. A good example of a direct install program is the one launched by British Gas in the United Kingdom in early 2008, which provides free energy conservation services to seniors over 70 years of age. These services include free attic and wall insulation—an offer in the U.K. worth around 600 British pounds. Under the program, attic and wall insulation is offered entirely free of charge to every homeowner in the U.K. who is older than 70.[178]

Southern Saskatchewan has enormous potential for solar applications because of our excellent sunlight resource with more hours of sunlight each year than any other part of Canada. Solar hot water and solar space heating systems are proven technologies that can readily be applied in urban and rural settings. In April of 2007 financial assistance was put in place by the Government of Saskatchewan for those installing solar systems for domestic hot water purposes. No assistance is available, at the time of writing, for those installing solar systems for space heating purposes, but this could be a logical next step. To prepare for and encourage a transition to solar energy, the provincial government could introduce legislation to protect the solar rights of all Saskatchewan residents who have installed solar systems on buildings they own. Municipalities could be encouraged to facilitate solar access through appropriate subdivision layout and design.

The use of district heating is one of the primary reasons why countries like Denmark, Germany and Sweden have a much lower greenhouse gas footprint than Canada. To implement district heating, you need water-based central heating in your buildings and a central distribution system to transport hot water to each building. A wide variety of low emission sources can be used to heat the water including wood pellets, solar energy, geothermal energy and waste heat from electricity generation stations.[179] District heating could be applied in new Saskatchewan neighborhoods and in the downtown core of our bigger cities where there is a more favourable economic case for installing a well designed district heating system.

Several European countries are using renewable energy sources for heating of buildings via a district heating system. In Sweden and Denmark, the use of wood pellets is widely applied for district heating. Germany has successfully piloted the use of solar energy and geothermal energy in district heating systems. Large scale solar projects have been constructed in communities such as Neckarsulm and Crailsheim with good results.[180] Heat from solar collectors on a wide array of buildings is collected and stored centrally in a large insulated tank and distributed as needed through the district heating system. Many communities in southern Germany and France have pursued geothermal energy by drawing hot water from deep underground water reservoirs and using it for space heating via a district heating system.[181]

In addition to its impressive solar resource, Saskatchewan is blessed with a geothermal resource that exceeds 60°C in much of southern Saskatchewan. The best geothermal conditions are south of Regina. In this part of Saskatchewan there are deep underground reservoirs containing large amounts of hot water. As one goes further south, underground water temperatures get hotter and in some places can reach 100°C.[182] These waters would be very suitable for use for space heating and hot water heating. Communities like Leader, Moosomin, Weyburn and Estevan are well positioned to make use of geothermal energy in the future.

SaskEnergy and SaskPower could work together with local suppliers and interested neighbourhoods and communities to pilot a variety of district heating projects that make use of the above mentioned renewable energy sources. This would be an example of an initiative that combines research and development, public awareness, and education and training policy components.

SETTING THE STAGE FOR DEEPER CHANGE
THROUGH THE USE OF DEMONSTRATION PROJECTS

Two Saskatchewan families, the Dumont family in Saskatoon and the Holzkaemper family in Regina, have already demonstrated that a new home can be constructed that consumes 11–20% of the energy of a conventional home. This can be done in a relatively cost effective way, with the initial investment easily being recaptured through energy savings over the life of the home. The Dumont home was built in 1992 and the Holzkaemper home was completed in 2007.[183]

In Edmonton and Prince Albert work is underway on the construction of net zero energy homes, residences that will produce as much energy from renewable energy sources as they consume.[184]

The Association of Refrigeration, Heating and Air Conditioning Engineers has set as a U.S. target that 70% of new commercial buildings in the USA will be net zero energy by 2015. In the United Kingdom, the national government has set a target of all new school buildings being zero carbon by 2016.[185]

These are very hopeful developments because they signal the potential for a fundamental transformation in building construction. However, in the midst of a construction boom in Saskatoon and Regina and many smaller urban centers across Saskatchewan in 2006, 2007 and 2008, there is little evidence that the knowledge that has been acquired to construct net zero energy homes is being applied. To facilitate the necessary transformation, the provincial government could provide home owner and home builder grants for the construction and ownership of Factor 9 Homes or Net Zero Energy Homes. Training programs in best practice applications to achieve net zero energy status should also be provided for home builders and their staff.

The provincial government could also partner with the Saskatchewan Home Builders to construct at least one net zero energy demonstration home in every Saskatchewan city and large town. Hundreds of thousands of Saskatchewan people would tour these homes and a large number of builders would gain practical experience in constructing them. This concept could be extended even further, so that in a partnership among the Province, Saskatchewan's towns and cities and the Home Builder's, entire subdivisions of homes would be constructed using renewable energy and achieving at least Factor 9 status.

GOVERNMENT SHOULD LEAD BY EXAMPLE
IN THE REDUCTION OF GREENHOUSE GAS EMISSIONS

If the provincial government wishes to see the widespread application of energy conservation and renewable energy, it must lead by example. First steps in the buildings sector have already been made. Saskatchewan Property Management has upgraded the energy efficiency of many existing provincial government buildings and set improved energy efficiency standards for new schools, hospitals and other provincially funded buildings.

One potential next step would be for the provincial government to model more progressive measures, such as the construction of all public buildings to at least LEED Gold Standards (Leadership in Energy and Environmental Design). Additional upfront capital costs would be recovered through energy savings over the first years of each building's lifetime. Going even further, the Province could set a date for all new public buildings to be carbon neutral and work towards this with the construction of several new net zero energy schools and health care facilities.

Meanwhile, all provincial government departments, agencies and Crown Corporations could be required to track their consumption of electricity, natural gas, gasoline and diesel fuel and to reduce it by at least 50% by 2020.

EDUCATION AND TRAINING

Saskatchewan can only embark on a transformation towards energy efficiency and renewable energy if it has the trained workforce to do so. Specialized training will be necessary in many areas. In the buildings and electricity sector, for example, training will be needed in energy efficiency retrofit, the enforcement of building code standards, the proper commissioning of new buildings, the positioning and installation of renewable energy technologies, and the integration of wind power into the provincial grid.

The provincial government could ask SIAST, the University of Saskatchewan and the regional community colleges to gear up appropriately to provide the needed training requirements. Saskatchewan curriculum programming would aim to take training to a level that meets North American standards. For example, all renewable energy installers would be trained to the standards of the North American Board of Certified Energy Practitioners.

VOLUNTARY PARTNERSHIPS

If Saskatchewan is to achieve a 32% reduction in greenhouse gas emissions by 2020, it stands to reason that one of the ideal places where an example can be set is at our post secondary institutions and research parks. These academic and applied settings are home to many talented faculty, students, engineers, architects, building managers, skilled tradespersons and members of the research community. Most of our institutions have physical space at their perimeters for locating renewable energy systems. By way of policy, the Provincial Government could invite interested campuses and research parks to enter into a partnership aimed at achieving a 50% reduction in greenhouse gas emissions by 2020. The Provincial and Federal Governments would need to provide the vast bulk of funding for the required initiatives. Each institution would provide the expertise and take responsibility for completing the work successfully.

Our SIAST campuses have excellent plumbing, heating, electrical and mechanical engineering programs on site. They are an ideal location to install solar hot water, solar space heating and solar photovoltaic systems on their buildings and model them for the community. Several of the SIAST campuses have space constraints, so solar energy combined with conservation measures could be an excellent place to begin.

Our University campuses and Research Parks have physical space for wind power installations as well as solar energy applications. Once again, conservation measures will be critical. Several new buildings on our campuses and research parks have already been built to LEED standards. What would be required under this new partnership is a major conservation retrofit of existing buildings. New facilities could be built to LEED Platinum or Net Zero Energy standards.

Each institution would draw on its existing strengths and opportunities. For example, the University of Regina campus and the Regina Research Park are well positioned to demonstrate a pilot in geothermal energy. There is a deep underground aquifer underneath Research Drive on campus. A geothermal energy project was partly completed at the site in 1979. A second well was never drilled, so the first well was abandoned, but sits beneath the surface of a parking lot on campus. The existing well could be re-established at a relatively low capital cost and a second well drilled. Hot water from the aquifer could be pumped to the surface and passed through heat exchangers to help meet the energy needs of buildings on campus.

The University of Saskatchewan already has many of the components of a well managed district heating system on campus, an asset that could be drawn on for renewable energy projects. The University and adjacent Innovation Place Research Park also have a significant and high profile land base that, subject to an environmental assessment, appears well suited to a small amount of wind power development.

There are exciting opportunities for our campuses to partner with other post secondary institutions in North America that are implementing impressive greenhouse gas reduction strategies. In Wisconsin, for example, the Governor has announced a plan to make four University of Wisconsin campuses energy independent with 100% of energy coming from clean sources such as solar, wind and biomass energy.[186]

These opportunities are just examples of what would be possible. Our institutions have enormous expertise and could work together in assessing the best available renewable energy opportunities, developing a plan and moving forward. The starting point, however, would be a partnership with the Government of Saskatchewan and a commitment from the provincial and federal governments to fund the work.

KEY EMERGING CHALLENGES AND OPPORTUNITIES

ANNOUNCED PLANS FOR CARBON CAPTURE
AND STORAGE AT THE BOUNDARY DAM POWER PLANT

As mentioned earlier in this paper, Premier Brad Wall's government has announced its intention to proceed with renovations at the Boundary Dam coal fired power station in order to capture some of its greenhouse gas emissions. The Boundary Dam Power Station is Saskatchewan's largest coal fired generating station with a capacity of 813 MW.[187] When the retrofit is complete, SaskPower expects to produce 100 MW of base load electricity using the carbon capture technology, with an expected reduction in greenhouse gas emissions of one million tonnes per year.[188] The carbon dioxide that is captured will be used for enhanced oil recovery. An investment of $1.4 billion is planned to undertake the retrofit. In late February of 2008 the federal government's budget provided $240 million to assist Saskatchewan with this initiative. SaskPower anticipates its Boundary Dam clean coal project will be the first of its kind to be brought online commercially in North America.[189]

The project will draw on Saskatchewan's experience gained in the Weyburn oilfield where the world's largest carbon capture project to date has been undertaken. A portion of the Weyburn oil field is operated by EnCana

Corporation. Since the year 2000, EnCana has been successfully injecting CO_2 underground to enhance oilfield production. The injection process has been monitored by the International Energy Agency GHG Weyburn-Midale CO_2 Monitoring and Storage Project, an international monitoring project that has been coordinated by the Petroleum Technology Research Centre on the University of Regina campus. Based on the monitoring work done to date, the geological formation into which the carbon dioxide has been injected appears to be well suited for long term geological storage of carbon dioxide.[190] Ongoing research work is being done by PTRC to further advance carbon dioxide storage and verification technologies.

To date, the world has limited experience with carbon capture and storage, so there is still uncertainty with respect to costs and outcomes. StatoilHydro ASA of Norway currently has four industrial-scale carbon capture projects in operation. Power Company Vattenfall AB is constructing a coal fired power plant in eastern Germany that will try to bury carbon dioxide in natural caverns beneath the earth. There are also important announcements of the intent to launch projects being made around the world. The government of Abu Dhabi has announced its intent to invest $15 billion in a network of carbon-capture and storage projects to pump greenhouse gases into oil fields. The British government announced in March 2008 its intent to make carbon capture readiness a requirement for all new electrical generating stations powered by fossil fuels. The Government of Australia has announced plans to amend its Offshore Petroleum Act to allow for seabed storage of carbon dioxide emissions from its coal-fired electricity generating stations.[191] In 2004 the Bush administration announced the construction of a carbon capture plant, FutureGen. After selecting an Illinois location in 2007, the administration pulled the plug on the project in early 2008 because of cost overruns.[192] The U.S. administration has said they will instead assist other groups across the U.S. that are working with carbon capture and sequestration technology.

Three issues to watch for as Saskatchewan pursues carbon capture and storage will be long term success in permanently storing carbon emissions, how much extra electricity will be used to remove the CO_2 from the coal plant's emission stream and the cost of the project. Some critics have expressed concern about the possibility that carbon dioxide emissions that will be stored underground could begin to leak back into the larger environment over time. This will need to be carefully monitored. A second consideration will be the amount of extra electrical power that will be required to remove carbon dioxide from the plant's emissions stream. The initial projected reduction in Boundary Dam's total output is in the range of 40 megawatts.[193] A third consideration will be cost relative to other greenhouse gas reduction solutions. This is an immediate issue for Saskatchewan. In 2007 SaskPower postponed plans for construction of a 300 MW near-zero emissions pulverized coal unit because the estimated cost had ballooned to $3.8 billion. The estimated cost of the new 100 MW project is $1.4 billion of which SaskPower's share is $758 million. There are also private investors. The federal government has made it clear that its contribution is capped at $240 million.

At the time of writing, that leaves the Government of Saskatchewan picking up cost overruns.

Carbon capture and storage is an important technology to invest in given the prevalence of coal-fired generating stations around the world. It is technology with promise. However, the Saskatchewan project is really a large scale demonstration project and given the costs involved, the project should be led by and very significantly funded by the Government of Canada. This is a project that will ultimately benefit all Canadian provinces that use coal fired electricity. It will also be of great interest to the international community. It thus makes sense for the Canadian government to provide more leadership and financial support than it is currently doing.

To meet provincial government greenhouse gas reduction targets, Saskatchewan must cut greenhouse gas emissions by at least 26 million tonnes of CO_2 equivalent per year by 2020. The clean coal retrofit at Boundary Dam Power Station will only account for 1 million tonnes per year of those savings.[194] Even if the project stays on budget, this is an exceptionally expensive endeavour for Saskatchewan. An equivalent investment in electricity conservation would produce triple the emission savings. This underlines the fact that in order to reach its greenhouse gas reduction targets, Saskatchewan will have to be strategic in where it makes its investments.

THE POSSIBILITY OF A NUCLEAR REACTOR IN SASKATCHEWAN

As mentioned earlier, Bruce Power is undertaking a feasibility study into a nuclear power station in Saskatchewan with the encouragement of the provincial government. Nuclear power offers the advantage of generating base load electricity while creating relatively small amounts of greenhouse gas emissions. To date, a reactor is being viewed as a potential addition to the generation network to meet our province's growing electricity demand.

The fundamental question to be asked is whether nuclear power is a better option for Saskatchewan than the conservation and renewable options discussed in this paper. At the end of the day, Saskatchewan taxpayers will have only a limited amount of capital to spend on new electricity generation, so difficult choices must be made. Three billion dollars spent on nuclear power is likely to be three billion dollars that is not spent on electricity conservation, wind power, heat recovery or small scale hydro, all viable options that also produce relatively small amounts of greenhouse gas emissions.

There are many reasons for Saskatchewan people to be cautious about nuclear power. The economics are not attractive. Reactor construction projects around the world often face large cost over runs. There are also enormous costs associated with decommissioning nuclear power plants after their operating life is over. For example, the nuclear power plant being built in Finland is still not complete, but is $2.5 billion over budget.[195] In Canada, Atomic Energy of Canada originally planned to build two small reactors (10MW plants to produce medical isotopes) for $140 million. The costs spiraled to $640 million and the project was ultimately abandoned.[196] In the United Kingdom, the cost of cleaning up aging nuclear power sites has risen from 12 billion pounds to 73 billion pounds.[197]

A nuclear reactor in Saskatchewan would produce new radioactive waste disposal problems for which Saskatchewan taxpayers would become responsible. The quantities of waste would be small, but the disposal problems are difficult to deal with. Both low level and high level radioactive wastes would be created. In Ontario, Macomb County Water Quality Board officials are strongly opposing plans for an underground repository to store low level wastes from 20 nuclear power plants. They fear drinking water contamination in the Great Lakes Basin in the centuries ahead.[198] Higher level wastes are produced in at least two ways. In the course of neutron bombardment inside a reactor, the structural materials in the core of the reactor become intensely radioactive. Upon demolition, hundreds of truckloads of radioactive rubble need to be securely stored for centuries into the future. The uranium fuel bundles inside the reactor are also transformed into intensely radioactive waste. These newly created wastes do not exist naturally and contain very dangerous and long lived radioactive isotopes such as strontium 90, cesium 137 and plutonium 239.[199] They must be kept out of the ground water supplies for tens of thousands of years to come. The global nuclear power industry and governments around the world have struggled to establish a functioning repository site for high level nuclear waste. They have faced intense public opposition and spiraling costs and to date have been unsuccessful.[200]

There is growing evidence that nuclear power plant operations increase the risk of childhood leukemia for children living near the plant. Research by scientists at the University of Mainz in Germany has found elevated leukemia rates among children under 5 years of age living within 5 kilometres of a nuclear reactor. In the United Kingdom, the Committee on Medical Aspects Of Radiation in the Environment found excess cancers within 25 kilometres of a nuclear reactor.[201] This is an area where more research is required, but the new studies suggest caution is in order.

The advantage of electricity conservation and renewable sources of electricity generation is that they do not create additional safety risks or environmental problems for current and future generations of Saskatchewan residents. Their economics are also more attractive.

Amory Lovins, a consultant to hundreds of private companies and government agencies around the world, has this to say about the economic comparison: "A kilowatt-hour of nuclear power does displace nearly all the 0.9–plus kilograms of CO_2 emitted by producing a kilowatt-hour from coal. But so does a kilowatt-hour from wind, a kilowatt-hour from recovered-heat industrial cogeneration, or a kilowatt-hour saved by end-use efficiency. All three of these carbon-free resources cost at least one-third less than nuclear power per kilowatt-hour, so they save more carbon per dollar."[202]

For the above mentioned reasons, those planning electricity generation expenditures in Saskatchewan should not make nuclear power one of their priorities for the decade ahead. Saskatchewan is blessed with other more attractive and safer alternatives for achieving at least a 32% reduction in greenhouse gas emissions.

SASKATCHEWAN POPULATION INCREASES

Most Canadian provinces have experienced population increases since 1990. As provincial governments and the Government of Canada set their greenhouse gas reduction targets, they must take account of population growth. So must all other signatories to the Kyoto Protocol.

Saskatchewan's greenhouse gas emissions rose sharply since 1990, the base year from which the Kyoto Protocol obligations are calculated. Emissions increased from 44.033 Mt CO2 equivalent in 1990 to 71.967 Mt CO_2 equivalent in 2006.[203] However, during this period there was almost no rise in provincial population numbers. The national census showed Saskatchewan's population numbers at 988,928 in 1991.[204] The Saskatchewan Bureau of Statistics reported Saskatchewan's population at 990,152 on January 1, 2007.[205]

However, 2007 was a major year of population growth for Saskatchewan. The province's population grew by 16,492 during the year, an increase of 1.7%, well ahead of the national average of 1.1%.[206] Further population increases are likely in the years ahead.

In planning to meet its target of a 32% reduction in greenhouse gas emissions by 2020, the Government of Saskatchewan will therefore need to take account of population increases and plan for even greater reductions in per capita emissions. The implementation of common sense measures such as an excellent energy efficiency code for new residential home construction would help reduce the impact of population growth. There are also potential opportunities that come with this growth. For example, the creation of new subdivisions in our cities provides an excellent opportunity to demonstrate renewable energy technologies for space heating, hot water heating and electricity. It is also an opportunity to take a more innovative approach to urban design by laying out new streets and homes to take maximum advantage of passive solar energy and by creating new neighborhoods that are less dependent on the automobile and more pedestrian friendly.

APPLYING THE POLICY MECHANISMS TO THE TRANSPORT SECTOR

The principles and policy mechanisms discussed above can be applied to other sectors of the Saskatchewan economy, as part of a Saskatchewan greenhouse gas reduction strategy.

For example, in the Saskatchewan transportation sector, which accounts for 16% of greenhouse gas emissions, the application of the policy mechanisms could make a substantial difference in emissions.[207] Transport illustrations for each of the policy mechanisms are very briefly described below.

USING LEGISLATION TO SET NEW DIRECTION IN SUSTAINABLE TRANSPORTATION

Saskatchewan lacks a unit within government that is focused on creating an environmentally sustainable transport system in our province. The Province could establish a Renewable Fuels and Sustainable Transportation Unit that is mandated to achieve a 32% reduction in GHG emissions in the transport sector by 2020 and is mandated to make Saskatchewan a Canadian leader in energy efficient transport.

IMPLEMENTATION OF VIGOROUS EMISSION CODES ON ALL NEW VEHICLE PURCHASES

The Saskatchewan Government could adopt California Vehicle Emission Standards for new vehicle sales. The regulations adopted by the California Air Resources Board will require a 30% reduction of greenhouse gas emissions by 2016 on new cars and trucks. Eleven other U.S. states have followed California's lead, including small states like Vermont, which has a population two thirds the size of Saskatchewan.[208] Several Canadian provinces have already expressed interest.

ADOPTION OF NEW REGULATIONS THAT APPLY TO THE OPERATION OF EXISTING VEHICLES

The Saskatchewan government could follow the lead of Ontario and require all commercial trucks operating in Saskatchewan to install speed limiters. The Ontario government has set 105 kilometres per hour as the maximum speed for commercial trucks in that province.[209] The Saskatchewan government could go further and reduce speed limits on divided highways back to 100 km per hour to reduce greenhouse gas emissions from highway travel.

A COMPREHENSIVE GASOLINE CONSERVATION PROGRAM USING FINANCIAL INCENTIVES

Provincial government rebates could be provided on the purchase of new and used hybrid cars and other environmentally friendly vehicles with ultra low gasoline consumption. At the same time, the Province could offer motorists financial incentives to turn in old, highly polluting vehicles. (At the time of writing, serious discussions are underway on the possibility of launching a vehicle scrappage program in Saskatchewan with the help of the federal and provincial government.)[210] The Saskatchewan government could also work with the private sector to provide tax credits for firms that make investments aimed at reducing transport related GHG emissions. Examples would be investments in video conferencing as an alternative to in-person meetings or an investment in employee home offices to permit employees to conduct work related business at home, thereby avoiding travel. In the commercial trucking sector, the Saskatchewan government could offer tax credits to trucking firms on the purchase of auxiliary power units. With such units there is no need to idle the truck to meet the driver's space heating, cooling and electricity needs when the truck is stopped; thus only one litre of fuel is typically consumed per hour versus eight litres for idling a large truck.[211]

ADOPTION OF RENEWABLE ENERGY OPTIONS IN THE TRANSPORT SECTOR

The Province could adopt a 1% mandate for biodiesel in Saskatchewan consumed diesel products. This would provide improved fuel economy, reduced greenhouse gas emissions and reduced engine wear, without having too much impact on the amount of Saskatchewan land available for food crops. The Saskatoon Transit Authority has been using 1% bio-diesel in all their buses for the past two years with very good results. Approximately 8 million litres of annual bio-diesel production capacity would be required in Saskatchewan to achieve a 1% bio-diesel blend.[212]

FUNDAMENTAL CHANGES TO THE WAY
THE TRANSPORT SYSTEM IS ORGANIZED IN ORDER TO REDUCE EMISSIONS

The Saskatchewan government could purchase the Regina-Saskatoon rail corridor (much of which is already up for abandonment at the time of writing). It could reestablish passenger rail service between Saskatoon and Regina. It could also work with the private sector to undertake a careful examination of all commercial truck traffic between the two cities in order to determine what portion of it could be efficiently moved back to rail. In general, CO^2 emissions are 5–10 times lower when rail is used instead of highway travel by truck.[213] However, transport impacts for each product line must be examined, including in-city emissions related to circumstances where goods would be transferred from truck to rail and then back onto trucks after intercity travel is complete.

SETTING THE STAGE FOR DEEPER CHANGES THROUGH DEMONSTRATION PROJECTS

One area with great potential for demonstration projects is the merging of sustainable transport and renewable electricity technologies. For example, the Province could work with a community interested in establishing a truck stop that supplies electricity to truckers from a renewable energy sources and that completely eliminates the need for idling trucks or operating auxiliary power units while they are parked. With the emergence of plug in hybrid cars, the Province could work with municipalities, post secondary institutions and large workplaces to identify locations where plug-in hybrids can be charged with an on-site renewable energy source. These sites could be designed not only for plug-in hybrids, but to meet an array of other local electrical needs. Plug-in hybrid vehicles will require kilowatt hours, but not kilowatts. Wind power and solar photovoltaic panels match this perfectly. The Province could also construct a wind turbine in both Saskatoon and Regina to supply the two SOCO Research Parks with electricity and produce hydrogen. A demonstration hydrogen filling station could be set up in each city, thus creating a hydrogen highway between Saskatchewan's two largest urban centres.

GOVERNMENT LEADERSHIP BY EXAMPLE

There are dozens of opportunities for government to lead by example. All new vehicle purchases through Saskatchewan Property Management could be eco-friendly vehicles. The public service could be asked to conduct inter-city travel by bus and by rail whenever possible. A Provincial Government department could pilot picking up its employees by hybrid van instead of each individual employee driving to work. It could encourage large private sector employees to also experiment with this option. The Province could formally establish anti-idling zones outside all provincially owned buildings and encourage school boards, universities, municipal governments and other bodies that receive provincial funding to do the same.

VOLUNTARY PARNTERSHIPS

The Provincial Government could establish a formal voluntary partnership with interested cities in Saskatchewan to advance GHG emission reductions. Common GHG emission reduction targets for urban transport could be set. Many specific projects could be worked on together. For example, the Province and each city could partner to ensure pedestrian friendly design of new neighborhoods, including good quality sidewalks, bicycle paths on arterial streets, well-planned bus service with shelters and centrally located grocery shopping services within easy walking or biking distance. Initiatives could also be designed around improving urban transit in existing neighborhoods. For example, provincial funding incentives could be put in place to help increase the frequency of service on city bus routes.

EDUCATION AND TRAINING

There are dozens of training needs that flow from the above mentioned initiatives. For example, there will be a need to train staff to plan for and implement each of the demonstration projects. There will be a need for logistics training to ensure the private and public sector have the resources to properly identify how goods can best be moved in economically practical ways that minimize emissions. There will be a need to train urban planners in pedestrian friendly design.

RESEARCH AND DEVELOPMENT

The Saskatchewan Research Council has been working intensively with the community of Nipawin to advance the commercial production of ethanol from wood wastes. This is one of many endeavors around the world to commercialize the production of ethanol from cellulose. It is expected that greenhouse gas emissions from ethanol produced from cellulose will be much lower than emissions associated with grain-produced ethanol.

FUNDAMENTAL CHANGES: CARBON TAX, MANDATORY EMISSION REDUCTIONS, CAPTURE OF FUGITIVE EMISSIONS, SAYING NO ENVIRONMENTALLY DANGEROUS DEVELOPMENT, REASSESSING ENERGY INTENSIVE ECONOMIC DEVELOPMENT

To successfully implement a comprehensive climate change strategy will require even more fundamental changes than have been discussed to date. The world will need to move as quickly as possible to greenhouse gas reductions that are in the 50–80% range and Saskatchewan will need to be part of that process. While part of this gap will be closed with new technology breakthroughs and innovative public policy, part of it will require bigger lifestyle changes and fundamental changes in how we operate our economy.

For example, in the policy arena many European countries have adopted a carbon tax. The Government of British Columbia announced a carbon tax in their February 2008 provincial budget, in effect taxing behaviour that pollutes.[214] The tax took effect on July 1, 2008 at $10 per tonne for carbon and increases by $5 per year until it reaches $30 a tonne by 2012. The tax is expected to raise $1.8 billion, all of which is scheduled to go back to consumers and businesses in the form of lower income tax and business taxes. By initiating a revenue neutral carbon tax in Saskatchewan, the provincial government could accelerate the adoption of low carbon technologies.

Saskatchewan's large industries, including its oil and gas sector will need to accept fundamental changes including firm caps on their greenhouse gas emissions and a timetable for mandatory, large scale emission reductions. Conventional coal fired electricity generation in Saskatchewan will need to be phased out over the next 25–30 years. The industrial, oil and gas, and electricity generation sectors, together account for almost 60% of Saskatchewan's total greenhouse gas emissions.[215] It will not be possible to achieve deep emission reduction targets in Saskatchewan without the above mentioned measures. Of special importance in the oil and gas sector is the regulation of fugitive emission sources, which in 2005 accounted for over 17 million tons of greenhouse gas emissions.[216]

In the industrial and electricity generation sector the federal government is moving forward with new regulations. At the time of writing, Prime Minister Stephen Harper government has announced its intention to require that coal fired power plants and oil sands plants that become operational in 2012 or later must adopt carbon capture and storage technology or a combination of other abatement technology and carbon credits by the year 2018. Ottawa has also announced its intention to regulate emissions from large industry and existing large coal fired electricity generation plants. The federal government's emission reduction schedule for existing plants will be intensity based—in other words tied to reduced emissions per unit of production.[217] There will be requirements for continuous improvement between now and 2020. This is at least a start and will result in emission cuts in several sectors. However, for industrial facilities and oil sands operations that are rapidly growing, it will not be adequate for the task ahead, since the intensity targets will allow total emissions at industrial facilities to continue increasing, if total production rises at a very rapid pace.

Climate change policies will need to be integrated into broader economic development policy. One dimension of this will necessitate all new economic development proposals being screened in the context of the climate crisis. This was clearly not done in the province of Alberta, when applications for oil sands projects were brought before government. Alberta oil sands operations now account for 50 million tones of CO^2 equivalent per year and are projected to grow rapidly.[218] The careful screening of oil sands development is a relevant example for Saskatchewan to consider as well, given Premier Wall's expressed interest in oil sands production in northwest Saskatchewan. Certainly, oil sands development in the way it has been practiced in Alberta is extremely greenhouse gas intensive and should not be permitted in Saskatchewan. If several large scale *in situ* oil sands developments were to proceed here, Saskatchewan's greenhouse gas emission reduction targets would not be met.[219] In the end, the wisest path may be for Saskatchewan to forgo oil sands development, at least in the near term, because of its environmental impacts. Not only are the excess greenhouse gas emissions very problematic, but conventional oil sands operations have large scale negative impacts from forest fragmentation, acid rain emissions, water pollution and damage to biodiversity.

Sir Nicholas Stern, author of the climate change assessment prepared for the U.K. government, has estimated that 2% of Gross Domestic Product will need to be invested each year to address the climate crisis. In this context, and given the exceptionally high level of emissions in Saskatchewan, the Saskatchewan and Canadian governments should plan to invest the equivalent of at least 1% of Saskatchewan GDP each year, a combined total of $450 million per year on measures in Saskatchewan that reduce greenhouse gas emissions.[220] This should be a sufficient sum to lever at least an equivalent investment from the private sector, bringing total annual investment to 2% of GDP. Given Saskatchewan's unusually high emissions, an even higher level of investment may ultimately prove to be necessary.

Although this chapter has focused on the leadership role the provincial government should play in tackling Saskatchewan emissions, the federal government also has a very large responsibility for public policy in this arena, and should be providing a substantial share of the necessary financial resources.

While major government investments, changes in lifestyle, shifts in tax policy and firm regulations will all be needed to tackle climate change, ultimately what will be needed above all is inspirational leadership. The Provincial Government should link itself and help link community leaders with jurisdictions around the world that are doing inspiring things to address climate change. For example, Germany, a country with less than half the sunlight hours of Saskatchewan, installed 100,000 solar photovoltaic systems in 2006.[221] California and Oregon are vigorously working to achieve their greenhouse gas reduction targets with aggressive solar programs, good building codes, comprehensive incentive programs and a willingness to regulate auto emissions. Vaxjo, a community of 78,000 people in Sweden, is half way to becoming a city entirely free of fossil fuels. 51% of its energy now comes from sources such as solar, geothermal and biomass energy.[222] The 46,000 people in the municipality of Thisted in Denmark are obtaining 82% of their heating and 92% of their electricity from renewable energy. Renewable energy sources include wind turbines, biogas, biomass, rapeseed oil, geothermal energy, solar energy and waste heat from industry. The municipality has over 250 wind turbines.[223] These are the kinds of jurisdictions Saskatchewan could work with as it seeks to fundamentally overhaul its energy and transportation systems in the face of the climate crisis.

Saskatchewan needs to do its share to ensure that future generations of Saskatchewan citizens and people across the globe can enjoy an inhabitable planet. We also need to act while there is still time to make a difference. Failure to reduce our greenhouse gas emissions sharply in the next two decades will mean that future generations will face a deteriorating natural environment, while at the same time being forced to cut their emissions even deeper than they would have otherwise needed to. This paper has demonstrated that a good starting point for achieving reductions in greenhouse gas emissions is to focus on energy efficiency and the application of renewable sources of energy.

ACKNOWLEDGEMENTS
I would like to thank Howard Leeson and Maureen Reed for the advice they offered in the course of my deliberations on this chapter. Thanks also to Kathie Maher Wolbaum, Puck Janes, Ann Coxworth and Roger Peters for their help and advice over the years in shaping policy ideas that made the preparation of this paper possible.

NOTES

1. Al Gore, *An Inconvenient Truth: The Planetary Emergency of Global Warming and What We Can Do About It* (New York: Rodale, 2006), 250–51.

2. Environment Canada, *National Inventory Report 1990–2006: Greenhouse Gas Sources and Sinks in Canada. The Canadian Government's Submission to the UN Framework on Climate Change* (Government of Canada, April 2008), 540 (Annex 10). Saskatchewan's greenhouse gas emissions accounted for 10.1% of Canada's total greenhouse gas emissions.

3. *Human Development Report 2007/2008—Qatar: The Human Development Index—Going Beyond Income* (United Nations Development Program, 2008). Refer to UNDP web site and to Country Fact Sheets—Qatar. The report lists Qatar's CO2 emissions per capita at 79.3 tonnes in 2004. It lists U.S. per capita emissions at 20.6 tones.

Hot Spots: *The Carbon Atlas* (United Kingdom: *The Guardian*, December 17, 2007). See graph "Highest Per Person CO_2 emissions, Top 20 plus UK, 2005, tones"). The graph reports on data prepared for the December 2007 United Nations Conference in Bali, Indonesia and uses the Energy Information Administration as its source. It cites world average per capita emissions at 4.37 tonnes, Canadian average per capita emissions at 19.14 tonnes, U.S. average emissions at 20.14 tonnes and Qatar average emissions at 61.94 tonnes. Varying estimates for Qatar's emissions are cited in the literature. This may be in part because data filed with the United Nations by Qatar appears incomplete. Qatar's emissions have risen extremely quickly since 1990 and population has risen quickly as well.

4. Presentation by Semida Silveira, Sustainability Expert, Swedish Energy Association, Stockholm, Sweden to a delegation of four Saskatchewan government representatives in February 2006."Sweden's Population Hits 9 Million" (Stockholm: Statistics Sweden, August 13, 2004). Framework Convention on Climate Change, National Greenhouse Gas Inventory Data for the Period 1990–2005, October 24, 2007. Refer to Table 4 on page 17. This data excludes emissions/removals from land use, land-use change and forestry. Environment Canada, *National Inventory Report 1990–2006*, 539 (Annex 10). The comparative data for Saskatchewan and Sweden are based on 2005 data for Sweden and 2006 data for Saskatchewan, the most recent data available at the time of writing.

5. "Past Decade the Warmest Ever, says UN Meteorological Agency" (United Nations News Centre, December 13, 2007).

6. T. Barker, I. Bashmakov, L. Bernstein, J.E. Bogner, P.R. Bosch, R. Dave, O.R. Davidson, B.S. Fisher, S. Gupta, K. Halsnaes, G.J. Heij, S. Kahn Ribeiro, S. Kobayashi, M.D. Levine, D.L. Martino, O.Masera, B. Metz, L.A. Meyer, G-J. Nabuurs, A. Najam, N. Nakicenovic, H.-H. Rogner, J. Roy, J. Sathaye, R. Schock, P. Shukla, R.E.H. Sims, P. Smith, D.A. Tirpak, D. Urge-Vorsatz and D. Ahou, "Technical Summary." In B. Metz, O.R. Davidson, P.R. Bosch, R. Dave and L.A. Meyer (eds.), *Climate Change 2007:*

Mitigation. Contribution of Working Group 3 to the Fourth Assessment Report of the Intergovernmental Panel on Climate Change (Cambridge: Cambridge University Press, 2007), 28.

7. B. Metz, O.R. Davidson, P.R. Bosch, R. Dave and L.A. Meyer (eds.), "IPCC, 2007, Summary for Policy Makers." In *Climate Change 2007: Mitigation of Climate Change. Contribution of Working Group 3 to the Fourth Assessment Report of the Intergovernmental Panel on Climate Change* (Cambridge: Cambridge University Press, 2007), 3.

8. Gore, *An Inconvenient Truth*, 63–67. National Oceanic and Atmospheric Administration, "Carbon Dioxide, Methane Rise Sharply in 2007" (USA: NOAA, United States Department of Commerce, April 23, 2008). In this release the NOAA reports that human activities pushed carbon dioxide levels up to 380ppm by early 2006. It also reports that by early 2008 the concentration of carbon dioxide in the atmosphere had risen above 384ppm. (Refer to graph entitled "Recent Global Months Mean Carbon Dioxide" published as part of the release. It states carbon dioxide levels in the atmosphere increased by 2.4 ppm in 2007.)

9. S. Solomon, S, D. Qin, M. Manning, Z. Chen, M. Marquis, K.B. Avery, M.Tignor and H.L. Miller (eds.), "IPCC, 2007: Summary for Policy Makers." In *Climate Change 2007: The Physical Science Basis. Contribution of Working Group 1 to the Fourth Assessment Report of the Intergovernmental Panel on Climate Change* (Cambridge: Cambridge University Press, Cambridge, 2007), 3. Tim Flannery, The Weather Makers: How We Are Changing the Climate and What It Means for Life on Earth (Harpers Collins Publishers Ltd., 2005), 30–31. David J. Hofman, *The NOAA Annual Greenhouse Gas Index (AGGI)* (NOAA Earth System Research Laboratory, 2008). Refer to "2007 Results" and chart recording nitrous oxide levels from 1978 to early 2008. (web site: www.esrl. noaa.gov/gmd/aggi/)

10. *IPCC 2007, Working Group 1*, 3. Official Website of the United States Environmental Protection Agency (Climate Change section), 2007. "Carbon Dioxide, Methane Rise Sharply In 2007," April 23, 2008). Refer to chart on methane increases from 2004 to early 2008.

11. Nicholas Stern, *The Economics of Climate Change* (Cambridge: Cambridge University Press, 2006), 5.

12. European Environment Agency, "Atmospheric Greenhouse Gas Concentrations (CSI 013)," April 2008. Refer to section entitled "Key Assessment." This assessment cites the overall concentration of the six Kyoto GHG's at 433ppm by the end of 2006. "Carbon Dioxide, Methane Rise Sharply in 2007, NOAA." David J. Hofman, *The NOAA Annual Greenhouse Gas Index*. Carbon dioxide levels increased from 380 ppm in early 2006 to over 384 ppm by the end of 2007. Nitrous oxide increased from 319 ppb in 2005 to over 320 ppb in 2007. Methane increased from 1774 ppb in 2005 to over 1783 ppb by the end of 2007.

13. Stern, *The Economics of Climate Change*, xvi (Summary of Conclusions). There is a growing number of scientists who believe greenhouse gas emissions need to be stabilized at a level of no more than 450 parts per million. One example is a group of over 200 well respected scientists who signed the "2007 Bali Climate Declaration By Scientists." They state "in the long run, greenhouse gas concentrations need to be stabilised at a level well below 450 ppm (parts per million; measured in CO_2-equivalent concentration)." The Declaration can be found on the web site of Climate Change Research Centre, University of New South Wales, Sydney, Australia.

14. Stern, *The Economics of Climate Change*, 219–21.

15 Ibid.,227.

16. *IPCC, 2007, Contribution of Working Group 3*, 3.

17. *IPCC 2007, Working Group 1, Technical Summary*, 25.

18. Flannery, *The Weather Makers*, 31.

19. David J. Hofman, "The NOAA Annual Greenhouse Gas Index." Refer to introduction to 2007 results (web site: www.esrl.noaa.gov/gmd/aggi/)

20. *IPCC 2007, Working Group 1*, 13. These figures represent "best estimates" of projected temperature increases by 2090–99 relative to the period 1980–99. The 1.8° C temperature increase is the best estimate for the low scenario which has a likely range of 1.1 to 2.9° C. The 4.0° is the best estimate for the high scenario which has a likely range of 2.4° C to 6.4° C.

21. Susan Joy Hassol, *Impacts of a Warming Arctic, Arctic Climate Impact Assessment* (New York: Cambridge University Press, 2004), 10.

22. Stern, *The Economics of Climate Change*, 8.

23. *IPCC 2007, Summary for Policy Makers*. In: *Climate Change 2007: Impacts, Adaptation and Vulnerability. Contribution of Working Group 2 to the Fourth Assessment Report of the Intergovernmental Panel on Climate Change* (New York, NY: Cambridge University Press, 2007), 10. Refer to "Ecosystems" subheading.

24. Stern, *The Economics of Climate Change*, 94.

25. Ibid., 114.

26. Gore, *An Inconvenient Truth*, 110.

27. Ibid., 82–84.

28. Ian Sample, "Rainfall the Worst for 200 Years … In Case You Hadn't Guessed." *The Guardian* (London), July 27, 2007.

29. "Flood Victims Fight for Food: Estimated 10 Million People Left Homeless, Stranded." *Saskatoon StarPhoenix*, August 7, 2007, B8.

30. CBC News. "Thousands Flee as Floods Inundate U.S. Midwest Cities: Officials in Iowa Irritated at 100-year Flood Every 4 Years," June 13, 2008. CBC web site: www.cbc.ca/world story/2008/06/13/iowa-flood.html; CTV News, "Flooding Leaves 20,000 Homeless in Iowa City," June 14, 2008. CTV web site: www.ctv.ca/servlet?ArticleNews/story/CTV News?20080614/fl…; Reuters. "Flooding Eases, Devastation Sets In," *Saskatoon Star Phoenix*, June 21, 2008, D5.

31. Stern, *The Economics of Climate Change*, 92.

32. Ibid., 78.

33. Gore, *An Inconvenient Truth*, 58.

34. *IPCC 2007, Contribution of Working Group 2 to the Fourth Assessment Report of the Intergovernmental Panel on Climate Change*, 13. Refer to the subheading "Africa."

35. Ibid., 14. Refer to subheading "Europe."

36. Miles Mittlestaedt, "How Global Warming Goes Against the Grain," *Toronto Globe and Mail*, January 24, 2007.

37. *IPCC 2007, Working Group 2*, 13. Refer to the subheading "Africa."

38. Stern, *The Economics of Climate Change*, 84.

39. Gore, *An Inconvenient Truth*, 117.

40. Stern, *The Economics of Climate Change*, 3.

41. "Larsen B Ice Shelf Collapses in Antarctica." Boulder, Colorado: National Snow

and Ice Data Centre Web Site, University of Colorado. Posted March 18, 2002 and updated March 21, 2002.

42. Stern, *The Economics of Climate Change*, 20.

43. *IPCC 2007 Working Group 2*, 12. Refer to subheading: "Coastal Systems and Low-Lying Areas."

44. Margaret Munro, "Northern Communities Brace For Disastrous Melt," *Saskatoon StarPhoenix*, October 7, 2006, E2.

45. Patrick Barkham, "Waves of Destruction," *The Guardian* (London), April 17, 2008.

46. Jeremy Page, "Climate of Fear in Sinking Country," *The Times* (London), February 2, 2007, 6.

47. "Press Conference by Alliance of Small Island States Addressing Climate Change." United Nations, Department of Public Information, February 12, 2008.

48. *The International Herald Tribune*, February 3, 2007, 2.

49. Cornella Dean, "Rapid Decline of Coral Leads to Restoration Efforts Worldwide," *The San Diego Union–Tribune*, May 17, 2007, E3.

50. *IPCC 2007, Working Group 2*, 11.

51. "Great Barrier Reef Could Die," *The International Herald Tribune*, February 3, 2007, 2.

52. *IPCC 2007, Working Group 2*, 12. Refer to the subheading: "Health."

53. Stern, *The Economics of Climate Change*, 87.

54. "World Health Organization Fact Sheet on Climate and Health, July 2005." World Health Organization Web Site.

55. "Fighting Climate Change: Human Solidarity in a Divided World." Press Conference on United Nations Development Programme Report. United Nations Department of Public Information. November 27, 2007; United Nations Development Programme, *Human Development Report 2007/2008: Fighting Climate Change: Human Solidarity in a Divided World* (New York: UNDP, 2007), 18.

56. Pamela Cowan, "Record Year for Cases in 2007," *Saskatoon StarPhoenix*, April 28, 2008, A4.

57. Geoffrey York, "Environmental Refugees: Mongolian Herdsmen No Longer Free To Roam," *Toronto Globe and Mail*, March 6, 2008, A10; Stefan Lovgren, "Climate Change Creating Millions of 'Eco Refugees' UN Warns," *National Geographic*, November 18, 2005.

58. Dan McDougall, "Time Runs Out for Islanders on Global Warming's Front Line," *The Observer*, March 30, 2008.

59. The Associated Press, "Ominous Arctic Ice Melt Worries Experts." CTV website: CTV.ca, December 11, 2007.

60. The Associated Press, "Ominous Arctic Ice Melt Worries Experts," CTV website: CTV.ca, December 11, 2007.

61. Marianne White, "Ice Melt Will be Once in a Million: Arctic Ocean Could See a Summer Free of Ice by 2010," *Saskatoon StarPhoenix*, November 16, 2007, A16.

62. *IPCC 2007, Contribution of Working Group 1 to the Fourth Assessment Report of the IPCC*, 15.

63. James Randerson, "Trees Absorbing Less CO_2 as World Warms, Study Finds," *The Guardian* (London), January 3, 2008.

64. Ian Sample, "Global Meltdown: Scientists Isolate Areas Most at Risk of Climate Change," *The Guardian* (London), February 5, 2008.

65. Juliette Jowit and Robin McKie, "Glaciers Melt at Fastest Rate in Past 5,000 Years," *The Observer*, March 16, 2008.

66. AFP, "Stern Review Author Paints Bleaker Picture on Climate Change." London: AFP, April 16, 2008.

67. Tony Harras (ed.), *Climate Change: Addressing Opportunities and Challenges* (Regina: Climate Change Saskatchewan, Keewatin Publications, 2007), 3.

68. Saskatchewan Corrections and Public Safety, "Chart of Provincial Disaster Assistance Program Historical Data 1975–2006." Provided to the Human Services Committee of the Saskatchewan Legislature in 2007.

69. Bruce Johnstone, "Government Prepared To Rein In SGI's Outside Business: Insurance Company Posts Profit of $35 Million in 2007 Despite Increase in Claims," *Saskatoon StarPhoenix*, 2008.

70. Government of Saskatchewan, "Government Supporting Flood Efforts at Cumberland House." Government of Saskatchewan News Release, June 29, 2005.

71. Visit by Peter Prebble with members of the RM of Arborfield in the summer of 2005 and tour of damage in the Rural Municipality caused by heavy rains and flooding; Kenyon Wallace, "Waldsea Lake Cabins in Peril," *Saskatoon StarPhoenix*, August 11, 2007, 3; David Hutton, "Province To Begin Draining Lake," *Saskatoon StarPhoenix*, July 19, 2007, A7; James Wood, "Flood-Damaged Cabins Ordered Demolished," *Saskatoon StarPhoenix*, August 14, 2007, 3.

72. "Flooding Eases On Northeast Saskatchewan Reserve." CTV News, CTV Web Site, April 23, 2007.

73. Remarks by Al Gore at an address at the Regina Exhibition Grounds on Monday, April 23, 2007.

74. Dave Sauchyn, Elaine Barrow, Ron Hopkinson and Peter Leavitt, *Aridity on the Canadian Plains: Future Trends and Past Variability* (Regina: Prairie Adaptation Research Collaborative, No. 03-01), 8.

75. Marc-André Parisien, Victor Kafka, Nadele Flynn, Kelvin Hirsch, Bernie Todd and Mike Flannigan, *Fire Behavior Potential in Central Saskatchewan Under Predicted Climate Change* (Regina: Prairie Adaptation Research Collaborative, Summary Document No. 05-01), 3.

76. Wendy Gillis, "Smoke from Forest Fires Forces More Evacuations," *Saskatoon StarPhoenix*, July 5, 2008, A9.

77. Bill Curry, "Native Towns at Risk of Going Up in Flames: More than 100 Remote B.C. Communities in Danger after Pine Beetles Create Huge Swath of Dry, Dead Timber," *Toronto Globe and Mail*, February 6, 2008, A5.

78. D. Sauchyn and S. Kulshreshtha, "Prairies." in D.S. Lemmen, F.J. Warren, J. Lacroix and E. Bush (eds.), *From Impacts to Adaptation: Canada in a Changing Climate 2007* (Ottawa: Government of Canada, 2008), 288, Figure 9 (a).

79. Ibid., 285.

80. Ibid., 319.

81. Ibid., 301.

82. "Saskatoon Soaked after Record-Breaking Rainfall," CTV News Web Site, June 18, 2007.

83. Sauchyn and Kulshreshtha, "Prairies,"307.

84. Ibid., 291, 293, 294.

85. Ibid., 295.

86. Ibid., 309. The authors report on comments made by elders at the "First Nations' Traditional Ways of Life and Climate Change: The Prince Albert Grand Council Elders' Forum," February 2004.

87. Ibid., 308.

88. Ibid., 293.

89. Ibid., 293.

90. United Nations Development Programme, "Fighting Climate Change: Human Solidarity in a Divided World." Press Conference on United Nations Development Programme Report, New York, November 17, 2007.

91. World Health Organization, "Climate Change Will Erode Foundations of Health: WHO Director-General Warns Vulnerable Populations at Greatest Risk of Projected Impacts." World Health Organization Web Site, April 7, 2008.

92. "Measuring the Human Cost of Climate Change," *The Guardian* (London), December 14, 2007).

93. Stern, *The Economics of Climate Change*, xv. Refer to "Summary of Conclusions."

94. Ibid., Chapter 9, 239.

95. Juliette Jowit and Patrick Wintour, "Cost of Tackling Global Climate Change Has Doubled Warns Stern," *The Guardian* (London), June 26, 2008.

96. Ashley Seager, "Avoiding Climate Change Disaster is Affordable, says PWC," *The Guardian* (London), July 3, 2008.

97. *IPCC, 2007, Contribution Of Working Group 3 to the Fourth Assessment Report of the Intergovernmental Panel on Climate Change 2007*, 27 (Technical Summary). Emissions of the fluorinated gases are estimated at about 1.1% of total emissions on a 100 year global warming potential basis.

98. United Nations Framework Convention on Climate Change "Status of Ratification" section. United Nations Framework Convention Web Site. Refer to the U.S. and Australia. Australia ratified the Kyoto Protocol on December 3, 2007, only weeks after the election of a national Labour Party Government.

99. "Australia Elected New PM," *Saskatoon StarPhoenix*, November 26, 2007, D10; Web Site of the United Nations Framework Convention on Climate Change. Refer to "List of Annex 1 Parties to the Convention–Australia." Australia ratified the Kyoto Protocol on December 12, 2007; Neil Sands, "Australia Comes in from the Cold on Climate Change." AFP. March 9, 2008 (http://news.yahoo.com/s/afp/20080309/wl_asia_afp/australiaclimate).

100. United Nations Framework Convention on Climate Change, "Status of Ratification" section, Refer to Canada.

101. "Harper Letter Called Kyoto a Socialist Scheme" (Canadian Press, January 30, 2007).

102. Hansard of the Saskatchewan Legislature, December 10, 2002, 2896–97.

103. Ibid., December 11, 2002, 2927.

104. Ibid., December 10, 2002, 2870.

105. Ibid., 2861.

106. Ibid., 2867.

107. Ibid., 2867.

108. Ibid., December 11, 2002, 2932.

109. Rick Patrick (Planning and Regulatory Affairs, SaskPower). Briefing Note entitled "SaskPower–Saskatchewan Renewable Energy," July 24, 2006.

110. "Seniors Housing Given Energy Assistance," *Saskatoon Saskatoon Sun*, January 6, 2002, 18; Colleen Silverthorn, "Government Opens Energy Conservation Office," *Regina Leader-Post*. September 17, 2002, B4; Andrew Ehrkamp, "SaskPower, City Sign Deal to Improve Energy Efficiency," *Regina Leader-Post*, October 18, 2002; Janet Nattress, "Energy Conservation Program Pays Off," *North Battleford News-Optimist*, December 8, 2002, 2; Barb Pacholik, "CO_2 Idea Given OK," *Regina Leader-Post*, November 16, 2002, B1; Neil Scott, "More Wind Power," *Regina Leader-Post*, August 28, 2003, B3; Murray Lyons, "More Wind Power," *Regina Leader-Post*, September 9, 2003, A1; Government of Saskatchewan, "Saskatchewan Mandates Energy Efficiency in Public Buildings" (Regina: Government of Saskatchewan News Release, December 15, 2003); Government of Saskatchewan, "PST Rebate on New Energy Efficient Appliances" (Regina: Government of Saskatchewan News Release, December 18, 2003; Government of Saskatchewan, "Increased Ethanol in Fuel May 1st, 2005" (Regina: Government of Saskatchewan News Release, June 10, 2004); Paul Hanley, "One-third Renewables Targeted for 2025," *Saskatoon StarPhoenix*, December 19, 2006, C2.

111. "Statistics from the Saskatchewan EnerGuide for Houses $2,000 Grant Program" Prepared by the Government of Saskatchewan as part of the "Saskatchewan EnerGuide for Houses Announcement," March 26, 2007.

112. Speech from the Throne, Hansard of the Saskatchewan Legislature, November 7, 2005, 2.

113. The Canadian Energy Efficiency Alliance, "Sixth Annual Ranking of Canadian Jurisdictions on Energy Efficiency." Canadian Energy Efficiency Centre web site, 2006), 4 (grade for 2005). The report was released on November 1, 2006 in conjunction with a press release. The report gives energy efficiency grades to each of the provincial governments and the national government from 1999 to 2005.

114. Government of Saskatchewan, *Saskatchewan Energy and Climate Change Plan 2007* (Regina: Government of Saskatchewan, June 2007), 4.

115. Government of Saskatchewan, "Green Future Fund Established With Proceeds From Sale of Share in NewGrade Upgrader" (Regina: Government of Saskatchewan News Release, September 5, 2007), and Media Backgrounder on the Green Future Fund, September 5, 2007.

116. Government of Saskatchewan, "Saskatchewan Energuide for Houses Extended and Enhanced" (Regina: News Release issued by Crown Investments Corporation citing Premier Lorne Calvert and Crown Investments Corporation Minister Maynard Sonntag, March 26, 2007).

117. Government of Saskatchewan, "Saskatchewan EnerGuide for Houses Announcement" (Regina: Government of Saskatchewan News Release, March 26, 2007).

118. Government of Saskatchewan, "Net Metering Program Announcement" (SaskPower News Release, October 1, 2007); remarks by Premier Lorne Calvert, Hon. John Nilson, Minister Responsible for SaskPower and Pat Youzwa, President and CEO of SaskPower.

119. Government of Saskatchewan, "SaskPower Eneraction Will Help Customers Save Money and the Environment" (SaskPower News Release, September 17, 2007).

120. Government of Saskatchewan, *Saskatchewan Energy and Climate Change Plan 2007*, 4.

121. SaskPower Web Site. Refer to "2007 Supply Decision"; Government of Saskatchewan, "Sustainable and Renewable Electricity Sources Will Power Saskatchewan's Future" (Regina: Government of Saskatchewan News Release, September 6, 2007).

122. Government of Saskatchewan, "Municipalities Benefit from New Energy Efficiency Initiatives" (Regina: Government of Saskatchewan News Release, August 17, 2007).

123. Canadian Energy Efficiency Alliance, "2007 Report Card on Energy Efficiency" (September 2008), www.energyefficiency.org/eecentre/eecentre.nsf/f562d7e5f28f9

124. James Wood, "Environment Group Seeks Ear of New Government," *Saskatoon StarPhoenix*, November 27, 2007, A9.

125. Paul Hanley, "Demise of Energy Conservation Office Rumoured," *Saskatoon StarPhoenix*, February 26, 2008, C2; Hansard of the Saskatchewan Legislature, April 22, 2008, 1053.

126. James Wood, "Wall to Work With Provinces on Conservation," *Saskatoon StarPhoenix*, January 30, 2008.

127. James Wood, "Emissions Goal Up In Smoke?," *Saskatoon StarPhoenix*, October 24, 2008, 3.

128. Ibid.

129. James Wood, "Wall Talks Up Reactors: Nuclear Dump Not on Agenda, but Uranium Plan Could Include Use of Small-Scale Reactors," *Saskatoon StarPhoenix*, December 11, 2007, 3.

130. CBC, "Premier Pushes for Uranium Enrichment in Sask." Canada: CBC News Tuesday, March 22, 2008.

131. James Wood, "Nuclear Among Options: Government Mulls Methods to Address Power Needs," *Saskatoon StarPhoenix*, April 23, 2008, 3.

132. James Wood and Randy Burton, "Sask. Nuclear Power Plant Still 'Long Ways Off': Boyd," Saskatoon *Star Phoenix*, May 8, 2008, A7.

133. Cassandra Kyle, "Bruce Power Eyes Nuclear Feasibility," Saskatoon *Star Phoenix*, June 18, 2008.

134. James Wood, "Premier Interested in 'Clean Coal' Development,"Saskatoon *Star Phoenix*, February 14, 2008, A4.

135. Government of Saskatchewan, "New Federal Funding Opens Door to Major Carbon Capture Demonstration Project in Saskatchewan" (Regina: Government of Saskatchewan News Release, February 27, 2008).

136. Government of Saskatchewan, "SaskPower Issues Request for Proposals for Carbon Capture Technology" (Regina: SaskPower News Release, August 20, 2008).

137. Saskatchewan Party, "Securing the Future: New Ideas tor Saskatchewan." Pamphlet distributed by the Saskatchewan Party During the October–November 2007 provincial election. Refer to section entitled: "A Sustainable Environment." The election commitment reads: "Require mandatory 2.5% bio-diesel blend on diesel fuels sold in Saskatchewan once provincial production capacity is capable of meeting demand."

138. Government of Saskatchewan, "Province Provides 20 Per Cent Rebate to 'Green'

Vehicle Owners" (Regina: Government of Saskatchewan News Release, April 7, 2008).

139. Government of Saskatchewan, "SaskPower Brings Award-Winning Project Porchlight Campaign To the Province" (SaskPower News Release, September 15, 2008).

140. Government of Saskatchewan, "Premier Commits to Exploring Oil Sands Potential" (Government of Saskatchewan News Release, December 12, 2007).

141. Premier Brad Wall, "Keynote Address, FirstEnergy East Coast Canadian Energy Conference," Waldorf Astoria Hotel, New York, March 13, 2008. Government of Saskatchewan Web Site, 2008. Please refer to Premier's speeches.

142. "It's About Time Wall Stands Up for Saskatchewan," Saskatoon *Star Phoenix*, October 14, 2008, 8.

143. Geoffrey York, "Isolated Canada Grudgingly Accepts Bali Deal," *Toronto Globe and Mail*, December 15, 2007.

144. "Alan Freeman, "Canada Blocking Consensus on Climate Change, Source Says," *Toronto Globe and Mail*, November 24, 2007.

145. United Nations Framework Convention on Climate Change, 1990–2005 Trends for Annex 1 Parties to the Kyoto Protocol. United Nations Web Site, 2008. This is part of a UNFCCC fact sheet on 1990–2005 emission trends posted on the web site of the United Nations Framework Convention on Climate Change; Environment Canada, Canada's 2006 Greenhouse Gas Inventory: A Summary of Trends. Environment Canada website, May 2008. 2006 data is the most current inventory data available at the time of writing.

146. Brian Laghi, "Tough New Green Plan Targets Oil Sands," *Toronto Globe and Mail*, March 10, 2008, A1.

147. *IPCC 2007, Contribution of Working Group 3 to the Fourth Assessment Report of the Intergovernmental Panel on Climate Change*, 3.

148. Ibid., 10.

149. Ibid., 13.

150. Ibid., 13.

151. Ibid., 10.

152. Ibid., 13–14.

153. Ibid., 19.

154. Government of Saskatchewan, *Saskatchewan Energy and Climate Change Plan 2007*, 6. The data is based on emission figures for 2004.

155. Database of U.S. State Incentives for Renewables and Efficiency: www.dsireusa. org/, 2008, Refer to Renewable Energy section for details on states with Renewable Portfolio Standards.

156. Presentation by Rodney McDonald, Sustainability and Standards Specialist, Special Projects and Evaluation, Manitoba Hydro in the summer of 2006 to Peter Prebble and Kathie Maher Wolbaum, representing the Government of Saskatchewan. Mr. McDonald has done extensive preparatory work for the Manitoba government on building codes; presentation by Jacob Worm, Manager of NewEnergy Denmark, Aarhus, Denmark in February 2007 to a delegation of four representatives from the Government of Saskatchewan (Peter Prebble, Lon Borgerson, Sandra Morin and Kathie Maher Wolbaum).

157. Meeting of Peter Prebble with John Rinella, Senior Policy Advisory, Conservation Branch, Office of Conservation and Strategic Policy, Ontario Ministry of Energy in the summer of 2007.

158. C40 Cities website, "Renewables, Rizhao, China: An Extensive Solar Program in China": www.c40 cities.org/bestpractices/renewables/rizhao_solar.jsp, accessed in 2008.

159. Ibid., www.c40 cities.org/bestpractices/renewables/Barcelona_solar.jsp, accessed in 2008.

160. Wood, "Nuclear Among Options," 3.

161. Presentations in the summer of 2006 by Lloyd Kuczek, Division Manager, Consumer Marketing and Sales, Power Smart, Manitoba Hydro; Lois Morrison, Manager of Marketing Programs, Manitoba Hydro; Rhonda Orr, Manager of Government Relations and Current Issues Co-ordination, Manitoba Hydro; Gerry Rose, Vice President of Customer Service and Marketing, Power Smart, Manitoba Hydro; Rick Patrick, Vice President of Environment and Regulatory Affairs, SaskPower and , Demand Side Management Unit staff, SaskPower. These presentations were made to Peter Prebble and Kathie Maher Wolbaum, representing the Government of Saskatchewan.

162. Meeting of Peter Prebble in July 2007 with Blair Hamilton, President, Efficiency Vermont; Scudder Parker, Senior Project Manager, Efficiency Vermont and Robert Ide, Director, Energy Efficiency, Department of Public Services, State of Vermont.

163. Danish Wind Industry Association web site. Refer to Sector Statistics–"Turbines in Denmark," accessed in 2008. The web site states that by the end of January 2007 there were 5,267 turbines in Denmark with a total capacity of 3,135 MW. These turbines not only provide for domestic consumption, but also for significant wind electricity exports; presentation by Preben Magegaard, Danish Folkcenter for Renewable Energy, at the World Wind Energy Conference 2008, Kingston, June 24-26, 2008. Mr. Magegaard estimated current Danish wind power capacity in 2008 at 3,200 MW; presentation by Hans Larsen, Head Systems Analysis Department, RISO National Laboratory, Technical University of Denmark, Copenhagen, Denmark to four representatives of the Government of Saskatchewan and subsequent discussions with the team of wind power researchers at the RISO National Laboratory in February 2007.

164. Presentation by Herman Albers, President of the German Wind Energy Association, 7th World Wind Energy Conference 2008, June 24–26, 2008.

165. Sustainable Energy Ireland, Sorne Wind, ENFOR, VRB Power Systems. "VRB ESS Energy Storage And The Development of Dispatchable Wind Turbine Output" (VRB Power Systems Web Site, 2007), 11–13; presentation by Dr. Eric Martinot at the World Wind Energy Conference 2008, June 24, 2008 on his "Renewables 2007 Global Status Report, Market Policy, and Investment Trends." Dr. Martinot states the future target for renewable electricity in Ireland is 13.2% by 2010.

166. Louise Radnofsky, "Wind Energy to Power UK by 2020, Government Says," *The Guardian* (London), December 10, 2007.

167. Presentation by Hugo Lucas, Institute for Energy Diversification and Saving, Spain at a Pre-Conference Workshop of the World Wind Energy Conference 2008, Kingston, Ontario, June 23, 2008.

168. SaskPower's web site notes that: "There is a technical potential of a few hundred megawatts of biomass distributed generation within the province which would come primarily from sawmill/pulp and paper operation wood residues. The amount of biomass that would potentially be used by SaskPower, however, will be less than the technical potential because some project and site specific characteristics may make some options economically impractical."

169. Presentation by Graeme Millen, Agri Energy Producers of Ontario, Panel on Canada's Renewable Energy Potential, 7th World Wind Energy Conference, Kingston, Ontario, June 24–26, 2008.

170. Presentation by Ludwig Dinkloh, Head of International Business, Schmack Biogas, AG, Germany to four representatives of the Government of Saskatchewan (Peter Prebble, Lon Borgerson, Sandra Morin and Kathie Maher Wolbaum) in February 2007; presentation by Gert Schultz, Manager (purchase of biomass), DONG Energy, Copenhagen, Denmark to Peter Prebble and Kathie Maher Wolbaum, representing the Government of Saskatchewan (February 2007); presentation by Thomas Siegmund, CEO of German BioEnergy Association, Berlin, Germany to four representatives of the Government of Saskatchewan in February 2007.

171. Presentation by Ludwig Dinkloh; presentation by Ken Kelln, P.Eng. and President of Kelln Solar Heating in Regina, Saskatchewan in May 2007.

172. Richard Blackwell, "Solar Power Heats Up With New Ontario Projects," *Toronto Globe and Mail, Report on Business*, January 22, 2008, B7.

173. Presentation by Herman Scheer, General Chairman of the World Council for Renewable Energy, entitled "The Winds of Change," 7th World Wind Energy Conference 2008, Kingston, Ontario, June 24, 2008.

174. Hawaiian Electric Company Inc. web site, "Sun Power For Schools Section." Sun Power for Schools is described as a voluntary partnership between Hawaiian Electric Company, Oahu's public schools and the community.

175. Presentation by Simon Clarke, Executive Vice President of Corporate Development, VRB Power Systems, Vancouver, B.C in the summer of 2007 to Peter Prebble and Kathie Maher Wolbaum, representing the Government of Saskatchewan; Jane Burgermeister, "Technology Advancements Allow Batteries to Store More Wind Energy." RenewableEnergyWorld.com Web Site. March 4, 2008.

176. Presentations by Melanie Chamberland (CANMET, Natural Resources Canada) and Roger Peters, Pembina Institute, Panel on Storage and Smart Grids: Enabling Renewable Expansion," 7th World Wind Energy Conference 2008, Kingston, Ontario, June 24, 2008.

177. Meeting of Peter Prebble with Michael Grainey, Director, and Mark Kendell, Senior Energy Analyst, Technology Development, Oregon Department of Energy in July 2006; meeting of Peter Prebble with Jack Layton, Leader of the New Democratic Party of Canada and former Toronto City Councillor in the summer of 2006; meeting of Peter Prebble with Peter Love, Chief Energy Conservation Officer, Conservation Bureau, Ontario Power Authority; Erika Lontoc, Program Manager, Commercial and Institutional Programs, Conservation Bureau, Ontario Power Authority in the summer of 2007.

178. Miles Brignall, "The Energy Offer That Really is a Dead Cert," *The Guardian* (London), January 12, 2008.

179. Presentation by Peter Dahl, Senior Manager, Economics and Marketing, Swedish District Heating Association, Stockholm, Sweden in February 2007 to four representatives (Peter Prebble, Lon Borgerson, Sandra Morin and Kathie Maher Wolbaum) from the Government of Saskatchewan; presentation by Kent Nystrom, Managing Director, Swedish Bioenergy Association, Stockholm, Sweden in February 2007 to four representatives from the Government of Saskatchewan.

180. Presentation by Marcus Braun, Office of the Mayor, Town of Crailsheim, Germany; Michaela Schoph, Renewable Energy Specialist and Project Leader, Town of

Crailsheim, Germany to four representatives of the Government of Saskatchewan, February 2007.

181. Presentation by Dr. Erwin Knapek, Mayor of Unterhacing, Germany in February 2007 to four representatives of the Government of Saskatchewan. Dr. Knapek led the installation of a geothermal system for electricity generation and space heating in the town of Unterhacing.

182. Telephone interview with Brian Brunskill, Helix Geological Consultants, Regina, in August 2007.

183. Telephone interview with Rob Dumont, Mechanical Engineer and Conservation Specialist in Saskatoon and owner of one of the most energy efficient homes in the world, August 2007; discussion with Rolf Holzkaemper at the opening of his Factor 9 home in Regina in the spring of 2007.

184. Ron Chalmers "Net-Zero Energy Home a First in City," *Edmonton Journal*, May 24, 2007; presentation by Rob Dumont, Mechanical Engineer and Conservation Specialist, Saskatchewan Research Council to the Energy Management Task Force of Saskatoon in February 2008; telephone interview with Janine Paul, Founder and Owner, Nexus Solar Corporation, Saskatoon, August 2007.

185. "All New Schools to be Zero-carbon by 2016," *The Guardian* (London), December 17, 2007; opening plenary session of the 2006 Annual Conference of the Solar Energy Society of the USA, July 2006, Denver, Colorado.

186. "Governor Doyle Announces Massive Five-Year Energy Plan: Citing Student Efforts, Wisconsin Governor Announces Major University of Wisconsin Clean Energy Initiative." Wisconsin Student Public Interest Research Group Web Site, September 29, 2006.

187. Saskatchewan Power Corporation, "Existing SaskPower Generating Facilities," Media Fact Sheet # 3, September 6, 2007. Saskatchewan's other coal fired power stations are Shand Power Station (267MW) and Popular River Power Station (572MW).

188. Government of Saskatchewan, "New Federal Funding Opens Door to Major Carbon Capture Demonstration Project in Saskatchewan" (Regina: Government of Saskatchewan News Release, February 27, 2008).

189. Jim Warren, "Clean Coal. Fuel for the Future," *Saskatoon StarPhoenix*, March 27, 2008, C5.

190. Harras, *Climate Change*, 10–11.

191. Michael Perry, "Australia Plans Carbon Storage Under Sea," *Toronto Globe and Mail*, March 20, 2008, B13.

192. "The Demise of FutureGen:The Cancellation of a Clean-coal Project Shows There's No Silver Bullet for Climate Change," *The Washington Post*, February 16, 2008, A 20.

193. Bruce Johnstone, "Plant's Clean-Coal Retrofit Would Cut Power Output: Generation Capability Would Fall by 40MW Due to CO_2 Capture," *Saskatoon StarPhoenix*, March 6, 2008, C8.

194. Government of Saskatchewan, "New Federal Funding Opens Door to Major Carbon Capture Demonstration Project in Saskatchewan" (Regina: Government of Saskatchewan News Release, February 27, 2008).

195. Harvey Wasserman, "New Nukes Not Ready for Prime Time: Nuclear Regulatory Commission Deals Devastating Blow to Nuclear Power Industry," *CounterPunch*, July 25, 2008.

196. Shawn McCarthy, "Scrubbed Reactor Plan May Cost AECL Millions," *Toronto Globe and Mail, Report on Business*, June 6, 2008; Janice Harvey, "Commentary," *New Brunswick Telegraph-Journal*, February 6, 2008.

197. David Shukman, "Nuclear Clean-Up Costs to Soar." London: The BBC, May 27, 2008.

198. Chad Selweski, "Down in the Dumps: Canadian Plan to Store Plants' Wastes Near Huron Provokes Outrage," *Macomb Daily*, June 8, 2008.

199. Gordon Edwards and Eric Notebaert, "Nuclear Power—Health And Safety Issues," August 9, 2008.

200. Mathew Wald, "As Nuclear Waste Languishes, Expense to U.S. Rises" (February 17, 2008); "Protestors Try to Derail Nuke Train," Australian News Network, March 28, 2001; Folkert Lenz, Reuters, Planet Ark, March 28, 2001. Wald reports that the U.S. federal government has already paid utilities $342 million for failure to dispose of high level radioactive waste, but is virtually certain to pay a total of at least $7 billion in the next few years. The Australian News Network reports that 30,000 police had to accompany a high level radioactive waste shipment by train for the purposes of disposal in Germany in 2001. Lenz puts the police presence at 20,000. Such unusual requirements for a police presence indicate both the level of protest and the state of division in society that nuclear waste disposal issues can create.

201. "Nuke-Plant Leukaemia Link?," *New Scientist*, February 9, 2008.

202. Amory B. Lovins, Imran Sheikh and Alex Markevich, "Forget Nuclear," *Rocky Mountain Institute Spring 2008 Newsletter*.

203. Environment Canada, National Inventory Report 1990–2006: Greenhouse Gas Sources and Sinks in Canada. The Canadian Government's Submission to the UN Framework on Climate Change. Environment Canada Website: April 2008), 539 (Annex 10).

204. Census of Canada, Chart entitled "Saskatchewan Census Population 1981–2006," prepared by the Census of Canada. Saskatchewan Bureau of Statistics Web Site, April, 2008.

205. Saskatchewan Bureau of Statistics Web Site (April 2008).

206. Government of Saskatchewan, "Huge Increase: Saskatchewan Grows by 16,492 in 2007" (Regina: Government of Saskatchewan News Release, March 27, 2008).

207. Government of Saskatchewan, *Saskatchewan Energy and Climate Change Plan* (Regina: Government of Saskatchewan, 2007), 6. Refer to Figure 1 (Saskatchewan Greenhouse Gas Emissions by Source: 2004)

208. Meeting held in July 2007 with George Little, Low Emission Vehicle Program, Department of Environmental Conservation, State of Vermont, USA.

209. Melissa Juergensen, "Ontario to Require Speed Limiters for Big Trucks," *Toronto Star*, July 2, 2007.

210. Environment Canada, "Vehicle Scrappage Programs." Vehicle scrappage programs are run in several Canadian provinces and cities for the purpose of reducing greenhouse gas and smog emissions. These programs receive financial assistance from Environment Canada. The Clean Air Foundation, the Saskatchewan Environmental Society, the Canadian Diabetes Association and the Government of Canada will be working together to launch such a program in Saskatchewan in 2009. Vehicles retired under these initiatives are recycled according to provincial environmental guidelines.

211. Meeting of Peter Prebble in the summer of 2007 with Don Struber, President of

Bison Transport; Arne Elias, Executive Director of the Centre for Sustainable Transportation in Winnipeg, and Terry Zdan, Policy Consultant in the Sustainable Transportation Development Unit of the Government of Manitoba.

212. Meetings held by Peter Prebble in the summer of 2007 with Jeff Balon, CEO of City of Saskatoon Transit Authority and Professor Barry Hertz, co-author of Saskatoon BioBus Project—Phase II Final Research Report.

213. Meeting held by Peter Prebble in May of 2007 with Reg Cox and Ed Zsombor of Saskatchewan Highways and Transportation. Variations in efficiency between rail and truck depend on the age of the truck and the locomotives.

214. Jeffrey Simpson, "B.C.'s Carbon Tax Sets a New Standard," *Toronto Globe and Mail*, February 20, 2008, A15; Justine Hunter, "Carbon Tax Focus of British Columbia Budget," *Toronto Globe and Mail*, February 20, 2008, A7.

215. *Saskatchewan Energy and Climate Change Plan 2007*, Figure 1, 6.

216. Environment Canada, "National Inventory Report: Information on Greenhouse Gas Sources." Environment Canada Website. Refer to Table A11-16: 1990–2005 GHG Emission Summary for Saskatchewan. See section on Fugitive Sources.

217. Brian Laghi, "Tough New Green Plan Targets Oil Sands," *Toronto Globe and Mail*, March 10, 2008, A1; Shawn McCarthy and Bill Curry, "Alberta Approves of Ottawa's New Emissions Rules," *Toronto Globe and Mail*, March 11, 2008, A11.

218. Erin Anderssen, "How Growth is Costing the Climate," *Toronto Globe and Mail*, February 1, 2008, A12. This article is part of a *Globe and Mail* series entitled "Shifting Sands: How Alberta's Oil Boom is Changing Canada Forever."

219. Paul Hanley, "Growth of Oil Sands Means Going Green a Fantasy," *Saskatoon StarPhoenix*, January 15, 2008, C2. *IPCC 2007, Climate Change 2007, Contribution of Working Group 3*; ibid., 268. The United Nations IPCC calculates that net emissions from oil sands are 15–34kg of carbon dioxide per GJ compared with 5–10kg of carbon dioxide per GJ for conventional oil. These numbers assume the production of transport fuel.

220. According to Statistics Canada, Saskatchewan's Gross Domestic Product was $45,922,000,000 in 2006. Refer to Statistics Canada, CANSIM, Catalogue no. 13-213-PPB and Statistics Canada Web site "Gross Domestic Product, Expenditure-Based, By Province and Territory 2002–2006."

221. Paul Gipe. "Germany Leads in 'Green Power' Technologies," *Environmental Science & Engineering Magazine* (March 2007): 46 (web site: www.esemag.com).

222. C40 Cities web site, "Renewables, Vaxjo, Sweden: Vaxjo is halfway to becoming fossil fuel free" (www.c40cities.org/bestpractices/renewables/vaxjo_fossilfuel.jsp, accessed in 2008).

223. Presentation by Preben Maegaard, Danish Folkcenter for Renewable Energy and President of the World Wind Energy Association from 2001–2005. 7th World Wind Energy Conference 2008, Kingston, Ontario, June 26, 2008.

APPENDICES

Appendix A: Electorial Results in Saskatchewan, 1905–2007

General Election — December 13, 1905				
Political Party	**Votes Cast**	**Percentage of Vote**	**Candidates Nominated**	**Candidates Elected**
Liberal	17,812	52.25	25	16
Provincial Rights	16,184	47.47	2424	9
Independent	94	.28	1	0
Totals	34,090	100.00	50	25
General Election — August 14, 1908				
Liberal	29,807	50.79	41	27
Provincial Rights	28,099	47.88	40	14
Independent-Liberal	394	.67	1	0
Independent	387	.66	2	0
Totals	58,687	100.00	84	41
General Election — July 11, 1912				
Liberal	50,004	56.96	53	45
Conservative	36,848	41.97	53	7
Independent	934	1.06	5	1
Totals	87,786	99.99	111	53*
General Election — June 26, 1917				
Liberal	106,552	56.68	58	51
Conservative	68,243	36.30	53	7
Non-Partisan	7,267	3.87	7	0
Independent	4,440	2.36	10	1
Labor	1,474	.78	2	0
Totals	187,976	99.99	130	59
General Election — June 9, 1921				
Liberal	93,983	51.39	60	46
Independent	46,556	25.73	35	7
Progressive	13,613	7.52	7	6
Conservative	7,133	3.94	4	2
Independent Conservative	6,295	3.48	3	1
Labor	6,034	3.33	3	0
Non-Partisan	3,735	2.06	3	0
Independent Labor	1,690	.93	1	0
Government	1,510	.83	1	0
Independent Non-Partisan	1,400	.77	1	0
Independent Pro-Government	Acclamation	—	1	1
Totals	180,949	99.98	119	63

*There were 54 seats contested at the 1912 election, however Cumberland was declared void and only 53 people were elected. A by-election was held on September 8, 1913, to fill the vacancy which existed in Cumberland.

General Election — June 2, 1925				
Political Party	Votes Cast	Percentage of Vote	Candidates Nominated	Candidates Elected
Liberal	127,751	51.51	62	50
Progressive	57,142	23.04	40	6
Conservative	45,515	18.35	18	3
Independent	8.703	3.51	6	2
Labor Liberal	4,704	1.90	1	1
Independent Liberal	2,653	1.07	1	1
Independent Conservative	1,545	.62	1	0
Totals	248,013	100.00	129	63
General Election — June 6, 1929				
Liberal	164,487	45.56	62	28
Conservative	131,550	36.44	40	24
Independent	32,729	9.07	17	6
Progressive	24,988	6.92	16	5
Liberal Labor	4,181	1.16	1	0
Economic Group	1,942	.54	3	0
Independent Liberal	1,160	.32	1	0
Totals	361,037	100.01	140	63
General Election — June 19, 1934				
Liberal	206,212	48.00	56	50
Conservative	114,923	26.75	52	0
Farmer-Labor	102,944	23.96	53	5
Independent	2,949	.69	3	0
Labor	1,420	.33	1	0
United Front	1,053	.25	3	0
Independent Liberal	133	.03	1	0
Totals	429,634	100.01	169	55
General Election — June 8, 1938				
Liberal	200,334	45.45	53	38
Co-operative Commonwealth Federation (CCF)	82,529	18.73	31	10
Social Credit	70,084	15.90	40	2
Conservative	52,315	11.87	24	0
Unity	9,848	2.23	3	2
Independent Labor	12,039	2.73	3	0
Labor Progressive	8,514	1.93	2	0
Independent	4,023	.91	2	0
Independent Conservative	828	.19	1	0
Independent Social Credit	228	05	1	0
Totals	440,742	99.99	160	52

General Election — June 15, 1944				
Political Party	Votes Cast	Percentage of Vote	Candidates Nominated	Candidates Elected
CCF	211,364	53.13	52	47
Liberal	140,901	35.42	52	5
Progressive Conservative	42,511	10.69	39	0
Labor Progressive	2,067	.52	3	0
Independent	705	.18	5	0
Social Credit	249	.06	1	0
Independent Liberal	5	.00	1	0
Totals	397,802	100.00	153	52
General Election — June 24, 1948				
CCF	236,900	47.56	52	31
Liberal	152,400	30.60	41	19
Social Credit	40,268	8.08	36	0
Progressive Conservative	37,986	7.63	9	0
Independent	11,088	2.23	5	1
Liberal-Progressive Conservative	9,574	1.92	3	0
Conservative Liberal	5,251	1.05	1	1
Independent Liberal	3,299	.66	1	0
Labor Progressive	1,301	.26	1	0
Totals	498,067	99.99	149	52
General Election — June 11, 1952				
CCF	291,705	54.06	53	42
Liberal	211,882	39.27	53	11
Social Credit	21,045	3.90	24	0
Progressive Conservative	10,648	1.97	8	0
Independent Progressive Conservative	1,542	.29	1	0
Independent	1,517	.28	3	0
Labor Progressive	1,151	.21	2	0
Independent Liberal	103	.02	1	0
Totals	539,593	100.00	145	53
General Election — June 20, 1956				
CCF	249,634	45.25	53	36
Liberal	167,427	30.35	52	14
Social Credit	118,491	21.48	53	3
Progressive Conservative	10,921	1.98	9	0
Independent	4,714	.85	2	0
Labor Progressive	536	.10	2	0
Totals	551,723	100.01	171	53

General Election — June 8, 1960				
Political Party	Votes Cast	Percentage of Vote	Candidates Nominated	Candidates Elected
CCF	276,846	40.76	55	37
Liberal	221,932	32.68	55	17
Progressive Conservative (PC)	94,737	13.95	55	0
Social Credit	83,895	12.35	55	0
Independent	1,417	.21	3	0
Communist	380	.06	2	0
Totals	679,207	100.01	225	54*
General Election — April 22, 1964				
Liberal	269,402	40.40	58	32
CCF	268,742	40.30	59	25
PC	126,028	18.90	43	1
Social Credit	2,621	.39	2	0
Communist	68	.01	1	0
Totals	666,861	100.00	163	58**
General Election — October 11, 1967				
Liberal	193,871	45.57	59	35
New Democratic Party (NDP)	188,653	44.35	59	24
Pc	41,583	9.77	41	0
Social Credit	1,296	.30	6	0
Totals	425,403	99.99	165	59
General Election — June 23, 1971				
NDP	248,978	54.99	60	45
Liberal	193,864	42.82	60	15
PC	9,659	2.13	16	0
Independent	189	.04	1	0
Communist	46	.01	1	0
Totals	452,736	99.99	138	60
General Election — June 11, 1975				
NDP	180,700	40.07	61	39
Liberal	142,853	31.67	61	15
PC	124,573	27.62	61	7
Independent	2,897	.64	5	0
Totals	451,023	100.00	188	61
General Election — October 18, 1978				
NDP	228,791	48.12	61	44
PC	181,045	38.08	61	17
Liberal	65,498	13.78	61	0
Independent	81	.02	2	0
Totals	475,415	100.00	185	61

*One seat declared void.
**One seat declared void.

General Election — April 26, 1982				
Political Party	Votes Cast	Percentage of Vote	Candidates Nominated	Candidates Elected
PC	289,311	54.07	64	55
NDP	201,390	37.64	64	9
Liberal	24,134	4.51	64	0
Western Canada Concept (WCC)	17,487	3.26	40	0
Independent	1,607	.30	8	0
Aboriginal People's Party	1,156	.22	10	0
Totals	535,085	100.00	250	64
General Election — October 20, 1986				
PC	244,382	44.61	64	38
NDP	247,683	45.20	64	25
Liberal	54,739	9.99	64	1
WCC	458	.08	9	0
Independent	358	.07	3	0
Alliance	237	.04	6	0
Communist	73	.01	1	0
Totals	547,930	100.00	211	64
General Election — October 21, 1991				
NDP	275,780	51.05	66	55
PC	137,994	25.54	66	10
Liberal	125,814	23.29	66	1
Independent	592	.11	8	0
WCC	46	.01	1	0
Totals	540,226	100.00	207	66
General Election — June 21, 1995				
NDP	193,053	47.21	58	42
Liberal	141,873	34.70	58	11
PC	73,269	17.92	58	5
Independent	712	.17	4	0
Totals	408,907	100.00	178	58
General Election — September 16, 1999				
NDP	157,046	38.73	58	29
Saskatchewan Party	160,603	39.61	58	25
Liberal	81,694	20.15	58	4
New Green Alliance	4,101	1.01	16	0
PC	1,609	.40	14	0
Independent	422	.10	2	0
Totals	405,475	100.00	206	58

General Election — November 3, 2003				
Political Party	Votes Cast	Percentage of Vote	Candidates Nominated	Candidates Elected
NDP	190,923	44.68	58	30
Saskatchewan Party	168,144	39.35	58	28
Liberal	60,601	14.18	58	0PC
Western Independence Party	2,615	.61	17	0
New Green Alliance	2,323	.55	27	0
Independent	1,997	.47	5	0
PC	681	.16	11	0
Total	427,284	100.00	234	58
General Election — December 11, 2007				
Saskatchewan Party	230,671	50.92	57	38
NDP	168,704	37.24	58	19
Liberal	42,585	9.4	58	0
Green Party	9,128	2.01	48	0
PC	832	0.18	5	0
Western Independence Party	572	0.13	8	0
Saskatchewan Marijuana Party	517	0.11	5	0
Vacant				1

Appendix B: Premiers of Saskatchewan, 1905–2007

1905–1916	T. Walter Scott (Liberal)
1916–1922	William M. Martin (Liberal)
1922–1926	Charles A. Dunning (Liberal)
1926–1929	James G. ("Jimmy") Gardiner (Liberal)
1929–1934	J.T.M. Anderson (Conservative/Coalition)
1934–1935	James G. ("Jimmy") Gardiner (Liberal)
1935–1944	William J. Patterson (Liberal)
1944-1961	T.C. ("Tommy") Douglas (Co-Operative Commonwealth Federation
1961–1964	Woodrow S. Lloyd (Co-Operative Commonwealth Federation)
1964–1971	W. Ross Thatcher (Liberal)
1971–1982	Allan E. Blakeney (New Democratic Party)
1982–1991	D. Grant Devine (Progressive Conservative)
1991–2001	Roy J. Romanow (New Democratic Party)
2001–2007	Lorne A. Calvert (New Democratic Party)
2007–	Bradley J. Wall (Saskatchewan Party)

Appendix C: Lieutenant Governors of Saskatchewan, 1905–2007

1905–1910	Amédée Forget
1910–1915	George W. Brown
1915–1921	Richard S. Lake
1921–1931	Henry W. Newlands
1931–1936	Hugh E. Munroe
1936–1945	Archibald P. McNab
1945	Thomas Miller
1945–1948	Reginald J.M. Parker
1948–1951	John M. Uhrich
1951–1958	William J. Patterson
1958–1963	Frank L. Bastedo
1963–1970	Robert L. Hanbidge
1970–1976	Stephen Worobetz
1976–1978	George Porteous
1978–1983	C. Irwin McIntosh
1983–1988	Frederick W. Johnson
1988–1994	Sylvia O. Fedoruk
1994–1999	John E.N. ("Jack") Wiebe
1999–2006	Lynda Haverstock
2006–	Gordon L. Barnhart

Appendix D: Past Presidents and Chiefs, Federation of Saskatchewan Indian Nations, 1958–2007

1958–1961	John Tootoosis
1961–1964	David Knight
1964–1966	Wilfred Bellegarde
1966–1968	Walter Dieter
1968–1978	David Ahenakew
1978–1979	Albert Bellegarde
1979–1986	Sol Anderson
1986–1994	Roland Crowe
1994–1998	Blaine Favel
1998–2003	Perry Bellegarde
2003–2006	Alphonse Bird
2006–	Lawrence Joseph

Index

Contributors

DAVID M. ARNOT attended the University of Saskatchewan and received his LL.B. Degree in 1975. He was appointed a Judge of the Provincial Court of Saskatchewan in 1981, sitting at North Battleford, Saskatchewan. In September of 1994, Judge Arnot accepted a secondment to the Department of Justice for Canada, as Director General of the Aboriginal Justice Directorate. In May 1996, Judge Arnot was promoted to the position of Special Advisor to the Deputy Minister of Justice and Deputy Attorney General of Canada. On January 1, 1997, he was appointed by the Federal Government to be the Treaty Commissioner for the Province of Saskatchewan for a five-year term. This term was extended for a further three years in 2002 and a further two years in 2005. Judge Arnot's work on the "Teaching Treaties in the Classroom Project" was specifically cited as a model for Canada by the United Nations Special Rapporteur on Racism in his report presented in March 2004. On January 15, 2009, Judge Arnot was seconded to be Chief Commissioner for the Saskatchewan Human Rights Commission for a five-year term.

BONITA BEATTY, PhD, is a member of the Peter Ballantyne Cree Nation. She is an assistant professor in the Department of Native Studies at the University of Saskatchewan. She has a doctorate in Political Science from the University of Alberta, specializing in First Nations governance and health administration. Her work experience has primarily been in health organization management and administration, policy-making and strategic planning, community development and training. She has also been involved in numerous projects and conferences promoting the importance of both post-secondary education and local knowledge. Prior to becoming faculty at the university, she was the Executive Director of Health and Social Development for the Federation of Saskatchewan Indians (2005–07); she served as a research associate with Family Medicine, College of Medicine at the University of Saskatchewan from 2002–04; was formerly the Executive Director of Peter Ballantyne Cree Nation Health Services from 1996–2002, and its Director of Community Development from 1995–96. Prior to PBCN Health, she was senior policy analyst with the provincial government, Saskatchewan Indian and Metis Affairs Secretariat, from 1991–95.

RAYMOND B. BLAKE is Professor of History at the University of Regina. His most recent book is *From Rights to Needs: A HIstory of Family Allowances in Canada, 1929–1992.*

JOSEPH GARCEA is an Associate Professor in the Department of Political Studies where he teaches courses in Canadian politics, local governance, public policy and public management. His areas of research and publication include local governance, immigration, citizenship, multiculturalism, and Indian urban reserves. He has co-edited books on municipal reforms, one entitled *Municipal Reform in Canada: Reconfiguration, Re-Empowerment and Rebalancing*, and the other entitled *Local Government Reform at the Turn of the Millennium: Australia, New Zealand, Britain, Ireland, Canada, and the United States*. He served as Chair and Director of Research and Analysis for the Saskatchewan Task Force on Municipal Legislative Renewal, as a member of the Métis Electoral Panel, and as a member of Saskatoon's Municipal Wards Commission.

THOMAS GUSA presently studies at the University of Windsor, Faculty of Law, and will graduate in 2010. He was born and raised in Spruce Grove, Alberta, and plans to return to Edmonton to begin the practice of law. Saskatchewan holds a special place in his heart and he is proud to descend from three generations of her history.

D. MICHAEL JACKSON was Chief of Protocol for Saskatchewan from 1980 to 2005; he established the provincial honours program, was executive director of Government House Heritage Property and coordinated ten visits of members of the Royal Family. He is the author of a number of articles on the Crown and of four educational booklets published by the Government of Saskatchewan. The Queen named him a Lieutenant of the Royal Victorian Order in 1987 and a Commander of the Order in 2005. He has B.A. and M.A. degrees from the University of Toronto and a doctorate from the University of Caen in France. He is now a research fellow at the Canadian Plains Research Center, University of Regina.

HOWARD J. LEESON was born in Lethbridge, Alberta, Canada in 1942. He received his MA and PhD from the University of Alberta in Canada. In 1977 he moved to Saskatchewan (where his mother's family had homesteaded) to work with the provincial government. He became the first Deputy Minister of Intergovernmental Affairs for the province in 1979, and was the Deputy in charge federal-provincial discussions which led to the patriation of the Constitution. In 1982 he joined the staff of the Department of Political Science at the University of Regina. In 2007 he was appointed Professor Emeritus in Political Science at the University of Regina, and in 2008 he was appointed Research Fellow, as well as Editor of the *Prairie Forum*, for the Canadian Plains Research Center. Dr Leeson has published numerous books and articles during his career, including *Canada Notwithstanding*, co-authored with Roy Romanow and John Whyte (a 25th anniversary edition of this book was just re-published in 2007), *Grant Notley: The Social Conscience of Alberta*, and *Saskatchewan Politics: Into the Twenty-first Century*, an earlier text on the politics of his home province.

GREGORY P. MARCHILDON is Canada Research Chair in Public Policy and Economic History at the Johnson-Shoyama Graduate School of Public Policy,

University of Regina. He previously served as executive director of the Royal Commission on the Future of Health Care in Canada (the Romanow Commission) from 2001 to 2002, and Deputy Minister to the Premier and Cabinet Secretary in Saskatchewan from 1996 until 2000. He is the author of *Health Systems in Transition: Canada* (University of Toronto Press, 2006) and the co-author of *Health Care in Saskatchewan: An Analytical Profile* (CPRC, 2007).

DAVID MCGRANE was born and raised in Moose Jaw and did his undergraduate degree in Political Science at the University of Regina and his Masters' degree in Political Science at York University in Toronto. In 2007, he completed his Ph.D. in political science at Carleton University in Ottawa. He began an appointment as a tenure-track Assistant Professor in Political Studies in July 2007 at St. Thomas More College and the University of Saskatchewan. He has published in the *International Journal of Canadian Studies*, the *Journal of Canadian Studies* and has a contribution in *Constructing Tomorrow's Federalism*, edited by Ian Peach (University of Manitoba Press). David frequently comments in the Saskatchewan media and he teaches classes in North American politics, Canadian political parties, federalism, multiculturalism, and provincial politics. His research interests include social democracy, Saskatchewan politics, Québécois nationalism, and western alienation.

TOM MCINTOSH (PhD, Queen's, 1996) is an Associate Professor of Political Science at the University of Regina. He previously held positions at the Institute of Intergovernmental Relations and the School of Policy Studies at Queen's, the Saskatchewan Institute of Public Policy at UofR and with Saskatchewan Health. He was a consultant to Saskatchewan's Commission on Medicare (2000) and served as Research Coordinator for the (Romanow) Commission on the Future of Health Care in Canada (2001/02). From 2004 through 2007 he was Director of the Health Network for the Canadian Policy Research Networks (CPRN) in Ottawa. He is the author or editor of eight books and numerous articles and research studies on Canadian politics and public policy.

KEVIN O'FEE, a graduate of the University of Regina in Political Science, is currently with the Johnson-Shoyama Graduate School of Public Policy's Outreach and Training branch. Prior to assuming his position with the JSGS he has held a number of senior policy positions with the Government of Saskatchewan. He is also a former Research and Policy Analyst for the Romanow Commission. he has since gone on function as a health policy consultant on a number of projects with the Institute of Intergovernmental Relations, Queen's University and the University of Regina. And co-authored the book *Health Care in Saskatchewan: An Analytical Profile* with Dr. Gregory Marchildon.

DAN PERRINS is currently the Executive in Residence and Senior Policy Fellow at the Johnson-Shoyama Graduate School of Public Policy, University of Regina. Prior to this, Mr. Perrins served in the Public Service of Saskatchewan for 36 years. He began his career as a frontline social worker and went onto hold a number of increasingly senior positions in Social Services, Health,

Education and Post-Secondary Education and Skills Training. In February 2001, Mr. Perrins was appointed as Deputy Minister to the Premier and the Head of the Public Service and served in that role until November 2007. He has lectured extensively on public administration, social policy and the machinery of government. Mr. Perrins has been awarded the Queen's Jubilee Medal, the Saskatchewan Centennial Medal and the Institute of Public Administration of Canada's Lieutenant Governor General's Medal for Distinguished Public Service. He is a graduate of the University of Saskatchewan and the School of Social Work, University of Regina.

MARILYN POITRAS has been working within the legal arena for 25 years. This experience includes work with every level of Indigenous government, provincial and territorial governments as well as federal government departments. She also works with Indigenous communities, institutions and government on issues of justice, governance, education, and culture as well as traditional Indigenous laws with Canadian Elders. Marilyn is an alumni of the Native Law Centre Program of Legal Studies for Native People, the College of Law at the University of Saskatchewan and has a Masters from Harvard Law School. She is the mother of four and currently lives in Saskatoon, teaching at the College of Law.

PETER PREBBLE has been active in the Saskatchewan environmental movement for more than 30 years. He was elected to the Saskatchewan Legislature 4 times and served as a Saskatoon MLA for 16 years. He served in Premier Lorne Calvert's Cabinet and retired from public life in October 2007. He is currently Director of Energy and Water Policy for the Saskatchewan Environmental Society.

MERRILEE RASMUSSEN, Q.C., acted as Legislative Counsel and Law Clerk advising the Saskatchewan Legislature for almost 15 years before moving to the private practice of law. Her MA thesis in 1995 focused on the decline of democracy in the Legislature and received the Governor General's gold medal. She has maintained her interest in parliamentary democracy in her law practice and has provided advice in relation to this area of the law to clients whose interests have been affected by the actions of the Legislature. She has also taught classes in Legislation and Law Reform at the University of Saskatchewan and Political Science and Human Justice at the University of Regina.

THE HONOURABLE ROY J. ROMANOW, P.C., O.C., Q.C. served as Premier of Saskatchewan from 1991–2001 and was first elected to the Saskatchewan Legislature in 1967. He served as Deputy Premier, Attorney General, and Minister of Intergovernmental Affairs where he was a key player in the federal-provincial negotiations that resulted in the Constitutional Accord and the Canadian Charter of Rights and Freedoms in 1982. In 2001, Mr. Romanow was appointed Commissioner on the Future of Health Care in Canada. He is an Officer of the Order of Canada, a member of the Privy Council of Canada, and has received honorary degrees from several universities. Starting in 2003, Mr.

Romanow received the Economic Justice Award from the Atkinson Charitable Foundation. Continuing in this capacity, he is the spokesperson for the Canadian Index of Wellbeing project and is the chair of the board. He also holds the position of Senior Fellow in Public Policy at the University of Saskatchewan.

ANDREA ROUNCE is a PhD Candidate in Political Science at Carleton University, focusing on the impact of public opinion on public policy formation, using an analysis of Saskatchewan post-secondary education spending. Her main research interests are post-secondary education policy (including access and affordability); public opinion; public sector governance (including university governance and university-community links); policy analysis; and quantitative and qualitative research methodology. She served as Principal Investigator for the 2006–07 McCall Review of Accessibility and Affordability in Post-Secondary Education (Saskatchewan) and has been a Lecturer with the Johnson-Shoyama Graduate School of Public Policy at the University of Regina.

DAVID E. SMITH is professor emeritus of political studies, University of Saskatchewan, and senior policy fellow, Johnson-Shoyama Graduate School of Public Policy, University of Regina. His most recent book, *The People's House of Commons: Theories of Democracy in Contention* (Toronto: University of Toronto Press, 2007) won the 2007–2008 Donner Prize.

GARY TOMPKINS is currently Associate Professor of Economics at the University of Regina and has been at the University of Regina since 1982. He received his B.A. (Honours) in Mathematics/Statistics and Economics from Queen's University and his M.A. and Ph.D. in Economics at the University of Western Ontario. His research interests include public finance, health economics and aboriginal economics. He has also participated in a number of governmental and other public bodies including being a member of two provincial review committees for medical diagnostic testing, the research director of the La Loche Community Case Study for the Royal Commission on Aboriginal Peoples, and a member of the Business Tax Committee of the Saskatchewan Urban Municipalities Association.

RYAN WALKER was born in Winnipeg and grew up both there and in St. Albert, Alberta. He has a BA from University of Lethbridge, an MA from University of Waterloo, and PhD from Queen's University at Kingston. In 2006 he moved to Saskatoon, in the region where his mother's side of the family was born and his great-grandparents homesteaded, to take a position as an Assistant Professor of Geography and Planning at the University of Saskatchewan. Ryan is a member of the Association of Professional Community Planners of Saskatchewan and is Chair of the University's Regional and Urban Planning program.

JOHN D. WHYTE is currently a Visiting Professor at the College of Law, University of Saskatchewan. For over twenty years, he was Professor of Law at Queen's Univerity and as well served as its Dean of Law from 1987 to 1992. During Canada's constitutional patriation process served as constitutional advisor to the Government of Saskatchewan and from 1997 to 2002 he was Saskatchewan's Deputy Minister of Justice. He has held appointments at the Yale Law School, Osgoode Hall Law School at York University, University of Toronto, the Saskatchewan Institute of Public Policy and the University of British Columbia.